The Inner Opium War

Printed in The United States of America

Index by Olive Holmes, Edindex

The Council on East Asian Studies publishes books in four series and, through the Fairbank Center for East Asian Research and the Reischauer Institute of Japanese Studies, administers research projects designed to further scholarly understanding of China, Japan, Korea, Vietnam, Inner Asia, and adjacent areas.

Library of Congress Cataloging-in-Publication Data

Polachek, James M.
  The inner Opium War / James M. Polachek.
    p. cm. – (Harvard East Asian monographs ; 151)
    Includes bibliographical references and index.
    ISBN 0-674-45446-4
    1. China–History–Opium War, 1840–1842.   2. China–Foreign
  relations.   I. Title.   II. Series.
  DS757.55.P65 1991
  951'.033–dc20   91-30657
                                                        CIP

ACKNOWLEDGMENTS

Research for this book was undertaken between 1977 and 1984 in the United States, United Kingdom, and Taiwan. My major debts for archival assistance are in the United States, in particular to the Yenching Library at Harvard University and to the Starr Library at Columbia University, whose staffs' patience with my endless and extended borrowings is much appreciated. Abroad, I am indebted to the staff of the National Palace Museum in Taipei for access to Chiach'ing, Tao-kuang, and Hsien-feng period memorials and related documents. I am also grateful, in the United Kingdom, to the Public Records Office for allowing access to its excellent collection of captured local-government materials from the Kwangtung provincial government.

On a personal level, I should like to offer my particular gratitude to the following mentors and colleagues for their help, encouragement, and criticism as this manuscript grew: Professors Frederic Wakeman, Philip Kuhn, Cyril Black, Robert Tignor, and Susan Naquin, and Dr. Mary B. Rankin.

CONTENTS

INTRODUCTION *1*
  Opium War Policies: Some Interpretations 3
  The Literati: An Anticipatory Overview 10

1 THE LITERATI RE-ASCENDANT *17*
  Who Were the Literati? 20
  Ideals of Career Patronage 23
  Constraints on Clique Politics 29
  The Hsuan-an Poetry Club as a Literati Faction 39
  As a Bureaucratic Patronage Clique 41
  As a Brotherhood of Aesthete-Connoisseurs 47
  Political Failure 50
  Aftermath: Lin Tse-hsu's Northern Reclamation Plan 59

2 THE RISE OF THE SPRING PURIFICATION CIRCLE *63*
  As a Personal Network 66
  As a Political Faction 73
  Ritual and Symbol 83
  Literary and Scholastic Philosophy 87
  The Ideal of "Moral Censure" (ching-i) Politics 95

3 THE POLITICS OF OPIUM SUPPRESSION *101*

The Case Against Embargo 103
The Legalization Initiative of 1836 113
The Failure of the Initiative 120
Intransigents Take the Helm 125

4 THE MYTH OF VICTORY IN KWANGTUNG *137*

Lin Tse-hsu and the Anti-Opium Campaign 141
Lin Tse-hsu versus Ch'i-shan 149
The Siege of Canton 159
San-yuan-li 163
Paramilitary Realities 169

5 THE DEBATE OVER THE CONDUCT OF THE WAR *177*

Ch'i-shan and the Tientsin Negotiations 181
The Case of Yao Ying on Taiwan 185
Wei Yuan and the Strategy of Defensive War 194
Yao Ying and Britain's Vulnerability in South Asia 200

6 THE KU YEN-WU SHRINE ASSOCIATION *205*

*The Mu-chang-a Government and Literati Political
   Influence 209*
Political Organization of the Association 217
Ritual and Scholastic Philosophy 225
In Search of a Political Program 231

7 THE END OF MANCHU DIPLOMACY *237*

The Second Victory of the Cantonese 242
Showdown 252
The Bonham Letter 254
The Crisis in Kwangsi 258
The Recall of Lin Tse-hsu 265

8 EPILOGUE *273*

NOTES *291*

BIBLIOGRAPHY *365*

GLOSSARY / INDEX *385*

Introduction

This book examines anew a question that has long absorbed the attentions of scholars of the modern period of Chinese history. That is the question of why the experience of decisive military defeat during the Sino-British, or "Opium," war of 1840 did not inspire a major overhaul of China's diplomatic and military posture toward the outside world. In searching for fresh insights into the logic of Chinese conservatism during this first phase of her encounter with nineteenth-century Western sea power, I have singled out for particular attention the decade-and-a-half between 1835 and 1850. This was an interlude that saw the Ch'ing empire struggling for the first time with an agenda of problems created specifically by the buildup of British commercial interests and military capabilities that had taken place in East Asia in the wake of the Napoleonic Wars: problems such as an expanding illicit trade in opium and silver bullion, the increased vulnerability of China's riverine defenses to Western naval penetration, and the unwillingness of most Chinese officials and scholars to perceive that a strategy of interim accommodation offered China her only chance for avoiding military humiliation. It was also a period marked by the first appearance of that typically late-Ch'ing phenomenon in foreign policy, the oscillation from harsh, xenophobic rigidity, to a collaborationist opportunism, and back again to rigidity—a phenomenon that would later become the despair of China's would-be foreign "protectors" and allies. Taken in combination, these twin features of the "Opium War interlude" (if thus it might be labeled)—the novelty, that is, of the new, "maritime" agenda in foreign relations, and the first anticipation of late-Ch'ing pendular indecisiveness in foreign policy questions—make it a particularly fascinating and fruitful period for anyone interested in reopening the question of imperial China's "non-response" to the nineteenth-century West.

But how is one to study it? And in what particular regards is the approach attempted in this book a new one? In one respect, what the reader will find in the pages that follow will seem not at all new, but rather a throwback of sorts to an older genre of history: the political narrative of Sino-Western diplomatic and military contact. This is, of course, the historiographical format through which China's "opening" used to be studied. I have come back to it in assembling my own insights into the period because we still possess no full English-language account of the 1835–1850 period in its entirety—none, at least, that incorporates the full range of relevant Chinese archives and published sources that have become available to the scholar since the 1950s. An updated narrative reconstruction in the tradition of Morse's, Costin's, Fairbank's, and H. P. Chang's studies of the Opium War period has thus seemed in order, and it is this that I have set out to accomplish.

In terms not of form but of analytical theme, however, I have consciously deviated in this volume from the outlook epitomized in the above-cited works and in other more recent studies dealing with the intellectual and political roots of Chinese conservatism during the later Ch'ing. While most of the above take as their central concern either the curious survival of the "Middle Kingdom" outlook on foreign relations or the distracting effect of the Taiping and ancillary rebellions on Ch'ing foreign policy during the Opium War interlude, I have chosen quite another focus. In this work I shall be devoting most of my attention to the little-known subject of central-government political dynamics as an influence upon Ch'ing military and diplomatic decision making. More precisely, I shall be concerned with the "court politics" of foreign policy—that is, with the making of key foreign policy decisions by the Ch'ing imperial government, and with the competition to influence these decisions. In particular, I shall argue that the Ch'ing deliberative system was too weighted down by the requirements of consensus, and much too open to interference by political adventurers bent on building up their own personal prestige, to generate effective diplomatic or strategic policies. I shall argue further that the country's rulers developed an acute awareness of this set of problems by the end of the first round of defeats and treaty exactions in 1842, but that, in spite of this perception, they remained unable, in the long run, to correct the weakness they espied, thus giving rise to the "policy oscillation" phenomenon alluded to above. Why this slippage took place—why no major restructuring of central-government political institutions or power relationships proved possible, in spite of the very considerable impetus for change provided by the 1840 war with Great Britain—forms the principal analytical question I shall attempt to answer in this book.

OPIUM WAR POLICIES: SOME INTERPRETATIONS

As should be clear from these preliminary remarks, then, this book is both a good deal more and a good deal less than a mere updating of earlier interpretations of Sino-British interaction during the period of the Opium War. Though it retells a well-known story, the events and actors will often be unfamiliar, as will also the approach, which emphasizes the inertia of the central-government political system as the chief obstacle to foreign policy change. One might justifiably ask why I have seen fit to attempt so radically different an interpretation of the causes and consequences of the Opium War. In particular, what are the shortcomings or insufficiencies in the existing literature on Ch'ing policy during this period that have prompted this effort at redefining our views of the problem? To answer, one must begin with the literature itself, within which one finds two somewhat divergent lines of interpretation, the one concentrating on the persisting influence of imperial Confucianist notions of state-craft, and the other on the displacement or distortion of a "rational" foreign policy as a consequence of the onset of the great wave of mid-century rebellions.

Within the first school, the dominant view remains that of John K. Fairbank, whose writings have relentlessly stressed the paralyzing effect that the "tributary system," and the "Sinocentric world order" that it expressed, had upon the diplomacy of the late empire. In Fairbank's view, this system—or, rather, this "ideology"—of foreign relations succeeded, even as late as the 1880s, in blocking Ch'ing perception of a need for competition with the maritime powers. Rather, the latter (and especially the British) were seen as participants *in* that system, aiding the equally foreign Manchu rulers of the Imperium as dependents or subordinates capable of supplying useful services, but in no case being regarded as equals worthy of emulation.[1] From this point of view, the explanation for the marginality of Chinese institutional innovation during and after the Opium War period lies in the tenacious strength and flexibility of the pre-nineteenth-century vision of a Sinocentric world order—a vision that could all too easily absorb the new phenomenon of Western "free-trade" imperialism without sensing in it any ultimate challenge to the political order in China.

Departing slightly (but not entirely) from Fairbank's argument is a second conceptual-determinist interpretation of Ch'ing nineteenth-century conservatism—albeit one concerned primarily with post-Opium War developments—in which the main issue is taken to be the irreconcilability of traditional Confucian political ideals with the statist or power-oriented spirit of late-nineteenth-century Western statecraft. According to this paradigm, which has found its most skillful articulation in the work of Benjamin Schwartz, the traditional ideals of statecraft and of elite political action dominant in the minds of the scholar-official class before 1895 were biased strongly against the kind of uncompromised glorying in state power that would later come to preoccupy reformist thought in the era of rapid institutional change. In this earlier period, the statist (or state-nationalist) rationale for change was simply not sufficiently developed in the "ortho-dox" Confucian approach to statecraft to justify any major acts of institutional reform—such as, for example, the abolition of the examination system.[2] Likewise, in the realm of economic organization, the traditional Confucian aversion to competition and the deeply ingrained habit of family loyalism have been seen as too powerful to be cast aside even in the government-controlled "modern" industrial complex that appeared in China in the 1870s and 1880s.[3] A radical and uncompromising break with the past was thus required before Chinese political elites would be free to undertake really ambitious structural reforms. And, quite naturally, such a break could not take place either quickly or without major disruptions.

Quite apart from these interpretations, which emphasize the influence of Chinese values and ways of thinking, one finds in two more recent works the basis for a second interpretation of China's mid-nineteenth-century inertia—an interpretation that might be labeled the domestic-distractions approach. I refer here to Frederic Wakeman, Jr.'s 1966 *Strangers at the Gate*, and to J. Y. Wong's 1976 administrative biography of Yeh Ming-ch'en, the Liang-Kuang viceroy responsible for provoking the "second" (1856–1860) Opium War. Admittedly, neither of these works is as concerned with Sino-foreign relations as with the social and administrative problems of southeastern China during the Taiping period. But they do bear a message concerning the domestic political origins of Ch'ing official xenophobia, a phenomenon they tie directly to the swiveling of official attention brought about by the advent of the Taipings. Both argue, in effect, that the ultimate consequence of this inward turn was to make otherwise fairly enlightened officials more inflexible and wooden in their response to British pressures than they would otherwise have been. Thus it is to the pressures and distractions of provincial government that we must look to discover the roots of Ch'ing government xenophobia during this period. Ideology seems to count for fairly little. In Wong's analysis, Viceroy Yeh, a figure usually offered up as exemplary of the spirit of Sinocentric ideological arrogance, becomes merely a harassed administrator, too preoccupied with the day-to-day problems of securing and funding his inland outposts to have time left for soothing British petitioners.

In Wakeman's study, the effect of these same inland distractions becomes somewhat more complex, and their result a more clearly irrational style of diplomacy, but it is still in them that we find the explanations for Ch'ing negotiative behavior. As Wakeman reconstructs the political situation in Kwangtung during the decade-and-a-half after the Treaty of Nanking (1842), it is the local scholar-gentry, rather than the officials, who were the really important actors. Well-armed but distinctly xenophobic, these tough-minded notables of the Canton hinterlands became, thanks to the near collapse of local order, the real arbiters of what could and could not be done in treaty dealings with the British. Try as they might, pragmatic conciliators like Ch'i-ying could not—and demagogues like Viceroy Yeh would not—enforce the new treaties; to do so was to write off virtually the only ally the government possessed as it struggled to suppress Taiping-inspired secret societies in the Pearl River delta. In the end, therefore, we find Viceroy Yeh not only sounding like a local gentryman in his vehement anti-foreignism, but apparently even believing his own claims—to disastrous result. This is perhaps further than Wong would be willing to go, but here too we see the needs of local control setting the tone of Ch'ing diplomacy, pushing it in a direction it might not have taken had there been no rebellion to worry about.

Though perhaps incomplete in some regards, the above seems to me to summarize the major explanatory themes that have been sounded, and still resound, on the subject of official anti-foreignism in nineteenth-century China. How well will they hold up as guides to the events of the period with which we are concerned in this book? That will depend in part on one's assumptions about where the really important decisions were made within the Ch'ing system—locally, or in Peking; and, even more, on how much influence and unity of outlook one is inclined to attribute to late imperial Confucianism. Supposing, however, that one makes no assumptions either way, it should be clear that much about the nature of early-nineteenth-century Ch'ing foreign policy conservatism still needs explanation.

Consider, for example, some of the possibilities that come to mind once we stop assuming that Ch'ing foreign policy behavior flowed inevitably from a fixed domestic ideological consensus. Was it necessarily true, then, that the Ch'ing could not embrace reform or collaboration with certain Western powers unless the majority of the traditional scholar class were first won over to a more positive view of the West itself? Did the Confucian utopianism of the traditional intelligentsia have to be replaced by a foreign-inspired one before significant institutional changes could occur, or before China could modify its mode of interaction with the outside world? In positing the need for this kind of massive intellectual readjustment, have we not wrongly dismissed the possibility that change could—indeed, logically ought—to have come through bureaucratic action undertaken in an elitist and pragmatic, rather than a utopian, spirit? After all, as the early Meiji foreign policy revolution reminds us, a practical interest in the centralization of power and in the enhancing of political unity could have supplied the inspiration for a program of change in China equally as well as the more utopian constructs that would later dominate the reformist thought of the late Ch'ing and early Republican periods. What if the early years of treaty diplomacy did in fact bring to the fore a nucleus of power-seeking court reformists of just such predisposition (a proposition I shall try to substantiate later in this volume), but they failed? Need we assume that this failure was guaranteed by the hostile ideological milieu in which they had to operate? Or might it have been unforeseen political difficulties that wrecked their efforts?

Our list of possible rejoinders to the "pull-of-tradition" interpretation of Opium War era Ch'ing diplomacy does not stop here, however. To it, I would add another more specific one, concerning the question of whether the Sinocentric or tribute-system ideology of Sino-foreign relations was really so deeply engraved into the mindset of the Ch'ing political elite as we have assumed? Was this really the only conceivable choice, or were there not alternative visions of China's global role, based squarely in China's earlier historical experiences, to which early-nineteenth-century Ch'ing emperors or their advisers could have turned *had they the will to launch out in new directions?* In a suggestive article on this general topic, Michael Hunt reminds us that the international Machiavellianism of the Warring States period and the expansionist cosmopolitanism of the early T'ang empire constituted just such ready-to-hand alternatives, and were consciously employed as such by late Ch'ing official reformers. Indirectly confirming Hunt's suggestion of an indeterminate, plural tradition, John Wills has recently proposed that early Ch'ing management of Sino-foreign relations, quite in contrast to its better known late Ch'ing mutation, partook very little of the tribute system ideology that had dominated Ming diplomacy.[4] None of this is to deny, of course, that the pompous "Celestialism" of the late Ch'ing court posed a very real problem for those who would have brought China more speedily into the modern world. But it will serve to remind us that there was an element of choice in insisting on this particular posture, and thus raise the question of why that choice was made—a question that cannot (save tautologically) be answered on grounds of ideology alone.

Thus far we have been concerned with the limitations of an ideological approach to the problem of Ch'ing foreign policy in our
period. Equally forceful objections can also be raised, however, to the
local-history or domestic-distractions approach, provided one is willing to question the idea that it was the provincial authorities rather
than court leaders who held the key to Ch'ing diplomacy in the early
days of the treaty system. For the pre-Taiping decades, at least, that
assumption demands to be questioned—particularly when the province under scrutiny is one as geographically remote from the centers
of Ch'ing imperial power as was Kwangtung.

But why so? For one thing, the regional center of gravity of the
Ch'ing imperial system was not in the southeast. It lay, rather, in
north and east-central China, two macroregions whose social structures and communications were a good deal more vulnerable to intim-
idation from the sea than were those of Kwangtung. The "center,"
therefore, ought logically to have been quite suspicious of intelligence and policy suggestions sent up from Canton, and to have
reserved for itself the privilege of responding to the same diplomatic
or military issues in ways very different from those advocated by the
Liang-Kuang viceroy. This, in fact, is precisely what happened during the Opium War itself, as we shall see in chapter 4. And it comes
near to being a description of what would occur again in 1857–1858,
during the early days of the second "Opium" war, when Peking simultaneously nurtured defiance in the hinterlands of Canton while agreeing to major treaty concessions in the Yangtze and in foreign rights
of access to the capital. A Kwangtung-based, or "local-history," interpretation of early treaty-period anti-foreignism thus seems quite
insufficient to explain why Ch'ing diplomacy as a whole moved in
the directions it did.

But even if the rebellion-fearing imperial agents in Canton did
eventually help push Ch'ing policy in a populist or xenophobic direction, how far back in time can we rightfully project this pattern?
One must not forget, after all, that Ch'ing authority in the south did
not really begin to crumble until after 1850, more than sixteen years
after Sino-British relations had become highly tense over opium and
free-trade issues. During the initial years of the Opium War interlude,
at least, the authorities in Kwangtung and Peking would have been
reaching decisions on foreign policy with no such domestic anxieties
to distort their judgment or distract their attention. If there are over-

tones of unrealistic intransigence and anti-foreign militancy in this earlier phase (and I shall argue that there are), how then are we to account for their presence? Not without a more careful scrutiny of the logic of foreign policymaking at the imperial *center*—a subject about which the existing literature on the Opium War period gives us little guidance.

We return, then, from our very hasty tour of the literature on mid-nineteenth-century Sino-foreign relations with a daunting list of explanatory possibilities as yet inadequately explored. It may well be, for example, that the mandarin scorn that British petitioners found so irritating (and inexplicable) in our period reflected a tradition of unwavering Sinocentric isolationism. But to argue thus is to leave unexplained why this particular brand of tradition was chosen, or allowed to dominate, at the expense of others. More simply, it is to ignore the politics behind that choice. By the same token, to posit that reform had to await the popularization of a Western-influenced utopianism among educated Chinese is to neglect the possibility that a practical *bureaucratic* interest in power (or power-enhancement) could also have supplied the motive for voluntarily opening China up to Western influences (as it does today), and thus to leave unexamined the intriguing question of why the Ch'ing bureaucratic class seemed unable to produce leaders strong enough to grasp this point and act upon it. Where, then, were the bureaucratic (or military) strongmen potentially sensitive to this opportunity, and why were they so weak, or so weak-willed? And, finally, how are we to explain the generally conservative drift of central-government leadership during the relatively quiescent—domestically quiescent, that is—years prior to the onset of the great rebellions of the Hsien-feng reign? The freezing effect of domestic disorder in Kwangtung has been well-documented, as we have noted. But until 1850, at least, it was Peking that made the critical decisions on foreign and domestic policy, and little can be learned, therefore, about the motives for these decisions by focusing upon events in the distant southeast. Rather, we must look for instruction to the configuration of politics at the center.

In this book, my point of departure and approach have been defined very largely by these several hitherto overlooked questions, and I have accordingly tried to provide a treatment of the period that will fill in some of the blank spaces identified in the course of the above reflections. Politics—the analysis, that is, of inter-group competition for power over foreign policy—forms our general subject; the pre-Taiping Opium War interlude (1835–1850), our time period; *central* government policymaking (and enforcement), our specific focus; and the rise (and demise) of a power-oriented pro-treaty-system leadership during the 1840s, the key narrative event toward which our story builds and which it seeks to explain. Since I have tried to come to grips with these issues in the context of writing a new narrative history of the Opium War period, it has been impossible to keep from straying at times into other matters—most notably that of provincial-level anti-foreignism in and around Canton (a subject that dominates fully two chapters of this book). Another very considerable digression occurs at the beginning of this work, where I delve at length into the pre-1835 history of "out-group" factional politics at the Ch'ing court, and examine the reasons why one particular class of elite political actors—the literati—seem so persistently to be drawn to this type of activity both before and during our period.

Apart from these two major detours, however, I have tried to keep this study focused as relentlessly as possible on the issues defined above: the processes and rivalries of Opium War era court politics, and the problems at that level of the system that kept pro-treaty forces weak while strengthening the hand of the isolationist ideologues ringed about them. By so doing, I hope, at the least, to have succeeded in laying to rest once and for all any notion that nineteenth-century China can be treated as an ideological monolith. If I am luckier still, this book will encourage greater attention to be paid in the future to such questions as the nature of political leadership at the apex of the late Manchu political order, and the direction in which it was evolving before the foreign impact became paramount in the early twentieth century.

THE LITERATI: AN ANTICIPATORY OVERVIEW

Historical narratives not usually benefiting from an overload of prefatory generalization, I shall not here attempt any systematic answers to the questions I have put forward in the preceding section. These can be reserved for the final chapter, where there will be time to consider them in the context of the events described in the middle sections of this book. There is, however, one particular theoretical component to this study that needs to be taken up before we become immersed in the story proper. That concerns the major political role I have assigned the "literati," a somewhat mysterious subgroup of the Confucian lettered elite who figure in this book as the inner core of the anti-treaty movement. In keeping with that judgment, I have digressed at the outset of this work (in chapters 1 and 2) in order to explore the full array of institutional and psychological issues that seem to have prompted this class's stubborn resistance to treaty concessions. My reasons for devoting so much space to the literati point of view will be clearer, however, if we pause here to anticipate certain of the conclusions about literati politics that will emerge from this digression, and consider such basic questions as who precisely the "literati" were, the range of concerns that drove them, and the particular political medium—that is, "factions"—through which they characteristically asserted themselves.

As regards the membership and motivational character of this group, a few words ought to suffice at this point, since we shall return to the matter at length in chapters 1 and 2. In defining the literati as a distinct subset of the much larger Confucian lettered elite—a seemingly arbitrary manipulation of terminology—I have in mind that particular subgroup of potential officeholders who sought career advancement through the recognition and friendship of fellow-spirits, rather than of their academic or bureaucratic superiors (the more conventional route). Although this might seem a highly subjective distinction, or one that most would-be officials of scholarly background would have denied existed (if only because it offended their self-respect), in practice there was a very real choice to be made, and never very many who were daring enough to choose the former path. Awareness of the exceptionality of such behavior is, I think, quite clearly reflected in the way in which nineteenth-century scholar-officials used the term *shih-ta-fu*—that is, to demarcate not all scholar-officials (its literal meaning), but rather those few who did as scholar-officials ought to do, particularly with regard to the selection of patrons and mentors. In keeping with this exceptionalist self-awareness, the literati approach to career-making and patron-hunting tended, as we shall see, to be self-consciously flamboyant and at times almost provocative, as if perhaps to advertise a collective scorn for the political order that was responsible for lowering the standards of the vulgar majority.

To this initial characterization it must immediately be added that the pursuit of the literati ideal, if undertaken collectively by any significant group of Han Chinese scholar-officials, was inherently controversial, even dangerous, and quite in violation of Ch'ing imperial thinking. In the context of our period, what was most controversial in the political style of the literati was their tendency to knit together into highly exclusivistic factions (*p'eng-tang*), functioning either to further the influence of a self-appointed few or to diminish the power of certain enemies. Inasmuch as such behavior threatened both the throne's disciplinary authority over the bureaucracy and the access to power of non-Chinese non-scholarly elites (a major concern under the ethnically foreign Ch'ing regime), it inevitably elicited the harshest and most furious of imperial condemnations. Yet, as long as factions of this sort remained the only vehicle capable of providing scholar-officials with some control over their personal fate, participation in them would continue to exercise strong appeal, even becoming (I shall argue) a progressively *more* influential phenomenon as the century wore on. The literati presence in late-Ch'ing high politics was, then, throughout our period intimately bound up with factional politics and with a mode of factional politics inherently controversial.

As for what motivated this persistent literati enthusiasm for "faction," it will be seen that I have emphasized two background issues in particular. The first, alluded to above, was the demand for more control by scholars over the terms of their progress into the ranks of the officeholding class. Under the Manchus, this demand took on certain implicitly "constitutional" overtones, since the issue was not simply freedom to seek support where one wished, but also the collective fate of the Han Chinese scholar-official "estate" as a whole—now but one of several broad elites competing for office and power. In addition to this quasi-constitutional grievance against the Manchu order, however, I have also sought to explain the appeal of "faction" in terms of certain persisting psychological and sociological features of lettered elite life by no means peculiar to the period of Manchu rule. These latter aspects of literati factionalism are discussed in detail in chapter 1, where I argue that the over-competitiveness of examination life tended in and of itself to breed a psychology of moral bravado and a taste for membership in close-knit loyalty groups, especially among scholars at the early, insecure stages of their careers. The picture that emerges from this discussion will in turn suggest that literati class identity was often a transitional affair—a momentarily assumed *persona*, as it were, appealing chiefly as a source of psychological reinforcement during certain more difficult passages in one's career development, but not necessarily likely to survive them. But we shall also see that, for some, it could be more than that: either a permanent alter ego of sorts, useful for senior officials in rallying the support of their juniors, or even a kind of lifelong vocation unto itself, as seems to have been the case with the famous poet-cum-factional-activist, Chang Chi-liang.

Two final points connected with the problem of literati influence in mid-century Ch'ing politics still remain to be commented upon before we can proceed. One concerns the precise range of behavioral attributes associated, in this book, with the concept of literati factions; and the other, the distortions in the overall image of Ch'ing high politics that may have resulted from my concentrating almost solely on the activities of literati political actors.

On the first point, it ought to be stated emphatically that literati factions or factionalism are *not* associated, in this book, either with political opportunism or with a presumed independence from any particular class or social base. In the political-science literature on twentieth-century China, at least, those are exactly the attributes that one would expect to encounter in factions, and that distinguish the latter from political parties. Here, however, no such connotations are intended. In fact, not only were literati factions extraordinarily non-opportunistic in their anti-treaty advocacy, but, as we shall also see, those factions most closely linked to this resistance were motivated by a very powerful sense of class-specific identity and values. There were, no doubt, many other patronage groupings alive and influential during our period that lacked this preoccupation with class and class values, but we shall be seeing very little of them—and not by accident either, for they seem to have played little if any role in the foreign-policy disputes with which we are concerned. *Faction*, therefore, is not to be read as a pejorative; to drive home that point, I have deliberately alternated the word with other more neutral terms, such as *party, circle,* and the like.

We come last, however, to the matter of omissions. Are there major political groupings or interests that have been ignored or pushed too far into the background as a consequence of this book's preoccupation with literati partisanship? The answer ought probably to be in the affirmative, with the leading contenders being the Manchus themselves. From the research of several American and Chinese scholars we have begun to take note of a complex of "Manchu interests" at work behind the facade of imperial Confucian bureaucracy, simultaneously policing that bureaucracy from the outside and displacing from its control major chunks of revenue and of job-patronage power. In terms of organization, this exclusively Manchu power preserve seems to have been anchored within several interlocking institutions: the imperial household bureaucracy (*nei-wu fu*), and the several trade monopolies, tax farms, and purveyance manufacturies under its jurisdiction; and the triad of superintendencies controlling grain transportation to the capital and maintenance of the necessary waterways. All these agencies would have found their powers and perquisites very much at risk whenever government policy moved toward war, and officials who headed them up were presumably very well situated to lobby effectively against whatever threatened them.

Why then do the powerful Manchus figure so minimally in the account of high policymaking offered here, while so much attention is lavished upon the politically more peripheral literati? For the not very satisfying reason, chiefly, that the sources do not conduce to righting the balance. Perhaps all historians are creatures of opportunity, lured to those subjects for which the documentation is most readily available, and deterred from those for which the sources are poor. However that may be, such considerations have certainly affected this study, whose shape has been much influenced by the fact that the published sources representing the literati side of the story are much richer and more easily available than those detailing the workings of the Manchu interest for our period.[5] This evidential imbalance may have produced an unbalanced account, one too lopsidedly informed by the literati perception of events. For the moment, however, there seems little alternative to relying primarily on literati sources for our impression of how the early-nineteenth-century Ch'ing political system actually worked; and so I have done, leaving for my successors the task of sorting out, if they can, what was afoot in the inner corridors of power where the literati never dared to go.

Such, then, are the problems and methodological eccentricities that the reader will confront in the study that follows. In conclusion it remains only to add a few explanatory comments concerning the structure I have employed for arranging the materials. Though the main interest of this study is how different political forces influenced decisions on foreign policy, only part of the discussion that follows (chapters 3, 4, and 7) is actually devoted to the topic of decisional politics in the narrow sense. In chapter 3 ("The Politics of Opium Suppression"), I examine the first and most dramatic of the foreign-policy decisions taken during this period: the 1838–1839 decision to interdict British trade at Canton in order to end the import of India opium into China, by which decision the 1840–1842 conflict with Britain was triggered. In chapter 4 ("The Myth of Victory in Kwangtung"), I follow the course of the debates over military policy that took place on the Ch'ing side during the 1840 war, focusing specifically on the search for a strategy to defend the key southeastern entrepot city of Canton. Finally, in chapter 7 ("The End of Manchu Diplomacy"), I examine the background to the 1850 removal from office of the leaders of the postwar reform party (Mu-chang-a and Ch'i-ying), focusing in particular on the role of the domestic-security question in aligning the monarchy on the side of the opponents of that group. In all three of the aforementioned chapters, the guiding interest is the competition between the leaders of literati opinion— who, in 1838, supported a trade cutoff; in 1841, backed the use of paramilitaries in defending against the British; and, in 1850, urged the toppling of the Mu-chang-a leadership—and their opponents entrenched within the bureaucratic and military establishments.

The remainder of the study that follows, however, is concerned, not directly with decision making, but rather with the formation of literati attitudes about the leading policy questions of the day. In the first two chapters ("The Literati Re-Ascendant," and "The Rise of the Spring Purification Circle") we shall be dealing primarily with the question of why the literati were able to assert themselves politically to such an impressive extent during the early decades of the nineteenth century. Along with this larger question, however, I shall also be considering the changing nature of the lettered elite's self-perception during this same period. There, I shall be concerned in particular with the problem of how the literati coped intellectually with the problem of their own political marginality under the Manchu dynasty. The principal conclusion is that dissatisfaction was rising, in pace, ironically enough, with the increasing dependency of the monarchy on their political cooperation after 1830. A heightened oppositional radicalism was the result—a mindset that was, in turn, to become important as a motive for resisting the treaty system and the accomodationist values it was seen to represent.

In addition to the introductory chapters, there are two others (chapter 5, "The Debate over the Conduct of the War"; and chapter 6, "The Ku Yen-wu Shrine Association") that are also concerned exclusively with the views of the literati, but now in the postwar decade. In the first of these, I examine attitudes on the military and diplomatic questions raised in the course of the Ch'ing wartime defeat. And, in the second, we shall see how lingering constitutional frustrations turned the literati with particular vehemence against the postwar peace party in Peking, whose key leaders were Manchus. These two shorter studies, in addition to explaining the 1850 overturn of the Mu-chang-a "peace" government, will also help, I hope, to illuminate the general nature of the sentiments that guided literati resistance to the treaty system in the nineteenth century.

The Literati Re-Ascendant

The Anglo-Chinese War of 1840–1842 might very well not have taken place had Foreign Secretary Palmerston, its principal enthusiast on the British side, applied himself beforehand to the study of contemporary Ch'ing court politics. Of course, as a flamboyant, populist Whig who thought himself adequately schooled in "the East" from a decade of experience in Mediterranean diplomacy, Viscount Palmerston was hardly the man to think such efforts necessary. And, even if he had, he might well have been disconcerted by the difficulties, for his was a time when European access to the inner political and intellectual life of the Manchu empire was at an all-time low, and credible information on the thinking of China's rulers almost impossible for a foreigner to obtain. Yet, had he or his agents been able to see through this formidable veil, their discoveries might well have cautioned them against expecting too much from the war they were about to fight.

One very considerable deterrent, one suspects, would have been the discovery that foreign affairs per se was a subject of virtually no interest in Ch'ing court circles, despite the havoc that international trade had been playing with China's monetary system since the early 1830s. Unlike the Japanese shogunate, which took care to monitor European political developments even as it proclaimed itself "secluded" from their influence, the Ch'ing central government apparatus made no provision for the gathering of intelligence on extra-Asian affairs. In this disinterest it was fully supported by the Confucian intellectual class, which by the early nineteenth century had come to think of "Western Learning" as no more than a branch of mathematics and astronomy, learned long ago from the Jesuits. Such an atmosphere was not even conducive to wrongheaded thinking about the foreigner, let alone its refutation or correction, and rendered the Ch'ing political establishment quite unprepared to digest the lesson of defeat that Palmerston stood ready to administer.

But, even supposing that this problem had been recognized and brushed aside, prolonged scrutiny of the Ch'ing political scene would have brought to Whitehall's attention another reason for caution. This was that the authority of the imperial court—its hold over the machinery of the state—was in the process of coming undone, just at the moment that Lord Palmerston proposed to burden it with the additional responsibilities of overseeing a humiliating surrender and enforcing an unpopular new system of commercial treaties. Behind this erosion of intra-governmental discipline lay the long-simmering discontent of the Chinese lettered elite with the terms of their relationship to the imperial Manchu state, the sources of which discontent would probably have been difficult for most outlanders to fathom, unfamiliar as they were with the preceding two centuries of imperial high politics. Some sense of the malaise that stirred these men could have been conveyed, however, by analogizing their struggle to that of constitutionalist middle classes of Louis Philippe's France or of post-Aufmarz Prussia; and, had these contemporary comparisons been pressed upon the Whiggish Lord Palmerston, it might well have raised questions in his mind about the political viability of the regime from which he proposed to wring concessions.

At the root of their dissatisfaction was a longstanding Manchu policy denying the Chinese scholar-official class the right (as a European, at least, would have seen it) to pursue political influence through private, intra-class collaboration. On this point, Manchu rulers were—or had been—quite adamant, at least up until the reign of the Chia-ch'ing emperor (r. 1796–1820), father to the monarch (Tao-kuang, r. 1821–1850) then upon the throne. Exceptions could perhaps be made for senior court favorites of lettered class background, who were from time to time allowed to lobby on behalf of their protégés or to represent their opinions to the emperor. But for Chinese literati at the lower rungs of the bureaucratic hierarchy, or still awaiting their first appointment—in other words, for the great majority—no such opportunities existed. For, as Ch'ing monarchs were fond of repeating, to tolerate such activity on a broad scale would be to guarantee perpetual factional warfare among rival bureaucratic cliques, thus making effective imperial rule impossible.

Such at any rate had been the dynasty's policy during the days when Manchu rule was most secure and effective, as it was under Chia-ch'ing's grandfather and father, the Yung-cheng (1722–1735) and Ch'ien-lung (1736–1795) emperors. But, had Lord Palmerston's hypothetical informants been somehow able to reconstruct developments over the preceding three decades, they would have learned that enforcement of this unpopular policy had been deliberately allowed to lapse, in practice if not yet by direct legislation. By the time our observers would have begun their inquiries, well-connected coteries of junior literati were regularly entering the political lists to challenge senior courtiers or their policies, very often displaying as they did so the signs of a lingering bitterness over the preceding century of repression. The implications of this new pattern, once spotted, ought not to have been too difficult to grasp. Ruled by monarchs who had begun to lose their nerve, and beset by literati dissent, the Ch'ing state was not likely to have much capacity for sustained ministerial leadership, or for durable policy reorientation. Yet it was precisely these abilities—or their absence—that would decide whether the empire could persevere in the new "liberal" course Palmerston expected to emerge from the war to come.

But of all this Lord Palmerston was cheerfully ignorant when he resolved, late in 1839, to attempt the "opening" of China by force, thereby committing Great Britain to two decades of frustrating and generally profitless friction with the Ch'ing authorities. It thus falls to the historian to uncover the political factors within China that would cause British policy to miscarry; and this, broadly construed, is the problem that shall concern us throughout this book.

Where then to begin? Building on the analysis suggested above, it would seem logical to start with the pre-history of the literati constitutional discontent whose disintegrative effect on Ch'ing leadership would become manifest during the foreign-policy crises of the 1830s and 1840s. No very satisfactory treatment of this subject is possible, however, without a backward digression into the period of the so-called high Ch'ing, when the straightjacketing of autonomous literati political activism first began to manifest itself as a fixed policy. We begin, then, in chapter 1, with a look at the early Ch'ing origins of this controversial policy. Who exactly were the Ch'ing literati, and why, and in what ways, had the pre-nineteenth-century Ch'ing state circumscribed their involvement in court politics? From these questions we shall move next to the question of why the straightjacket began to loosen during the first decades of the new century. What accounts for the Manchu throne's curious reversal of attitudes after 1800, and what were its political consequences? With these background questions behind us, we shall be ready, in chapter 3, to take up the analysis of Ch'ing foreign policy decision making during the 1830s, wherein the aftereffects of this unsuccessful attempt at repression are very much in evidence.

WHO WERE THE LITERATI?

If, by literati, we mean all junior members of the Chinese examination elite in a position to follow, or have an opinion about, central-government affairs—a broad definition of the term—how large a group are we talking of? And who ought to be included within it?

There is no precise way to answer these questions, since the Ch'ing government itself neither recognized nor licensed membership in any such community. What can be said, however, is that this group never represented more than a very small subsection of the empire-wide degree-holding class. Although by late Ch'ing times as many as perhaps one million men (approximately one-half percent of the entire male population) held examination degrees corresponding to one of the three levels at which the state examinations were traditionally administered (county-prefectural, provincial, and metropolitan), that portion of this larger group capable of ongoing participation in any aspect of the political or intellectual life of the capital was necessarily small, for relatively few of these men could support themselves for very long away from their native communities.[1] Yet, short of actually residing in Peking or in some other higher-order cultural center (Yangchow, for example), there was simply no way to keep abreast of the changing intellectual fashions and rumors of political intrigue that were the staple of eighteenth-century "news," for China had as yet no periodical press to circulate this sort of information.

Given the difficulty for most scholars of meeting this locational requirement, it seems safe to say that no more than twenty-five thousand or so of their number qualified even potentially as literati-activists, the actual number being of course much smaller.[2] Most of these men would have been holders of the provincial (*chü-jen*) degree, which certified the candidate for the privilege of taking the triennial metropolitan examinations in Peking and, also, for the receipt of various public and private subsidies to cover travel expenses to and from the capital. Again to somewhat oversimplify, we might consider this provincial-graduate subgroup as defining the larger or outer elite corps from which activists in national-level political movements might be expected to emerge.

However, narrowing our radius still further, we might wish to call attention to a much smaller degree-delineated subgroup within the larger, outer elite, composed of those whose degree status and/or social-occupational connections encouraged prolonged residence in the capital city itself. As of the nineteenth century at least, there was in common usage a set of phrases denominating this narrower subgroup, which was known as the Southern City (*nan-ch'eng*) set, or, alternatively, as the Hsuan-nan set (the place names in question referring to the southern, Chinese part of Peking where lower-grade officials of Chinese examination elite background usually resided).[3] Forming the solid core of this "inner" examination-elite group of perhaps one thousand or so metropolitan degree-holders who had advanced sufficiently far up the examination ladder to enter on to one of the official career tracks of the Peking bureaucratic establishment.

The Peking offices available to such new graduates were, however, very largely ceremonial or sinecurial in nature. (For this reason, in fact, the incumbents described their jobs as *ch'ing-hsia*, "pure and leisured.")[4] They thus allowed or even encouraged the officeholder in question to keep up his ties with non-official colleagues, fellow examination graduates, and co-provincial student sojourners in the capital, and with the occasional visitors from his native province or county who wended their way to the capital for the triennial competitions. These "leisured" junior officers of the Southern City accordingly provided a kind of social bridge, spanning the gap between the contact-hungry information seekers of the outer examination elite on the one hand, and the cultural and bureaucratic magnates of the Peking establishment on the other. By virtue of this mediational role, they inevitably played a key part in attempts to mobilize the larger examination elite for concerted political action undertaken during the nineteenth century.[5]

Breaking down this inner core of Southern City official sojourners into even smaller subsets, we would probably wish to mark off one particular group of ceremonial and sinecurial functionaries as the most promising source of leadership for examination-elite political networks. This was the pool of Han-lin Academy graduates—or the Han-lin "Club," as one recent author has dubbed it.[6] The Han-lin (literally "forest of quills") was in late imperial times the most prestigious career way station that existed for scholars of metropolitan degree status who had scored firsts in the series of examinations administered in the capital. As a reward for this achievement, attained by only a few dozen men in each triennial sitting, the inductees into the Han-lin club were sidetracked upon graduation into a series of high-prestige, rapid-advancement, but still primarily non-administrative jobs in the capital. It was exclusively from the ranks of Han-lin Academy alumni, for example, that the court selected the officers entrusted with the supervision of provincial-level examinations. And it was likewise from this same exclusive club that the throne recruited the staff for the Grand Secretariat (Nei-ko), the vestigial cabinet and still-functioning depository for state archives that had been inherited from the Ming. Since the functionaries of the Han-lin owed their precociously won official status entirely to success in the examinations, and since, moreover, their first taste of power and influence came in the acquisition of assignments as examiners, they tended more than any other office-defined subgroup within the inner examination elite to be the most alert students of current, examination-related intellectual and literary trends in the capital. This accreditation in turn made them the natural leaders and pacesetters in the world of Southern City politics and patronage. For it was inevitably to such men that other examination graduates turned when looking for future patrons or for up-to-the-moment advice on the preferences of influential examiners.

The only other officeholding group within the inner examination elite equally valued as a conduit into the world of examination fashions was to be found within the ranks of the secretaries of the Grand Secretariat (Nei-ko *she-jen*). According to Ch'ing usage, this purchased office could be filled by scholars of very low examination degree rank provided that they could capture the personal endorsement of one of the six grand secretaries. Thanks to the close personal connection provided by this recommendation procedure, the *she-jen* were commonly understood to be useful informants about the pedagogical and literary predilections of the secretaries, whose role within the Peking examinations supervisorate was a very considerable one.[7] Together, therefore, with members of the elite Han-lin club, the Nei-ko *she-jen* were highly useful for outsiders hoping to read the trends of intellectual fashion correctly. Within the rumor-filled milieu of Southern City career life, these two subgroups (the Han-lin and the *she-jen*) persistently figured as the magnets to which newcomers almost always wished to attach themselves.

IDEALS OF CAREER PATRONAGE

The foregoing generalizations about the hierarchies observable within the examination elite itself hint at our next question, which concerns the models of obligation and of loyalty that could be invoked as ambitious scholars sought out the aid of their betters in the scramble for success. The all-consuming passion of the lettered class was, of course, to pass the examinations. And with the odds so heavily weighted *against* success (one estimate suggests a 3000/1 fail rate),[8] and the substance of the examination questions so notoriously susceptible to arbitrary judgment, it was but natural that special relationships would be cultivated with knowledgeable and influential men in order to smooth the way to the top. The models that were imitated as such personal relationships were forged are not just of interest, however, as curious relics of a bizarre institution. They also merit our attention because they served as templates for more ambitious kinds of network building, such as occurred when the literati mobilized for independent political action. Rather than commonalities of political ideology, class program, or religious faith, it was instead shared ideals of how personal patronage should be offered and accepted that tended to draw the lettered elite into durable units of political cooperation. To properly comprehend the mentality of nineteenth-century literati political mobilization requires, therefore, that we preface our inquiry with some remarks about the models of interpersonal loyalty available to our protagonists.

Our first point relates to a negative attribute of the system, one that was often criticized and resented by idealists even as they participated in it. Patronage was not claimed or awarded on the basis of deep or lasting relationships. Quite the opposite: By late Ch'ing times at least, such boons as the sharing of inside information, commendation to the attentions of a high-ranking examiner, or even the loan of money for personal expenses tended normally to be offered on the basis of exceedingly superficial and short-term contacts.

No better index of this practice exists than the prominence of coincidental ties in structuring the flow of many important career-aiding services.[9] The mere fact, that is to say, of having passed an examination in the same year as another degree-holder or in a sitting when so-and-so happened to be examiner; or the happenstance of hailing from the same county or of being the offspring of a scholar attached to another member of the examination elite by this same sort of bond—purely *coincidental* relationships such as these provided perhaps the most familiar matrix within which ambitious candidates for degrees and for offices expected to obtain help. The conventionalized modes of address used to make the approach when bidding for support on these grounds themselves betray just how impersonal and weak these affinities were felt to be. Thus, the newly successful candidate characteristically introduces himself to a previously unknown examination reader as "your pupil"; the graduates of the same examination address each other as "your same-year younger brother" (*nien-ti*), while a son calling upon a same-year fellow-graduate of his father might recognize the latter as his "same-year uncle" (*nien-po*). The insistent reference to more intimate models of support-yielding relationships (teacher-pupil, fraternal, avuncular, and so on) amounts, however, to a confession that the coincidental tie was felt instinctively to be very unconvincing grounds for claiming favor. In the eyes of the more self-conscious literati public, moreover, such conventionalized mock-intimate politesse was considered vulgar and embarrassing, at least when used merely to disguise the opportunism inherent in this sort of relationship.[10]

These frequently expressed scruples notwithstanding, it is nonetheless evident that the great majority of examination candidates regularly swapped favors on just such artificial grounds. To enumerate but a few examples, we find in the papers of successful nineteenth-century scholar-officials a great many instances in which "coincidence" friends and patrons helped finance such basic services as payment of doctors' bills, family funeral expenses, or fines incurred through official malfeasance; or provided the basis for useful letters of introduction to third parties who had it within their power to name candidates to teaching or examination-reading positions.[11] Given that most higher-degree-holders had taken and passed a great many examinations (each of which in turn generated several hundred successful candidates); and given also that many successful competitors were themselves the progeny of higher-degree-holders, the range of potential patrons to whom one might turn must have been unimaginably broad. This was truly a promiscuous elite.

A second point concerns the prominence of literary or aesthetic fellowship (*wen-tzu chih chiao*) as a model in the forging of patronage relationships. Although, as we have noted, coincidental bonds tended to provide the latticework used for negotiating or claiming assistance in career-making, within this larger, rather impersonal framework, it was generally the case that commonalities of aesthetic or literary interest (however superficial) had to be established before help would be forthcoming. This was as true, we might add, in the public world of examination patronage as it was in the more private realm of personal assistance. Why then did these ties matter?

One possible answer is that the range of dependency relationships encountered by the successful lettered-class career maker in late imperial times was simply too broad for rapport to be established on the basis of more exacting kinds of affinities, such as moral or philosophical brotherhood. To judge from the few available cases where a full record survives of all personal acquaintanceships struck up during the span of a career of examination-taking and officeholding in the Ch'ing, the scholar entering the bureaucratic establishment via the examination path probably counted between three hundred and six hundred men as "mentors and friends" (*shih-yu*) — that is, as his benefactors and beneficiaries.[12] The transitory flavor such freewheeling patterns of association necessarily imparted to all relationships must have made it difficult to conceptualize them as outgrowths of the Confucian practice of treading together down the path of self culti-vation. For, according to traditional standards at least, the latter would normally have entailed prolonged collective immersion in the deciphering of canonical or philosophical texts or in mutual ethical surveillance. The presupposition that all encounters were fleeting and but a small part of the larger experience of elite life, however, tended to make the moral-philosophical mode of friendship seem somewhat too ponderous. Aesthetic fellowship was an ideal simply much better suited to the needs of the man on the run.

Apart from the functional appropriateness of belletristic friend-ship to the needs of elite life in the later imperial era, however, there must also be taken into account certain institutional and technical developments of the late Ming (1368–1644) and Ch'ing periods with-out which this particular model of fellowship would not have caught on quite to the extent that it did. One such development was the har-nessing of printing as a medium for the diffusion of model examina-tion essays during the late sixteenth century. Though this practice may have begun simply as a response to the broadening of the lower tiers of the examination-taking class that resulted from the rapid urbanization of the economy in this same century, it soon left its mark on the culture of the upper, and more established members of the examination elite as well. By the 1620s or 1630s, it had evidently become common practice for promising young scholars to constitute prose-composition drill groups or clubs (*she, wen-she*) for the specific purpose of publishing the model essays of members, thus bringing their "genius" to the attention of the examination bureaucracy in the capital.[13] If not yet quite the same thing as aestheticism, this develop-ment at least tended to re-focus the language of elite intercourse around stylistic rather than interpretive, philosophic, or ethical issues.

Probably more important as a formative influence bearing on the texture of nineteenth-century examination-elite culture, however, was the boost given the ideal of aesthetic fellowship as a result of the expansion of the role of verse composition in the imperial examina-tions during the mid-eighteenth century. Though the exchange of occasional verses had been a major pastime of the examination elite since at least T'ang and Sung times, verse writing itself had not played a major role in the examination system of the late imperial era until the Ch'ien-lung emperor chose to reintroduce it into the examinations through a series of changes undertaken between 1751 and 1760.[14] The effect of this new departure was apparently to spark a revolution in miniature in the curriculum of elite examination studies; and, in tandem with this, in the ideals of literati fellowship. For example, Weng Fang-kang (1733–1818), a northern Chinese scholar-official who had begun his climb up the examination ladder in the 1740s, records that he had to devote an additional ten years to his studies in order to master the "new" subject; for the better-educated and more cosmopolitan literati of the lower Yangtze region the gap may not have been quite so great.

Consciously or not, in shifting the emphasis in the examination system toward verse, Ch'ien-lung had acted to complete the aestheticist reorientation of patronage and friendship models among the examination elite. Personal convergence and intimacy henceforth would tend to find their ultimate expression in the sentimentality or lyricism of poetry, and not in the didacticism of prose expression. Perhaps the single best token of the effects of this mid-eighteenth century poeticization of the elite cultural curriculum is the emergence, in step with it, of a new genre for the collecting and recording of poetry itself. From the late-eighteenth century onwards, we begin to find members of the scholar elite experimenting with a new kind of anthology, knit together from samples of verse culled solely from the works of "mentors and friends" encountered in the course of the anthologizer's own life. The original models for this sort of collection were provided by two late-seventeenth-century scholar-aesthetes, Ch'en Wei-sung (1626–1682), and Wang Shih-chen (1634–1711), the works of the latter the better known of the two. However, Wang's anthology (the much-celebrated *Kan-chiu chi*, or "Collection of [verses of friends] remembered nostalgically") was not actually circulated in printed form until 1752, a fact that suggests in turn that the model did not catch on until after Ch'ien-lung's examination curriculum reform had spurred a broadening of interest in verse as a medium for recording the day-to-day events of elite intercourse. However, in the wake of its mid-eighteenth-century publication, Wang's *Kan-chiu chi* very visibly set in motion a trend toward the merging of the hitherto distinct realms of examination-system-derived friendships and the more private modes of association traditionally linked with the pursuit of aesthetic interests. By 1803, for example, the great Ch'ien-lung court litterateur, Wang Ch'ang (1725–1806), could actually publish a collection of "poetic biographies" ordered according to examination degree ranking and year.[15] Clearly, aesthetic fellowship, or the cult of aesthetic elegance (*feng-liu, feng-ya*), as it had now come to be called, had by the nineteenth century become *the* dominant mode through which men confirmed common values within the interstices of public life.[16]

The preceding observations bring us to a third, larger point concerning the ideals of patronage informing nineteenth-century lettered-class political activism. Throughout the period that occupies our attention in this and succeeding chapters, one can detect an ongoing quest for more exclusivity in the defining of key patronage relationships. The ideal of "discretion in one's public intercourse" (*shen-chiao*) exercised perennial appeal in the late Ch'ing, as indeed in earlier periods. Though one might question whether this ideal did not function more often as a way of protesting against the inescapable realities of literati life than as a guide to action, there were, nonetheless, both in the early and in the late Ch'ing, a good number of men who chose to take it seriously even at the cost of decreased chances for advancement into government office.[17] To some extent, no doubt, such behavior required the bracing of an idiosyncratic psychology, or the presence of other highly situational forces that are hard to document. Yet, at the same time, the ideal of exclusivism was very much a continuing presence within the mainstream of elite friendship culture—a perennial ideal, as it were, that was bound to flourish so long as the real patronage relationships experienced in actual life continued to be compromised by opportunistic and excessively subjective aesthetic values.

The idealization of exclusivity, moreover, was a dimension of lettered elite psychology that tended to carry over into the world of political activism with remarkable persistency throughout the late imperial era. In mid-seventeenth-century Soochow, for example, one particularly active league of literati actually named their group the Shen-chiao she, or "discretion-in-intercourse club," by which name they called attention to the fact that the league refused to accept for automatic membership the sons of established local literati families.[18] Here, quite obviously, exclusion of the favored native-son candidates from league participation was regarded as a first step toward some stronger sense of mutual loyalty, such as would be necessary if a confrontative approach to political competition in the capital was to be attempted. Likewise, early in the nineteenth century, when the style of club political cooperation was making a comeback, one finds in the writings of one of the emerging new leaders, P'an Tseng-i (1792–1853), virtually identical thoughts about the need for narrowing and deepening the basis of elite patronage contacts. Calling one day upon a grand secretary (Sung-yun) who had been an official acquaintance of P'an's father, the younger P'an was greatly vexed (or so he claimed) to find himself being offered a chance for official advancement solely on the grounds of the old "friendship" between his father and the man who sat before him as his host. "His excellency [Sung-yun] has assumed," Tseng-i wrote in his diary, "that this was the reason for my call. It had not occurred to him that there are those in this world who did not make such requests!".[19] Here again, one can hardly fail to note the close connection between the desire for more authentic patronage relationships on the one hand, and the impulse to form cliques or factions, such as the Hsuan-nan Poetry Club, which P'an was to help organize in the 1820s, on the other.

CONSTRAINTS ON CLIQUE POLITICS

If the impulse to form exclusivistic patronage cliques dominated the political imagination of the lettered elite, how then did the Ch'ing state define its position regarding the legitimacy of such activity?

At least until the governmental reverses of the early nineteenth century began to diminish their self-confidence and their independence of the Chinese lettered elite, Ch'ing rulers had been quite strongly committed to reining in such behavior. Resistance to the building of cliques (*p'eng-tang*) within the examination elite's ranks was in fact one of the most frequently reiterated political ideals of the Ch'ing monarchy. It served in Ch'ing propaganda to define one of the supposed major advantages of Manchu rule, and to contrast the current dynasty on favorable terms with its predecessor, the Ming, whose administration had been greatly troubled (some said ruined) by such behavior.[20]

The Ch'ing monarchy's devotion to eradication of clique politics did not mean, of course, that patronage networks had ceased to operate in the examination and appointments system. Quite the contrary.

The Ch'ien-lung emperor, who was one of the three mid-Ch'ing monarchs most strident in his attacks on exclusivistic groupings among the lettered class, seems consistently to have encouraged the formation of patronage groups "from above," as it were, as a means of hemming in potentially dominant bureaucratic power-wielders. During the middle years of that monarch's personal rule, for example, a clique of northern Chinese scholars had been elevated to positions of power within the examination system as a means of under-cutting the influence of a much-feared minister of southern Chinese background (Chang T'ing-yü), inherited from the previous reign. And, later on in his life, Ch'ien-lung seems knowingly to have tolerated the growth of a rival, Manchu-led clique (under the leadership of the much-vilified Ho-shen) as a force within the examinations and job-allocation system, perhaps in order to counterbalance the influence of the northern scholar group.[21]

Yet, in condoning and in using such vertical networks for imperial purposes, the Manchu state was not really contradicting itself. Rather, it was confirming what its ideologues consistently maintained — namely, that loyalty groups of this sort were attractive to scholars and bureaucrats only for selfish and degraded motives. There was no room, in such sponsored cliques, for a sense of exclusive superiority or honor, as one recent student of mid-Ch'ing factions has pointed out. And when, as sometimes happened, an occasional scholar or official took it into his head to claim such higher ideological status for his affinity group, over and against all others, he could expect to be firmly denounced and punished as a warning against any further slippage back in the direction of Ming literati behavior.[22]

Though some twentieth-century scholars have seen this Ch'ing aversion to cliques as part of a sustained dynasty-long pattern of attacks on Chinese elites, it is fairly clear that no single, overarching policy guided government attempts to control lettered-elite political behavior in this area.[23] In fact, three somewhat disconnected episodes of anti-*p'eng-tang* institutional and normative legislation can be identified. The first, which unfolded during a nine-year period (1651–1660) in the very early Ch'ing, took place against a background of bitter political warfare within the newly ascendant Manchu conquest nobility. During this period, we see a rapid proliferation of rules banning such "Ming-inspired" practices as the formation of local literary societies, the "idle" founding of local academies, the congressing together of lower-degree-holders for purposes of challenging local officials, or the submission by lower-degree-holders of opinions on government matters during examinations or at any other time. The concern in this generation of legislation, one notes, seems very largely to be with the threat of literati misbehavior in a *local* political setting. And one suspects that the reason for it is that both the emperor and his Manchu aristocratic rivals in the power struggle were jockeying to prevent each other from collaborating with Ming-remnant local scholar groupings in the newly conquered south.[24]

A second assault on literati-clique activism, beginning in the late K'ang-hsi reign (1661–1722), and extending into the reign of his successor, the Yung-cheng emperor, appears to have been provoked by literati involvement on the losing side of a prolonged struggle over the succession that raged from 1708 to 1723. As a young ruler, we might note with some irony, K'ang-hsi had made felicitous use of *wen-she* loyalty networks among the southern literati to weaken the influence within the bureaucracy of his rivals, including a former regent and his allies among the pre-conquest Chinese collaborator class.[25] However, in 1708, when certain important literati leaders refused to join the emperor in breaking with the first-named heir-apparent, Yin-jeng, institutional changes were introduced to block such potential support from evolving into a full-fledged legitimist faction aligned with the discontented ex-heir-apparent. One of the more important of these changes was the elimination of the so-called "joint nominations" (*hui-t'ui*) procedure for deciding on promotions among the higher-level officials. This procedure, which had its roots in the Ming practice of diffusing authority over personnel evaluations into the hands of several competing official agencies in the capital, had provided for the participation of a wide circle of official actors in all such promotional decisions. Not just ministry chiefs, but also the staff of the Metropolitan Censorate, a general oversight body, had been allowed to voice their opinions, in the hope that attention might thus be called to instances of ministerial collusion aimed at screening miscreants from exposure. However, in 1712, as factional bickering over the succession reached a peak of intensity, K'ang-hsi suddenly terminated the *hui-t'ui* procedure. Though it might not have been foreseen that the change would endure, the old procedure was in fact never revived; and indeed, by 1730 or so, a new highly secretive inner palace secretariat, called the Grand Council (Chün-chi-ch'u) had begun to take over from the board chiefs the business of deliberating over important appointments.[26]

A third round of moves intended to discredit or control the literati's clique-building instincts came under Ch'ien-lung. This time, however, the brunt of the attack fell neither upon local *wen-she* nor upon the personnel-selection system in the capital, but rather upon the censorate itself, an institution whose powers had already been somewhat curtailed under K'ang-hsi. A slightly closer look at the evolving role of this body is here required, therefore, in order for the full significance of Ch'ien-lung's ideological onslaughts against the "abuse" of censorial power by literati cliques to become comprehensible.

In the rhetoric of late imperial politics, the office of censor was often described as embodying the ideal of providing a "pathway for words" (*yen-lu*) to the throne.[27] Were this avenue open, it was believed, words critical of imperial or high bureaucratic policy that ought to be heeded might instead be systematically suppressed by the imperial executive establishment. Under the impress of this ideology, the sixty-eight senior and junior censors who served the late Ch'ing throne in the capacity of "speaking officials" (*yen-kuan*) were encouraged to regard themselves as transmitters of rumor or hearsay (*feng-wen*)—that is, of information about officials and their behavior that came to them through informal channels, rather than through the vertical channels of regular bureaucratic documentation.[28] The monarchy was by no means willing to concede that all such gossip was legitimate as a basis for complaints against specific employees of the government, and Ch'ing rulers could on occasion be quite abusive and vindictive in their response to scholars who took their mission as censorial muckrakers too literally.

Yet, even at its mid-eighteenth-century zenith of power and success, the Ch'ing monarchy was still prepared to recognize a role for literati rumor networks within this censor-mediated information-gathering process. The recruitment policies used for appointing new censors demonstrate this role. Even though approximately half of all such appointees were Manchus (and thus men who lacked local or, in most cases, even examination-system connections), a significant proportion of the Han Chinese quota for appointments was always filled directly from the Han-lin Academy.[29] Since such men would have had no previous exposure to regular bureaucratic administration, and were, presumably, without "old friends" among the higher officials, they could have discharged their office as imperial monitors only through making use of private connections among examination-system friends or kinsmen. More explicitly still, the court from time to time even undertook to establish that kinship and same-province (*t'ung-hsiang*) networks among the examination elite were legitimate sources of hearsay by punishing Han Chinese censors who had failed to report rumors about corrupt local officials. Thus, in 1724, after the Shansi governor, Sa-ha-liang, and an assistant had been proven guilty of extracting heavy bribes from their subordinates (thereby forcing local officials to squeeze the taxpayers for the extra revenue), a Shansi-born censor, Lu Ping-chang, was punished for failing to submit an indictment before the scandal had come to light. As a native of Shansi, Ch'ien-lung argued, Lu must have been aware of these goings on. His silence therefore betokened complicity.[30] Similarly, in 1786 and 1793, several more censors lost their posts or were demoted in rank for failing to transmit hostile comments on certain local officials presumed to have been current among their fellow-provincials at home and in the capital before the miscreants were brought out into the open by other means.[31] Comments by the emperor in connection with these cases indicate, in addition, that he had a quite specific notion of how the gagged censors ought to have received the intelligence in question. Neighbors and relatives or "friends" who had arrived in the capital from the home province, or corresponded with these censors, surely must have been talking endlessly of the dismal goings-on in local administration, Ch'ien-lung noted sardonically. How then could the censors in question plead ignorance? Thus, as Censor Lu learned, perhaps too late, it was anticipated that informal examination-elite friendship networks would equip the "speaking officials" for their role as imperial watchdogs.

This continuing commitment to an institutionalized role for literati informational networks in exposing bureaucratic corruption brought with it, however, a major headache for the monarchs of the middle Ch'ing period. How was the throne to protect against the possibility that such channels would be preempted by the literati for purposes of pushing an out-group examination clique into power? Moreover, if the throne remained attracted to the tactic of ruling the bureaucracy by playing patronage cliques against each other, what was to prevent leaders of ousted cliques from using examination cli-

ents among the censors as mouthpieces for vengeful campaigns directed against those who had robbed them of their glory?[32] It was this
particular dilemma that troubled the Ch'ien-lung emperor virtually
from the beginning to the end of his reign, and led to his ceaseless propaganda campaign against the "Ming-inspired" excesses he pretended
to keep discovering in the attacks emanating from the censorate.
Under Ch'ien-lung, as indeed under his son, we therefore find the censorate becoming the target of ever stricter normative vigilance, with
individual censors being forced to accept ever more demanding standards of evidential support, even at the cost of compromising the utility of the *yen-lu* itself.

A few examples will suffice to convey the flavor of this imperial
paranoia, and to suggest the kind of negative influence it must have
had. Consider, first, Ch'ien-lung's response to the censor Ch'ien
Feng's impeachment of the Manchu governor of Shantung, Kuo-t'ai,
in 1782, and to the follow-up impeachments provoked by this action.
During the 1780s, when Ch'ien entered office as a censor, the imperially condoned Ho-shen clique was very much dominant in the
upper echelons of the bureaucracy. The Han Chinese northern
group, then out of power, had been trying for several years, without
success, to produce evidence of maladministration by one or more of
its rivals. Finally, in 1782, Ch'ien managed to put together a strong
case against the governor of Shantung, Kuo-t'ai, who was known to
be in the Ho-shen camp. By carefully coordinating with a certain Liu
Yung, then vice-president of the censorate, Ch'ien was able to make
the charges stick, and Kuo-t'ai was dismissed and eventually executed.[33]

Censor Ch'ien, however, had several very close literati friends and
patrons in Peking who were clients of the northern clique, while Liu
Yung was the son of Liu T'ung-hsun, the patriarch of that latter
group. The emperor was thus never quite able to bring himself to follow to their source the leads that Ch'ien had revealed, fearing that, if
he did so, he would be playing into the hands of those hotter heads
among the opposition who wanted a total, Ming-style witch hunt
against the Ho-shen faction.

The kind of fears that Ch'ien's actions had sown in the bosom of
the emperor were soon afterwards to be publicly articulated, when
another Han Chinese censor, Ch'in Ch'ing, dared to suggest to the
throne that the tactic of squeezing subordinates for which Kuo-t'ai

had been punished was in fact universal, and was producing widespread instances of embezzlement of reserve accounts by local magistrates who needed quick sources of "gift" money. Ch'in was bluntly asked what specific evidence he had against individual malefactors. And, when it turned out that Ch'in had no specific cases in mind, he was treated to the following highly revealing torrent of abuse:

His submission consists entirely of empty talk, and is of no practical use. Its example must not be allowed to be imitated. Previously, in the matter of Ch'ien Feng's impeachment of Kuo-t'ai, . . . Kuo-t'ai was punished only after a special investigatory commission had found certain of Ch'ien's charges accurate. Moreover, We had long since been hearing unpleasant things of this Kuo-t'ai. Our immediate action upon his impeachment was therefore not merely in response to Ch'ien Feng's submission. Then, too, there have been other cases [of corruption], such as those of Wang Lin-wang and Ch'en Hui-tsu, where word had been circulating for some time about the guilt of the parties involved. Although we fervently hoped that there would be an exposure by the censorate, none was ever forthcoming. . . . How well this shows that, where Han Chinese graduates of the examination system are involved, officials will always protect each other, and the scandal will never be brought to light! Had Kuo-t'ai been a Han Chinese, We suspect that even [so righteous a fellow as] Ch'ien Feng might never have gotten around to censuring him!

And then came the inevitable cadence about how such falsely righteous cliquishness, if allowed to go unchastened, would swiftly bring down the dynasty, as it had the Ming:

The evil practices of the censors of the late Ming had their beginnings in just this kind of manufacture of claims of corruption with no real evidence, by which method rival cliques set about making things hot for each other. Once this had begun, the opponents leagued themselves into parties, each trying to exclude the other from power. Before long, they ceased caring about whether their actions benefited the state, and even came to prize the experience of being subjected to beatings at court as evidence of their own righteousness. This kind of thing is the seed of plague! It must not be allowed to happen in a properly ruled state, and We cannot condone it![34]

What Ch'ien-lung was really saying, in effect, was that he saw it as more dangerous to let Chinese examination-system cliques, such as Ch'ien Feng's, acquire the lustre of a righteous opposition proven correct, than to tolerate a certain amount of corruption among his Manchu and Chinese courtiers. Hence the refusal to allow Ch'ien Feng to be seen as a hero of censorial idealism; hence the quashing of successor impeachments building upon Ch'ien's revelations; and hence (though it is not mentioned in the edicts from which we have quoted) the cautious avoidance of any actions that might produce unwanted censorial martyrs for oppositional idealism to feed upon. And hence also the consistent and angry refusal to look any further into the matter of Ho-shen's squeeze networks and the effect they were having upon provincial government finances.

Another example of how the effectiveness of the censorate was undercut by this imperial determination to prevent it from being used as an instrument of moralized combat between rival examination cliques occurred only a few years later, in 1799. As might have been predicted, the Ch'ien-lung emperor's obsession with avoiding a full-scale inquiry into the misdeeds of Ho-shen (lest he thereby encourage a witch-hunt among Ho's enemies) led before long to runaway corruption on the part of the condoned court cabal. Shortly after the Ch'ien-lung emperor's death, in 1799, it was revealed that Ho had amassed a fortune equal to two years' regular government expenditures by packing key posts in the provincial bureaucracy with self-compromised protégés and then extracting huge bribes from them as a price for guarding them against disciplinary action.[35] To make matters worse, this spreading conspiracy of corruption had occurred at a time when, unbeknownst to Ch'ien-lung, the state was no longer able to condone it without exposing itself to serious risks of rebellion. The same protective links to the Ho-shen clique at court that had secured the tenure of so many provincial officials could also, it was soon discovered, be used for screening from the throne embarrassing disclosures about unsuppressed lawlessness, ineffective military action against rebels, or revolt-prompting official transgressions. The White Lotus Rebellion that tore apart the western provinces of Szechuan and Shensi for eight years (1796–1804) and cost the government three years' revenues to suppress, was widely believed by critics to have been encouraged by practices of this kind.[36]

Upon taking power in 1799, therefore, Ch'ien-lung's son, the Chia-ch'ing emperor, found himself faced with an even tougher test of his political ideals than his father had faced in the Kuo-t'ai case. Should he respect the arguments that kept coming in from officials serving in the western provinces, which blamed the government's problems on the disruptive influence of the chiliastic White Lotus cult, and which played down the provocative role of official squeeze, mistreatment, and cover-ups? Or should he heed the words of the censorial and Han-lin opposition, led (as ever) by men with close personal ties to the northern-scholar clique, which emphasized the culpability of the corruption-tainted bureaucracy?[37] According to this latter group, only a small number of the rebels were true religious fanatics. The great majority, they claimed, had been driven into the arms of the insurgents by magistrates who were compelled by their superiors in Ho-shen's clique to squeeze the people mercilessly. If the emperor wanted to end the rebellion, therefore, he would have to launch a massive purge of the bureaucracy, both in order to remove guilty officials and to send a signal to those who replaced them that such a lapse in the standards of official morality would not be tolerated.[38] Acting in the hope that this latter position would be accepted, the Han-lin compiler Hung Liang-chi took the daring step of relaying to the throne through his former examiner, Chu Kuei, as well as through other contacts, an impeachment containing the names of over forty active and retired high-ranking officials. And he even criticized the new emperor for having taken no action of his own to punish the men named in the indictment.[39]

Though the background and the concrete issues at stake were new, the choice was not really that different from what it had been in the Kuo-t'ai case: to condone corruption (within limits), or to risk a frenzied war of factions by granting the critics the high moral stature that came with total vindication of their charges. Not surprisingly, considering the traditions in which he had been raised, Chia-ch'ing chose the former course, though not without some hesitation. If Hung's list of accusees were targeted for investigation, Chia-ch'ing pontificated, a spirit of vindictiveness would be automatically encouraged, and the destructive contentiousness of late-Ming politics would be revived.[40] Worse still, Hung had lobbied for the purge he wanted by self-consciously identifying his fellow critics as the true representatives of literati cultural ideas. "Sometimes these days," Chia-ch'ing complained, "baseless tales are circulated through poems or belletristic prose documents, the author of which puffs himself up with pride in the conviction that he is a 'literary man of fashion.' How can We endure that at a time of maximum glory of Our empire, such as the present, there should be a reversion to the despicable habits of the late Ming, when [the literati] took to echoing each other's opinions as if they alone had truth on their side?"[41] Therewith, Hung was banished to the western frontier as a caution to others, and the emperor resolved to narrow the compass of the purge to only the most egregiously corrupt.[42]

Such, then, were the ground rules that the Ch'ing had devised in order to forestall the dangers it saw implicit in literati factionalism. There remains, of course, the question of just how effective state propaganda really was in persuading the literati that the way of "cliques" was indeed so perverse. One modern scholar has argued that many late-eighteenth-century literati really did come, tacitly, to accept the notion that exclusivistic cliques could only represent selfish or clandestine interests.[43] Support for his view, moreover, can be found in the testimony and behavior of the elder leaders of the northern scholar group—men such as Weng Fang-kang or Chu Kuei. Even during the ascendancy of the Ho-shen cabal, for example, Weng had continued to decry the false righteousness of Ming-style literati oppositionism.[44] And Chu, who came eventually to orchestrate Chia-ch'ing's minimalist purge of the post-Ho-shen bureaucracy, was widely reported to have made it his principle to avoid moralistic rhetoric or vindictiveness when dealing with the small number of cases that actually came up for inquiry. Instead, his preference was for keeping as many as possible of the former party in power, while meanwhile insisting on the feasibility of their self-redemption. It would seem from all this that Ch'ien-lung's preachings had not been entirely without effect, and that the literati had in fact been somewhat discouraged from idealizing late-Ming politics.[45]

Yet it can be misleading to confine our attentions to these few and rather elderly power-holders in the early Chia-ch'ing bureaucracy. Even among their protégés within the next generation, there was no shortage of scholars who took just the opposite view. For example, Yao Nai, who was one of the non-officeholding literati associated with Weng Fang-kang ever since the 1760s, wrote a widely read tract sometime early in the nineteenth century in which the Ch'ing government was taken to task for its failure to encourage a spirit of outspokenness among the students at the Han-lin.[46]

Even more openly critical of the Ch'ing position, however, was the scholar-official Wang Ch'ang, whom we have previously encountered as the spokesman par excellence for the aesthetic-fellowship ideal of literati patronage relations. According to one of his biographers, Wang responded to the exposure of Ho-shen in 1799 by a deepening of interest in earlier, Ming-era traditions of literati moral protest, and by complaining to his friends and protégés of the "spinelessness" and "lack of character" common among the lettered elite of the current age. Out of this vexation was conceived the project of compiling a history of the Tung-lin Academy, the southern Chinese philosophical center from which late-Ming partisan movements had taken their scholastic cue. And from this in turn grew the idea of assembling a register of all of the empire's academies, as a prelude, it would seem, to a reform of the curriculum so as to revive respect for the Tung-lin's traditions.[47]

For Wang, one is forced to conclude, the Ho-shen affair had been proof that the official Ch'ing views on factions now needed to be reversed by a more sympathetic reevaluation of the late Ming epoch. From this might come an alternative and more positive vision of literati political cohesion. To judge from the interest shown in Wang's project by others in his entourage, views identical to Wang's own were becoming fairly widespread by the early nineteenth century. Here, perhaps, was the sign that a new beginning was about to occur, that an attempt would be forthcoming to infuse factional activism with moral idealism and political legitimacy once more.

THE HSUAN-NAN POETRY CLUB AS A LITERATI FACTION

In the wake of the Ho-shen's demise, as the reactions of Hung Liang-chi and Wang Ch'ang so well illustrate, the leaders of literati fashion had already begun to overcome some of the awe that had inhibited independent, idealistic collective political action by members of their class during the heyday of Ch'ing rule. It is therefore hardly surprising to discover that the overall position of literati loyalty networks within the Ch'ing political system began to change and to acquire a much more positive and idealistic character as we move forward into the early decades of the nineteenth century.

The first instance of an ideologically self-confident literati grouping asserting itself at the national political level came in the closing years (roughly 1814–1820) of the Chia-ch'ing reign. At the center of this pioneering movement was a group that called itself the Hsuan-nan Poetry Club (Hsuan-nan shih-she), a quasi-literary association of Southern City officials and Han-lin scholars that for a time was able to exercise considerable influence over the determination of candidates for key posts within the provincial mandarinate. It is this network and its activities that will be the object of our attention for the remainder of this chapter.

Before launching directly into the analysis of the Hsuan-nan Club, however, we ought to take careful note of the fact that the Club was only a first step, and not in itself the culmination of a trend. A fuller flowering of literati activism, more truly kindred in spirit to the tabooed Tung-lin Party of the late Ming, was to come only after the Club's influence had waned, and its particular political strategies and scholastic ideals had lost their grip upon the imagination of the Hanlin and the junior officials of the capital. It is only with the emergence, in the 1830s, of a successor group—the so-called "Spring Purification" circle (see chapter 2)—that we begin to observe all the telltale symptoms of Ming literati activism: factional recruitment within the interstices of the examination system itself; the prescription of a narrowed curriculum of study to which aspirants for membership were expected to conform; and, most symptomatic of all, the development of an oppositionist power base through the exercise of influence within the metropolitan censorate.

Though still too cautious for such tactics, the men active in this inaugural phase of late Ch'ing literati self-assertion were to pave the way, through their efforts—and, most important, through their failures—for this shift toward a more radical, more Ming style of political mobilization in the second phase. The key link here indeed is failure: the failure, that is, of the relatively modest program of bureaucratic retrenchment that came, during the 1820s, to constitute the principal political goal of this Hsuan-nan Club "party" within the bureaucracy. As a consequence of that setback, there would take place a fundamental shift in attitudes about how independent literati influence might be used to "revive" the condition of the dynastic government—as the goal was usually expressed. The patient, "participationist" approach of the Hsuan-nan Club activists, who had sought power within the responsible administrative roles of the territorial bureaucracy, thus would yield eventually to a more aggressive oppositional strategy, geared to pressuring the bureaucratic establishment from the sidelines. And the climate would thus be created, by the early 1830s, for a full-blown revival of the late Ming model of literati political activism.

The longer term significance of the Hsuan-nan Club, then, is that of an experiment that failed. And, in our analysis, we shall accordingly concentrate on the background to this failure, emphasizing in particular how political obstacles within the Ch'ing governmental system snarled the efforts of one unusually vigorous Club member, Lin Tse-hsu, at reform of the bureaucracy from within. The impact of this failure will be taken up in chapter 2.

AS A BUREAUCRATIC PATRONAGE CLIQUE

Several of the crucial distinguishing features of the Hsuan-nan Club patronage network, as it functioned during the zenith of its power in the late 1810s and early 1820s, have already been remarked upon. They might here be usefully reiterated, however, as prelude to the analysis that follows.

As a self-conscious literati political faction, the Hsuan-nan Club dates from 1814, although, as we shall see, the patterns of association that linked its members together date back into the last years of the Ch'ien-lung period. The participants in this nexus modeled their enterprise, in outward form as in self-conception, after the aesthetic fellowship circles dominant in Ch'ing examination-elite culture since at least the middle of the preceding century. In functional terms, however, the purpose of this grouping was unambiguously careerist. It was to help both Club members and their friends gain inside-track consideration for transfer into middle-level posts within the territorial administration, a sector of the Ch'ing bureaucracy that had been thrown into turmoil in the aftermath of a second White Lotus Rebellion in 1813.

Two points that need to be noted about the Club concern, once again, the choices made by its leaders with regard to collective political strategy once affiliates had begun to acquire a significant degree of influence within the mandarinate. First, participation in, rather than moral censure of, the territorial administration was seen as the most effective tactic for purging it of corrupt influences. Second, there was a tacit agreement to avoid involvement in examination-system politics. No recorded effort was made to forge a new intellectual orthodoxy or to use the examination system to recruit new members into the circle. In effect, the Club did not plan its own reproduction. Accordingly, its political influence waned rapidly after 1827, the year of the failure of the Club's first and only major confrontation with hostile entrenched bureaucratic interests.[48]

Of all the features we have enumerated, perhaps the most unusual, given the perennial attachment of the literati to oppositionist causes, is the enthusiasm for jobs in provincial government. Accordingly, let us begin with some consideration of the range of factors that made this collective goal seem so attractive.

One circumstance that goes far toward explaining this peculiarity of the Hsuan-nan Club was the exceedingly close set of patronage relationships binding clubmen of the Hsuan-nan circle to the older generation of literati-courtiers we have dubbed the northern-scholar clique. Altogether, almost half of the thirteen Southern City literati-officials who banded together to form the Hsuan-nan Poetry Club in 1814 counted themselves as students of Weng Fang-kang, Chu Yun, or Chu Kuei—the three longest-lived of the men who had originally made up that earlier circle of northern Chinese litterateurs.[49] In the normal course of events, perhaps, such connections would have counted for little, for the influence of such imperially sponsored literati cliques seldom survived the death of the ruler who had created them. However, Chu Kuei's northern clique was to prove the outstanding exception to this rule. Their credit having been established by two decades of prolonged resistance to Ho-shen, the venerable Chu and his compeers became, under Chia-ch'ing, a kind of semi-secret in-group at court, to which the emperor habitually turned whenever he wished to bypass entrenched bureaucratic evaluations.[50] In this manner, a closed literati friendship network came gradually to control the loyalties of many of the new young talents just then beginning to make their mark within the regular bureaucracy. Against such a background, the hopeful young men of the Hsuan-nan Club, themselves also firmly locked into this same northern-clique patronage network, came naturally to look to the territorial service as a setting where their own collective ambitions could best be realized.

In chronological terms, the influence of the northern-scholar patronage network within the job-allocation procedures of the regional administration can be seen as having developed in two somewhat separate phases. First was the Chia-ch'ing "restoration" itself—a modest effort at restaffing certain key middle-level slots in the provincial administrative hierarchy with virgin Han-lin talent recruited through "northern" literati connections that lasted from 1799 until about 1805. From the cohort of literati-bureaucrats drawn into office during these years there was eventually to emerge a new circle of senior provincial officials whose names are now perhaps forgotten, but who, in their day, were perceived as heralds of a new era of literati ascendancy within the provincial managerial establishment—men such as Chiang Yu-hsien, Juan Yuan, Sun Yü-t'ing, and Tung Chiao-tseng, to list only the best known.[51]

A second phase was ushered in in the last decade of the Chia-ch'ing reign (1810–1820), when this initial nucleus of literati reformers achieved sufficient bureaucratic seniority to take over as power-brokers within the world of private literati patronage. Occurring more or less simultaneously with the eruption of a second major political crisis at the Chia-ch'ing court (this one prompted by the White Lotus Rebellion of 1813–1814), this coming of age of the Chia-ch'ing restoration generation was ultimately to bring about a further massive expansion of the influence of literati networks within the recruitment procedures of the territorial bureaucracy. The formation of the Hsuan-nan Club itself in 1814 was one expression of this new influence.

Skipping, in the interest of brevity, over the first of these two episodes, we can more profitably begin our scrutiny of this gradual buildup of northern-clique power by examining the pattern of leadership exercised by the veterans of the 1799 restoration during the second phase, as they themselves climbed astride the seat of power during the twilight years of the Chia-ch'ing era. We shall here concentrate, in particular, on the figure of Chiang Yu-hsien (1766–1830), the first in this restoration cohort to be promoted to the rank of viceroy. In 1811, Chiang, still only eleven years past his graduation from the Han-lin Academy, was elevated to the office of governor general of Kwangtung and Kwangsi provinces—an astonishingly quick rise up the ladder of success for a Han Chinese official.[52] From this vantage, moreover, Chiang at once set about the business of promoting into office under him a string of Southern City literati-officials brought to his attention through a network of Peking "friends" and "mentors" tracing back, ultimately, to Chiang's own examiner, Weng Fang-kang. As this particular recruitment connection began to acquire visibility and permanence in the closing years of the Chia-ch'ing period, a small band of Weng's Southern City disciples, led by Ch'en Yung-kuang and Wu Sung-liang, organized themselves to act, in effect, as Chiang's agents in the capital, thus bringing the Hsuan-nan poetry circle into existence.[53] Here, however, our immediate concern is with the range of background factors that allowed Chiang to carve out such an ambitious role for himself, and with the influence of his particular style of leadership upon the ideology of reform eventually to be embraced by the Hsuan-nan clubmen.

Of crucial importance in facilitating the emergence of this talent-spotting system was the shock administered by the 1813 rebellion, and the emperor's attendant decision to undo some of the snarl of regulations that normally kept control over the appointments firmly in the hands of the ministry chiefs in Peking. Without getting too deeply involved here in the technicalities of the Ch'ing appointments and promotions system, we might characterize its modus operandi under pre-1813 conditions as depending upon a careful balance of power between the regulation-obsessed staff officials in Peking and the task-oriented anti-regulationist executives who oversaw the operations of regional government in the field. Though acknowledging the rule books to be grievously overloaded with regulations affecting personnel administration, Ch'ing emperors nonetheless preferred to deal with requests for waivers on a case-by-case basis, rather than by permanent cutbacks in the volume of the procedural regulations.[54]

In 1813, however, the outbreak of a second major northern Chinese religious rebellion, developing within less than a decade of the suppression of the first, seems to have brought home to the throne the real danger of continuing on with such an unrealistically demanding arsenal of procedural norms. Post-mortems on the second rebellion were unanimous in their verdict that the rebellion's leaders could have been exposed and the uprising perhaps even preempted had officials been under less pressure to doctor their reports and court logs so as to stay out of trouble with iron-fisted "rule" men in the capital.[55] Acknowledging the validity of this complaint, Chia-ch'ing quickly announced a suspension of several major personnel review criteria, and promised to have the Board of Civil Appointments review the entire inventory of rules with an eye to making more deletions still.[56]

Along with this stunning retreat from a control emphasis in the personnel-evaluations system, moreover, Chia-ch'ing also began, after

1813, to show an increased tolerance for literati network influence in the selection of new Southern City talent for first-job positions in the provincial mandarinate. Mid-Ch'ing administrative practice governing such appointments had been geared here too, as in the evaluations system, to minimizing the possibilities for the exercise of such influence by the gubernatorial executives themselves. Tradition had limited to a mere handful each year the number of entry-level positions in the middle tiers of regional government available to Southern City officials. Furthermore, qualifications for such appointments were exceedingly strict and seniority-biased. There had not, therefore, usually been very much room for favoritism.[57] However, under Chia-ch'ing's direction, the final ten years or so of that emperor's rule saw a dramatic reversal of this policy, too. Now, vastly expanded annual cohorts of Han-lin alumni began to swarm into the regional intendancies and prefectureships that dominated this important middle level of provincial administration, and from there to rise quickly into top-level supervisory positions directly under the gubernatorial executives.[58]

As this stream turned gradually into a torrent, moreover, there began to appear unmistakable signs that these new assignments were being made in secret consultation with an in-group of high-level officials, including Chiang and several other northern-clique protégés occupying court positions in Peking.[59] The precise thoughts that had stirred the aging Chia-ch'ing to go along with this kind of privatization of recruitment practices remain unclear, since there was never any public announcement that assignment policies had in fact shifted in favor of the literati. However it seems fairly clear that there was a close relationship between deregulation within the personnel evaluations system and privatization of sub-gubernatorial assignment procedures. With the discretionary privileges of the top provincial executives so markedly on the rise, perhaps the monarchy had come to accept, also, that the quality of personnel occupying middle-level positions would inevitably become more critical to the smooth operation of the personnel system—for it was the intendants and prefects, as Chiang pointed out to the emperor late in 1813, who would now have to fill the vacuum in the evaluations system that had been created by the attenuation of the formal review regulations.[60] Bowing before this new necessity, Chia-ch'ing seems to have resigned himself after 1813 to the need for consultations with his inner literati advisers before approving any further nominees for these crucial assignments. And, at one juncture, that weary ruler had even allowed himself to be publicly lectured by Governor General Chiang on the legitimacy of the court's going along with such a remarkable degree of privatized influence inside the recruitment system. From Chiang's point of view, at least, such an arrangement was not to be confused with "factionalism" (*tang-yüan*) in the traditionally perjorative sense. Rather, it was to be understood as "cooperation motivated by admiration," designed, as Chiang put it, to ensure that "like-minded men would come to the fore, improving each other by mutual example, just as the entwined roots of the miscanthus come up from the ground in bunches when the stalk is pulled."[61] In the aftermath of 1813, it would seem, even such venerable Ch'ing beliefs as the assumed moral depravity of literati cliques were going by the boards.

To return, however, to the Hsuan-nan Club, there is much evidence to link the appearance of this organization in 1814 to the growth of Chiang Yu-hsien's influence as an insider within the Southern City job-allocations system. In point of fact, Chiang's emergence as an invisible eminence within that system was tied to the simultaneous elevation into high court office of two other Weng Fang-kang examination protégés: Ying-ho (1771–1839) and Ts'ao Chen-yung (1755–1835).[62] Late in 1813, as part of a general renovation of the Peking ministries, Ying-ho and Ts'ao were both given major promotions, and Ts'ao was made a grand secretary. Their joint assumption of high positions in the capital, coming hard in the wake of Chiang Yu-hsien's rise to top office in the provinces, had now brought into existence a very remarkable power alignment, whereby the disciples of a single, senior literati-courtier (Master Weng) now simultaneously occupied powerful patronage roles at court and in the territorial bureaucracy. With the emperor himself now very much inclined to bypass regular promotion procedures, the opportunities for literati network-building and influence within the processes of official recruitment were now more open than they had been in anyone's memory.

The Hsuan-nan Poetry Club, one must conclude, was brought into existence late in 1814 to exploit these opportunities. More explicitly, the point of the Club's founding must have been to regularize social contacts between Weng's many students in the capital, including, on the one hand, five of the nine Southern City officials and

Han-lin who actually joined the Club at its inception, and, on the other, the three senior officials (Chiang, Ts'ao, and Ying-ho) who were now clearly privy to the emperor's inner councils when decisions on promotions and transfers into the provincial bureaucracy were to be taken. Weng himself, still alive and healthy at the time the Club came into existence, was presumably to act as a shared focus of loyalty.[63] But the real point of the Club, we may infer, was to give permanent shape to the new northern-clique protégé network now firmly entrenched in the center of power. The Hsuan-nan Club was to be, in effect, a clearing house for news and evaluations of prospective literati talents between the several individuals tied together in this Weng-student grid: Chiang, in Kwangtung; Ying-ho and Ts'ao Chen-yung in the palace; and Weng's disciples Ch'en Yung-kuang and Wu Sung-liang in the Southern City. Using the conventionalized literati media of laudatory couplets inscribed upon paintings, or dedications to collections of their friends' literary works, the Weng-student network would henceforth seek to keep itself well-informed, under the guise of purely belletristic activity, about the more promising Southern City candidates for provincial office.[64] The literati of the Hsuan-nan Club were thus in the enviable position of enjoying access to an inside track in the provincial appointments system. It was scarcely to be wondered, therefore, that they would look to this particular sector of the imperial bureaucracy as the obvious place to organize themselves as a loyal party of reform.

AS A BROTHERHOOD OF AESTHETE-CONNOISSEURS

So far, we have stressed the network functions of the Hsuan-nan Club, and we have presented it as a kind of informational grapevine for spreading word of the merits of approved Southern City candidates to contacts within the Weng Fang-kang student nexus so as to help influence their prospects for transfer into the regional administration. The Club was more, however, than a network. In line with the general early-century trend toward investing literati patronage activities with an idealistic character, the leaders of the Hsuan-nan Club devoted much attention, as well, to the elaboration of a particular set of cultural models, intended to idealize the activities upon which they had embarked. The adoption of the club (*she*) or "aesthetic fellowship" format in 1814 was itself, for example, very much related to the desire to project a specific model of how literati in general ought to interact with each other. And this same need for idealizing images of high literati friendship traditions seems also to explain the care Club leaders displayed in choosing a calendar of regular meeting days and an agenda of poetic topics for verse composition.

Taking up, then, the question of how the Peking "central" of this Hsuan-nan Club network sought to project and legitimize the image of its activities, we can distinguish at least two different levels of self-conscious symbolic statement.

At the most obvious level, Club rules provided for an artificially small and fixed number of guests to be included at the group's regular gatherings, thereby conveying the message that the men therein conjoined were a closed circle, and not much interested in recruiting newcomers. As we survey, for example, the rosters of several meetings held during the initial years of the Club's existence, we note that only seven "poets" were called upon to attend any one gathering.[65] A Club commemorative scroll prepared in 1824 tells us that the ritual number of participants had by then been increased to nine. But this was still a trifling assembly, compared, for example, to the huge throngs that assembled when examiners feted their students at the Chiang-t'ing pavilion, in the southern part of the Ming Hsuan-nan ward.[66] The impression that they intended to convey, of course, was one of politically unthreatening aloofness from the hurly-burly of examination system patronage seeking—an impression that seems, in fact, to square with the non-self-reproductive character of the Hsuan-nan nexus itself. A lofty superiority to the vulgar world of examination-clique politics was one conception, then, that screened the Hsuan-nan Club from identification as a "faction."

As we penetrate a bit deeper into the world of Hsuan-nan Club ritual, however, we uncover a second layer of symbolic statement—this one addressing the problem of how literati culture itself, rather than any particular group, might be justified in assuming a role within elite politics. The issue was tackled, as ever, through allusion to specific historical model personalities, rather than through direct statement. But the selection of literati heroes that the clubmen chose to venerate seems to reveal a very self-conscious attachment to the scholastic and personality values that had been favored by the northern-clique scholars of the Ch'ien-lung court. In these values was a second source of legitimacy. Let us see if we can discover what it was.

There were in fact only four model literati figures that appeared as frequent objects of Hsuan-nan Club veneration or collective imitation. The first was Cheng Hsuan (127–200), the Han-dynasty scholar commonly accepted, in Ch'ing times, as the founder of the discipline of textual studies (*k'ao-chü*). According to a number of different sources, one of the original seven members of the Club, Hu Ch'eng-kung (1776–1832), had taught his fellow clubmen the habit of celebrating the supposed early-August birthday of this scholarly giant each summer.[67] The point of this celebration was not, however, to associate the Club specifically with Han-dynasty literati culture so much as with the scholarly currents (indirectly traceable to Cheng Hsuan) that had flourished in the late eighteenth century, thanks to the influence of Weng Fang-kang, Chi Yun, and other northerners active at the late Ch'ien-lung court.[68] As a result of the impact of the imperially sponsored Imperial Manuscript Library (Ssu-k'u ch'üan-shu) project and of other equally grandiose bibliographical and connoisseurial enterprises undertaken by Ch'ien-lung, the philological disciplines such as etymology, paleography, phonology, and the like—known collectively as Han Learning—had come very much into fashion in this earlier period. In paying tribute to Master Cheng, therefore, the Hsuan-nan clubmen were in effect declaring themselves the intellectual heirs to Weng and his circle of late Ch'ien-lung court philologists. Such an identity, one must assume, was to be treasured because, of course, Weng and his fellow northerners had emerged as the "loyal" party after the long, dark night of the Ho-shen dictatorship. To be a devotee of Cheng Hsuan and of Han Learning was, in other words, to be on the side of honor and probity.

Resonances with the tastes and values shared by the late Ch'ien-lung literati oppositionists appear, also, in the choice of the other three literati personalities honored by the Club: Su Tung-p'o (1037–1101), whose birthday (just before the lunar new year) provided the other great occasion for Club gatherings; and the early Ch'ing poet-erudites Chu I-tsun (1629–1700) and Wang Shih-chen (1634–1711), whose collections of verse provided the *topos* for a great many Club poetry bouts. All three of these figures had also been models, in one way or another, for Weng Fang-kang—though the intellectual values that had made them appealing had related perhaps more to aesthetic than scholastic concerns. Su Tung-p'o, for example, had supplied the name for one of Master Weng's literary studios, Su-chai, while Wang and Chu had served as exemplars of the "erudite" or neo-classical style of verse composition for Weng during his formative years.[69] Perhaps more important, though, than the Weng pedigree was the specific personality type represented by all three men. Su, Wang, and Chu, we cannot help but notice, all seem to fit the same mold. All were polymaths and eclectics—summarizers of earlier beaux-arts traditions and of other forms of learning, but still above full dedication to any one of these traditions. In short they were dilettantes, in the best sense of the word: men too large and too flexible, that is, for squabbling over narrow claims, or for recommending rigid dogmas of literary right and wrong.[70]

The resonances here, then, would seem to be not so much with the scholastic as with the aesthetic and personality ideals of the Ch'ien-lung court literati. Through the cult of these three latter-day poets and erudites, in other words, the Hsuan-nan clubmen meant to identify themselves in retrospect with what they regarded as the most valuable features of Ch'ien-lung literati culture: dispassion, eclecticism, and aesthetic versatility. Looking at the same set of ideals from a political (rather than aesthetic) point of view, however, one cannot fail to notice another more subtle meaning. Yes, they seem to want to tell us, we are in truth a superior lot, a minority specially deserving of power and recognition. But our spirit is not one of idle contentiousness or self-infatuated vanity. We are men of tolerance, men who might be trusted to use power with a maximum of sympathy for those who differ with us.[71] In this way, then, did the poets of the Hsuan-nan Club wish to be understood by their literati compeers. And in this way, through these particular ideals, they found the political legitimacy that was needed to cleanse their party of the negative associations of "faction."

POLITICAL FAILURE

In the demanding atmosphere of traditional examination-elite politics, compromisers and eclectics, such as the Hsuan-nan Club literati openly boasted themselves to be, were perhaps inevitably doomed to leave the stage under a cloud of opprobrium. And, indeed, later in the closing years of the Tao-kuang reign (1820–1850), the voices of criticism were already noisy in their disapproval of the cosmopolitan and dispassionate spirit they saw as having informed the scholarship of the Hsuan-nan Club generation. To one such critic, the retired intendant Yao Ying (himself, ironically, indebted to Club sponsorship for his rise through the ranks), the stress on philology and the devaluation of earlier traditions of Confucian moral pedagogy that had been a hallmark of the Weng school could even be held responsible for the collapse of Ch'ing resistance during the Sino-British War of 1839–1842.

I reflect with regret [Yao wrote, in a bitter retrospect on the Ch'ing defeat], how long it has been that scholarship has been in decline. Since the Imperial Manuscript Library was organized, all the great court ministers have been preoccupying themselves with textual studies and with pure erudition, and no longer can we find any who are absorbed with ethical studies. In fact, if someone should happen to say a kind thing about a Confucian scholar of the Sung, Yuan, or Ming, he becomes the object of ridicule. For this reason the morals [of officialdom] and the people's loyalty decline with each passing day. No one any more has the slightest notion of propriety, righteousness, restraint, or shame. . . . The enormity of our dynasty's disgrace seems to mean nothing. Have we not been brought to this pass by the errors of those "worthies" so eager to disparage the Sung Confucians?[72]

Yet, though Yao Ying and others would later portray the passing of the northern clique era as a consequence of the bankruptcy of its leaders' intellectual orientations, the facts speak otherwise. At the critical moment of Chiang Yu-hsien's downfall (1830), for example, one highly regarded and influential Southern City man of fashion, Ch'eng En-tse, saw the setback more as the consequence of narrow-minded, petty bureaucrats fighting back against an idealistic leader, and not (as Yao would later have it) as the result of an excessive inclination to compromise.[73] Taking our cue from Ch'eng's remarks, we shall here accordingly propose that intra-bureaucratic clashes provoked by the reform strategies of Club-affiliated officeholders (such as Chiang) were the immediate precipitants of the Club's demise. Intellectual discreditation thus shall be interpreted as the consequence, not the cause, of that fall from grace.

So saying, we are obliged to turn our attention next to the enormously complicated matter of intra-bureaucratic reform as an issue on the agenda of early Tao-kuang politics. By way of introducing this topic, we might best begin with some general comments on the conceptual and political limitations hedging in virtually all participants in this great game of imperial bureaucratic reform in the early nineteenth century. When the Hsuan-nan Club rose to preeminence in late Chia-ch'ing, Ch'ing bureaucratic leaders had already been wrestling for nearly twenty years with the problem of how to bring state revenues into line with seemingly out-of-control levels of expenditure.[74] That they had achieved no major breakthrough is to be explained in large measure by the extraordinary narrowness of the conceptual world within which all reform planning took place. The underlying causes of Ch'ing administrative deterioration—problems such as over-population, economic stagnation, ecological decline, and exhaustion of the labor-absorbing potential of the traditional rural economy—none of these problems seemed to have been considered as within the range of effective bureaucratic action. Rather, as if by some fear-inspired agreement, lest the sheer intractability of these difficulties overwhelm the governing elite in despair, the typical activist mandarin of the Chia-ch'ing and Tao-kuang reigns tended instead to focus hermetically on problem areas within the bureaucracy itself where retrenchment seemed possible. Aware in a vague sort of way that the state bureaucracy itself was badly overextended, the bureaucratic reformists of this period in China's history never seriously discussed the possibility that more, not less, government might be necessary.[75]

Beyond these general conceptual limits, however, there were other, less universally accepted *political* limitations hemming in early-nineteenth-century Ch'ing statesmen as they struggled to prop up the tottering imperial bureaucracy; and it was in coping with these limitations that the Hsuan-nan Club reformers ultimately came to grief.

In essence, these restrictions might all be understood as deriving from the state's commitment to a careful balance of power within the governmental system in order to secure central government interests. The problem was perhaps a perennial one in dynastic politics, but in the late Ch'ing it was compounded by the fact that an ethnically foreign elite was asymmetrically concentrated, as a bureaucratic consumer class, at the central level. Under the Ch'ing, Peking and its immediate environs were the home of several hundreds of thousands of nearly idle Manchu functionaries, stipendiaries, and soldiers who drew their sustenance wholly or in part from grain and silver transferred to them by other, much harder working bureaucrats stationed in the provinces. How to protect the interest of this "foreign" central-region establishment thus developed into an especially thorny problem for Ch'ing rulers.[76]

To guard against the danger of official sabotage from the empire's other centers of power, the Manchu dynasty had perpetuated and improved upon an elaborate arrangement providing for a careful balance of supervisory powers within the provincial administrative apparatus. Cutting across the command lines of the regular regional bureaucracy, whose responsibilities were organized within fixed geographic units, were three functionally specialized superintendencies that reported directly to the court. These were, respectively, the tribute-grain administration (in charge of collecting and forwarding Peking's food supply tax to the capital); the waterway-conservancy administration (in charge of the upkeep of the Yellow River and of the intersecting portion of the Grand Canal, over which this tax grain was shipped); and the salt-monopoly tax administration (in charge of collecting payments from the patented salt wholesalers who distributed salt manufactured at government-run salterns along the coast into the interior).[77]

All three of these superintendencies required cross-provincial coordination. But that was probably not the most basic reason for their continued existence as agencies at once separate and aloof from the regional administration proper. More to the point, the services they provided were of vital strategic interest to the center, and were thus believed to be too important to be entrusted solely to unchecked regular provincial administrators. This was obviously the case with the grain tax and waterway superintendencies, whose extractive fiscal orientation and transport-oriented (rather than flood-control-oriented) hydromanagerial disposition quite clearly conflicted with the interests of the fund-starved and flood-victimized local bureaucracy. But it was true as well of the salt superintendency, whose proceeds tended to service imperial needs (such as military campaigns or major river control projects) and not local ones, and whose very existence in itself guaranteed a profitable livelihood for well-organized gangs of salt smugglers—the bane of local administrators everywhere in China on account of their endlessly diversified criminal activities and habitual involvement in rebel movements.[78]

Naturally enough, in a period of intense administrative overburdening and strain in almost all areas of government, this kind of socially and economically costly division of managerial authority tended to come in for harsh criticism. The result was a string of suggestions urging the partial or complete dismantling of all three of the problematic superintendencies—either by reassigning their tasks to the regular territorial administration, or (more dramatically) by eliminating them altogether through a total restructuring of Peking's arrangements for extracting food supplies and salt tax revenues.[79] Yet here, too, the court was to prove extraordinarily resistant to change—in this case, it would seem, because no Ch'ing monarch wished to grant unchecked authority over these important tasks to a single chain of command rooted in the provinces.

The boundaries restricting the options available to reform-minded bureaucrats in the Chia-ch'ing and Tao-kuang periods were not, then, entirely conceptual ones. Political considerations were at issue, also. And where they were, there was considerable room for disagreement. How much disagreement came ultimately to figure in the demise of the Hsuan-nan Club nexus is the tale to which we must now turn.

At the heart of the conflict that was, in the end, to drive Chiang Yu-hsien from office and destroy the collective influence of the Hsuan-nan clubmen was the latters' covert adoption of a program aimed at dismantling the superintendencies fully or in part in order to lighten the loads borne by the regional bureaucrats in the south. For a few short years during the middle and late 1820s, a constellation of clubmen at the peaks of their careers assumed control of virtually all the regular line positions in the key revenue-generating provinces of Kiangnan and Kiangpeh. As ambitious bearers of the literati-reformist torch, however, they were not content, once installed in these positions of power, to limit themselves merely to reforms in the personnel administration—the mandate under which Peking had transferred them there.[80] In addition, Chiang Yu-hsien and his colleagues developed an attachment to the idea that much more telling gains in the efficient use of bureaucratic talent and funds could be secured by disassembling the huge and wasteful superintendency bureaucracies in charge of shipping Yangtze tribute grain over the man-made waterways to the capital. In their place, it was proposed to substitute a privately run maritime delivery system under the control of the regular provincial officials, thus saving the government untold sums in reduced delays and waterway maintenance costs.

To urge such change was already to step well beyond the conventional limits of provincial executive initiative. But even more risky was the reformers' choice of covert, almost conspiratorial methods to implement this bold idea. Knowing well that appealing directly to the throne for authority to make these changes would not work, Chiang and his allies in the Liang-Kiang (Kiangsu, Anhwei, and Kiangsi) bureaucracy sought instead to smuggle them through under cover of the exercise of the discretionary powers normally afforded to high-level regional officials. When bad luck revealed their project for what it was, Tao-kuang quite understandably grew suspicious. The influence Chiang and the Club network had been able to exercise within the assignments system thus quickly lapsed, ending with it political prospects of the Club as a vehicle for collective literati activism.

How the Chiang party got into position to attempt so ambitious a maneuver is a tale too complicated to recount in full. Perhaps the most important contributory development, however, was the decision resolved upon by the newly enthroned Tao-kuang emperor, late in 1820, to root out the illegal practices that had been draining funds from local government treasuries at a frighteningly accelerating rate, even as the paper accounts sent up to Peking continued to indicate full deposits. In spite of a noble effort by Grand Secretary Ying-ho to persuade the new ruler that insufficient revenues were the basic problem, Tao-kuang allowed himself in the end to be convinced by Chiang and the incumbent Liang-Kiang viceroy, Sun Yü-t'ing, that a tax increase was impossible, and that only improved discretionary management from below could resolve the problem. Once having lent his approval to this further expansion of gubernatorial managerial freedoms, however, Tao-kuang was obliged to concentrate the best, most loyal, and most trusted middle-level administrative talent available to him in the upper level offices of Kiangnan and other provinces where the fiscal stakes were high. As this concentration proceeded, Club influence within the Liang-Kiang administration inevitably grew until, by 1825 or thereabouts, Club alumni or their close Hanlin mentors and friends controlled virtually all the key posts in the regular bureaucratic hierarchy.[81]

This slow buildup of direct personal command influence in the provinces of Kiangsu and Anhwei was to provide the immediate backdrop for the Hsuan-nan Club bureaucrats' assault, late in the 1820s, upon the entrenched powers of the tribute-grain and waterway-conservancy superintendencies. These provinces lay at the crossroads of the highly commercialized and highly taxed lower Yangtze agricultural zone and the artificial north-south transport artery that carried the food-grain surpluses of this region up to the capital. And the fiscal leaks that Chiang and his followers had been called in to plug were very much a product of the transfer onto local government officials of the cost overruns incurred by the managers of this inland transportation system.[82] Under such circumstances, it was virtually inevitable that there would be conflict between the regular provincial-level administration, on the one hand, and the transport and grain-tax superintendencies, on the other. The real question, however, was how far the new provincial leadership would be willing to venture in fighting back against the corruption in the transport agencies that was bleeding dry the local government treasuries.

Before long it would become clear that the clubmen now making the decisions in Kiangsu and Anhwei were inclined to go very far indeed—much further, in fact, than any of their recent predecessors had ever dreamed of going.[83] The strategy upon which Chiang and his supporters settled by 1827 involved the resurrection of a method of grain transport that had been used as an interim device when (as often happened) the inland waterway system had to be closed down for major repairs. On such occasions in the past, supply of the capital had been by sea—an expedient that had become ever more attractive in the Ch'ing with the development of a thriving commercial junk fleet trading between Shanghai, Tientsin, and Manchuria that could be easily pressed into service on a commission basis.[84] Chiang, however, became soon convinced by his subordinates that this procedure could be made permanent, even without Peking's consent. With the canals thus rendered largely redundant, the next step would be the phasing out of the huge, 12,000-junk canal fleets and their expensive crews. And this could be followed in turn by major reductions in annual government outlays for the maintenance of the Yellow and Huai rivers, whose upkeep was traditionally rendered much more complicated by the requirement for coordination of maintenance and repairs with the annual northward passage of the tribute-grain fleet.[85]

This was an astonishingly bold program, at least within the context of Ch'ing bureaucratic politics. Yet, for a few short months in 1826 and 1827, at any rate, circumstances seemed to favor the scheme—as did, for that matter, the concurrent emphasis on broadened discretionary powers for the provincial gubernatorial executive.

First, the Yellow and Huai rivers had, by 1826, fallen into a condition of disrepair that seemed highly likely to become permanent, thus making the north-south waterway system largely unusable whatever the southern mandarins might have thought about the wisdom of adhering to the traditional canal-transport formula. In 1824, a rash attempt at repair of a key feeder reservoir near the junction of the Canal and the Yellow River had so badly disrupted the hydraulic engineering arrangements needed to keep the system working that repair seemed very nearly impossible.[86] Between that time and Chiang's transfer south as Liang-Kiang viceroy in mid-1827, three successive administrators had lost their jobs because overly ambitious schemes to reconstruct the old system had been aborted.[87] And, in 1825–1826, during one of these reconstruction attempts, the court had been forced to authorize use of the coastal route as a makeshift alternative to canal transport.[88] The climate was a perfect one for delay (in the name, of course, of prudent conservatism) while at the same time ironing out the kinks of the sea-shipment procedure. Before very much longer, it could be expected that Peking would have to accept the new arrangements as a *fait accompli*. And, at this point, the institutional demolition of the hated superintendencies could begin.

For the moment political conditions also seemed propitious. The northern-clique protégé network, if perhaps somewhat weakened by the Chiang/Ying-ho confrontation of 1820, was still apparently strong enough to lubricate central-local cooperation in the planning of the supposedly temporary coastal shipment experiment. (Grand Secretary Ying-ho was, in fact, specially deputed to oversee things at the Peking end of the delivery system, thereby helping immeasurably to promote efficient coordination with the officials at the other end.)[89] More important still, the throne seemed as yet very much committed to the highly liberal approach to central-regional supervision that had marked the last years of the Chia-ch'ing reign and the inaugural phase of the current one. Chiang could have reasonably assumed that his own misgivings about undertaking any further grandiose schemes of waterway reconstruction would be heeded. Before long, the sea junk fleets would have become established as the more reliable carriers of the grain tribute.[90]

But then, when all seemed most hopeful of success, things suddenly began to go wrong. By sheer fluke, the ever-unpredictable Yellow River managed, somehow, to unclog its lower course temporarily in the summer of 1827, and then to fall to a new record low late in the following autumn, allowing, as if by miracle, the reservoir sluices at the Canal head to be opened up for the first time in three years.[91] However, Chiang and his second-in-command, the Kiangsu governor, T'ao Chu, remained blinded by their own dogged determination to surge ahead with the prearranged sea-shipment plan, and thus refused, till 11/4 (21 December), to recognize that their scheme no longer had any justification. As edicts and responding memorials flew back and forth between Kiangsu and the capital during the final phases of the deliberation, it became clear that considerable distrust of the reformers' intentions was creeping into the emperor's thoughts. Thus, on 9/10 (29 October), Tao-kuang accused Chiang outright of attempting without authority to turn sea shipment into a standing procedure; and then on 9/30, when T'ao Chu tried once again to defend the sea-shipment plan, he was bluntly charged by the emperor with "acting in cliquish collusion" with Chiang.[92]

By the time the reformers finally admitted defeat on the sea-shipment initiative, they had lost more than just an opportunity for a quick solution to the irrationalities plaguing the Kiangsu provincial government.[93] They had also lost much of their credibility as loyal and trustworthy servants of the Tao-kuang emperor. This was to be unmistakably demonstrated, a little more than two years later, when Chiang Yu-hsien became caught up in what normally would have been considered a very minor scandal growing out of the escape from justice of a salt smuggler reported to have been arrested in northern Kiangsu—an affair, moreover, for which Chiang had not been personally responsible.[94] The punishment meted out was far in excess of the crime. Chiang was peremptorily removed from office and sent into retirement, so badly shocked and humiliated that illness and death followed within several weeks. For T'ao Chu and for Ch'eng En-tse, this sudden fall from grace was to be traced to the machinations of court officials representing the vested interests of the corrupt tribute-grain bureaucracy.[95] Be that as it may, there were also serious differences between the goals of the clubmen and those of the Manchu court itself, particularly on the question of how much ought to be risked to save the ancestral institution of transporting tribute grain by inland canal to the capital. These discrepancies, exploding out into the open in the winter of 1827, brought upon the Hsuan-nan Club leaders a setback from which they were never able to recover.

AFTERMATH: LIN TSE-HSU'S NORTHERN RECLAMATION PLAN

Though the political power of the Hsuan-nan club network was damaged beyond repair by Chiang Yu-hsien's downfall, the curtain had not quite yet been rung down on the struggle to break the power of the superintendencies. The idea continued to preoccupy one particular clubman who somehow survived Chiang's departure from the scene to emerge during the 1830s as a lone champion of this cause—a Chu-ko Liang, as he himself put it. That man was Lin Tse-hsu, governor of Kiangsu for the better part of the decade, and key intermediary as well in the transfer of power from the Hsuan-nan Club to the Spring Purification circle, its successor as the standard-bearer of literati activism.[96]

In the end, Lin's plans likewise came to nothing. But this second failure was to have consequences of considerably greater import than the first. Whether because he was far younger and more energetic than his Club confreres had been at the time of *their* setback in 1827,[97] or whether because conditions in the mid-1830s were just that much more depressing and desperate, Lin did not take his rebuff fatalistically. Instead, he fought back in the time-honored manner of literati officials unwilling to accept their own political sidelining—that is, through political adventure. Much of the desperate energy that Lin was later to invest in his collaboration with the Spring Purification oppositionists and with their crusade against the opium traffic seems in fact to have flowed from this mid-career taste of frustration and from the desire to revive the legitimacy of the retrenchment cause. The present chapter might fittingly be concluded, therefore, with a brief afternote of Lin's one-man campaign, during the 1830s, to carry on with the battle for a less wasteful supply system.

Soon after his promotion into the office of Kiangnan governor early in 1832, Lin began to busy himself with a plan intended to secure the dismantling of the canal-borne grain transport fleet by means more gradual and less controversial than those attempted in 1827.[98] The idea on which Lin drew was certainly more far-fetched than that of converting to a coastal grain-transport system. But it had the enormous political advantage, relative to that earlier scheme, of posing no conceivable threat to the smooth supply of the capital as the reform went forward. And that, no doubt, is why it seemed so attractive to Lin.

Rather than attacking the wastefulness of the supply system at the transport end in the south, Lin proposed, instead, to start by developing altogether new sources of food-grain for delivery to the capital, and to do so in the north—in fact, in the very suburbs of Peking. A wealth of historical documents existed to prove that irrigated-field agriculture had, in past times, been practiced even in the dry, rainfall-deficient climate of the North China plain, where the capital was situated.[99] Engaging the services of two scholars native to the seat of his governorship, Soochow (one of them, incidentally, the Hsuan-nan Club activist, P'an Tseng-i), Lin commissioned the compilation of these documents into a long position paper, completed sometime in 1836.[100] This elaborate production seems to have been intended for presentation to the throne on the occasion of the audience granted pro forma to all high provincial officials when they were rotated between offices, for we know that Lin took the finished volume north with him when he left Kiangnan for re-assignment, early in 1837, to the Hupeh-Hunan governor-generalship.[101] Judging, furthermore, from the contents, it seems clear that Lin had in mind the possibility that the throne might be won over to the idea of launching a trial paddy-field reclamation effort in the marshlands just southeast of Peking. If this first experiment were successful, the government's investment in loans to tenant reclaimers was to be recouped through taxes, and recycled into a second round of reclamation efforts, continuing on thus until sufficient irrigated acreage had been created to guarantee a reliable local supply of grain equal to the amount traditionally extracted from the Yangtze provinces. In step with each consecutive advance, however, the equivalent of the new increment in local tax grain was to be subtracted from the existing southern tribute-grain quota. Thus, the corruption-bloated transport superintendencies could be cut back in a gradual and orderly way, without the slightest risk to the food supply of the capital.[102]

Here, then, was the master plan for another, last try at reform from within. Much more cautiously tailored to suit Ch'ing political realities than the first, it provided for dismantling the troubled tribute-grain system only at a slow pace and under the careful control of the authorities in the north.[103] Yet even this carefully thought-out compromise was unable to get the hearing Lin had been hoping for. Through the diligent lobbying efforts of the Manchu Chihli governor general, Ch'i-shan, who apparently feared for his job and perhaps for the patronage that would be lost with any reductions in the superintendency staffs, the proposal was not even allowed to come before the emperor during Lin's 1837 audience.[104]

More would be heard from Lin on this, but, for the moment at least, the verdict must have seemed all too clear. The hope that had spurred the young literati of the Hsuan-nan Club generation onward, the faith that office and power within the regional government system could be turned to positive result, had now been revealed as illusory. It was time to look for a new model for literati political action.

CHAPTER TWO

The Rise of the Spring Purification Circle

Even before the reverses of 1827 and 1830, the appeal of the Hsuan-nan Club among the Southern City avant garde had clearly begun to slip.[1] Within only a year or two of the 1827 debacle, moreover, a new literati party was already beginning to coalesce in the capital, its reputation gradually coming to be established thanks to the spring purification gatherings (*chan-ch'un ch'i*) that it hosted annually in the capital from 1829 onwards. Totally different in spirit from the Hsuannan Club, the new Spring Purification circle that succeeded it as the standard-bearer of literati political aspirations understood itself from the start as a moral opposition, and enthusiastically professed an admiration for the Tung-lin party of the late Ming. This more radical ideal of literati politics was still ascendant when the Ch'ing skidded into its first "modern" diplomatic and military crisis, late in the 1830s, and affected quite profoundly how the government dealt with that crisis. A close scrutiny of this ideal's rise to popularity is thus in order. Accordingly, in this chapter our purpose will be to identify the changes in the political milieu that made such a stance seem feasible and legitimate, and to probe the self-perception of the men who became its spokesmen.

Some time very soon after the winter of 1823–1824, the Peking branch of the Hsuan-nan Club simply stopped meeting. An exhaustive search through the surviving papers of the Southern City examination elite of the 1820s fails to reveal any record of continued regular gatherings by any groups of seven or nine scholars on the occasion of Su Tung-p'o's birthday—the distinctive hallmark of the Hsuan-nan Club's ritual activity—past that date.[2] The next episode in the history of broad-knit literati organizational efforts inside the Ch'ing political system began in the spring of 1829, when a group of twenty-four men were invited to the first in a series of so-called Spring Purification banquets at the T'ao-jan-t'ing Pavilion in the southern (Chinese) city of Peking. The hosts at this gathering were two Han-lin compilers: Hsu Pao-shan (Han-lin class of 1820) and Huang Chueh-tzu (Han-lin class of 1823). Until Huang left the capital at the end of 1838, this pair continued regularly to convene annual spring banquets and other, somewhat smaller, mid-summer and late fall gatherings.[3]

As we turn, now, to probe the range of ties that drew together the participants in these affairs, we shall discern certain basic continuities with the Hsuan-nan Club, both in terms of personal connections and of belletristic values. The contrasts, however, seem far more striking, and it is largely on them that our analysis will focus. Unlike the Hsuan-nan Club, the Spring Purification circle was intended, from the start, to engage the political activism of the outer rim of the examination elite, and to build a following among provincial degree-holders who were just starting their sojourn in the capital. To these men, the Hsu-Huang network provided service as a kind of literary gateway for reputation building within the salons of certain of the capital's leading examiner-politicians, notably the grand secretary P'an Shih-en. Thus, unlike the Hsuan-nan parent group, from which it had been spawned, this renewed literati political network of the 1830s sought to build up power within the examination-system recruitment process, a direct step backwards, as it were, toward the resurrection of the late-Ming political style.

A second contrast with the Hsuan-nan Club lay in the attachment of this new network to the fortunes of a rising and ambitious senior Peking politician, P'an Shih-en (Han-lin class of 1793), who was competing during the early 1830s for power within the metropolitan bureaucracy. As the result of this connection, the Hsu-Huang circle was to become very much a creature of high-level factional politics, though it was also to be a good deal more than that. Here again, we seem to be moving away from the spirit of the Hsuan-nan Club literati, who had invested their energies chiefly in finding ways to profit from the success of their senior brethren, not seeking openly to promote that success.

A third contrast with the Hsuan-nan Club comes in the realm of ideology. In the aesthetic and philosophical discourse of the new group, we encounter a much more strident and doctrinally intense approach to literary style and taste than had ever been popular in the waning years of northern-clique influence. The eclecticism that was pervasive in the world of late-Chia-ch'ing literati thought began to be replaced by coherent dogma, based squarely on the doctrines of a particular type of aesthetic and literary criticism known as the T'ung-ch'eng school. In step with the move into examination-system politics, then, the influential literati leaders of the 1830s were also engaging in a third type of activity very reminiscent of late Ming high politics: that is, campaigning for Confucian philosophical rectification.

Finally, there seems to be a significantly more positive evaluation of the idea of the literati as critics of, rather than participants in, the work of government. Unlike the Hsuan-nan clubmen, who saw the provincial administrative world as the logical area for their activism, their successors in the Spring Purification circle tended to prefer the role of the critic of bureaucracy. Consistent with this alteration of perspective, they sought to exert oppositionist influence through their personal ties within the censorate. This too, of course, was a move back in the direction of late Ming politics, and serves as a fourth point of contrast with the more moderate style of the Hsuan-nan Club generation. How, then, did these changes come about?

AS A PERSONAL NETWORK

Much can be learned about the reasons for the turn toward a more defiant ideal of literati political participation in the late 1820s by examining the informal patterns of association that drew together the founding members of the Spring Purification circle. Quite unlike their predecessors in the Hsuan-nan Club, these men were not brought into contact with each other (with one or two exceptions) through mutual connection to an influential examination-system patron. Rather, the dominant pattern is one of friendships developed in the course of reaction against failure, non-recognition, or outright career interruption. To be sure, there were important variations in experience and in mood between the various informal friendships that were to be welded together in 1829 under the aegis of the Spring Purification circle. Yet all of these groups seemed to share a common sensibility, inasmuch as the participants had all been denied the kind of smooth passage through the system that they had once assumed would be theirs. Coping with disappointment or adjusting to a world suddenly turned inhospitable—such are the themes that seem to assert themselves most frequently in the ideals of friendship that brought this particular generation of activists to the fore.

At the upper, more conservative end of the spectrum of private friendships from which this new circle was ultimately to grow was a small clique of three or perhaps four Han-lin classmates conjoined by their precocious mastery of Chia-ch'ing era aesthetic and belletristic fashions. Hsu Pao-shan, the eldest of the four, was the son of a late-eighteenth-century official, Hsu Hung-ch'ing, who had spent long years in the secretarial service of the great late Ch'ien-lung scholar and patron Pi Yuan (1730–1797). From this paternal influence, the younger Hsu had acquired a certain competence in imitating the poetry of the early Ch'ing greats, Wang Shih-chen and Chu I-tsun, and access to the poetry salon of the Hsuan-nan clubman, Wu Sung-liang.[4] Huang Chueh-tzu (1793–1853), the second in this Han-lin aesthete clique, was a child prodigy whose uncle, Huang Hsi-yuan (Han-lin class of 1802), had studied poetry under Weng Fang-kang during the latter's term as Kiangsi educational intendant (1786–1789). Through his uncle's influence and connections, Huang Chueh-tzu, too, had been introduced into the circle of Wu Sung-liang's poet friends in the capital and had won that latter personage's approval as one of the Southern City's most promising up-and-coming young poets.[5] Li Yen-pin (Han-lin class of 1823) the third in this Han-lin graduate group for whom we have good information, was equally well placed to absorb the influence of northern-clique aesthetic fashions, inasmuch as his elder brother, Yen-chang (1794–1836), had been one of Weng Fang-kang's favorite students and the editor of several of Weng's poetry and prose anthologies.[6]

Of the private dimensions of the relationship between these men, we know little or nothing. But of their social activities, we have ample records. These seem to have begun in or around 1826, when Hsu and Huang first began to host parties for litterateurs and poets visiting the capital. We know, too, that both men turned up regularly from 1826 onward in the company of Tseng Yü (1760–1831), a poet and anthologist who had been for many years an intimate of Weng Fang-kang, but who was now living in retirement in Peking, whiling away his last years pursuing his lifelong passion for verse and helping newcomers of whom he approved to establish their reputation as poets.[7]

What sent Hsu and Huang forth from this relatively secure nook in Peking society and out onto the stage of literati politics? Certainly not any documentable disillusion with the traditions of aesthetics and poetry writing they had mastered. The impetus seems, rather, to have come from anxiety over the fate that awaited their particular brand of poetic fashion with the impending death of Tseng Yü and Wu Sung-liang. Without these elder statesmen of Peking's poetry circles to help, Hsu, Huang, and Li faced together the unappealing prospect of losing entrée into the world of poetry banquets that brought younger, promising officials into the company of potential senior patrons. For these particular members of the graduating Han-lin class of 1826, then, entry into the world of political entrepreneurship was prompted by the withering away of key family connections within the elders of Peking's social and political world.[8]

In addition, however, to this small in-group of Han-lin aesthetes, the Spring Purification circle was also eventually to incorporate three other informal clusters of friends who had never enjoyed anything even so good as the temporary proximity to the leaders of Southern City fashion that Hsu, Huang, and Li had once known.

The first among these three was a coterie of central Yangtze scholars—including Kuan T'ung (1780–1831), Mei Tseng-liang (1786–1856), and Ma Yuan (n.d)—aligned, by virtue of their common literary prejudices, with the so-called "ancient prose" (*ku-wen*) school of belletristic criticism. This latter school, which stressed utilitarian and nonconformist values in its approach to poetry and to prose alike, had been markedly out of fashion in the Ch'ien-lung and Chia-ch'ing periods. And, as a result, these three men had gotten their start in Peking only after many initial rebuffs, and a late-career rescue by two well-connected Anhwei governors (T'ao Chu and Teng T'ing-chen).[9] It was, therefore, as men suddenly, and late in life, given the recognition they believed long deserved that these friends gradually drifted back up to the capital between 1829 and 1832. Not surprisingly, they chose, on their arrival, to settle in as scholars and teachers of *ku-wen* to the next generation. And it was from this small circle of aging literary comrades-in-arms that the belletristic leadership of the Spring Purification circle was to emerge. One can well imagine that the shared years of exile, and the late restoration to belletristic favor, must only have reinforced the inclination (always latent in *ku-wen* thought) to indulge in the rhetoric of revival and to return to simple, direct moralism in letters.[10]

Another set of literati friendships that eventually drew a number of eccentric or rebellious literati types into the Spring Purification circle revolved around the remarkable personality of a junior provincial official, Yao Ying (1785–1852). As with the literati of the *ku-wen* group just discussed, the great preoccupation of Yao Ying's life and career was failure and self-redemption. In Yao's case, however, vindication was pursued not as a scholar seeking office and reputation in the literary society of the capital, but as an idealistic local official, resolved to bear up under the strains of a job that was unrewarding and dangerous until, one day, recognition would be his. No doubt there were a great many scholar-officials in early nineteenth-century China who shared this dream. But Yao Ying was not just a minor official with a vision. He was also a belletrist of considerable self-confidence, owing to his kinship and pedagogical links with the T'ung-ch'eng school—the major interpreter of the *ku-wen* doctrine in the Ch'ing period. (Yao was a grand-nephew of Yao Nai [1732–1815], the last great interpreter of the T'ung-ch'eng tradition.)[11] His decision to devote himself to a career of idealistic service in county-level office, therefore, was made against a background of other options. For example, in 1808 (the year he passed the metropolitan examinations), the 23-year-old Yao willfully refused to call on his grand-uncle's student, the Hsuan-nan clubman Ch'en Yung-kuang, to improve his chances of placing into the Han-lin Academy.[12] The result was that he wound up being assigned to the waiting list for county magistrates, whence, finally, in 1816, he was given a post in Fukien province.[13]

The next five years were to be spent in a series of low-level positions in that province and in Taiwan. But this period of employment came abruptly to an end with Yao's dismissal, nominally for mishandling a lawsuit, but (according to Yao himself) actually for incurring the irritation and jealousy of his less high-minded superiors.[14] During the following decade, Yao was reduced to eking out a living by taking on odd secretarial jobs thrown his way by an assortment of co-provincials holding office in Fukien and Taiwan.[15]

Between jobs, however, Yao managed to make two trips to the capital (1825–1827, and 1830–1831), in the hope of gaining reinstatement. Finally, in 1831, his tenacity was rewarded when admirers in Peking managed to get him assigned to northern Kiangsu as a magistrate-designate in charge of flood-relief operations. In Kiangsu, Yao had, at last, the kind of higher bureaucratic support that a magistrate needed in order to advance his career. Accordingly, he rose rapidly. By 1836, at age 50, he was promoted to the office of salt controller at Yangchow. And, within but two years of that promotion, he received special recommendation for transfer to the important post of Taiwan intendant.[16] Once again, stubborn adherence to principle had been rewarded, and in a way that must have generated a very special sense of self-importance as a moral example to other aspiring officials.[17]

Yao Ying's long pilgrimage, however, is of interest to us here chiefly for the set of friends, admirers, dependents, and followers that it drew together around him along the way. As we have noted, Yao was not just a junior official struggling to make an official career; he was an avid belletrist in the *ku-wen* mold. Belletrists having an unquenchable thirst for literary friends and for renown, Yao had gone out of his way to aid the careers of a considerable number of struggling scholars, including such men as the T'ung-ch'eng pedagogue, Fang Tung-shu, the out-of-office Fukienese scholar-official Cheng K'ai-hsi, and several promising literati with local roots in the vicinity of Yangchow—all of whom were to follow Yao onward into the ranks of the Spring Purification circle in the 1830s, often as provincial correspondents.[18]

But by far the most important of Yao Ying's discoveries, from the point of view of the history of the Spring Purification circle, was a very young Fukienese poet, Chang Chi-liang (1799–1843), whom Yao had met in Foochow in the early 1820s.[19] Virtually from the moment of their encounter, these two men perceived each other as kindred spirits; and, though shared literary tastes may have had something to do with this (Chang, like Yao, had begun as a *ku-wen* talent), the really telling dimension of the relationship seems to have been a mutual recognition as souls given to flirting with political ruin in the hope of winning ultimate glory on their own terms.[20] In a letter to Chang, written in 1823, for example, Yao praised his new protégé as a man of such talent that he might "choose the path of eccentricity (*ch'i*) without any danger of excess." "Your trials," he continued, "are inflicted on you only so that Heaven can come to your aid."[21] This impression of Chang's character, one suspects, was also very nearly Yao Ying's own self-conception, and it must have infused into the relationship something of that rare intimacy known only to men who see their poetic self-image mirrored perfectly in another. Not surprisingly, therefore, we find Yao Ying going to considerable trouble to introduce Chang Chi-liang into the polite world of Peking poetry banquets, first by bringing his works to the attention of Ch'en Yung-kuang, and then by shepherding Chang around the capital in 1826 and 1827 as Ch'en's poetry friends grew more and more interested in this curious young man from Fukien.[22]

Thus launched into Peking society, however, Chang lost no time in displaying the eccentricity Yao had so esteemed. He first publicly insulted that grand patriarch of poetic connoisseurship, Tseng Yü, at a banquet Tseng held in Chang's honor; then he retired to a temple in the Western Hills of Peking after it had become clear that no influential examiners wanted to have anything to do with such perversity.[23]

Nevertheless, it was not at all rare that a man who had discarded a chance for examination success came thereby to enhance his reputation in the world of letters. And that seems clearly to have been what this act of defiance achieved for Chang Chi-liang. By 1828, he was fast becoming the new standard of taste among the younger literati-poets of the capital. During the years that followed, his particular brand of emotional, direct, even perhaps primitive poetic expression became very much the model for the literati of the Spring Purification circle.[24]

From Yao Ying and his entourage of non-conformist admirers we come to a fourth group of literati rebels to associate themselves eventually with the Spring Purification circle. This group seems best described as Han Learning eccentrics. It included four or possibly more men in early middle-age whose youthful reputations had been secured through a precocious mastery of the Han Learning disciplines, but whose impulsive personal temperaments accorded poorly with the patient, skeptical, and non-imperative values normally associated with that same particular tradition of scholarship. Becoming good friends during the course of fairly long and unrewarding terms as *she-jen* in the Grand Secretariat, these dissident scholars impressed themselves upon their Southern City compeers as perhaps a bit too ambitious in their determination to claim urgent, practical uses for the modes of scholarship they had mastered. But, perhaps for that very reason, their presence was to be welcomed eagerly by the bitterly anti-philological T'ung-ch'eng school partisans within the emerging Spring Purification circle. For what could be better evidence of the degeneracy of pure erudition than the fact of its having provoked a utilitarian mutiny from within its very own ranks?

Two of the aging prodigies included in this clique of Han Learning eccentrics had hereditary scholarly pedigrees (as was normally the case with Han Learning erudites), but two others were self-taught latecomers. In the former category were Kung Tzu-chen (1792–1841) and Wang Hsi-sun (1786–1847). Kung descended from a scholar-official family with roots in the sophisticated cultural heartland of Kiangnan. Taking advantage of his father's several tours of duty in Peking, he had developed a precocious proficiency in paleography, and, somewhat later, under the instruction of his maternal grandfather, the Han Learning scholar Tuan Yü-ts'ai (1735–1815), in etymology as well. Later in life, however, he experienced a run of bad luck in the metropolitan examinations that he characteristically blamed on the scholastically bland "conformism" of the grand secretary Ts'ao Chen-yung. Kung's search for fame then drew him increasingly to the composition of poetry and short, compelling, quasi-scholarly essays on current affairs—such as his famous pieces of 1820 and 1829 urging the extension of provincial administration westward into the Central Asian fastness of Sinkiang.[25] Wang Hsi-sun like-wise came into his Han Learning expertise more or less through fam-ily inheritance, his father being the noted bibliographer and historical geographer Wang Chung (1745–1794). But he too had a sec-ond side to his scholarly personality, originally manifested in a youth-ful intoxication with poetry and, later on, in a growing absorption with the problems of fiscal reform bedeviling the Ch'ing government in his own day. By the early 1830s, Wang's short, pithy, and often uto-pian essays on how the empire might rebuild its agricultural base were to circulate in the capital as a kind of manifesto of the emerging oppositionist movement.[26]

Wei Yuan (1794–1858) and Tuan-mu Kuo-hu (1773–1837)–the oth-er two Han Learning renegades in this set–traveled in the opposite direction, that is, from letters *to* Han Learning. But their desire to make something more vital and compelling of the arid scholasticism they found (and mastered) in the capital was not reduced by their late arrival. Wei began as a poet prodigy, and only developed an enthusi-asm for classical philology when studying in Peking. From here, how-ever, he had quickly moved on to his ultimate métier, which was as a specialist in the institutional history of the Yuan (1279–1368) and Ch'ing periods. The significance of this choice of fields lay, of course, in current events, for the mid-Ch'ing and Mongol periods had been eras of peak military success for imperial arms, contrasting hugely (and, for Wei, lamentably) with the militarily debilitated condition of the present government.[27] Tuan-mu Kuo-hu, like Wei, had also established his youthful reputation as a poet, and then later immersed himself in philology under the influence of his patron, Juan Yuan. Late in life, however, his interests were shifting again, this time in the direction of a newly discovered enthusiasm for *ku-wen* prose, with which he filled the time between scholarly excursions into the interpretation of the *I-ching* (Classic of changes).[28]

Consistent with the iconoclastic nature of this Han Learning study clique, its incorporation into the larger Spring Purification cir-cle was accomplished through personal connections based on affinities of personality, and not of learning. The men responsible for linking this group into Huang Chueh-tzu's circle were Huang's inti-mate, T'ang P'eng (1801–1844), and Yao Ying, neither of whom had any particular taste for the academic pursuits of this foursome, but both of whom admired the "heroic intensity" of their personalities.[29]

Yao, coming up to Peking in 1826 for the first of several attempts to mend his career, seems to have made the initial introductions.[30] But Yao was no admirer of textual studies, and, as he tells us, it was really the "eccentricity" of this particular band of scholars that made them seem worthy of his friendship. That point in itself, however, is of interest. For it reminds us, once again, of how great a gap loomed between the melodramatic ideal of friendship now coming into its own among the Spring Purification literati and the more austere, more imitative, more conformist mode of friendship that had been celebrated by the Hsuan-nan clubmen. The mood among the literati of the Southern City was very obviously in flux. And it is time now to ask just why so radically different a concept of literati brotherhood could take root in the political world of the early 1830s.

AS A POLITICAL FACTION

In analyzing the evolution of the Spring Purification circle, we have characterized it as a patchwork of out-of-fashion literati academic and friendship groups, woven together by the experience of career frustration and a common inclination toward unconventionality. As we move on, now, to examine the political functions gradually assumed by this originally rather loosely knit social network, we are confronted at once with an apparent anomaly. Everything we have so far observed about the normative milieu of Ch'ing elite politics would seem, on first sight, to have militated against any meddling in organized political activity by such a group of dissident, hyper-intense personalities. For not only was the system extraordinarily intolerant of literati political activity; it was particularly hostile to the idea of alliances based on academic schism or the notion of moral superiority. Yet here was a collection of rebellious souls who outspokenly rejected the self-doubting spirit of eighteenth-century elite culture, and who envisioned the "man of heroic intensity" as the appropriate model for literati emulation. How, we ask, could such a clique propose to assert itself politically without fear of self-destructing?

In attempting to resolve this apparent anomaly and to clarify the nature of the political goals pursued by the literati-politicians of the Spring Purification group, we shall here focus on two rather unusual aspects of the elite political scene during the 1830s. First was the race for power at court sparked by the approaching retirement of the Tao-kuang emperor's favorite Chinese grand councillor, the elderly Ts'ao Chen-yung (d. 1835). As early as 1828, one of the two Chinese contenders for Ts'ao's position, P'an Shih-en, began to seek out the support of the emerging leaders of the Spring Purification circle, and to exert himself as an examination official on behalf of candidates they brought to his attention. This collaboration grew even closer during the mid-1830s, as P'an maneuvered openly to embarrass his rivals (chiefly Juan Yuan) by directing the moral protest energies of the Spring Purification literati against these men and their bureaucratic clients.

A second event that helps explain how the dissidents of the Spring Purification set could organize openly for political power was the unsettling effect on the bureaucracy of a half-decade of unusually bad weather in the vital food-producing areas of South and Central China. The years between 1830 and 1835 were plagued by almost annual floods and droughts in the Yangtze valley, and by an attendant rise in lawlessness and social banditry with which the bureaucracy appeared almost completely unable to cope. As an exceedingly nervous emperor struggled to maintain surveillance over his badly demoralized provincial officials, he inevitably found reason to tolerate or even to encourage the moral vigilance of the emerging Huang-Hsu clique as a means of keeping up the pressure for bureaucratic responsibility. Operating in a mutually reinforcing way, these two political developments greatly facilitated expansion of the Spring Purification group's power in the early 1830s. They also prompted its leaders to engage in two characteristic patterns of political activity: the recruitment of a provincial-scholar clientele through patronage within the examination system, and the use of that network to collect information on abuses in provincial administration.

At this point, however, it is necessary that we delve a little more deeply into the specifics of these two political events. The first of the developments of the Tao-kuang reign that smoothed the way for the Spring Purification clique's entry into politics was, as we have stated, the aging of the emperor's trusted senior grand councillor, Ts'ao Chen-yung (1755–1835) and the emergence of a Kiangnan examiner politician (we might say "literocrat"), P'an Shih-en (1770–1854), as a contender for the position about to be vacated. As we have noted in discussing the rise of the Hsuan-nan Club, Ts'ao was one of the two senior men connected to the Weng Fang-kang student network who had risen suddenly to power at court in the wake of the 1813 rebellion. Becoming a grand secretary in 1814 and a grand councillor in 1820, he had accumulated nearly unrivaled power as a trusted adviser on personnel and staffing problems during the first decade of the Tao-kuang reign (1820–1830).[31]

The basis of this power lay, however, chiefly in Ts'ao's extraordinarily extensive experience as a provincial and metropolitan examiner.[32] With Chinese Han-lin and *chin-shih* occupying ever more prominent roles in provincial administration, an official with such rich experience as an examiner could be counted on to offer the throne reliable judgments on the personality of the principal contenders for high office.[33] Ts'ao had been eminently suited to this role, but his aging and enfeeblement as the 1820s drew to a close (he celebrated his 70th birthday in 1825) made it obvious that a successor would have to be groomed for the job. By the late 1820s, it was becoming clear that there were only two real contestants: Juan Yuan (the current Yunnan-Kweichow governor general) and P'an Shih-en (currently acting president of the Board of Rites and Chinese rector of the Han-lin Academy).[34] Of the two, P'an had something of a lead in the area of examination experience, thanks to his Peking-based official career. (Juan, by contrast, had seen only provincial service since 1810.) And it was this advantage upon which he attempted to capitalize when he returned to the capital in 1828 after a prolonged leave of absence.

P'an's overt maneuvering to capture the position about to be vacated began with a quick move to build up an examination clique under his own control, but dominated ideologically by his old proté-gé, Huang Chueh-tzu. In the autumn of 1828, P'an used his position as examiner of candidates for assignment as provincial examiners to steer Huang into the key job of administering the provincial examinations for Kiangsu and Anhwei provinces.[35] Then, beginning the next year, when P'an served his first tour of duty as palace examiner, he began to collect advice from Huang and several others in the Spring Purification set on the new talents Huang had discovered in the Kiangnan examinations, and on the styles in poetry and composition that these men preferred.[36] At the same time, P'an Shih-en's two sons, Tseng-shou and Tseng-ying, began in 1828 to turn up regularly in Huang's company; in the following year, they appeared at the first Spring Purification gathering.[37] What all of this indicates is that P'an Shih-en had decided, as of 1828, to extend his help as an examination official to Huang Chueh-tzu and to the several cliques of dissident literati close to Huang. These men were to be allowed to nominate admired poets and belletrists on the outer edge of the examination class and to bring them to P'an's attention—whence, if possible, they were to be helped through the upper reaches of the metropolitan examinations.[38]

Very good indication of the importance of P'an Shih-en's examination sponsorship to the political ambitions of the Spring Purification circle is supplied by the record of its meetings during the years 1829–1838). The dates of these gatherings and the number of men in attendance are listed in the two right-hand columns of Table 1, below. On the extreme left, I have indicated the fluctuations in P'an Shih-en's position within the metropolitan examination bureaucracy, and have also tabulated those occasions on which P'an's rivals (Juan Yuan and Mu-chang-a) were included in the examination directorate. As will be immediately observed, the really large assemblies of 1829, 1832, and 1836 (which included significant numbers of kung-ch'e examination candidates) were held when P'an was in the best position to influence the outcome of the examinations (that is, as a primary examiner, or as a secondary examiner on good terms with the preeminent primary examiner, as in 1829). On the other hand, when there were no examinations, or when P'an's rivals dominated the primary examination, gatherings were not usually scheduled at all, or, if they were, they were apparently small affairs (as in 1830 or 1838). Whether or not the Spring Purification gatherings were used for the exchange of hints about how to bring one's examination paper to P'an's attention is difficult to say. In some instances (as in 1829 and 1838), when meetings occurred before the palace examination, this might well have been one of the purposes of the meeting. In other cases, however (as in 1832 and 1836), the gathering followed the examination P'an had supervised, and probably was given over, instead, to felicitating successful candidates, encouraging those who had not passed, and poring over the examination essays and poems that had been written. In any case, however, it was clearly the Peking chin-shih examinations and the kung-ch'e candidates' interest in gaining P'an Shih-en's favor that determined the scheduling and attendance levels of the Spring Purification gatherings.

The very visible dependence of the circle's leaders on P'an Shih-

TABLE 1 Correlation of Spring Purification Meetings and
P'an Shih-en Examination Offices (1829–1838)

	P'an Shih-en Post	Mu-chang-a	Juan Yuan	Date/Number of Participants in Spring Purification Meeting (source: HPSWCCNC)		
1829 (TK 9)	Pa, C*			3/28	24	
				6/26	16	
1830 (TK 10)	(no exam)			4/9	15	
				9/19	22	
1831 (TK 11)	(no exam)			(no meetings listed)		
1832 (TK 12)	Pr	Pr		5/29	24	(23 attend)
1833 (TK 13)	C*		Pr	(no meetings listed)		
1834 (TK 14)	(no exam)			5/1	16	(13 attend)
1835 (TK 15)	C	Pr		(no meetings listed)		
1836 (TK 16)	Pr		Pa	4/4	42	
1837 (TK 17)	(no exam)			(no meetings listed)		
1838 (TK 18)	Pa, C	Pr		3/30	(no enumeration)	
				6/15	(no enumeration)	

Legend:
* In these years, Ts'ao Chen-yung was one of the primary examiners
Pr primary metropolitan examiner (source: *Ch'ing-pi shu-wen*)
Pa palace examiner (source: *SL-TK*)
C court review examiner (source: P'an Shih-en, *Ssu-pu-chai pi-chi*, 6:7b–8a)

en's patronage raises, in turn, the question of what sort of obligations these men perceived themselves as incurring, and of how they discussed their political collaboration with that elder statesman. References to this issue usually go no further than to repeat hoary clichés about helping the high-minded minister advance "great talent" into office. Another strain, however, appears from time to time in the record of interactions between P'an and the Huang-Hsu set, and involves the idea that the latter's promotion of talent within the examination system was to be viewed as part of a process of mobilizing literati criticism against bureaucratic neglect or laxity. For example, in 1828, as Huang Chueh-tzu was about to depart on a tour as examiner in Kiangnan, P'an Shih-en's son, Tseng-shou, urged Huang to pay special heed to literati talent from the flood-wracked northern part of Kiangsu. Here, the younger P'an observed, "The waters of the Yangtze and Huai spill out for miles around, while crows and frogs feed upon the carcasses"; thus it was crucial that the upright scholarly spirits from this mismanaged corner of the empire be brought into positions of influence, where their words of protest might be heeded.[39]

Given the prominence of this same protest theme (of which more presently) in the political philosophy of the leaders of the Spring Purification circle, it is apparent that P'an's call for the sponsorship of outspoken talent caught on, and came, before long, to define one of the self-acknowledged purposes of the circle. Through such rhetoric, P'an Shih-en's interest in building a literati following and in controlling information on bureaucratic mismanagement was brought into resonance with the impulsively anti-bureaucratic psychology of the Spring Purification literati. To help P'an in his quest for talent, was, in short, to echo Yao Ying's call for men who would "jolt" the age.

The other dimension of the aberrant political milieu of the mid-Tao-kuang years was the agricultural and social crisis. P'an Shih-en's ambitions and encouragement notwithstanding, it is extremely unlikely that the Spring Purification group would ever have succeeded in carrying its moral crusade directly into the arena of factional politics had it not been for the administrative chaos and imperial panic created by the terrible five-year period between 1830 and 1835. Under more stable circumstances, one can easily imagine the quixotic idealism of a Chang Chi-liang or a Yao Ying getting the group into real trouble, perhaps by triggering a furious impeachment of its interference in the examination system. But with famine spreading, banditry on the upswing, and the provincial administration apparently loosing control of the situation, the emperor seemed to believe that he had no alternative but to throw the machinery of bureaucratic self-policing into high gear—even if that meant risking the revival of Ming-style factional politics. Responding to these circumstances, Hsu Pao-shan and Huang Chueh-tzu drew the Spring Purification circle ever more vigorously into the business of scourging and uprooting the "degenerates" of the territorial administration;

and, in late 1835, Huang was even decorated and promoted for his efforts in this regard!

Behind this series of rather spectacular political shifts was a five-year run of natural catastrophes of rather extraordinary severity, even for catastrophe-prone late Ch'ing rural society. Materials assembled by Chinese scientists in the 1960s on the history of floods and droughts in the province of Hupeh indicate that the decade of the 1830s ushered in forty years of extraordinary irregularity in weather patterns, the worst times coming at the beginning of this period.[40] More recently, a Taiwanese scholar, Huang Chien-hua, tabulated authorizations for famine relief for the period 1820–1850 as an indicator of fluctuations in harvest. Huang found that the years 1832, 1833, and 1835 ranked as the top three in terms of nationwide frequency of major natural catastrophes reported.[41] Since years of bad harvests would have created food shortages of much greater severity than isolated bad years, it seems clear enough that Ch'ing rural society was subjected to abnormally intense pressures on its food supply for at least the first half of the 1830s. An upsurge in organized food seizures and in unemployment-generated criminal or insurrectionist activity was widely reported as having resulted from this prolonged period of bad harvests, and there is little reason to doubt the validity of the connection between rising food prices and escalating violence claimed by many contemporaries.[42]

Our concern here, however, is not so much with the social as with the political consequences of the 1830s agrarian crisis. The most significant dimension of the crisis was the remarkably sluggish and evasive response it drew from the civilian bureaucracy. As much as it possibly could, the bureaucracy ignored the waves of violence that private sources tell us were cresting over south and central China in this period. It responded only by doing its best to understate the seriousness of the disorders in its reports to the throne. It did so, first, because it had neither the coercive nor the economic resources necessary for effective action against the troublemakers, and, second, because the open defiance of authority manifested in many of the incidents threatened, if reported, to trigger angry imperial demands for the arrest of largely unarrestable "bandit" leaders or for the exemplary punishment of local officials who were no worse than the average.

Evasion, however, was a dangerous game. To many outraged local notables, and to their friends and kinsmen in Peking, it seemed only to encourage the professionalization of social banditry and its link-up with folk-religious movements and minority dissidence.[43] On the other side of the coin, the more sophisticated and enlarged insurrectionary networks created by de facto official tolerance were increasingly likely to brave public showdowns with government authorities, thus insuring that soldiers would have to be sent in and the throne informed. Almost every year between 1831 and 1837 there occurred just such an outbreak, with the throne becoming palpably more nervous and vindictive on each occasion.[44] From this accumulating paranoia came, in turn, an increasing inclination to encourage bureaucratic criticism by the censorate. Reflecting this new trend toward a more active role for the literati as overseers of the bureaucracy, the annual frequency of censorial impeachments for laxity in bringing criminals to justice shot suddenly upward in 1830, and stayed at unprecedented high levels until the end of the decade.[45]

From the point of view of the instinctively anti-bureaucratic and politically bloodthirsty literati associated with the Spring Purification circle, a shift toward official encouragement of literati vigilance in overseeing the bureaucracy was bound to be received as good news. And so it was. In 1835, for example, Ch'en Fang-hai wrote to Huang Chueh-tzu (one of the first two men in the circle to become a censor) to congratulate him on his successes as a "speaking official," and to urge him on with the injunction that vast realms of the empire would benefit from the removal of "each and every rotten official" in the upper reaches of the territorial bureaucracy.[46]

But perhaps the most revealing insight into the way the Spring Purification group viewed the new liberal policies of the 1830s appears in the reaction to the Hsu Pao-shan punishment case of January 1833. Hsu had been elevated to the office of censor along with Huang late in 1832, thus giving the clique its first opportunity to enter the arena of accusatory politics. This promotion came at a time when the fires of anti-bureaucratic wrath were being stoked by concern over an unexplained and apparently unsuppressible Yao aborigine rebellion that had started in southern Hunan province in January 1832. As the spring went by and a protracted campaign by government troops still failed to bring report of victory, the emperor had grown unmistakably suspicious. On 23 April, an imperial clansman, Hsi-en, was dispatched from Peking to investigate the progress of the fighting. Then, on 20 June, his fears further aroused by signs of worsening drought

in the vicinity of the capital, Tao-kuang had issued an edict of imperial penitence, condemning himself for inadequacy as a ruler. In the
traditions of Chinese political ritual, this gesture amounted to a call
for criticism of the ruler and his high bureaucratic minions; and, on
6 July, the emperor did, in fact, display unwonted cordiality when a
censor, Ch'iu Yuan-chün, presented him with a tedious and largely
useless catalogue of practically all the current trouble spots in the
realm. In response, Tao-kuang set out the equivalent of an emergency
charter. Local officials were, he declared, to be evaluated according to
"public opinion" (*yü-ch'ing*, meaning, of course, the censorate), while
their immediate superiors were to be judged by how well their subordinates did in this respect.[47]

All of this had left as yet unresolved the question of how far up
the hierarchy of authority the censorate's finger was to be allowed to
point. But a gathering imperial disinclination to protect senior
officials had been evidenced with the removal of the Liang-Kuang
viceroy, Li Hung-pin, from his post in mid-September for covering
up the passivity of his soldiers in the Yao campaign. When, one
month later, a string of former and current high-level officials in
Hunan had also been punished for failure to report the troubles there
much earlier, it must have seemed that any and all officials were fair
game.[48]

Returning, however, to Hsu Pao-shan and his friends in the Spring
Purification group, we can well imagine the excitement prompted by
this first great crack in the wall of upper bureaucratic prestige. By the
spring of 1832, Chang Chi-liang was already assembling whatever
bits of information he could piece together on the Yao rising, and
was confidently informing his friends that both Lu K'un (the governor general with jurisdiction for Hunan) and Li Hung-pin (his
counterpart for Kwangtung) were "petty, shortsighted, without any
vision at all, and simply unworthy of trust."[49] By January 1833, Hsu
had clearly been convinced that Chang was right. On 1 February
1833, newly promoted, he accordingly submitted a lengthy indictment of virtually all phases of official conduct during the Yao crisis,
implicating both Li Hung-pin (already dismissed), and his successor,
Lu K'un. Lying and misrepresentation were alleged in almost every
detail. And, for good measure, Hsu threw in a few allegations about
high-level corruption in the metropolitan province of Chihli, where
there had been a recent, though much smaller, uprising.[50]

Hsu's gesture was a brave one, to say the least, for the imperial clansman Hsi-en had just exonerated Lu K'un of any wrongdoing, while Ch'i-shan, who was the ranking official in Chihli province, was perhaps the most respected Manchu officeholder in the provinces and very much a contender for a high future position at court. Moreover, as was soon to become evident, neither Hsu nor his friends had any concrete evidence to back up their charges. If this became clear, Hsu might have been punished as a fabricator of tales and agent of mischievous factional politics.

Yet, miraculously, this first attempt at open defiance of the system ended happily (or very nearly so) for Hsu. In fact, Tao-kuang's final disposition of the affair seems, if anything, to have encouraged the Spring Purification literati in their belief that the trends of the times favored their cause as moral vigilantes. True, the emperor's first response was harsh. On 2 February 1833, Hsu was ordered stripped of all his offices and rank and given a caustic lecture on his misdeeds. But four days later, Tao-kuang inexplicably backed down and reinstated Hsu to the Han-lin Academy—letting him off, in effect, with a simple demotion—while announcing that it would be a poor example to punish a "speaking official" so drastically.[51]

The hint of toleration contained in the emperor's final decree was noticed at once, and turned forthwith into a cause for great celebration in Hsu's circle. P'an Te-yü, for example, wrote at once from his home in north Kiangsu to congratulate Hsu on his pardon and to urge upon him the extraordinary significance of what had just happened. News of the affair, P'an gushed, had "flooded his inner soul with a rare sensation—as if it had been suddenly released from its shackles, as if the thick ice of winter had suddenly melted into water, as if the thick clouds had broken up to reveal the clear sky." With this example before them, P'an continued, many more brave souls would now be certain to speak out. And if they did not, "one could only blame the censors for betraying the court; not the court for belittling censors."[52] The Hsu Pao-shan affair could thus be seen as a triumph for the cause of literati oppositionism and as a stunning setback for the bureaucracy. The emperor had been driven by his own suspicions to make common cause with the spirit of literati vindictiveness. And Hsu and his friends knew it.

To recapitulate, the emergence of the Spring Purification circle as a self-confident political force early in the 1830s was facilitated by two peculiarities of the larger political situation. Backing from P'an Shih-en, one of the competitors in the race for Ts'ao Chen-yung's seat on the Grand Council, provided both the means and political support needed to venture into examination-system politics. And indulgence by a nervous ruler, badly frightened by the crumbling of bureaucratic authority during the agrarian crisis of the 1830s, guaranteed unprecedented ease of access to the channels of remonstrance.

Almost as if to remind everyone of the changed complexion of Peking politics, the emperor took the unusual step, late in 1835, of simultaneously promoting four particularly outspoken censors to prestigious posts in the capital bureaucracy.[53] Among the four was Huang Chueh-tzu, P'an Shih-en's most pre-eminent disciple, and, by this point, the de facto leader of the Spring Purification party. At almost the same time, P'an himself assumed the coveted office of chief grand councillor, following the long-expected death of old Ts'ao in February 1835.[54] Within but six years of their appearance as an identifiable clique, the brothers of the Spring Purification circle were firmly lodged in the seat of power.

RITUAL AND SYMBOL

The political world of the Spring Purification circle was so far removed from that of the Hsuan-nan Club in its values that one scarcely expects to discover any continuity between the two groups in their self-legitimating rituals or symbolic activities. Yet, a good deal of the ritual of the later circle seems deliberately modeled after the ceremonial practices of Weng Fang-kang and his students in the Hsuan-nan Club. The birthday of Su Tung-p'o was regularly honored, in keeping with the Ch'ien-lung-era tradition begun by Weng. That of Huang T'ing-chien, another Sung-dynasty poet who had likewise been imitated by Weng, was also celebrated each summer. And impromptu affairs were from time to time gotten up in imitation of the social rites popularized by the early Ch'ing literati Wang Shih-chen and Chu I-tsun—also men who had been idealized by Weng and his followers.[55]

As we attempt to interpret this somewhat surprising choice of ceremonial practices, two different layers of meaning emerge. The first is the pursuit of what might be termed imitative or associative legitimacy. As with the Hsuan-nan Club itself, the meaning of group rit-

ual in these cases seems to derive from the desire to replicate the conventions of a respected literati political grouping of the preceding generation. By adhering outwardly to the ceremonial traditions of the
Hsuan-nan Club, the Spring Purification literati thus, in effect,
sought to have themselves understood as successors to the political
legitimacy that former group had enjoyed. A second layer of meaning is revealed in the subtle changes of emphasis imposed on these
inherited rituals: the new prominence afforded the cult of Ou-yang
Hsiu, a writer and statesman of the Sung only occasionally honored
by Weng and his compeers; the abandonment of the birthday celebration for Cheng Hsuan, the patron saint of the Han Learning scholars; and the lavish attention on the political (as opposed to purely
literary) activities of the early Ch'ing literati-aesthete "greats."
Through these transpositions, the literati of the Spring Purification
circle seem to have deliberately adjusted the ceremonial traditions of
the Hsuan-nan Club so as to bring them into line with their own preference for ku-wen literary philosophy, distaste for Han Learning values, and nostalgia for the late-Ming/early-Ch'ing political style of
open factional manipulation of the examination system.

In the realm of self-consciously pursued imitation of the traditions of the Hsuan-nan Club, we might note that the great spring
gatherings from which the Spring Purification circle acquired its
name had their roots in an allusion to one of the all-consuming connoisseurial enthusiasms of the late Weng Fang-kang. In 1803, Weng
had published a lengthy textual study of the various extant medieval
rubbings of a now lost specimen of calligraphy produced in the year
353 by one of early China's most revered calligraphers, Wang Hsi-
chih (A.D. 321–379).[56] The original masterwork, entitled the "Preface
to the Spring Purification Festival at the Orchid Pavilion," had com-
memorated a poetry banquet organized by the calligrapher and a
number of his friends among the courtiers of the Chin state. This
scroll had long since been lost, but before its disappearance an early
T'ang emperor and one of his courtiers had arranged to have a facsimile carved into stone. This facsimile had then been used for the manufacture of rubbings, which had been copiously distributed to court
favorites who in turn employed them as models for the production
of their own stone inscriptions from which still other, less authentic
rubbings were made. The cycle of facsimile making and reprinting
had continued until, by the eighteenth century, the curio market was

virtually flooded. Yet so cherished was the fine calligraphy of Wang Hsi-chih's "original," and so powerful was the magnetism of this first great age of literati aestheticism, that the search for the authentic version had become a virtual occupation for collectors and bibliophiles. With the support of that great beaux-arts patron, the Ch'ien-lung emperor, Weng Fang-kang had brought his search to what seemed its final culmination in an 1803 study. His conclusion was that the most authentic version was the so-called Ting-wu-pen copy, which had been reproduced from a calligraphic copy of the original executed by the early T'ang courtier Ou-yang Hsun (A.D. 547–631). Weng, however, had apparently never seen an original of this version.[57]

Kung Tzu-chen's discovery of a Ting-wu-pen original in 1824 in one of the antique shops of the Southern City, and its subsequent purchase for installation in a temple just outside the city, provided the occasion for the first Spring Purification celebration held by the Huang Chueh-tzu circle. By this act, they assumed from Weng the mantle of high connoisseurship, thereby conferring upon their group the redeeming outward appearance of continuity with the imperially approved scholarly enthusiasms of the northern-clique courtiers.[58]

There were also practical considerations. The results of the first stage of the metropolitan examinations were announced just before the April-May flowering of the trees ordained the season proper for the Spring Purification party. Not surprisingly, though, one finds only a few references to this aspect of the choice to emulate the Orchid Pavilion gathering. In an identification with Weng Fang-kang and with the aesthetic fraternity tradition Weng had so loved, here alone was safety.[59]

Several other aspects of Spring Purification circle ceremony also took their meaning from the replication of northern-scholar practices. For example, Huang Chueh-tzu and Li Yen-pin seem to have held Su Tung-p'o birthday gatherings in Peking in the last weeks of every lunar year, just as had the Hsuan-nan clubmen (though there was no longer a fixed number of participants). Similarly, the mid-summer gatherings of the circle (see Table 1) were described, somewhat inexactly, as honoring the birthday of Huang T'ing-chien, a Sung period Kiangsi poet whose natal day celebrations had been first marked by Weng Fang-kang in 1788.[60]

Yet there was more to the structure of the circle's ritual than mere recapitulation of venerated Hsuan-nan Club traditions. Missing en-

tirely is the late-summer Cheng Hsuan celebration that had been intermittently observed by the Han Learning scholars within the club. In
its stead appears an enthusiasm for the Sung dynasty belletrist, Ou-
yang Hsiu (1007–1072), whose place in the pantheon of ancient scholar-
exemplars was based mainly on his fame as a *ku-wen* revivalist.[61]

A second shift of nuance that seems to reflect important differences is in the way the circle dealt with the memory of the early Ch'ing
literati. In the poetry gatherings of the Hsuan-nan Club, it will be
recalled, the cult of poets Wang Shih-chen and Chu I-tsun had generated a great number of themes for poetry compositions. To some
extent, the cult of Wang Shih-chen as a model aesthete was carried
over into the gatherings of the 1830s, there to cast its spell over the
taste of some of the participants. But Chu I-tsun vanishes entirely,
condemned, by Hsu Pao-shan, as a "mere" Han Learning pedant. In
Chu's place, there appears, instead, a new-found fascination with the
great K'ang-hsi court literocrat, Hsu Ch'ien-hsueh (1653–1694).[62]

The Spring Purification circle's interest in Hsu Ch'ien-hsueh
seems to have been prompted, in the first instance, by Hsu Pao-shan,
a sixth-generation descendant who studiously imitated his renowned
ancestor's habit of taking into his home young scholars newly arrived
in the capital from the south.[63] In 1826, Hsu went one step further
and began to turn his ancestor into a subject for group imitation and
ritual veneration by circulating a scroll showing his great-great-great-
grandfather holding an Orchid Pavilion flower-viewing and drinking
party at the Sui-yuan Garden near his home in K'un-shan in the
spring of 1694. From the frequency of this same scroll's reappearance
as a conversation piece in the circle's "art talk" gatherings, it seems
clear that Hsu's 1694 banquet picture soon came to take its place
alongside the original Orchid Pavilion rubbing as a source of inspiration for the new circle.[64]

But why Hsu Ch'ien-hsueh? To answer that question, we shall need
to go beyond the scroll's image of him as a partying retired scholar-
aesthete (*wen-jen*), and to place him back in Peking, during the heyday of his political career. In the years before his retirement, Hsu had
been one of a small group of new-generation southern literati personally sponsored by the K'ang-hsi emperor during the 1670s as an examination patronage clique intended to balance off a more senior clique
of northern Chinese and Manchu politicians. The great event in the
history of this Southern clique (Nan-tang) had been the authoriza-

tion, in 1679, of a special metropolitan examination, for which "erudite" candidates had been nominated directly by the leading lights of this same group, Hsu of course included. Through this examination a very considerable number of men from southern literati families, which had participated actively in the factional politics of the Ming and had been debarred from the bureaucracy early in the Ch'ing conquest, succeeded in re-entering the official elite.[65]

We do not have to look far to notice the parallels between Hsu Ch'ien-hsueh's Southern Clique and the political project on which the Spring Purification literati had embarked: that is, using the examination system as a way of building up a scholar's network within the bureaucracy. Indeed, the parallel may be drawn still more closely, for Huang Chueh-tzu and Hsu Pao-shan referred on occasion to the postexamination banquets of 1679 as models for their own similar celebrations, several times expressed the hope of persuading the Taokuang emperor to hold another "erudites" examination, and late in 1835, actually memorialized the emperor (though without success) on behalf of this pet project. The cult of Hsu Ch'ien-hsueh, therefore, seems to express a departure from the Hsuan-nan Club's enthusiasm for the early Ch'ing as an age of poet-aesthetes, and a turn instead toward an interest in examination politics. For within the longer reach of Ch'ing history, here alone could be found a precedent for monarchical indulgence of the Ming style in elite politics.[66]

LITERARY AND SCHOLASTIC PHILOSOPHY

The ghost of late Ming literati politics, lurking just out of sight behind the outer forms of the Hsu Ch'ien-hsueh cult, provides a fitting thematic bridge into our next topic: the Ming-style literary and political philosophy current within the Spring Purification circle. It has been observed in an earlier section of this chapter that much of the political energy of this Hsu Pao-shan/Huang Chueh-tzu clique went into mobilizing complaints against a "lax" and "morally lazy" provincial administration, and that the spirit of bristling impatience undergirding this crusade tended to spill over into a preference for recruiting "upright" literati whenever the opportunity presented itself for dabbling in examination politics. By way of rounding out our history of the reassertion of literati political power in the decades before the Opium War, it seems worth examining just how this protest spirit so much in evidence in the political activities of the Spring Purification circle affected the *intellectual* dimensions of literati life in the early 1830s.

The truly distinctive feature of the literary and philosophic views that were on the rise in this period was their tendency to stake out a dogmatic "orthodox" position and to deny alternate ideals of literary taste or scholastic philosophy. The contrast is, of course, with the inclusivistic eclecticism of the intellectual world of the northern-scholar era. And here I would suggest that this disavowal of the more cosmopolitan intellectual habits of their Chia-ch'ing elders was indeed one of the major issues in Spring Purification literati thought, perhaps best understood as an attempt to translate into the realm of philosophic discourse some of the same enthusiasm for oppositionism that stirred the *political* imagination of these scholars. The problem then becomes, of course, to understand how these new, more rebellious spirits rising to prominence in Southern City intellectual life in the early 1830s perceived—or misperceived—the intellectual values of the outgoing generation, and how they rationalized their attack upon them.

Again, some brief background is in order. Thematically speaking, the central philosophic issue that runs through almost all Southern City aesthetic debates in the early nineteenth century is that of how elevated taste and literary proficiency related to the assumed moral superiority of the literati as activists in public life. Was the cult of elegance (*feng-ya*) a kind of acid test of character, allowing only the best men to survive its tough standards? Or was style perhaps only a reflection of personal greatness that had its roots elsewhere? Characteristically, the Hsuan-nan Club intellectuals had equivocated on this issue. From the T'ung-ch'eng school they had borrowed the idea that the refinement of literary style consisted chiefly in eliminating the clichéd, distracting, and cluttering elements in writing that blocked the expression of true feeling. Since only men of sincere natures could or would push their literary self-improvement to this point, "letters" became in a sense subordinate to moral character, the cultivation of which, it could be argued, had to be pursued in the *non*-aesthetic realm of moral philosophy.[67] At the same time, however, Weng Fang-kang had developed his own theory of taste, which analogized the mastery of poetry and other literary forms to the pursuit of textual studies, thereby attributing to it something of the same vir-

tue in forging character ideals (patience, breadth, aversion to dogma-
tism, and so forth) as had been ascribed to the Han Learning disciplines.[68]

That both positions could have been maintained simultaneously
seems, at first, confusing. But within the broader context of Ch'ien-
lung/Chia-ch'ing-era philosophy of learning, it was in fact logical
that both views be acknowledged. To these thinkers, the broader
realm of learning (*hsueh*) was naturally divisible into three self-con-
tained fields: *k'ao-chü* (philology); *i-li* (moral philosophy); and *wen-
chang* (belletrism). Within this triple-curriculum framework, the
eclecticism of Hsuan-nan Club aesthetic philosophy would have been
expressed in the form of a statement to the effect that the moral value
of literary composition might inhere either in the writer's ability to
infuse his work with the spirit of moral philosophy (the T'ung-ch'eng
approach), or with the moral sensibility of philological objectivism
(the Weng Fang-kang approach). Ultimately, however, since the ideal
of the scholar was inclusiveness, both approaches were necessary and
appropriate, in order that *i-li, k'ao-chü*, and *wen-chang* might all be
sustained.[69]

The intellectual reaction of the 1830s was to hold that the Chia-
ch'ing-period insistence on the validity of all elements in the triple curriculum was the quintessential shortcoming of the elder generation.
The starting point for revision was the idea that all fields of "learning" were not equally exalted. Rather, borrowing (ironically) from
another favorite conception of eighteenth-century thinkers, the res-
tive iconoclasts of the 1830s harped constantly on the theme that
dominant trends in scholarly life tended inevitably to shift between
certain fixed possibilities, and that it was only by identifying with
the incoming or nascent trend that the scholar could acquire a truly
forceful moral presence. By the late 1820s or early 1830s, several of
the literati connected with the Spring Purification circle were independently converging on the same general notion that *k'ao-chü* (and,
for some, *wen-chang* as well) had lost its vitality, and was about to be
replaced by *i-li* as the dominant field of scholarly attention.

Thus, writing in the 1830s to a circle acquaintance, P'an Te-yü
declared that for at least several decades neither philological nor belletristic studies had produced any literati capable of "bringing to life
the spirit of the Sages." According to P'an, the former had begun
with the intention of helping to explicate the Classics, but had ended

up getting mired in trivia; while the latter had declined into a vain competition for reputation and influence in the world of literary fashions. This, of course, left moral philosophy as the ascendant area—though, interestingly, P'an (himself a poet of considerable repute) was not quite willing to renounce belletrism completely. Instead, he insisted several times that the *i-li* revival could be carried over into the world of letters.[70]

Moving along a nearly parallel trajectory, Mei Tseng-liang (another serious belletrist) put forward the idea in 1824 that the *k'ao-chü* emphasis of the Ch'ien-Chia era was now about to be replaced by moral philosophy for precisely the same reasons that the former had originally replaced the latter in the eighteenth century. Philology, Mei insisted, had originally been promoted by "men of high moral ambition" (*yu-chih chih shih*) in reaction to the "emptiness and narrow-mindedness" of the scholarly fashions of the late K'ang-hsi era, when study of the Sung Neo-Confucian commentaries on the Classics (the very core of *i-li* scholarship) had become merely something to be "aped" in order to fit in with current fashion. Now, however, *k'ao-chü* studies had been reduced to much the same kind of vulgar imitation of the "rage of the times." From this it followed that *i-li* scholars were now to inherit the coveted status of "being above seduction by the vulgar fashions of the age," and were about to emerge as custodians of the true Way.[71]

Having thus decisively broken with the eclecticism of the tri-discipline formula, and having determined that moral philosophy was the wave of the future, how then did these men come to grips with the category of letters? In general, P'an Te-yü's formula—the synthesis of letters and moral philosophy—was the one adopted by most. The real problem arose, however, when it became necessary to state just what the fusion of these two disciplines might mean in practice.

One way of handling the question involved falling back on the for-mulae of the T'ung-ch'eng *ku-wen* school, according to which literary accomplishment was merely the objective manifestation of the au-thor's progress in self-cultivation. Thus, for instance, Mei Tseng-liang described the excellence of poetry and prose alike as inhering in the "truthful intensity" (*chen*) of the writer; while P'an Te-yü argued along similar lines, substituting the ideal of sincerity (*ch'eng*). The tag word *sincerity* immediately brings to mind the vocabulary of Sung

Neo-Confucian self-cultivation, thus providing us with a link between the worlds of moral philosophy and letters.[72]

A somewhat different approach involved claiming that greatness in *wen-chang* depended on the urgency and usefulness of the message conveyed by the text. In praising the censorial memorials of Huang Chueh-tzu, for example, several of his friends described them as having captured the essence of *wen-chang* by cogently setting forth the wrongs of government and the need for reforms. Or, to consider another example, P'an Te-yü at one point attempted to reduce the entire problem of evaluating *ku-wen* prose to that of determining how much of the verbiage it contained "could not be left unspoken"– again implying, it would seem, that immediate relevance to public affairs (*shih-wu*) somehow imparted a greater-than-usual literary intensity to a given specimen of writing.[73]

The exhortation to judge literary craft on the basis of its evident sincerity or utility was not, however, an adequate formula for dealing with one critically important sub-category within the world of letters. This was the category of poetry. Being an allusive and nonlogical medium, poetry could not be as readily held to these same standards. Thus it became necessary to engage in further explication of the *i-li*-as-*wen-chang* formula, this time in the context of devising a vocabulary for discussing the ideals of *poetic* composition.

Two men within the Spring Purification set seem to have been particularly preoccupied with this task—both of them poets of repute: Chang Chi-liang and P'an Te-yü. Their common point of departure was the literary philosophy of Wang Shih-chen, the early Ch'ing poet and critic who will be remembered as having been apotheosized by Weng Fang-kang out of regard for his extraordinary command of the pre-Ch'ing poetic tradition. What attracted these two later Ch'ing poets to Wang, however, was not his excellence as an anthologist, but rather his advocacy of the idea of poetry-as-intuition. In fact, as Richard Lynn has pointed out, Wang's ideas on the value of intuition in poetry were very largely lifted from the *Ts'ang-lang shih-hua*, a Sung-period work on the poetics written by Yen Yü (1180–1235), who had himself derived his ideas very largely from Zen (Ch'an) intuitionalism. In Wang's elaboration, the key value of poetry had been posited as inhering in the vaguely defined idea of *shen-yun*, a phrase that connoted something like "personal mood, atmosphere, or tone, expressed in an indirect, tenuous way."[74] The nearest equivalent of *shen-yun* in the original Yen Yü text is the phrase *ch'ing-hsing*, or "the intuitive power of discernment" of the poet—an idea that is balanced off against the learned aspects of poetic art.[75] In the discourse of the poet-philosophers of the Spring Purification group, we notice at once that the contrast between "personal sensibility" or "intuition" (now rephrased as *hsing-ch'ing*) and "studied art" (*hsueh*) was quite central to almost all discussions of poetic taste and value, clearly reflecting the influence of Wang Shih-chen.

This, however, is but half of the story. For both P'an and Chang saw themselves as Confucian activists, not as Zen mystics, and both were eager to find in poetry a medium for passionate political expression. They could not, therefore, easily identify with the quietist component of Wang Shih-chen's aesthetics, nor with his ideal of tenuous expression. What they did, therefore, was to preserve Wang's valuation of the intuited, while rather subtly infusing that concept with Sung Neo-Confucian moral philosophy.

Perhaps the most revealing (because most inadvertent) example of how Wang Shih-chen's "intuition" came to be reworked as a Neo-Confucian moral construct (*i-li*) occurs in P'an Te-yü's *Shih-hua* (Remarks on poetry) and in his prefaces to the poetry anthologies of other literati in the group. Thus, for example, in constructing a hierarchy of values according to which poems might be rated, P'an tells us that the highest sort of poetry expresses the individual's *hsing-t'ien* (moral nature endowed by Heaven). Next is *ko-yun*—the learned or studied formal features of poetry. This hierarchy already introduces a Neo-Confucian twist into Wang Shih-chen's dichotomy, but P'an does not stop here. Going even further in the direction of moralizing Wang's original idea of intuition, P'an next comments that this same highest type of poetry has the attribute of "clarifying and explaining moral principles" at the same time that it expresses "those matters that appertain to our inner mind."[76]

The same transformation of artistic intuition into Neo-Confucian *moral* intuition occurs in Chang Chi-liang's poetics. For example, Yen Yü's *ch'ing-hsing* becomes, in Chang's formula, *hsing-ch'ing* (one's moral nature and its expression), the communication of which is supposed to be the ultimate goal of poetry.[77] Or, again, following P'an Te-yü, Chang divides all poets into three categories according to the kind of natural disposition (*ch'ing-hsing*) displayed in their works, and places the "poetry of the man of moral resolve" (*chih-jen chih shih*) above "poetry of the man of study" (*hsueh-jen chih shih*).[78] Here *chih-jen* carries the weight both of the idea of inspiration (hence the contrast with *hsueh-jen*), and of the idea of energetic moral impulse, as in *chih-ch'i*, or the "courageous sense of moral resolve."[79] Starting with a stress on artistic intuition, then, P'an and Chang gravitated almost unselfconsciously toward the idea that the essence of poetic expression is the ability to convey intuited moral apprehension (*i-li*).

But what exactly did all of this mean in practice? How *did* the mysteries of the poetic imagination acquire a moral character? The best clues to how this would have been answered emerge from the writings of Chang Chi-liang, who was the only one of the poets of the Spring Purification circle to really venture beyond the blurred abstractions of Neo-Confucian vocabulary to attempt a description (albeit metaphorical) of how the poet actually experienced such moral intuitions.

Sifting through Chang's image-filled comments on the nature of such experience, we come at once to two core ideas: first, that of the poet as a man of super-ordinary but thwarted ambition; and second, that of "tragic empathy" (*kan*), a special capacity possessed by such exalted personalities.

Perhaps the key idea in Chang's self-representation is that of the *chih-shih*, a phrase that normally connoted a type of knight-errant personality (*shih*) driven by his impetuous temperament (*chih*) to righteous deeds of the sort that most men would never attempt. However, for Chang the poet too could be a kind of eccentric moral hero, acquiring superhuman stature by confronting his fate, to which, in his greatness, he refuses to yield. Interestingly, Chang devotes little space to explaining why some men should respond in this way to frustration, and others not. It was enough merely to observe that only where some true greatness of character already exists will such a reaction follow. But where it does exist, and is thwarted by the failure to gain worldly recognition, it is as though "the waters of the river [are blocked] and stirred up, and must find a way to vent themselves lest they spill over onto the plains."[80]

Here we come to the second key idea in Chang's search for a moralized understanding of his own poetic intuition. The vent through which such thwarted feelings are released will vary with the times, Chang tells us. But when this perturbation spills over into poetry, it possesses an almost supernatural capacity to arouse empathy in people far removed in time or space:

[When the *chih-shih*] vents his inner troubles and his long pent-up emotions, his heroic intensity causes him to stare up at heaven and down at the earth, and to sing out his lament as if in self-mockery, or as if in self-mourning, or as if in self-consolation. Thousands of hundreds of years later, those who come across the words will feel as if they were inside his body, and had shared his fate. They will breathe out a sigh in mournful commiseration, or sadly shed tears for him.

Poetry coming from any less grand a spirit can have no such power to excite tragic empathy (*kan*) at such distant remove.[81]

At this point, Chang's discourse comes to an end, still somewhat shy, perhaps, of convincing a dispassionate reader that this young man's popularity as a poet necessarily demonstrated the moral fitness of Master Chang and his friends for a privileged political role. But Chang's words were not written for a dispassionate readership. They were written for an audience of examination candidates themselves looking for a way to vent their own feelings of entrapment, and for a way, also, to link this exercise to the higher moral mission of oppositional activism. For such an audience, one may well imagine, the "tragic-empathy" standard of poetic excellence must have been appealing indeed, inasmuch as it offered an emulative model for political protest. For, after all, if the poets of the Spring Purification circle had, like Chang, been endowed with a gift for conveying tragic emotion, were they not then ipso facto suited equally well to the job of conveying to their friends in the capital some sense of the "mournfulness" or "sadness" they encountered in roaming the empire in their trips back and forth to Peking? And was not the empathetic infection of Peking society with these same feelings the first step, then, toward their alleviation—since, as everyone knew, such sadness among the people of the empire could only be explained by the neglect or the misdeeds of the officials?

Inserting ourselves into the perspective of Chang's audience, then, we can perhaps better understand why, for Chang and his admirers at least, poetic intuition could actually seem a moral thing, a benefactor of the public condition, and not merely a manifestation of subjectivity or eccentricity. And we can grasp, as well, why, in the more troubled political milieu of the 1830s, with the oppositionist tide rising, this, and not the more eclectic and learning-inclined views popular in the Chia-ch'ing era, should have triumphed as the key to poetic aesthetics. Here indeed was a useful new literary orthodoxy to have at one's command as one prepared to tilt against the complacent old men of the bureaucracy.

THE IDEAL OF "MORAL CENSURE" (*CH'ING-I*) POLITICS

Rounding out our survey of the issues preoccupying the opinion makers among the Spring Purification literati, we come last to the subject of the Ch'ing "constitution," if such it might be termed.[82] At the heart of the new faith that was sweeping the Southern City in the early 1830s was a conviction of the inappropriateness of the current dynasty's prohibitions against direct political participation and expression by non-officeholding literati. Quite unlike their immediate forbears in the Hsuan-nan Club, the activists of the Spring Purification circle were eager that this issue be addressed directly and openly and that as many restrictions as possible be removed. How they argued the case for such liberalization is the problem to which we now turn—a problem of no small dimensions, since the questions at stake necessarily involved a re-examination of traditional Ch'ing claims about the depravity of the late Ming political elite.

To hark back to our earlier review of Ch'ing official doctrine on this question, it will be recalled that the cautionary example of factions undermining Ming political unity had been frequently invoked to justify prohibitions against direct literati participation in politics. Out of the presumed lessons of late-Ming (and also early-Ch'ing) experience had emerged a variety of detailed institutional and normative constraints that had made it difficult or impossible for literati networks to assert influence independent of formal bureaucratic channels. Students in government schools or academies in both the provinces and Peking had been banned from protesting official actions; scholars taking examinations were prohibited from organizing to write diatribes against officials unless specifically asked by the examiner for their opinions; and even the metropolitan censors, their official responsibility for criticism of the bureaucracy notwithstanding, had been placed under a variety of powerful normative constraints against "wild accusations," "factional intrigues," and the like on account of their linkage with examination-system patronage networks in the Han-lin and in the higher tiers of the bureaucracy.

In the political discourse of the Spring Purification literati, there was no single unifying concept for this array of restrictions. But there was a unifying word for the kinds of political expression that had been repressed under this Ch'ing system. *Ch'ing-i*, literally, "moral censure," was a phrase whose meaning derived from two passages in the Confucian Classics in which were asserted the propriety of non-officials (*shu-jen*) speaking out in censorial protest when and only when the higher authorities "manifested injustice in their application of rewards and punishments to officials." *Ch'ing-i* thus came to refer to the range of literati political privileges enjoyed in the Ming and denied under the Ch'ing. It was in the hope of reviving a polity tolerant of *ch'ing-i*, akin to that of the late Ming, that the Spring Purification literati applied themselves as they lashed out at the Ch'ing order.[83]

In the interest of brevity, we can here pass over the considerable body of literature produced by these scholars on the historical details of late-Ming politics.[84] This was, significantly enough, a subject that drew considerable attention. But our principal interest here is in how exactly the enthusiasts of late-Ming political culture addressed the thorny problem of justifying what amounted to a direct attack on the Ch'ing political constitution. It must be emphasized from the start that this was as difficult intellectually as it was controversial politically. For these men had been brought up to associate *ch'ing-i* politics and its quintessential late Ming manifestation—the Tung-lin clique—as enemies of political stability. The scholars of the Ming were "arrogant," Kuan T'ung remembered as having been told; while another Spring Purification commentator, Fang Tung-shu, reported having heard from his friends and elders that the Tung-lin was "excessive in its moral self-confidence" (*feng-ch'i t'ai sheng*), and had not paid sufficient attention to the realities affected by its policies.[85] How then could a return to *ch'ing-i* politics be advocated without precipitating a decline back into wild subjectivism, "arrogance," and factional division?

In the end, there was never a direct answer to this problem. But there did develop a roundabout solution, involving the notion that the restrictiveness of the Ch'ing system had, by the time of the Chia-ch'ing reign, produced dangers that were even greater than those of factionalism. Three scholars—Yao Ying, Kuan T'ung, and Lu I-t'ung—produced the most elaborate arguments for such a position. As we scrutinize their remarks, we notice a very close echo of the line of argument pursued in the attack on *k'ao-cheng*: namely, that "fashions" or doctrines (in this case, the ideals of reserve and reticence among the scholar elite) were appropriate only for limited periods of time, and were bound to be superseded as the cyclical momentum of history moved forward. The Ch'ing system had been appropriate in its time as an antidote to the excesses of the Ming, but current conditions had now made it out of date, and it was time to move back in the opposite direction.

Yao Ying stated the case for a cyclical-determinist approach to literati political ethics the most cogently, so we may begin with a summary of his position. Echoing the *ku-wen* doctrine that the state of "letters" mirrored the cyclical pattern of dynastic government, Yao proposed that all dynasties moved through a three-phased sequence. First came the phase of "inauguration" (*k'ai-ch'uang chih t'ien-hsia*), then the era of mid-dynastic "inherited stability" (*ch'eng-p'ing chih t'ien-hsia*), and, finally, an "era of troubles" (*chien-nan chih t'ien-hsia*)—in other words, of political disintegration.[86] The problem then became to determine what sort of talent and literati personality were to be encouraged by the state in each of these three periods.

Gliding over the "era of inauguration," which seemed to have no relevance for the present, Yao proposed that under conditions of mid-dynastic stability the emphasis ought to be on cultivating in the elite the virtues of personal quiescence and amiability of manner. A non-contentious collective elite personality would in turn act as a kind of invisible ordering influence on the rest of society, thus helping to maintain the general orderliness and peace prized by the age.

But, Yao continued, the Ch'ing had now obviously passed beyond its calm middle age. Symptomatic of the entry into a "time of troubles" were a whole list of developments, many of which were bound up with the troublesome trend toward lawlessness and social turbulence. The empire was now overpopulated and could not be fed adequately; the state's military machinery no longer inspired awe; the "people's temper" was "unquiet"; "treacherous and fraudulent" social leaders were running about unchallenged; the state's revenues were exhausted; power was slipping into the hands of "those below"; officials were frightened of the people under their charge; and there was a growing population of men without stable livelihoods. These were all symptoms of a "disease in the body politic" (*t'ien-hsia p'ing*) that made the "cautious," "decorous," and "modest" literati values of the past clearly outdated. What was now required was the cultivation of a new type of scholar-official personality, referred to by Yao as the *chih-shih*—by which was meant very much the same sort of heroic personality as Chang Chi-liang had revered in his poetics.[87]

At this point, unfortunately, Yao ends his discussion, leaving some uncertainty as to what institutional changes he would advocate. But the inference seems to be that a move back toward the spirit of the Tung-lin and toward the *ch'ing-i* style of literati political participation was now considered appropriate, if only as a way of weening scholars from their obsolete habits of passivity and reserve. In "times of trouble," in other words, the pliable scholar-official mentality was a political risk. And expanded literati participation in political discussion would have value as a way of spreading the *chih-shih* spirit among the officials of the future.

Though not quite so respectful as Yao was of earlier Ch'ing norms, both Kuan T'ung and P'an Te-yü offer a very similar set of justifications for tearing down the normative barriers standing in the way of a *ch'ing-i* revival. In both cases, the crucial point seems to be the presumed cost in social turbulence that the dynasty now pays for sticking to its ideal of the close-mouthed, non-contentious scholar. For Kuan T'ung, the ultimate consequence of the current dynasty's ban on *ch'ing-i* is that the lettered elite has lost its will to resist the "wicked" and the "bullies" of the countryside.[88] For, today, the scholars and the officials have been so infected with the vices of accommodation and servile flattery that they are incapable either of remonstration with careless superiors, or of setting an example of strict rectitude that would inspire or overawe their social inferiors. As a warning of where this trend promises to lead, if unchecked, Kuan then reviews the details of the 1813 uprising, pointing out that even officials in the Palace had been unable to resist the blandishments of the rebel leaders because of their lack of spiritual backbone.[89] To save itself, therefore, the dynasty must act to break down the love of flattery and the dislike of mutual criticism and remonstrance that now permeate literati and official culture. And the only way to do this, Kuan insists, is to regenerate *ch'ing-i* politics, not just allowing but positively requiring censors, students, and even minor officials to criticize their colleagues and their betters.

Very much the same thread of cautionary reasoning runs through Lu I-t'ung's treatment of the problem of *ch'ing-i* as well, though Lu seems somewhat more sympathetic with the spirit, if not with the cause, of social insurrection.[90] Echoing Yao Ying, he agrees that the Ch'ing has now descended into an era of "sickness," the problems of which are compounded by the blandness of elite culture and the consequent unwillingness to "shock" or to "stir things up" by pointing to the symptoms.[91] The presumed influence on the lower orders of this elite aversion to "honest speech" is then diagnosed in a rather remarkable formula on the nature of social discontent. These days, Lu complains, even in the villages, even among kinfolk, no one dares to be anything but accommodating and uncritical toward their friends and elders. How much less likely, therefore, that inferiors might seek to remonstrate with their superiors within the bureaucracy, or with the emperor!

But, Lu continues, it is inevitable that men of subordinate social or bureaucratic station will feel ill-will toward their betters, and will seek to "express this discontent" in one way or another. If these sentiments are not allowed to vent themselves through righteous statements or through "moral firmness" (*kang-chih*), then they will find their outlet in "evil" or "cunning." The secret of good government, Lu concludes, is to find ways to channel discontent into "moral intensity" and to prevent it from manifesting itself in underhanded and devious behavior. And social insurrection is nothing more than the consequence of failure to teach people how best to express their feelings of moral indignation toward their betters.

Since "those below" had by now become so accustomed to habits of furtiveness, secrecy, and lawlessness, it behooved "those above" to take measures to revive a more honest spirit. Censors, minor officials, and, inevitably, "the humble scholars of the backwoods" were to be encouraged to speak out—or, more specifically, to vituperate against injustices. And "speaking officials" who persisted in their timid and evasive ways were to be punished by the loss of their jobs, or worse. Thus, everyone would be inspired with a spirit of courage (*yung*) and the danger of smouldering resentments exploding into full-scale rebellion would be finally dissipated.[92]

The consensus was that the conservative values of the mid-Ch'ing scholar had become not only outdated but positively dangerous in this new age of political disintegration and unrest, and that only a rapid termination of policies that suppressed *ch'ing-i* could retrieve the situation. To these men, the opportunity for the scholar to speak out in moral censure of officials was essential to the inculcation of a new spirit of moral firmness and outspokenness in the elite. Since the dynasty had now to choose between the regeneration of literati morals and extinction, it followed that *ch'ing-i* had now regained a legitimate place in the political system. The rehabilitation of Ming political ideals, at least in the eyes of these Chinese literati, was now complete.

CHAPTER THREE

The Politics of Opium Suppression

On 13 February 1840, *The Times* (London) published some observations purporting to explain why the Ch'ing government had of late been acting with renewed truculence on the matter of British imports of contraband opium into China. According to that article's author, whose poor understanding of the contemporary Chinese political scene appears about average for its day, this recent shift in the direction of belligerence was to be explained as the result of the newly gained ascendancy within the emperor's councils of a "set of grey-haired Torries that would surprise even the good people of Queen Anne's time" with their stubborn conservatism.[1]

The analogy, aimed of course at a British public and informed by Whig-liberal prejudices, is not really appropriate. Yet, almost by accident, it does seem to highlight certain of the more telling features of the new political leadership (the Spring Purification party) that had recently captured control over the court's foreign-trade policies— provided, that is, that we substitute the Tories of Walpole's time for those of Queen Anne's. Like these latter, the men now in control of the empire's policies were surest of themselves as men of letters, and as idealizers of the role of personality and of true friendship in government. And like them, also, they were perhaps better suited to an oppositionist role. In office, by contrast, they were exceedingly unsure of themselves, and much inclined, therefore, to political adventure and militance, perhaps as a diversion from the more serious and more intractable problems of the day.

Without overstraining the metaphor, then, we can extract from it one useful point that can serve as a prelude to the argument to be elaborated in this chapter: That is, that the Ch'ing government, and *not* the British, took the really active role in forcing a diplomatic and military showdown over the drug question in 1840; it did so under the influence primarily of *internal* political pressures, and not foreign economic or military threat. This internal pressure, we shall further argue, arose out of the desire of the Spring Purification party (in alliance with Lin Tse-hsu) to establish more firmly the legitimacy of its rather unorthodox power base within the Ch'ing system. The Ch'ing government's inability to work out a satisfactory policy on the control of foreign trade provided these ambitious but insecure political leaders with an issue where they felt a great gamble might well be worthwhile, if only for the rewards that would accrue in terms of increased political legitimacy to their own party. From this largely internal impetus, and not from any ineluctable *raison d'état*, emerged the bellicose trade restrictions that *The Times* was to complain about. And from these restrictions, in turn, were to come the acts of provocation that gave the British their excuse for military action. In this chapter our concern will be to illuminate how, why, and with what consequences, these Chinese "Torries" interjected themselves into the debates on trade policy, in the end pushing the Ch'ing state into a war it was grievously unprepared to fight.

THE CASE AGAINST AN EMBARGO

As background to the consideration that follows of the role of the Spring Purification party in the trade debate of 1836–1838, we might best begin with some evidence on the insufficiency of the *raison d'état* approach as an explanation for the Ch'ing decision for a restrictive trade policy in 1839.

The unsentimental wing of the "China-as-victim" school of historians (represented, most recently, by Hsin-pao Chang's excellent study of the diplomatic background to the 1839 war) has long contended that China undertook her rather daring attempt to close off foreign trade in 1839 as a last-ditch effort to protect a monetary system that was being ruined by the outflow of bullion for drug purchases.[2] This analysis, if substantiated by evidence that a significant number of official actors on the Ch'ing side believed a trade cutoff threat held the answer to the monetary question, would support quite well the idea that Ch'ing China was forced into war by foreign pressure. However, such evidence does not exist. In fact, available evidence on the question suggests, to the contrary, that the men in charge of policy up until 1838 – supported by the great majority of officials and even, in part, by the emperor – did not regard trade embargo (aimed at ending drug imports) as an effective solution to the disintegration of the Chinese currency then in progress. Some saw domestic monetary reform options as more likely to work. Others preferred legalization of the drug to reduce its price and to bring down the volume of imports. Still others, including the Tao-kuang emperor, seem to have believed that nothing but strict trade controls could work, but were not convinced that China had the military clout to enforce such controls against a feared maritime enemy. Though disagreeing among themselves, these different actors (who, together, comprised the vast majority within officialdom) nevertheless had reached agreement, by the late 1830s, that interrupting foreign trade with Britain did not hold the real answer to the domestic fiscal woes arising from China's dwindling supply of silver specie. If their views had prevailed, there probably never would have been an opium war.[3]

But let us look a little more closely at the range of considerations that had spread so pessimistic a view of Ch'ing foreign-policy options among the bureaucratic elite on the eve of the 1836–1838 debates.

First was the problem of deciding just how much of the silver famine—as it was called—was actually attributable to the outflow of specie to pay for opium. On this, official opinion remained ever divided. But a significant number of mandarins and publicists continued, to the end, to stress the preponderant influence of domestic currency management deficiencies, and to argue that domestic currency reform therefore was the key to solving the financial crisis.

To begin with the silver famine itself, it is clear that the early 1830s did in fact witness a serious decline in the availability of silver bullion, and that this had a decidedly negative effect on the public as well as the private sectors of the economy. As of the early nineteenth century, China's monetary and financial system was relatively primitive and inflexible. It was dependent on the maintenance of stable rates of exchange between the state-minted copper coins used in small, daily market transactions, on the one hand, and the unminted silver sycee (nearly pure bullion) used for the settlement of larger accounts. Fiat or paper instruments of credit were underdeveloped, and tended to be held in suspicion by "metalist" state ideologues; moreover, it is doubtful that the public would have trusted its largely unaccountable bureaucratic rulers sufficiently to accept state-issued notes at face value. When, therefore, the government became aware (during the mid-1820s) of a trend toward "cheap" coins and "dear" silver, it had to take this development with the utmost seriousness, inasmuch as parity instability of this sort affected inter-regional and public-private economic transactions in too many sectors to allow a do-nothing response.[4]

But it is far less clear that the awareness of rising silver prices turned all official eyes automatically in the direction of illegal drug imports as an explanation for the phenomenon. For one matter, it was not evident that the drug traffic was the sole or even the major cause of the silver famine of the late 1820s and 1830s. Devaluation of the coinage had also been hastened by the lowering of government quality standards and by a wave of counterfeiting, and with coins thus debased it was but natural that there would be a quickening demand for silver and an attendant decrease in the availability of the latter. Then, too, Chinese awareness of uniformity of foreign-minted silver dollars and of the savings in assay fees that accrued to the businessmen who used them allowed foreign silver coinage to circulate in China at an above-face-value premium, in turn drawing purer unminted Chinese sycee out of the country. As many pointed out, both these problems could have been managed without a frontal attack on the drug traffic, and the Ch'ing government might have gone far toward restabilizing the bimetallic exchange rates if it had turned its energies to improved control of copper-coin minting and to the production of a reliable silver coinage.[5]

A second set of considerations tending to dissuade Ch'ing officials from contemplating foreign-trade controls as a realistic solution to the silver-price problem had to do with the onshore policing requirements of cutting off trade. For good practical reasons, an embargo on foreign trade—whether conceived as a pressure tactic to elicit British voluntary renunciation of the drug trade or as a permanent measure—could not easily be divorced from a policy of tough action against the Chinese distributors who ferried the opium (and outward-bound silver) between the foreigner and the Chinese consumer. As many officials were to warn the emperor, to impose a trade cutoff without simultaneously uprooting the native traffickers would be merely to drive the smugglers and legal traders alike into illegal channels. By the mid-1830s, at least, this had begun to happen anyway, even without any actions having been taken by the Ch'ing government to restrict the authorized trade at Canton (China's sole legal port of call for European ships), and customs revenues were beginning to be lost as a result. Obviously, more pressure at Canton would only accelerate the trend.[6]

Why not, then, go after the native, tax-evading smugglers? But when they considered such a step, Ch'ing provincial officials could not but feel profound misgivings. As of the 1830s, the majority of senior provincial officeholders had already been through many unpleasant experiences in conjunction with attempts to control outlaw organizations who were well entrenched in the local social infrastructure or who catered to victims not willing to police themselves. From such encounters, they had learned that smugglers of almost any commodity were simply beyond the reach of efficient prosecution, owing to the government's lack of an independent police force. Whenever the mandarins attempted to bring such criminals to justice, they had to depend on civilian informants. But the information supplied by such witnesses was more likely than not to have been contributed by parties themselves actively involved in the same line of business, and eager to have the law chase their rivals from the field. To pursue the Chinese middlemen in the opium traffic could thus pile bureaucratic evils on top of existing social ones. Few had the stomach for such action. Yet, without it, as everyone admitted, it would be self-defeating to talk of quarantining China's foreign trade.[7]

The third consideration that argued against trade control as a potential cure for China's monetary woes was the lack of confidence in the Ch'ing military to enforce such controls effectively. If a total trade embargo were imposed, did the Ch'ing imperium possess the military means to drive off well-armed foreign smuggling ships? And could its land forces face down possible British naval reprisals against Ch'ing cities and fortifications? No one knew for sure in the early 1830s, when debates over the trade-embargo sanction first began in a serious way, but, as the decade wore on, first the mandarins in Canton, and then even the court itself, began to have uneasy suspicions that British naval and artillery power might prove irresistible.[8]

As this particular issue was to return to haunt the "trade-embargo" party during and after the hostilities of 1840–1842, we might here digress briefly to document just how the court had come to look upon the military question on the eve of the Spring Purification party's intervention in the debates. Though most public pronouncements on this question were fuzzy, there was one incident when both words and actions revealed the emperor and his advisers to be quite unsure of their military leverage. This occasion came in 1834, some five years before serious hostilities actually developed. But, as there was no effort in the interim to modernize Ch'ing armaments, one can fairly assume that the same lack of self-confidence continued to trouble the counsels of the emperor, and thus to add to the catalogue of negatives already discouraging talk of closing off foreign trade.

The incident in question began with the decision of the British Foreign Office, under pressure from parliamentary Free Traders anxious to liberalize Sino-British trade from both ends, to dispatch Baron William John Napier to Canton as a kind of envoy extraordinary. There he was to inform the Chinese of the recent abolition of the East India Company's monopoly on the carriage trade between Canton and London; provide for the upgrading of British representation at Canton now that this China station was under crown, not company, protection; and, if possible, attempt to gain a direct audience at the "court of Peking," in order to plead for the opening of additional trading ports.[9]

In the event, none of these ends were to be gained, chiefly because Napier had not been assigned the naval and marine forces that would have been needed to force the Ch'ing into yielding on any of these issues. But Napier did have two frigates—*Andromache* and *Imogene*—at his disposal, and these he was determined to use to the fullest possible effect.

Not even waiting for the Chinese to give him cause, Napier had set immediately about the business of manufacturing a provocation so as to be able to administer as quickly as possible the salutory "whiff of powder" he believed alone capable of bringing the "Celestials" to their senses. Immediately upon his arrival in the Gulf of Canton, late in July 1834, he had proceeded straight to the factory (that is, foreign-warehouse) area just outside of Canton without first applying for the customary harbor-entry papers. Naturally, such impetuousness had not endeared him to the protocol-conscious viceroy, Lu K'un, and Napier thus found himself quite unable to gain access to Lu or any other local officials. After several weeks more, with the Chinese still pretending he did not exist, Lord William felt the time had come for action. *Andromache* and *Imogene* were ordered forthwith to attempt the run of the Bogue estuary as far as Whampoa, in order to let Lu feel a little more pressure. On 7–8 September, to everyone's amazement, the ships succeeded in navigating this perilously shallow stretch of water. Even more ominously for the Ch'ing, moreover, the two English ships managed to give the supposedly formidable Ch'ing shore batteries resisting their advance en route very much the worst part in an exchange of cannon fire that went on for several hours.[10]

In the end, to be sure, the benefits Napier was able to extract from this "lesson" were few, since Lu soon divined that the British could not follow up on their initial gains. By cleverly playing upon the embargo threat to turn the British trading community at Canton against their governmental representative, Lu was able to force Napier to retreat in disgrace from the Bogue. And, by 11 October, Lord Napier was dead of a fever in Macao.

Nevertheless, the actions taken by the court during and immediately after this contretemps reveal that Peking had become convinced of its military vulnerability, even in the supposedly easily defensible inner reaches of the Pearl River estuary. Informed of the details of the early September naval engagements just inside the Bogue, the emperor and his councillors seem to have grasped quickly that a real military showdown might well result in a dangerous humiliation for the Ch'ing. "It seems that all our forts have been emplaced to no purpose. They cannot beat back even two barbarian ships," the emperor is reported to have exclaimed. "How ridiculous. How detestable!"[11]

At the same time, moreover, Governor General Lu was immediately put on a very short leash, so as to forestall any risk of further provocations to the British. He was not to "bicker over some trifling tariffs" or to "push the civilian traders to the wall merely because of the intransigence of their chief," and all talk of a punitive embargo by the Ch'ing was to be stopped the moment the barbarians agreed to the restitution of the diplomatic status quo ante. Lu was not to try to lever any further concessions from the British with this threat.[12]

The dynasty, having experienced at first hand the kinds of military reprisals it might face in a trade embargo, had thus shown itself extremely unsure that it could control the situation. Here was a third barrier to action, for what possible good could come of trying to save, by a trade embargo, silver that would only be lost again through defeat in war?

Over and against all these dissuasive considerations, there was, to be sure, at least one concern weighing heavily on the minds of the emperor and his advisers that still argued strongly for the notion of cutting off foreign trade. But this was a concern that was not directly related to the monetary issues that had originally sparked the debate. It was the fear that the Ch'ing military, the inevitable accomplice to any well-organized drug-distribution system, were themselves becoming debilitated through opium consumption, thus leaving the empire's southern flank dangerously exposed to the threat of civil insurrection.[13] Touching, as it did, upon a nerve that had been throbbing since 1813, and still more painfully since the onset of the agricultural crisis of the early 1830s, this particular anxiety had shown itself capable, on one occasion at least, of driving the emperor to such heights of desperation that the more rational level of policy debate, outlined above, had been abandoned, and serious discussion had been launched of initiating an embargo, come what may. After all (the argument must have gone), why not risk prompting a rebellion through crackdowns on the import networks if not to do so would be to guarantee that insurrection would take place anyway, and on terms of near certain disaster for the government? Yet, this particular justification for a trade embargo did not address the currency scarcity that had been responsible for debate in the first place. And, what is more, this somewhat hysterical argument did not prove itself capable of sustaining court enthusiasm for a trade cutoff policy for very long.

The episode that brought this fear of military debilitation out into the open and into the debates over foreign trade policy had taken place in 1832 and grew out of the Yao aborigine rebellion along the Hunan-Kwangtung border that we have already noted in conjunction with the Hsu Pao-shan impeachment controversy.[14] The reader may recall that the Liang-Kuang governor general, Li Hung-pin (Lu K'un's immediate predecessor), lost his post and had his career wrecked by the incredible slowness and passivity of his troops in mounting a campaign against the Yao sanctuaries in the hill country of inland Kwangtung. The reason why Li's columns had moved so slowly and fought so poorly was that they were comatose with opium—a circumstance that had been ascertained beyond a doubt in mid-1832 by the imperial clansman, Hsi-en, who had been sent to investigate the delay. To make matters more frightening still, however, the high addiction rate was not to be explained merely by the miseries of camp life or the horrors of living and fighting a guerrilla war in a malaria-infested, inhospitable part of the empire. The real reason for the prevalence of the drug habit among Li's troops was that, just before the Yao wars, they had been stationed along the coast, near Canton, where they had been engaging systematically in squeezing and protecting the smuggling trade, and, of course, indulging themselves in the forbidden pleasures of the drug. Of this, too, the emperor was eventually to be apprised.[15]

But there was yet another twist to the story of how Li's army had been ruined by Bengal opium, one that helps to explain the court's desperate response to the affair. Li himself had known what was going on, and, in spite of instructions from Peking, had done nothing about it. In November 1829, Li Hung-pin had submitted to the emperor a secret memorial accusing the British of drug trafficking in the Gulf of Canton on a scale that no official had ever before suggested.[16] In July 1831, a censor named Feng Tsan-hsun had revealed to the emperor that, despite Li's earlier frank admissions, the governor general had in the interim been doing nothing to impede this illegal trade. Or almost nothing. For some of the trade was beginning to move upcoast, as foreign opium cruisers developed new contacts

with native receivers operating out of Amoy, Tientsin, and the Leichow Peninsula. But the bulk of the illegal merchandise was still passing right up into the Pearl River, Feng claimed. How could this
traffic be moving so easily past the checkpoints established in the
channel? Only with the complicity of the patrol forces themselves,
whom Feng accused of being on the payroll of the Chinese "thugs"
who controlled the drug business onshore. A tighter policing of the
policemen themselves was thus very much in order.[17]

The court had heartily agreed. Feng's evidence had been passed
along to Li at once, accompanied by exhortations that action must
be taken immediately to force the British to desist, even (if necessary)
by threatening a total trade embargo. In response, Li had promised to
bear down harder. No need, he assured the emperor, for an embargo:
The job could be done by stricter inspection of incoming British
cargo vessels and by tougher action against the native "fast crabs" that
ran the drug ashore from the foreign depot ships anchored off Lintin
Island, in the Gulf.[18]

Yet, here it was 1832, a year later, and what had Li done about all
of this? Obviously, nothing, since most of his soldiers were now
themselves addicts! To Tao-kuang, the message that all of this conveyed could not have been more disturbing. Chinese soldiers were in
open complicity with underworld traffickers: taking their bribes,
smoking their drugs, and revealing the impotence of the military
arm of the state. Even so awesome and trusted an official as the Liang-
Kuang viceroy, Li Hung-pin, appeared to be unwilling or unable to
move against the source of this evil, the arrogant English barbarian,
lurking just out of sight, off the coast, smug beneath the protection
of his fast ships and deadly cannon.

For a moment, it appears, Tao-kuang lost his head. Or perhaps it
was just that things now seemed so bleak that other considerations
hardly seemed to count any more. Li, needless to say, was immediately removed from office. His successor, Lu K'un, was ordered to
Canton in a whirlwind of instructions that made it incontrovertibly
clear that strict control of Kwangtung's foreign trade was to be the
order of the day:

We now reflect: This opium arrives from overseas, but it collects in Kwangtung.
If the source is to be stopped up, then efforts must begin with Kwangtung. . . .
After Lu K'un reaches Kwangtung, he must conduct a full investigation of how

the drug manages to come onshore and into the interior. Then he must devise means for stopping this. There must be a "pulling up of the roots and a blocking of the source" (*pa-pen sai-yuan*). One final, all-out effort must bring an end to this evil. Accordingly, we are ordering copies of Feng Tsan-hsun's memorials to be sent to Lu for perusal. If he has any other plans for dealing with this matter, let him deliberate carefully and apprise Us. We shall be certain to keep a careful eye upon the way in which these measures are implemented. LET LU NOT TAKE HIS INSPIRATION FROM LI HUNG-PIN, MERELY MUDDLING ALONG WITH HIS GAZE WRAPT ONLY UPON THE IMMEDIATE TASKS AT HAND, AND ENTIRELY OBLIVIOUS TO THE LONGER-TERM INTERESTS OF THE STATE![19]

Obviously, Lu still retained some discretion over how to drive the opium hulks from Kwangtung's shores. But the reference to a "final, all-out effort," and to a "pulling up of the roots," indicated plainly that any amount of risk was now considered legitimate, even if it came to a total shutdown of all foreign trade.

But for how long would the emperor stand behind such a fearsome order? Lu K'un, for one, seems to have believed from the start that cooler heads at court would soon prevail. He therefore moved at a desperately slow pace, on the one hand drowning the court in a flood of documents reporting the success of his mopping-up operations against seemingly endless enclaves of inland insurrectionaries (so perhaps, then, the military had not after all lost its sting!); and, on the other, doing little or nothing to provoke the British—in the hope, obviously, that in time the emperor would realize the enormous dangers involved in the use of the trade sanction and would desist.[20]

And, of course, in the end he was to be proven absolutely correct, though there were a few frightening moments along the way.[21] We have already noted the sobering influence exercised upon the court by the encounter with the *Andromache* and the *Imogene*, late in the summer of 1834. And we will recall, as well, that one of the first orders that had gone out to Lu K'un had been the warning to steer clear, at all costs, of the trade-cutoff threat. In our first review of the Napier episode, that injunction had perhaps sounded oddly out of place, considering the success Lu had just scored in using this very threat to turn the British merchants against their temperamental ambassador. But it had been one thing to suspend trade in order to secure merely a return to the pre-Napier diplomatic status quo ante.

It was quite another to employ this same highly risky weapon aggressively, and for the much more ambitious goal of forcing the British to yield their hugely profitable stake in the India opium-import business. In such an attempt, it seemed, the court would have no part, even if it meant that the opium epidemic among the imperial soldiers continued to rage. And, as if to confirm that the court had regained its senses, Governor General Lu was authorized, later in that same year, to confine his control efforts to a token action, every now and then, against the native opium smugglers, so as to impose at least "some sense of restraint" upon them.[22]

The point, then, is that even so compelling a public interest as the preservation of the reputation and prestige of the imperial military was to prove, in the end, insufficient to override the broad bureaucratic consensus against a trade embargo. Based on the lessons they had gained in the field, the mandarins influential in provincial governance had been moving for some years prior to 1836 in the direction of discarding the idea that trade sanctions held hope of restoring fiscal and monetary health to the Ch'ing empire. Though perhaps never fully persuaded, by 1834 the emperor himself had nonetheless also been won over to the view that the trade weapon was not the answer. Even when confronted with evidence that the drug problem was rotting his southern armies, Tao-kuang had been only momentarily enthusiastic about an embargo, an enthusiasm soon dispelled by Lord Napier's guns.

There was, in short, no longer any significant constituency for the trade-control sanction—at least within the bureaucracy itself—when the great foreign-trade and opium-policy debate began in earnest, early in 1836. The awesomely destructive impact of the opium trade—socially, economically, even militarily—simply had not supplied a motive sufficient to force the Ch'ing government into a war-risking adventure of an embargo for political ends. Our conclusion, then, can only be that the impetus of the eventual turn back toward trade warfare in 1839 came from outside the mainstream of bureaucratic opinion—that is from the literati themselves—and expressed a mode of thinking about foreign-policy questions not informed by conventional notions of risk and benefit. With this point in mind, we turn, next, to look more carefully at the 1836–1838 debates themselves—debates from whose resolution was to issue one final, and fatal, wave of enthusiasm for terminating Sino-British trade. What, then, moved the leaders of literati opinion to take up this unpopular cause? What ends did they have in mind beyond the remedying of the monetary and military decrepitude inflicted by the spread of opium consumption? (For, clearly, there must have been other matters on their minds to have drawn them into embracing a position already so broadly discredited.) And how were they able to convince the emperor to give them the chance to try out their ideas? What was it about the structure of Ch'ing politics in the late 1830s that made it possible for so marginal a group to gain a hearing over the heads, as it were, of the entrenched bureaucratic hierarchy? These are the questions we shall now seek to answer, as we redirect our attention to the actual processes of decision making that led up to the fateful return to restrictionism in 1839.

THE LEGALIZATION INITIATIVE OF 1836

Our study of how literati opinion deflected Ch'ing policy back in the direction of rigid trade controls begins with their resistance to an attempted liberalization of policy in 1836. One might anticipate that mounting bureaucratic disillusion with other alternatives would eventually incline Ch'ing leaders to consider the idea of legalizing the drug traffic. In addition to lowering import prices and encouraging domestic replacement of foreign sources of supply, such a move would also have the clear advantage of removing the Ch'ing military from its prestige-eroding role in the sheltering of a contraband product, and might thus even help reduce consumption among the troops.

In fact, Lu K'un had already been pressing hard for such a policy change at the time of his inopportune death in office, late in 1835. His idea, moreover, was to be picked up and renewed by Lu's bureaucratic and examination-system mentor, Juan Yuan, early in 1836, and it was to be strongly supported, by Lu's successor in office, Teng T'ingchen.[23]

Yet the outcome of these efforts from within the bureaucracy was not as expected. In mid-1836, just as the advocates of legalization seemed on the verge of success, a vigorous resistance suddenly blossomed forth from the censorate, spearheaded by the Spring Purification circle, and backed by considerable informational resources that this network of literati politicians possessed. Taking skilled advantage of these resources, as well as of the political fluidity and renewed indecisiveness of the emperor following the death of Grand Councillor Ts'ao Chen-yung, in early 1835, the opposition was able to thwart legalization. It was, in time, even able to build upon this initial victory to win imperial backing for a new attempt at solving the opium problem through trade controls—this time to be supplemented by a prior crackdown against onshore consumers.

The demise of the 1836 legalization initiative thus provides a convenient starting point for our scrutiny of how the Ch'ing court was turned aside from the more realistic course it had seemed prepared to follow in the wake of the Napier affair. It marks the forceful entry onto the stage of foreign-policy debate of an organized literati-oppositionist constituency in Peking—an opinion group that would acquire, over the next few years, even greater influence over foreign and military policy. Perhaps even more important, it brings to light evidence of the relative weakness of establishment forces within the Ch'ing administrative system (in this case, the senior provincial bureaucrats)—a weakness that would likewise become more pronounced in the ensuing half-decade. Taking this latter observation as our cue, we might usefully begin our review of how the legalization plan was deliberated by focusing, first, on the political circumstances that made effective literati resistance possible, as well as attractive. We shall then move on to examine the details of the legalizationists' case, and the methods used by the opposition to discredit them.

In a sense, the failure of the provincial bureaucracy to win firm imperial support for the abandonment of opium import controls in 1836 flowed from the anarchic and disputatious character the central government's decision-making system had acquired by the late 1830s. Normally top-heavy and dominated by one or two powerful grand councillors and their clients within the territorial bureaucracy, that system had been showing signs of increasing susceptibility to assault by Southern-City interlopers since at least the early part of the decade, thanks primarily to Tao-kuang's growing obsession with the prospect of rebellion and his corresponding disinclination to turn back challenges by the censorate to the actions of senior provincial personnel. The trend toward inclusivity and broadened Southern City participation in policy review was to receive considerable new impetus, however, in early 1835, from the departure from the Peking political scene of Ts'ao Chen-yung, the last of the truly awesome incumbents to fill the office of grand councillor in the late Ch'ing.

With the death of the irreplaceable Ts'ao, Tao-kuang would become even less willing than before to trust his bureaucratic establishment, and thus—for the moment at least—all the more determined to use rival networks within the metropolitan bureaucracy to control it. This concern to counterbalance the weight of vested bureaucratic interests is nowhere more in evidence than in the personnel choices Tao-kuang would make during the years 1835 and 1836, just as the renewed debate over trade and drug policy in the southeast was getting under way. So perfect, in fact, was the power equilibrium that would emerge from this reshuffle that administrators in Kwangtung (such as Teng T'ing-chen) and their backers in the capital (notably Juan Yuan) never really had much of a chance of beating back the predictable counterattack that their Southern-City rivals launched against their liberalization scheme. A brief look at how Tao-kuang replenished the ranks of his consultative staff in Peking after Ts'ao's death—just as the opium question was about to be reconsidered—will help to confirm how difficult a fight the legalizationists faced as they confronted their critics in 1836. The pattern revealed by these new consultative appointments seems in fact to reflect a conscious determination to give equal place to senior representatives of the Kwangtung provincial administration, on the one hand, and to their foes within the literati-dominated censorate, on the other.

The first of these two groups of newly appointed policy referees was headed up by the 71-year-old Juan Yuan, the oldest provincial bureaucrat of the Chia-ch'ing restoration era still active in affairs of state. (As of January 1835, Juan was serving as viceroy in charge of the two southwestern provinces of Yunnan and Kweichow). As qualifications for the advisory role, however, Juan could point to more than just a long and honorable record as a provincial official. He could also look back upon ten years (1817–1826) of experience as chief administrator of Kwangtung and Kwangsi (Liang-Kuang viceroy), credentials that made him without doubt the empire's most practiced veteran of still untarnished reputation in dealings with the English. In this latter office, moreover, Juan had also acquired valuable firsthand experience with the intricacies of the coastal smuggling trade, and in the engineering of protective fortifications to guard against naval attack. All of this added up to a very impressive set of qualifications for advising a now insecure emperor on the veracity of the reports coming from Canton. Accordingly, within only several weeks of Ts'ao Chen-yung's death, the emperor recalled Juan permanently to the capital, bestowing upon him the office of full grand secretary (effectively minister without portfolio).[24]

It was not just an insider's knowledge of "barbarian affairs" however, that Tao-kuang was acquiring with his transfer of Juan to the capital. Knowingly or not (and I suspect very knowingly), the emperor was introducing into his inner councils a representative of the realist point of view on the trade question—a perspective that had been gaining increasing influence over the past several years among the mandarins in service in Canton. We have already remarked upon Lu K'un's lack of enthusiasm for confronting the British over the Gulf of Canton opium traffic, as well as that same official's support for the idea of legalization of the drug. However, what needs to be added is that, once recalled to Peking, Grand Secretary Juan became Viceroy Lu's behind-the-scenes supporter. Lu was, in fact, one of Juan's examination-system pupils, and probably also a beneficiary of Juan's bureaucratic patronage—meaning, in context, that the two men must have been carefully coordinating their views on the trade question on the eve of Juan's elevation to his advisory office in the capital. (And, indeed, Juan was later to boast to an old Southern-City acquaintance that Lu had "imitated" Juan's own approach to the barbarian problem in Kwangtung.)[25] In bringing Juan to Peking as a kind of informal foreign-policy adviser, therefore, Tao-kuang was probably attempting to give the fairest possible hearing (albeit at one remove) to Lu's opinions and to the cause of legalization.

Balancing off this "old-Kwangtung-hand" advisory group, however, was a second and very differently inclined consultative corps whose role in the deliberations was to be formalized by imperial order somewhat later in 1835. This group, recruited entirely from the staff of the metropolitan censorate, received its mandate to comment on trade policy questions through a highly unusual decree issued by the emperor on 15 October 1835. In this edict, Tao-kuang singled out for honorary promotion en bloc a group of four censors whose reports on administrative corruption during the preceding several years had much impressed the throne with their "accuracy" and "practicality." In reward for their warmly praised activism as bureaucratic watchdogs, the four were to be promoted to the capacity, in effect, of ombudsmen-extraordinary. They were, the emperor instructed, to speak out "fearlessly" in criticism of provincial officials and of their policy suggestions. In context, this meant that they were to feel free to challenge the legalizationists, although this was not stated specifically.[26] The emperor seemed inclined, instead, to present his gesture as little more than a continuation of the trend toward imperial encouragement of literati vigilance in the oversight of regional governance. Yet there can be no missing the additional suggestion that Tao-kuang was here seeking to balance off the influence of the rather conservative old-Kwangtung-hand opinion group.

The date of the preferment of the court censors coincides with the receipt of news at court of Lu K'un's death and with the naming of a successor in whom Tao-kuang clearly wished to inspire a sense of uncertainty about how the political winds were likely to blow at court.[27] Moreover, three of the four individuals singled out for this distinction had already achieved some prominence as commentators on drug and monetary problems. Feng Tsan-hsun, for example, will be remembered as one of the censorial gadflies who had stubbornly tormented the Liang-Kuang viceroy, Li Hung-pin, with his well-informed reports on the continuing illegal opium traffic in the Gulf of Canton. Tseng Wang-yen had played an analogous role in making things difficult for Lu K'un, though he had had perhaps somewhat less success.[28] Huang Chueh-tzu, the third in the group, was the guiding hand behind the Spring Purification clique. But he had also achieved, by 1835, a reputation as something of a censorial expert on currency problems in the Yangtze valley, most likely thanks to the broad range of connections among the Kiangsu examination elite that he had gained as a provincial examiner for that province in 1828.[29]

The fourth censor drafted by Tao-kuang for his special surveillance role, Chin Ying-lin, does not appear to have made any contributions to the trade-policy debate prior to 1835. But he was known to be exceedingly well versed in the problems of Ch'ing judicial procedures owing to six years' experience as a junior staff official in the Board of Punishments. This, one suspects, was probably the reason for his inclusion in the censorial referee group, inasmuch as problems of equity in the enforcement of existing laws against Chinese distributors were coming to occupy a prominent place in the arguments of the legalizationists just at the time the commission-of-four was created. Also a possibility, however, was that the emperor wished to have at his side a scholar-official with social roots in the highly commercialized Yangtze region (Chin was from Hangchow), where monetary contractions would be felt most immediately, so as to insure that the currency-control aspects of the trade problem would continue to receive due attention.[30]

On the eve of the legalizationist initiative of 1836, therefore, major changes had suddenly been introduced into the normal procedures for the referral of policy questions having to do with foreign trade at Canton. Lapsing into a bout of insecurity and indecisiveness in the wake of the loss of his venerable inner-palace confidant, Ts'ao Chen-yung, the Tao-kuang emperor had in effect acted to reduce the amount of automatic influence in trade-policy deliberations traditionally enjoyed by the Liang-Kuang viceroy by virtue of his unmatched expertise in "barbarian affairs" and his command of the archives of diplomatic correspondence. To achieve some safety from the danger he now foresaw of being maneuvered, from below, into injudicious policy decisions, merely to suit the convenience of certain of his bureaucratic servants, Tao-kuang had installed around him a carefully balanced committee of expert councillors, representative alike of bureaucratic and literati-censorial points of view. As a result, political outsiders, operating through the networks of the censorate, had gained a vastly more influential role in trade policy than they could have expected to exercise under more normal circumstances. Ts'ao Chen-yung's death had inadvertently opened the way for Huang Chueh-tzu and his followers to exploit this influence for their own political purposes.

Before seeing how the Spring Purification opposition used this power to thwart the realist party, however, there is perhaps one more observation pertaining to the unusual condition of the policy-review mechanisms of the Ch'ing court circa 1836 that needs to be put forward. That is, that both sides in the new balance of forces in the capital had access to a broad array of private literati contacts within the academy system of Canton, the Kwangtung provincial capital. Through these connections, teachers and students affiliated with the more elite institutions of that city's educational establishment were to be drawn directly into the trade controversy of the next several years. The bitter polarization of Cantonese literati opinion that arose out of this involvement in the Peking debates over legalization would continue on, in fact, well into and after the 1840–1842 fighting. Delaying our elaboration of that particular theme until the next chapter, however, we can here confine ourselves to a brief glance at how such academy support was sought out by both sides.

On the legalizationist side, it is clear that Juan Yuan, Lu K'un, and the latter's successor as Liang-Kuang viceroy, Teng T'ing-chen, all collaborated closely with the newest and most official of Canton's four principal academies, the Hsueh-hai-t'ang. From this institution they solicited advice and support in favor of their cause. The Hsueh-hai-t'ang, it perhaps needs to be added, was without doubt the most illustrious surviving incarnation of the northern-clique era's academic values. It had been founded in 1820 by Juan himself, in cooperation with several prominent Chinese foreign-trade merchant-philanthropists, as part of a campaign to plant the ideals and erudition of the Han Learning movement in a rather insular terrain where pre-Ch'ienlung intellectual patterns still dominated. Having achieved considerable success in this project, Juan's personal involvement in the affairs of this school had naturally continued even after his departure from Kwangtung in 1826. And it was on account of this ongoing close personal connection with the Hsueh-hai-t'ang that Juan was able, during the late 1830s, to align the expertise of its scholars in support of the generally cautious line he was advocating in foreign policy.[31]

On the other side of the debate, the oppositionists, mobilized around Huang Chueh-tzu, were able eventually to draw information and support for their arguments from the sizable body of academy students and teachers living in Canton who took umbrage at the imported intellectual fashions in vogue at the Hsueh-hai-t'ang (or who, for other reasons, felt uncomfortable with the liberal approach to trade and drug policy that seemed to be in favor at that institution of learning). Moreover, since the Han Learning party was the newcomer group, and was somewhat tarnished by its identification with allegedly corrupt mercantile interests, the local support, in Canton, available to the Spring Purification leadership seems consistently to have outweighed that available to the Juan party in the capital.[32] This disadvantage, along with the general slippage in mainstream bureaucratic influence at court, was to have a pronouncedly negative influence on the prospects for the legalizationist movement, as we shall see below.

THE FAILURE OF THE INITIATIVE

Early in 1836, Napier's successor as overseer of British trading interests in Canton, Captain Charles Elliot, began to hear from reliable Chinese mercantile sources that the Celestial Court was on the verge of a momentous decision. According to Elliot's informants, Taokuang had been persuaded by Juan Yuan to undertake the "remarkable" measure of legalizing both the import of India opium and the domestic production of the drug as the most realistic policy for slowing the efflux of silver that was so sorely troubling trade and tax collection through China. Indeed, so convincing was the evidence of an impending change of heart in Peking that not only Elliot, but knowledgeable academy circles in Canton, and even the governor general, Teng T'ing-chen, thought that the emperor had already been brought around to sanctioning the idea.[33] True, it had not been Juan himself, but rather a middle-ranking Southern City official, one Hsu Nai-chi, who had requested formal change of the laws in a petition submitted to the emperor on 17 May. But that could be explained as a face-saving device, aimed at protecting both Juan and the prestige-conscious emperor from too visible a role in this difficult decision by allowing the matter to be referred to a committee of precedents experts selected from the Board of Punishments. The next step, undoubtedly, would be a positive committee report, to be followed up quickly by a terse edict of authorizing the change.[34]

In the end, the prognostication proved entirely wrong, but the details that had been leaked to Elliot concerning the court debate in the spring and summer of 1836 seem on the whole to have been quite accurate. As far as can be ascertained, it was indeed at the instigation of Juan Yuan, or at the very least with his tacit approval, that the legalization plan had been offered up as a final solution to the problem of trade controls. Juan's involvement was evidenced, for one thing, by the Hsueh-hai-t'ang provenance of the formula upon which Hsu Nai-chi's arguments had been based. The essayist whose works had inspired Hsu was a certain Wu Lan-hsiu (1808 *chü-jen*), a Kwangtung-born graduate and co-director of the academy, and a longtime scholarly favorite of Juan, going back to the days of the latter's term as Liang-Kuang viceroy. Under these circumstances, it is almost inconceivable that Hsu could have availed himself of "pupil" Wu's studies on the legalization question without Juan's approval.[35]

Furthermore, as the enemies of the grand secretary and of his model academy did not hesitate to point out, there were probably personal reasons why the continuation of the government's on-again off-again campaign against the drug trafficking made Juan and his party among the Cantonese quite nervous. After all, the money that had been paid for the Hsueh-hai-t'ang's construction and its endowment was very largely donated (or, perhaps more accurately, squeezed) from the coffers of the government-licensed foreign-trade monopoly guild merchants of the city of Canton. To such men, of course, the possibility of a trade stoppage was not a cheering one. And, what is more, there was even the possibility that a serious crackdown against the racketeers would bring to light cohong merchant complicity in the drug trade—a possibility Juan and his scholarly dependents in Canton could scarcely have looked forward to with anything but alarm. Howqua II, the famous cohong plutocrat who had so generously "contributed" to the Hsueh-hai-t'ang project, and to other of Viceroy Juan's philanthropies, had in fact already been implicated once before in just this sort of illegal transaction. To make things more difficult still, Juan himself was widely suspected of having turned a blind eye to the British stockpiling operations at Lintin that had begun during his term as viceroy.[36]

From Grand Secretary Juan's point of view, therefore, there was excellent reason to want to bury, once and for all, the foolish idea of trade control—and to do so quickly, before anything further transpired that might damage the reputations of worthy men. Legalization, in addition to offering the most certain practical benefits of any of the entertained options, was also a way to guarantee that the tiresome idea of interdicting foreign trade would not be heard of again.

As for the arguments Juan and his allies advanced in favor of the deregulation scheme, the emphasis fell, predictably, upon the host of administrative dysfunctions arising out of attempts to enforce existing laws that provincial officials had been complaining about for years. Going perhaps one step beyond these purely pragmatic considerations, however, the Juan forces also seemed to be making a kind of philosophic case against inflated notions about human nature or the capacity of the government bureaucracy for social action. As these latter sentiments were, later on, to help confirm the contrary views of the Spring Purificationists, we might here take brief cognizance, as well, of the philosophic underpinnings of the legalizationist cause.

Looking first at the practical arguments mustered against perpetuation of the old drug-control laws, we may cite briefly from the 1833 memorandum on the question written by the Hsueh-hai-t'ang director, Wu Lan-hsiu. For it was this document that gave Hsu Nai-chi his inspiration. To begin with, in attacking the much-discussed embargo policy, Wu noted, first, that it would not work unless all foreign trade and traders were banned from Chinese shores. Otherwise, the smuggling would simply be shifted from British to American or other national fleets. Such a total shutdown of China's export trade would, however, threaten the livelihoods of hundreds of thousands of transport workers and small growers who earned their meager livings from the legal (tea and silk) and illegal (opium) business with the foreigners. Then again, to close down Canton to British ships alone would probably only encourage the British to seize one or more offshore islands as a base for new shipping networks. Most problematically of all, the "total" approach, to be successful, would require a Draconian police effort onshore in order to break up the highly mobile and elusive native distributor networks. Bitter experience had taught that the imperial bureaucracy simply did not possess a sufficiently reliable police apparatus to pursue these distributors. Regulations of the sort that would have to be enforced, Wu claimed, were "but toys in the hands of corrupt government functionaries." The tougher the regulations, the worse the blackmailing of innocents would become, while the traffic itself would not be the slightest bit interrupted. The government agents and soldiers assigned to such cases would merely report one or two arrests and seizures, and whatever else they confiscated would simply be resold.[37]

At the root of Wu's skepticism about trade control, therefore, was a worldly-wise sense of the practical limits of the Ch'ing state's internal enforcement capacities. Of course, Wu was conspicuously ignoring one way out of the enforcement dilemma that would naturally have recommended itself to the more idealistic among the Confucian scholar elite. This was the possibility that society itself, under the leadership of a morally renovated scholar class, might be able to take over from the government the responsibility of policing the onshore native dealers out of business. But the omission itself is revealing. For, as Wu makes quite clear, it was based on his fundamentally negative assessment of the ability of the elite to persuade the masses to turn against drug users and their suppliers. (A social consensus against drug use, Wu argues elsewhere in this same tract, could only be created by the experience of "satiation" and "penitence"—just as with children learning by bitter experience to avoid excesses of diet, drink, and sex—and not by command or influence from above.)

Yet even here, cynical though it might perhaps sound, Wu's position does not seem inconsistent with the kinds of assumptions the Han Learning orientation would have inclined most literati-bureaucrats of Juan's generation to accept. And if such skepticism about the scholar class's social leadership potential was indeed the majority position within the bureaucracy, one can well see why Wu and Juan would have thought the enforcement issue sufficient to silence the restrictionists once and for all.

Such, then, was the thinking behind the policy to which Grand Secretary Juan almost succeeded in winning Tao-kuang's assent in 1836. Almost. For although the legalization plan that went before the throne in mid-May 1836 was supported at court with sufficient eloquence to elicit an order that it be referred to the Kwangtung authorities for their comment (a step which, in context, virtually guaranteed that it would be carried, since Teng was strongly in favor of legalization), the whole idea was mysteriously dropped even before that viceroy's highly enthusiastic endorsement arrived back in Peking on 12 October.[38]

What, then, had gone wrong? We have no way of knowing just what words, uttered within the protective silence of the Summer Palace, might actually have turned the emperor around once again. But certainly part of the difficulty can be traced to a last-minute set of revelations, indirectly implicating the legalizationists in illegal currency dealings, that seems to have its origins in the efforts of the anti-Hsueh-hai-t'ang faction in Canton. Still more to the point, this last-minute assault from Canton seems to have been encouraged and coordinated by Huang Chueh-tzu and the Spring Purificationists in the capital, with a view toward gaining supreme power within the emperor's foreign-policy counsels. Such a strategy was, at any rate, fully consistent with the kind of oppositional game Huang had been playing prior to the debate, and it would have suited P'an Shih-en's ambitions as well to dislodge Juan from Peking. Moreover, as we have already mentioned, the Spring Purification party had for some time been cultivating its own following among the academy pedagogues of Canton. It seems certain that these ties with the regional anti-legalizationist movement provided the channels through which the disruptive new disclosures about illegal trading were to reach the capital.

To come back, however, to the specifics of the attack, it is evident that Huang Chueh-tzu's friends in Canton had been keeping close tabs for some time on the doings of the cohong merchants, in the hope of finding information that might sabotage the credibility of their patrons within the legalizationist party. Using the information thus obtained, Huang Chueh-tzu and his fellow oppositionists were able to muster two timely impeachments against the "old-Kwangtung-hand" lobby and its favorite philanthropist, Howqua II, for alleged complicity in the opium- and silver-export traffic.

Huang Chueh-tzu himself was the first to make use of this evidence from Canton with an eye toward sullying the reputation of the Juan party. On 30 October 1835, a full year earlier, Huang had submitted a plea against a change of policy. To this he had appended (in the form of a secret memorial) a list of allegations of large-scale involvement by the Howqua family firm in opium transactions. For some reason, this report seems never to have come to the emperor's attention. But then, nine months later, while the Hsu Nai-chi proposal was under review by Governor General Teng in Canton, another Spring Purificationist, Yao Yuan-chih, supplied the emperor with a second and longer list of charges about misdeeds within the cohong. This document had the most telling effect. Reading Yao's memorial on 5 August, the emperor was sufficiently impressed by the charges that he immediately issued an order demanding investigation and punishment of the offenders.[39]

Inevitably, the prestige of the cohong-linked Juan faction fared badly in the wake of these nasty revelations. During the following several weeks, as more rebuttals of the legalization scheme continued to pour in from the censorate, the tone of the answering edicts swung ever more over to the side of the critics.[40] By the time Governor General Teng's positive report on the Hsu Nai-chi proposal actually arrived in Peking in mid-October, there was already so little interest left in the idea that the document was not even graced with the usual referral to committee deliberation. Tao-kuang, it seemed, had once again changed his mind on the trade-control questions, this time persuaded by an increasingly well coordinated literati opposition movement. And so the "remarkable measure" that had aroused so much hope in Captain Elliot fell by the wayside, never to be revived.

INTRANSIGENTS TAKE THE HELM

On 16 October 1836, Teng T'ing-chen, the cautious but scrupulous mandarin now in charge at Canton, received fresh instructions from the court that must have been exceedingly disheartening. Without having yet even seen Teng's carefully drafted brief in favor of the suspension of the anti-opium laws, Tao-kung had ordered Teng to begin deliberations anew on how to cut off the opium trade at its Kwangtung "source."[41]

To the politically astute Teng (as indeed to most other provincial chiefs), the meaning of this reversal was immediately clear. The emperor was reverting to his 1832 posture of insisting on total suppression of the opium traffic in the Canton vicinity. Teng would now be expected to find ways of expelling the opium business from the Kwangtung coast, no matter what the consequences. And, being a prudent man, that is exactly what Teng set about doing.[42]

For officials at court associated with the victorious Spring Purification party, however, the question of where to go next was not so easily resolved. An embargo was not a solution to more general problems of controlling foreign trade. Spring Purificationists' actions had guaranteed that the matter of Kwangtung's external trade would be back in the middle of court politics and that the responsibility for finding a workable means of controlling that trade would now lie with the opposition leadership—with Huang Chueh-tzu, with his Southern City literati followers, and with Grand Councillor P'an Shih-en, who had no doubt been egging Huang onward. Unless they wished to surrender the political gains so recently won, these men would themselves have to find a way past the numerous practical difficulties that for years had been discouraging attempts to bear down upon the existing maritime trade arrangements.

But how exactly was this to be done? How could the elusive and dangerous British opium clippers be chased away from the shores of Kwangtung without provoking a major war? How could pressure be brought to bear on opium without immediate escalation to a full trade embargo that would endanger so many livelihoods onshore? And, still more to the point, what was to be done about controlling the native end of the drug-distribution system? How was this particular sub-sector of the trade to be assaulted without creating massive opportunities for blackmail and fraud by corrupt government agents and their underworld accomplices?

These hurdles must have seemed, if anything, even more formidable to the newly triumphant Spring Purificationists than they had to Grand Secretary Juan. For the ideas on foreign trade current among most of Huang Chueh-tzu's friends in the capital at the time of the campaign against legalization were apparently quite simplistic, and offered no real guidance. Even the self-professedly practical Kung Tzu-chen could only suggest, as of 1838 or so, that *all* foreign trade be terminated—a view that merely echoed the notion derived from Inner Asia policies of punishing misbehaving nomads by cutting off their profitable trade access to the settled Chinese economy.[43] Under the circumstances, then, it is no wonder that nearly two more years were to elapse before the Spring Purificationists could come up with their own set of answers.

The "new" answer to the trade control dilemma, broached by Huang Chueh-tzu in a famous memorial of 2 June 1838, must have impressed many by the ingenious simplicity of the detour its author had found around all the old difficulties. Without beating around the bush, Huang and associates (the document had been collectively authored) confessed at the outset that the embargo weapon was absolutely useless.[44] There was simply no way to wean the British away from their lucrative smuggling traffic, the profits of which far outstripped those accruing from legal commerce, simply by the threat of closing down authorized trade at Canton. Nor, the memorial allowed, could the Ch'ing hope for much success by mounting a sustained drive against the Chinese dealers. Rather, the imperial bureaucracy ought to apply pressure against the smuggling trade by striking at the most vulnerable link in the chain—the Chinese consumer! Through a stepped up campaign to punish the addict—a campaign to be given teeth by the passage of a death-penalty provision for unrepentant users—the market for imported legal opium was to be made so small that prices would plummet, and neither English nor Chinese dealers would have the incentive to persist in their noxious profession.[45]

It must all have seemed so logical. And not just logical but fair as well. For, barring the unpleasantness of the executions (a moral question that itself probably would have raised few eyebrows among the elite), there was, as Huang pointed out, a real element of justice in directing the weight of the law against the consumer, rather than the distributor. By this change, Huang proposed, in effect, to strengthen the moral probity of the government's position, inasmuch as the addicts, unlike the dealers, betrayed their guilt to the world through readily observable symptoms. In enforcing the law primarily against the consumer, then, the mandarins would no longer have to agonize over the reliability of their informers. And, for those whose consciences still bothered them, Huang added yet another provision: namely, that no executions were to take place for a year. In the meanwhile, medicine was to be distributed, and all users were to be given the chance to surrender their pipes and drugs, and make a fresh start. What possible objections could now remain to prevent plunging ahead with a "final" campaign to wipe out the opium blight?[46]

And yet, supremely practical and just though it sounded, there was one small but quite important detail in the emerging Huang plan that was not quite consistent with the rest. That was, that it assumed major enforcement efforts in Kwangtung province alone, there to be orchestrated by an official loyal to the Spring Purification party. That official, it was soon revealed, was the current Hu-Kuang governor general, Lin Tse-hsu, whose enthusiastic endorsement of Huang's plan (arranged prior to its presentation to the throne) was in the end to swing the emperor into supporting it. And, as events progressed, it was to become evident that Lin had volunteered for the job of implementing the anti-drug crusade in Kwangtung, where he was to be dispatched before long as special imperial agent.[47]

We have suggested that this particular provision for concentrating enforcement in Kwangtung alone introduces a somewhat false note into an otherwise plausible scheme. But why so? In the first place, of course, because it tells us that Huang still did not believe he had found an answer that the bureaucratic majority would support—for, otherwise, what need would there be for a special commissioner to oversee the campaign?

But, still more confusing, why had Huang and his allies singled out Kwangtung? Why not, instead, concentrate upon Kiangsu, for example, or upon other areas where opium use had grown to much larger proportions? (In Soochow, for example, an estimated 40 percent of the city's 250,000 residents were estimated to be on opium by the early 1830s—a much larger population than could have existed anywhere in the much less urbanized southeast.)[48] And, even if the market for the drug in Kwangtung could be destroyed, given the huge potential market still remaining upcoast and in the interior provinces, what was to keep the smugglers from simply shifting their route of penetration?

One looks in vain to the official documents of 1838 for clarification of these curious anomalies in the Huang plan. Neither in Huang's memorials, nor in Lin's do we find any mention of special commissioners for oversight of enforcement in Kwangtung or elsewhere. Nonetheless, when considered within the larger context of continuing bureaucratic suspicion of the utility of trade controls and of the ongoing post-1835 struggle for influence within court consultations, this resort to a strategy of high-profile localized enforcement of the anti-user laws seems to be remarkably well suited to the immediate political and ideological concerns of the Spring Purification faction. Pursuing this idea, let us see what sense we can extract from the specifics of the enforcement methods ultimately relied on by the Huang–Lin coalition.

One concern addressed by the limited enforcement scheme, as shall be presently documented in more detail, was to find a means of attacking the drug import system that would not require broad official cooperation up and down the length of the China coast. Such cooperation, it was well understood, was not likely to be forthcoming—a point that became unmistakably clear after the great majority of officials consulted in the course of the 1838 poll on the death-penalty law refused to lend it their support. Implementation of the new legislation, then, had necessarily to be concentrated in one or two pilot provinces, and placed under the direct authority of officials loyal to the Spring Purification group and to its goal of total eradication of opium imports. And it would have to take as its aim the limited goal of inducing only a momentary collapse of the drug market, pending the relocation of the smuggling traffic northwards. In the end, then, the hopes of the Spring Purificationists turned on the prospect that the commercial panic induced by such a temporary collapse would give Lin the leverage needed in order to pressure the British authorities into sacrificing the drug trade to salvage the profits of legal commerce. That being Lin's intent, it made very good sense that the enforcement effort should focus on Kwangtung—for that particular location would afford the maximum amount of foreign publicity to the campaign, thus presumably hastening the collapse of British resolve and bringing the affair to a conclusion before the limited nature of the Ch'ing suppression drive could be ascertained. If, in short, the Ch'ing had to bluff, Kwangtung was the logical place to do it.

The other concerns informing the Spring Purificationists' confusing choice of enforcement strategies appear, however, to be more political than practical in origin. First among them, one suspects, was the desire to project the anti-opium crusade as an undertaking that would give expression to the ideal of direct action by the scholar class—an ideal the Spring Purification circle had helped propagate among Southern City literati earlier in the decade. An all-out crusade against drug consumption—however localized—would have the virtue of requiring the active involvement of the local examination elite as a condition of its success, for the degree-holding elite offered the Ch'ing bureaucracy the only effective means at its disposal for bringing pressure to bear on offenders within the middle classes of local society where drug abuse was most concentrated. From the point of view of the legitimacy-obsessed ideologues who dominated the Spring Purification party, the opportunity to mobilize the academic elite for such highly moral purposes must have seemed so exhilarating that the shortcomings of the anti-user strategy could easily be brushed aside.

Then, too, we ought to consider the possibility that Lin Tse-hsu himself most likely preferred that the final drive to end drug imports be undertaken in only one province, and under his own specially commissioned leadership. As we have already had occasion to observe, Lin's reasons for collaboration with the Spring Purificationists on this matter had much to do with his own quest for increased personal and political credibility at court. By bravely leaping into the fray, where other high officials had hung back, and by emerging (it was hoped) with the long-sought prize of a written British promise to end their involvement in the opium trade, Lin would establish his fitness for the reward of a transfer to the Liang-Kiang governor generalship. And, once emplaced there, he would at last be able to embark upon the long contemplated scheme for reforming the tribute-grain transport system. Who then could dare impugn his motives? And who would then dare offer resistance to the measures he had been planning for the agricultural reclamation of the north? In this way, Governor General Lin's own political concerns likewise fed into the choice to pursue a localized policy for drug control in the south.

But let us now review, more closely, the evidence for each of these several points. It is noteworthy that the Spring Purification coalition, its strength in Peking notwithstanding, never even tried to secure an order extending strict enforcement of the anti-consumption laws beyond the two southeastern provinces of Kwangtung and Fukien. Lin's self-requested dispatch to Kwangtung early in 1839, and the subsequent assignment of Huang Chueh-tzu on a parallel mission to southern Fukien early in 1840, may both be taken as indications that the Spring Purificationists were determined to see the new anti-user laws implemented with as much severity as possible in these two provinces.[49] But there is no sign of any further effort by the Spring Purification leadership to extend the network of special agents beyond this remote corner of the Chinese coastline.

No doubt one of the more compelling reasons for this reluctance was surely the overwhelming evidence of official displeasure with the idea of executing addicts that had surfaced in the course of the 1838 debates over Huang's proposal. Nineteen of the twenty-six high-ranking provincial officials consulted refused categorically to lend their support to this plan. Even Lin's old ally and patron, the aging Liang-Kiang viceroy, T'ao Chu, disapproved of the "excessive harshness" of the new law (as well he might, considering the huge population of addicts within his bailiwick). Others, such as the Chihli governor general, Ch'i-shan, were even more insulting, and made little secret of their unwillingness to put teeth into the campaign within their own administrative jurisdictions.[50]

Faced with such powerful opposition, Lin and his backers among the Spring Purificationist party had, therefore, no choice but to confine their crusade to the southeast where Lin himself could supply the kind of vigorous, committed leadership needed to insure that the new laws would be enforced to full effect. As to how Lin proposed to guarantee that such a limited effort would bring results, we can reasonably infer from Commissioner Lin's subsequent actions, undertaken upon his arrival in Canton, that much hope rode on the possibility that the British could be enticed into renunciation of their offshore opium trade if presented with a precipitous decline in local demand for the drug. In part, the enticement was thus to be a commercial one. First would come a drastic fall in drug prices, as the distribution system contracted. By stepping in with a vague promise of compensation for surrendered opium and by guaranteeing contin-

ued access to the profits of the tea trade (conditional upon the promise of no further complicity in the India drug traffic), Lin evidently
believed that he would be providing the British traders with an opportunity preferable to continued involvement in the declining drug
business.

But Lin's strategy did not rest on commercial incentives alone.
Equally prominent in his calculations was the presumed effect on the
foreigner of unexpectedly resolute moral action from the Ch'ing side.
From the start, Lin seems to have assumed that the English had espied the same moral timidity in the Ch'ing bureaucratic elite that the
Spring Purificationists were so fond of indicting, and that a demonstration that this timidity was not all-pervasive would thus have a
devastating effect. The famous opium burning in June 1839, attended
by scores of foreign witnesses, is perhaps the best known symbol of
the impact Lin believed his own determination would achieve. But,
even before this, Lin was already sounding quite confident about the
effect of his own personal moral courage. Within but a few days of
his arrival at Canton, and just barely established in his new quarters,
for example, Lin was already writing proudly to Tao-kuang to announce that the very rumor of his impending arrival had been
sufficient to scare the opium "king," Jardine, from the coasts of the
empire. The incredibly fast-paced timetable he was to pursue in following up the first opium surrenders with a demand for signed guar-
antees of no further drug trading is further indication of how much
Lin's plan was predicated on the assumed impact of resolute actions
upon a disbelieving barbarian audience.[51]

The impetus behind the enforcement strategy elected by the
Spring Purificationist bloc was not, however, simply practical in
nature. Political and ideological concerns figure equally prominently,
among them—as we have stressed—the desire to enact a policy that
gave full expression to the *ch'ing-i* ideal of direct engagement of the
scholarly moral conscience in the work of governance. The very idea
of anti-consumption legislation was in itself, in a sense, an invitation
to scholar class vigilantism on the local scene—for, as we have already
noted, the state's authority was perceived even by its own highest representatives as too flimsy and too poorly disciplined to be trusted
with responsibility for broad-scale drug-law enforcement. But the
call for the punishment of opium users appealed to literati idealism
in another capacity as well—that is, as a vehicle for probing the very

moral fitness of the scholar class as an independent leadership elite. Because there were, quite obviously, simply too many drug consumers for there to be any thought of arresting them all, and because use was concentrated among the middle classes of local society, it was recognized from the outset by leaders of the Spring Purification movement that prosecution would have to take aim at scholar-class offenders first. Within this group, at least, the identification of offenders would be simple, involving nothing more than an extension of the usual character-guarantee methods traditionally employed in controlling access to examinations and to government schools. Furthermore, powerful sanctions, such as the threat of permanent denial of degree-holder status, existed to help ensure compliance without any need for immediate recourse to the death penalty.

Not surprisingly, in light of what we have already seen of the Spring Purificationists' obsession with reviving the social authority of the lettered elite, this prospect of putting the lower ranks of the degree-holder class to the test came as a most welcome opportunity. Just how much enthusiasm such an enterprise was capable of stirring up is perhaps best revealed by the remarks that appear in an 1838 tract written by Yao Ying's close friend, the T'ung-ch'eng scholar, Fang Tung-shu. Noting, first, that critics of the anti-consumption legislation frequently alluded to the examination-rank status of offenders as a major obstacle to its enforcement, Fang here argues, in reply, that this very circumstance might equally well be construed as offering the best possible grounds for pushing ahead with the proposed law. The control of moral offenses, unlike the control of violent crime, depends, Fang insists, on making punitive example of offenders in high station—in other words, of the literati. Moreover, a full panoply of status-reducing penalties, or "penalties of shame," exist for this purpose: penalties such as dismissal from official or secretarial service, or lifelong debarment from the examinations.[52] An all-out attack on lettered-elite drug users was therefore not only appropriate, but feasible as well.

From the point of view of the Spring Purification leadership, then, the problem to which the new legislation was construed as an answer was not just that of ending drug use. Equally important, it was that of reestablishing the moral fitness of the degree-holding class as a social elite—a cause that had long been high on the literati reform agenda. Following quite consistently from this perception of the problem was the answer of a localized, model enforcement effort, to be conducted under the baton of an official championed by the Spring Purification circle, and to be assisted by a select ensemble of Cantonese scholars recruited through connections within Canton's academic world. As we shall see in the next chapter, the success of Governor General Lin's campaign in Kwangtung was predicated on the ideological mobilization of the local elite as a replacement for unreliable local government functionaries in the surveillance effort. More revealingly still, the initial wave of user arrests was designed to close in, first, upon the users of lettered-class status—upon those, that is, whose leadership ought to have been exemplary, and had not been.[53] The planned crusade against drug consumption, in short, gained much of its validity from its resonance with the idea of model social leadership by the scholar elite. And if, perhaps, some of the Spring Purificationists were a little blind to the defects of their scheme, the blindness may well have resulted from an excessive attachment to this symbolic aspect of their formula.

Finally, however, we come to the question of how Lin had been persuaded to throw his support behind the Huang plan. Our analysis suggests that Lin had been won over by the implicit promise that, if successful, he would gain for himself the office and prestige needed to revive the northern reclamation plan. But let us see what evidence exists for this interpretation.

The place to begin is, perhaps, with the nature of the understanding that had been worked out between the death-penalty advocates in the capital and Lin. That there was such an understanding is suggested by a number of apparent coincidences that, added together, hardly look coincidental at all. For one thing, there is evidence that a move was afoot within the Grand Council (almost certainly supported by P'an Shih-en) to remove Teng T'ing-chen from his post as the chief of the two Kuang provinces just before the June death-penalty proposal went before the emperor. The point of the move (which was not, for the moment, successful) was presumably to clear the way for Lin's appointment as Teng's replacement after the legislation had been pushed through. For another, Lin's extraordinarily positive endorsement of the Huang memorial of 2 June, which Lin had composed in reply to the throne's referendum on the feasibility of the death-penalty measure, was, as we have seen, sent off with breathtaking speed.[54]

Clearly, then, Lin had had prior intelligence concerning the capital-punishment initiative, in all likelihood relayed to him by his son, Ju-chou, who was then in the capital to sit for the 1838 metropolitan examinations.[55] Moreover, in a secret appendix attached to his official reply to the death-penalty referendum, Lin took the rather extraordinary position that there now could be no going back on the capital-punishment idea, since the proposal had already been made public, and to retreat from it at this point would be to send a clear signal to native and foreign lawbreakers alike that the Ch'ing government simply lacked the will power to act.[56] The inference one must draw from all this is that Lin had long since been converted to the idea of a great crusade against the drug, and was now merely looking for ways to make the case for such a crusade more compelling.[57]

Nevertheless, there still remains one final mystery surrounding Lin's action late in 1838. What did Lin hope to achieve by this gamble? We have speculated that Lin hoped for the Kiangnan-Kiangpeh governor generalship, from which T'ao Chu was soon due to retire, and a chance to tackle the unfinished business of the tribute-grain transport. That there was some sort of deal struck during Lin's interviews with the emperor early in 1839 is attested by what happened soon after Lin departed the capital for Canton. Though no mention of it occurs in the official record, it is evident that Tao-kuang was so impressed with Lin's optimism on the prospects for a quick resolution of the drug question that he did promise Lin an immediate transfer. Thus, on 22 April 1839, only weeks after Lin's retinue had arrived at Canton, Lin was named concurrently to the office of Liang-Kiang viceroy, with the post to be assumed once the current business in Canton had been finished.[58] Moreover, on 12 August of the same year—with Lin still in Canton, and the diplomatic crisis growing daily more serious—the emperor was to refer to "the Liang-Kiang Governor General Lin" a detailed plan for the reform of the tribute-grain system, drawing from Lin, in reply, a lengthy proposal urging the reinstatement of coastal transport, and the quick commencement of an experimental reclamation project in the Peking vicinity.[59]

It was, then, very much with the next step in mind that Lin had accepted the perilous assignment to Canton as the emperor's hand-picked plenipotentiary charged with awing the British into giving up their noxious traffic in India opium. Just as much as Huang Chueh-tzu, Lin was playing at the game of foreign policy essentially for domestic political purposes, and for the sake of expanded credit within the internal processes of Ch'ing politics. And, indeed, so hypnotizing, so captivating was the prospect of capturing these internal political prizes that the real dangers about to be encountered were never adequately reflected upon. Thus entranced by the glory that was to be theirs, the Spring Purification party led Tao-kuang into a war he had been told would never take place.

The Myth of Victory in Kwangtung

It is one of the more curious aspects of the Sino-British war of 1840–1842 that the Ch'ing defeat and surrender failed in the end to achieve any lasting impact on how that government conducted its foreign relations. Literati beliefs about the economic and military self-sufficiency of the empire remained fundamentally unshattered, in spite of the seemingly indisputable military verdict. And, what is more, the Ch'ing monarchy was to prove unable to exclude literati political initiatives for very long from the realm of diplomatic deliberations, no matter how irresponsible the literati role had been in the policy debates of the late 1830s.

Why was this? In this and three subsequent chapters, we shall be considering a number of internal political developments whose influence converged to assure this particular outcome. But first, we shall focus on the events of the war itself. More particularly, we shall be interested to see how these events came to encourage the literati in their belief that the 1842 defeat was not conclusive evidence of the bankruptcy of the existing political and military system.

The line of explanation to be pursued leads us somewhat away from the main theatres of conflict, for, as the literati themselves would later understand it, this was was actually two conflicts, whose outcomes were quite different. In the Yangtze and off the central China coast, there had been defeat after defeat. But in the southeast, and particularly at Canton, where the principal action of this part of our story unfolds, the verdict was believed to have been much more positive for the Ch'ing side. Indeed, even as the final peace negotiations were getting under way at Nanking in August 1842, vigorous protests began to pour into Peking from all across the empire, urging that the triumphs allegedly scored by "loyal" Ch'ing subjects in Kwangtung had established that concessions were not necessary, and that Ch'ing belligerence ought therefore to be perpetuated. Moreover, over the next several years, this same claim of an overlooked Ch'ing triumph in Kwangtung continued to serve as a rallying point for those many scholars who wished to undo the new treaties. Having proven that the means existed to resist, the victories at Canton thus called the literati onward, to a renewed struggle against the barbarian.[1]

To contemporary British observers (as, indeed, to many Manchus), all this was to seem terribly perplexing. Conditioned to expect that responsible governments could recognize when they had been defeated in the field, and confident that the recently demonstrated British capacity to seize key Yangtze communications centers had established the fact of Ch'ing incompetence to continue the war, they could not account for the perverse claims of a Ch'ing victory in the southeast.[2] But, equipped as we now are with a background in high Ch'ing politics, we are perhaps in better position to grasp how such a view could have spread. The really crucial factor was, of course, the special intensity of literati political involvement in the conduct of military operations in the southeast, a circumstance that arose, in turn, directly out of the decision to concentrate opium enforcement efforts within the provinces of Kwangtung and Fukien, and to assign Lin Tse-hsu to oversee them.

These efforts did not influence Captain Elliot and his government in quite the manner intended. And, by late 1839, Lin was thus to be compelled to tighten a full tourniquet around the Canton trade, in turn prompting the dispatch of a large expeditionary force from India. Whether they had foreseen it or not, therefore, Lin and his local scholar accomplices in Canton had found themselves in charge of a full-scale war. Or rather, if not quite in charge, then at least responsible for it.

The matter of responsibility was certainly, in fact, the crucial one. And, indeed, a great deal of what was to transpire at Canton during the period of hostilities (at least on the Ch'ing side) will only make sense when understood as the outgrowth of a concern, shared by Lin and by his supporters alike, to cleanse their reputations of the all-too-likely charge of irresponsible warmongering. The only way to do this, once the fighting had actually begun, was to win: or, at least, to avoid too obvious a setback in the places (Canton and Amoy) where literati activists occupied command positions. Thus, from virtually the moment bullets began to fly, one begins to see maneuvering of the most extraordinary sort at Canton, intended to convince the broader Ch'ing political elite that, whatever else had happened, the Ch'ing had not lost the war in the Pearl River delta. And to show as well, one might add, that such reverses as had occurred at Canton had been the fault solely of Governor General Lin's arch-rival within the bureaucracy, the "cowardly" Manchu commissioner, Ch'i-shan. Had Lin been left in charge of Canton's defenses, it followed, even these temporary routs (from which local forces were said to have quickly recovered) would never have occurred.

Needless to say, those who chose to credit this version of events had also to overlook certain basic features of the campaign the British had just fought and won. In retrospect, it should have been clear to all, as it certainly was to some of the emperor's palace advisers, that Her Britannic Majesty's fleet had never targeted the Pearl River estuary as its major objective. Under explicit instructions from London, it had instead determined to ignore Canton and to strike northward, closing in upon China's great transport artery, the Yangtze River, where the Ch'ing empire's own supply lines were most vulnerable to waterborne assault and where postwar trade prospects were the most exciting.[3] In a vague sort of way, this marginality of the southeast to the British war effort was eventually to become an accepted tenet of Manchu generalship—which explains why, after

May 1841, the dynasty's best field units were invariably detailed to the lower Yangtze and to Tientsin. But for Lin and his venerators, the British remained, from beginning to end, but another species of "pirate" "marauder" (*hai-k'ou*), incapable of sustained penetration of the empire's inner fastness, and tied, by their own immediate needs for cash and supplies, to the smuggler-dominated southeastern littoral. That they had not succeeded in seizing and holding Canton (or any other major city in this latter quarter, for that matter) therefore could be certainly taken as proof that China's coasts were defensible, if the defense were only properly organized and led.

Yet it was not just literati *amour propre*, or a convenient miscomprehension of British strategy, that won for the saga of Cantonese resistance so large a following among the lettered elite. There was yet another aspect to the appeal of this legend—an aspect that will, in fact, require the better part of the chapter before us to explicate properly. That is, the service it performed in justifying the takeover, by local elites, of military powers formerly monopolized by the bureaucracy and by the Manchu court. The "victory" at Canton, as we shall presently discover, was never presented to the political public as a victory of Ch'ing imperial arms. Rather, it was consistently credited to the zeal of local scholar-notables in undertaking to rally loyal paramilitary forces to the support of the Ch'ing cause just when the officials and the generals had brought the city to the brink of disaster.

To grasp just why this dimension of the war should have figured so significantly in popularizing the myth of "Canton unconquered" requires a multi-layered analysis of the events transpiring in and around Canton in 1841 too complex to be easily summarized here. The major outlines of our interpretation can perhaps still be anticipated, if only schematically. Certainly one of the most telling factors was the unanticipated strain imposed on virtually all key coastal cities by the rapid transfer there of hand-picked troops under mainly Manchu command. In Chekiang and Kiangsu, no less than in Kwangtung, these "guest" legions were to prove much more a scourge of the local population than were the British themselves. The myth of paramilitary, civilian-led resistance successfully challenging the British where the regular military had failed carried with it the implicit lesson that the court should abandon its traditional predilection for fast-paced, manpower-intensive armies sent in from the outside, and leave military arrangements to local elites.

Within this context, however, the scholar-generals of Canton had a very noteworthy contribution to make. For it was really only in Kwangtung that there existed the social conditions conducive to large-scale scholar-led military mobilization independent of the bureaucracy. What such private mobilization actually entailed, in order to be effective, was the prior existence of an elite-controlled property base capable not only of financing a private self-defense force, but also of simultaneously benefiting, managerially, from its deployment. Perhaps nowhere in coastal China, outside of the Pearl River delta, did such conditions exist. But even if that was true, the efficiency of civilian mobilization efforts in Canton was nonetheless attractive elsewhere as a demonstration that the hated regulars were unnecessary to the war effort.

So here, then, was another layer to the grand appeal of the idea that there had been two wars, and that the struggle in Kwangtung had been victorious. The scholar-led militia units of Canton were credited with successful resistance against the British, and, by virtue of that claim, they automatically confirmed local elites elsewhere in their conviction that the "generals" ought not be allowed to fight this war.

LIN TSE-HSU AND THE ANTI-OPIUM CAMPAIGN

As will be evident from our introductory remarks, the truly unusual feature of the events that were to unfold in Kwangtung during the 1840–1842 war was the extraordinarily prominent role of the Cantonese scholar-elite. Because of the depth of local elite involvement in military (and, for that matter, diplomatic) affairs in that province, our history of the war in the Kwangtung theatre divides into two separate stories, only at the end fusing back into a single strand. First is the official level, where Lin and then his successors as theatre commanders-in-chief (Ch'i-shan, Ch'i Kung, and I-shan) were nominally in charge—in coordination, naturally, with the court. But, in the end, the direction that events were to take in Kwangtung was to be decided as much by the actions of the upper crust of the local degree-holding class. At this second level of activity, the activists were academy pedagogues and their pupils—the finest of the Cantonese urban scholar-elite. Through both their fanatic loyalty to Governor General Lin, and, later on, their growing concern to insulate their native city from the ravages of British *and* Ch'ing soldiers, these scholars were to be propelled into the thick of local diplomatic and military deliberations. Once established there, moreover, they were not to be evicted easily, as a succession of postwar provincial official appointees were to learn to their dismay. Our story of the resistance at Canton thus naturally takes as its starting point the problem of just how these men managed to involve themselves in the business of international warmaking—a business that, strictly speaking, was not theirs to engage in.

As we shall presently see, formal military leadership passed into private scholarly hands only beginning with the March-May 1841 siege of Canton, owing mainly to the collapse on that occasion of regular government forces in the area, and to the need to fill the attendant military vacuum on the Ch'ing side. However, as we shall also see, the scholars of Canton were more than ready for their chance when that occasion presented itself. Scholar-commanded auxiliary units already were in the field. Moreover, the leaders of these forces already possessed a kind of ad hoc organizational base within the academy hierarchy of the city, capped at its upper end by a special coordinating bureau (*chü*) located at the Ta-fo-ssu Temple.

This latent organizational matrix alerts us to the fact that the Cantonese academy elite had been moving, gradually, into the sphere of public affairs even before the eruption of hostilities accelerated the pace of their intrusion. And it suggests, as well, that we must trace the beginnings of this involvement at least as far back as the anti-drug campaign of early 1839, from which campaign the Ta-fo-ssu Bureau first emerged as a center of local elite organizational influence.

The idea of mobilizing the Cantonese scholar class in the struggle against drug consumption was, of course, an inspiration of Commissioner Lin's, and began to manifest itself virtually from the moment Lin set foot in Canton. Within two weeks of his arrival (on 10 March 1839), Lin's diary indicates he had begun to consult with what might be described as the academy-class scholars there. And from these discussions Lin was to move directly to the creation of an independent, scholar-run opium-control operation headquartered in the Ta-fo-ssu Temple compound inside the city. The membership, we note from Table 2,[4] came almost exclusively from among the ranks of the pedagogues then occupying leadership roles within the academy establishment of the city.

According to a lengthy manifesto issued by Lin to explain the ex-

Table 2

Name	Academy Office
Chang Wei-p'ing	Board of directors, Hsueh-hai-t'ang
Ts'ai Chin-chuan	Current academy head in Hui-chou prefecture
Teng Shih-hsien	Head, Yueh-hua Academy
Ch'en Ch'i-k'un	Head, Yang-ch'eng Academy
Yao Hua-tso	Hunan prefect-designate, home on leave of absence

act nature of this non-official body, the mission of this Ta-fo-ssu Bureau was to receive deliveries of surrendered opium and smoking equipment from individual offenders in the city, and to distribute medicine to those turning in their supplies. At the same time, the bureau chiefs were to maintain surveillance over the members of the local degree-holding class known to them from their teaching activities, to recommend upright scholars in each of the suburban areas to oversee parallel sorts of activities in their own neighborhoods, to enroll all examination scholars in pledge groups sworn to abjure opium smoking, and to hand over offenders within their own ranks. Through the mobilization of the hierarchy of academic institutions from above, in other words, Lin was hoping to gain voluntary self-enforcement of the consumption prohibition within the examination-taking elite. Presumably, since degree-holders seem to have constituted a major category of offenders, this would quickly reduce local demand for the drug.[5]

A second aspect of the opium drive that also called for scholar-elite assistance involved the identification of Chinese distributors, and the ferreting out of corruption in the water-patrol forces and other local government agencies responsible for the toleration of smuggling activity. This was a more delicate operation, politically, than arresting consumers—since suspects displayed no visible symptoms, and those arrested in the past were often known to have been innocents framed for purposes of extortion or to divert attention from the real culprits. Yet Lin's need to induce a quick collapse in the drug market made it absolutely necessary that these middlemen be attacked too. And, since regular government agents could not be trusted with such a job, Lin found himself calling, inevitably, upon the scholar class.[6] No doubt other, more cautious officials would have balked at such a step. But here we must remember that Lin was now acting in collaboration with the Spring Purificationists, a group fanatically committed to the idea that scholars were fit for—in fact, needed—such responsible social-managerial roles. In effect, Lin was here only acting on an assumption that had been latent in the drug-crusade idea from the start.

Thus the acceptance of consumer surrenders, the overseeing of group pledges within the scholar-class, and the production of reliable information on the elusive middlemen in the smuggling traffic and on those who helped them from within the government itself—these key tasks fell to the scholars.

This sharing of administrative labors was only one aspect, however, of a much more far-reaching attempt by Lin to penetrate into what might be called academy politics in Canton. At the same time that Lin was calling for scholar-gentry aid, he was self-consciously moving to win for himself and his cause an identity and a loyalty that transcended the immediate issue of drug suppression. The core of scholar activists who moved in to occupy the key roles in the Ta-fo-ssu Bureau were drawn into this activity not simply by anti-opium fervor, but also by Commissioner Lin's adroit linking of his campaign to the promotion of a belletristic revival (*hsing-wen*) movement in the upper ranks of the academic elite itself.

In doing so, no doubt, Lin had very good practical reasons. For, as we have suggested, the kinds of services Lin was demanding from the local scholar class required a very high level of integrity to be of real value. And that, in turn, required that the developing campaign be associated as closely as possible with scholastic or belletristic "renovation"—that perennial source of elite moral optimism. Yet, whatever his reasons (and one suspects, perhaps, that there was also a good measure of literati vanity in Lin's inspiration), the decision to link the anti-drug effort to a revolution in local academic fashion was to have consequences that quite outlasted the campaign from which they had originally sprung. Inadvertently—or, perhaps, not so inadvertently—Lin was thereby to install in key roles a nucleus of firmly loyal souls, who would thenceforth connect their own survival as leaders within Cantonese academic life with the preservation of Commissioner Lin's prestige as a policymaker. Here, as it was later to develop, were the true seeds of local elite involvement in the diplomatic and military realms—an involvement that was to get under way as an outgrowth of scholar-class determination to sabotage those peacemakers trying to discredit Lin's policies.

But we have digressed somewhat from our immediate concern, which is here merely to document the ideological and personnel changes within Cantonese academy life introduced by Commissioner Lin in conjunction with his anti-opium crusade. Let us see if we can reconstruct more precisely just how this association of opium suppression with belletristic revivalism actually looked in practice.

The place to begin is with a quick synopsis of the divergent intellectual trends current in Canton on the eve of Lin's arrival—for scholarly "renovation," in Canton as in Peking, inevitably meant a readjustment in the relative status of these different schools, from which in turn was to come the energy for a new effloresence in letters. We have already dwelt, in passing, on one such trend, the philological-positivist or Han Learning school. This current of scholarly thought, as we noted, had been introduced into Canton by the former governor general, Juan Yuan, early in the 1820s. Its temple was, of course, the Hsueh-hai-t'ang, though even Han Learning scholars never enjoyed a complete monopoly in shaping the curriculum there.

Indeed, as we have noted, Han Learning had bitter rivals, even during Juan's tenure of office, as a claimant on the scholastic loyalties of the Cantonese pedagogical class. During the late 1830s, in pace with the changes in intellectual fashion then sweeping the capital, these rival schools began to combine under renewed official patronage to form a countercurrent quite bitterly critical of the Han Learning orthodoxy. Lin had, in the end, to do little more than give his own personal blessing to this reorientation (and to confirm it through additional personnel changes within the academies) in order to establish himself as a revivalist.

For our present purposes, the list of these rival academic influences can be confined to two, though there was clearly a plenitude of lesser, indigenous schools that also existed in some tension with the newer Han Learning, even if less capable of offering a challenge to it.[7] The first was a local variant of the Weng Fang-kang school of poetic aesthetics, called the White Cloud Mountain (Pai-yun-shan) school. To be sure, in Peking, the Weng school had been closely associated with Han Learning. But that association was much less clear-cut in its Kwangtung counterpart, seeded, originally, by Master Weng during a mid-career term as schools commissioner there. Weng's ideas had been reworked at the hands of Cantonese followers recruited on this and later occasions, and had eventually been reduced to little more than a new consciousness of broader, Peking-generated currents in poetry fashion, centered, inevitably, upon the study of the works of Wang Shih-chen. All seemingly quite inconsequential, perhaps. But the White Cloud Mountain group, inheritors of this local transformation of northern-clique aesthetic ideals, had nonetheless come to occupy a distinct, and distinctly proud, role within the Cantonese academy system. Chang Wei-p'ing (1780–1859), its most famous proponent, had been so respected a local lecturer even in Juan Yuan's day that he had been assigned a place in the Hsueh-hai-t'ang. At the same time, Huang P'ei-fang (1779–1859) and T'an Chin-chao (*chin-shih* of 1817), two others associated with the White Cloud Mountain school, had been floating, somewhat dissatisfied, in and out of local academy posts for well over a decade as of the moment Commissioner Lin came sweeping into Canton, early in 1839.[8]

Also affiliated, if indirectly, with this lingering northern-school aesthetic group was Ch'en Hung-ch'ih (*chin-shih* of 1805; Han-lin), the master of the Yueh-hua Academy since 1834. A somewhat eccentric character, Ch'en had somehow derailed after a promising start as a protégé of the great northern-clique literocrat Chu Kuei. By the time he arrived in Canton, moreover, he had decided (for unexplained reasons) that he disapproved of the cold-blooded approach to learning that was the hallmark of Hsueh-hai-t'ang scholasticism. As one biographer was to remember him, during his declining years as a Canton academy head, Ch'en had acquired the habit of spending all his time in the company of a few favorite students,

. . . arguing over their judgments of [actions recorded in] the *Book of History* and the [post-classical] histories, his emotions rising and his words pouring out with vehemence. Or, on other occasions, he would discourse upon the words and deeds of officials of reputation and of great scholars of the Ch'ien-lung and Chia-ch'ing period; or he would talk excitedly and with indignation of the issues of the day. On such occasions, he would rise to great heights of feeling, and would often compose a poem on the spot. . . .[9]

Such an approach was most decidedly a tilt away from objectivism, and toward the "urgent-words" end of the academic spectrum—thus really more akin to the spirit of the T'ung-ch'eng school than to that of Han Learning.

The second intellectual current ready to challenge the dominant Han Learning fashion in Canton was, in fact, the *ku-wen* (or T'ung-ch'eng) party itself. This school had been popularized in Canton chiefly through the efforts of Fang Tung-shu (1772–1851), a T'ung-ch'eng native (and, incidentally, a close friend of Yao Ying) who had taught for several years in Canton in the 1820s under the somewhat unwelcome patronage of Juan Yuan himself. Fang, however, had never quite approved of his patron's intellectual lineage, and so had not stayed long at his post. It must therefore have been with great eagerness that he returned to Canton, early in 1837, this time at the behest of a governor general whom he could respect as a longstanding patron of the T'ung-ch'eng school, Teng T'ing-chen.[10]

We must return now to the realignment of official scholarly patronage patterns in Canton in the late 1830s, from which the literary renovation of Lin Tse-hsu was to spring. A perceptible shift seems to have set in just after the 1836 rejection of legalization, perhaps commencing with Governor General Teng's decision to summon Fang Tung-shu back to Canton in 1837, nominally to oversee the composition of a gazetteer of the Cantonese maritime customs authority. At around the same time, moreover, Teng was taking steps to bring Ch'en Hung-ch'ih into his inner circle—first (in 1836) consulting with him on the opium-control question; next, asking Ch'en to nominate a favorite pupil as tutor to Teng's son; and then in 1838, appointing another of Ch'en's star pupils, Ch'en Li, to the board of directors of the Hsueh-hai-t'ang.[11]

Thus, the tide of official scholarly favor had already begun visibly to shift, even before Lin's dramatic entry into the "city of rams," early in March 1839. What Teng had initiated, however, Lin was to push much further. As his first gesture toward the local rivals of the Han Learning establishment, Lin began with the symbolic step of making his official residence in the Yueh-hua Academy (until recently, under Ch'en Hung-ch'ih's leadership), and not, as one would have expected, in the Hsueh-hai-t'ang. This choice was immediately followed by the announcement of a special examination intended to "fathom the local scholarly climate." Such examinations were a normal part of the tenure-inaugurating ritual of a newly arrived high provincial official. But what was unusual about these examinations (held 20 August 1839) was that Lin excluded the students of the Hsueh-hai-t'ang from the competition, asking only those enrolled in the other three top-ranking academies of the city to participate. In the examination itself, Lin went to some lengths to associate himself with the anti-Han Learning forces. The poetic theme was a reference to the great T'ang dynasty *ku-wen* belletrist, Han Yü, who had once, like Lin, been "exiled" to the malaria-infested Ling-nan frontier, and whose presence was supposed, "for one evening to have rolled the miasmic mist . . . away."[12]

The final indication of which way the Lin regime would swing was to come in the form of the simultaneous elevation of two of the White Cloud Mountain set (Huang P'ei-fang and Chang Wei-p'ing) to positions of prominence within the city's academic establishment. Late in 1838, just prior to Lin's arrival, Teng T'ing-chen had already elevated both these men to the Hsueh-hai-t'ang's board of directors, while giving Huang a simultaneous honorary appointment as head-master-without-salary at the Yueh-hua and Yang-ch'eng academies.[13] Lin seemed determined to continue this course. It was Chang and a friend who were first among the local scholar class to be ushered in to meet the commissioner on his arrival, early in 1839; Chang Wei-p'ing's son alone for whom Lin endeavored to win a pass on the 1839 provincial examinations; and Chang, again, who was the only local scholar to be afforded a private interview by Lin as the latter left Canton in 1841. Needless to say, Chang also served as an original member of the Ta-fo-ssu Bureau; while Huang was likewise asked to join somewhat later on. By contrast, none of the surviving pedagogical greats of Juan Yuan pedigree still active in the city (Chang Shao, Tseng Chao, or Fan Feng, for example) were asked to participate in this body as long as Lin remained in office.[14]

How this frantic juggling of academy directorships, and signaling of new official scholarly allegiances, affected the morale of the local lettered elite is a matter that requires some guesswork. But the outward signals of a great enthusiasm among the benefited scholarly majority are certainly there to be observed. Some hint of how feelings were running is already apparent in an exchange recorded by the new Yueh-hua headmaster, Liang T'ing-nan, as having taken place between himself and Lin late in 1839, just as Lin was making ready to shift his lodgings from the Yueh-hua Academy to the governor general's yamen. When Lin began his valedictions with an apology for having inconvenienced the scholars of the academy by his long stay, Liang cut him off abruptly. "The scholars of this school," Liang riposted, "have long held Your Excellency in high esteem."[15] But even more dramatic a demonstration of the loyalty Lin had won for himself was to appear late in 1840, when Ch'i-shan's eleventh-hour peace plan caused the court to remove Lin from his offices in Canton. The list of well-wishers coming to commiserate with Lin on the eve of his departure was practically endless; and Lin's usually terse diary halts to reel off, one after the other, the names of all the high-ranking scholars, academy heads, and recent degree-winners from the city's schools who turned out *en masse* to present him with a set of eight matched hanging scrolls.[16] Why they had all come was suggested, in part, by the wording of these scrolls: to Governor General Lin for his "teaching and renewal of literary culture" (*chiao-yü hsing-wen*).[17] At least for those present at this meeting, that dimension of Lin's efforts seemed to rank on a par with his other great accomplishments: "Justly and loyally promoting the honor of the state," and "scattering the [opium] smoke over the malarial seas."

Unless Lin had masterminded a gigantic fraud, therefore, our impression must be that scholarly mobilization against the opium traffic had indeed been a success, and that it really had fused, in the minds of many, with the drama of a renewal of letters. From these tremors of local scholarly excitement were to arise, in time, the faith that the war Lin had started really could be carried forward. And from that conviction came, in turn, the idea that the scholars themselves could defend Canton.

LIN TSE-HSU VERSUS CH'I-SHAN

If the soul of Cantonese scholarly militarization was already latent in Governor General Lin's literary revival and anti-opium campaign, the corporeal manifestation of that spirit was not to assume its final form until well after those particular episodes had long been forgotten. In between came another set of events, unfolding, this time, mainly within the interstices of the imperial bureaucracy rather than the confines of Cantonese academic politics. The main protagonists were not local scholars but high-ranking provincial officials, and the prize over which they fought was of far greater magnitude than the mere control of local academic office. The stakes were nothing less than the control of the empire's policy toward Great Britain as the principals—Lin Tse-hsu and Ch'i-shan—settled down to battling it out during the winter months of 1840–1841 well knew.

Yet the outcome, and even the progress, of this contest was to have consequences of the most immediate sort for the nascent scholar-generals of Canton. Even as this miniature drama unfolded, the scholars were already being drawn into it, thanks, originally, to Lin's efforts to drum up support from all possible quarters in order to block the Manchu commissioner Ch'i-shan's peace initiative. With the resolution of this struggle in Lin's favor, Canton itself suddenly came under direct foreign threat. Having themselves had a role in precipitating the British decision to attack, the scholars of Canton could hardly stand aside and watch their city fall, without resistance, to the enemy. Thus, the road for the scholar-activists of Canton was to lead, with unforeseen swiftness, from political mobilization in defense of Lin, to military mobilization in defense of their native city.

For the moment at least, however, our narrative must be concerned first with the details of Lin Tse-hsu's contest with Ch'i-shan over foreign policy—the event from which all else was, in a sense, to spring. The motivating force in this confrontation—the source from which all its bitter energy flowed—was Commissioner Lin's passionate desire to divert blame from his own initial recklessness. Having steered the Celestial Empire into a major military confrontation that he had refused until the last minute to see coming, Lin was now left in the awkward position of having to find a formula—some formula—by which he could persuade himself and others that war was not indeed too terrible a risk for the Ch'ing side as most had imagined. That formula, naturally, would have to present the new enemy in the shape of other past seaborne threats that had been successfully resisted by continental imperial governments—such as, for example, the so-called Japanese marauders (*wo-k'ou*) of the mid-sixteenth century, or the Taiwan-based fleets of the half-Japanese Coxinga (Cheng Ch'eng-kung), who had raided the Ch'ing coastline during the third quarter of the seventeenth century. And so the British were placed in the manageable category of maritime raiders, who, everyone knew, unlike legitimate states, lacked the stamina to fight for political objectives, and thus could be controlled simply by prolonging the struggle to the point where material profits (through commerce or looting) had been exhausted.[18]

As he struggled to breathe life into this misleading formula during the waning months of 1840, Lin ran into a succession of nasty hitches, occasioned, first, by Elliot's own refusal to act in conformity with Lin's plan; and, second, by the realization on the part of certain Manchu leaders in Peking that Lin's view of British strategic limitations and motives had been entirely wrong.

But here we must back up several steps to review the progress of diplomatic and military affairs until immediately prior to Lin's moment of truth, in the fall of 1840. Lin's problems began with the mid-1839 collapse of his scheme to extract a permanent guarantee of no further involvement in the India opium traffic from the British superintendent of trade, Captain Elliot. From this setback emerged, in turn, a bellicose last-minute embargo on all British trade and provisioning, and the concomitant British decision to resort to arms. Though there is much to suggest that the liberal war party in London and Manchester was already primed for a fight even before the guarantee issue arose, it is also true that Lin's precipitate actions in dealing with this particular aspect of the opium negotiations helped greatly to unify British commercial opinion behind the hawkish Free Trade lobby and the equally hawkish Palmerston. Up until he began to push for such an agreement, involving a possible capital sanction against all future offenders, Lin had been able to make some progress in his second-hand negotiations with the British representative. Under pressure from steeply falling opium prices (induced, however, as much by importer over-speculation as by diminishing Chinese consumption), the traders and Elliot had seen some virtue in agreeing to surrender existing stockpiles through Elliot, if Lin would agree to compensation. Without clarifying his position on the latter issue, Lin had nonetheless eagerly accepted the offer, and, in June 1839, at Chen-k'ou, near the Bogue, he proceeded to put all the 20,000 chests he had received to the torch (apparently unaware that he was destroying crown property). Further than this, however, Elliot simply would not go. And when Lin then proceeded to demand "voluntary bonds" (again, in unknowing violation of Western legal practice), he found his counterpart increasingly intractable. That left but one option: the trade cutoff sanction. And, accordingly, on 5 January 1840, the court, dragging along behind Lin, agreed to promulgate the necessary edict. Such an order, even with Lin's enthusiastic efforts at local enforcement, could do little but drive the fence-sitters among the British trading community into the arms of the war-intent Elliot.[19]

And so began Lin's period of trials. Yet, perhaps more costly still than the injudicious provocations offered to Elliot was the commissioner's grave miscalculation about how the British would strike back. Did Lin believe the assurances he had been sending Peking of the relative weakness of the British position, in spite of the other side's superiority in ships and gunnery? Lin certainly seems to have convinced himself that the enemy he faced truly was of little more account that the sea marauders of earlier imperial times, and from this drew the inference that the British would have to focus their anticipated attack upon Canton, the only coastal city "near" their home bases in the "Southern Seas" whose trade and stockpiled wealth were sufficient to provide "booty" to cover the costs of fighting so far away from home. By contrast, the upcoast stations (such as the Chusan islands, off the mouth of the Yangtze, or Tientsin), where British admirals really were planning to strike, seem never to have figured in Lin's thoughts as likely targets. (No doubt part of the problem for Lin was his lack of comprehension of the financial arrangements normal to European wars that permitted much greater freedom of action in the field that Lin's own spoils-financed concept of maritime warfare allowed for. Liang T'ing-nan, one of Lin's military advisers and one who was certainly in every other regard eager to portray Lin as a sympathetic figure, nevertheless has Lin later confessing his own original mistake on this point, but only after it was too late to correct. In all likelihood it was this oversight in particular that explained why Lin was so sure that Canton would be the enemy's prime military objective.)[20]

Thus, Lin had badly miscalculated the way in which the fighting would be likely to develop. Moreover, acting on the basis of this miscalculation (and perhaps also out of a desire to avoid alarming Peking unnecessarily), Lin had delayed alerting the court as to the possibility of attack in the north until the last possible moment. For almost an entire year (from mid-1839 to mid-1840), as he waited in Canton for the enemy to come to him, Lin had confined defense planning entirely to the Kwangtung coast. Anticipating an attempt to sack Canton, or perhaps to force the reopening of trade at gunpoint, Lin had here undertaken the usual range of preparations for a pirate raid.

Chains had been stretched across the mouth of the Whampoa; fireships made ready; and improvements ordered in the fortifications in the vicinity of the Bogue, including even some test casting and firing of newer, foreign-style bronze cannon. But beyond these local initiatives, there had been not a whisper of activity anywhere else along the coast, nor even any warning from Lin that such activity might be necessary.[21]

The result of all this was, of course, that Elliot's forces—22 warships, 27 transports, and 3,600 Scottish, Irish, and "Native" infantry—were able to achieve complete surprise when they descended, in the summer of 1840, upon their two preselected objectives: the fortified city of Ting-hai, in the Chusan Islands; and Ta-ku, the strongpoint guarding the river approach to Tientsin and Peking. Ting-hai fell, without resistance, on 5 July 1840. And, at Ta-ku, to which a reduced version of the British expeditionary force repaired on 11 August (a mere eight days after word had finally come from Lin that there would be an attack!), the governor general in charge of the defenses, Ch'i-shan, could do little more than offer his services as a mediator between Elliot and the court, in the hope of thereby delaying a repetition of what had just happened at Ting-hai. (The British engineer, Ouchterlony, who had accompanied Elliot to Ta-ku in August, records that the Chinese were frantically throwing up earthenwork defenses as the British flotilla drew near!).[22]

Ch'ing abilities to resist, minimal as they perhaps were, had barely been tested before Elliot was practically at the gates of Peking and ready to start pressing his demands. To Lin Tse-hsu, this eventuality was doubly painful: first, because Lin had himself been very much to blame for the failure to forewarn his colleagues in the north; and also because, as word began to reach Canton of the substance of the ongoing Tientsin parleys, it was becoming clear that Ch'i-shan intended to convince the emperor that the whole business about the opium could have been settled peacefully, if only Lin had not been so unreasonable.[23]

Obviously, Lin could not afford to disown his own diplomacy now, for, to do so at this point, would be to admit that his earlier claims about British vulnerability had been misinformed, even self-seeking. He thus grew, if anything, even more rigid in his insistence on the British-as-pirates, directing his persuasive efforts first to the throne and, when that failed, to personal friends within the bureaucracy. The great battle for self-vindication was now about to begin.

The first approach, naturally, had to be to the emperor, whom Lin still clearly hoped to persuade of the feasibility of continued military resistance (the obvious tactic, since, after all, there had been no real test of arms so far). Thus, upon hearing of the loss of Ting-hai, Lin wrote hastily to Peking asserting that the British forces there were weak, demoralized, and easily assaulted and that the island might easily be retaken by sneak attack from the onshore Chinese population. Simultaneously, a sea-raid on the British flotilla operating off the mouth of the Pearl River was promised by Lin as a way of drawing the expeditionary force away from the northern coastal station. Tao-kuang, however, was not impressed, and noted unkindly that Lin seemed to be trying merely to cover himself for the "bungling" in Kwangtung that had brought on the loss of Ting-hai in the first place.[24]

But Lin was not yet ready to quit, and on 11 October he sent off an eloquent and impassioned plea for the continuation of his own unyielding diplomacy. He had, Tao-kuang was now told, "long since" expected that British frustration at Canton would lead to raids elsewhere along the coast; Ting-hai's seizure had thus been entirely predictable, since the barbarians needed to sell their opium and buy their tea in order to pay for the costs of the war they were now fighting. However, Lin reported, the enemy garrison on Ting-hai was weak and sick, and an uncooperative populace had undermined their trade. "Thus even if we now do not engage them on the high seas, but confine ourselves to 'resolute defence of our strongholds,' we have the means to bring them to self-exhaustion." No concessions should be made in the forthcoming negotiations, therefore; for "the prestige of the state" was at stake in the maintenance of the opium prohibition, and the means were at hand to stand by this higher order of principle. To back down now would be only to invite more demands and added arrogance from the other side.[25]

The arguments were, however, too late: for, already on 28 September, the emperor (now under Ch'i-shan's spell) had decided that Lin would have to be replaced, and that Ch'i-shan would have to go to Canton if there was still to be any prospect of a non-military resolution of the conflict. "Totally senseless and disgusting stuff," was his comment on Lin's latest proposals. "You say that the barbarians are only making an empty show of force to test our resolve. But it seems to Us that, if anyone has learned from their tricks, it is you, who are trying to frighten Us just as the English try to frighten you!"[26]

The closure of Lin's direct line of communications to the court by no means discouraged him, however, from carrying on, now as an oppositionist, in the hope of gaining a hearing for the idea that the war should be continued. This Lin was quite well equipped to do, provided as he was with an array of admirers both within the government bureaucracy (where a number of former subordinates now occupied key positions), and, more important still, within the world of the Southern City literati. His case drew additional˙ strength, moreover, from the fact that his rival, Ch'i-shan, was now in the unenviable position of having to mediate between Peking and a suddenly much more aggressive Elliot. As the negotiations got under way outside Canton in November 1840, Lin was able to keep himself informed through loyal scholarly acquaintances and ex-subordinates on the trade-expansion and territorial demands Elliot was now advancing—demands that predictably ran well ahead of what Ch'i-shan was willing to relay to Peking. He was also able to watch, grimly, from the sidelines as Elliot unilaterally seized Hong Kong and stormed the outer Bogue forts in January 1841, in order to keep up the momentum of negotiations. Naturally, all of this made excellent material for Lin's developing campaign to oust Ch'i-shan and to resume the war.

Thus, on 26 January 1841, Lin (still in Canton), wrote to ˙his former subordinate, the Kiangnan governor, Yü-ch'ien, to complain about the sad drift of events in the south since Ch'i-shan had arrived to take charge. Yet, he admited sadly, the stories were true that Yü-ch'ien must have been hearing about how the key forts guarding the mouth of the Canton River had fallen, several weeks before, to British attack. But this was owing to Ch'i-shan's cowardly refusal to prepare for renewed fighting—all in the vain hope of avoiding provoking Elliot's suspicions about Ch'ing bad faith. Of course, Lin continued, Ch'i-shan had continued to blame all his troubles on Lin's mishandling of the opium question, but this was all so much nonsense. "He did not care to reflect," Lin commented acidly, "that these rebellious barbarians had not dared before this to venture an attack [in the river] because our defenses were then tight, and our unity of spirit made us as impregnable as a rampart. . . . , and so he turned our arrangements upside down, broke our morale, sabotaged our soldiers' spirit, stiffened the [enemy's] resolve, and brought insult to our military prestige."[27] If the Ch'ing were now suffering military setbacks, in other words, the blame was not Lin's, but Ch'i-shan's: Lin's measures for quarantining the key strongholds had been sound and would have stood the test of battle had Ch'i-shan not sabotaged them to "buy" enemy favor.

And then, on 18 February, Lin wrote to his former metropolitan examiner, Shen Wei-ch'iao, in Peking, giving the "true" history of the current imbroglio—in which history, naturally, Ch'i-shan, rather than Lin, proved to be the real bungler. Everything had been under control and the enemy's arrogant spirit tamed, Lin insisted, until the Ch'ing court's indecisiveness over the issue of voluntary bonds had revealed to the British that "we were not as one in our purpose." Acting on this perception of Ch'ing internal dissension, the British had taken to probing for weak points along China's coastline. Naturally, Lin, at Canton, had foreseen that this might happen, and had not only erected "impregnable" defenses in his own theatre, but had urgently warned Peking of the threat that now confronted Ch'ing fortifications all along the empire's maritime frontier. However, the Chihli viceroy, Ch'i-shan, had refused to take these warnings seriously. He had thus been caught in a condition of embarassing unpreparedness by Elliot's squadron. To extricate himself, he had determined upon a policy of appeasement—the same policy he was (at the time Lin wrote) still stubbornly pursuing at Canton, against all hope of success. For the nature of these English barbarians was such that conciliation would lead only to more arrogant demands, as the foolish Ch'i-shan had since discovered. Thus, Ch'i-shan had compounded his initial error of military negligence with an injudicious kind of diplomacy. And the Ch'ing cause had suffered an irreversible setback.[28]

There must, of course, have been a good deal more of such apologetics in circulation during the winter of 1840–1841, either directly from Lin's own hand, or from the hands of his literati admirers in Peking. For, barely had the *pourparlers* gotten under way in Tientsin than all sorts of savage revelations began to surface before the emperor concerning Ch'i-shan's double-dealings—most of them having some substance. For instance, starting on 8 November and continuing intermittently over the next several months, the metropolitan censorate erupted forth with a succession of reports (originating,

ultimately, from Huang Chueh-tzu in Amoy) designed to cast suspicion on Ch'i-shan's claims that he had managed to lure the British
from Ting-hai. Not only had there been no such agreement, but
(Huang and his agents in Peking insisted) the British were now actually fortifying the place and preparing for a long stay. Under such circumstances, it was hardly appropriate that the talks planned at
Canton should be allowed to get under way![29]

Even more telling, however, than the help Lin's campaign had elicited from the Spring Purificationists was the support it drew from
former protégés within the provincial bureaucracy. In mid-February
1841, the Soochow governor, Yü-ch'ien, catalyzed by the news Lin
had been forwarding from Canton, submitted to the court a damning
impeachment of Ch'i-shan's actions from the initial talks at Tientsin
to the currently stalemated negotiations in Canton. This was an
important break for Lin, since Yü-ch'ien, being a Mongol, was just
the sort of official who might be given command if military action
revived. His intervention against Ch'i-shan thus greatly simplified
the emperor's problems in considering what to do next.[30]

Another loyal ex-subordinate, the current Kwangtung governor, I-
liang, entered the fray soon afterward with revelations perhaps even
more damning than Yü-ch'ien's had been. Angered not just by what
had been done to Lin but also by his own exclusion by Ch'i-shan
from the secret talks with Elliot, I-liang decided to break to the
emperor the news that Ch'i-shan had been playing with the idea of
offering recognition of the status quo in Hong Kong in return for
immediate retrocession of Ting-hai. And, in the same dispatch,
which reached the emperor on 26 February, he included a British-
prepared Chinese translation of a proclamation informing all Chinese living on that island (Hong Kong, that is) that they were now
under British crown law![31]

This last bit of evidence clearly destroyed whatever faith Tao-
kuang had still retained in Ch'i-shan and in the negotiations at Canton. For had not Ch'i-shan been explicitly warned that there were to
be no concessions of territory? And why had Ch'i-shan never mentioned in his dispatches so much as a single word about the British
determination to hold Hong Kong? Within hours of the arrival of
the damaging document from I-liang, therefore, the order had gone
out for Ch'i-shan's arrest and recall to the capital.[32] And within but
a few more weeks, with the prospect of resuming war now before

him, Tao-kuang was at last to relent and offer Lin a qualified pardon. Lin was to be assigned to the lower Yangtze front as a "deputy," there to assist Yü-ch'ien (newly named as theatre commander) to improve the defenses along the eastern Chekiang coast, just across from Ting-hai. Thanks to the fanatic loyalty of his friends within the government establishment, Lin had won. And the war would now be taken up again, where it had stopped.[33]

There is, however, one last aspect of the Lin/Ch'i-shan duel that needs to be mentioned, before we turn back, again, to our narrative of events at Canton. That is the role the scholars of Canton themselves had played in helping to plead Lin's case and to damage Ch'i-shan's. Their aid bore perhaps only indirectly upon the outcome of the struggle, but the vehemence of its delivery reveals quite unmistakably the hold Lin had acquired on the imaginations of many in this group. In February 1841, just as the fate of the negotiations hung in the balance, a scholar-led protest demonstration suddenly exploded inside the city, adding further to the pressure that was eventually to impel I-liang to take the field against his colleague. The immediate background to this protest was the circulation in the city of news of Ch'i-shan's cession of Hong Kong and of the acting governor general's uncertainty over whether or not to forward the evidence of this unauthorized action to Peking. Excited by this news, a certain Teng Ch'un called a meeting of "the collected scholars of the prefectural schools" in order to get up a petition urging I-liang, the viceroy, to go through with the impeachment.

Then, however, the crowd moved on to Ch'i-shan's yamen. "Several tens [of the students] went in," recounts Liang T'ing-nan, "and Ch'i-shan had to explain to them that the peace concessions [meaning the cession of Hong Kong] were in accord with the emperor's will, and that perhaps the gentlemen were not very familiar with the realities of the situation." Before the unpopular Ch'i-shan could clear his office of unwanted guests, however, he had to endure an afternoon of lecturing on just how the barbarians ought to be dealt with.[34]

Was this but a random, spontaneous venting of naive student emotionalism? Possibly it was. But one can hardly fail to note that Teng Ch'un, the organizer of the affair, was himself a member of the White Cloud Mountain clique that had originally been tapped by Lin for the talent needed to oversee the opium-suppression drive, and was also a close friend of the current Ta-fo-ssu Bureau commissioner,

Huang P'ei-fang.[35] More likely, then, the demonstration had been an insiders' affair, prompted by the scholar-commissioners' deliberate leakage to the students of the information about I-liang's impending decision. The scholars of Canton had now taken their stand. And it had been for Lin, and for war.

THE SIEGE OF CANTON

From the point of view of the scholar-activists of Canton—now about to be plunged almost over their heads into the treacherous currents of war—the news of the toppling of Ch'i-shan and the redemption of Lin was no doubt very gratifying indeed, at least initially. Gone at last was the hated Manchu commissioner, who had almost succeeded in laying low the man they so revered and who had gratuitously insulted the scholars with his abrasive reminders that they had no particular grasp of the issues at stake in the conflict. True, Lin had still not been given a full pardon. And true, also, Lin would soon be leaving Canton for good. But the word about Lin's replacement that reached Canton co-terminously with the order for Ch'i-shan's arrest must have compensated at least partly for the loss. The new governor general, it was learned, was to be a Han Chinese official, Ch'i Kung, who, while not himself a Han-lin, was of a Han-lin family, and who had already an established reputation for consulting very closely in government decisions with the leaders of local scholar opinion. Furthermore, Ch'i had recently served a six-year term in the Kwangtung governor's yamen, so that he would need little prompting when it came to deciding just who the representatives of local elite opinion were.[36] For a fleeting moment, at least, it must have seemed as if the pro-Lin scholar faction in Canton was about to have its way on both of the issues that concerned them: The war would go on, as desired, and here in Canton the local elite, not the Manchus, would be in control.

But then, gradually, a new, and much more ominous trend began to develop, arising from actions initiated by both the British and Ch'ing sides, and quite out of the control of the Cantonese elite. First was the decision, taken in Peking and without any consultation with local officials in Canton, to transform the Pearl River delta into the major arena for decisive military action against the British. The Manchu military spirit had now clearly asserted itself in the capital, and the price in suffering and loss of autonomy for the officials and people of Canton was to be high indeed. Some 17,000 soldiers were en route to the Kwangtung front where they would have to be maintained at the expense of the provincial government and the citizens of the provincial capital—until, that is, they could complete their attack upon the newly gained British island fortress in Hong Kong.[37] The top command over military operations in the Pearl River theatre, moreover, had been assigned to a prince of the blood, I-shan, whose only experience in government life had been fighting Muslim rebels on the plains of inner Asia.[38] To the scholars of Canton, who had already had quite enough of Manchu arrogance and highhandedness during the run-in with Ch'i-shan, these developments could hardly have boded well. And for those of them (such as Liang T'ing-nan) truly convinced that the war could actually be fought as a war of attrition against a pirate enemy, the whole operation must have seemed pure folly from the start. What sense could it make to squander limited Ch'ing resources on a one-shot try for glory, when the object of the struggle was to wear down the enemy?

But worse news was still to come, this time from the enemy quarter. Quite unintimidated by the Ch'ing decision to begin a military buildup in Canton, Elliot determined, late in February 1841, that he had enough of the conference table and it was time to resume military pressure. After but a week of a naval action in the vicinity of the Bogue, British forces were already in full command of the outer ring of forts guarding the water access to Canton. There they had halted for ten weeks, after the interim Ch'ing commander, Yang Fang, agreed to allow the season's trade in teas and silks to be concluded. But by 17 May, after the new purchases had been safely removed from the Canton river channel, the British were on the move again, slowly tightening the noose around the provincial capital. The Ch'ing, it seemed, were to be taught a lesson, so as to end once and for all any illusions about British naval power.[39]

It was against this suddenly very somber background that the first overt moves developed to bring the scholars of the Ta-fo-ssu Bureau directly into the organization of local self-defense. The initiative arose at least as much from the viceroy's yamen as from the scholars themselves. From all available accounts, it would seem, in fact, that Ch'i Kung was the really active spirit at this initial stage of local elite paramilitary mobilization. Either because he too completely distrusted I-shan's military skills, or because he resented having to govern, in effect, as the Manchu general's paymaster, the new governor general showed himself from the start most anxious to work with the Lin faction among the city's scholarly leaders in order to build up a second, civilian-led line of defense. Thus, two of the three men the new governor general took as his initial advisers were scholars of the "renovated" academy directorate: Liang T'ing-nan (Lin's 1840 choice to head the Yueh-hua Academy) and Huang P'ei-fang (an 1838 Teng appointee to the Hsueh-hai-t'ang). A third, Yü T'ing-kuei, was probably an academy student of Huang's—we have insufficient biographical information to be sure.[40] Through Liang, in turn, Ch'i Kung seems to have come to some sort of understanding with the retired Han-lin scholar Li K'o-chiung regarding the raising of a private, local elite-funded army to be based in Fatshan—a suburban manufacturing city some 10 miles southwest of Canton. This army was presumably to guarantee a sanctuary for the retreating provincial government should it prove advisable to abandon the capital.[41] Finally, Ch'i Kung, in collaboration, again, with the academy elite, turned to the question of defending Canton itself. Sometime late in April or early in May 1841, Huang P'ei-fang arranged for the Ta-fo-ssu Bureau directors to raise funds for a special "water-brave" force for river operations. The commander of this unit was Lin Fu-hsiang, a low-ranking scholar from Macao and a student of Huang's. Through Lin, in turn, were recruited some 500 men from the outlying counties of the delta well-versed in the terrain around Canton and in the ways of river fighting.[42] Through this entirely private force, Ch'i Kung acquired in effect an autonomous capacity for military operations in the Canton suburbs. Perhaps indicating his low opinions of I-shan's generalship, Ch'i stationed this force north of the city, away from the front where I-shan was preparing for his all-out attack on British forces on the river.[43]

Meanwhile, as Ch'i Kung moved to align the civilian administration in Canton increasingly with the Ta-fo-ssu commissioners and so provide himself with a civilian-led reserve force, Generalissimo I-shan was acting with increasing aloofness vis-à-vis these same scholar-strategists. Liang T'ing-nan recalled, with some vexation, that the Manchu held himself remote from the Ta-fo-ssu Bureau's affairs, and consistently refused audiences with its leaders, or with any other scholarly military experts, for that matter. The generalissimo was, in his own words, "too busy" with preparations to waste his time listening to such advice. And why should he listen to it, knowing full well that it was rooted in the "fantasies of bookworms" and "lacking in relevance to the realities"?[44] More infuriatingly still, even after it had finally dawned on the Manchu prince that his grandiose plans for a water assault against the British fleet would require some sort of independent river force to move his troops and to gather intelligence, I-shan would still not accept Liang's suggestion that he make use of the scholars to recruit such a force from among the boat people of the delta. To entrust such a role to the Cantonese, he believed, would be to create just so many more spies for the enemy—for who, after all, could trust these perpetually "traitorous" people of the Pearl River coast? Far better, instead, to hire men from the adjacent province of Fukien, even if it did require more time. The result was that I-shan still had no river navy of his own when the final showdown with the British came.[45]

As the battle for Canton approached, therefore, the command structure had already split into two clearly demarcated camps. In nominal control of operations was the "insurgent-quelling generallissimo," I-shan, together with his subalterns, Lung-wen and Yang Fang, and his 17,000 unpopular "picked" troops from the interior. Already quite visible as a nascent second layer of military organization was a civilian-led force under the joint command of the Ta-fo-ssu Bureau scholars and the provincial viceroy, Ch'i Kung. Just how this latter force might be used, and what its goals might be should the struggle move yet further upriver, was still probably quite unclear to its leaders. But one thing its commanders knew for certain: They desperately wished to be rid of I-shan and of his brutal, costly, and useless army. The version of the events would reflect this aim in most unmistakable form. In it, I-shan and his legions were (not without justice) to figure as the bunglers of Canton's defenses, while, equally predictably, the scholar-paramilitaries were (with far less accuracy) to appear as the last-minute rescuers of their native city. The paradoxical myth of victory at Canton was about to be born, but it was to be a myth that communicated little sympathy for the Manchu-led military establishment.

SAN-YUAN-LI

The final episode in the tragi-comic battle for Canton—occurring in the closing weeks of May 1841, and climaxing with a Ch'ing government decision to ransom the city for 6 million dollars—was of little practical significance for the outcome of the larger Sino-British struggle just then beginning to get seriously under way. Moving off from the Pearl River estuary, British forces were soon to regroup for a second push northward, this time with the intent of penetrating into the central reaches of the Yangtze valley where Ch'ing imperial supply lines seemed to be the most exposed.[46] As this new effort progressed, bringing the British closer to the political victory and trade concessions they sought, the events at Canton must have seemed more and more a sideshow, a diversion on the road to bigger and much more consequential engagements.

But the memory of that same fight was not to be so quickly obliterated from the minds of the men who had the worst of it. On the Ch'ing side, at least, the British agreement to withdraw for a price came quickly to be understood as proof that Elliot had lost his nerve. He had been daunted, in the end (as the story now came to be told), by the "people" of the city and by the great hordes of villagers that had followed their scholar-leaders out onto the field of battle. More astonishingly still, by the end of the year, this version of events was to attain the status of proof that the war ought to be turned over everywhere to civilian-led irregulars. And even the emperor would for a while flirt with the idea of doing just that, though in the end he would not be entirely convinced of its feasibility.

How this was to happen is only partly explained by the details of what took place in the final days of the siege. For the rest of the story, to which we shall turn in a moment, it will be necessary to trace the actions of the officials and scholars here and elsewhere along the coast who determined to make of this minor affair a case in point to back their demands for the withdrawal of Manchu-led regulars from the war. We shall need to begin with the specifics of what actually did occur at Canton in the last days of the fighting. In particular, we shall need to take cognizance of an incident that took place just north of the city, when British troops clashed briefly with peasant village guards. This was the so-called San-yuan-li incident—an incident that, with official and literati support, was soon to be offered to the

Ch'ing political world as a demonstration of what "the people" could do against the enemy.

The affair occurred on 30–31 May 1841, at the village of San-yuan-li, just a few miles above the city of Canton, near whose walls General Gough's forces were waiting for the outcome of the discussions about ransom terms. Frederic Wakeman's perceptive study of the evidence concerning this engagement has helped to establish a number of interesting points about what actually took place. The sudden appearance in the field of some 10,000 village militiamen and their brief success in isolating a column of Sepoys during a flash rainstorm were not, he has shown, the results of any prearrangement with the scholars or officials inside Canton. What Gough had unknowingly blundered into was a tradition of village confederation for self-defense. The villagers of the San-yuan-li area had been keyed up by reports of grave-desecrations and rapes by British and Indian soldiers. Responding in accordance with time-honored traditions of reciprocal aid against a shared outside threat, they had marched forth, in the first instance, in the hope of intimidating the invaders by a show of massed manpower. To accomplish this, 100-odd villages mobilized more than 7,000 primitively armed men in several hours' time. When the British stood up to this force and tried to scatter it with rocket fire, things got uglier than had perhaps been intended. At this point, a sudden thunderstorm caught a detachment of Sepoys and their British officers out in the paddies, unable to use their drenched muskets. The column was immediately set upon by the peasant "braves," and, before it could be rescued by reinforcements, it had suffered some 15 wounded and one killed. The next day, the British forces still stubbornly refusing to withdraw from the area, an even larger force of village volunteers began to collect. By now, however, the ransom agreement had been signed in Canton, and the Ch'ing military command, determined to prevent renewal of the fighting, dispatched the Kuang-chou prefect, She Pao-shun, together with several subordinates, to the scene to instruct the leaders of the village militia forces to call their men away.[47]

That was about the extent of the affair—except perhaps for a few mysterious episodes of angry placards being posted within the city itself to warn the British against coming back to the San-yuan-li vicinity. Nothing more had been proved, apparently, than that angry peasants would fight to defend their homes and villages from a perceived threat. Certainly neither Elliot nor Gough had taken the matter very seriously.

Yet virtually from the moment of its occurrence, both the scholar-generals of the city, and their allies in the province's civil administration, seem to have decided that the villagers' attack had established that the militia could deter the British, where I-shan and his troops could not. Reworking the several different versions of the story they had obtained, they soon had produced a convincing array of proclamations describing the unknowing village notables of San-yuan-li actively threatening to throw the British into the sea, together with the "cowardly" mandarins and "rapacious" soldiers who had fled before them during the recent fighting.

Actually, it seems to have been the scholars of the Ta-fo-ssu Bureau who first were inspired with the idea of borrowing the voice of the San-yuan-li militia chiefs for this particular set of propagandistic purposes. Probably what had put this idea into their heads was the short, 300-character manifesto the villagers really had pasted up in public places inside the city to deter an expected punitive attack by the "vengeful" British barbarians. But this former manifesto (or "Scolding of the Foreign Devils," as it was called) had been a pretty rustic affair, filled with colloquialisms and "keep-away-from-our-turf" bravado, not much concerned with the subtleties of scholar-versus-bureaucrat rivalries inside the elevated world of Canton military politics.[48] By contrast, in the three city-scholar productions that were later posted, the language was much more elegant and classical. And the point of the invective was also different, with the emphasis switching from the "fierceness" of the villagers to the fecklessness and ineptitude of the generals. From here, the argument sweeps, irresistibly, toward the conclusion that the "righteous people" (*i-min*) must be allowed to run the war in their way—that is, without the ruinous presence of the hated extra-provincial regulars.[49]

Thus, in a "Proclamation Addressed to the English Barbarians . . . from the People of the Countryside Residing in Canton," the writers assert that "in our passion for revenge all of us are alike aroused; what need have we, then, to trouble our high officials to 'raise their spears' [in our defense]? Waving our arms and giving a great shout, we certainly have the power to crush the [English] beasts without anyone else's aid!"[50] Or, in the "Tears of the Pearl River," another of these anonymous placards, the writer insists on two separate occasions that the government soldiers have been more cruel and caused many more deaths to the local people than the "devils" or the "barbarian people." And he then moves on to indict the authorities in Canton for making the people of the city part with huge sums of money for the ransom, and for "barring" the people of the villages from defending themselves (the reference here being to the prefect's interference at San-yuan-li on 31 May).[51] Finally, in the longest and most eloquent of these city-produced manifestoes, the authors twice repeat (in their threats) that the "official soldiers" (*kuan-ping*) of the province will not be needed should hostilities resume. Instead, "We shall only call on the people of the countryside," and "we ourselves" shall take up arms to kill off you [British] pigs and dogs until there is not one of you left."[52]

Obviously, the preoccupations reflected in these latter documents are those, not of the village defensemen, but of the urban scholarly strategists who had for so many months been fuming at the carryings-on of I-shan's expeditionaries. They can only have been authored, then, as expressions of the version of recent events that the scholars of Canton themselves wanted publicized to a broader political world. And, indeed, one of these productions (the "Tears" manifesto) even admits as much, when it calls upon "benevolent gentlemen" to spread its message about everywhere, "so that a courageous official in the capital might report its sentiments to the throne."[53]

Scarcely surprising, then, that during the next several months, the manifestoes of the braves of San-yuan-li did indeed find their way to Peking and to other quarters as well, speeded there by literati correspondence networks, as well as by the vigorous lobbying efforts of officials, like Ch'i Kung himself, bitterly hostile to the kind of war the Manchu government seemed determined to fight. Chang Wei-p'ing, the White Cloud Mountain poet and Ta-fo-ssu Bureau headman, seems, for one, to have been quite exercised that the world should learn of the true significance of San-yuan-li. And to make sure that it did, he composed a short and moving poem on the affair, echoing the sentiments of the Canton manifestoes, that was to circulate widely through scholar poetry networks.[54] Meanwhile, in the Southern City, the Cantonese Han-lin Lo Ping-chang, newly returned to the capital from home leave in the fall of 1841, distributed among his friends a large collection of popular ballads about San-yuan-li and other recent goings-on in Canton, all terribly persuasive on the subject of the people's bravery and the cowardice of I-shan's regulars.[55]

That these endeavors by Chang, Lo, and others achieved their intent is demonstrated by the broad readership the San-yuan-li manifestoes appear to have gained among scholars outside of Kwangtung, even before the year was out. Thus, we observe Fang Tung-shu (now back again in his native T'ung-ch'eng) recording in a poem that he had finished poring over some of these documents during the autumn of 1841 and had been greatly moved by them. And even in out-of-the-way southern Chekiang, Sun I-yen, a Southern City officeholder living temporarily at home in Jui-an, was to be roused to verse later in that same year after similar materials had come into his hands.[56]

At the same time, moreover, as the poets of Peking and elsewhere were helping to spread the gospel of San-yuan-li, so also were the civil officials of Kwangtung and other coastal provinces. This too was understandable, considering that the commencement of the British Yangtze invasion in the fall of 1841 had brought with it a sudden rash of additional Ch'ing troop transfers into the same region—much to the consternation of provincial governors like Liu Yun-k'o and Yen Po-t'ao (in Chekiang) and Liang Chang-chü (in Kiangnan), who now had to face precisely the same problems Ch'i Kung had been living with for months. How very natural that, under such circumstances, there should be a great expansion of mandarin interest in what had happened at San-yuan-li. Yet, even so, the audacity certain of these newly converted official enthusiasts displayed in lobbying for court accreditation of the San-yuan-li saga is quite remarkable.[57]

It was probably Wang T'ing-lan, a sub-gubernatorial official in the Canton civil administration, who was the first to attempt to spread official interest in the story beyond the confines of Kwangtung province. In mid-1841, Wang wrote to a same-year graduate, the Fukien financial commissioner, Tseng Wang-yen, with the full inside story of the San-yuan-li battle. From Wang, Tseng and his fellow officials learned that the villagers had surrounded an enemy force of "one thousand or more," killed "eighty or ninety" of them, wounded innumerable others, and would doubtless have exterminated the whole lot if only I-shan had sent in his reinforcements to help. Instead, however, the generalissimo had become fearful that the recently signed truce agreement would fall victim to British wrath. He had thus done nothing, letting slip a great chance for victory. But this, Wang told Tseng, was just what one would expect from someone so inept and cowardly.[58]

The preaching did not, however, end there. Tseng immediately brought Wang's letter to the attention of his superior, Governor General Yen Po-t'ao, who in turn sent it on, with an enthusiastic cover letter, straight to the emperor. And when Tao-kuang then asked the newly appointed Kiangnan governor, Liang Chang-chü, for his opinion on the tale (Liang, we should note, had just been transferred from Kwangsi, immediately upriver of Canton, where he would have been able to collect his own information on events in progress in the Pearl River theatre), the answer he received was even more euphoric than Wang's letter in its praise of the village fighters. So convinced was Liang, in fact, of the truth of the claims about these peasant corpsmen, and so eager, too, to have the emperor share his conviction, that the Kiangnan governor even presumed to enclose an original of one of the San-yuan-li manifestoes in his report.[59]

The really significant decision about the credibility of the San-yuan-li story would still, however, have to be made by the court. It was one thing for a provincial official to wax eloquent on the formidable peasant soldiers of Kwangtung. But it was quite another matter again to expect the emperor, merely on the basis of such claims, to rein in his strategic impulses, call back his generals, and withdraw his elite troops from the Yangtze gateway provinces. But what exactly did Tao-kung and his inner-palace advisers make of all this? And, if they too believed, what would they do? In particular, would they accede to Ch'i Kung's recent precedent-setting request for permission to withdraw for good the remains of I-shan's army and to substitute for it a standing force of 36,000 local militiamen?[60] Would such a precedent, even in Kwangtung, be acceptable to a government that had traditionally refused to share military power with the local scholar class?

In the end, in fact, there never was to be a final ruling by the court on any of these questions. But, in two limited regards, at least, the changes in strategy desired by the San-yuan-li propagandists actually did take place. First, and most important, was the decision not to replace I-shan's shattered army with fresh outside troops. On 31 October 1841, the Manchu commander-in-chief of the Nanking military theatre, Hai-ling, petitioned the emperor in the strongest possible terms to dispatch at once to the southeast a new field army assembled from Manchurian garrison units. This was necessary, Hai-ling argued, in order to inject fresh life back into the campaign in Kwangtung (a concern that must have loomed large for the general, since his own troops were about to come under attack). With the Yangtze now facing another British onslaught, it was critically important that the Ch'ing renew the pressure against the British rear in Hong Kong. And for such fighting, Hai-ling insisted, only the best northern troops would be adequate.[61]

But Tao-kuang would have none of this. And then, as if to add a larger strategic gloss to his veto, the emperor six days later (on 5 November) promulgated a remarkable document, conceding as a matter of principle that irregulars ought to be mobilized everywhere along the coast, not just in Kwangtung, so as to reduce the need for any further shifting about of elite units. In fact, this new ruling was still not quite the same thing as a decision to turn the war over to scholar-led militia forces. Tao-kuang nowhere makes mention in it of actual withdrawals of transferred units. All that it really signified, in fact, was that the court was now too worried about a possible attack on Tientsin or Manchuria to be able to spare any more first-class troops for the south. The trials of the lower Yangtze civil officials were still far from over.[62]

Yet, from the vantage point of the officials and scholars of Canton, this 5 November edict could be read in the most positive sort of way. At the very least, there would be no more incoming troops from the north or from the interior. And the "principle" that irregulars were of value in the fight against the British invaders had at last been recognized. These were both major political triumphs in their own right. But they were triumphs, no less, for the myth that the scholars of Canton had created: the myth of a "victory" at San-yuan-li.

PARAMILITARY REALITIES

By way of bringing to a conclusion our narrative of the strange second war the Ch'ing side fought—or thought it had fought—in the southeast, it will be necessary here to document one last sequence of events that were to occur at Canton. These arose out of the actions of Governor General Ch'i Kung and the Ta-fo-ssu Bureau scholars, not in the realm of political lobbying outside of the province, but rather in connection with the reorganization of the government's actual military disposition in the vicinity of Canton itself. During the fall and winter of 1841–1842, more or less in pace with the advancing repute of paramilitaries in the strategic rhetoric of the court, the authorities in Canton undertook to transform the claims of local elite loyalism and spontaneous popular hostility to the British with which they had been bombarding Peking since 1841 into a tangible, independent military force supported and manned exclusively by Cantonese themselves. In this effort they were to be quite remarkably successful. By the war's end, somewhere approaching 40,000 regulars (the equivalent of nearly half the province's regular quota of government-maintained soldiers) were to have been added to the ranks of the forces theoretically available to resist another British attack.[63] Further, they were to be concentrated exclusively in the neighborhood of the provincial capital, where, by 1842, it was no longer Green Standard regulars, but rather these new detachments that had absorbed responsibility for patrolling the labyrinthine inlets and creeks of the Pearl River estuary. Canton, in short, was to be virtually independent of the military bureaucracy and come almost entirely under the paramilitary control of local elites, a situation not paralleled anywhere along the empire's coastline during or after the war. How this was accomplished, and how Peking would perceive the strategic significance of this switch (in terms of its own wartime objectives), are the questions we must now address. For, quite obviously, both matters would have great bearing in the postwar years on how the authorities in Peking and Canton would dispose themselves on the question of paramilitary demobilization—one of the most ticklish postwar political issues in this particular part of China.

In the wake of the British retreat from the Canton river in June 1841, the truce arrangements agreed upon by Elliot and his Ch'ing counterpart, Prince I-shan, had mandated a pullback some twenty miles from Canton of all Ch'ing regular units remaining under arms in the area.[64] The military vacuum created by this redeployment, the effect of which was compounded by the defeat-induced demoralization of those troops under the government's banners and by fear of looting and of banditry, had made it imperative that some sort of arrangements be made by the civilian authorities and the local elite to police the city and its rural suburbs.[65] The random and ad hoc militia structures created by the bureau in Fatshan and elsewhere during the siege, in other words, would now have to be replaced by some more regularized structure of armed control. But how exactly was this to be done?

In theory, of course, there was no reason why this could not have been accomplished merely by systematizing and extending into all precincts the kind of village guard arrangements that had worked so well at San-yuan-li and in other village clusters dotting the hill country just north of the provincial capital. There the traditions of village self-defense had shown themselves well enough entrenched to bring out a huge force of peasant guardsmen whose morale had been sufficiently high even to withstand a brief test by British rocket fire. Presumably, such village guard-force units could have easily handled the threat from within, and done so, moreover, without the expense or political controversy attendant upon the raising of a fully professionalized constabulary force.

As subsequent developments were to demonstrate, however, such informal methods of militia organization as these simply were not sufficient to service the more ambitious kinds of local security needs Ch'i Kung and the Ta-fo-ssu Bureau leaders had perceived and were intent on meeting: needs that included protection both against foreign attack and against well-organized native mobsters and racketeers who had always controlled certain of the more socially complex reaches of the delta.[66]

In the first place, it is evident that the new military planners at Canton really were quite frightened of the prospect of another "looting" of Canton by the British, and were determined to make such a return as costly for the enemy as they could. Such a concern alone can explain the huge amount of effort that went into building new river forts and into emplanting all sorts of obstacles (stone-filled boats, pilings, chains, and so forth) at practically every point of entry into the delta.[67] To man these fortifications and patrol the barriers, however, Ch'i Kung would need some kind of permanent standing army, available at all times, and not just during emergencies. Then, too, funds would have to be raised to finance these new riverine defenses—funds that could scarcely be squeezed out of villages already well protected by their own volunteer guards.[68] And, finally, there were certain parts of the delta where internal security needs could not be met by local communities themselves. Such areas included the walled city of Canton and its satellite towns, such as the great manufacturing center of Fatshan (population 200,000), ten miles to the southwest. But they also included large stretches of rural terrain as well—notably the esturarine shoal-fields (*sha-t'an*) reclaimed from the salt marshes of the delta. Here transient tenant-laborers, duck herders, and boat people, rather than settled villagers, were the principal inhabitants. In such stretches of the estuary—where, incidentally, many urban academies held rent-bearing properties—communities were too atomized, and secret-society-run protection syndicates too active, to allow patrol arrangements to be entrusted to local volunteers.[69]

All these considerations persuaded the responsible authorities in Canton that they would have to create a delta guard force of a fully professionalized and centralized character to supplement the San-yuan-li type self-defensive arrangements that existed in certain upriver portions of the delta. In fact, Ch'i Kung's initial report to Peking on military reorganization following the lifting of the siege of Canton (submitted in September 1841) had already spoken plainly of this necessity. (Though, we might add, the explanation given—that the village guardsmen of the kind that had fought at San-yuan-li were "reluctant to campaign" away from their homes—told only part of the story).[70] But, in December, in a second report written after the November 1841 edict authorizing irregulars universally, Ch'i Kung was able to be more straightforward about the arrangements he had been implementing. There were now, Peking learned, over 30,000 mercenaries (*chuang-yung*) on the payroll, recruited from the seagoing folk of Ch'ao-chou, Hsiang-shan, Shun-te, and Tung-kuan, and gathered together in garrisons of from several hundred to a thousand to guard various key points throughout the ditch- and canal-filled delta.[71]

The huge scale of this private army leads us to the question of how such a force was paid for, and thus to our next point, which concerns the fee-earning services it performed for scholar-controlled corporate landowning bodies (mainly academies) holding rent-producing properties in the shoal fields themselves. Sometime during the fall or winter of 1841, Ch'i Kung seems to have been talked into letting the Ta-fo-ssu Bureau in Canton assume responsibilities as a kind of overlord licensing agency for authorizing and controlling shoal-field exploitation within the lower delta. As this system came eventually to function, interested urban and suburban corporations holding plots within these areas were to purchase licenses recognizing their rights as landlords from this new, centralized militia authority in Canton. By virtue of such recognition, the landholding agency would then be guaranteed the right to protection by the Bureau's patrol forces—protection both against rival strongman organizations run by the secret societies and against unruly tenants and graziers themselves. The Bureau, for its part, would receive yearly fees for the licenses that would help pay for the patrol forces.[72]

From this modest beginning, the authorities in Canton moved on, late in 1842, to an even more ambitious project involving the issuing of licenses for new reclamation projects in the outer reaches of the Whampoa channel—these likewise to be managed by the Canton Bureau and policed by its soldiers. The provincial government, it now seemed, was intent on bringing the subcontracting and policing of nearly all reclamation in the delta area under the control of a single, scholar-run centralized authority in the provincial seat.[73]

The point was, clearly enough, to coax funding for military reorganization from the pockets of the delta's landlords without at the same time stirring up tax protests. And, given that particular goal, the arrangement was eminently practical, offering as it did an improved security of control to absentee landlords in return for the surcharges that they paid into the coffers of the Ta-fo-ssu Bureau. Moreover, from the provincial government's point of view, regardless of how effectively the shoal patrols might or might not fight against the British, the system was already justified solely on the basis of the contribution it made to internal order. For now, at least, Ch'i Kung had nearly 40,000 well-paid and well-armed gendarmes to assert government authority in the Triad-infested waterways of the delta. As measured against the dangerous state of affairs that had existed in mid-1841—and even, for that matter, against the fairly anarchic circumstances that had obtained during the prewar years, when corrupt, underpaid regulars had exercised this function—this must have seemed a considerable gain for the cause of local law and order. So much an improvement, in fact, that it might be worth a few exaggerations to Peking in order to keep the new "army" in the emperor's good graces.

All of which will serve to bring us, in due course, to the matter of how this ambitious program of military restructuring was represented to Peking, and how Peking, for its part, was disposed to regard Ch'i Kung's quite unorthodox innovation. From the very outset, of course, Ch'i Kung was intent on portraying his measures as an important contribution to the Ch'ing government's military efforts against the British. This the governor general had to do, since one of the primary reasons for establishing the legitimacy of the paramilitaries was, as we have seen, to get Peking to withdraw its field armies from the city. Under such circumstances, it was a foregone conclusion that the new army would have to be a more formidable opponent of the enemy than I-shan's had been. And so, in fact, the emperor was told.[74]

Moreover, at least initially, there seems even to have been a genuine readiness on the part of the emperor to credit these claims, if only perhaps because there was (after November 1841) no real alternative to rebuilding the Kwangtung units from the outside. The emperor's willingness to believe, however, was to be gradually eroded by his disappointments at the inertia of the new "army" during the winter of 1841–1842, when, suddenly, it became critically important to Peking that an offensive of some kind be undertaken against Hong Kong. The background to this decision to call out Ch'i Kung's irregulars for an assault on the British main base in the south was the approaching military showdown in the lower Yangtze theatre. There, in a last-ditch attempt to stem the enemy's relentless advance upon the Grand Canal and Nanking, the court had ordered one final counteroffensive. For this it had gathered together some 30,000 troops (including 10,000 elite and aborigine fighters from the interior provinces) for a grand three-pronged attack against British positions in the eastern Chekiang promontory.[75] However, awareness ran high, in Peking and at the front in Chekiang, that prospects of success would be greatly aided if the British fleet, or part of it, could be drawn off by the necessity to relieve pressure upon Hong Kong. For such a job the Cantonese irregulars ought to have been perfect, since they were natives of the region, and, according to what Tao-kuang had been told, were adept at "water warfare." What could have been more appropriate, then, but to throw these intrepid marines against the British forces on Hong Kong island – perhaps in a daring nighttime raid, backed up by a mutiny from the island itself, prearranged with the Chinese coolies and servants who kept the colony running?[76]

But, though a veritable flood of edicts descended upon I-shan and Ch'i Kung in Canton, arguing, imploring, demanding such an attack, it never took place. I-shan explained this first as a matter of local military priorities. The Kwangtung command would have to wait until the delta's defenses had been made invulnerable before going on the offensive. Otherwise, he insisted, the irregulars could not march (or sail) into battle confident that their own rear was safe from British counterattack. But, by January 1842, I-shan was willing to be a little more forthcoming. The Cantonese irregulars, he admitted, simply "had no stomach" for confronting the British on the seas—or even, apparently, in Kowloon harbor. But that itself ought not to be taken as a negative comment on their utility to the Ch'ing, since a successful defensive action at Canton was a better way of engaging the enemy than a direct attack upon his strongest positions. Moreover, at least according to I-shan, the spectacle of Ch'ing military preparations advancing so rapidly just across the bay from Hong Kong had put considerable fear into the new British plenipotentiary, Pottinger, and had forced him to deploy more warships in Hong Kong harbor, where they now sat, wasting supplies and unable to help their own campaign in the north.[77]

To Tao-kuang, all this was greatly vexing, since, at the moment he received this report, Ch'ing armies in Chekiang were dissolving in disarray, broken by the enemy's formidable naval firepower. Reluctantly, he began to come to two difficult conclusions. First, the opportunities for negotiations would again have to be explored. For this purpose the Manchu general Ch'i-ying was ordered to Hangchow in April 1842. Second, the irregulars of Canton, having proven themselves worthless, would have to be pared back. On 13 April, I-shan— whose claims about enemy ships lying idle at Hong Kong were now openly scorned as "absolute nonsense"—was accordingly ordered to start taking these actions. The stage had thus been set (however inadvertently) for a clash between the court and the government authorities at Canton over the fate of the new Kwangtung "army."[78]

But, to the Cantonese, and even to I-shan, this struggle still seemed very far in the future. As late as October 1842, when the generalissimo was about to depart for the north, he could still tell the emperor that the "scholars and people of Canton" were gratified to him for allowing the "raising of irregulars to defend the citizenry," thereby sparing "their province alone" from the savagery of the enemy.[79] The Cantonese, at least, had still to admit that they had not won a "unique" victory over the British.

CHAPTER FIVE

The Debate Over the Conduct of the War

One of the principal arguments of this book—that literati political ambitions fostered an inward-looking intellectual rigidity during the period of the Opium War crisis—seems almost flatly contradicted by the extraordinary effusion of literati interest in wartime defense and diplomatic policy that erupted in 1842. Scarcely a single anthology of the works of politically active literati resident in Peking during the last months of the war or the years immediately following the Treaty of Nanking is without its bitter poetic lament over the humiliation of the empire's armies, or its passionate tract urging one or another formula for the quick recovery of military self-confidence.

Nor was this sudden burst of enthusiasm for discussing and study-ing "maritime affairs" confined to occasional essays or poems, soon to be forgotten once the shock of the treaty—with its alarming provisions for new trade ports and for the cession of Hong Kong—had passed. The immediate postwar years were also to see the publication of several major works by literati on coastal defense and on the geography and political economy (however poorly understood) of the European trading empires, and the circulation in manuscript form of others. Yao Ying's well-received *Record of a Mission to Tibet (K'ang-yu chi-hsing)*, and Wei Yuan's even more broadly cited *Illustrated Gazetteer of the Maritime Nations (Hai-kuo t'u-chih)*, for example, were both immediate products of the shock of defeat, as were several other somewhat less widely distributed volumes on military and geographical subjects, such as Huang Chueh-tzu's *Illustrated Compendium on Maritime Defense (Hai-fang t'u-piao)*, or Hsu Chi-yü's *Short Account of the Maritime Circuit (Ying-huan chih-lueh)*, a vaguely pro-European work suppressed until its 1866 reprinting. Then, too, there were a number of careful studies of the recent war itself—both as an episode in diplomacy and as a case study in military planning—including, most prominently, Wei Yuan's *Record of the Campaigns and Pacification of the Foreign Fleets (Tao-kuang yang-sou cheng-fu chi)*, and its rival, the more defeatist *Record of Pacifying the Barbarians from Afar (Fu-yuan chi-lueh)* of Huang En-t'ung.[1]

In comparison with the political and intellectual milieu of the immediate prewar years, this in itself seems a startling change: a realization, as it were, of the intractable reality of international military competition, or a confession that the prewar ministerial leadership had blundered into its confrontation with England too much blinded by internal political causes to pay adequate heed to the problems of external defense. As Yao Ying, the passionate Ming-revivalist literati leader of the prewar political scene, was to put it, the scholars of the 1830s had been too enclosed in their narrow, domestic world— Yao himself included. Writing to a friend in 1846 or 1847, Yao blamed this political and intellectual introversion in no uncertain terms for the disaster that the Ch'ing had just suffered:

The techniques of the barbarians have never been greatly superior to those of China. Moreover, in terms of strategic geography they fight in violation of the precepts of military science [i.e., by operating so far from their bases]. Why, then, have we panicked and retreated whenever they have landed on our shores? Surely the reason is that the book-bound scholars of China have been too glued to immediate concerns, and too inattentive to planning for "that which lies distant." In the days preceding this crisis, our scholars paid no heed whatsoever to the study of the interstate relations or domestic affairs of these barbarians from beyond the seas. And thus, when their great ships suddenly hove into view, [our scholars] were as terrified as if they had just seen a ghost or spirit; and as frightened as if they had just been struck by a thunderbolt.[2]

It was now time, Yao seemed to be saying, for the literati to give their undivided attention to matters external.

Nor does the impression of a sudden outward redirection of literati interest change when we examine the political alignments and controversies that came to dominate the Peking political scene during the 1840s. For these too seem to have been very much the product of disagreements within the elite over the external affairs of war and diplomacy. As is well known, the major political rivalry in the capital during the years immediately following the Nanking negotiations pitted the Manchu grand councillor, Mu-chang-a, who had backed the policy of retreat at court, against the Han Chinese grand councillor, Ch'i Chün-tsao, who (supported enthusiastically by his many adherents) had been the most vigorous opponent of the surrender policy.[3] Moreover, in the final showdown between these court factions, climaxing in 1849–1850, diplomatic and military issues were to play a highly visible role, as we shall discuss in chapter 7. After 1849, for example, the opposition party was to make much of the fact that the British had not resorted to war (as their rivals insisted they would) over Ch'ing refusal to admit foreigners into Canton. This, they claimed, proved what the more enlightened students of barbarian affairs had been saying all along—that the British were too overextended in south Asia and Nepal to risk another conflict in distant China. And in 1850, when the Mu-chang-a government finally fell from grace, the emperor himself was to declare its leaders unnecessarily timid on the Canton question, and to present this as a major reason for the decision to throw them out.

To all outward appearances, then, the literati had now fully committed themselves to greater attentiveness in the realm of what they called maritime affairs. Concern within the political elite over foreign policy questions had developed to the point that it eclipsed other issues as a source of disagreement and spur to political competition. This would seem, indeed, to be a very different, and much more extroverted, political climate than that of the 1830s, when fairly trivial bureaucratic reforms and controversies over the Ch'ing political constitution had been the main fare of high politics. And if the political milieu was still not quite ready for a major commitment to military or economic modernization, surely the greater sensitivity to foreign affairs that had been induced by the war would, before long, begin to move things in that direction.

Yet in the end, matters did not develop this way. The newfound literati fascination with the external world did not lead to great self-consciousness or to a positive appreciation of the military and economic institutions that had enabled the enemy to triumph. It led, instead, in precisely the opposite direction: backward, toward a renewed conviction that Lin Tse-hsu really had been right, and that the maritime West really was, for all its formidable exterior, only an empty threat, not a challenge requiring major institutional reforms. War-provoked alarm, though deep, nevertheless ended up binding the literati all the more closely to the old ideas of Chinese strategic self-sufficiency.

In this chapter and in the next, our inquiry will concern itself with why this view triumphed at the expense of others. For the purposes of the chapter at hand, however, we shall be interested in one feature of the mid-century Ch'ing political milieu that had a direct bearing on literati consciousness of the war and its implications. This was the consciousness-molding influence exercised by the Spring Purification circle and other loyalty networks that had been built up by the literati in the prewar years. As we proceed with our analysis of literati opinion formation in the postwar era, we shall have occasion to observe over and over again how the channels through which views about the war were diffused were dominated by the prewar literati party, and how, as the result, the self-exculpatory enthusiasm of the literati leaders responsible for the war came to be inserted into almost every popular account of what had taken place. Needless to say, the legend of San-yuan-li and of paramilitary triumphs over the British figured quite prominently in these accounts. For after all, that particular affair (or rather, the distorted publicity given it) had been in part a product of the determination to vindicate Lin Tse-hsu's insistence on the practicality of military resistance.

But it was not simply the claims of an overlooked victory in the south that captured the postwar literati political imagination. Also prominent in this literati war literature were themes of betrayal and of internal sabotage. The tremendous amount of hostile publicity

Lin had stirred up against Ch'i-shan, for example, became one of the great influences on how the literati were to understand the war in retrospect. And there were other, parallel instances, where the residue of wartime policy quarrels and the appeals they had prompted to Southern City friends and supporters provided postwar commentators with convincing evidence that defeat really had come from within—such as, for instance, in the famous Taiwan case of 1843 that will be discussed below. The impact of these bitterly *ad hominem* productions on literati willingness to believe that military success had truly been within reach cannot be overrated. For, when presented against a background of lurid intrigues by cowardly Manchu generals and timid mandarins, the claims of an overlooked victory at Canton acquired just that much more plausibility.

Our attempt to interpret the influences bearing upon postwar literati political consciousness begins, then, with the analysis of how the literati loyalty networks built up during the immediate prewar period determined what kinds of information about the details of the 1840–1842 war would achieve the broadest currency. Stories of betrayal, of officials and generals in league to thwart the serious belligerents, had a major place in this inner literati view, if only because so much of this private literature had its origins in the efforts of literati leaders to dishonor their opponents. Let us therefore launch our review of this loyalty-network literature by reconstructing, as best we can, two of the best-known betrayal legends: Lin's victimization by the Chihli governor-general, Ch'i-shan; and, the impeachment of the Taiwan intendant by the Amoy commissioner, I-liang.

CH'I-SHAN AND THE TIENTSIN NEGOTIATIONS

Without a doubt, the most widely circulated and accredited tale of bureaucratic betrayal was the episode of Lin Tse-hsu's removal from office and his replacement as imperial commissioner at Canton by Ch'i-shan late in 1840. To review briefly the course of events that led up to that particular episode, we shall recall from the previous chapter that the removal of Lin had been precipitated by Elliot's arrival at Ta-ku near Tientsin in August 1840 with a supporting naval squadron in tow. This surprise move caught the Chihli governor general, Ch'i-shan, and the court, totally unprepared. Although it is uncertain whether the Ta-ku forts could have been held even under more advantageous circumstances, the hue and cry that followed was to focus instead on whose fault it was that there had been no effective defense preparations at Ta-ku.[4]

From Ch'i-shan's point of view, and from Tao-kuang's as well, there did not at first seem to be much doubt about who had been in the wrong. As we have already had occasion to note, Lin Tse-hsu had withheld all mention that the British might attack the north until it was virtually too late to take any precautionary actions. And he had done so because he simply had not expected this move.

Lin, however, had (or was soon to develop) other views on the matter. In one of his more broadly circulated self-defenses (his February 1841 letter to Shen Wei-ch'iao), he set forth his own side of the affair, in terms that introduced two new (and entirely false) claims about what had taken place. There had in fact been warnings of possible attack, Lin was now to insist. If they had not been taken seriously, that was to be attributed to the timorousness or sluggishness of the Chekiang and Chihli authorities. Second, Elliot's choice of Tientsin as his main target now became, in Lin's reworking of history, a "feint" or a "bluff"—a probe to search out the weak point in the Ch'ing defense system—that had occurred only because Lin himself had frustrated their primary purpose: the seizure of Canton. There is no convincing basis for either of these claims. But let us pause a moment to hear Lin's version, for it was soon to become the "official" view of the opposition:

At first, these barbarians were terrified of our celestial majesty, and at once handed over the entire stock of opium from their hulks. We had no need to deploy a single soldier or shoot a single arrow. . . . [But later when we backed down from our resolve to force them to sign promises of no further imports], they craftily perceived that our will was not as one. . . . Thereupon their ships began to glide like phantoms along our shores, and rumors began to fly forth from all quarters. Fortunately, in the Kwangtung region we had made vigilant defense preparations, and were able to drive them off several times. [And we were further aided] by the embargo edicts that then authorized us to terminate all their trading. *I then anticipated that their response would be to raid other provinces along our coast, and I accordingly sent in no fewer than five reports asking that orders be issued for defense preparations to be made. And I even managed to discover in advance and to report that they planned to occupy the Chusan [Islands] and to descend upon Tientsin.* . . .But the Chihli governor general, having earlier reported that a fleet need not be built [to guard that province], now found himself in a panic when the barbarian ships approached. So as not to humiliate himself as had the Chekiang authorities, he resolved to speak soft words and be generous with gifts, and thus appease their anger and delight them. *Thus would he insinuate his way out of the danger [he now faced]. He never anticipated that this would only whet their dog-like appetites, making them even more insatiable than they had been before.* [Italics added].[5]

The facts contradict Lin's claims. In the first place, we know from the testimony of Lin's own military adviser, Liang T'ing-nan, that Lin had chosen to disbelieve early (spring 1840) reports about the dispatch from India of a large British naval force. His so-called "warning" of April 1840 in fact consists of little more than a list of arguments against worrying too much about the "rumor" Lin is reporting on British plans to send a fleet upcoast. And, still more to the point, the choice to make Tientsin the pressure point instead of Canton had been made in London, not at the China front, and had begun to be prefigured in Palmerston's correspondence as early as October 1839.[6] It is thus ridiculous for Lin to claim to have "driven off" the enemy fleet, and equally absurd for him to argue that the enemy's singling out of Ta-ku was connected to a decision to probe for weak points away from Canton.

Yet on these two ungrounded claims Commissioner Lin staked his self-defense, and these claims soon became the basis of a great deal of literati gossip about the affair—indicating, unmistakably, that it was Lin's account that had determined these men's views.

But let us examine some specific instances of this literati version, inspired by Lin himself, of the commissioner's purge. One widely circulated rendering of it occurs in an often-quoted letter composed by Lin's friend and wartime correspondent, the Mongol Han-lin Yü-ch'ien, to a fellow spirit within the bureaucracy, in the spring of 1841. Writing just after the ransoming of Canton, in May of that year, Yü-ch'ien analyzed the British strategy:

In the preceding two years [i.e., since Lin's arrival at Canton in the spring of 1839] the defenses of Kwangtung had been well organized, and there was no possibility of [the British] finding a strategy for seizing [the provincial capital]. Therefore the barbarians attacked and occupied Ting-hai. But their intentions remained firmly fixed upon Kwangtung. Their next step therefore was to concoct a treacherous plan. The most gullible [of the coastal governors and governors general] was singled out as the victim of their deception. Accordingly, they proceeded to the headquarters of the Chihli governor general at Tientsin and submitted a plan for the reconciliation. At the same time, they told Ch'i-shan: "If

your Excellency goes to Kwangtung, our two sides can live in everlasting peace."
[Ch'i-shan] was ignorant of strategy and of the barbarians' nature alike, and so he
was taken in. Boldly he took matters into his own hands. Upon reaching Kwangtung, [as a sign of good faith] he promptly dissolved the naval force and water
braves [Lin had assembled].[7]

And so the city of Canton fell into English hands.

To another literati commentator, Hsia Hsieh, who had learned of
the intrigue from Yü-ch'ien's account, the matter amounted to
nothing more than an exercise of the most elementary of military
strategies: taking by ruse what cannot be taken by direct assault:

> The rule of fighting is that, if you attack the enemy's weak point, then his strong-
> est position becomes no better than a weak point itself. Behold how [Palmer-
> ston's] letter was handed over at Tientsin; how Lin and Teng were cashiered; how
> Grand Secretary Ch'i-shan was transferred to Kwangtung; and how the fortifica-
> tions at the Bogue were removed and Canton left exposed "like an open sack,
> inviting all to pilfer." [It is manifest] that Elliot had no intention of negotiating
> a settlement, but only sought to utilize Grand Secretary Ch'i-shan to unlock the
> door to Canton.[8]

In this ingenious manner, then, Elliot had succeeded in prying his
two most formidable opponents (Lin and Teng) from office, and the
Chinese side, taken by surprise by Elliot's seizure of the Bogue forts
the following spring, had soon thereafter to acquiesce to an evacua-
tion of all its troops from the Pearl River estuary.

The hypnotizing spell of Lin's own history of this complex affair
is here evident, both in the assumption that Canton had all along
been Elliot's principal target, and in the portrait of Ch'i-shan as the
all-too-willing victim of Elliot's ingenious outflanking maneuver.
And those very same assumptions inhabit the war memoirs of a great
many other contemporaneous literati activists as well—many of
whom seem like Hsia Hsieh to have gotten Lin's story via Yü-ch'ien
correspondence. Thus, for example, late in 1842 a young scholar
from Kwangsi named Wang Hsi-chen passed around to his friends in
the capital a draft letter to the grand councillor, Ch'i Chün-tsao,
which dwelt, as had the accounts of Yü-ch'ien and Lin, upon the element of cunning in British strategy. This cunning, Wang earnestly
warned the grand councillor, had been evidenced, *inter alia*, in the
treacherous methods the British had used to "fulfill their designs"
upon Canton, and to "implicate" Lin. Let the current government

therefore take note, and not again be caught unawares by such arrant trickery.[9] At about the same time Wang was handing around his letter, moreover, another much better established Southern City personality, the censor Chu Ch'i, was coming to much the same conclusion as he reflected back upon what had happened at Tientsin. In a lengthy and emotional poem on the war written in mid-1842, he has the British, once again, "launching a treacherous subterfuge," sailing north to "set the [frightened officials in that quarter] to vilifying Commissioner Lin," and then ungratefully violating their promises to Ch'i-shan after he helped them get rid of Lin.[10] Nearly everyone, it would seem, had been seduced by Lin's tale.

As the result, therefore, of Lin's spirited self-defense and the publicity it got, the explanation that was to dominate postwar literati commentary on why the Ch'ing had been overwhelmed in the first phases of the war was to be an entirely self-determined, inward-looking one. Elliot's first northern campaign and the British decision to try the peace ruse upon Ch'i-shan were proof only of the strength and ingenuity of Lin's defense arrangements at Canton. And if such wiles had been successful, it was because, quite plainly, the Ch'ing bureaucracy had allowed too many spineless officials, such as Ch'i-shan, to clamber into high office. From this it was but one small additional step to the conclusion that perhaps the whole war, and not just the opening rounds, had been deliberately sabotaged by mediocre bureaucrats, intent upon safeguarding their jobs from the risks of a war they had not wanted. As one Southern City official very much under Lin's influence was to write, directly after the Nanking negotiations had ended, the whole sorry performance of the Ch'ing government in the recent war could be ascribed to the "premeditated treachery" of such officials. The government, it seemed—or at least most of its agents—had been merely going through the motions of waging war, meanwhile secretly hoping that Lin and the activist party would wreck themselves as quickly as possible. With such an attitude crippling the Ch'ing side, even the empty bluster of these "island barbarians" could easily carry the day.[11]

THE CASE OF YAO YING ON TAIWAN

If Lin Tse-hsu's 1840–1841 campaign against Ch'i-shan had first popularized the suspicion that the war had been lost through self-defeating treachery, that same conviction was to be given even more appeal by a second great literati *cause célèbre*: the attempt to save the Taiwan intendant, Yao Ying, from "revenge" by his British and Manchu enemies in 1843. Very few episodes connected with the war received quite so much publicity among the Southern City literati as this particular affair. And not surprisingly, either: Yao, we might remember, was one of the great moving spirits behind the original Spring Purification caucus in Peking, and had been accumulating enthusiastic scholarly dependents for over a decade by the time his own career was caught up in (and almost ruined by) the 1840 war. Moreover, like Lin, Yao had been a party to most of the political maneuvers that had precipitated the war—a circumstance that compelled him to act, throughout this affair, with maximum regard to maintaining the appearance of his own wisdom and honorability, whatever the realities of the situation might actually be.[12] Finally, and adding still more fuel to the fires of controversy that Yao's actions were to ignite, was his own personal identification with the core values of *ku-wen* belletrism. To leave posterity words that conveyed a vivid moral example, and to act as if one were already between the covers of a "praise-and-blame" history text—such values were, to Yao, as to others in the T'ung-ch'eng school, the cardinal ideals of the scholar-official's life.[13] This particular mind-set was to render Yao even more willing than Lin to propagandize in his own self-defense. And it was to guarantee, as well, that the story of Yao's victimization would create even greater faith in the "self-defeat-through-intrigue" version of the war than had Lin's sufferings at the hands of Ch'i-shan and Elliot.

But at this point some background is in order. What brought about Yao's spectacular run-in with the Ch'ing authorities late in 1842 was the action he had taken as a wartime commander in co-charge of the defense of the island of Taiwan. The history of these actions began in the autumn of 1841, a crucial juncture in the progress of the war, when the British, under new leadership, were initiating the second and final round of assaults on Chinese coastal and riverine defenses that would take them to the walls of Nanking by the following spring.

For the purposes of our current narrative, several events related to that campaign can be seen in retrospect to have been of vital consequence for the outcome of the "Taiwan case." The first was the fall of Amoy on 26 August 1841, with no significant resistance by its defenders. Amoy was the first city to be occupied by British soldiers in this renewed round of fighting, and its loss (by contrast with the allegedly successful defense by Teng T'ing-chen in 1840) prompted an immediate and irate response from the court. I-liang, at the time Liang-Kuang governor general, and by reputation a militant, was assigned on 30 September to investigate the causes of the debacle. And on 19 October he was issued the seal of an imperial commissioner with responsibility for the defense of the province of Fukien. British garrison forces having evacuated on 5 September in order to avoid depleting their main attacking force, I-liang was spared the unpleasant task of having to recapture the lost port. But a flotilla of foreign craft remained anchored off Kulangsu Island, within sight of the city. And British forces continued to use that island as a staging point and supply base for their naval operations further to the north.[14]

At around the same time, a British troop ship, *Nerbudda*, carrying a complement of several hundred Sepoy troops for deployment in the Yangtze campaigns, was blown off course and shipwrecked off the port of Keelung, in Taiwan. A large number of Indian soldiers were taken prisoner by the Ch'ing authorities and an appeal was sent to Peking for permission to execute them as invaders.[15] While the matter was being deliberated at court, a second British vessel, the brig *Ann*, ran aground and went to pieces near Ta-an harbor—a port slightly further to the south—and its crew (this time including 18 British officers) likewise fell into the hands of the local authorities.[16] By June 1842, the intendant's jail in Tainan contained 149 Sepoys and 19 "white" foreign soldiers. In the meantime, Yao Ying had received authorization to put the entire lot to death. These instructions were dutifully carried out on 12 or 13 August 1842, after interrogations had been completed. Only 9 of the castaways (mostly white, with the exception of two Cantonese pilots) were spared.[17]

Though none of these events was particularly decisive for the outcome of the war then being fought, in combination they conspired to put the Amoy commissioner in a difficult position. According to a later report submitted by him, the August raid by the British on Amoy had resulted in the loss of all of the heavy-draught war-junks assigned to defend that port and the nearby Pescadores. The funds at his disposal, according to this same report, were not adequate to support even so unambitious a naval construction effort as would have been required to replace them.[18] The expulsion of the British from the Fukien coast–including Kulangsu and the Pescadores–was nevertheless expected of him. I-liang's already onerous burden could scarcely have been lightened by the news from Taiwan. It must certainly have been made heavier still by the receipt of word, in two successive edicts from Peking (dispatched on 18 and 19 January 1842), of the anticipated arrival of British naval reinforcements and of I-liang's own elevation to the post of governor general of Fukien and Chekiang provinces.[19]

Adding to the pressure all of this placed on I-liang, it may well be imagined, was at least a twinge of jealousy over the enthusiasm his subordinates on Taiwan had succeeded in eliciting from the court. Coming in the wake of a string of military disasters–including the loss of Amoy (26 August 1841), Ting-hai (1 October), and Ningpo (13 October)–Yao's report of the "sinking" of the *Nerbudda* roused Tao-kuang to transports of martial enthusiasm. The imperial ecstasy, it appears, may well have been unfounded; for the *Nerbudda*–as Yao himself was later to confess–seems to have run aground without the help (claimed by the Taiwan command) of a direct hit on her mizzenmast by Chinese shore batteries. Of this, however, Tao-kuang as yet knew nothing. "Reading this news, my felicity knows no bounds," reads his endorsement of Yao's "victory" memorial. And to signify that his excitement was more than rhetorical, the habitually miserly emperor had authorized an immediate advance, from the Foochow treasury, of 300,000 taels to strengthen Taiwan's defenses against anticipated British retaliation.[20] "Does the Taiwan intendant," I-liang is reported to have exploded, "think that he can challenge destiny with his bare hands?"[21]

As the war entered its climactic phase, therefore, there was already considerable tension between the Manchu governor general, I-liang, in Amoy (the nominal theatre commander), and the difficult-to-control intendant in charge of Taiwan. The final showdown between these two competing officials was not to come, however, until Yao himself had independently solicited (and received) imperial permission to execute the survivors of the two British shipwrecks. This was a step that I-liang had already urged Yao not to take, since (as he had told Yao) the British commandant on Kulangsu, across the harbor from Amoy, had discovered what Yao was up to and threatened an invasion of Taiwan if the deed was done.[22] Not deterred, Yao had

gone ahead anyway, leaving I-liang no doubt enraged, but too preoccupied with other matters to act. Thus things stood as the war came
to an end.

At this point, however, events began to unfold that were soon to
leave Yao and his supporters convinced that there had been Ch'ing
official intrigue against him ever since his first "victories" had won
imperial praise. In the fall of 1842, Sir Henry Pottinger, Elliot's
replacement as British plenipotentiary in China, brought the matter
of Yao's war crimes (for such indeed they were, in British eyes) before
the Nanking viceroy, Ch'i-ying, his opposite number in the recently
concluded peace negotiations. Ch'i-ying, as one of the emergent
heads of the peace party, was not reluctant to prosecute the investigation Pottinger demanded. Nor, for that matter, was I-liang. All manner of proofs were thus hurriedly assembled by the two Manchus to
establish that Yao had in fact knowingly misreported the way in
which prisoners had come into his hands.[23] And, with this evidence
before him, Tao-kuang had felt obliged to give way and, on 11 January 1843, to order a formal judicial inquiry into the charges against
Yao and Ta-hung-a, the Manchu garrison commander on Taiwan,
commenting acidly:

If the matter is actually as [Ch'i-ying says], have not [these two] deceived their sov-
ereign, misdirected the government, and brought disaster upon the people? How
can their crime be exonerated?[24]

Within but two more months, both were in jail in Peking, awaiting
their sentences—sentences that were, however, to be quite lenient,
since Tao-kuang never really had much liking for the affair, and was
acting mainly to placate the ever-worrisome British. (Yao had, in the
end, merely to serve for three years or so as a minor official in the
remote western reaches of Szechuan province.)[25]

This, then, was the background against which Yao made his own
rather spectacular counter-moves, aimed at establishing that his actions had been honorable, and that Ch'i-ying and I-liang were the vil-
lains. Strangely enough, Yao did not deny that the claim of sinking
the enemy's ships was false. Rather, his tack was to dismiss it as a
mixup resulting from his failure to verify his sub-commander's
reports, while simultaneously insisting that his own inclination to
believe what he had been told was motivated by the loftiest and most
honorable of concerns. Yao was to stress over and over again, in his

voluminous correspondence on the case, that there had been a critical morale-building need for a Ch'ing naval triumph—a need that
overrode the particulars of the method in which the *Nerbudda* and
Ann had actually come to grief. And there had, likewise, been a need
for at least one mandarin who would openly defy the prospect of
British reprisals, if only to inspire kindred spirits on the mainland
with the will to continue the Ch'ing resistance.[26]

But here let us let Yao speak for himself. In the winter of 1843,
soon after his release from prison, Yao explained his actions to a sym-
pathizer (Liu Hung-kao, the Fukien governor) in the following terms:

> The destruction of the barbarian ship at Keelung [*i.e.*, the transport *Ner-
> budda*, reported by Yao to have been sunk by shore batteries] seems to have
> resulted from her hitting a reef. And the destruction of the barbarian ship at Ta-
> an [*i.e.*, the *Ann*, supposed to have been destroyed by Yao and Ta-hung-a in coop-
> eration with a force of local fishermen-militiamen] was said to have resulted from
> her running aground. But [at the time of these actions] the men-in-arms through-
> out Taiwan were unrelenting in their vigilance at the parapets. And the righteous
> people were all eager to engage the enemy . . .

> Moreover, at the time [we received the reports of the two sinkings] the bar-
> barians were [fighting] with full fury. Despoiling several provinces, they had been
> laying waste to our people and murdering our generals. The court had designated
> several [officers] as imperial commissioners with sole responsibility for chastising
> them. But in the provinces there was not a single army that could report a vic-
> tory. [His Grace] fretted and agonized day and night, and the loyal and conscien-
> tious [men at court] gnashed their teeth [in frustration]. Therefore, when the
> reports reached [Tan-shui] of the sinking of the barbarian ships and the capture
> of the barbarian [prisoners], everyone clapped their hands to their foreheads and
> exclaimed their congratulations, and said that [the sea spirit] Hai-jo had per-
> formed a miracle [in order to] help our officers and people extirpate the ghoulish
> breed [of invaders]. The opinion of all was that we ought to memorialize at once,
> both to bring solace to Our Sovereign's worried and angry heart, and to inspire
> our armies to rebuff the barbarians . . .[27]

The significance of Yao Ying's consciously contrived actions, then,
had been to bolster the morale of a sagging Ch'ing officialdom and of
the island's staunch paramilitaries. And if Yao had seemed, perhaps,
to be acting shabbily in murdering so many prisoners just to keep
the deception secret, surely the world must by now have realized that
the deception itself had been undertaken at great personal peril, and
thus could only have been honorable in its intentions.

Good military leadership, then, was mainly a matter of keeping up a bold front. And, after all, hadn't the lie worked, inasmuch as the scholars and people of Taiwan had never lost their nerve, and as the British had been thereby deterred from attack at least until the declared war was over?

That, at least, seemed to be the other implicit justification offered by Yao in his letters on the incident. For, in this correspondence with his friends in Peking and elsewhere on the mainland—a correspondence that had already made him something of a hero even before his arrest in 1843—Yao returns ceaselessly to the point that his own personal bravery, and not much more, had kept up the courage of the militiamen and mandarins on the island, in spite of the terrible danger they faced. In a mid-1841 letter to a fellow Spring Purificationist (Mei Tseng-liang) in the capital, for example, Yao had reminded his old friend that the situation on Taiwan was even more perilous than it was on the mainland. For here, one had to fear not just the barbarians but also the very real prospect of a local uprising. "The secret is in not showing that one is perturbed, and in facing down these threats with pure *sang-froid*," Yao had reflected.[28] Or, again, in mid-1843, just before his jailing, Yao was to write to Fang Tung-shu that there were "all too few" within the official world who were truly capable of "forgetting their fears for themselves," or of "winning the confidence of the soldiers and people" by their "heroic and resolute energy." But obviously, Yao had been an exception.[29]

But if wise official leadership thus consisted of daring to keep up appearances and thereby helping them to become realities, then, by the same logic, the cautious realism of I-liang and Ch'i-ying had, like Yao himself, been a little more willing to believe in their own strength and a little less concerned with previous setbacks, then who could say what might have been accomplished?

Of course, being a man of principle, Yao would himself name no names. (On just one occasion did he appear to hint that I-liang had been acting our of jealousy over the acclaim Yao had won, but that slip was not to be repeated.)[30] At his trial in Peking, he typically refused to confound his Manchu accusers, preferring instead to confess his "crimes" and go silently to his punishment.[31] But, Yao's reticence notwithstanding, the problematic behavior of his rivals had not gone unnoticed by the intendant's many admirers among the Southern City literati. And, for that very reason, almost all secondhand accounts that were to circulate among the literati about the affair during 1843 and 1844 dwell obsessively upon the conspiratorial malice of Yao's persecutors, as if to argue, by implication, that the war really might have been lost because of the very bad examples that these men had set.

Thus, for example, Hsia Hsieh's very long account of the Taiwan imbroglio zeros in quite mercilessly upon I-liang's cowardice, while quite overlooking the possibility that Yao's bravery might have been a good deal more damaging for the Ch'ing:

Earlier [Hsia moralizes], when Governor General I-liang was serving [as governor of] Kwangtung, he had been opposed to negotiations. As soon, however, as he was promoted to the Min-Che governor generalship, he began to fear a repetition of previous events at Amoy. His lifelong [sense of honor] suddenly deserted him, and he did not mind the loss. He [then] covered up for the barbarians and suppressed the people, and passed the blame [onto the shoulders] of his subordinates.[32]

When, therefore, the equally feckless Nanking governor general, Ch'i-ying, and the (Manchu) grand councillor, Mu-chang-a, had decided that Yao had to go, I-liang had been an all-too-willing accomplice.[33] Similarly, for the Spring Purificationist Lu I-t'ung, the lesson of the tale was clearly that the Ch'ing had had far too few wartime leaders like Yao, and far too many like I-liang. "Had all our leaders at the front been of Yao's caliber, *willing to risk all on a dare and never looking back*, we might perhaps still not have triumphed every time. But at least then there might have been some reasonable chance of a favorable outcome" (emphasis added).[34] But there had been practically no others like Yao, and all too many like Ch'i and I-liang, who would not gamble or bluff. And so, inevitably, defeat had resulted, and the chance for victory had been tossed away.

The examples here quoted do not begin to exhaust the huge number of earnest commentators who agreed with Yao and Lu.[35] Rather than merely enumerate more examples, it might be more to the point to give some anecdotal sense of the scale of publicity Yao's little drama was to achieve. When, for example, the intendant, now in chains, was rumored to be about to arrive in Peking, in the spring of 1843, practically the entire Southern City officialdom seems to have trekked out to the suburbs to meet him. According to one account, a certain rather elderly Southern City official, Wang Hsi-sun, "almost went blind" from the grief he experienced listening to Yao relate what had happened. On the same note, back in Peking itself, I-liang's brother was described as fretting, daily and nightly, about what "future generations who read of this in the histories" would have to say about the way his brother had acted during the affair.[36]

Upon his release from jail at the end of the year, moreover, Yao was to become even more of a fascination for the younger and bolder spirits of Southern City society than he had been before his trial, since he now could be invited to proper literati gatherings and his story recited at length. Hardly averse to such celebrity status, Yao seems to have relished the opportunity to lecture at these affairs. Through the memoirs of Feng Kuei-fen, a burgeoning Han-lin talent who happened to attend one such meeting, there is preserved an account suggesting just what effect Yao exercised upon his enthralled listeners:

After Master [Yao] was set loose from prison, I joined with several of my friends to throw a banquet for him at his lodgings. Then someone in the group asked him to give us the full story of what had happened on Taiwan [during the war]. He did so, but with great modesty, never boasting at all of the things he had done, but going into great detail about the terrain and about the stratagems that had been used. Then, however, when we were all half tipsy with wine, he suddenly stroked his beard and straightened his gown. "No fear that our state is lacking in men of talent," he said to us. "Affairs of state such as this are not yours to be concerned about. Yet I see that your hearts are bursting with intensity as I talk, as if this were all your own personal grievance. . . . How true it is, then, as the saying goes, that "men of spirit can surely find a way!" I might be old and no longer capable of very much, but is there anything that cannot be accomplished in this world [by men such as yourselves]? It is up to you gentlemen! Keep up your pride! Keep up your pride!" Whereupon all of us who had been listening suddenly cast down our gaze with shame.[37]

How, then could anyone in the Southern City believe that this war had really been unwinnable, when the victims of Ch'ing self-sabotage were so near at hand, so familiar, so persuasive, and so eloquent in their own defense? No, surely, a way could have been found, if only there had been more men of spirit. That it had not could only be explained by the scandalous intrigues of the bureaucrats and the courtiers who now seemed to be controlling the throne.

WEI YUAN AND THE STRATEGY OF DEFENSIVE WAR

Having been persuaded by Lin and Yao that treachery from within was to blame for the Ch'ing defeat, commentators on maritime affairs were predisposed to find great validity in the traditional strategic formulations that had guided these literati-generals in the field. Not too long after the fighting had ended, Lin Tse-hsu's ideas about exhausting the "pirate" enemy through defensive warfare, and the supposed lessons of the paramilitary "victory" at San-yuan-li, were to be woven eloquently together by Wei Yuan into a formula for a war of attrition that relied almost entirely on non-Western military techniques. And, not too many years after that, Yao Ying himself would undertake to compile a volume on the South Asian "weak flank" of the British empire, from which information he would adduce that his own earlier, wartime notion of waiting "imperturbably" for the enemy to overextend himself had been entirely correct. The impact of these authors and the strategies they found validated by wartime experiences was enormous—a fact that should not surprise us, since the ideas and case materials that went into their work already enjoyed the advantage of broad prior circulation through the Spring Purification war-party grapevine. Then, too, the ideas that Wei and Yao now set forth profited from the fact that they had themselves originated (ultimately) from a common fund of favorite literati military-historical readings. These included, most notably, the *True Record of Troop Training* of the late Ming pirate-queller, General Ch'i Chi-kuang (1528–1587); and the *Illustrated Discourse on Maritime Defense* of Cheng Jo-tseng (fl. 1505–1580), another official likewise active in these same mid-sixteenth-century campaigns against Japan-based corsairs. For most literati readers, therefore, the strategic truths that could be gleaned from Wei's and Yao's works were practically *deja vu*, and, for that reason, all the more plausible. And finally, as if to guarantee the receptivity of the intended audience, there were the well-known stories of blundering Manchu generalship in Kwangtung and in the lower Yangtze counteroffensives to show that the dynasty's military commanders had indeed not heeded the lessons Wei and Yao had now distilled.[38]

But let us now take up, briefly, the work of these two highly influential summarizers of the literati version of the war, noting, as we do, how the various sources we have mentioned—the reportage on Lin's and Yao's defense planning; the tales of paramilitary heroism at Canton; the sixteenth-century pirate-suppression texts; and the angry critiques of Manchu strategy in the offensive phases of the war—flowed together to produce a persuasive impression of how Ch'ing strategy could have defeated the enemy. We begin with Wei Yuan and his powerfully argued brief for paramilitary and defensive warfare as the overlooked keys to effective resistance.[39]

It is not fully clear when and with what expectations Wei decided to undertake his two major works on the 1840 war (the *Illustrated Gazetteer of the Maritime Countries*, completed in January 1843, and published in 1844; and the *Record of the Campaigns and Pacification of the Foreign Fleets*, published in 1846).[40] But internal textual evidence suggests strongly that the former work, at least, was intended as a counter-polemic, directed against those within the official world—and particularly those within the new diplomatic leadership in Canton—who had begun to question the veracity of the accounts of San-yuan-li that had circulated during the war. In his rebuttal, Wei (deterred not at all by the fact that he had never been to Canton) seems intent on proving that the disparagers were wrong, that the paramilitaries of the southeast had indeed scored major triumphs (and not *just* at San-yuan-li!), and that, furthermore, the defensive strategy that had made their actions so effective had been foolishly ignored by the Ch'ing high command elsewhere, thus explaining the sad outcome of the Yangtze campaigns.[41]

But here some background is in order concerning the debate that had begun over the Kwangtung militia and its role in the recent war. That question, naturally enough, had come up for close scrutiny when the "peace" government, in power in Peking and Nanking since mid-1842, had decided to demobilize the Cantonese irregulars as part of a broader effort to insure the smooth implementation of the new treaty agreements. The principal agent on the spot responsible for this task was a certain Huang En-t'ung, who had been transferred from Nanking to Canton late in 1842 at the instance of the chief "peace" diplomatist on the Ch'ing side, the Nanking governor general, Ch'i-ying.[42] As an official who had seen considerable action at the lower Yangtze front (he had been one of the officials in charge of the undistinguished defense effort at Nanking), Huang had already been quite skeptical of the value of paramilitary warfare and militia forces even before his arrival in Canton. His skepticism was only intensified by the experiences he encountered upon taking up his duties in that city, where his arrival had been met by a vicious placard campaign aimed at spreading the idea that the demobilization scheme was a mandarin "trick" intended to speed the "selling" of the city to the barbarians. Genuinely irritated by the falsification, Huang had taken the unusually courageous step of launching a propaganda counteroffensive in Peking, in the hope of revealing the opportunism of the militia leadership for what it really was. To Chiang Hung-sheng, a friend in the capital currently serving as a censor, he had sent a summary of his own findings on the Cantonese irregulars—findings that hardly fit at all with the stereotypes popular among those in the Southern City inspired by the example of San-yuan-li. According to Huang, the militia chiefs who had instigated the placards against him were nothing better than "one or two barely literate fellows, upstarts in disposition, entirely ignorant of [political] realities, and totally lacking in concrete ideas. All they are capable of doing is waving about their claims of 'loyalty to the dynasty' so as to indulge their rhetorical vanity." In practical military terms, they could do absolutely nothing to frighten off the foreigner—who, in any case, had long since "seen through their petty tricks." In setting the record straight, Huang hoped, clearly, to smooth the way for a quick restoration of government control over the Kwangtung militia forces.[43]

Huang's words had been directed, in the main, not at the Ta-fo-ssu Bureau scholars themselves, but at the carpetbagging scholar-adventurers—men like the Chekiangese licentiate Ch'ien Chiang—who had flocked to Canton in the later months of the war in search of jobs and glory.[44] But, to the majority of the literati in the capital and elsewhere outside of Kwangtung, still under the spell of the war advocates, the assault seemed a challenge to the very idea that irregular warfare had a legitimate place in the empire's maritime defenses. (And, indeed, in another set of essays, published in 1846, Huang would openly attack the "hackneyed" works of Ch'i Chi-kuang and other paramilitary enthusiasts of the Ming period, whose influence upon current war-party thinking he found pernicious.)[45]

Coming back, however, to Wei Yuan's two volumes, it was evidently with the intention of refuting the peace party's insinuations about the Kwangtung militia and about the impracticality of the Ch'i Chi-kuang formulas that Wei decided to write the true history of the war. And to write it not once but twice. For in both his works, Wei devoted a considerable amount of space to raking over the literati-grapevine accounts that he had acquired of the doings at San-yuan-li and elsewhere in the southeast, and to extracting from them a quite believable picture of civilian self-defense forces and irregulars effectively thwarting the enemy advance.

Thus, in his *Pacification of the Foreign Fleets*, Wei set out for his readers a version of the San-yuan-li tale more inspiring than anything that had come out of wartime Canton. To begin with, not merely "eighty or ninety," but now "more than two hundred," foreign soldiers turn out to have been killed by the villagers. And even Admiral Bremer somehow entered into the action (under the somewhat garbled name of Bremer-Becher), managing to lose his "command baton," and double-barreled pistol, and his head ("as big as a one-peck measure").[46] But there is still more to come, for now it appears that the Fatshan "braves" of the Ta-fo-ssu Bureau had also been in the field during the last days of the siege of Canton, and had not merely "blinded" the British garrison in a nearby fort with an ingenious application of poisonous smoke, but had also "wrecked" a fleet of enemy sampans sent in to relieve the defenders.[47]

Though this latter information, it turns out, has been clipped from one of the reports of Generalissimo I-shan, and thus might not be entirely reliable, another item in the same account certainly does have the the ring of authenticity to it. That is the obligatory citation from the San-yuan-li manifestoes, one of which was quoted *in extenso* just as Wei brings his narrative to a close. And what particular themes should be featured in the quoted section? What else but the "stealth" of the British (who never dared attack the city when Lin was in charge, but instead cajoled an "intriguing minister" of the Ch'ing into dismantling Lin's defenses); and the determined "loyalty to the great Ch'ing" of the Cantonese people, who hereby swear that they will "fill the river with stones, catch up the British in an encirclement, and wipe them out with fire-ship attacks" should the enemy ever again try to penetrate up the Canton river.[48]

For Wei, apparently, this last bit of documentation virtually clinched the argument about whether or not the paramilitaries had been of use to the Ch'ing side in the battle for Canton. At any rate, in the remainder of the *Pacification*, and in the maritime defense essays of his *Illustrated Gazetteer*, Wei was no longer concerned so much with clearing the name of the San-yuan-li militiamen as with showing that the strategic formula used in Kwangtung had a much wider applicability, the true significance of which had unfortunately been inadequately grasped by the Ch'ing high command elsewhere. And what was this formula? In the postface to the *Pacification*, Wei describes it simply as "neither attacking, nor negotiating, but concentrating singlemindedly upon defense."[49] If the Ch'ing had everywhere substituted a "concentration on defense" for full-scale war, he continues, it could have availed itself not only of "righteous volunteers" (such as at San-yuan-li), but even of the help of underworld folk-military professionals and of the seafaring people of the coast, who knew everything about the British from their long history of illegal commercial dealings with them. For, after all, in a *jujitsu*-like war of retreat (which is more or less what Wei seems to mean by "defense"), there would be all kinds of opportunities for catching the enemy out by deceptions and tricks—just the sort of thing the "heroes" of the criminal and secret-society worlds were so adept in, and that, for adequate reward, they would be eager to undertake on behalf of the government.[50]

And so the argument runs, too, in the introductory essays to the *Illustrated Gazetteer.* Conjuring up, in these latter pieces, a most believable picture of the Cantonese irregulars and of Yao Ying's Taiwan militiamen holding the British at bay by means of the retreat strategy, Wei then launches into a bitter denunciation of the generalship of the lower Yangtze commanders and of I-shan, whom he describes as having been over-preoccupied with "reckless offensives" (*lang-chan*). The Mongol Yü-ch'ien, for example, who had been in charge of the east Chekiang front in the first days of the British Yangtze campaign of 1841–1842, comes in for particularly harsh criticism in this regard, since Wei (who had himself briefly served in eastern Chekiang) was quite well-informed about that ill-fated commander's strategic doctrines, and did not hesitate to bare them to the world as an example par excellence of the kind of military wrongheadedness he believed had cost the Ch'ing the war.[51] For Yü-chien, as Wei shows, the possibility of fighting a war of step-by-step retreat into the middle reaches of the Yangtze had been ruled out from the start. The easy navigability of that river for British oceangoing warships, the Mongol had decided, simply forbade any effective inland defensive actions in that theatre. Instead, Yü-ch'ien had believed that the war had to be carried to the enemy, by seizing and holding Ting-hai Is-land—just as I-ching was later on to believe that the Ch'ing had to attack British onshore bases in the east Chekiang promontory. And, of course, I-shan had made the very same mistake in his reckless assault on British positions downriver of Canton.[52]

All of this, Wei continues, had been terribly ill-advised, inasmuch as it had exposed Ch'ing forces directly to the enemy's formidable shipborne firepower. But an even more deadly flaw in this strategy that stressed offensive action had been the requirement it had im-posed for concentrating huge numbers of men, weapons, and sup-plies in order to gain the manpower advantage needed for offensive combat. The assembly of such gigantic "forward" armies had necessi-tated, in turn, the massive influx of extra-provincial manpower and material resources from the interior, so as to avoid depleting the de-fensive positions the Ch'ing was still committed to holding all along the coast. During the important campaigns of the war, Wei notes bit-terly, there had thus been no real "strategy" (*yung-ping*) but only the fruitless "shifting about of reserves" (*tiao-ping*):

When the barbarians attacked Kwangtung, we shifted troops from elsewhere into Kwangtung. When they next attacked Chekiang, we then shifted troops from [Kwangtung and] elsewhere into Chekiang. And when they attacked Kiangsu, we then [again] shifted our troops into Kiangsu.[53]

Of course, state treasuries and peasant taxpayer patience could hardly be expected to hold up for long under the dreadful fiscal weight of such a wasteful strategy.[54] And thus, perversely, the Ch'ing had fought a war of attrition, not against the over-extended British, but against itself, and had failed miserably to make proper use of the one supreme advantage it did enjoy: short supply lines.

Thus, from his reaffirmation of the accomplishments of the para-militaries of Kwangtung, Wei moved, inexorably, back toward the same strategic macro-conception that Lin Tse-hsu himself had first put forward in the early days of the war. The enemy, for all his much-touted advantages in weaponry ("stout ships and fierce guns") was nonetheless extraordinarily vulnerable to attrition tactics, since he must trade as he fights, and must meet his war costs out of the profits of local commerce and looting. Ch'ing strategy ought therefore to have been designed to exploit this weakness, and should, as with the campaigns against the *wo-k'ou* marauders of the 1550s (to whom Wei makes frequent allusion), have been geared to extending the war until there was no more trade, and no more easy booty, for the enemy to batten upon.[55] For this, obviously, the defensive style of fighting, and a reliance on locally recruited and locally supplied paramilitaries, would have been much better advised than the squandering of precious Ch'ing revenues on offensive campaigns by expensive, incompetent elite units. And so, appropriately, in the first published version of the *Illustrated Gazetteer*, the first two chapters are entitled "On Defense." Here was one overlooked formula by which the British could have been defeated. And, if anyone doubted, had not the Ch'ing effectively won by precisely such tactics in the southeast?

YAO YING AND BRITAIN'S VULNERABILITY IN SOUTH ASIA

Our brief summary of Wei Yuan's two studies of the 1840 war does not do justice to their full and very rich contents. In particular, it neglects Wei's interesting treatment, in the *Illustrated Gazetteer*, of the problem of offensive warfare, wherein he takes up the question of rearmament; urges the construction of dockyards and arsenals in the spirit of Peter the Great's innovations in seventeenth-century Russia; and even, quite presciently, foresees a need to link naval development with maritime commercial expansion, so as to provide it with a revenue base and a trained manpower pool.[56] However, our omission is also, to an extent, a contextually appropriate one. This is so, first, because, for Wei, Ch'ing competence in offensive war is by no means accepted as a final determinant of how foreign policy ought to be modulated. As long as the Ch'ing could conduct an effective defense—a requirement that, for Wei, could be met without any naval or weaponry modernization—there was no reason, he argues, for it to abandon its original goal of forcing the termination of the opium-import traffic.[57] And, in the second place, as shall become clear in a moment, Wei shared with his fellow strategist and historian, Yao Ying, a grand faith that British colonial vulnerabilities could be exploited as a substitute for a Chinese offensive capacity. For both these writers, but especially for Yao, the final push that (in the next war) was to force the British into retreat along the China coast was to come, not from Ch'ing armies, but from the mutiny of other conquered or threatened peoples long exposed to and resentful of British imperial hegemony in south and central Asia. At this point, there-fore, we might take leave of Wei, and turn, instead, to Yao Ying's 1846 *Record of a Mission to Tibet* (*K'ang-yu chi-hsing*), the other of the triad of war-inspired works on strategy and strategic geography that seem to have had the greatest influence on the literati perception of the Ch'ing state's military predicament.[58]

Like so many other of the strategic brainstorms that we encounter in the literati war literature of this period, Yao's ideas on British impe-rial vulnerability trace their origin back to a wartime initiative that (like San-yuan-li) had somehow failed to gain the recognition it should have had from the Ch'ing central government establishment. In this case, moreover, the initiative had been Yao's own, or at least partly his, so that the author had every confidence that he knew what he was talking about.

It had been only in the last months of the war, apparently, that Yao had become aware of the fact that the British, like the Ch'ing, were an imperial power, possessing all of the imperial paraphernalia of subject peoples, racial prejudice, and a fondness for using native sol-diers for military jobs that the British themselves were not eager to take on (such as, for instance, the fighting in China). We know, in fact, precisely when Yao learned this; during the long spring months of 1842, when Yao's Sepoy and British prisoners moldered in their cells in Tainan, awaiting the arrival of their death sentences from Peking. Perhaps because he had begun to notice the tensions between the white officers and their black soldiers and camp-followers (some 240 of the latter had been left behind to drown in the first of the two shipwrecks, and only 150 made land), Yao decided that he ought to find out more about the background of this latter group.[59] Accord-ingly, he had set about interrogating Captain Denham (of the *Ann*) on the details of the British raj. One may doubt that he learned very much of actual use, but whatever else, he evidently convinced him-self that there was indeed much bad will here, and that it might be exploited.[60]

The ideas that this new knowledge about India and the other Brit-ish colonial outposts in maritime Asia had set astir in Yao's mind did not, however, take on strategic significance until very near the end of the war, when news had begun to trickle across the Taiwan Strait that the Ch'ing government was about to commence negotiations. At this point, Yao seems suddenly to have "heard," from his surviving prisoners, of a Nepalese (or "Gurkha") revolt in progress against the British across the southern flank of Tibet. (In fact there was no revolt, though there were strains arising from British India garrison probes toward Tibet. In February 1841, the Gurkhas, who were nominally tributaries of the Ch'ing, had in fact sent an emissary to Lhasa to ask for help in repelling the invaders, though no help had been forthcoming. This latter episode was doubtless one of the sources of Yao's information.) Seizing on this, and making use, as well, of his somewhat inexact expertise on Indian geography, Yao had dashed off dispatches both to Governor General I-liang in Amoy and to the court in Peking to propose that the Ch'ing act immediately to back the Nepalese. Through such action, he insisted, the flames of insurrection could be quickly spread into "neighboring" Calcutta, the heartland of British power in India. And the British, at the moment closing in for the kill at Nanking, would have to send their troops back to India forthwith.[61]

I-liang never received the long and persuasive dispatch Yao reports having rushed off to him on 1 July. Nor did the emperor receive his copy. But, even if they had, it is doubtful that much interest would have been shown. For the court was now resigned to ending the war as quickly as possible, and therefore not likely to be much interested in a scheme that would only prolong it.[62]

But, for Yao at least, the grand design of striking the British from their vulnerable Indian flank could not be put so easily aside, even after the treaties had been signed. During 1844 and 1845, as the former intendant served out his punishment of exile to western Szechuan as a minor official, he had grown increasingly obsessed with the idea. And increasingly persuaded that here was the great solution to the unsolved problem of Ch'ing offensive weakness. From this conviction, there was to develop, first, a vigorous correspondence with Wei Yuan and other literati now engaged in writing the history of the war on the subject of British imperial over-extension; and, second, Yao's own 1846 work on the peoples and terrain of Tibet, Nepal, and India.[63]

We can here easily pass over the specifics of Yao's "geography," for this compilation was innovative only with regard to the new information it provided on recent events in Tibet and Nepal. In other respects it offered only a reworking of already out-of-date Jesuit sources and Wei Yuan's *Illustrated Gazetteer*. Moreover, like Wei's parallel work on the maritime components of the British empire, Yao's volume all but ignored the institutions of the homeland from which British power had sprung.[64] Harder to pass over, however, was the influence that Yao's work, together with the preparatory puffing and publicity, had upon Southern City opinion. Wei Yuan, for one (at least according to the not unsympathetic Cantonese scholar, Ch'en Li [1810–1882]), was so persuaded by the Gurkha-insurrection fantasy that, under its influence, he conceived the idea of using the American, French, and Russians (like the Nepalese, also under British threat) as potential allies in the next war against Britain. Lin Tse-hsu, with whom Yao and many of his friends in the capital kept up a correspondence all through the 1840s, was similarly impressed by Yao's argument. And, as a fitting comment on the amount of interest aroused by Yao's work, the second edition of Wei Yuan's *Illustrated Gazetteer*, brought out in 1847, added to its original chapters, *inter alia*, a whole new section on the history of recent European colonial expansion and competition in India and Central Asia.[65]

Of such stuff, then, was constituted the new knowledge—the new outward orientation—that Yao had praised himself so inordinately for helping to popularize. Or, at least, what Yao, Wei, and others thought of as new knowledge. For, in fact, as one can hardly fail to notice in reading through all of this material, practically nothing has been allowed to creep into either Wei's or Yao's presentations that might question the truth both men were so determined to establish: that, even without new military techniques, the Ch'ing could, and should, have been able to fight its maritime enemy to a draw. The outward turn, and the new literature that chronicled it (or at least that literature that got read), was thus not much more than a polemic, a polemic whose purpose was to absolve the leaders of the Spring Purification war party of blame for the debacle that had followed from their actions.

The Ku Yen-wu Shrine Association

Earlier in this study, we raised the general question of why the apparently irrefutable evidence of Ch'ing strategic vulnerability along the empire's maritime frontier called to light by the events of the 1840 conflict did not register more profoundly upon the nerve centers of that system and upon the way it would conceive and execute its foreign policy thereafter. Though we have yet to explore fully those limited modifications that did occur (a problem that will be taken up in this present chapter), part of the answer should by now be apparent. At the root of the problem was the stranglehold that the Spring Purificationists and their heroes within the bureaucracy had upon the news-collecting mechanisms of the Southern City elite. The tales of wartime intrigue that these men would consume and believe, and the particular brand of maritime-defense literature that they would credit, these perception-forming literatures were products of the literati correspondence networks controlled or influenced by the Spring Purification war party. The views on maritime defense and diplomacy that would emerge from this highly selective exposure to information were thus in a sense predetermined. They would have to serve, in most loyal fashion, the political ambitions of the Spring Purification leadership.

The ingrained habits and loyalties of prewar examination-system politics, however, were not to exercise a blinding influence on Ch'ing postwar diplomacy just through the encouragement of a false perception of China's strategic predicament. They were to affect the course of diplomatic deliberations at yet another, perhaps even more insidious level: that is, by providing a model and a constituency for opposition to the peace government now in power in the capital. During the six years immediately following the conclusion of the Treaty of Nanking, as we shall presently see, maritime policy was to be set almost exclusively by a small handful of Manchu courtiers, ex-generals, and bureaucrats, whose power stemmed directly from the emperor and from his often expressed concern to avoid another war with Britain. In Peking, where this group was the most strongly entrenched, the new Manchu leadership was led by Mu-chang-a, the premier grand councillor, who had managed to displace his Chinese rivals, Wang Ting and P'an Shih-en, from influence during the closing days of the war. In the provinces, where its hold on power was perhaps always more tenuous, the Mu-chang-a party was nonetheless able to control the staffing of the new diplomatic "commissioner" posts that now existed in Canton, Tientsin, and Nanking, and thus to assure that men inclined to its own point of view retained a degree of influence within local administration.[1] All things considered, therefore, the new government commanded considerable authority. It was not one to be easily challenged even by bureaucratic war enthusiasts, let alone by the politically marginal Southern City literati.

Yet, commencing late in 1843 or thereabouts, a literati-bureaucratic opposition did, in fact, begin to coalesce and to acquire a highly visible organizational form: the so-called Ku Yen-wu Shrine Association (*Ku T'ing-lin hsien-sheng ssu-hui*). Moreover, in little more than six years' time, this same opposition was to gain a stunning victory. By December 1850, it succeeded in ousting from office both Mu-chang-a and his principal provincial diplomatic agent, Ch'i-ying, and in gaining an imperial declaration to the effect that the throne had been persistently "misled" by these men's advice on foreign policy.

What made these challengers so surprisingly effective? The question will require the better part of this and the following chapter to answer in adequate fashion. More to the point, it will oblige us to scrutinize not just why scholars heeded its call for resistance to the Mu-chang-a peace leadership, but why the monarchy did also. Our argument in the chapter at hand will begin by focusing on the way in which the lingering influence of the idealization of literati loyalty-group politics that had been so important a feature of political life in the 1830s was, in the postwar years, to provide the anti-treaty forces with both a model for oppositional action and a broad and academically varied constituency of followers within the upper ranks of the lettered class. It will become apparent that the Ku Shrine Association self-consciously associated itself with the forms and with the patronage ideals that had been popularized by the Spring Purification circle during the prewar decade. Perhaps even more important was its ability, through that identification, to capture for the anti-treaty movement an association with the venerable cause of "moral-censure" politics—with the cause, that is, of securing a recognized position within the Ch'ing political constitution. During the dark and depressing days of the Mu-chang-a regime's dominance at court, that latter identity was, in turn, to become critically important to the anti-treaty movement, since there was little the opposition could do to challenge the government directly in the realm of foreign policy. However, by managing to acquire a second personality—that of heir to the Spring Purification circle as guardian of the literati political interest—the Shrine Association party was able to continue as an active force through the grim years of enforced silence on the foreign-policy question. That it could do so was in turn a tribute to the success the earlier group had enjoyed in propagandizing on behalf of this same cause.

But there is a second strand that runs between the idealization of literati loyalty politics in the 1830s and the resiliency of the anti-treaty opposition in the 1840s. This one involves continuity, not in the ideology of opposition, but in the constituencies to which the new challengers could appeal: constituencies that were to be surprisingly variegated in their intellectual makeup. Among the ranks of the

Ku Association oppositionists, there will be encountered not just our familiar old acquaintances of *ku-wen* or Neo-Confucian pedigree. Equally prominent was a scholarly group that, in terms of the logic of prewar academic debates, ought not to have been there at all. This was the Han Learning party, distinguished in the prewar years by its association with the diplomatic realism of the old Kwangtung hands, Juan Yuan and Lu K'un. Yet now, quite suddenly, representatives of this same patronage group appear very prominently among the ranks of the defenders of the policies of Lin Tse-hsu and Yao Ying! Juan Yuan himself, for example, was to be numbered among the behind-the-scenes supporters of the Ku Association, while his son (Juan Fu) and several of his favorites (such as Ho Shao-chi and Chang Mu) were to be openly active within it.[2] Lurking in the background of this anomalous political fellowship, however, was a consideration that, for the moment at least, seemed either to bridge the particular disagreements that had troubled the truth-seekers of the prewar decades or to render such disagreements irrelevant. That was the perception that unless the Mu-chang-a government was driven from power, the very idea itself of scholarship-based patronage within the examination system would be lost. This idea, which had formed so basic a part of the prewar political and intellectual environment, had come under attack when the new chief grand councillor, Mu-chang-a, successfully wrestled control of examination-system patronage from his Chinese colleagues. The losers in this development included all prewar scholarly affinity groups whose prospects for continued access to upper-echelon official patronage were now dimmed—not just the Spring Purificationists. Thus, the cause of rescuing scholastic idealism itself could take its place, alongside that of defending literati political privilege, as a war cry for the anti-government opposition. In this way, the scope of the anti-treaty (or, rather, anti-treaty-maker) movement would be still further broadened.

To sum up, then, the resistance to the Mu-chang-a government, starting originally as propaganda against the peace negotiations spread by the Spring Purification group, quickly evolved into a much broader affair. Under the influence of ideas about moral-censure politics and about scholarly influence within the examination system, the counteroffensive soon became transformed into a conservative movement embracing literati of widely varied intellectual background. The full reconstruction of the anti-treaty movement's appeal thus leads us back, ultimately, to the exploration of its continuities with the structure of literati-clique politics in the 1830s. The analysis of these continuities will be the larger purpose of this chapter, as we now turn to take a closer look at how the Ku Yen-wu Shrine Association came into its own as the leading organizational vehicle of the anti-treaty movement.

THE MU-CHANG-A GOVERNMENT AND LITERATI POLITICAL INFLUENCE

Our introductory remarks on how literati opposition to the Mu-chang-a peace cabal was to be organized in the 1840s suggest that government repression of criticism and its attempts to manipulate patronage within the examination system had great bearing upon the ability of the challengers to reach out to a broad literati constituency. Taking our cue from these observations, we might logically begin our sketch of how oppositional organization developed during the postwar decade by exploring why and to what extent such repression occurred. So doing, let us start with the matter of Manchu preponderance in the peacemaking process, which seems to have been the root cause of much of this unpopular crackdown on lettered class political privilege.

It has long been recognized that the Ch'ing peace diplomacy that emerged at the end of the 1840 war was largely of Manchu inspiration and execution. Even at the time of the Nanking negotiations, British agents were struck by the fact that the men heading the imperial delegation across the table from them were "Tartars," not Chinese. Their memoirs invariably contrast the realism and flexibility that these men brought to their task with the obstinacy and arrogance of the Han Chinese officials with whom they had previously dealt.[3] This same dominance of Manchu bureaucrats in postwar diplomacy was also noticed by the Southern City men who kept Lin Tse-hsu informed of events during his long (1842–1845) punitive exile in Turkestan. For, in one of the cryptic notices of the postwar political scene reaching Lin from one source late in 1842 or early in 1843, we read that "all but one" of the high provincial officials in office along the coast were now non-Chinese.[4]

And, of course, both of these assessments were in substance correct, though the institutional details and logic informing the Manchu intervention and the displacement of Chinese officials merit more comment than we can obtain from such partisan sources. On the losing side of this reshuffle can be identified at least three vice-regal-echelon officials of Han Chinese/literati background. Lin Tse-hsu, demoted from the governor generalship of Kwangtung and Kwangsi in late 1840, had been nevertheless kept at the front (in eastern Chekiang) until July 1841. But in March 1842, he had finally been packed off for Ili (in Central Asia) upon the court's becoming persuaded that the war could not be continued. His commissioner's seal, empowering the holder as a diplomatic plenipotentiary of sorts, went first to Ch'i-shan, then to I-li-pu, and finally to Ch'i-ying, late in 1843. All were Manchus.[5] Teng T'ing-chen, governor general of Chekiang and Fukien until his removal and punishment as a Lin supporter in late 1840, was clearly another victim: His job fell, first to another lettered-class official, Yen Po-t'ao, but then, late in 1841, into the hands of the Manchu I-liang. Similarly, the Hupeh-Hunan governor general, Chou T'ien-chueh, a Lin protégé and vigorous enthusiast of opium suppression and protracting the war, had been named, late in 1839, to the post of Chekiang and Fukien viceroy, but then mysteriously ejected from it in the wake of what appears to have been a politically motivated impeachment.[6] Chou remained in Canton during most of 1841, aiding Ch'i Kung in the organization of Canton's defenses, and perhaps expecting to resume his post in Fukien. (As late as July 1842, rumors were circulating in Nanking that Chu Kuei, the grand patriarch of the northern clique, had appeared in a seance in the capital to recommend Chou's reappointment along with Lin's!).[7] But this was not to be, for the Fukien-Chekiang job, as we have seen, was to stay in the grasp of Yao Ying's old enemy, I-liang.

The other institutional detail lurking behind this reshuffle that deserves brief consideration involves the expanded use of the irregular office of imperial commissioner or plenipotentiary (*ch'in-ch'ai ta-ch'en*)—now, for the while, a strictly Manchu designation—as a means of yet further removing Han Chinese provincial officials from any role in maritime diplomacy. The first such use of this designation may well have been in the spring 1842 dispatch of the Manchurian Tartar general, Ch'i-ying, to eastern Chekiang, where he and I-li-pu (co-designated as commissioner) were empowered to probe the possibility of negotiations; no such authority was given the mercurial provincial governor, Liu Yun-k'o. This arrangement continued down to the culmination of the 1842 Yangtze campaign, with Ch'i-ying and I-li-pu—and not the regular provincial officials—taking the lead in making the approach to the British.[8] A still more interesting variant was to occur in Kwangtung shortly after the close of the war. For Kwangtung, unlike the Yangtze provinces, was an administrative region where the maintenance of local order and good relations with the scholar-elite bulked considerably larger than any perceived strategic interests of the dynastic center. That meant, in practice, that no attempt would ever be made to remove the locally revered Chinese official, Ch'i Kung, from his post of governor general (at least so long as he was fit for duty). But, even so, the court would not consign responsibility for treaty enforcement to this unpredictable man. And so, much to Ch'i Kung's chagrin, the aging I-li-pu was sent down, late in 1842, to serve as commissioner for maritime affairs in Kwangtung. And when I-li-pu himself was taken ill, early in the next year, the seal passed, not to Ch'i Kung, but to Ch'i-ying.[9] Obviously, officials of literati background could not be trusted to be fully sensitive to the court's new-found concern to settle the war and keep the peace. Or so the emperor and his chief councillor, Mu-chang-a, seem to have thought.

This displacement of high-level officials, of which Lin's informants complain, was, however, only the beginning of what was to turn out to be a much broader postwar peace-government attack on the literati as a collective influence group in Ch'ing politics. Following hard upon the purge of Lin, Teng, and Chou, there was soon to materialize a string of further-reaching initiatives aimed, now, at trimming back the influence of the lettered elite in more subtle ways, so as to provide still more security for the new treaty system against possible literati sabotage.

This quiet, inner purge would take its first casualties even before the war had ended. The initial victims were two senior Han Chinese literocrats, of pro-war inclination, whose very considerable retinues of examination-system protégés made them particularly dangerous as potential saboteurs of the negotiations. The 70-year old grand secretary, T'ang Chin-chao (a Juan Yuan protégé) was the first to go. On 2 May 1841, he was demoted to a relatively minor office in the capital for trying a bit too hard to get Lin recalled as Ch'ing theatre commander in Kwangtung.[10] Greatly vexed, T'ang had chosen, the next year, to resign all his posts. But he had stayed on in the capital nonetheless—hoping, it would seem, that a sudden, last-minute reversal of policy might allow him to resume office on terms of somewhat greater trust.

Then, in June 1842, came the somewhat more spectacular removal (if such it was) of Wang Ting, the septuagenarian grand councillor (and third-ranking of all the senior examiners of the capital, in terms of the number of sittings he had overseen) who had, late in the war, assumed leadership of the cause of continuing the military struggle. Though the old and ailing Wang had no doubt been losing ground for some time to Mu-chang-a in the ongoing court discussions on war policy, he had stubbornly refused to take a leave of absence to regain his health, evidently fearing that his absence would leave Mu-chang-a virtually without outspoken rivals in the emperor's inner councils. The strain of work, however, (or was it something more sinister?), soon overtook him; and, after several weeks of uninterrupted duty in the palace, he fell dead in his office on 8 June— leaving behind him, it was said, a furious testamentory memorial excoriating the decision to reopen talks with the British. The memorial's fate is not clear. But word quickly spread that Mu-chang-a had had Wang poisoned before he could submit the completed document to the emperor. And threats were reported against Wang's son (Wang Hang), who, as a Han-lin compiler and graduate of the 1840 metropolitan examinations, was a figure likely to come under heavy pressure.[11]

The removal of the two chief pro-war literocrats from the scene was soon followed by a pair of even more blatant maneuvers intended to intimidate those younger Southern City and provincial officials owing allegiance to these men, or for other reasons aligned with the belligerent party.

The first of these maneuvers occurred early in 1843. It came in the wake of a fortuitous discovery that the Board of Revenue's Peking treasuries had been quietly drained of over 9 million taels (three quarters of their current nominal deposits, and approximately one quarter of the entire budgeted yearly revenue intake of the bureaucracy!) since their last thorough audit, late in the eighteenth century. The oversight of these deposits had been the ongoing responsibility of a rotating committee of metropolitan censors, prominent among whom were to be found the stars of the Han Chinese examination elite. The revelation of the huge embezzlement could therefore hardly have been more timely, since it implicated at a stroke a huge number of middle-ranking Han Chinese literati-officials who had risen into office via the censorate, as well as an ever larger number of still active censors. The opportunity for crushing this potentially troublesome network of officials was not let slip. On 25 April 1843, a committee of four non-Han investigators, under the Mongol president of the Board of Works, Sai-shang-a, completed a new audit. And on 6 May, another committee, under Prince Ting and likewise containing no Chinese, recommended a schedule of fines to be levied without exception upon all men who had been, or were currently, in office as censorial treasury-auditors.[12] Suspicions immediately swept the Southern City that Grand Councillor Mu-chang-a was making use of the investigations for the express purpose of ruining T'ang Chin-chao's protégés within the bureaucracy, since T'ang was widely known to have blocked an earlier exposure of the deficits.[13] Whatever the truth of this, the stiff fines—which had to be paid before the implicated official could resume office—just happened to pick off three key middle-rank officials who had been active in lobbying for the vigorous prosecution of the war. These were Huang Chueh-tzu, leader of the Spring Purification party; Tseng Wang-yen, a veteran of the 1835 censorial commission (who, during the war, had passed Wang T'ing-lan's San-yuan-li report to Yen Po-t'ao); and Lo Ping-chang, the Cantonese academy head and censor who had also played a major role in forwarding to Peking the evidence about the San-yuan-li engagement.[14]

At around the same time as the followers of T'ang Chin-chao and other pro-war literati were being rooted out of the censorate, moreover, still another thunderbolt crashed down upon that stronghold of literati political influence, this time from the hand of the emperor himself. It took the form of a shattering rebuke administered to Su T'ing-k'uei, a censor who was an examination pupil of Huang Chueh-tzu, and who had himself been active in Spring Purification circles in Peking during the 1830s. Early in April 1843, perhaps stirred to anger by the spectacle of so many literati heads rolling at once all around him, Su had daringly undertaken to bring into the open the lettered elite's resentments over the way that they were being throttled by Mu-chang-a. In two separate memorials, he had called for the removal of the offending grand councillor, and for the promulgation of a penitential edict by the emperor himself. Referring to a string of recent portents (one in each of the three realms of Chinese cosmology: heaven, earth, and man), Su had claimed that interlinked disorders of this variety indicated a fault at the level of the Son of Heaven, whose role was supposed to be that of mediator between these three jurisdictions. The recent "running amok" of the English barbarians, the serious ruptures in the Yellow River's dikes in 1842, and the appearance in the skies of a long white comet trailing toward the east—all of these signaled, he thought, a disjuncture in the natural harmony of things for which the emperor had to take the blame. By implication, too, such portents suggested that the sage ruler was being "blocked," or his vision "obscured," by disloyal ministers. This, Su claimed, justified the immediate removal of the offender (Mu-chang-a), and a simultaneous request by the emperor for "straightforward" criticism of the throne by the literati.[15]

This series of requests had not only been categorically denied, but Su T'ing-k'uei and several of his comrades had received a stiff tongue-lashing from the throne, intended to make it clear that the court wanted no more meddling by the literati in the review of its "barbarian" policies. There had been, Tao-kuang insisted, no arbitrary muzzling of the voice of the literati. At least two of Su's former Spring Purification circle comrades, T'ang P'eng and Wu Chia-pin, had been granted the extraordinary honor of an imperial perusal of their written opinions on the war, even though, strictly speaking, they had lacked the privilege of submitting such documents directly to the emperor. But the court would now insist on its privilege of discountenancing proposals that "clung to antiquity without recognizing the changed circumstances of today"; or that "merely played upon empty words, and offered no substantive advice for the improvement of governance or for the welfare of the people." In other words, there was to be no more impractical talk of invoking the stratagems of the past for solving the problems now confronting the empire along her maritime borders. Traditional solutions simply did not apply.[16]

With this unmistakably clear pronouncement, according to the *Ch'ing-shih*, "morale again lapsed and the 'path of speech' of the literati became mostly silent."[17] Similarly, the correspondence of Lin's Peking agents records (perhaps a bit hyperbolically) that even in the teahouses and wine shops of the Southern City could be found large signs warning customers "to avoid discussing current affairs"—meaning, of course, as the context makes clear, the diplomatic policies of the government.[18] And such, likewise, is the sense conveyed by a popular broadside illustration, brought to the capital sometime in 1843 or 1844 from Soochow, where it had apparently been selling in great quantities. On this sheet was sketched the figure of the (former) champion of the war party, P'an Shih-en, his mouth sealed shut by a great chain and his hands and feet bolted down by great iron nails.[19] With the emperor now having ruled literati opinion out of order on diplomatic and military affairs, even the venerable P'an, it now seemed, would have to be silent.

But even with the censorate now firmly under control, still the relentless Mu-chang-a would not rest. Intent on blocking even the possibility of criticism, the head of the peace party pressed also for control over the examination system itself, so as to make sure that Chinese coming into office would be of appropriately cautious persuasion on matters of foreign policy. Starting in late 1841, and continuing at least until 1847, Mu-chang-a was to claim for himself the all-important job of (Manchu) co-chancellor of the Han-lin Academy, while placing the compliant P'an Shih-en in the parallel post reserved for Chinese.[20] From this roost, he was evidently able to control job patronage at least for Han-lin graduates (the most troublesomely self-confident members of the lettered elite). And, for those who refused to submit to his inspection and approval, rumor had it that there would be very little chance of winning a job as provincial examiner—an all-important prize sought anxiously by all newly matriculated Academy "students."

The kind of rage that was provoked by such blatant interference in the Han-lin patronage system—by an unscholarly Manchu at that—is well illustrated by an anecdote that made the rounds of the Southern City after the war, concerning the allegedly punitive removal of the Han-lin Lo Tun-yen from just such an examiner's assignment:

Lo [Tun-yen] of Shun-te [Kwangtung], Chang [Fei] of Ching-yang [Shensi], and Ho [Kuei-ch'ing] of Yunnan were all same-year graduates of the [1835] metropolitan examinations, and entered the Han-lin still under 20 years of age. All three, moreover, shared the same sub-examiner, the sub-department-director of the Board of Revenue, T'ang P'eng [a former Spring Purification circle leader].
[However,] at the time, the Grand Secretary Mu-chang-a dominated the government. And "those who warmed their hands over his brazier felt no cold." Their Excellencies Chang and Ho both gave their allegiance [to Mu], but [Lo] steadfastly refused to have anything to do with him. As the result of the first

examiner-assignment test held after their graduation from the Academy, each of the three was awarded a provincial assignment. . . . After his commission had been announced, [Lo] paid a courtesy call on P'an [Shih-en]. P'an asked him whether or not he had seen Grand Secretary Mu, to which Lo replied that he had not. [P'an] was very much upset and said: "It is very risky for you to come to see me before you have paid your respects to Grand Secretary Mu." But Lo was young and full of self-confidence. Refusing to heed P'an's advice, he never did go round [to see Mu]. The next day, with no warning, an edict was promulgated that declared, "Lo Tun-yen is too young to attend properly to the duties of examiner. Let him remain in the capital. Let so-and-so go in his stead." Everyone knew that Mu was responsible for the change. . . . Of such magnitude, then, was Mu's imperiousness.[21]

One may doubt, of course, that Lo's defiance was the sole or even the main reason for his loss. But the important point is the willingness of Lo's Southern City compeers to believe that Mu was the villain. This willingness, one suspects, had its roots in the shared concern of a great many pre-1842 Han-lin matriculators who, like Lo, had reached the top of the examination system on the basis of the impression their scholarly skills and seriousness had made on the high-ranking literocrats of the capital (as Lo had, for example, upon P'an Shih-en). But with Mu-chang-a determined to control the inner processes of the Han-lin patronage system, such scholarly salience would now count for little. Indeed, it might become a liability by marking one out as too intimate with one of the literocrats that Mu had purged. A real nervousness thus seems to have greeted the new ascendancy of the Manchu chief minister within the examinations establishment, of which the popularity of Lo's tale gives ample evidence.[22]

In this manner, then, the desire of the postwar Manchu leadership to secure its control over diplomacy led, step by step, to an ever-widening assault on the literati. Though only a relatively small number of scholar-officials had originally been associated with the Spring Purificationist war party, many more were humiliated, harassed, or chased from office because of Mu-chang-a's anxieties about the possibility of literati sabotage of the treaty agreements. More ominously still, the prestige of the censorate—since the 1830s the fortress of collective literati influence within the political system—was now apparently once again on the decline. And the structure of literocratic patronage itself had been significantly altered and centralized, much to the vexation of the academically more sophisticated members of the Han-lin elite, who perceived their chances of continued official patronage to have worsened considerably. These challenges would arouse feelings of consternation perhaps even more intense than had the tales of wartime intrigue and discarded opportunities for victory. And they would help cement together in the minds of many Southern City activists the cause of resisting the treaties, on the one hand, with that of resisting the political incursions of the treaty-makers on the other. As a result, those die-hard Spring Purification opposition-ists still willing to fight on now had a ready constituency waiting to follow them back into the field. To see how this protest movement took shape, however, we have to examine the structure of the political organization around which it coalesced: the Ku Yen-wu Shrine Association.

POLITICAL ORGANIZATION OF THE ASSOCIATION

On 12 April 1844, a group of fourteen prominent scholars and junior academic officials residing in Peking assembled at the compound of the Tz'u-jen Temple, near the booksellers' market in the Southern City. Their purpose was to inaugurate what was to become a regular tradition of thrice-yearly meetings to pay homage to the early Ch'ing dynasty Han Learning scholar Ku Yen-wu (1613–1682), whose portrait had just been installed on a small altar inside the temple compound.[23] As the ranks of the participants gradually swelled during the remainder of the decade, however, it was to become evident that the purposes that had brought these men together went considerably beyond the rekindling of interest in Master Ku's particular brand of Han Learning scholarship. Among those who assembled to burn incense at the newly completed shrine, we will find only a handful of men previously noted for their devotion to textual studies scholarship. Chang Mu (1805–1849), the son-in-law of the junior grand councillor, Ch'i Chün-tsao, was one; and so, certainly, was Ho Shao-chi (1799–1873), protégé of the recently retired grand secretary, Juan Yuan. But the more visible intellectual influence within this group was, rather, that of the *ku-wen*-oriented Spring Purification circle, from whose ranks came five of the fourteen Southern City scholars present at the inaugural gathering in the spring of 1844: Ch'en Ch'ing-yung, Chu Ch'i, P'an Tseng-wei, Su T'ing-k'uei, and T'ang P'eng.[24] The odd blending of intellectual affiliations encompassed indicates, rather, that the Ku devotees were paying allegiance to something more basic than any particular scholastic cause. This was the defense of the principle that scholarship itself should matter in the recruitment of talent into the higher reaches of the examination elite. That fundamental ideal of literati politics was seen as under threat, thanks to the efforts of Mu-chang-a and his accomplice, the "gagged" P'an Shih-en. To resist, the Ku-libationers intended to do everything in their power to advance the political prospects of Mu-chang-a's one active rival in the Grand Council, Ch'i Chün-tsao. And, for this purpose, the revival of the traditions of the Spring Purification circle—which was how this group tended to discuss the significance of its actions—was the all-important first step.

But here we need first introduce a bit more detail about the preparatory actions that had paved the way for the initial gathering at the Ku shrine. A close examination of the immediate background activities of the scholars who attended the first several meetings of the Shrine Association in 1844 reveals, in fact, that two somewhat separate efforts had gotten under way, shortly after the Treaty of Nanking, to build a new coalition of literati oppositionists in the capital. These twin enterprises would eventually converge in the 1844 founding of the Ku Shrine Association.

One such flurry of renewed activity, undertaken quite without support at the higher levels of the Peking bureaucratic establishment, emerged from within the depleted ranks of the Spring Purification partisans still active in postwar Peking. Here, our old friends Yao Ying and Chang Chi-liang had the major roles, though the circle of ku-wen students surrounding Yao's intimate friend, Mei Tseng-liang (a circle that included, most notably, the censor Chu Ch'i), also appears to have played an important part in recruiting new members. The inspiration for this renewal was Chang Chi-liang's death late in 1843, amidst symbolic circumstances evocative of the spirit of earlier literati protest actions famous in Chinese history. Buoyed up by the admiration Chang's action seems to have elicited from all quarters in the capital (and by the fame it guaranteed his poetry), his former Spring Purification associates undertook to return to the realm of symbolic protest politics, first by collecting funds for a shrine to Chang himself, and later by rehabilitating the cult of the Ming xenophobe and martyr, Yang Chi-sheng, with whom Chang had deliberately identified himself during his last days.

That the 44-year-old Chang Chi-liang would recognize the opportunity for a tragic gesture, and seize it to advantage, might almost have
been predicted. From our earlier encounter with Chang and his poetic
ideals, we will remember a still youngish man, obsessed with his own
sense of personal eccentricity, and determined to find redemption
through verse and defiantly idealistic conduct. It was not, however,
until the Southern City was rocked by the story of Yao Ying's victimization in the "Taiwan Case" that Chang found the moment for acting
simultaneously, and dramatically, on these twin ideals.

Chang happened to be in the vicinity of Nanking in the spring of
1843 when word began to spread that the British had brought charges
against Chang's friend and patron for murdering the prisoners of war
incarcerated in the prison at Tainan. At once aroused by this obvious
injustice, Chang had undertaken to deliver a public tongue-lashing to
a fellow Fukienese who had helped confirm the British charges, and
then to follow his mentor to Peking, there to appeal his case, if need
be, to the metropolitan censorate. From this course he was eventually dissuaded by the more prudent Yao, who evidently realized that
the punishment would only be a token one. But Chang still insisted
on promising Yao that, should the sentence be exile to Ili (as originally threatened), the two men would make the trip to the frontier
together.[25]

Then came the release of Yao from prison and his partial reprieve,
early in the winter of 1843. Chang Chi-liang, we are told, was delir-
ious with joy; but also, apparently, somewhat aggrieved at the loss of
the chance for a self-sacrificial show of devotion. He thus chose the
next best course, moving in with Yao when the latter, now free and
ever attentive to the symbolic possibilities of his own situation,
decided to set up interim lodgings in the half-ruined Southern City
villa of the Ming martyr Yang Chi-sheng (1516–1555). This site had
been selected for its xenophobic associations, inasmuch as Yang had
died protesting a plan to appease Mongol aggressors along the northern border by ceding them additional horse markets. To Yao and
Chang, the circumstances of Yang's 1555 protest seemed to offer a perfect analogue to those of the present. (There were always, it seems,
perfect historical analogues available for men of Yao's persuasion!)
But during the cold Peking winters it was no fit place to live, particularly for one suffering (as Chang apparently was) from tuberculosis
or some other serious respiratory disease.[26]

Yet Chang insisted in following Yao into his new quarters and in participating in the succession of congratulatory banquets that followed (one of which has been described in the preceding chapter). The combination of the cold and the strain soon took their toll, as we learn from Yao Ying's recollections of the poet Chang's last days:

I called a doctor to look after his illness. But I was particularly apprehensive about the cold, and so I ordered a double-lined robe to be made for him. I insisted he [take the side of the house] facing the sun and warm himself with the brazier. But day and night his cough continued. There was much phlegm, and it had a putrid [smell] and green color. [Chang] was disgusted. The doctor said his lungs were paralysed. . . .

On the 5th day of the 10th month [of 1843], he suddenly lost his voice. He was startled and declared that this meant that the end must be near. In a great rush he gathered together the drafts of his recent poems, and commissioned my cousin to make a fair copy. He himself indicated the order in which [the poems] were to be bound, and where the reading marks were to be placed. After four days of this, he got up early one morning and summoned me, asking me to call the censor Chu Ch'i to his sickroom. [When] Chu arrived, [Chang] produced a printed anthology, 10 chüan in length, of his own poems, which [he wished] to re-edit. [Chu] wielded the brush and went through them asking [Chang's decision on each]. When he wished to keep a poem [in the anthology], he gave a slight nod. If he wanted a poem deleted, he shook his head. They worked from dawn, and by noon the job was done. [Chang] then brought up several matters he wished us to attend to after his death. [Chu and I] signified our assent. By then his energy was even more depleted. That evening he died.[27]

As the last minute frenzy of editorial revisions and deletions so well attests, Chang had made up his mind to project his own death in poetic context. It was to be an embodiment of his lyric conception of the chih-shih, hero loyal to forlorn causes; a last testament to the pathetic power of the poet's vision; and, of course, a pointed allusion to the uncompromising anti-barbarian belligerence of Master Yang.

A romantic self-indulgence? Perhaps. But Chang's eye for the appropriate gesture had always been a sharp one. (Recall, for example, his attention-grabbing insult to the aging Chia-ch'ing poetry critic, Tseng Yü). And there is every reason to suspect that, here again, Chang had spotted a critical symbolic need—this time for clearing the name of the Spring Purificationists of the stain of facile opportunism. For the truth was that not one of the original war party had met death in the field or gone down (even in suicide) with any of the myriad cities that had fallen to the British. Among the ranks of the

Manchu and Mongol commanders, there had been no lack of such martyrs. The Mongol official Yü-ch'ien, for example, had drowned himself after the fall of Chen-hai; and the Manchu Hai-ling had ended his own life after the loss of the Grand Canal junction city of Chinkiang, in mid-1842.[28] There had even been a handful of Chinese generals who had died gloriously, as attested by a recently erected Peking shrine, put up by Chekiangese scholar-officials in the capital, and dedicated to the memory of Ko Yun-fei and other Chekiangese soldiers who lost their lives in the lower Yangtze fighting.[29] But of literati heroes, there were none, not even among the virulent war-enthusiasts of the Spring Purification party who had, after all, started the whole thing.

To this lack, however, Chang Chi-liang's reckless self-sacrifice supplied a kind of answer. Even if there were still no literati war heroes, at least there would be no doubt that the Spring Purificationist leaders were courageous enough as individuals, and quite capable of sacrificing their lives for a principle. Moreover, the specific cause for which Chang had abandoned his life—scholarly loyalty to a friend in adversity—was one that had its own particular appeal under the circumstances. For it indicated that the Spring Purificationists, whatever their shortcomings, were men who could keep faith with one another in times of declining fortunes. Whatever guilt these scholars might have felt over their role in the recent war could thus be assuaged by a return to that most fundamental literati ideal of all—true friendship.

Did Chang's gesture succeed? Apparently it did. For, in the first place, there followed, hard upon the heels of his death, a string of renewed fund-raising efforts that drew many of Chang's former associates back into the domain of symbolic protest politics. Paying for the deceased poet's funeral expenses was a start. But this was soon followed by the raising of a subscription from erstwhile Spring Purificationists and assorted other friends to build an altar to Chang in the capital, early in 1844. And then, three years later, came another subscription effort clearly inspired by Chang's death: the assembling of funds to rebuild Yang Chi-sheng's decrepit villa itself, as a kind of joint memorial to Yang's vigilance in resisting the conciliationists and to. Chang Chi-liang's remarkable modern-day replication of Yang's gesture.[30]

Chang's action seems to have succeeded on another front too—

that of renewing the political self-confidence of the *ku-wen* belletrists (Yao included) whom we see, shortly after Chang's death, suddenly reemerging as a leadership nucleus within the regathering opposition party. Was it perhaps that the "urgent words" of Chang Chi-liang's poetry were now, again, the rage in the Southern City? Or was it perhaps that one of the current leading lights of the Southern City—the censor Chu Ch'i—had been the man asked by Chang to tend to his literary estate? Whatever the specific reason, we cannot fail to notice that the ranks of the Ku Yen-wu Association were soon to be populated by a very considerable number of young scholars trained up in the art and ideology of *ku-wen* belletrism by Mei Tseng-liang, formerly of Spring Purification circle renown.[31] As a side note, we might also observe that this particular scholastic affiliation was to be responsible for the recruitment of a distinct regional wing of the Shrine Association whose political contributions to it were to be of crucial importance at the moment of its triumph in 1850. From the culturally isolated provinces of Hunan and Kwangsi, where "ancient-prose" studies had their largest following, were to be drawn, via this connection, an impressive list of Shrine Association activists, including the famous scholar-general Tseng Kuo-fan and the brave band of Kweilin (Kwangsi)-born literati who were to first alarm the Peking government about the nascent Taiping Rebellion. But the details of these latter accomplishments will have to wait until the next chapter.[32] For the moment, we need observe only that the tradition of *ku-wen* belletrism was to survive the wartime reverses suffered by the Spring Purificationists, and that it was to do so in large measure as a comment on the brilliant aptness of Chang Chi-liang's actions.

In addition to the group rallied by Chang Chi-liang and his admirers, however, there was a second nascent oppositional party in the process of forming in postwar Peking—this one under considerably more exalted leadership. The man whose influence figured most prominently in this parallel effort to launch an anti-Mu-chang-a coalition in the capital was the grand councillor, Ch'i Chün-tsao, who has already come to our attention as the only remaining advocate of continued belligerence within the council at the conclusion of the Nanking agreements. Ch'i's convictions on this matter seem to have been acquired during the course of an 1840 mission to Amoy to inspect defense preparations and the progress of the opium-suppression effort. His partner in that trip had been Huang Chueh-tzu, the

Spring Purification circle leader, with whom Ch'i seems to have developed a close friendship. Huang's militant attitudes evidently made a lasting impression, for we find Ch'i soon thereafter throwing himself into the campaign to oust Ch'i-shan and, soon after that, emerging as an outspoken advocate of the paramilitary defensive-warfare formula for prosecuting the war. No doubt Ch'i carried these views with him into the Grand Council upon his elevation into that body, late in October 1841. For we have evidence of a trail of continuing correspondence on the militia and defense questions in progress between Ch'i and several Southern City scholarly admirers, lasting well into the winter of 1842.[33]

A record of impressive verbal belligerence during the 1840 war was not Ch'i's only claim to leadership of the opposition now coalescing in Peking. Probably equally important in this regard was his identity as the patron of a coterie of extremely proficient Han Learning scholars around whom, in turn, could be rallied the numerous angry victims of Mu-chang-a's heavy-handed rule in the Han-lin Academy. The most important figures in this scholarly entourage were Ch'i's son-in-law, Chang Mu (1805–1849), Miao K'uei (1783–1857), and Hsu Han (*chü-jen* of 1835).[34] Though none of these three were Han-lin alumni themselves, they all enjoyed a considerable following among the membership of that institution, owing in large measure to their previous employment by Ch'i and others as provincial examination readers in Kiangsu and Chekiang during the 1830s. On the basis of that experience, they had naturally acquired influence over the trends of scholarship current in these academically sophisticated provinces. The prestige that this gave them in the eyes of the Han Learning enthusiasts of the academy (coupled, of course, with their reputation as intimates of Grand Councillor Ch'i) would in turn acquire major political significance in the postwar period, since, in the aftermath of Juan Yuan's (1838) retirement and the ouster of T'ang Chin-chao, the partisans of Han Learning no longer had an obvious patron in high places. Thus, almost inevitably, they found themselves drifting, during the 1840s, first into the company of Chang, Miao, and Hsu, and then, through them, into the academic entourage of Grand Councillor Ch'i. And, for this same reason, many of them would wind up in the camp of the anti-treaty movement—a movement which, if successful, promised to install Ch'i in Mu's place as dominant influence in the examination politics of the capital.

In addition to Ch'i's trio of examination readers, at least six lower Yangtze scholars of Han Learning background seem to have been ushered into the ranks of the opposition through this particular route. (These were Chang Yueh-sun, Chao Chen-tso, Chuang Shou-ch'i, Chu Yu-ts'un, Feng Kuei-fen, and Lu Hsien-chi.)[35] But, numbers aside, the emergence of such a clearly defined scholastic resistance to the new regime in Peking, possessing its own connections at the upper levels of the metropolitan bureaucracy, was perhaps even more important for the additional encouragement it lent to the newly recovered Spring Purification group. For here was a way both to broaden the anti-treaty resistance already inaugurated by Chang Chi-liang and, at the same time, to anchor it once again in the high politics of council debates and perhaps even of examination patronage.

Or so, apparently, the Spring Purificationists seem to have persuaded themselves. For, in the spring of 1844, the decision was suddenly taken to combine forces with the Ch'i Chün-tsao/Han Learning faction. The existence of this alliance was to become evident for the first time at the Ku Shrine dedication ceremony itself, which was originally planned by Chang Mu and the Ch'i party, but attended by five former members of the Spring Purification group. These links were confirmed a second time, later in that same month (April 1844), when a commemorative tablet for Chang Chi-liang was set up inside the compound just constructed by the Han Learning oppositionists to honor *their* hero, the erudite Ku Yen-wu. And it was to be saluted, once again, in 1847, when both groups again joined forces, this time to rebuild the Sung-yun-an villa, where Chang Chi-liang had spent his last days in 1843.[36]

Thus, within but two years of the rise to power of the Mu-chang-a peace party at court, the leaders of that new regime had managed to alienate the Han Chinese lettered elite so thoroughly that even the bitterest of scholastic rivals could now see their way to cooperation. Where once that elite had been polarized by academic disputes, it now found itself united in common opposition to the ascendant Mu-chang-a power group at court. Whether or not all those connected with this Han Learning wing of the new opposition were quite as convinced as their Spring Purification counterparts of the folly of the government's policy of retreat, that issue had become largely immaterial. For the moment at least, there was a clear overriding reason for wanting to join together to undermine the current, pro-treaty government, for only in this way could scholarship be restored to its rightful role in public life. This latter purpose provided a common goal that could bring together the elite of the Southern City as perhaps no other, and which could guarantee that there would be vigorous and enduring support for the Shrine Association's crusade to break the power of the emperor's current favorites. It remained only to establish a new set of symbols and of ideas about scholarship appropriate to this new, highly diverse constituency. And that was precisely what the Ku Yen-wu Shrine Association was to set about doing.

RITUAL AND SCHOLASTIC PHILOSOPHY

We need not linger at great length over the subtleties of the ritual and philosophical apparatus erected by this new generation of oppositionists as they marshaled for combat with the bureaucratic establishment. The leitmotifs we encounter here are entirely predictable—and fairly superficial as well. At the symbolic level, the main preoccupation of the Ku Yen-wu libationists was to establish an identity as heirs to the Spring Purification party, which was now viewed (with the convenience of retrospect) as having represented the political ideals of the lettered class as *a whole*, and not merely of one portion of it. And, in the realm of scholastics, the principal concern became to establish that the Han Learning and *ku-wen* traditions really did have certain basic ideals in common. In the prewar years, such claims would have seemed no doubt quite unconvincing. But it is a fitting measure of the changes the Mu-chang-a terror had wrought in the climate of Southern City intellectual life that such a unifying ideal of the true scholar could now be proclaimed, and that a new synthesis could emerge, based on the belief that scholarly authenticity needed only the credential of resistance to reigning intellectual fashion for its verification.

But let us begin, first, with a few remarks about the effort to portray the Ku Shrine Association as sharing the same intellectual lineage as the earlier Spring Purification circle, since it was this claim that gave rise to the need for proving that the belletrists of the former grouping and the Han Learning pedants of the latter were really of one mold.

The lineage from which the Ku Shrine Association leaders wished to believe themselves descended began with the Spring Purification circle, whose high-minded spirit of independence was frequently hailed as a model for the literati activists of the current, more degenerate age. That this identity was self-consciously cultivated can be seen from the remarks that appear in a series of Shrine Association verses compiled by two Huang Chueh-tzu students, Yeh Ming-feng and K'ung Hsien-i, on the occasion of a second (1856) reconstruction of the Ku shrine compound:

In days of yore, the venerable [scholar] of Fu-chou [i.e., Huang Chueh-tzu]
Had held his "Orchid Pavilion" gatherings each spring at the Chiang-t'ing
    Pavilion.
The lofty spirit of these gatherings has now long since lapsed.
Their memory is now over twenty years behind us,
Like a towering peak crumbling into forgetfulness. . . .

But, Yeh continues, there still survives among us one of the scholarly greats of those bygone times (Lu I-t'ung). And we can be proud that he is with us this day, helping us to remember that original occasion, now thirty years past (in 1826), when the "Venerable of Fu-chou" had convened the first Spring Purification banquet.[37]

This same claim of continuity is underlined by the stubborn retention of the Spring Purification festival day itself as a focus of group social life. Lacking the influence within the examination system that the original Spring Purificationists had enjoyed, the Ku Association literati had no particular reason to coordinate their meetings with the examination calendar. But they did so anyway, holding their prime annual banquet day toward the end of the third lunar month, just as had the Spring Purificationists.[38] Was this perhaps a confession of impatience—an admission that being on the sidelines was not, after all, so desirable a circumstance to find oneself in? Perhaps so. But it was also a reminder that the chain leading back to the happier days of the 1830s was, for these men, still an unbroken one.

There was, however, one significant addition to the conventions of Spring Purification ceremonial—an addition that seems, indeed, to be quite specifically directed to this problem of making do with outgroup status vis-à-vis the examination-system establishment. That was the decision to use the Tz'u-jen Temple, rather than the suburban Chiang-t'ing Pavilion, as the site for meetings and for the Ku and Chang Chi-liang altars. This latter location, it will be recalled, was in

Ch'ing times the traditional setting for examiner-pupil banquets, and had served as such since the great literocrat-patrons of the mid-K'ang-hsi had used it for entertaining the participants in the 1679 "by-invitation-only" special examination.[39] It had also been, of course, the place where the Spring Purification circle had convened its yearly spring banquets. For the Ku Yen-wu libationers, however, the idea of meeting at a spot where the loathed Mu-chang-a or P'an Shih-en might suddenly appear with their flocks of sycophantic hangers-on was obviously unacceptable. Another site therefore had to be found. And the one on which they settled—the Tz'u-jen Temple—was chosen deliberately for its history as a place to which high-minded recluses, eager to avoid the vulgar traffic of examination-calendar socializing, had traditionally repaired.

To the informed nineteenth-century man of letters, the Tz'u-jen Temple, lying just inside the Hsuan-nan precincts, would have at once recalled the stories of the founding ancestor of Ch'ing poetics, Wang Shih-chen, who had frequently fled to this particular temple compound during its book fairs to take refuge from the press of favor-seekers.[40] But, even more to the point, it would also have recalled the actions of the Ku Shrine Association's patron scholar-deity, Ku Yen-wu, when he visited Peking in the late 1660s. For, like a good many members of the latter-day association, Ku had had ready access to the current grandees of examination-system politics, including his nephew, the Southern Party patron, Hsu Ch'ien-hsueh. But he had most certainly not wished to avail himself of that kind of patronage. As Ku had repeatedly made clear, he had regarded his influential kins-man as too much obsessed with power and far too little concerned with the serious cultivation of learning.[41] According to seventeenth-century anecdote, therefore, Ku had refused Hsu's offer of lodgings, and had instead chosen to put up at the much shabbier Tz'u-jen Tem-ple compound. To Ho Shao-chi, one of the 1844 founders of the Ku Association, the gesture seemed to catch quite perfectly the spirit that the oppositionists of the 1840s wished to convey through their own actions:

In those times, the temple book fair was so grand an occasion!
When the stalls were set up, one could find charts and scrolls collected from
   every [corner] of the empire.
The venerable scholars of these first years of our dynasty

Gathered here to pass their leisure time in company.
Master [Ku] had countless close friends [among the greats of the capital],
But he lived [here] in borrowed lodgings, with only a brazier in the winter, and
a paper fan in summer.
Even today, in the shadow of the two noble pines guarding this temple,
It is as if one can still see his inkstone lying there.[42]

So here, then, was a comment of sorts on the plight in which the literati oppositionists of the 1840s found themselves, thanks to their loss of influence in the examination system. Responding to that unwelcome state of affairs, the scholars of the Ku Association elected to put the best possible face on it by regarding themselves as latter-day emulators of Ku Yen-wu, taking refuge in the Tz'u-jen Temple from the vulgar world of examination-system politics that seemed to preoccupy everyone else in the capital. Thus, out-group status in the capital was (through its association with the memory of Ku Yen-wu) given the appearance of an idealistic choice. And the cause on behalf of which this choice has been made was Master Ku's cause of preserving true scholarship in a world where its survival was threatened by the examination system itself.

But if the defense of such scholarship was the ideal to whose service these angry critics of the government had pledged themselves, what then was the Han Learning virtuoso Ku Yen-wu doing as its emblem? Apart from his nose-thumbing at the greats of his day, what made this particular scholar the obvious spokesman for an ideal of scholarly commitment behind which all true scholars could rally?

At first glance, this choice does in fact seem somewhat puzzling, inasmuch as Ku was best known in Ch'ing times as a paragon of Han Learning erudition, and not as a broad synthesizer of different traditions of scholarship. Indeed, to Chang Mu (whose lifelong interest in Ku seems to have prompted the idea of selecting him as an emblem for the new opposition), it was quite specifically for his contribution to quintessentially Han Learning fields that Ku was respected: phonetics, etymological studies, and historical geography. Moreover, transcending the particulars of these fields, Ku had helped establish a *method* of inquiry (epitomized in his *Record of Daily Knowledge,* or *Jih-chih lu*), that had set the tone for mid-Ch'ing Han Learning scholarship by emphasizing the patient accumulation and verification of isolated bits of factual knowledge about the past.[43]

Yet Chang Mu's perception of Ku was not the only way in which it was possible to claim kinship with that much-regarded early Ch'ing scholar. As several other Ku Association scholars would point out, Ku's methodology had itself come into existence as a kind of protest against the prevailing habits of the lettered elite of Ku's own day. In this respect, Ku's scholarly style could be seen as vigorously iconoclastic and rebellious, and very much out of sympathy with the conformist and quietist values that had later become associated with Han Learning in its mid-Ch'ing manifestation. For most of the eager young spirits that rallied to the Shrine Association banner in the 1840s, it was this particular aspect of Ku's scholarly personality—this triumphant defiance, that is, of the intellectual mainstream of the day—and not the specifics of his philological research that aroused admiration and a sense of intellectual affinity. Here, then, is where we must look to uncover the broader significance of Ku's election as the hero for the literati of the 1840s to emulate.

We have perhaps already glimpsed this controversial side of Ku's temperament in his handling of his relationship with Hsu Ch'ien-hsueh and in his refusal of office under the Ch'ing. Here, however, it might be added that this same penchant for battling against his age had prompted Ku to compose a series of essays bitterly critical of the institutionalized cynicism he found in the Ming and early Ch'ing governments' treatment of the literati-bureaucratic class. In this *T'ing-lin wen-chi*, as well as in the *Jih-chih lu*, Ku had mobilized his knowledge of China's medieval past to berate the regimes of his own day for a whole string of offenses. In Ku's eyes, these late imperial governments were guilty of knowingly overpopulating the ranks of the degree-holding class; of vulgarizing the curriculum of the educational and examination systems; and of ruining the psychological condition of the officeholding class by undercutting even healthy particularistic attachments (such as, for example, to one's native place, where official tenure was forbidden). Through polemics such as these, Ku had, if inadvertantly, anticipated the sentiments and even the discursive style of the mid-Tao-kuang *ku-wen* revivalists, who had likewise found their mission in the regeneration of the lettered elite, and who had similarly used interdynastic comparisons to attain critical perspective on the present.[44]

Our point is, then, that the intellectual values latent in Ku Yen-wu's Han Learning scholarship were indeed quite far removed from the quietist and self-critical values of the eighteenth-century Han

Learning establishment to which the T'ung-ch'eng belletrists of the Spring Purification party had once taken such violent exception. And, by the same token, they could indeed be understood as consistent with the vigorously nonconformist spirit of the mid-Tao-kuang *ku-wen* party. If this did not yet produce any positive agreement on exactly what scholarship was, it at least provided a kind of consensus about what it was not. Thus we arrive at the core ideological formulation of the new oppositionists: that true scholars could be found anywhere that there was resistance to the degraded, other-determined intellectual fashions of the times, even if that resistance happened to take the form of the previously condemned Han Learning pedantry.

Thus, for example, the dedicated Shrine Association *ku-wen* belletrist Chu Ch'i—a man entirely without expertise (or even interest) in philological subjects—could nevertheless now recognize a kindred spirit in Ku Yen-wu, and thus (by implication) in the Han Learning scholars he found gathered around him at the yearly Tz'u-jen Temple rites:

Thinking back to the first years of the Our Dynasty—how gloriously was the study of the Classics advanced!
Retired and venerable scholars [i.e., Ku] were in those times often urged to come to the capital
But the mores of the literati had been long since degraded: how could they be revived [simply by men like Ku taking office]?
How right, then, was [Master Ku] for applying himself instead to the promotion of "unadorned studies"![45]

Refusal of position; dedication to reform the "mores of the literati"; and pursuit of "unadorned" (that is, Han Learning) studies here fuse quite comfortably in an ideal of the scholar that even the *ku-wen* revivalist Chu could understand and admire.

On the other side of the divide, the Han Learning scholars in the Shrine Association were now also eager to join in this discovery of a previously unobserved sympathy with the ideals of the *ku-wen* revivalists of the 1830s. Thus, here again is Ho Shao-chi, dedicating the Ku Shrine in 1844 with some verses setting forth, in his poetic portrait of Ku Yen-wu, this transfigured impression of the model Han Learning scholar:

Thinking back, I recall the last years of the Ming
When the age was embittered by the battles of snakes and dragons.
The moral integrity and earnestness of the scholar [class] were then at their peak
But as soldiers or generals [attempting to guard the Ming regime in the south],
   these men were lacking in training.
What could a humble, bookish Confucian scholar hope to accomplish in such
   times?
Vulgarized schools of learning competed, and, in competing, each fanned high
   its own flames.
The records of the sayings of the Sung Neo-Confucians had been degraded to
   empty phrase-mongering.
While the belletrists vied with each other in pursuit of superficial glory,
Master Ku held firmly to the task of reviving the Way.
Delving through the records of antiquity, he linked together the recent past
   with earlier times.
And dissected exhaustively each of the Classics and histories until he commanded
   them all,
Gaining a grand overview of the celestial and of the human . . .
Who but this "man among the rushes"
Could have forced open the eyelids of a blind age?[46]

For the philologist Ho Shao-chi, then, as equally for the *ku-wen*
enthusiast Chu Ch'i, the abrasive and cautionary spirit of Ku Yen-wu
could be seen as bridging the previously warring schools of early-
nineteenth-century intellectual life. By emulating this aspect of Ku's
scholarly personality, diligent philologists and passionate belletrists
could once again see themselves as united in a common ideal of scholarship. From this conviction it was, in turn, but a short step to the
belief that the Shrine Association somehow represented all serious
scholarly endeavor. As Ho Shao-chi was himself to put it in another
poem in honor of the Ku Shrine, the ceremonies that had been
launched in 1844 had drawn in all the "great Confucian scholars and
talented students of the realm, *both those who pursue unadorned studies,
and those who are adept at [ku-wen] prose.*"[47] The authentic scholars of
the empire had found their common ground; thus braced by their new
conviction that all defiant scholarly spirits were their allies, they could
now issue forth together to challenge the hated Mu-chang-a.

IN SEARCH OF A POLITICAL PROGRAM

But how then was true scholarship to be restored to its rightful place?
We have already observed, earlier in this chapter, just how thorough

had been Mu-chang-a's demolition of the political institutions from which the Southern City literati could normally expect to draw their power. Independent literati control of Han-lin patronage, and tolerance for freewheeling censorial criticism of administrators and their policies (especially where diplomatic issues were concerned)—both these sources of collective power and influence had now vanished. Nor was there any reasonable hope of reversing this new powerlessness. For, so long as Tao-kuang continued to be the prisoner of a numbing fear of confrontation with the British, there was little likelihood he could be induced to distance himself from Mu-chang-a. And Mu-chang-a would certainly not back down now. How could the literati opposition reclaim its lost political influence, when the circumstance that had caused the loss of that influence in the first place—the emperor's fear of the costs of diplomatic irresponsibility— remained beyond its ability to alter?

For the best part of a decade, this problem would remain essentially unsolved. Nonetheless, throughout the seven years of enforced silence on questions of foreign policy that followed, there did persist a kind of faith that the oppositional coalition would ultimately find its way back into the emperor's good graces. Predictably enough, the conviction on which this optimism was grounded derived from the very same idea that had originally legitimated the expansion of literati power in the 1830s. That was the conviction that the Ch'ing state would not dare to risk the kind of dampening of lettered elite loyalism that would occur if it persisted in debarring the literati from political participation. If the present regime was allowed to continue in power, the Shrine Association's leaders warned each other in solemn tones, there would certainly be recrudescence of the same passive, conformist, and indolent mentality that had paralyzed the elite in the days of Ho-shen and of Ts'ao Chen-yung. Unless the scholars and scholar-officials were jolted from this mood by the bracing experience of active participation in censorial politics, moral debilitation would overtake them rapidly. And, in that torpid condition, they would be of no service to the dynasty as a bulwark against social anarchy and rebellion.

Within the Shrine Association itself, the most eloquent exponent of this cautionary theme was the Kwangsi scholar Chu Ch'i—a Mei Tseng-liang student who had come under the influence of the T'ung-ch'eng school. According to Chu's own later testimony, his views on the question of literati morale had been formed very much under the

spell of Kuan T'ung's famous 1821 essay on rectifying popular mores—
the same document that had so much influenced the Spring Purification literati in their own espousal of a revival of *ch'ing-i*, moral
censure.[48] In that essay, it might be recalled, Kuan had linked the rise
of popular rebelliousness to the dampening influence of the Ch'ing
system on the temper of the scholarly elite. With this diagnosis Chu
agreed most heartily as he reread Kuan T'ung's essay in twenty years'
retrospect. The remedy? Obviously, to revive the institutions of scholarly participation in government. Unless this were done quickly,
Chu warned, the drift he had espied toward complacency and conformism would not be reversed in time to avert another major challenge to the dynasty from below.

Elaborating on this same theme in another essay (entitled "On
Language and Substance"), Chu harped despondently on the mood
of passivity that he saw spreading among the elite since the ascendancy of the Mu-chang-a government. Colorless and over-cautious
bureaucrats dominate the examination system, strangling stillborn
the spirit of indignation and bold non-conformity. Men seeking success in such a system inevitably adopt the values of their seniors, and
become mere yea-sayers; while men of unusual character are perforce
pushed to the side:

We are told that a great tree is not discarded on account of a minor blight, and
that defects in a thoroughbred, such as the habit of bolting or kicking, do not
make it useless for riding. The talents of the ambitious, the aggressive, and the
opinionated are often employable. But what finds praise in today's world are [the
virtues of] considerateness, restraint, and modesty. . . . He who possesses these virtues not only assures himself a tranquil career, untroubled by fear, but procures
for himself, as well, an exquisite reputation.[49]

The ascendancy of such timid and complacent souls, Chu complains, cannot but pose great danger for the survival of the dynasty:

As they wend their way through the corridors of the court, dressed in their
resplendent hats and robes, their superiors do not hold them in suspicion and criticism does not fall upon them. [They appear] imperturbable, thoughtful, and profound beyond measure. But should a great crisis one day arise, they will become
flustered and paralyzed, tongue-tied and lock-jawed, and will dare not utter a
word. At such junctures, their so-called "considerateness, restraint, and modesty"
turn out to be totally useless.[50]

The need for building a more heroic mode of elite personality, then, supplies the ultimate justification for undoing Mu-chang-a's and P'an Shih-en's newly gained control over the government, and for again "opening wide the avenues of (literati) comment," as Chu was to urge in yet another essay on literati mores.[51]

Though in a slightly less ambitious fashion, Tseng Kuo-fan, another Mei Tseng-liang student, was to advance precisely the same argument early in 1850, this time in the form of a public appeal to the newly enthroned Hsien-feng emperor. At present, Tseng opined, official morale was suffering from four afflictions, each the product of the Ch'ing over-correction of earlier traits in elite culture. Timidity is now generally taken for prudence; and passivity for respectfulness. (Afflictions 1 and 2.) Metropolitan officials have become shrinking and petty. (Affliction 3.) And provincial officials are given over to equivocating and muddling along, concerning themselves only with conforming to appearances, and systematically sacrificing future needs for immediate peace and quiet. (Affliction 4.) The only way to correct this exceedingly dangerous trend, Tseng concluded, was to bypass entirely the entrenched bureaucratic patronage establishment in Peking. Instead, the emperor ought to open the gates of the palace to hear what the literati themselves (as represented by the entire corps of capital officials, not just the grand councillors) think about the current parade of officeholders, high and low.[52]

This, of course, amounts to a slightly different formula than Chu's for reviving the outspokenness of the lettered elite, for it limits their comments to the realm of personnel evaluations. But ultimately Tseng's argument is really very much the same as Chu's, and might be taken as equally representative of the kind of opinions on the legitimacy of ch'ing-i that were current in Shrine Association circles in the 1840s. Bureaucratic society had simply become too tame and insipid, thanks to so many years of saturation by Ch'ing values. And the only way to shock it loose was by giving non-bureaucratic networks immediate access to the emperor as a kind of compensating spiritual influence upon the system. Once again, in other words, the case for independent literati political influence is made to rest on a perceived need for bolstering the state's defenses against the dangers created by a passive elite. And once again there waited in the wings a band of true scholars whose unusual dedication to the values of heroic non-conformity were believed to qualify them to lead the literati back into high politics.

We must here, however, take leave of the Shrine Association leadership without, for the moment, discovering what the effect of Tseng's argument was to be upon the Hsien-feng emperor. For, with the submission of Tseng's petition, in April 1850, the Shrine Association's quest to renew the institutional power of the lettered elite had brought that issue back once again into the domain of public decision making. What would happen next would thus be determined, not by literati rhetoric, but by the new monarch's assessment of the changing needs and priorities of the central government. Ultimately, as we shall see, Hsien-feng would conclude that a stronger literati presence in Peking policy debates was in the best interest of the court. But to understand properly the background of that decision, it will be necessary, first, to consider the range of developments beyond the world of the court itself that influenced the emperor—developments, that is, in the realm of diplomacy and in the area of domestic control.

CHAPTER SEVEN

The End of Manchu Diplomacy

If the leaders of lettered-elite political opinion had been outcasts at the court of Tao-kuang during that emperor's declining years, their fortunes were to take a remarkable turn for the better upon the accession of his 18-year-old son, the Hsien-feng emperor, on 25 February 1850. On 11 May of that same year, word came from the palace that the first steps had been taken to recall Lin Tse-hsu to high office. On 16 May, yet another surprising order issued forth, this one summoning Yao Ying to the capital, apparently for a similar reinstatement. And this was to be swiftly followed by news that Su T'ing-k'uei—the censorial enthusiast of a trans-Himalayan military alliance against the British and the would-be purger of Mu-chang-a in 1843—would also be reinstated to his original post in Peking, along with two other of his Shrine Association compeers, Chu Ch'i and Ch'en Ch'ing-yung.[1]

Even more pleasing still would be the action that the new monarch was to take on 1 December of this same year. In a single thundering edict that fills several pages of the official court chronicle, Hsien-feng not only stripped his father's two chief advisers on maritime diplomacy, Mu-chang-a and Ch'i-ying, of all their government offices, but he went further, specifically condemning the role these two had played in ruining Lin Tse-hsu and Yao Ying, and in "cowing" the throne with stories of how dreadful the consequences would be if the British were not placated at every turn.[2] The significance of these shifts in imperial favor could hardly have been clearer. The literati, mobilized under the leadership of the Shrine Association oppositionists, were now obviously back in a position of influence over the empire's maritime relations. And their reappearance as a force to be reckoned with in this domain had an immediate effect at the very highest levels of the Ch'ing system.

All these rather spectacular developments, moreover, took place as a consequence of aggressive political maneuvers initiated by the literati themselves, and were not merely a reflection of the new monarch's instinctive bellicosity in foreign-policy matters, as has sometimes been asserted. The key initiative from which almost all else sprang, as we shall presently see, turns out to have been Tseng Kuo-fan's 13 April 1850 appeal to the newly enthroned emperor, urging that a broad range of Peking literati-officials be consulted about worthy candidates for office. To be sure, the kind of temporary suspension of bureaucratic normalcy here requested was a boon frequently (indeed, almost automatically) offered by incoming emperors, under the pretense that it was necessary to inaugurate a new reign by encouraging the talent presumably stifled at the lower layers of an ossified civil service. This had been a regular practice earlier in the Ch'ing, and thus, except for the slightly more ominous language of Tseng's request, his petition might not have seemed of more than ritual significance at the time it was first made public.[3] But that impression was soon enough to be dispelled. For, from the poll Tseng had requested, there was to emerge, first, a demand for the recall of Lin Tse-hsu and Yao Ying to high office (to which Hsien-feng ultimately assented despite Mu-chang-a's furious objections); and then, almost inevitably, the removal of the Manchu courtiers who had originally hounded them into disgrace.

That the new emperor should thus have chosen to bow before the demands of an organized literati opposition, thereby putting his empire once again at diplomatic risk, seems at first sight astonishing. For, after all, if there had been any significant changes in the direction of Ch'ing external policy after the peace of 1842, the support for those changes had come, as we have seen, from the monarchy and from its own hand-picked agents within the bureaucracy. Even if the British successes in the 1840–1842 war had not much impressed the literati, they had registered sufficiently on the Manchu power elite ringing the throne to warrant a reorganization of the deliberative and executive structures that governed Ch'ing diplomacy and to bring about a concentration of power in the hands of that same narrow group. And, with these new structures locked in place, a new, specifically Manchu style of diplomacy had developed. The guiding principle of that diplomacy had been to avoid at all cost any action that might provoke a new military confrontation. And its fruit had been a string of treaties and indemnity settlements that, while outraging Chinese literati opinion, had indeed helped keep the peace: the British commercial and tariff treaties of 1842 and 1843; and French (LaGrene) treaty of October 1844, granting toleration for the Catholic religion; and the Medhurst settlement of 1848, whereby the Ch'ing government, under Ch'i-ying's guidance, agreed to compensate three British missionaries for wounds suffered during an unauthorized foray into the Shanghai hinterlands.

Yet, in the first months of the new monarch's rule, this one significant structural change in the conduct of Ch'ing foreign relations was to be undone. And it was to be undone, moreover, at the hands of the monarchy itself, now openly seeking to conciliate literati resentments against the Manchu diplomatic directorate that had overseen the implementation of the new system. What, then, had brought about this sudden change of heart? What was it about the mid-century political milieu (both internal and external) that had catalyzed this reassessment of Manchu diplomacy? And what, more specifically, can we discover about the changing political circumstances of the monarchy itself at the mid-century mark that might illuminate its baffling decision to abandon its earlier policies, after having earned so much enmity by imposing them in the first place?

One important element, no doubt, was chance: the coincidence, that is to say, of the accession of an 18-year-old prince to the throne in February 1850, just at the point when the Manchu idea of diplomacy was about to be put to its toughest test. But the other major events in the story were not quite so adventitious. Their origins lay in the structural weaknesses of the Ch'ing political system—weaknesses we have already encountered earlier in this narrative, which were to reappear, once more, at mid-century, fatally compromising the throne's ability to adhere to the new course it had just set.

The first of these weaknesses was the old problem of lack of control—or, more accurately, lack of inclination to exert control—over the particulars of policy implementation throughout the southeastern littoral as a whole. Such laxity already had a considerable tradition behind it by the time it was again to become a source of difficulties during the 1840s. We saw it, much earlier in this narrative, as a problem in the framing of trade policy, hampering the emperor from imposing his own ideas on the reluctant Liang-Kuang governor general, Lu K'un. During the 1840–1842 war, we saw the same disposition asserting itself once again, now in the military arena, where the court decided with surprisingly little resistance to allow Ch'i Kung to build up a semi-private military apparatus much more powerful than the centrally controlled military forces in the area. This arrangement had clearly violated the spirit of traditional imperial administration, and would have been inconceivable in the north or in the Yangtze heartland of the empire except under the most extreme of circumstances. Yet, in Kwangtung, the court had allowed it to occur with very little effort at controlling the outcome.[4]

This same preference for avoiding close control over the direction of diplomatic and military strategy in the southeast was, moreover, to survive the war largely unaltered, in spite of the best efforts of the Manchu peace party in the capital. In this postwar decade, however, the outcome of such continued laxity would be a challenge to central government policy itself. In 1849, the weak central government presence in Kwangtung would facilitate a rather extraordinary experiment in military bluffing by the mandarins and scholars of Canton, whereby they sought successfully to defy the treaty provisions authorizing foreign residence within that city. Presented with this stunning *fait accompli*, which bore all the hallmarks of the wartime literati line on defense and diplomacy (mobilization of paramilitaries, and so forth), the monarchy could hardly remain unaffected. Two different policies for handling maritime affairs thus soon achieved currency in court pronouncements on the treaty-enforcement question: the conservative, anti-provocationist position of the Manchu diplomats, on the one hand; and the blustering, populist style that had been vindicated in the 1849 "victory" at Canton, on the other. Though the throne did not allow itself to be forced to choose between the two strategies, the fact remained that the unfaltering allegiance Mu-chang-a had once commanded for his policy of diplomatic prudence was no longer there. And with its loss, there disappeared one of the main props supporting the edifice of Manchu postwar diplomacy.

The second weakness of the Ch'ing governmental system that would reappear on the scene at mid-century to undercut the Mu-chang-a leadership was the ever-dangerous phenomenon of rural insurrection along the southern, sub-Yangtze flank of the empire. This threat had been, of course, one of the forces that had shaped the pattern of Ch'ing politics in the 1830s, when it had pushed the emperor into conceding unprecedented influence to the representatives of Southern City opinion in order to guarantee the support of the Chinese lettered elite in the government's battle against disorder.

However, if the energies of the Chinese social elite were now again to be effectively coordinated with bureaucratic efforts to restore control, the power-brokers of the Southern City would once more have to be given a stake in political cooperation. The price that such cooperation would entail would certainly include the loosening of Mu-chang-a's stranglehold over examination patronage and over bureaucratic promotions. As this realization dawned upon Hsien-feng in the spring of 1850, he lost no time in showing his willingness to make the necessary concessions—first, by bowing to Tseng Kuo-fan's April 1850, call for a special polling of elite opinion on talent within the bureaucracy, and then by yielding to the majority wish that Mu-chang-a's victims (Lin Tse-hsu and Yao Ying) be recalled and put in charge of the impending campaign to bring the rebellion in the south under control. To regain the loyalty of the scholar class, in other words, Hsien-feng would prove all too happy to override his chief councillor, even if this meant reinstating literati leaders whose views on maritime policy were frighteningly provocative. By this means, a second nail would be driven into the coffin of the new diplomacy of the post-1842 years.

To be sure, in none of this—neither in the flirting with the Kwang-tung model of anti-treaty defiance, nor in the sacrifice of Mu-chang-a to appease Southern City sentiments—was there any notion of imposing a new set of goals in the management of maritime policy. As far as the court was concerned, the Ch'ing commitment to enforcing the treaties still stood, at least as a matter of general principle. There was to be no planned campaign to reverse any of the commercial or tariff concessions already made, nor any scheme for deliberately testing the resolve of the British elsewhere along the coast. A change mainly in atmospherics, and not really in policy, would be the principal consequence of Mu-chang-a's fall. Indeed, things could scarcely have been otherwise, with the government itself about to be reduced to a congeries of isolated local regimes holding scattered pockets of territory against the Taiping rebels. Yet the failure of Mu-chang-a's opponents to produce a clear alternative to his policies was probably not so important, in the long run, as the message his fall would inscribe in the history books—that the Ch'ing monarchy was simply too fragile, too insecure domestically, to be able to sustain an unpopular foreign policy. If Ch'ing rulers would hereafter be chary of identifying themselves with such policies, the lesson of Mu-chang-a's failure would surely be one major reason for their caution.[5] But now we must examine more closely just why this decision to undo the new, postwar diplomatic leadership was made.

THE SECOND VICTORY OF THE CANTONESE

Insofar as changing perceptions about the Ch'ing empire's military vulnerability influenced the 1850 departure from the tenets of what we have been calling Manchu diplomacy, then it was certainly the April 1849 British retreat at Canton that was the critical turning point. What happened, quite briefly, was this. According to the provisions of the Treaty of Nanking, the British believed themselves to have secured the right to reside within the precincts of five specified Chinese cities, henceforth to be designated as "treaty ports" (*kang-k'ou*).[6] At four of these five, they were eventually to have that right recognized. But at Canton there was trouble from the start. The problem arose (or so the mandarins claimed) from the unwillingness of "the people" to countenance a foreign presence inside the walls of this great provincial capital. Baffled by this resistance, the British had let the matter go unresolved for five years, mainly because they were too preoccupied with trade and trade-related diplomatic questions elsewhere along the coast to bother with this comparatively minor difficulty at Canton.

Then, however, in the spring of 1847, having been provoked by the Cantonese on a variety of other issues, the British plenipotentiary, Sir John Davis, turned to military action. Once again British forces quickly reduced the Ch'ing fortifications guarding Canton from sea attack, leaving the city totally vulnerable. Bowing before this display of *force majeure*, the Ch'ing emissary, Ch'i-ying, agreed to let the British in after the expiration of a two-year moratorium. However, in April 1849, when the time was up, Ch'i-ying was no longer on the scene, and had been replaced by two Chinese officials whose sympathies lay very visibly with "the people" of Canton. As the deadline for implementing the 1847 agreement approached, these two officials, Hsu Kuang-chin and Yeh Ming-ch'en, mobilized the Cantonese irregulars for a last-ditch stand, and ordered the cessation of all trade. Though the court fully expected that this show of bravado would lead to another military showdown, and tried to call off Hsu and Yeh at the last moment, its voice was not heeded. At that point, however, the British, amazingly enough, chose to yield, and agreed not to press their demands for entry. The Ch'ing had, it seemed, won a stunning diplomatic victory, simply by pitting the people against the enemy's superior firepower. The script could have been lifted straight from Wei Yuan's "Maritime Defense" tracts![7]

Of course, the reality of what had taken place at Canton was by no means consistent with the boasts of a great triumph for popular military forces that soon came to inform the accounts of the affair reaching the capital from Hsu and Yeh. But in a sense, that did not matter. For this time (unlike in 1841) there really had been a British retreat. Any remaining doubts were soon dispelled by the somewhat pathetic British appeal directed, in the spring of 1850, to the Ch'ing authorities at Shanghai and Tientsin requesting that the decision of the officials at Canton be overruled. When, once again, the British proved unwilling to use force to prevail on this issue, the case for unreflective adherence to the Mu-chang-a line in Sino-British diplomacy—that provocations must be avoided at all cost—suffered yet a further blow. And so, in the end, did the prestige of its author.

For the moment, however, our concern lies with the background to this second showdown at Canton, and not with its consequences. Clearly, there is much that needs to be explained in this affair. How,

one wonders, could such an adventurous maneuver as that attempted
by Hsu and Yeh have taken place at all, given the (apparently) firm
grip of the Manchu peace faction on policymaking, and its hold over
the commissionerships in the coastal provinces? Why had the confrontation not been averted by Ch'i-ying or by the emperor, both of
whom were quite convinced at the time of the final showdown that
there was real risk of war? Why, in a word, had the court's guidance
of policy been so weak, so easily ignored?

Part of the answer, as we shall presently discover, lies in the unusual militance that the Cantonese were themselves to demonstrate in
blocking the full enforcement of the treaty terms. Here, as in no
other of the new treaty ports, both merchants and scholars would
join together, by 1847, under the banner of resistance to implementation of the entry and residence provisions of the treaties. That formidable partnership of business and academic elites, encountered
nowhere else along the coast during the 1840s, would have been quite
difficult to oppose even had the court been fully determined to do so,
since it controlled important military as well as economic resources
needed by the government for its day-to-day functioning. But—and
here is the really crucial point—during the postwar years the central
government had never been really determined to enforce its own
ideas upon the Cantonese. Alongside of the control strategy, which
was to reach its maximum effectiveness during Ch'i-ying's four-year
stay at Canton (1843–1847), there had always co-existed a cooptation
strategy, aimed at maintaining the loyalty of local elites through the
mediation of benevolently disposed Han Chinese mandarins. As a
result, Manchu diplomacy at Canton had never been implemented in
such a way as to force an unwilling local populace to go along,
against its will, with the prevailing policies.

The circumstances that encouraged Hsu and Yeh, in 1849, to try
their hand at bluff arose directly from this policy of avoiding confrontation with the Cantonese over diplomatic questions. First, late in
1847 the court had decided to restore to Han Chinese officials full
control over the conduct of diplomatic affairs at Canton. And, second, the two officials who had benefited from this decision—Hsu
Kuang-chin and Yeh Ming-ch'en—had realized that their continuation in office depended entirely on their ability to maintain the good
will of the leaders of local public opinion. Intransigence had been
the inevitable result. Thus, in the end, it was not really oversight or

neglect, but rather the very deeply ingrained habit of loose supervision over policy enforcement in peripheral Canton, that prepared the way for the initial departure from the conciliationist diplomacy of the immediate postwar period.

Our analysis of the history of the exclusionist triumph of 1849 properly begins, therefore, with the question of why the court remained averse to asserting full control over diplomacy in Kwangtung—for, had Peking been otherwise inclined, it is doubtful that the leaders of popular opinion in this region would have felt so free to challenge central-government policy on treaty enforcement. We have already seen, in our study of wartime military planning, that the Manchu government's own sense of strategic priorities tended to draw its attention to the Yangtze valley and the Peking-Manchuria coastal corridor. Here was where government revenue interests, supply sources, and elite military strength were most concentrated. Kwangtung, by contrast, had traditionally figured as unimportant in the conduct of central administration. Only a small Manchu garrison was stationed there, and revenue transfers to the capital and the Yangtze provinces were confined mainly to the extraction of maritime customs revenues. In the postwar milieu, moreover, even this latter interest waned, since the customs collection returns that would be produced by the direct Yangtze trade, through Shanghai, could be expected soon to overtake those of the bypassed southeastern entrepot city of Canton.[8] Thus, the particular strategic vulnerability of the Yangtze that had been revealed by the 1840 war, compounded now by the further diminution of Canton's importance as a revenue source, pointed toward a much greater emphasis on central-government control over Yangtze coastal diplomacy than over the conduct of foreign relations at Canton.

And, indeed, as one reads through the records of Ch'ing diplomatic dealings on the Canton front during the 1840s, one sees reflected precisely such an assumption of strategic marginality. It was not, for example, until almost a full year after the cease-fire at Nanking that the chief Ch'ing negotiator, Ch'i-ying, was dispatched to Canton—principally, it would seem, because the court expected that the critical issues in postwar diplomacy and military planning would arise in connection with British attempts to penetrate the Yangtze via Shanghai, and not at Canton. Or, to consider another manifestation of the same attitude, we might note that Manchu officials, (first Ch'i-ying, then Pi-ch'ang) were kept in charge of the territorial administration in the Yangtze theatre until mid-1847, expressing, no doubt, the throne's concern to see that postwar Sino-foreign interactions were here supervised with a maximum of regard for the dynastic center's concern to avoid renewal of fighting. In Kwangtung, by contrast, control over the regular government stayed always in the hands of Chinese administrators, even during the brief three-year interlude (1844–1847) when Ch'i-ying was nominally in command as governor general.[9]

To be more specific, throughout the 1840s one sees, in the pattern of sub-gubernatorial appointments within the regular provincial bureaucracy, a cautious insistence on retaining in office at least one high-level Han Chinese official of examination-elite background and known sympathy to the Cantonese paramilitary leadership. Thus, until his death in 1844, Governor General Ch'i Kung—the original guiding spirit behind the Cantonese defense force—remained firmly in control of the regular civilian administration. And, upon his demise, a string of rather independent-spirited Chinese Han-lin were shifted into the provincial governor's yamen in Canton. First came Ch'eng Yü-ts'ai (in office from early 1843 to early 1845), who had been a vocal wartime advocate of the paramilitary strategy and of a war of attrition.[10] Then came Hsu Kuang-chin—a Chinese of *chin-shih* parentage who would later show himself decidedly eager for a fight with Ch'i-ying. And finally, in 1848, came Yeh Ming-ch'en, a Han-lin whose brother (Ming-feng) was actually one of the leaders of the Shrine Association in Peking![11] By contrast, the peace party was unable to get more than a shallow toehold in the regular provincial bureaucracy. In 1843, Ch'i-ying's adjutant, the Han Chinese "pacifist" Huang En-t'ung became sub-governor in charge of judicial affairs, and even, for a brief interlude (1845–1846), governor, At the same time, Ch'i-ying himself, as we have mentioned, was able to appropriate the office of governor general for himself for a three-year period (1844–1847). But that was all. The bulwark of official resistance to the local anti-treaty movement was thus very fragile indeed. And, for that very reason, the likelihood was that much greater that the mandarins would condone or run before it, rather than resist it.

But, of course, official attitudes, and the absence of a strong guiding hand from Peking, only partly explain the dangerous showdown with the British at Canton in 1849. The other important factor was the existence of deep-seated mercantile and scholar-class grievances against the new diplomatic order that Ch'i-ying and the treaty system had imposed upon the Cantonese from above. Coming together during the panic created in the aftermath of the British raid of 1847, this pair of grievances was to bring into the field an unusually strong coalition of local elites determined to block full implementation of the treaty provisions. And it was that coalition that would eventually bring down Ch'i-ying and annul the agreement he had made with the British in 1847.

The more volatile of the two disaffected groups in postwar Canton was undoubtedly the merchant (or, more accurately, the merchant-artisan) class of that city—a group that was perturbed over the way Ch'i-ying and the (largely) Manchu negotiating team at Nanking had bartered away its previously privileged position in China's export trade. In all likelihood, anti-Manchu sentiment among this segment of the populace was already running strong, even before the end of the fighting. It had, after all, been a Manchu general—I-shan—who had pushed the city to the front lines of the war, and who had then, in defeat, squeezed its wealthy to pay the ransom the British had demanded.[12] But, however strong such sentiments had been in 1842, there is no doubt that they grew stronger still in the wake of the Manchu government's decision to accede to the opening of the tea-exporting entrepot of Foochow, and of the Yangtze, in 1842—concessions that opened the way for a rerouting of the tea and silk export trade away from Canton.[13]

The disaffections created by this latter concession had already given rise to a series of ugly clashes with both officials and foreigners in the vicinity of Canton in the immediate postwar years. But much worse was still to come. For, in the early months of 1847, the city's economy sustained even more damage as the influence of the London financial panic of 1845 gradually caught up to the Sino-British trade and bit into what remained of Canton's export business. And then—as if to guarantee that the flames of resentment would burn more brightly still—came the invasion scare of April 1847, touched off by Major D'Aguilar's reoccupation of the Bogue forts. To a great many Cantonese, the significance of this renewed military action by the enemy could only be that the British were planning to penetrate directly into Canton's West River hinterland, so as to capture for themselves the profits of the inland transport trade running between Kwangtung and the Yangtze valley. These fears were increased, moreover, by the news that Ch'i-ying had agreed to lease warehouse space to the foreigners inside the city itself, and by the information (in this case, false) that the authorities had also promised to sell the British land in the upriver suburbs of Canton for the construction of unspecified additional facilities. All through the summer months of 1847, therefore, the city continued to buzz with rumors of the hated Manchu governor general's complicity in yet further concessions. And, in the meanwhile, a committee of urban merchants and shopowners was constituted, quite without the permission of the government, in order to raise a band of militiamen for defense. The merchants of Canton would fight, if they had to, to prevent any further outrage.[14]

In the end, however, it is doubtful that the antipathies of the tradesmen and artisans of Canton alone would have been sufficient to unseat Ch'i-ying, had it not been for the encouragement that these urban leaders received from a second aggrieved local constituency—the scholarly militia directors of the city's academy system. For, without the help of this latter mediating group, it would have been vastly more difficult for the anti-Ch'i-ying forces to approach the high officials in Canton itself, and to come to an understanding with those among them who shared in the hostility to the governor general.

Why the scholars of Canton should have wished to throw in their lot with the movement to expel Ch'i-ying is, however, the problem that must first be addressed. The origins of the hostility that Ch'i-ying was to face from this second quarter can be traced back to the campaign which that unhappy Manchu diplomat had launched in 1842 (through the medium of his local agent, Huang En-t'ung) to pare down the paramilitary units under the control of the Ta-fo-ssu Bureau. These attempts were not successful, since, in the first place, Ch'i and Huang never possessed authority adequate to force the local officials to cooperate with them, and since, also, the local mandarins were in no mood to risk a collapse of law and order merely to serve the abstract purposes of the new diplomacy. But the effort itself was sufficient to stir up considerable suspicion about Ch'i-ying's motives among the scholars who had become involved in managing the new paramilitary units during the last months of the war. The discontent provoked by Ch'i-ying's actions in this regard was to surface in 1847, when the scholars would help fan the flames of protest against the Manchu governor general's conduct.

Initially, perhaps, Ch'i-ying simply had not appreciated the degree

to which local security needs had become intertwined with the perpetuation of the wartime militia arrangements. Or perhaps, acting
out of traditional Manchu military prejudices, he had convinced himself that it was simply unwise for there to be so strong a force of men
at arms under local elite control, when regular government forces in
the area were still weak and demoralized.[15] Whatever the case, the
signs are unmistakable that he and the peace forces in the capital and
in Canton resolved upon an all-out campaign to dissolve the paramilitaries very soon after the treaty agreements were signed at Nanking.

The crackdown on this "Canton army" had begun in October
1842, when a new Tartar general, the 74-year-old imperial clansman
I-li-pu, was ordered to proceed to Canton to replace the outspokenly
pro-militia I-shan.[16] I-li-pu had brought with him, as his adjutant, the
notoriously pacifist (and anti-milita) Chinese official Huang En-
t'ung, whom we have previously encountered as the writer of the
tract on the outmodedness of traditional strategic formulae on maritime defense that provoked Wei Yuan's ire.[17] It had not taken long for
Huang to swing into action. Soon after his arrival in Canton, a series
of complaints began mysteriously to pour forth from the censorate
in Peking decrying the way in which the Cantonese defense forces
had been abusing their power. On 26 September 1842, an unidentified "someone" in Peking had brought to the court's attention that
the mercenaries of the Canton new army had been allowed by the
officials and gentry nominally in control of them to "routinely terror-
ize" the boat people of the delta (the tenants, that is to say, who
worked the licensed reclamation holdings under the Canton bureau's
authority). These militia were, it now seemed, little better than a
gang of bullies who ought to be reined in or demobilized.[18] Then, on
12 November, just on the eve of I-li-pu's arrival in Canton, another
mysterious someone in Peking brought forward yet further hearsay
evidence concerning the activities of the Cantonese irregulars. Their
two principal leaders. Huang P'ei-fang and Hsu T'ing-k'uei, were
widely believed to be peculating from the purchase of rations; the
army itself consisted almost entirely of hired ruffians and not (as
reported) loyal village peasants; and the entire community of knowledgeable and respectable people in Canton were said to hate Hsu and
Huang for the harm that their actions had brought upon the city.[19]
Though there is no satisfactory evidence of precisely what if any
actions had resulted from this latter impeachment, the charges seem

at least to have finished off Hsu and Huang, neither of whose names appear on rosters of the leadership of the irregulars at Canton during the remainder of the decade.[20] And then, finally, had come demobilization itself—or at least, partial demobilization—of the professionalized contingents of Canton's defense force. Again, it is not clear exactly when or on what scale this took place. But Liang T'ing-nan, one of the Canton academicians in charge of the irregulars, indicates that some demobilization did occur, and that the immediate result was a noticeable increase in banditry in the suburbs of the city.[21]

At that point, however, the campaign had run into local official resistance. The reason seems to have been the very same outbreak of lawlessness that Liang and other chroniclers of local events noticed as one of the first consequences of demobilization. By weakening the coercive machinery that had enforced the scholar-gentry version of law and order in the delta's shoal-fields while simultaneously injecting thousands of unemployed military professionals into the ranks of the local underworld, Ch'i-ying had, of course, greatly encouraged such a development. (Though, one might add, increases in tenant-and underworld-organized violence seem to have been ubiquitous in those parts of the coast where there had been serious fighting, probably reflecting the loss in government prestige occasioned by the systematic defeat of its soldiers.)[22] The response of the local authorities, logically enough, had been to help the scholars reorganize the patrol forces, if perhaps in a slightly more decentralized fashion than had been the case earlier. Governor Ch'eng Yü-ts'ai had been the one to take the first step in this direction, in 1844, when he licensed the formation of a so-called Sha-Chiao vigilante league in the southern and eastern suburbs of the city. (The name was an abbreviation for two jurisdictions in P'an-yü county—Sha-wan and Chiao-t'ang—where problems of underworld lawlessness were particularly severe.) Moreover, during the next two years, at least five more such impromptu organizations had been established in the more outlying reaches of the Pearl River estuary, likewise with the approval of the civil authorities.[23] Thus, Ch'i-ying's efforts to reduce the paramilitaries had not failed to produce results, but they had taught the scholars and dissident local officials the habit of collaborating against Peking's leadership in the interest of advancing their own idea of how local order ought to be maintained.

The enmity of this latter law-and-order constituency was to prove particularly problematic for Ch'i-ying during the crucial days of the so-called real-estate panic touched off in the city of Canton by the 1847 British seizure of the Bogue forts. Protest placards and scholar petitions, later recovered from the Liang-Kuang governor general's yamen by the British, reveal that the Sha-Chiao league—that reorganized version of the Ta-fo-ssu Bureau—was the principal organizational vehicle behind the mob violence that broke out in the city in June and July 1847. The Sha-Chiao League directorate seems also to have been active in spreading fears of British-inspired land confiscation well out into Canton's western (upriver) suburbs, and in perpetuating rumors of a projected foreign real-estate grab within the city even after Ch'i-ying had publicly announced that no sales or other agreements would be made. But, most ominously of all, these same confiscated records reveal that the Leaguers had undertaken these acts of sabotage against Ch'i-ying with the full consent and encouragement of the recently appointed governor, Hsu Kuang-chin, and of his second-in-command, Yeh Ming-ch'en.[24]

Whether Hsu and Yeh were acting merely in defense of what they perceived as enlightened local official interests, or whether there is more to it than that (Yeh's brother was, after all, a Shrine Association leader), is difficult to say. But, whatever the exact motives behind this partnership, the effect it wrought upon Ch'i-ying and his policies could not have been more devastating. Aware, at last, that his earlier demobilization blunder had created dangerous levels of resentment among the militia leaders, Ch'i-ying now hurriedly tried to repair the damage. In mid-June, he wrote to the emperor to suggest that it would be wise to bring "respectable" academy directors from the city and suburbs directly into all future negotiations with the British, so as to head off any further needless rumormongering. However, as Tao-kuang was quick to realize, it hardly made sense to keep that unpopular Manchu official in Canton as the court's emissary if the management of local diplomatic affairs was henceforth to be overseen by a scholar-official commission. Ch'i-ying had, after all, a very bad record in his dealings with local "public opinion" in the past. The report of the formation of the new commission (received in Peking on 9 September) thus led quite swiftly to a court decision to begin edging the venerable Manchu diplomat out of his seat of power.[25] On 6 December, a highly irregular secret edict was dispatched directly to Ch'i-ying's subordinate, Governor Hsu Kuang-chin, empowering him to submit his own evaluation of Ch'i-ying's diplomatic chief-of-staff, Huang En-t'ung, and to replace him if so desired; and instructing Hsu, at the same time, that "quieting the people's feelings" (that is, appeasing the scholar-gentry) was henceforth to be considered a higher priority than meeting British demands. Hsu, in other words, was to begin taking over the conduct of future negotiations. On 3 February 1848, the new situation was formally recognized with the recall of Ch'i-ying "for an audience" in Peking. The Manchu grasp over Canton diplomacy, never very sure, had now been surrendered for good.[26]

SHOWDOWN

This sudden change in the complexion of local diplomatic authority left unresolved one crucial problem: Was the Ch'ing still bound to honor Ch'i-ying's 1847 agreement to throw Canton open to British residence in April 1849? Nor was this so simple a matter as Hsu and Yeh seem originally to have thought. For, in spite of the highly confident tone of the new diplomatic commission's reports to Peking, the emperor and his advisers remained stubbornly convinced that it would be folly to test British resolve anew. Over and over Peking continued to caution Hsu and Yeh on this point, and to urge them to offer the British some sort of face-saving gesture (such as a walk, perhaps, inside the city!), even while assuring the scholar-commissioners that no real change in the exclusionist status quo had taken place.[27]

Yet, in the event, the glory-seeking Hsu and Yeh were ultimately able to deal more firmly with Bonham. First, they flatly refused to comply with the 1847 agreement, then they mobilized the "loyal militia" of Canton and the suburbs as a demonstration that the Ch'ing side was willing to use force to back up this new policy. Finally, they encouraged merchant guilds to organize a total trade boycott in order to redouble the pressure on Bonham to back away from his demand.[28]

What had persuaded the local authorities to step out onto this apparently dangerous course of defiance was the perception, reinforced by American-supplied intelligence, that the British were not in fact prepared to use military force again in the Canton Gulf, as they had been in 1841 and 1847. All through 1848, Hsu had been receiving reports through merchant channels that the current business depression in England and the increase in Anglo-French tensions following the collapse of the July monarchy in France were sure to render Britain much less willing to gamble on another war in far-off China.[29] Hsu's confidence in his calculation that Bonham would not resort to force seems to have been further strengthened, at the last minute, by an American report that London had just ordered Bonham not to go to the hilt on the Canton question. Rather, he was to hoard diplomatic and military capital for more important questions, such as the planned exchange of Foochow and Ningpo for better-situated ports in the Yangtze valley.[30] Interestingly, this latter bit of information was not passed on to Peking. But it apparently emboldened Hsu to proceed with still less caution in his confrontation with Bonham, even to the point of forging an imperial edict representing the abrogation of the 1847 agreement as a matter of court as well as local policy.[31] Just as expected, Bonham, under instructions not to push the matter, had then yielded with only a pro forma protest about the "bad faith" of the Ch'ing side.

Of such stuff, then, was made that second great triumph of popular resistance in Kwangtung. As Hsu and Yeh knew quite well, there never really had been much of a chance that their bluff would be called—which is probably why they decided to take the risk in the first place. Nor, of course, had there been any real test of the paramilitaries. But these trivial details did not seem at the time to detract from the larger truth that had just been demonstrated about British strengths and weaknesses. It was, after all, just as Wei Yuan and Yao Ying had said it would be. The British truly were an over-extended imperial power, as their unwillingness to shift troops back out to China had just proven. And the cooperation the Ch'ing had secured from the Americans had revealed for all enlightened men to see that the barbarians were not united, and that Britain's maritime rivals could be enlisted in the cause of Ch'ing China's defense.

Thus, the reports that went up to Peking to announce the news of the Ch'ing triumph did not hesitate to speak most encouragingly of the higher principles of diplomacy that had just been reestablished. The British retreat, Tao-kuang was given to understand, was proof final that this enemy feared "the people," even if he did not fear the emperor's armies. So long as the court was able to command the uncompromised loyalty of its subjects (the loyalty, that is, of the lettered elite), it would be able in the end to "trim the [British] arrogance, and render them dependent on us."[32] And, lest the significance of the recent events at Canton be missed, Hsu and Yeh enclosed in their dispatch announcing Bonham's "surrender" a copy of the "public letter of admonition" that the "scholars of Canton" had addressed to Bonham on the eve of the May 1849 showdown. It could have been written in 1841 under the influence of the excitement over San-yuan-li. The "unity of the people had become strong as a rampart." How, the scholars then asked rhetorically, could the tiny British garrison of two or three thousand on Hong Kong dare to throw themselves against the several millions waiting to fight them at Canton? And if there really were to be a war, would that not mean "precipitously transferring soldiers from the [British] empire's other entrepots, and taxing the merchants [of these other colonies] to pay for it—in effect, sacrificing the important for the trivial?"[33]

Out of the disturbances created by Ch'i-ying's futile confrontation with the elite of Canton, there had thus evolved by mid-1849 two serious setbacks for the cause of Manchu diplomacy. First, Ch'i-ying himself had been humiliated and ousted from Kwangtung, left in the lurch by an emperor who did not regard the outcome of the negotiations at Canton as sufficiently important to warrant going to the aid of his chief representative. And, second, through the testimonials of Governor General Hsu, the literati had been given their cue to revive once again the Wei Yuan strategy for dealing with the foreign threat. This latter development was perhaps the more threatening of the two, at least from the standpoint of the conservative peace party leaders still nominally in control of policy in the capital. For now, under the influence of this renewed literati belligerence, the monarchy appeared ready to slide back into its earlier, more opportunistic approach to foreign-policy questions. If that was not yet obvious from its handling of the Canton imbroglio in 1849, it would soon be demonstrated all too clearly in the way that the court would choose to dispose of the Bonham appeal of May 1850.

THE BONHAM LETTER

The effect upon Mu-chang-a's political fortunes of the 1849 coup at Canton, though not yet decisive, was nonetheless highly detrimental. The loss of influence that he and his policies had suffered in the wake of Hsu Kuang-chin's triumph was to become clear almost immediately from the new, independent tone that crept into the Hsien-feng emperor's pronouncements during the brief flurry over the so-called Bonham Letter, delivered to the court in May 1850, in protest against Ch'ing policies over the Canton question. Suddenly, there began to creep back into the imperial utterances on foreign relations some of the same lack of caution and apparent self-confidence that had, on the whole, been missing since 1842. True, behind this shift back toward intransigence lurked other, perhaps more fundamental domestic concerns, to which we shall presently come. But there were also unmistakable signs that the surprising British retreat over the Canton question in 1849 had sown serious doubts in the new ruler's mind about the wisdom of the unqualified conciliationism that Mu-chang-a had continued to advocate all through this crisis. A brief glance at how this second, 1850 scare was handled will bring to light just how much Hsu's triumph had transformed the court's outlook on the question of the Sino-British treaties to the disadvantage of the chief grand councillor and his policies.

The Bonham Letter was, in fact, a production of Foreign Secretary Palmerston, and had been sent to Hong Kong on 18 August 1849, after word had reached London of the Ch'ing government's revocation of the 1847 understanding on the Canton question. In this letter of protest, which had been duly translated into Chinese, and addressed to the "ministers for foreign affairs" Mu-chang-a and Ch'i-ying, Palmerston asked for an imperial reversal of Hsu Kuang-chin's exclusion decision, and for a cancellation of a Cantonese gentry project to erect a tablet of honor to Hsu and his subordinate, Governor Yeh Ming-ch'en. On the assumption that Hsu Kuang-chin could not be trusted to communicate these demands to the capital, the British plenipotentiary, Sir George Bonham, had been instructed to convey them in person to the Shanghai intendant. If that still failed to secure their transmission to Peking, Bonham was to fetch them to the mouth of the Pei-ho for submission to the court under the implied (but unsupported) threat of a naval action against Peking itself.[34]

In the event, the mere threat of another British naval intrusion into the Gulf of Chihli proved sufficient to induce the "great officers" at Shanghai to relay the letter post haste to Peking, where it arrived on 28 May (followed, two days later, by the arrival of the sloop HMS *Reynard* off the mouth of the Pei-ho, carrying Interpreter W. H. Medhurst with a duplicate copy). Nevertheless, a full two weeks were to expire between the receipt of the protest and the peaceful departure of the *Reynard* (on 11 June). During this interlude the new monarch was clearly worried that he was faced with another very real threat of war, as becomes obvious from a number of retrospective references to actions taken in this two-week period that turn up in later imperial edicts. And that was precisely the impression Bonham intended Medhurst's excursions to the Pei-ho (with its overtones of Elliot's fateful trip to Tientsin in August 1840) to supply. On the other hand, if Bonham was only bluffing—and there were those at court who claimed that he undoubtedly was—then how far should the throne be willing to go in testing him?[35]

It is obvious, too, that during this same two-week interval, Mu-chang-a was doing his very best to portray Hsu Kuang-chin as a mindless provocateur and to win the emperor over to reinstating Ch'i-ying. This becomes evident, in the first place, from the fact that, on 18 June, just after tensions had begun to abate, the emperor ordered the Grand Council to assemble for his own perusal a full transcript of Ch'i-ying's and Hsu Kuang-chin's past memorials on Kwangtung diplomacy, commencing from the time of the April 1847 raid by D'Aguilar on the Bogue forts, and continuing on down to the moment that the Bonham Letter reached Peking. How had the two rivals opined on the Canton entry question, the emperor now wanted to know? And was it really the case (as Mu-chang-a claimed) that Ch'i-ying was the more responsible of the pair? Moreover, in December, within the text of the damning edict that cast both Mu-chang-a and Ch'i-ying from imperial grace, there was to appear yet further confirmation of how Mu-chang-a had tried to reimpose Ch'i-ying upon the emperor. Things had even progressed to the point of a special private audience, arranged by Mu-chang-a, for the purpose of impressing upon the emperor the Manchu version of events that had recently transpired in the south.[36]

Yet, in the end, there was no reinstatement of Ch'i-ying. And Hsien-feng decided, after all, to go his own way—sitting tight and refusing to make any immediate concessions until it could be established for sure that Bonham had been authorized to use force. "These barbarians," an edict of 3 June instructed the nervous Chihli governor general, Norjinga, "have violated the treaties in coming here. Their intent is but to cow us with empty threats." If Medhurst wanted only to take up the Canton question again, he was to be sent packing; there was nothing to discuss. Of course, there was still a certain amount of hedging in all this—for Hsien-feng was not yet quite sure of himself as a diplomatist. If the British brought more ships to Pei-ho, or if Medhurst had other, more "reasonable" demands, then talks might be conducted. But, no matter what the case might be, Hsien-feng had decided he was not going to overrule Hsu on the Canton-entry matter or to encourage the British to think that a Manchu prince might be a softer touch than his Chinese servants in the south.[37] And when, at last, the *Reynard* finally weighed anchor and departed again for Shanghai, confirming that Bonham had been bluffing, the exultant emperor permitted himself his first truly extravagant gesture of bravado. On 12 June, but one day after Medhurst's leave-taking, a top-priority message went out reiterating the emperor's summons of Lin Tse-hsu to the capital, and ordering the officials in Fukien not to let reports of Lin's weakened physical condition be an obstacle to his resumption of office. Two days after that, a confident edict was rushed off to all coastal governors general and governors, instructing them to undertake appropriate preparations for defense. The Ch'ing would show that it was not scared by the prospect of war.[38]

Did this mean, then, that a decision had been taken to alter the basic direction of Ch'ing diplomacy? Hardly. For, in spite of all the apparent belligerence in his management of the Bonham Letter affair, Hsien-feng was still not in the mood to attempt any positive new departures on his own. Mu-chang-a was to survive for another half year as chief councillor, and it would be months before the new emperor would allow the censors to gush forth with their opinions on what should come next.[39] But a new conviction had nonetheless been implanted into the young emperor's mind—one that augured poorly for the future of Mu-chang-a's brand of diplomacy. That was the conviction that the British would not lightly undertake another war in China, no matter what Mu-chang-a might say to the contrary. Following the example set by Hsu in Kwangtung, Hsien-feng had now tested the enemy's resolve and found it weaker than expected. If nothing else, this meant at least that Hsien-feng would not be nearly so concerned as his father had been to curb the literati for fear of provoking another fight with Britain. The authority of the peace government had thus suffered its first serious blow—all thanks to the valiant militiamen of Kwangtung.

THE CRISIS IN KWANGSI

If the hold of the Manchu diplomatists in Peking had been first loosened by events moving out of control along the empire's maritime periphery, it would be the uncontrollability of the inland periphery—of the turbulent sub-Yangtze provinces—that would administer the *coup de grace*. There, in the famine-wracked mountainous reaches of Kwangsi and southern Hunan, was the second dangerously exposed flank of the authoritarian leadership that had been in the ascendancy in the capital since 1842—a second corner of the Ch'ing empire where events could easily get out of hand in a way that would cast doubt upon the wisdom of the chief councillor's policies. Only this time, the embarrassment for Mu-chang-a and his followers would be considerably more dangerous, politically, than that incurred over the Canton question. What was at stake here, in this second distant periphery, was nothing less than the internal security of the Ch'ing empire itself. This was an area of government where there could be no indulgent condoning of mistakes, no cautious waiting to see how the dust would settle. Once the alert was sounded, the court would be obliged to act fast. And the remedy that would have to be invoked was not one that could be easily administered with an unpopular and elitist Manchu cabal still holding on to power at court. This remedy was to arm the literati—a group implacably hostile to the Manchu interest at court and only too eager to exploit this second of its weaknesses in order to drive that interest from power.

The embarrassing flimsiness of Mu-chang-a's control over the situation in this inland periphery resulted, in a sense, from the same administrative minimalism that had vitiated government authority in Kwangtung during the crisis of 1849–1850. Kwangsi province, where the trouble began, was another of those administrative units marginal to the empire's supply and revenue systems. In fact, it was even more marginal than Kwangtung, and normally required major injections of funds from other provinces (chiefly from Kwangtung) to maintain the government's constabulary forces. Such a commitment of external revenues was not likely to be forthcoming from a tax-starved postwar government in Peking concerned mainly with the security of the Yangtze and northern coastal regions—any more than it had been forthcoming for Kwangtung during the critical second phase of the 1840–1842 war.[40]

At the same time, however, Kwangsi—like the southernmost portion of Hunan that it abutted—had to cope with problems of economic, social, and agricultural dislocation in the postwar period that were far more severe even than those faced by the authorities in next-door Kwangtung. Heavy concentrations of shiftless and volatile immigrants; dense aboriginal populations, implacable in their resentment of Han interlopers; a miserable marketing and transport infrastructure that made food distribution and prices a perennial problem; and a heavy dependency on unstable secondary occupations like opium smuggling or porterage—all these circumstances conspired to make of nineteenth-century Kwangsi an administrative nightmare, and a difficult place to control even in the best of times.[41]

The late 1840s were very far from being the best of times for Kwangsi. First, there were a whole rash of new problems brought on, in one way or another, by the 1840–1842 war and the economic changes that followed it. One was the opening of the Yangtze (and of the tea-producing hill country of Fukien and Chekiang) to direct access by British buyers or their agents. By virtue of this new arrangement, much of the seasonal transport work—the fetching of Bohea teas and of Taihu silks over the Meiling Pass—that had traditionally supported the poorer peasants in this province was suddenly eliminated. The British navy's imposition of a tough new law-and-order regime along the shipping lanes of the southeast also hurt Kwangsi. It produced a steadily growing influx of an unsavory population—uprooted smugglers, pirates, and other outlaws—who now settled down in the province to prey upon the commerce of the interior.[42]

But perhaps even more disruptive than these war-induced dislocations was the succession of crop failures that blighted the entire rural economy of the sub-Yangtze south in 1847, and again in the winter of 1849–1850. By the final months of 1849, this wave of natural disasters had already sufficiently crimped the food supply in southern Hunan to precipitate another Yao aborigine rebellion, whose development proceeded along a trajectory remarkably similar to that followed by the Yao insurgents of 1832. Routed by local militia and government troops, the rebels (headed by Li Yuan-fa) had been forced to flee their native counties in Hunan and had swept into neighboring Kwangsi, where the local elite was militarily weaker, and thus easier prey. Settling down in this new terrain, Li and his followers had joined the river pirates of Lo Ta-kang in raiding the river commerce of inland Kwangsi and in wreaking general havoc upon the province. In the wake of this second "bandit" intrusion, gangster rule is reported to have inundated as much as 70 percent of the territory of the province by the time the Hsien-feng emperor came to the throne, early in 1850.[43]

Yet, faced with this galloping disintegration of its authority—soon to result in the rise of a fanatic Christianized army that would conquer and hold the vital Yangtze region under the standard of the "Taiping Heavenly Kingdom"—the high officials in the provincial capital of Kweilin seemed surprisingly inert. Complaints from local magistrates and delegations of scholars from the outlying county seats got no results. Stubbornly, seemingly uncaringly, the provincial governor, Cheng Tsu-ch'en, refused to dispatch his garrison units much beyond the vicinity of Kweilin itself. Nor could he be persuaded to make a full report to Peking about the need for such broader patrols, so that reinforcements and extra funds might be sent in from Hunan and Kwangtung. Why was the response so lethargic?[44]

For the answer to this question, we must digress briefly to discuss the strategic and financial problems that were preoccupying the Manchu reform government in the capital at the same time as this unfavorable situation was developing in Kwangsi. For it was ultimately these problems of the central government that hamstrung Governor Cheng, preventing him from taking decisive action lest the Peking authorities be forced to divert additional scarce revenues in his support. The Peking government had, in the first place, to keep the central government bureaucracy running smoothly, the soldiers of the metropolitan garrison fed, and the Canal transport system operating—all with transfer revenues from the provinces virtually stopped and with the level of deposits in the Peking treasuries at an all-time dynastic low. The 20-million-tael indemnity imposed by Great Britain and the roughly equal amount that had been drained off in military expenditures during the war took their toll also, since they had depleted the few public and private concentrations of liquid resources still intact at the beginning of the fighting. Then, too, so had the Board of Revenue embezzlement cases, which had revealed to alarmed authorities that 9 million taels believed to be on deposit in the capital were really not there at all. And, finally, there had been the predictable demands of the Yellow River conservancy. That river, allowed, apparently, to go somewhat under-maintained in 1841, had paid back the oversight with a disastrous series of ruptures in the summer of 1842. The repairs required still further outlays from the provincial treasuries, and thus ate more deeply still into the revenue surpluses normally available for remittance to the capital.[45]

These losses had naturally placed great strains upon the managers of the empire's central-government finances. Indeed, for one terrible moment in the spring of 1843, the emperor had even been forced to consider cutting back on the stipends of the banner soldiers on duty in the metropolitan garrisons. Moreover, on top of all of this, the court was determined, come what may, to do something to improve coastal defenses. Or to improve them, at least, in the vicinity of the capital, in order to prevent another sudden scare at Tientsin. Even if skimping elsewhere, the Mu-chang-a government did manage to come up with 1 million taels for the outfitting of the Ta-ku forts with new, heavy brass cannon and for the creation of a new, 6,500-man cavalry squadron for mobile warfare along the flat Chihli coastline. Moreover, it fully intended, too, that the lower Yangtze provinces (Kiangsu, Chekiang, and Anhwei) should have their fortifications rebuilt as well, and that, if possible, the river navy should be improved in order to protect the tribute-grain fleet from attack.[46]

Intent on meeting these twin objectives—restoration of central government finances, and rearmament in the north and the Yangtze valley—the postwar reform leadership in Peking was to show itself ruthlessly determined to force the provincial administrators of northern and central China to reassume their long-ignored statutory levels of revenue deposits and of yearly transfers to the capital. So determined were they in this matter, in fact, that in 1848, a special revenue-dunning commission (almost entirely Manchu in its membership) was constituted in the capital to handle the paperwork and to dish out the appropriate fines and punishments to tardy officials. And who but the ever unpopular Ch'i-ying (now back in the capital after his failure in Canton) should have been asked to serve as head of this commission?[47]

The consequences for government policy toward the mounting crisis in Kwangsi were predictable. As the better informed literati of that province would soon become aware, law and order in Kwangsi had become a minor priority for the government in Peking, and would readily be sacrificed by Mu-chang-a and his allies if other needs arose. More specifically, the scholars of Kweilin would realize that Governor Cheng himself had been under orders for some years to avoid any actions or reports that might signal a need for help from the outside. For Mu-chang-a wanted no further burdens imposed upon his already inadequate fiscal machine—least of all from this miserably isolated and marginal corner of the empire. And that was why the appeals for action, and the local elite petitions for a more vigorous campaign against the "bandits," had failed to bring any results.

At this point, however, we might profitably turn our attention to the documents that record how local elite opinion in Kwangsi (and Hunan) was coming to view this perplexing behavior on the part of the central government. The perspective from this particular quarter is of special interest to us here because it would ultimately be from this source that the opposition leaders in Peking would draw their most compelling evidence against the Mu-chang-a regime. Chu Ch'i, Lung Ch'i-jui, and Wang Hsi-chen—to list only the most prominent figures among the Kweilin scholarly elite—were all active in the Ku Shrine Association. And, as pupils of Mei Tseng-liang, they would naturally have been in close touch with Tseng Kuo-fan as that latter leader organized the challenge to Mu-chang-a in the spring of 1850. Furthermore, Lung was an examination protégé of Tu Shou-t'ien, former tutor of the new emperor and a very important man at court during the inaugural years of the new reign.[48] The scandal that these Kwangsi scholars had begun to sense in the way the bureaucracy was hiding the disorders in Kwangsi thus would quickly come to the attention alike of the Southern City opposition and of the emperor himself (through Grand Secretary Tu). Much of the correspondence that conveyed to the capital the details of what was going on still survives; and we ought therefore to pause here, briefly, to see what it tells us about the literati viewpoint at this critical juncture.

A letter of Lung Ch'i-jui to his mentor, Mei Tseng-liang (probably dating from late 1850), is the richest in this series of documents, so we might begin with a sample of the opinions it had to offer concerning the current state of affairs. Lung was at the time on home leave in Kweilin, but he had obviously been taking considerable interest in the progress of the rebels, and had been asking a great many questions about why Governor Cheng had been so inactive. Here is what he had to relate to Mei:

The county-level official has little discretionary authority. But there is certainly enough power here to discover the activities of those treacherous types who swear followers to their cause and organize bands. Yet when this information is passed upward to the province, [the authorities at this higher level] . . . are content to tolerate it and cover it up. And if there are one or two aggressive and capable subordinates [who persist], they will be reprimanded and scolded. Thus they are given to realize that their [chief] wants them to desist. Yet even the provincial officials do not necessarily believe that this is the ideal state of affairs. . . . Sitting over them is the "prime minister" who indirectly signals his intentions to them. His message is that floods, droughts, and lawlessness are not to be routinely reported [to Peking], for such tidings will "trouble the Imperial Concern." And, besides, there are limits to the funds available to the state; you should not [suggests the minister] be asking for outlays on every minor pretext. . . . Now the province chiefs are all of scholar [i.e., examination-system] background . . . and they depend on influence [in the capital] to win their transfers and promotions. They thus cannot do without the help of the "prime minister." If they act without first consulting him, their project will fall through. . . . So, when they are forewarned, none will dare take up such matters again.

Now the [disturbances that produced the] rebel band in Chin-t'ien [i.e., the Taipings] date back to 1834–1835. . . . The governor then was [Liang Chang-chü]. He used to amuse himself day in day out with poetry and drinking expeditions in the hills. His successor was likewise unwilling to do anything about the lawlessness. The man who succeeded him [Cheng Tsu-ch'en] is the one I have described as "shaping his actions to the wishes of the prime minister."[49]

The inaction of the authorities in Kweilin, in short, was clearly perceived as the result of policy directed from Peking. And this state of affairs was directly tied to the revenue-obsessed biases of the "prime minister," Mu-chang-a.

Somewhat earlier, however, Lung had already been in touch with several other of his friends and mentors in the capital. To his examiner, Tu Shou-t'ien, he had imparted the following observations during the final days of the Yao rebel invasion of Kwangsi, early in 1850:

As of this moment several [government] detachments are combining their operations [against the invaders from Hunan]. It should not be difficult for us to wipe them out completely. But what I fear is that these insurgents have in the past descended [by surprise] from mountain passes and set upon their targets. If our forces concentrate in the plains and open areas, there is no way we can maintain contact with them. But if we follow them over the hills, they will hold the advantage in tactics . . . and we will have a hard time defeating them.

Even more worrisome are the indigenous bandits in the outlying prefectures and counties. They now gather in bands of several thousand, and lay waste to villages and towns in clear daylight. The young and strong are forced to join up with them, while the old and feeble are forced to flee or allowed to starve to death. Villages have been stripped of dogs and chickens. When the time for spring plowing came, neither water buffaloes nor seed were left. When, soon after, the bandits retreated, there was simply no way to get the plowing [and seeding] done. . . . This is the situation that now exists in Kweilin, P'ing-lo, Hsun-chou, Liu-chou, Ssu-en, and Nan-ning.

The high officials in the province are hamstrung because the number of soldiers is limited, and there isn't much available in the way of funds [to support field operations]. . . . They are attempting to be liberal [i.e., not chasing after every band of insurgents]. They have a good idea of the strengths of the enemy and have been thorough in trying to contain them, but they can't solve the problem of how to procure more funds. Further, [they complain] that, since there are currently no county seats under [bandit] occupation, they cannot ask for the mobilization of a field army from the outside, for this would entail huge expenditures. They also [seem to] be concerned to remember the warnings of the past [i.e., Grand Councillor Mu-chang-a's warnings].

As for the local bandits, they are an ingenious lot. They realize that, if they seize the county towns, they will draw down on themselves a full imperial army. So, wherever they pass, they content themselves with stripping the villages and towns practically bare, and do their best to avoid contact with government soldiers. . . .

The officials in charge of the province work day and night on their strategy. [But they cannot get around the fact that] if they bring many soldiers into the field, they won't be able to pay for them. Whereas if they keep them in their garrisons, each unit will be [too] weak [to act].[50]

In tandem with these private letters of Lung, moreover, there also converged upon the capital a whole stream of angry petitions carried up from the south in the spring of 1850 by the Kwangsi scholars arriving for the triennial examinations.[51] The effect of these petitions can be glimpsed from the remarks of another Shrine Association scholar, the Hunanese Sun Ting-ch'en, who wrote back to Kweilin, in mid-1850, to report (in verse) how strong an impression they had made, and to urge Lung to set out at once for Peking to help push the protest movement forward:

There is new fighting at the K'un-lun Pass
The jackals and wolves have not yet been cleared from the mountain fortresses,
They raid into T'ien-chou [in Ssu-en-fu, Kwangsi] and then into Ho-chou.
The wail and lament [of the people] shakes the fringes of the empire, where the yellow clouds scud,
The militia lies demobilized, and cannot fight.
The county magistrate's head has been severed, and none retrieve it,

The Emperor Hsien-feng sits now upon his throne,
And summons his ministers to audience to inquire about the woes of his
subjects.
The examination candidates have been summoned by imperial order from the
distant reaches,
They moan out their grievances, but show no anger.
A pity that [Master Lung] has not yet been summoned [to court],
But lives still in his cottage, by the reeds in the icy stream.
When you [examination candidates] get back, go converse with our censor
[Chu Ch'i],
Tell him that he must hurry his return for the sake of the people.[52]

Within but weeks of the new emperor's accession, therefore, Southern City rumor circuits were abuzz with angry whispers about the way in which the diplomacy interest at court had been condoning the spreading anarchy along the Kwangsi-Hunan border. Though more than purely local grievances against the emperor's chief minister lay behind this rumor campaign, the important thing for the moment was that the specifics of the accusation were entirely accurate. Mu-chang-a apparently really had elected to sacrifice the province of Kwangsi as a pawn in his larger game. Control really had been knowingly allowed to lapse on the assumption that it probably did not matter very much in the long run whether the government or the secret societies ran the Kwangsi countryside. What the "prime minister" had not counted upon, however, was the speed with which this lawlessness would spawn a military threat capable of spilling over into the more important provinces to the north—a threat taking the form of the dread legions of the Taiping Heavenly Kingdom. As the enormity of the danger gradually dawned upon the new emperor, his resolve would grow ever more firm. Mu-chang-a would have to be abandoned. And abandoned in a way that would leave no doubt about the emperor's determination to make his peace anew with the leaders of literati opinion.

THE RECALL OF LIN TSE-HSU

Having brought into focus the predicament of the Mu-chang-a government as of early 1850 and the threats that confronted it in the realms of foreign policy and domestic security, we are now in position to return, with somewhat sharpened insight, to the matter of

Tseng Kuo-fan's April 1850 petition for a broad referendum on bureaucratic talent. Though Tseng's proposal bore all the outward signs of a purely ritual gesture, the motives that lay behind it were eminently political, as we shall see. What Tseng intended, in thus applying to the emperor for a show of inaugural benevolence to the literati, was to prepare the way for a whole series of opposition-planned *démarches* whose purpose would be to extract the maximum amount of damage from the revelation of Mu-chang-a's complicity in hushing up the situation in Kwangsi. The chief councillor's guilt was perhaps sufficient to cause his removal in any case, but Tseng and the infuriated dissidents of the Ku Shrine Association wanted to do a good deal more than simply remove him. They were determined, too, to embarrass his foreign policies by spreading the taint of deceit onto them. Their strategy turned, therefore, on tying the decision about reversing course in Kwangsi as closely (and as embarrassingly) as possible to the question of whether or not to proceed with the dis-mantling of the no-provocations foreign policy so favored by the chief councillor.

The first inkling that this would be the opposition's plan of attack was to appear in the very un-random sampling of talent that the responses to the April referendum produced—ostensibly as recom-mendations for possible leaders of the government's war against the Kwangsi rebels. The leading vote-getters—Lin Tse-hsu, Yao Ying, and Chou T'ien-chueh—were without exception individuals who had the most terrifying sort of reputation as diplomatic intransigents. Then, too, they were all well known as darlings of the Mu-chang-a haters in the Southern City. That being the case, the chief councillor could hardly stand quietly by and allow their triumphant return to power—even if he could, somehow, resign himself to a defeat on the matter of dealing with the Kwangsi rebels. He could thus be counted on to raise diplomacy-related objections to any talk of restoring Lin to high office—and to raise such objections in the most vociferous manner possible. But by so doing, he would, of course, only be digging the grave that much deeper for the cause of diplomatic prudence. By December, the emperor would himself become persuaded that his chief minister was merely using diplomacy as a pretext to save his own face. And the slate would thus be wiped clean, both of Mu-chang-a and of his policies.

In addition to Tseng Kuo-fan himself, it is evident that this ingenious strategy had the support, as well, of P'an Shih-en and Tu Shou-t'ien. That, at least, is the impression afforded by the returns these two ministers submitted in response to Tseng's talent referendum, the originals of which are preserved *in toto* in one of the Ch'ing government's state record books.[53] Paging through these documents, we find that the first mention of Lin Tse-hsu occurs on 8 May, when P'an Shih-en, as ever the bellwether of the Peking political scene, put Lin's name forward together with that of Yao Ying. And we discover also that Grand Secretary Tu had seconded the recall of Lin three days later—this time explicitly for the purpose of assigning him bandit-quelling responsibilities. Tu's endorsement, moreover, obviously carried weight. For on the very day that his seconding recommendation came before the throne, the decree went out recalling Lin to the capital. (So also, we might add, did an order summoning Chou T'ien-chueh, another man Tu had nominated).[54]

As expected, Mu-chang-a had immediately sensed in all of this a challenge to his control over foreign policy, and had accordingly fought back stubbornly. Although he could not directly hold up the reinstatement of Lin, he could at least urge the emperor to move cautiously, and to consider carefully the consequences. That strategy, moreover, apparently brought him temporary success. Of this, we have the testimony of the emperor himself, who, on 1 December, would recall with considerable bitterness that Mu had raised all sorts of objections to Lin's reappointment, including the matter of his alleged poor health. And we have, additionally, the evidence of the second recall edict, issued on 12 June, just after the worst days of the Bonham Letter crisis had passed—an edict that, presumably, would not have been necessary had there not been some signaling of indecision to the provincial authorities in the interim.[55] Obviously, then, Mu-chang-a had been able to exploit the sense of panic produced by Medhurst's arrival off the Pei-ho to successfully persuade the emperor to take no immediate action on the Lin recall matter.

But, if diplomacy had saved Mu temporarily in June, it would not prove able to do so again in October, when the chief councillor apparently tried again to block Lin's reassignment to office.[56] Quite the opposite. For this time, the appeal to consider the empire's diplomatic needs had the result of turning the emperor against the very idea of diplomatic necessity itself. What ultimately caused this second effort at obstruction to come undone was, of course, the ever worsening news that kept coming in from Kwangsi. From the emperor's point of view, the continuing deterioration of the government's position in that province seemed to underscore the point that action could no longer be postponed. Moreover, it raised in the emperor's mind the distinct possibility that Mu-chang-a had been using the diplomacy issue all along to prevent the embarrassment and removal of his client, Governor Cheng Tsu-ch'en. This latter suspicion was reinforced, we might here add, by a certain amount of extra prodding from that veteran Mu-chang-a-hater, Censor Lo Tun-yen, whose impeachment of Cheng on 17 October provided the final impetus in resolving the emperor upon sending Lin to Kwangsi.

But by now the rebellion itself was doing the Shrine Association's work for it, and, in the end, that is what goaded Hsien-feng into action. This fact becomes clear if we look at the exact sequence of events surrounding Lin's appointment as Kwangsi commissioner (on 17 October). The appointment of Lin had in fact been preceded by the receipt of a full series of reports highlighting the mismanagement of Governor Cheng's administration. Against the background of the steady deterioration in the government's position revealed by these reports, Mu-chang-a's continued caution on the recall of Lin, and his stubborn refusal to acknowledge that a real crisis existed in Kwangsi, must have looked increasingly suspicious. Diplomatic concerns, the emperor would now come to believe, had been the smokescreen behind which the chief councillor had hidden the proof of his own irresponsibility.

The stratagem, then, had worked more efficiently and more devastatingly than anyone could have foreseen in May, when the Lin recall referendum had first surfaced. The cause of Manchu diplomacy had become, by November, inextricably linked with that of deception of the emperor and of concealing a dangerous threat to the empire's internal security. It would thus be necessary to denounce the diplomats themselves and to phrase the rebuke in the most unambiguous language, so as to insure that no doubt remained about where Hsien-feng's priorities lay.

The decision to undertake such a verbal assault was apparently made some weeks before the promulgation of the grand edict of 1 December—and was held up, in its implementation, chiefly by the derailment of the young emperor's first plan of action. In his hasty search to contrive a plausible public case against Mu-chang-a's and Ch'i-ying's foreign policy, Hsien-feng had hit, first, upon the idea of basing the accusations on the role Ch'i-ying had played (with Mu-chang-a's help, of course) in smoothing the way for the 1844 acceptance of the French demand for the toleration of Roman Catholicism in China. There was no question but that Ch'i had been the guiding force behind the decision to give way to this request. The evidence of that diplomat's activities concerning this matter was readily at hand in the Grand Council's archives. Once that material had been made public, moreover, there would be no difficulty in establishing the connection between the Mu-chang-a government's condoning of the rebels at home (the Taiping were Christian rebels) and its appeasement of the maritime barbarians abroad. However, the young emperor's enthusiasm for the soft-on-Catholics strategy seems to have diminished soon after his initial order calling for a search of the Ch'i-ying papers—perhaps because he had found out, in the interim, about the specifically Protestant genealogy of the Taiping faith. It would never be mentioned in public edicts on foreign policy, and we learn of it today only because the documents attesting Ch'i-ying's role in the toleration treaty of 1844 survive, together with the orders for their assembly, copied neatly in the Council's monthly record book for October-November 1850.[57]

But, even without the Christianity issue to link together the doomed ministry's foreign and domestic policies, there would still have to be a public denunciation of Mu-chang-a's diplomacy. And so there was, on 1 December, when the emperor revived the older theme of "deceiving the emperor" to prove to his own satisfaction that Mu-chang-a's handling of the barbarians and his behavior in Kwangsi were manifestations of the same evil. Announcing, at long last, the removal of the two officials—Mu-chang-a and Ch'i-ying—from all of their posts, the emperor lit in with particular ferocity on the "deceitfulness" of his father's favorite—a flaw he now saw as the unifying cause of every mistake Mu had made since 1842:

Formerly, when the coastal problem [i.e., the 1840 war] was at its height, Mu-chang-a spared no effort in purging his opponents in a most despicable fashion. Loyal and energetic men like Ta-hung-a and Yao Ying were obstacles to his monopoly of power, and so he insisted on bringing them down. [At the same time] he defended, with uncompromised enthusiasm, the shameless and unconscionable actions of Ch'i-ying. Truly a case of "the wicked coming to the aid of the wicked." Similar instances of his abuse of favor and power are too numerous to recite.

[Moreover, since Tao-kuang's death] he has become even more obnoxious in his abuse of Our Graciousness, and has shown not a sign of repentance. During the days following Our Accession in the first months of this year, he equivocated on every major issue and refused to speak out. But after several months had elapsed, he began again to try his old tricks. When the English ship [bearing Bonham's letter] arrived at Tientsin, for example, he sought to have Ch'i-ying reinstated as a confidential adviser [on diplomatic affairs] so as to further his own purposes. In his unspeakable treachery he would have Our Subjects once again trod under [by the barbarians].

[Moreover] when P'an Shih-en and other ministers recommended Lin Tse-hsu, he reiterated many times that Lin had been weakened by poor health, and was not capable of bearing up under the pressures of office. Furthermore, when We personally were considering dispatching Lin Tse-hsu to Kwangsi to take charge of exterminating the insurgents in that province, Mu-chang-a many times voiced his doubts about whether or not Lin was capable of leaving his sickbed. By his distorting and misleading falsehoods, he kept Us ignorant of affairs outside the capital. In this respect his guilt is beyond argument.[58]

The same pattern of deceit was discovered and decried in the actions of Ch'i-ying—and particularly in his habitual discouraging of provocations in dealing with the English:

As for Ch'i-ying—his cowardice and ineptitude are truly astounding. Is not his predilection for compromising the people, truckling to the barbarians, and turning his back on the dignity of his state established beyond a doubt by his argument [two years before] in favor of allowing [the English] to enter the city of Canton? . . . Fortunately, Our Imperial Father saw through his mendacity [during the crisis of 1847] and promptly recalled him to the capital. But he was not punished forthwith, since it was Our Father's policy to be unhasty [in such matters]. Yet, when he was granted an audience with Us this year, he remarked repeatedly how terrifying the English are, and how it behooved us to placate them at every turn, thus deliberately deceiving Us in the belief that we would not notice his perfidy, and in the hope that he might guarantee anew the security of his emoluments and of his office. The more he argues, the more manifest becomes his total lack of scruples. His talk sounds like the yapping and snarling of a dog. Yet he shows not a sign of contrition.[59]

The message was as unequivocal as Hsien-feng dared make it. Here was a clear disavowal, both of the Manchu diplomats, and of their deceitful, risk-exaggerating style of dealing with diplomatic crises. What this denunciation might portend for the future of Ch'ing maritime policy remained, of course, still to be determined. But, as a gesture of conciliation to the leaders of Southern City opinion, its meaning was unmistakable. The emperor had resolved not to forget the one lesson that had been learned from the agonies of the 1840 conflict. No longer would the empire's external relations be considered too important to be subjected to the vicissitudes of literati opinion.

CHAPTER EIGHT

Epilogue

The spectacular uprooting of the Mu-chang-a power group in the capital described in the preceding chapter can be seen in retrospect as having brought to a close an important episode in late Ch'ing political history. The distinct hallmark of this period—one that sets it off markedly from the post-Taiping Rebellion decades—was the prominence of the Manchu-Mongol service aristocracy as a kind of praetorian guard of reform. They had first advocated, for example, the uselessness of military resistance to British demands in 1842. More significantly still, it had been Manchu princes and court officials, and not Chinese bureaucrats, who perceived that controversial institutional changes (such as greater centralization of decision making and finances) would be needed to preserve the peace and to make the post-treaty order profitable to the Ch'ing state.

The kind of vigorous, consensus-defying reform leadership displayed by the courtier-elite in the days of Mu-chang-a and Ch'i-ying, however, was not a prominent feature of the political landscape after the mid-century mark. Indeed, during the final third or so of the century, it became almost axiomatic among foreign diplomats in China that the Manchu court and its hangers-on were exercising a woefully negative influence on the prospects for self-strengthening.[1] While this judgment was somewhat unfair, we can appreciate the circumstances that encouraged it. Although signs of a readiness to innovate begin to appear, after 1861, in virtually all of the aspects of institutional life vital to the renewal of Ch'ing China's international prospects, in no case (except possibly that of diplomacy itself) will we find the court taking the key entrepreneurial role in promoting the necessary adjustments. Instead, guidance tended to come increasingly from Chinese elites, often of only marginal bureaucratic status. In some cases, moreover—and especially in the crucial areas of military and fiscal reform—the prestige and power of the court was exercised to conservative and obstructive effect.[2] Forsaking its earlier, activist commitment to promoting change, then, Peking's leadership would gradually develop, after 1850, into a force largely hostile to reform.

Why this happened is a question only partially answerable on the basis of the events analyzed in this book. Nevertheless, Hsien-feng's decision to retreat from diplomatic and political reform can be seen, in its own right, as having helped push the court one step closer toward the negative role it would later permanently assume.

One regard in which this connection with later events can be readily identified is that of military modernization. Here, the court's virtual abdication from a positive leadership role in foreign relations meant, inevitably, that the key inaugural experiments in the use of Western weaponry would be undertaken by military leaders situated at the margins of the Ch'ing power structure, and not by the banner command of the capital region. Matters could scarcely have been otherwise, considering that the procurement of access to foreign weaponry—and to the finances needed to pay for it—necessarily premised a willingness to engage openly in diplomatic bartering with the treaty-port powers. Having forsworn this option in 1850, Peking could only sit back and watch, with misgivings, as Han Chinese military plenipotentiaries, locked in combat with the Taiping in central China, turned in desperation to just such tactics after 1860. The experience in the use of up-to-date artillery and small arms acquired by these new-style units in the victorious pacification campaigns of the post-1860 decade, moreover, gave them a permanent edge in fighting technique over the banner soldiers of the capital region. Ever wary of this superiority, the Manchu military elite turned increasingly, after 1870, to harassment tactics and to the obstruction of further modernization in order to keep the gap from widening.[3] Here, then, was the first unfortunate legacy of the 1850 *volte face*—the conversion, that is, of the banner military elite into a vested interest intent on limiting rearmament to an absolute minimum.

A second area where the impact of the 1850 retreat seems to linger on is in the increasingly consensual basis of dynastic self-legitimation during most of the remainder of the century. Here, Hsien-feng's return to a "popular" foreign policy, anchored firmly in literati support, clearly foreshadows the pattern of monarchical legitimation through anti-Western conservatism that would come to prevail under the long reign of the Empress Dowager Tz'u-hsi (r. 1861–1908). One can, in fact, see intimations of this novel use of consensus politics from virtually the moment the coup d'état of 1861 propelled Tz'u-hsi into power. Passing over the details of that complicated incident, we need here observe only that Tz'u-hsi's successful capture of leadership in 1861, as well as her subsequent retention of it, rested very largely on her ability to reconcile the reality of a new set of treaty concessions abroad, with the appearance of enhanced respect for literati sensibilities in treaty and reform questions at home. This was accomplished, in part, by her alliance with an outsider in the Manchu princely establishment (I-hsin, usually called Prince Kung). To this able but isolated reformer was entrusted the thankless task of institutionalizing the system of foreign diplomatic representation in the capital promised by China after her defeat by Britain and France in 1860. Prince Kung's solution to this tricky problem—the Tsung-li Yamen, or "office for international affairs"—was never, in fact, to win much approval in Southern City circles. But, from the vantage point of the literati, Prince Kung's politically dependent regime was clearly much preferable to the aggressive princely leadership group that had flourished in the days of Mu-chang-a, and again, though with reduced clout, in the late 1850s.[4] The appeal of the new arrangement of power was further broadened by the Empress Dowager's solicitude in finding posts for veteran literocrats, such as Ch'i Chün-tsao, for-

merly associated with the restoration of Southern City influence in
1850. Upon the occasion of her 1861 accession, for example, both
Ch'i and Wo-jen (another hero and beneficiary of the 1850 *volte face*)
were granted prominent positions in the metropolitan bureaucracy
and installed as the new boy emperor's tutors.[5] As a third prop of her
consensus-building policy, moreover, Tz'u-hsi made it her habit to
encourage literocratic rebukes of Prince Kung's alleged apostasy
against Confucian tradition whenever he pressed her too hard for
institutional reform at the central-government level.[6] For venerable
opposition leaders (like Ch'i Chün-tsao), who remembered all too
well the unchecked abuses of power of the late 1840s, this careful cir-
cumscribing of Prince Kung's authority must have evoked welcome
echoes of Hsien-feng's inaugural rebuke to the power-hungry Mu-
chang-a.

By such actions as this, the precedent set by Hsien-feng's restoration of literati prerogatives was ingeniously translated by the Empress
Dowager into a permanent new aspect of imperial self-legitimation.
Admittedly, under Tz'u-hsi, the underlying rationale behind this policy of propitiating Southern City opinion was no longer quite so
directly related as it had been in the Tao-kuang and Hsien-feng periods to the need for literati support in the battle against heterodox
rebellion. Of much more immediate concern, in this later era, was
the frightening power of the new, modern army commanders—a
power the monarchy sought to check by counter-mobilizing literati
traditionalism.[7] Nonetheless, the pattern of insistence on Southern
City literocratic support was one that resonated unmistakably with
the Hsien-feng emperor's "restoration" of the power of the literati
some eleven years earlier. Here was a second capacity in which the
volte face of 1850 proved a decisive influence in the later trend toward
abnegation of leadership at the center.

To study the later evolution of Ch'ing politics is, then, to be
reminded of just how crucial a divide was crossed in 1850, concomitant with the court's decision to step aside from an active leadership
role in guiding the adjustment to China's changed international circumstances. This abdication of responsibility did not, of course,
fully preclude institutional change. Nor, after 1861, was it intended
to. It sufficed, however, to guarantee that the specifically Ch'ing
dimensions of the imperial power structure—the monarchy and the
Manchu-Mongol service aristocracy—would thereafter view diploma-

tic and institutional modernization chiefly as a threat to be diverted
or contained, rather than as a force that could be harnessed to rebuild
the waning power of the monarchy.

By shouldering the problems of refashioning Ch'ing foreign policy only to fail under their weight, then, Mu-chang-a and his comrades among this inner Ch'ing elite did not merely postpone the job
until the 1860s. They may also, however inadvertently, have added significantly to the constraints under which future central-government
leadership would have to operate throughout the entirety of the self-
strengthening era.

With our brief look into the future forewarning us of how crucial
an event the mid-century deflection of court reform leadership
would turn out to be, it seems appropriate that we should, in conclusion, review what has been learned in this book about its causes. As
I have tried to make clear, these were only partly situational in
nature. In certain other regards, what happened in 1850 flowed logically, even inexorably, from the peculiarities of the Ch'ing central
political system itself, and it is upon this latter range of influences
that our attention can most profitably be focused at this point. What
then were these peculiarities, and what lay behind them?

An obvious place to begin is with the curiously persistent weakness of the bureaucratic "interest" in the making of early-nineteenth-
century Chinese foreign policy. There was in Ch'ing politics no such
thing, of course, as a purely official point of view on foreign-policy
questions, any more than on domestic ones. But, within the administrative elite as a whole, there were clearly certain officials whose policy views were shaped primarily by systemic or centrist concerns
(Was a policy likely to prove universally enforceable? Would it
enhance or undermine central-regional coordination?); and others
who tended to be influenced more by regional or consensual
considerations—such as local or Southern City literati. In this sense
one may speak of a gap between the bureaucratic (or bureaucrat-
centrist) outlook and its opponents within the Ch'ing political system. And, in this sense also, one might validly characterize most of
the foreign-policy disagreements we have studied as direct outgrowths of this gap—as was, for example, in the 1850 tug-of-war between Mu-chang-a and his opponents that Hsien-feng had to arbitrate
upon coming to the throne. The saliency of this particular political

fault line comes as little surprise, given the longstanding ethnic and administrative tensions dividing the bureaucratic center from other, competing nuclei of power within the system.[8] What *is* surprising, however, is the regularity with which leaders on the bureaucratic end of these policy disputes went down to defeat—this in spite of the more direct access they often had to the emperor than did their opponents; in spite, also, of their enjoyment, as a rule, of ethnic insider status; and in spite, usually, of the superior reasonableness of their specific arguments. But here we might do well to recall the particulars of the debates and defeats in question, if only to remind ourselves of the curious regularity of the pattern.

Far and away the most stunning defeat for the centrist approach came in 1850, with the removal from power of Mu-chang-a and Ch'i-ying—two statesmen whose notion of foreign policy had pivoted on insuring the security of the capital and its supply links to the lower Yangtze region, and whose chosen instrument for achieving this had been a centrally policed system of "pacifying" treaty concessions, to be forced, if need be, down the throats of the disgruntled Cantonese. Almost from its inception, however, this policy had been difficult to impose. The sticking point, as we have seen, was that new treaty arrangements could not possibly work without the disarming of the xenophobic irregulars who had become the principal guardians of law and order in and around the city of Canton during the last year of the Opium War. For obvious reasons, neither officials nor literati with an ongoing stake in the region found this step acceptable, whence the mounting challenge to the enforcement of the residence provision of the new treaty system. Here, then, was a clear test of the policies and strength of the centrists. But the victory had gone to their opponents.

Nor was this an unusual outcome for our period. On at least two other occasions, as well, the bureaucratic impulse had extended itself into foreign-policy deliberations, only to be dealt a decisive reversal at the hand of literati-intermediated oppositional coalitions. The first of these analogous setbacks had occurred in 1836, when a quartet—ironically enough—of Han Chinese statesmen (Grand Secretary Juan Yuan and three Kwangtung officials: Lu K'un, Teng T'ing-chen, and Hsu Nai-chi) had temporarily held the initiative on trade and opium-control matters. Taking advantage of this opportunity, the Juan party had attempted to bring some consistency and enforceability back into Ch'ing coastal-control regulations by proposing a limited import-legalization plan. Though clearly unattractive in its moral implications, such a reform would probably have helped in the short run to stanch the outward drain of silver that was then seriously disrupting Ch'ing tax administration. More important, it would certainly have simplified the task of keeping tabs on the behavior of coastal officials. In these twin regards, it bespoke a highly bureaucratic, rather than consensual, orientation in foreign policy. But, as we have seen, Juan's proposal proved extraordinarily vulnerable to challenge from below, very largely because its spirit was so purely elitist and managerial.

Mutatis mutandis, this was the weak point, too, of the third major centrist initiative we have studied in this narrative: the 1841 decision to seek a quick end to the fighting through concentrated onshore offensives in Kwangtung and Chekiang. Resented from the outset by the civil officials and local dignitaries through whose terrain the attacks were to be pressed, this decision nonetheless made a good deal of sense from the point of view of the Manchu-Mongol strategists who dominated court military thinking. If successful, it promised a quick termination of hostilities; and (though this was never stated) if not, its costs would be so dramatic as perhaps to bring the emperor around the more quickly to an appreciation of the benefits of peace. Then too the offensive strategy had the advantages of temporarily diverting the main military action away from the capital area and the Grand Canal, and of minimizing the role of potentially dangerous irregulars. All in all there was a formidable menu of arguments in its favor. Yet here, again, the nay-sayers—in this case a coalition of literati and threatened local officials—were able to compromise the plan quite seriously, if not to disrupt it altogether. As we have seen, I-shan's Kwangtung offensive was all but sabotaged before it could begin by Governor General Ch'i Kung, and his forces eventually harried out of the province, to be replaced by a strictly local muster. Only in Chekiang did the operations go forward as planned—too late, as it turned out, to draw the British away from their advance upon the Canal.

A curious insufficiency of power thus seems repeatedly to have hampered those who would steer policy in a centrist or bureaucratic direction—be they Manchu or Chinese, generals or diplomats. Curious because, in the first place, this had not been a feature of Ch'ing generalship or diplomacy in earlier periods; and curious, too, because the logic of dynastic survival seems, in retrospect, to have pointed in the direction of more, and not less, central orchestration of policy than in the past. Yet even so determined and so well situated a leader as Mu-chang-a would not overcome this peculiar feature of the early-nineteenth-century Ch'ing political system. Consensualist and regionalist impulses, one is forced to conclude, were simply too deeply embedded within the system to be pushed aside for foreign-policy purposes.

But why was this the case? Why was the distribution of power so bottom-heavy, so remarkably advantageous to those set upon resisting the centrist will in policymaking? So asking, we come at once to a second persisting peculiarity of the system: the strongly centrifugal political orientation of the Southern City literati throughout the period we have surveyed. Owing to this predisposition and to the influence—or, more accurately, the veto power—wielded by these Southern City literocrats, regional administrative or elite interests at odds with the center could usually be sure of support "at court," so to speak, for their efforts to resist unwanted new policies. To be sure, there were very real limits on how, or how effectively, this kind of lobbying power could be exercised. Much always depended on the momentary predisposition of the emperor, on his receptivity to being advised by "impractical" Chinese literati. Moreover, in foreign-policy matters at least, there are signs of a lingering distrust of any Han Chinese advice—a circumstance that perhaps explains why the leaders of the Shrine Association had to push so hard on the Kwangsi cover-up issue in 1850. Yet, for all of this, the Southern City voice was one that was heeded with surprising regularity in Opium-War-era Peking; and, when it was, the beneficiaries usually proved to be provincial officials or elites, as the following reconsideration of instances previously noted in our narrative will remind us.

Recall, for example, the dilemma Lin Tse-hsu faced in early 1841, and how vigorous a lobbying effort his Southern City allies were able to mount on his behalf. Though one would hesitate to describe Lin as a parochialist, it was nonetheless his refusal to consider the dangers to which his trade-interdiction policies exposed the central power apparatus that had turned the emperor against him in 1840, and had brought Ch'i-shan to Canton as his replacement. To be cashiered under such circumstances, one would think, would have been enough to discourage almost any official. Yet Lin was able, as we have seen, not only to fight back, but even to hound his successor from office, thanks principally to the spirited campaign of personal vilification Huang Chueh-tzu was able to whip up in Peking against Lin's powerful Manchu adversary. By the time this assault had been successfully concluded, no fewer than ten memorials of Southern City provenance had come before the emperor—two from Huang's own hand, and eight more from anti-Ch'i-shan censors under Huang's personal influence. True, Ch'i-shang's naive underestimate of British war aims had made it that much easier for Huang's shafts to find their target. And true, also, the victory was both incomplete and short-lived, with Lin never gaining the permanent reinstatement to his post in Canton that he and his supporters had hoped for. Yet, in the larger perspective, what is most important in all of this is that a regional official of only median rank and seniority had been able to count on, and receive, very effective backing in the capital, thanks entirely to literati lobbying efforts.

Though Lin's successors in Canton could never be assured of quite this degree of loyalty, we have seen that they too were able to manipulate literati opinion in the capital to advantage in the fight to wriggle free of central-government guidance. Ch'i Kung, for example, had played this game masterfully in his effort to keep control of local military forces from passing into Manchu hands during the later stages of the war and after. We shall remember, to cite but one instance of this, how the events of the siege of Canton (in February-May 1841) had been altered by Ch'i's academy-scholar associates into a tale of victory by local militiamen thwarted only by the cowardice of the Manchu commander on the spot, I-shan, and the regulars under his command. Through the intermediation of Chang Wei-p'ing and Lo Ping-chang, two Cantonese literati with excellent Southern City connections, this version of the battle had then been circulated throughout the capital, where it had helped create a climate of opinion favorable for Ch'i's next move: the construction of a huge private military apparatus under local gentry control. Similarly, Hsu Kuangchin, Ch'i Kung's successor but one as Liang-Kuang viceroy, seems to have bet heavily on Peking literati support during the showdown phase of the Canton entry crisis of 1849, for he took measures to insure that Chang Mu, the guiding spirit behind the Ku Shrine Association, received constant updating on developments in Canton as the final confrontation with Bonham approached. Having thus guaranteed a maximally euphoric Southern City reception for the news of his victory, it became fairly easy for Hsu and his assistant, Yeh Ming-ch'en, to greatly inflate its significance, and thus to convert Canton into a virtually autonomous bastion of diplomatic authority for the next decade.

Nor was the pattern confined to intra-bureaucratic conflicts over foreign policy. The same centrifugal orientation that drew Southern City activists onto the side of beleaguered official actors in the south could also elicit support for private interests, particularly where local security issues were at stake. A desire to aid the beleaguered gentry-academicians of Canton, for example, is plainly visible in much of the pro-militia mythology we have summarized from the war chronicles of Wei Yuan and others. A much better example of this specific type of advocacy, however, is the Shrine Association-engineered exposé of governmental neglect in Kwangsi during the first months of Hsien-feng's reign—an action undertaken very much in response to the fears and complaints of that province's threatened scholar-gentry elite and in outright defiance of the regional bureaucracy. That the gentry of Kweilin could make use of indirect channels to lay their case before the emperor himself attests again to the unusual responsiveness of Southern City opinion to complaints of this order. For, as we have seen, Tseng Kuo-fan and Tu Shou-t'ien were willing to press the case even before they or anyone else had any idea of the full dimensions of the scandal their efforts would eventually bring to light.

It would seem, then, that, if the Ch'ing central political system of our period was peculiarly responsive to eccentric interests within that system, including both adventurist or parochialist regional administrators and civilian law-and-order activists, much of this is to be traced to the sympathetic predisposition of the literocrats of Peking, and to the considerable powers of influence these men commanded. Such sympathy could be as telling in domestic-policy conflicts as in foreign, as the Kwangsi affair reminds us. But its effect within the latter realm is what concerns us here, and there it cast a very long shadow indeed, facilitating, as we have seen, a succession of triumphant revolts against court insider control over foreign policy.

Having reminded ourselves of the indispensibility of the Peking literati as guardians of this peculiarly downward-responsive style of foreign-policy management (or, perhaps more accurately, of policy mismanagement), we confront, finally, the question of underlying intent. To what degree did the pattern of literati partisanship we have described find sanction in higher-level ideals? Looking beyond the merely political dimensions of literati rebelliousness—the fears, jealousies, ambitions, and hatreds that often seem the chief grounds for their anti-ministerial intrigues—do we discover the signs of a higher purpose behind these actions? And, if we do, wherein lay the underlying concern: foreign affairs or domestic governance? Are we dealing here, in other words, with a compelling vision of how relations with culturally inferior outsiders ought properly to be conducted? Or might it not be more accurate to interpret the literati role in Opium-War-era politics as the expression of some higher domestic aspiration—as, for example, the desire to restore the Chinese scholar-official class to a position of secure collective power such as it had once enjoyed under the Ming?

The question cannot be answered categorically. But it can be argued, I think, that a sense of domestic political purpose—sometimes high-minded, and sometimes not—forms the most consistent guide to literocratic politics in our period. Conversely, a coherent alternative program for dealing with the foreigner and his perplexing military power seems to appear only fairly late in the game, and then chiefly as an afterthought, a second exhibit, as it were, in the case for a greater lettered-elite role in policymaking.

To enlarge somewhat on the point, let us begin by reflecting for a moment on how Southern City opinion first solidified its place in nineteenth-century Ch'ing politics. This had occurred, we recall, during the Chia-ch'ing reign, well before there was any sign of a crisis in Sino-foreign relations, and had long since evolved its own particular rationale (in the form of a self-extolling analogy with Ming moral-censure politics) by the time the debate over opium smuggling was ready to begin. The opening wedge, we will further recall, had been a quintessentially domestic issue: unpoliced rebellion at the doorstep of the capital; and, right down to 1850, this issue remained the surest card in the literati suit, their most reliable claim to a voice in politics.

Moreover, though there were obvious practical reasons for playing this card whenever possible, there were equally persuasive programmatic ones. As we have seen, Spring Purificationist true believers like Chang Chi-liang or Yao Ying, for example, had as their ultimate purpose nothing less than the total transformation of the personality ideals of their class, in the interest (as they would have it) of better immunizing the social anatomy against moral infection. From their point of view, sounding the alarm over the breakdown in social order was practically a mission unto itself, entering even into the new literary dogmas they pressed upon their colleagues. Other, more modest reform proposals likewise regularly linked to the "rebels-in-the-hills" issue included calls for enhancement of the managerial and fiscal autonomy of local officials (the claim being that this would facilitate a more conscientious attack on the roots of disorder) and—another frequent favorite—institutionalized protection of censorial whistle-blowers (the policemen, as it were, of the police). The point is, then, that something approaching a fixed strategy and agenda—*both anchored firmly in the soil of domestic governmental concerns*—had come to shape literati involvement in politics during the two decades before the opium crisis, and continued well thereafter.

By contrast, no such prior clarity of objectives or program is visible in connection with foreign affairs. As we have been at pains to show, Commissioner Lin and his Spring Purification sympathizers in the capital were drawn into the debate over opium control almost inadvertently, the immediate objective being the enhancement of Lin's personal standing at court. Not until overwhelmed by the 1840 war and its unhappy domestic political aftermath did literati independents like Wei Yuan get around, belatedly, to formulating and documenting their own theories, so to speak, of Sino-foreign relations. And, when they did, what emerged was in many regards an echo of refrains long since audible in the domestic sphere. Wei's own preoccupation with arming the civilian population and the enlistment of errant heroes on the government side sounds, for example, extraordinarily like a reworked version of the social-control ideas favored by the Spring Purificationists in the 1830s. So, too, do his (and Commissioner Lin's) enjoinders that the British be dealt with as "mere" pirates—a breed of enemy already commonplace in the literati coastal-control literature of the late Chia-ch'ing.

Belated in their appearance and derivative in their content, literati solutions to the British question thus do not suggest much capacity or inclination to think about foreign affairs in isolation, even by the end of our period. That is not to say these views carried no weight at all, for they did in the end provide the rationale for the diplomatic hardening that set in after 1850. They tell us little, however, about why this change was so urgently sought. For this, we must look instead to the domestic program evolved by literati activists during the 1820 and 1830s, whose chief goals (administrative decentralization and censorial free speech) stood little chance of realization so long as an authoritarian Manchu peace party ruled in Peking. Therein, our evidence suggests, lay the most persistent incitement to militancy.

All of this leaves us with one last piece of ground to be explored: that of the unexpressed biases or ethnic tensions helping to shape literati views on the foreign-policy questions of our period. Though such feelings are harder to identify than the programmatic concerns with which we have been dealing so far, they may have been just as important, or even more so; for, in a closed, multi-ethnic political system, it would be surprising indeed if unadmitted ethnic or status-group jealousies did not play a role in most major policy struggles. Reading between the lines, I think we shall discover a very considerable list of such prejudices at work in the foreign-policy debates of the 1830s and 1840s, foremost among them being something I would term the "class chauvinism" or "cultural chauvinism" of the Han Chinese lettered elite: the feeling, that is, that they could best define and implement the changes needed to rescue the empire, and ought to be allowed to do so with a minimum of interference. Complementing this "literophilic" sensibility seems to have been an enormous faith in the value of literati friendship and mentorship ties as politically restorative forces—whence came, in turn, the predisposition to support politically troubled Han-lin veterans virtually without regard for the policy issues at stake. However indirectly, these sub rosa biases could often have a dramatic effect on literati views, even in conjunction with foreign-policy questions of only marginal programmatic interest in their own right.

A case in point is Lin Tse-hsu's evolution, first into a trade-control hardliner, then into an apostle of treaty abnegation, largely under the impress, I would argue, of the intramural class-chauvinism he shared with other members of the Chia-ch'ing generation of literati reformers. It will be recollected that Lin began his career in the bureaucracy as one of a tightly knit cluster of ex-Han-lin fast-risers catapulted into high provincial office under the patronage of Chiang Yu-hsien during the 1820s. While generally eschewing any open pretensions to a special right of leadership, this cohort of literati reformists had nevertheless felt free to challenge covertly traditional Manchu-imposed administrative priorities whenever adherence to them threatened to obstruct the provincial-level improvements in which they were engaged. Thus, for example, Chiang Yu-hsien and T'ao Chu had planned—and nearly secured—a permanent curtailment of canal-shipped tribute-grain deliveries in 1827, in clear disregard of announced court policy. And thus did Governor Lin himself embark during the 1830s on a five-year crusade—likewise unsuccessful—to reduce the huge tax load imposed by early Ch'ing rulers upon the Kiangnan heartland. So controversial a sequence of undertakings could only have been prompted by the conviction that Chinese literati officials were somehow better equipped than others within the bureaucracy to judge where and how reform should proceed—an attitude that seems only to have been reinforced by the rebuffs both these initiatives suffered en route.

This "literophilia," already implicit in Lin's approach to domestic affairs, became an influence as well on his foreign-policy views virtually from the moment of his arrival in Canton. As has been shown, Lin took up his duties in that southeastern port city determined to accomplish much more than his instructions called for. Not only would he bring the illicit drug trade under control, but he would do so promptly and permanently—all this as a demonstration of what shih-ta-fu zeal could achieve, and as a pathway back into a position of trust at court. Given such a mindset, it is not difficult to see why Lin took so extreme a position on trade control. Nor, in retrospect, is it surprising that he would lay the blame for his wartime failures at the feet chiefly of Manchu rivals within the bureaucracy: first Ch'i-shan, then I-shan, and ultimately Grand Councillor Mu-chang-a himself.

Once aroused by Lin's actions, moreover, the class egotism of the Han-lin literati remained a powerful influence upon their foreign-policy views for years to come. Juan Yuan's puzzling postwar defection to the side of the anti-treaty militants, for example, seems explicable only in these terms, for he had certainly evidenced little programmatic sympathy for the hardliners during the 1830s, when Han-lin veterans still occupied the heights of power. What seems to have turned him around was Mu-chang-a's postwar attempt to dominate virtually all literocratic patronage and to uproot all groups capable of resisting him, irrespective of their particular scholastic underpinnings. This, from Juan's point of view, must have looked like a throwback to the

Ho-shen years; and, if fighting back meant re-aligning himself with the dishonored war party, then a militant he would be. A similar, class-centered logic seems latent in Tseng Kuo-fan's 1850 cooperation with the Shrine Association, for he too had been expressing grave doubts about Lin's policies only a few years earlier.

There was, in short, a kind of unwritten agenda beneath the surface debates over foreign policy we have studied: an unspoken "inner" agenda shaped, ultimately, by the insecurities to which all lettered-class Chinese were subject as they struggled with the problems of career-making in a still Manchu-dominated world. By "inner," I do not mean "most fundamental" or "determinant," for this particular dimension of literati political consciousness—this "Han-lin chauvinism"—was by no means the sole or most compelling argument for Southern City resistance against the post-Opium War treaty system. Additional boosts in this direction were provided, as we have seen, by a tradition of attachment to decentralized policy enforcement (hence aversion to the legalistic uniformity promised by the new arrangements); by a predisposition (scarcely reconcilable with modern treaty diplomacy) to favor the dispersal of police power into private hands; and, above all, by an awareness that persistent monarchical paranoia on the home front made resistance to treaty-making strongmen like Mu-chang-a a practical political goal. Here was already a very rich inner (in the sense of domestic) agenda, one that would probably have sufficed in and of itself to guarantee literati opposition. Yet it may not have been the innermost. In the end, no full explanation of this extraordinary hostility to the treaty system seems possible without taking into account the wounded class vanity of the Chinese lettered elite, from which sprang a nearly reflex willingness to believe the very worst about the Manchu statesmen who had guided the new system into being. That such feelings came so readily into play suggests to me that the sides in this dispute had already been chosen before the issues yet existed; that the parties knew instinctively whom they would be arguing against, before there were yet grounds for disagreement. It is in this double sense that the conflict we have studied seems rightly characterized as an "inner" Opium War.

Notes
Bibliography
Glossary/Index

N O T E S

Introduction

1. See John K. Fairbank, *Trade and Diplomacy on the China Coast*, esp. pp. 464–468; "Synarchy under the Treaties," pp. 204–231, esp. pp. 216, 222, and 225; "The Early Treaty System in the Chinese World Order," and "The Creation of the Treaty System," esp. p. 217.
2. Benjamin I. Schwartz, *In Search of Wealth and Power: Yen Fu and the West*, pp. 10–18. See also Joseph R. Levenson, *Liang Ch'i-ch'ao and the Mind of Modern China*, pp. 109–122, for the related idea that traditional elite culture and nationalism were antithetical. Much the same notion—i.e., that the belatedness of the intellectual "transition" explains the delay of reform prior to 1895, then the quick acceleration thereafter—informs the more recent work of Chang Hao (*Liang Ch'i-ch'ao and Intellectual Transition in China*). See, in particular, pp. 30–31 for the suggestion that a Neo-Confucian-inspired commitment to "the orthodox political goals of the Confucian state" outweighed the "peripheral" ideal of wealth and power as legitimate goals of state policy until some time in the 1870s or 1880s.
3. This is the principal argument in Albert Feuerwerker, *China's Early Industrialization: Sheng Hsuan-huai (1844-1916) and Mandarin Enterprise.*
4. Michael Hunt, "Chinese Foreign Relations in Historical Perspective"; John E. Wills, Jr., "Maritime China from Wang Chih to Shih Lang."
5. With the important exception of the hoppo, none of the key individual or

institutional actors within the Manchu-interest camp (as it functioned during the 1800–1850 period) has bequeathed us his state papers. The best source on Manchu politics for the 18th century is the *Shih-liao hsun-k'an* (*SLHK*) series, published by the Peking National Palace Museum during the 1930s. However, it contains nothing very informative concerning how specifically Manchu agents influenced court opinion in the 1830–1850 decades — with the exception, again, of the hoppo. The same applies to the *Ming-Ch'ing shih-liao* (*MCSL*) series published in Taiwan in the 1960s. Imperial Household and other uncatalogued archives in Peking will presumably help us to fill this gap. Without such resources, there is no satisfactory way to penetrate the facade of the imperial persona as presented in the *Veritable Records*.

1. The Literati Re-Ascendant

1. For the size of the degree-holder population ca. 1800, see Chang Chung-li, *The Chinese Gentry*, p. 164.
2. Chang Chung-li, pp. 125–126, estimates the total population of provincial degree-holders (*chü-jen*) at 18,000, and the average number of candidates sitting for each metropolitan examination at roughly 8,000. This latter figure is confirmed by Fa-shih-shan in his *Huai-t'ing tsai-pi*, 2:11a. To the larger of these two figures must be added the between 500 and 1,000 men of sub-*chü-jen*-degree status holding purchased offices in the capital, and another 3,000–4,000 *pa-kung* (licentiates by special selection) who were also eligible to compete in Peking examinations (Chang Chung-li, p. 129), plus the sons of civil officeholders serving in the capital.
3. Hsuan-nan was the name of a Ming-dynasty ward; in Ch'ing times, the northern part of the city was reserved for bannermen. For the two phrases, see, for example, Feng Kuei-fen, *Hsien-chih t'ang chi*, 5:60a, and Ch'en Yung-kuang, *T'ai-i-chou wen-chi*, 3:4a. The latter reference makes the point that residence closer to or in the Summer Palace (Yuan-ming yuan) would have been required for officials needing to be present at court. In poetry, Nan-ch'eng is often reversed as Ch'eng-nan: cf. Wu Sung-liang, *Hsiang-su shan-kuan ch'üan-chi*, 10:11 ff.
4. These included mainly: the Han-lin Academy; the vestigial Supervisorate of Imperial Instruction; the apprentice (*hsueh-hsi*) posts of the 6 staff ministries (civil appointments, revenue, ceremonies, war, public works, and punishments), including the offices of *lang-chung* or department director, *yuan-wai-lang*, or assistant department director, and *chu-shih*, or 2nd-class secretary; and the secretaries (*chung-shu*, or *she-jen*) in the Grand Secretariat. The distinction between what I here call administrative and non-administrative posts was one emphasized by the upper literati themselves. Perhaps the most common mode of identifying the two types of offices is that used by Kung Tzu-chen, who refers to them respectively as *cheng-yao* ("governmentally essential") and *ch'ing-hsia* ("pure and leisured") posts. See his *Kung Tzu-chen ch'üan-chi*, p. 32. Interestingly, the idea of "purity" (*ch'ing*) seems to have been persistently coupled with service in non-administrative offices, imply-

ing, apparently, that responsibility tended to corrupt or confuse the spirit. For a clear instance of *ch'ing-hsia* in this latter sense, see Lin Tse-hsu, *Yun-tso shan-fang shih-ch'ao*, 2:12a.

5. For an excellent survey of the literature on the general topic of late-19th-century political-action groups, see Mary B. Rankin, "'Public Opinion' and Political Power: *Qingyi* in Late Nineteenth Century China." On pp. 460–461, she discusses this class of officials as social intermediaries.

6. J. P. Dennerline, *The Chia-ting Loyalists*, p. 18. This and the following analysis of the role of Han-lin graduates follows Dennerline, pp. 17–20. Cf. also Chang Chung-li, p. 122, for the continuation of the Ming system under the Ch'ing.

7. For the Grand Secretariat under the Ch'ing, see Yeh Ming-feng, *Ch'iao-hsi tsa-chi*, pp. 24–26; and Juan K'uei-sheng, *Ch'a-yü k'o-hua*, pp. 30–31. The connection with a grand secretary generally required to gain appointment to the *she-jen* posts could also be used to gain promotion from *she-jen* into the post of secretary to the Grand Council, in turn an entrée into high provincial office. For example, see *ECCP*, p. 75 (biography of Chao I). For *she-jen* as fashion-setters, see *HCSH*, 2, 7:71.

8. Miyazaki Ichisada, *China's Examination Hell*, p. 122. This computation measures the chances of a lower-degree-holder (*sheng-yuan*) to become a metropolitan graduate (*chin-shih*).

9. I am indebted for the concept of coincidental connections to Andrew Nathan's typology of political relationships in the late Ch'ing and in early Republican political culture. He sees them as the equivalent of ascriptive ties, "established at an early stage in a young man's career by virtue of a combination of circumstances and choice . . . [thus lacking any real] element of contractualism." See Nathan, "'Connections' in Chinese Politics: Political Recruitment and *kuan-hsi* in Late Ch'ing and Early Republican China," pp. 8ff.

10. Cf., for example, Hsu Pao-shan, *Hu-yuan ch'üan-chi, tsa-chu, kuo-t'ing lu*, 8b; Wu Ching-tzu, *The Scholars*, p. 6; *TCFC, wen-lu*, 6:18a–20a.

11. For funeral expenses, see, for example, Chiang Yu-hsien, *Sheng-i-chai nien-p'u*, 1:25a; and Chang Chi-liang, *Chang Heng-fu ch'üan-chi, wen*, 3:6a. For medical-expense subsidies and old-age welfare collections through same-year or examiner-student ties, see, for example, Hsu Pao-shan, *Hu-yuan, tsa-chu*, 32b–33a. Lo Ping-chang, *Lo-kung nien-p'u*, p. 31, gives an example of "coincidence" friends paying off a fine. *HPSW*, 19:21b–22a, and Chang Chi-liang, 3:22a, give examples of a co-provincial's recommendation for examination-reading and secretarial positions.

12. Wang Shih-chen, *Yü-yang shan-jen kan-chiu chi*, 1:9, notes that this late-17th-century scholar-official saved poetic mementos of 333 such friendships. Wang Ch'ang, *Hu-hai shih-chuan*, preface, 1a, records that "in excess of six hundred" poetic partners of the same sort traded verses with this late-18th-century scholar-official. Liang Chang-chü records "over 260" friendships of the same variety in his *Shih-yu chi* of 1845 (author's preface, 1a).

13. William S. Atwell, "From Education to Politics: The Fu She," pp. 336–337; Dennerline, pp. 31, 309.

14. For the use of poetry in the examination system of the T'ang, see Liang Chang-chü, *T'ui-an sui-pi*, 6:14b. For the same in the Sung, see Li Cheng-fu, *Sung-tai k'o-chü chih-tu chih yen-chiu*, pp. 14ff. For the discontinuation of verse in the Ming, and its replacement by the eight-legged essay, see Shen Chien-shih, *Chung-kuo k'ao-shih chih-tu shih*, p. 150. Sources differ as to when exactly verse was reintroduced. The *Ch'ing-pi shu-wen*, 6:22a, says that this occurred for provincial and metropolitan examinations in 1757. Fa-shih-shan's *Huai-t'ing tsai-pi*, 2:13a, says sub-provincial examinations began regularly to test for versification skills in 1760. Chu Kuei, *Chih-tsu-chai wen-chi*, 1:12a, however, records that a poetry test had been standard in the court review examination (*ch'ao-k'ao*) from the early Ch'ing, and that the Ch'ien-lung emperor personally began to stress this as a Han-lin admittance criterion in the 1751 examinations. Both Chu Kuei and Weng Fang-kang (*Fu-ch'u-chai wen-chi*, 4:11a, 12a, 22a)—two exceedingly important literati-courtiers of the later Ch'ien-lung—indicate that they did not systematically study poetry until 1751, but thereafter devoted much time to it. This evidence suggests that 1751 was the critical year for the return to an emphasis on poetry composition. Chang Chi-liang, 3:14a, retrospectively recalls that the habit of "making a reputation" through poetry was a peculiarity of the Ch'ien-lung and the Chia-ch'ing eras (1736–1820).

15. For the influence of Ch'en Wei-sung's *Ch'ieh-yen-chi shih-jen hsiao-chuan* and of Wang Shih-chen's *Kan-chiu chi* as pioneering models, see Wang Ch'ang, *Hu-hai*, preface, 1a. For the delayed publication of Wang Shih-chen's work, see his *Yü-yang shan-jen kan-chiu chi*, 1:3–4.

16. Wang Ch'ang's work, for example, was imitated by Fa-shih-shan in the latter's *P'eng-chiu chi-chien lu*, a work that in turn seems to have been in great demand in Peking in the early 19th century. See *LCCW, #3*, 1.7b–8a; and Fa-shih-shan, *Ts'un-su-t'ang wen-chi*, Suppl., 1:10b. Wu Sung-liang's *Shih-ch'i-fang shih-hua*, apparently written in the 1820s, was also based on Wang's work, which Wu had annotated. (See Wu Sung-liang, *Hsiang-su, shih-hua*, preface.)

17. See, for example, Lynn A. Struve, "Some Frustrated Scholars of the K'ang-hsi Period," p. 348; and James Polachek, "Literati Groups and Literati Politics in Early Nineteenth Century China," pp. 463–464.

18. Dennerline, pp. 308, 310.

19. P'an Tseng-i, *Hsiao-fu-shan-jen shou-ting nien-p'u*, 23b–24b.

20. For the best treatment of this theme, see David S. Nivison, "Ho-shen and his Accusers: Ideology and Political Behavior in the Eighteenth Century," esp. pp. 218ff.

21. For Ch'ien-lung's problems with Chang T'ing-yü (and his Manchu counterpart, O-erh-t'ai), see Nivison, pp. 228–230; and *ECCP*, pp. 55–56. No monograph as yet exists on imperial sponsorship of Han Chinese factions under Ch'ien-lung. But my own tentative analysis identifies a clique beginning its rise in 1750 or so, with the forced retirement of Chang T'ing-yü. The Shan-tung scholar-official Liu T'ung-hsun was the man responsible for the first impeachment of (the southerner) Chang, in 1741 (see *ECCP*, p. 55). In 1747, Liu in turn "passed" a group of three unusually young scholars from the

Peking area through their provincial examinations: Chi Yun (1724–1805), Chu Kuei (1731–1807), and Weng Fang-kang (1733–1818). These three, together with their "teacher" Liu, Liu's son Liu Yung (1720–1805), and their examination-system protégés and Han-lin friends, shall be hereafter described as the northern clique. (For Liu, Sr., as 1747 examiner, see *Ch'ing-pi shu-wen*, 6:7a. For his patronage relationship with Chu Kuei and with the latter's younger brother, Chu Yun, see *LCCW*, #1, 3:14b; and #2, 7:15b–16a; also Yao Yung-p'u, *Chiu-wen sui-pi*, 2:2b. For the close friendship that developed between Liu's three 1747 star pupils, see Chu Kuei, *Chih-tsu-chai shih-chi*, 8:19). Imperial interest in Liu's protégés (possibly based on regional concerns) began early and continued throughout the entire reign, as evidenced in a string of unusual honors and dispensations. (See, for example, *ECCP*, p. 120; and *LCCW*, #1, 3:6b–7a.) But the most important token of imperial recognition was the Imperial Manuscript Library endeavor, begun in 1773 at the suggestion of Chu Yun, and completed in 1782 under the editorship of Chi Yun. (*ECCP*, pp. 198–199; and Yao Yung-p'u, 2:6a.) That the Ho-shen clique may have been allowed influence in the examination system to reduce that of the northern group is suggested by an abrupt change of rules governing the testing of Han-lin for provincial examination assignments that took place during the 1770s. In 1777 the results of the test were for the first time kept secret, and this became a regular practice after 1779. (*LCCW*, #1, 3:7b.) Since Ho, presumably, had a stake in helping the less impressive scholars in the Academy, such a procedure would have been advantageous. Susan Mann Jones, "Hung Liang-chi," pp. 190–193 (footnote 16), documents how Ho used the control this gave him to place underqualified favorites as provincial examiners. There are also many anecdotes from the 1780s and 1790s that show northern-clique scholars refusing to beg for Ho's patronage. See, for example, Yao Yung-p'u, 2:3b; and Li Yueh-jui, *Ch'un-ping-shih yeh-ch'eng*, 45–46, for T'ang Chin-chao; and *LCCW*, 1, 1:19b–20a, for P'an Shih-en (a Liu Yung protégé).

22. Nivison, pp. 230, 232.
23. For a good English-language summary of modern Chinese scholarly literature on the general pattern of Manchu repression of Chinese lettered-class political influence in the Ch'ing, see Huang Pei, "Aspects of Ch'ing Autocracy: An Institutional Study, 1644–1735," esp. pp. 5–9, 25.
24. The best discussion of Manchu elite politics in this period (in English) is Robert B. Oxnam, *Ruling from Horseback*, pp. 38–63. For the connection between factionalism among the conquest nobility and the legislation against "Chinese" or "Ming" style lettered-class political habits, see p. 55, esp. note 52. See also Lynn A. Struve, "The Hsu Brothers and Semi-official Patronage of Scholars in the K'ang-hsi Period," p. 258, for the Ch'en Ming-hsia case and the legislation in question.
25. For an excellent analysis of the K'ang-hsi emperor's use of rival "northern" and "southern" Chinese lettered-class groups (each, however, under Manchu leadership) in the 1670s and 1680s, see Harold Lyman Miller, "Factional Conflicts and the Integration of Ch'ing Politics, 1661–1690," pp. 100–173.

Silas Wu, *Passage to Power*, pp. 43ff. explores K'ang-hsi's recruitment of the southern faction through appointment to the South Library (Nan-shu-fang), a kind of informal tutorial body charged with instructing the ruler on moral and historical themes. Dennerline, pp. 304ff., following Hsieh Kuo-chen, argues that the southern network built upon connections going back to the late Ming examination-system patronage group known as the Restoration Society (Fu-she).

26. For the prolonged succession crisis of 1708–1723, see Silas Wu, pp. 112–183; for 1712 as a turning point, see pp. 152ff. For the 1712 termination of the *hui-t'ui* procedure, see *WHTK*, p. 5371; and Wang Ch'ing-yun, *Shih-ch'u yu-chi*, 1:46a–47a. For the role of the Grand Council in nominating high-level officials in the post-1730 period, see *Ta-Ch'ing hui-tien* (1818), 3:3b.
27. See, for example, *SL-CC*, 277:31.
28. In the Ch'ing, all censors were capital officials, and were known collectively as *k'o-tao*. Charles O. Hucker, *The Censorial System of Ming China*, pp. 47–54, translates the full titles of the two tiers of officials abbreviated in this binome as "supervising secretaries" (*chi-shih-chung*—each responsible for a *k'o*, or staff organ) and "investigating censors" (*tu-ch'a yü-shih*—each nominally responsible for a provincial circuit [*tao*] jurisdiction). I hereafter simply refer to these two levels of censorial office as senior and junior censors. This is more appropriate to the Ch'ing usage, wherein only seniority, not duties, differentiated the two.
29. See Su Shu-fan, *Kuo-ch'ao yü-shih t'i-ming*, pp. 263ff.
30. *SH-CL*, 88:4b.
31. *SH-CL*, 89:6.
32. Nivison, pp. 226–227, cites several edicts reflecting a specific concern with the possibility of losers in power struggles targeting their assumed victimizers for criticism. This kind of behavior in particular seemed to bother Ch'ing rulers because it implied a belief that the monarchy was not really in control of appointments.
33. The outlines of the Ch'ien vs. Kuo-t'ai case are taken from *ECCP*, p. 150, and Nivison, pp. 233–236. Nivison's analysis, however, fails to spot the examination-system network operating on the oppositionist side of the affair. Ch'ien Feng can be tied to the northern clique through two sets of connections. First, he is described as a member of a poetry club organized by the Mongol Han-lin Fa-shih-shan (1753–1818) in the 1780s. (See Wu Sung-liang, *Hsiang-su, shih-hua*, 1:9; and Chu Ch'i, *I-chih-t'ang wen-chi*, 3:6b.) However, Fa's group (for which, see *LCCW*, #2, 7:15a) was a direct extension of the northern-clique network. The senior poet in it, Ch'ien Tsai (1708–1793), was a same-year Han-lin (entering class of 1752) together with Weng Fang-kang, and was to become, in fact, the principal poetry teacher and inspirer of that latter northern-clique leader. (See Weng Fang-kang, *Fu-ch'u-chai wen-chi*, 4:11a; and Yao Yuan-chih, *Chu-yeh-t'ing tsa-chi*, 5:16b–17a.) It also included Chu Yun, brother of Chu Kuei (*LCCW*, #2, 7:15a). Ch'ien is also described as having been introduced into Peking society by his (provincial) teacher, Yao Nai (1732–1815), who was another close Han-lin friend of Weng's. (See

ECCP, p. 900, for Yao and Weng; and Mei Tseng-liang, *Po-chien shan-fang wen-chi,* 10:13a, for Ch'ien as a pupil of Yao.) Fa-shih-shan's own connection with the northern clique might have grown out of an examination-system connection, at one remove, with Weng Fang-kang. (See Liu Ssu-wan, *Shang-chiung-t'ang shih-chi,* 50:1b.)

34. *SL-CL,* 1173:17b–18a; see also 1173: 14b–15a, for the first response to Ch'in's impeachment. The date of the case is 1783.

35. According to the well-informed testimony of Wu Hsiung-kuang (1750–1833), an experienced late-18th-century provincial official on the outs with the Ho faction, the institutional device most commonly employed by Ho involved the threat of exposure of unauthorized depletions of government revenue payments on deposit in provincial and sub-provincial treasuries. Wu himself was assigned as a sub-gubernatorial official to Shantung in 1797 on the understanding that he would collect evidence of such misdeeds against the provincial governor. (Wu Hsiung-kuang, *I-chiang pi-lu,* 1:25a.) Wu also claims that this practice began in 1780, when the Yunnan provincial authorities were caught by Ho with huge depletions in their accounts, and used Ho's good offices to get Peking to agree to a schedule of repayment (1:34b).

36. See Susan Jones, "Hung Liang-chi," pp. 140–141, 172–173, 176–177.

37. The role of the northern clique in channeling information on the rebellion into the hands of opposition leaders in the capital involved the use of several different sets of personal networks. Susan Jones, "Scholasticism and Politics in Late Eighteenth Century China," pp. 40–41, documents that patronage and cooperative relationships forged in conjunction with the Imperial Manuscript Library project were one vehicle for bringing such information up to Peking. This project had been dominated by two northern-party scholar-officials, Chu Yun and Chi Yun. A second set of northern-clique connections that were engaged by the would-be exposers seems to have involved the Fa-shih-shan poetry circle, which we have shown to have begun as an offshoot of the northern clique patronage network. (Above, note 33.) By the late 1790s, this circle had come to include Ch'in Ying (1742–1821), Ho Tao-sheng (1766–1806), Hung Liang-chi (1746–1809), Kung Ching-han (1747–1809), and Wang Ch'i-sun (1755–1818). See Wang Ch'i-sun, *T'i-fu wei-ting kao,* 2:13a–19a, and 6:6a–7a; and Ch'in Ying, *Hsiao-hsien shan-jen wen-chi,* 2:51a. At least two of these men had excellent sources at the west China front where the White Lotus Rebellion took place. Kung Ching-han had himself served as secretary to Governor General I-mien in Shensi between 1796 and 1799 (*ECCP,* p. 446). Wang Ch'i-sun's brother, I-sun, was a Hupeh magistrate actively involved in the fighting to contain the rebels. (Jones, "Hung Liang-chi," p. 135.) But probably the most important northern-clique relationship in this campaign was that between Chu Kuei and his protégé, Hung Liang-chi. For this relationship, see Jones, "Hung Liang-chi," p. 142; *LCCW,* #1, 2:17b; and Kung Tzu-chen, p. 520, which emphasizes the closeness of Chu with the "class of 1790," a class that included Hung.

38. The opposition position is summarized from Lo Chen-yü, comp., *Huang-Ch'ing tsou-i,* Suppl., 1:17ff; 2:1ff; and Susan Jones, "Hung Liang-chi," p. 140.

The arguments of the bureaucratic establishment have been reconstructed from the rebuttals presented by the critics whose works are contained in the above sources.

39. For Hung's submission—which took the irregular form of a letter, in triplicate, to Chu Kuei and two other high officials (one, Prince Ch'eng, being the current emperor's brother)—see *ECCP,* p. 374, and Jones, "Hung Liang-chi," pp. 161–178. Hung's letter was apparently also circulated privately in handwritten copy by Hung's son, I-sun. See Ch'ien I-chi, *K'an-shih-chai chi-shih-kao,* Suppl. 6:30b.

40. *Ta-Ch'ing hui-tien shih-li,* (1899) 22:17091, edict dated Chia-ch'ing (hereafter, CC) 4.

41. *THHL,* 8:17b. Here Chia-ch'ing still complains of the danger of a revival of Ming censorial contentiousness, and in particular of the "recent" habit of copying and circulating censorial submissions in private copy.

42. *ECCP,* p. 374. The limited nature of the post-Ho-shen purge is discussed in Philip Kuhn and Susan Jones, "Dynastic Decline and the Rise of Rebellion," pp. 108, 116–117.

43. Nivison, p. 232.

44. Weng Fang-kang, *Fu-ch'u-chai wen-chi,* 3:4a.

45. For Chu Kuei's role in (and reasons for) blocking a factional purge, see Yao Yung-p'u, 2:3a. Another sample of privately expressed (and therefore believable) lettered-elite criticism of the Ming style of idealistic factional partisanship is quoted in *TCFC, wen-lu,* 6:10ff (citing a letter from Lo Han-chang). Chao-lien, *Hsiao-t'ing tsa-lu,* Suppl., 2:55b, gives an interesting variation on the standard critique of Ming literati activism, blaming it on the excessive influence of the intuitionalist school of classical studies (*li-hsueh*) and on the lack of respect for careful textual analysis of the Confucian Classics and histories.

46. For the original, see Yao Nai, *Hsi-pao-hsuan shih-wen-chi, wen-chi,* pp. 3–4. For its quotation by early-19th-century scholars, see for example Liang Chang-chü, *T'ui-an sui-pi,* 4:7b–8a; and (an unacknowledged quote) Chu Ch'i, 4:13.

47. Wang's views might be taken as representative of attitudes among the northern-clique-affiliated scholars at the turn of the 19th century. Wang's own connection to the northern-scholar group seems to go back at least as far as 1768, when he was implicated (along with Chi Yun) in an attempt to protect the salt official and bibliophile Lu Chien-tseng. See *ECCP,* pp. 120, 806. *LCCW,* #1, 8:2a, says that Wang and Weng Fang-kang were neighbors and constant companions in Peking in 1760 and 1761. Weng Fang-kang's *Fu-ch'u-chai wen-chi* (4:13a) confirms this. Wu Sung-liang, *Hsiang-su, shih-hua,* 1:15b, notes that Wang served sometime later in Ch'ien-lung's reign as literary secretary to Tseng Yü, the Yangchow salt commissioner, where Hung Liang-chi and Sun Hsing-yen (two of Ho-shen's impeachers) were his coworkers. For the pan-imperial register of academies (which survives in manuscript in the National Central Library, Taiwan), see *T'ien-hsia shu-yuan tsung-chih,* passim. The same work, 1:164–179, devotes considerable coverage to

the Tung-lin Academy. Page 154 gives the last year mentioned in these volumes (i.e., CC 4, or 1799), and notes this date as marking the reconstruction of the Ch'ing-ch'i Academy in Ch'ing-p'u county, Kiangsu, which was Wang's home county. I attribute the authorship to him on this basis. Yen Jung, *Shu-an hsien-sheng nien-p'u*, 2:22b, describes the register having been published in 1802. Ch'in Ying, 5:40, records that Wang asked Ch'in to help him search for documents on the Tung-lin Academy, and that the help was forthcoming.

48. For the secondary literature on the Hsuan-nan Poetry Club, see: Hsieh Cheng-kuang, "Hsuan-nan shih-she k'ao"; Hsieh Kuo-chen, "Chi Hsuan-nan shih-hui t'u-chüan"; James Polachek, "Literati Groups," pp. 157–206; and Wang Chün-i, "Kuan-yü Hsuan-nan shih-she ti chi-ko wen-t'i." For the 1814 inauguration of the Club, see Polachek, "Literati Groups," pp. 169ff., citing Hu Ch'eng-kung, *Ch'iu-shih-t'ang ch'üan-chi, wen-chi*, 4:23; and Wang Chün-i, pp. 221–222. The other points covered in this summary will be documented below.

49. Five of the thirteen men who participated in the Hsuan-nan Club for the first five years of its existence were men who had studied poetry and poetry criticism under Weng Fang-kang in Peking. These were: Ch'en Yung-kuang (1768–1835), Li Yen-chang (1794–1836), Liang Chang-chü (1775–1849), Liu Ssu-wan (n.d.), and Wu Sung-liang (1766–1834). See Liang Chang-chü, *Shih-yu chi*, 1:14b; and Wang Chün-i, p. 235. A sixth, Lin Tse-hsu, appears to have made his way in Southern City society in the late 1810s on the basis, in part, of his father's status as an examination pupil of Chu Yun, brother of Chu Kuei. See Lin Tse-hsu, *Yun-tso shan-fang wen-ch'ao*, 2:18b and *Yun-tso shan-fang shih-ch'ao*, 2:11a. Liang Chang-chü's father-in-law, Su Kuang-ts'e, was a 1779 provincial graduate passed by Chu Kuei. Chu also passed Liang's elder brother in the metropolitan examination of 1799, and Liang himself in the 1802 palace examination. See Liang Chang-chü, *Kuei-t'ien so-chi*, 4:8a, 6:2a. For the remaining members (Ch'ien I-chi, Chu Chien, Hsieh Chieh-shu, Hu Ch'eng-kung, Huang En-t'ao, T'ao Chu, and Tung Kuo-hua), see Polachek, "Literati Groups," pp. 170–171.

50. Chu and his northern-scholar nexus can be identified as having performed two somewhat irregular tasks for the Chia-ch'ing emperor during the years immediately following Ho-shen's overthrow (in 1799). First was the collection, through examination connections, of informed lettered-class opinions on the honesty and honorability of officials in important offices, or being considered for them. The Honan governor, Ching-an, for example, is reported to have been spared punishment for failure to drive the White Lotus rebels from his province because one of his former subordinates, who happened to be on good personal terms with Chu Kuei, vouched for his probity in a private conversation with that latter figure. See Ch'ien I-chi, 1:11a–12a. Fei Ch'un, who was one of the first officials to advance under the new, post-Ho-shen regime (he became Kiangnan governor general in early 1799) was an examination protégé of Chao I (1727–1814), a northern-party scholar-official who had risen in office in the mid-Ch'ien-lung under the sponsorship of Liu T'ung-hsun (see *ECCP*, p. 75; Chao I, *Ou-pei shih-hua*,

pp. 65–66; *Ou-pei hsien-sheng nien-p'u,* 12b, 31b, and *mu-chih-ming,* 6b). For the emperor's high esteem of Fei Ch'un, see *THHL,* 2:28b, and *SH-CC,* 27:9a (edict of 1799, 5th lunar month). These passages suggest that Chu Kuei, under Chao's influence, had been speaking up on Fei's behalf. On some occasions, Chia-ch'ing seems to have used informal examination-grapevine information to establish the trustworthiness of a lower-level official, and then used this as a basis for evaluating the credibility of senior officials by scrutinizing their evaluations of this same trusted junior officeholder. The handling of the case of the Anhwei magistrate Tso Fu (1751–1833) is a good example of this technique. Tso, who was a former subordinate of Chu Kuei's in Anhwei, was under investigation for financial mismanagement when Chu was summoned to Peking in 1799 to become grand secretary and 1799 metropolitan examiner. From T'ang Chin-chao, a provincial graduate in Peking for the 1799 examinations who had passed through Tso's current jurisdiction (Ho-ch'iu county) on his way north, Chu confirmed that Tso was a popular and respected official. (*CHLC,* 196:33b. For T'ang Chin-chao as a Chu Kuei pupil, see Chao-lien, Suppl., 2:44b. For Tso's background, see *CHLC,* 196:28ff.) Tso was reinstated to his original post and rank, and then promoted. The governor who had launched the disciplinary action against him, one Ch'en Yung-fu, did not long survive in office, however, since the court now believed his judgment faulty. The same fate was to be met by Ch'en's successor at one remove, Wang Ju-pi, in 1805, probably for the same reason. See Wang Hsien-ch'ien, 6:38a.

The other capacity in which the northern party helped Chia-ch'ing was in "guaranteeing" new (mainly Han-lin) talent for mid-level provincial posts, often themselves important as platforms for scrutinizing the behavior of high-level officials. At least three successful early Chia-ch'ing provincial officials can be identified as having entered the territorial administration by this route: Sun Erh-chun (1770–1832: 1805 Han-lin); Chiang Yu-hsien (1766–1830: 1781 Han-lin); and Juan Yuan (1764–1849: 1789 Han-lin). For Sun as a Chu Kuei pupil and bureaucratic client, see Chao-lien, 7:26a. Chiang was a provincial examination pupil of Weng Fang-kang and a metropolitan examination pupil of Chi Yun. (*HCSH,* #1, 9:66a; Chiang Yu-hsien, 1:6a.) For the "spy" role of Chiang's first provincial appointment, see Chiang Yu-hsien, 1:12; and *SL-CC,* 68:31a–33b. For Juan Yuan as a client of Chu Kuei, see Chao-lien, 8:27b, which claims Juan was transferred directly from the Han-lin Academy to the governorship of Chekiang in 1799 on Chu's recommendation. For Juan as a special imperial agent, see Wei Peh-t'i, "Internal Security and Coastal Control: Juan Yuan and Pirate Suppression in Chekiang, 1799–1809," esp. p. 85, note 5; and *SL-CC,* 68:29a–30a. Another variation of this method of planting northern-clique nominees in provincial surveillance roles is suggested by Wang Yin-chih's biographer, Wang Hsi-sun (1786–1847). Wang Yin-chih (1766–1834: *chin-shih* of 1787) was a 1786 classmate of Juan Yuan, Sun Hsing-yen, and Chang Hui-yen, all of whom were closely associated with Chu Kuei, and with the opposition to Ho-shen. In 1807, probably through the sponsorship of his same-year friends, Wang was given the rare honor of direct assignment to the post of education commissioner in Honan without prior participation in the test usually used for picking candidates. Arriving at his post, Wang then submitted secret reports to the emperor concerning unspecified abuses in administration, which reports were then relayed to the provincial governor for action along the lines suggested by Wang. See Wang Hsi-sun, *Ch'ieh-chu-an wen-chi*, 7–8. For a memoir of contemporary scholar-official awareness of how the Chu Kuei connection was being used by the Chia-ch'ing emperor, see Wu Sung-liang, *Hsiang-su, chin-t'i shih*, 4:14b.

51. For more details on the 1799–1805 turnover in the provincial bureaucracy, see (in addition to prior footnote) Chao-lien, 7:26a, and esp. 8:24b–28a. For Chiang, Juan, Sun, and Tung as the stars of the new administrative generation brought to the fore by Chia-ch'ing's shake-up, see Wu Hsi-ch'i, *Yu-cheng-wei-chai ch'ih-tu*, 2:25a.

52. For Chiang's advance, see Chiang Yu-hsien, 1:28b. For an example of a more typical pattern of Han Chinese career development within the provincial bureaucracy, see *ECCP*, p. 684, and Sun Yü-t'ing, *Yen-li-t'ang chi, nien-p'u*, 6b–30a. Sun Yü-t'ing, the eldest in this Chia-ch'ing restoration generation of provincial officials, waited thirty years (1786–1816) after gaining his first post-Han-lin provincial office before reaching the same vice-regal rank, though we must subtract from this a period of mourning leave of nearly three years.

53. For details, see below.

54. For an excellent general discussion of the Ch'ing government's standard procedures in the evaluation and disciplining of local officials, see Thomas A. Metzger, *The Internal Organization of Ch'ing Bureaucracy*, pp. 233–417. For the problem of conflict between central government (i.e., Board of Civil Appointments) regulationism and the preference of the top-level provincial officials for a more flexible approach to rule enforcement, see Metzger, pp. 239–240, 245, 269–275. In the Ch'ien-lung and early Chia-ch'ing reigns, the emperor (or the emperor and his councillors) seemed inclined to distrust requests from below for waiving promotion-impeding penalties bearing upon local officials. See *Ta-Ch'ing hui-tien shih-li*, (1899) 63:3a–7a, esp. 6b–7a (edict of CC 5), and *SH-CC*, 28:2a (edict of CC 11).

55. For a general study of this uprising, see Susan Naquin, *Millenarian Rebellion in China: The Eight Trigrams Uprising of 1813*.

56. For the impact of the rebellion—and the disclosures of the investigative commission—on the Chia-ch'ing emperor, see James Polachek, "Literati Groups," pp. 30–31; and Chao-lien, 4:44a–63a, esp. 59b, for the matter of official negligence. For the conviction that overly rigid enforcement of performance controls tended to undercut local official willingness to expose dissident bands and religious sects, see *SL-CC*, 285:15a. For the suspension of one review criterion (i.e., the number of *yin-kung ch'u-fen*, or demerits incurred through routine errors or oversight) in evaluations for the promotion into *t'i-tiao* posts (i.e., those county-level positions for which candidates were recommended by provincial officials), see *THHL*, 11:30b–

31a; and *Fan-ssu ting-li hui-pien*, Chia-ch'ing, 19, 2:15b. For the order for an additional review and reduction in the number of disciplinary regulations, see *SL-TK*, 7:24b–26a. See also *SCTI*, 2:289, for confirmation that *yin-kung ch'u-fen* continued to be disregarded for *t'i-tiao* promotions as late as 1833.

57. Polacheck, "Literati Groups," p. 80, table 3, shows (based on data from Chu Ju-chen, *Tz'u-lin chi-lueh*) that, during the Ch'ien-lung reign, only about 3 Han-lin graduates per year were promoted to entry-level positions in provincial government. During the late Chia-ch'ing and early Tao-kuang periods, however, the number rose to between 10 and 12. For the tendency to promote the most senior eligible capital officials into such entry-level vacancies, and for the negative effect on morale of such appointments, see *CSWP*, 13:63a–64a (memorial of Chiang Yu-hsien, 1813).

58. On the dating of this sudden boom in the recruitment of Han-lin into first-job middle-level posts in provincial administration, see Polacheck, "Literati Groups," p. 80, table 3. The data collected in this table (i.e., the number of Han-lin entering provincial administration in decades from 1736–1745 onward) show the greatest increase between the 1786–1795 and 1796–1805 groups. However, the grouping is done on the basis of the year of *entry* into the Han-lin. Since an average of ten years normally elapsed between then and first provincial appointment, the change in policy would have come between 1805 and 1814. Note also that the number of new Han-lin entrants per annum leapt up in 1799 (see p. 176, table 5), which allows us to guess that the early 1810s were the moment of transition to preferential recruitment of Han-lin. See also *HCSH*, #1, 10:33a, which records a controversial 1813 utterance by the northern scholar Han-lin Pao Kuei-hsing, to the effect that Chia-ch'ing had committed himself to substitute Han Chinese for Manchus in high-level provincial posts. This statement might reflect the beginning of the trend that we have remarked.

59. The evidence for this is circumstantial. Two official biographies, however, record that Chiang Yu-hsien was able to steer first-appointment Han-lin into posts under his authority. See *ECCP*, p. 716, for Chiang's recruitment of the 1801 Han-lin, Teng T'ing-chen; and *CHLC*, 197:2a, for Chiang's induction of the 1796 Han-lin, Chao Shen-chen, in 1812 as circuit intendant in Kwangtung. Gubernatorial-level officials normally were allowed to recommend only subordinates in this fashion, based on evaluation of service completed under their own scrutiny. Here, however, Chiang is vouching for the names of Southern City officials whom he had no way of knowing, save through the good offices of fellow northern-clique scholar-officials in Peking. In the case of Teng, the Hsuan-nan Club connection was via Ch'en Yung-kuang, a Weng student and Club member, who was Teng's in-law. See Wu Sung-liang, *Hsiang-su, chin-t'i shih*, 7:6a. In the case of Chao Shen-chen, the connection in question seems to have run through Chao's provincial examiner, Ch'ien Feng, who was (see above, note 33) a northern-clique activist. Chao was recommended for the *pa-kung* (licentiate by special selection) degree in 1789 by Ch'ien Feng, who was provincial director of studies for Hunan. See *CFTCC, Tung-ming wen-chi, hou-chi*, 12:7a. Through

Ch'ien, apparently, Chao was introduced to Weng Fang-kang, Chiang's mentor. (See Weng Fang-kang, *Fu-ch'u-chai*, 6:8a.) See also note below for T'ao Chu, Liang Chang-chü, and Lin Tse-hsu as other first-job Han-lin beneficiaries of Chiang's patronage.

60. Polachek, "Literati Groups," pp. 113–116, based on *CSWP,* 13:62a–65a.
61. *CSWP,* 13:64b–65a.
62. For Ts'ao Chen-yung as a Weng poetry student and examination pupil, see Weng Fang-kang, *Weng-shih chia-shih lueh-chi,* 36a; and Liang Chang-chü, *Shih-yu chi,* 111:18a. For Ying-ho's connection with Weng, see *HCSH,* #1, 9:67a; *LCCW,* #1, 9:12a; and Liang Chang-chü, *T'eng-hua yin-kuan shih-chao,* 7:21b–22a. Ying-ho may not in fact have been an examination pupil of Weng's. But he seems to have been one of Weng's literary executors and inherited a large portion of Weng's curio collection. For Ying-ho's rise to "cabinet"-level office after heroism in suppressing the 1813 revolt, see *CHLC,* 39:26. *CHLC,* 38:2a, notes that Ts'ao was advanced to adjunct grand secretary on 10 October 1813, two days after the uprising. For his examination patronage relations with Hsuan-nan Club members, see Wu Sung-liang, *Hsiang-su, shih-hua,* 2:5a; and Ch'en Yung-kuang, "T'ai-i-chou shih-tz'u-ch'ao," 3:16 (1935) p. 3.
63. For the role of Weng's pupils in the Club, see above, note 49. For the contact that developed between Weng's students and Ts'ao, one might note, for example, the couplets exchanged between Weng, Ts'ao, Ch'en Yung-kuang, and Liu Ssu-kuan (the last-named both Club members and Weng pupils) on the occasion of the new (1817) class of Han-lin being formally presented to the Academy's (Chinese) director, Ts'ao Chen-yung. See Ch'en Yung-kuang, "T'ai-i-chou shih-tz'u-ch'ao," 3:3 (1934) p. 2; and Liu Ssu-wan, 50:1. See also Liang Chang-chü, *T'ui-an sui-pi,* 6:24a, which notes that Liang had preserved calling cards from Ts'ao and Ying-ho.
64. The best example of how this Weng-student network operated to bring candidates to the attention of Chiang Yu-hsien is that of T'ao Chu (Han-lin, class of 1802), who won his promotion to a first provincial office (intendant in eastern Szechuan) in 1819 through Club connections. T'ao was not himself a Weng pupil. However, T'ao's fellow clubman, Liu Ssu-wan, was, and had been in contact by letter with Chiang (now Szechuan governor general) on the eve of T'ao's advancement. See Liu Ssu-wan, 52:2a. For the colophoned painting (of T'ao, as a censor, breaking up ice in the Grand Canal) that Liu probably passed along to Chiang, see Liang Chang-chü, *T'eng-hua,* 8:1a. The reverse correspondence—from Chiang to Liu, or to other Weng students—clearly helped T'ao learn enough about conditions in Szechuan and about Chiang's administrative goals to make an excellent impression on the Chia-ch'ing emperor during an 1819 pre-appointment interview. See *TWIK,* 58:8a. More indirect evidence suggests that the Chiang connection was also used to get first-job appointments for two other Club members: Liang Chang-chü and Lin Tse-hsu. See Liang Chang-chü, *T'ui-an sui-pi,* 5:12a; and Lin Tse-hsu, *Yun-tso shan-fang shih-ch'ao,* 4:1a–2b. For some general comments on Chiang's role as a patron within the bureaucracy, see Yao

Yung-p'u, 2:11b; *HCSH,* #4, 6:26b; and Shao I-ch'en, *Shao Wei-hsi i-wen,* 60b–61a. The role of Ts'ao Chen-yung in backing Weng-student-grapevine nominees is suggested by the comments that survive about Ts'ao's intimate knowledge of personnel at the middle and higher levels of provincial administration. See, for example, Chang Chi-liang, *Chang Heng-fu, shih,* 20:33b.

65. See, for example, *TWIK,* 53:35b, 54:7a, 55:35b, 55:43b, 60:5b–6a; and Liang Chang-chü, *T'eng-hua,* 8:2.

66. For the nine-man gatherings, see Liang Chang-chü, *Shih-yu chi,* 6:2; P'an Tseng-i, *Hsiao-fu shan-jen,* 20b–21a. For an example of the 40- or 50-man banquets often convened at the T'ao-jan-t'ing or Chiang-t'ing Pavilion during examination sessions, see Wu Sung-liang, *Hsiang-su,* 6:1a.

67. Yoshikawa Kōjirō, "Ko Shōkyō," in *Yoshikawa Kōjirō zenshū* 16: 263; Wang Chia-chien, *Wei Yuan nien-p'u* p. 15, note 3; P'an Tseng-i, *Kung-fu hsiao-chi,* 7:12b; Liu Ssu-kuan, 52:3.

68 For the role of Chi Yun (chief director of the Imperial Manuscript Library project) in spreading interest in the textual studies disciplines, see Yao Yung-p'u, 2:6a. Weng's influence as a court patron of the Han Learning (i.e., textual studies) tradition can be better documented, since Weng's papers survive in more complete form. *LCCW,* #1, 3:9, sees Weng and his poetry-group friends (Ch'ien Tsai, Ch'en Chin-fang, and Yao Nai) as the key link in diffusing the study of inscriptions through the Imperial Manuscript Library project. Weng Fang-kang, *Fu-ch'u-chai,* 7:6b–19a, gives the fullest discussion of Weng's rationale for the pursuit of *k'ao-chü.* It is to be noted, however, that Weng saw *k'ao-chü* as complementary to and reinforcing of the rival classical scholarly tradition of intuitive moral philosophy (*i-li*). See, for example, Weng, 4:20b, and 11:14a–15b.

69. For Su Tung-p'o birthday gatherings (12th lunar month, 19th day), see *TWIK,* 55:43b, and Liang Chang-chü, *T'eng-hua,* 8:2. Weng's enthusiasm for Su is noted in *ECCP,* p. 857. For Chu I-tsun as a subject of study and imitation (for Weng), see Liu Ssu-wan, 43:9; and (for the Hsuan-nan Club members) Ch'en Yung-kuang, *T'ai-i-chou wen-chi,* 6:25b and Chang Hsiang-ho, *Hsiao-chung shan-fang ch'u-kao, shih,* 4:1ff. For Wang Shih-chen in the same capacity, see (for Weng) Weng Fang-kang, *Fu-ch'u-chai,* 3:5b, 9a–10a; 8:3a, 6b; and 15:13b; and (for the Hsuan-nan clubmen) Liang Chang-chü, *T'eng-hua,* 7:17, 9:4b–5b; Ch'en Yung-kuang, "T'ai-i-chou shih-tz'u-ch'ao," 3:7 (1935) p. 2; and Liang Chang-chü, *T'ui-an sui-pi,* 21:23b–24b.

70. Chu I-tsun's reputation as a scholar rested mainly on his painstaking collecting of earlier works on classical exegesis and on his collection of primary sources for the history of Peking. See *ECCP,* pp. 183–184. Wang was respected for his critical evaluation of pre-Ch'ing poetry and for his allusion-filled "erudite" verse. See *ECCP,* p. 832. Yao Ying (*CFTCC, Shih-hsiao-lu,* 6:16a) notes that Su was known in early-19th-century China as a kind of literary dilettante, not as a serious Confucian moralist. I am indebted to James T. C. Liu, of Princeton University, for this general point concerning Su.

71. The point about the value (and superiority) of the non-contentious person-

ality is made quite directly by Weng Fang-kang in his *Fu-ch'u-chai*, 7:15b–17b.
72. *CFTCC, Tung-ming wen-chi, wai-chi*, 1:34.
73. *HCSH*, #1, 10:53b–54a, citing Ch'eng En-tse, who was a Hsuan-nan Club member (see P'an Tseng-i, *Hsiao-fu shan-jen*, 21a).
74. At least three major debates took place in the period 1799–1820 over revenue shortages (and what to do about them). For the first (in 1799), see *THHL*, 7:42b, 43b–44a; and *CHLC*, 29:36a. For a renewed debate in 1813–1814 (now focusing on the search for alternatives to the sale of offices), see Hsu Ta-ling, *Ch'ing-tai chüan-na chih-tu*, pp. 52–53, citing *SL-CC*, 282: 7b–9b; and Ying-ho, *En-fu-t'ang nien-p'u*, 58b–64a. For 1820–1821, see *SL-TK*, 4:18b–10a, 5:1b–3a, 7:37a–38a, 10:12a–14a, 10:25a–27a, 10:28a–30a; and Sun Yü-t'ing, *Tsou-su*, 1:40a–47a.
75. For a good English-language account of the ecological problems of the early 19th century, see Kuhn and Jones, pp. 108–113, 154. For a general overview of the failure to meet these new pressures with adequate fiscal reforms, see Suzuki Chūsei, "Shin-matsu no zaisei to kanryō no seikaku," pp. 191–203; and Suzuki Chūsei, *Shin-chō chūkishi kenkyū*, pp. 29–83. A good example of how early-19th-century scholar-officials insisted on blaming the government's managerial debilitation on the patterns of behavior *within* the government, rather than on environmental strains, occurs in *CSWP*, 21: 7a–8a (1800 essay of Hung Liang-chi).
76. For the perennial competition between grain-consuming military interests in the north and the scholar-official elite of the grain-supplying lower Yangtze, see, for example, Dennerline, pp. 40–41, 332 (footnote 80), for the Ming period; and James Polachek, "Gentry Hegemony: Soochow in the T'ung-chih Restoration," pp. 223–224, for the center-regional conflict over grain supply in the 19th century.
77. Kuhn and Jones, pp. 109–128.
78. For the pattern of conflict over north-south waterway upkeep between provincial and central bureaucratic interests in the early 19th century, see Polachek, "Literati Groups," pp. 263–271, and esp. pp. 360–364. For the military use of loans raised from the salt-monopoly merchants, see Thomas Metzger, "T'ao Chu's Reform of the Huai-pei Salt Monopoly (1831–1833)," p. 3. Metzger (p. 5) and *HPSW*, 22:6b, suggest that, by the early 19th century, provincial officials were openly pessimistic about their ability to control or arrest smugglers.
79. The obsession of early-19th-century lettered elite reformists with the superintendencies is betokened by the ubiquitousness of the river/grain transport/salt tax rubric in the descriptions of statecraft studies carried out by these men. See, for example, Chang Hsiang-ho, "Kuan-lung yü-chung ou-i pien," 3a (speaking of Chang's in-law, Wu Tzu-ho); and Ch'u Chin, "Tao-kuang hsüeh-shu," pp. 269–270 (speaking of scholar-official reform thought in general during the 1820–1850 period). During the 1814–1827 period, when Hsuan-nan Club interest in reform of the superintendencies developed, three scholar-officials of marginal position within the bureaucracy, but connected to the northern-scholar network, were writing prolifically

about this subject. They were: Ch'en Wen-shu (1775–1845), a Juan Yuan protégé (see *ECCP,* p. 104); Pao Shih-ch'en (1775–1855), a Chu Kuei protégé (see Hu P'u-an, *Pao Shih-ch'en hsien-sheng nien-p'u,* 5b–8a, 16a); and Wei Yuan (1794–1856), a T'ang Chin-chao pupil (see Wang Chia-chien, *Wei Yuan nien-p'u,* p. 7). For Ch'en's influential 1810 and 1825 proposals to dismantle the canal transport system in favor of a coastal transport one, see Ch'en Wen-shu, *I-tao-t'ang ch'üan-chi, wen-ch'ao,* 1:1a–18a; and 9:29a–36b. For his 1826 essays on river conservancy and salt-administration retrenchment, see ibid., 12:1a–12b, and 12:21a–26b. Pao Shih-ch'en's most influential contributions to this literature take the form of a set of essays, published in 1826 under the title *Chung-ch'u i-shao,* urging conversion to coastal transport. See *ECCP,* p. 610. For Wei Yuan's studies, see his *Wei Yuan chi,* 1:398–410 (1825) on grain-shipment reform; ibid., 2:421–437 (1839) on salt-administration reform; and 1:365–378 (1842) on river-conservancy retrenchment. Wei was adviser to Ho Ch'ang-ling and to Chiang Yu-hsien during the 1827 attempt to implement coastal grain transport; see below and Wei, 1:421–425. Ho Ch'ang-ling, *Nai-an tsou-i ts'un-kao, shih-ts'un,* 3:4 (poem of 1827), indicates that Ho, Wei's employer, was already committed by 1827 to the elimination of the canal and salt administrations.

80. According to Wei Yuan (*Wei Yuan chi,* 1:405), the five-prefecture "province" of Kiangnan—i.e., Soochow, Sungkiang, Chen-chiang, and Ch'ang-chou prefectures, and T'ai-ts'ang department—generated about 1.6 million piculs of transported tribute grain per annum, or about 40% of the entire empire-wide total. This and the rest of Kiangsu and Anhwei were in the early Tao-kuang (ca. 1821–1830) targets of major clean-up campaigns aimed at uncovering hidden deficits in provincial- and county-level treasury deposits, and at preventing their recurrence through improved surveillance of local officials. For details, see the following note.

81. For the 1820 reform decision, see *SL-TK,* 4:18b–20a, 5:1b–3a; 7:37a–38a; 10:12a–14a; 25a–27a, and 28a–30a. Anhwei and Kiangsu were two of the three most deficit-troubled provinces as of 1821 or so. (Suzuki, "Shin-matsu no zaisei," pp. 195, 197.) Suzuki (p. 212 note 37, and 213–214) documents the orders for audits and for a general clean-up in Kiangsu in 1821 (completed in 1823) and in Anhwei (completed in 1824). The concentration of Hsuan-nan Club members in posts in these provinces seems to have begun, in 1821, in conjunction with this campaign, with the assignment of T'ao Chu to the office of financial commissioner of Anhwei (*ECCP,* p. 710). By 1826–1827, the following clubmen or Chiang Yu-hsien protégés were in gubernatorial-level office in these provinces: Liang Chang-chü, Kiangsu financial commissioner (*ECCP,* p. 500); T'ao Chu, Kiangsu governor (*ECCP,* p. 710); Teng T'ing-chen, Anhwei governor (*ECCP,* p. 716); and Chiang Yu-hsien (appointed Liang-Kiang governor general on Tao-kuang (hereafter TK) 7/5/11 (see *SL-TK,* 117:18a).

82. For this, see Wei Yuan, *Ku-wei-t'ang wai-chi,* 7:9a–11b; Kuhn and Jones, p. 121, and Yamaguchi Michiko, "Shindai no sōun to senshō," p. 59.

83. Kuhn and Jones, pp. 122–123, citing the work of Hoshi Ayao, describe the

debates concerning the possible use of the coastal route for grain transport that took place in 1803, 1810, and 1815. In all three cases, the proposal debated was for permanent redirection of part of the shipment (see, for example, Chiang Yu-hsien, 1:24a–25b); the measure was referred collectively to the affected bureaucrats for their opinion; and the regional officials vetoed it. In 1827, by contrast, as we shall see below, the proposal emanated from the provincial bureaucracy itself, and was put forward ostensibly as an interim measure, thus avoiding the necessity for referral.

84. See, for example, *CSWP,* 48:11, for the plan to use coastal shipment in 1700 when a major repair of the Canal was about to be undertaken. For the development of the Shanghai-Manchuria coastal shipping trade in the Ch'ing, see Yamaguchi Michiko, pp. 56–72.

85. This was the position advocated by Wei Yuan and Ho Ch'ang-ling in an 1827 letter to Chiang that seems to account for Chiang's subsequent actions. See Wei Yuan, *Ku-wei-t'ang wai-chi,* 7:41a–42a; and Ho Ch'ang-ling, *Nai-an, wen-ts'un,* 6:17. For the idea of separating the management of river control and transport problems from each other as a means of improving and simplifying the administration of each, see Wei Yuan, *Wei Yuan chi,* 1:324. The same idea was developed again by Feng Kuei-fen in 1867, see his *Hsien-chih-t'ang chi,* 5:59.

86. For the 1824 Kao-yen disaster, see Polachek, "Literati Groups," pp. 207–220.

87. These three were the Liang-Kiang governor general, Sun Yü-t'ing (see *ECCP,* p. 684) in 1824; his successor as governor general, Ch'i-shan (in office from 1825–1827: see *ECCP,* p. 127); and the director general of Kiangsu waterways, Chang Wen-hao, who lost his post in early 1825 (see *Ch'ing-tai ho-ch'en chuan,* p. 161). For the unsuccessful attempts to repair the Canal/Yellow River junction between 1825 and 1827, see Polachek, "Literati Groups," pp. 232–259.

88. For the supposedly temporary 1825 sea-shipment plan, which was originated by the Grand Secretary Ying-ho (a Peking official), see Ho Ch'ang-ling, *Chiang-su hai-yun ch'üan-an,* 1:12a. Fifty percent of the southern rice was shipped by sea to Peking; the other 50% was commuted into silver, and used to pay for repair of the canal.

89. For Ying-ho's role in the 1825 experiment, see Ying-ho, 105a; and Ho Ch'ang-ling, *Nai-an, wen-ts'un,* 6:5a. Late in 1827, another official in Chiang's protégé network, Ho Ch'ang-ling (see Ho, *Nai-an,* 6:14a–10a for the relationship with Chiang) wrote to Ying-ho's newly named successor (and examination pupil) as grand councillor, Mu-chang-a, to plead the case for continuing sea shipment (Ho, *Nai-an,* 6:1a–2b). In 1830, T'ao Chu (*TWIK,* 41:39b) wrote to his "teacher," Ying-ho, in a manner suggesting that Ying-ho had favored the permanent sea-shipment plan. One problem that undercut the 1827 reform might have been the mid-1827 political ruin of Ying-ho. See Ying-ho, 108b–109a.

90. For Chiang's request to renew sea shipment in the autumn of 1827, see *SL-TK,* 125:3b–4a. For his alerting the throne to the dangers of any precipitate attempt at canal repair, see *SCTI,* 1:199–203, and *SL-TK,* 131:25b.

91. *SL-TK*, 120:3a–4a; and 125:26ff.

92. *SL-TK*, 125:14ff (for edict of TK 7/9/10); and 126:31a (for edict of 9/30).

93. For the termination of the sea-shipment plan (on 11/4) and the emperor's final condemnation of Chiang's strategy, see *SL-TK*, 129:12a–13b.

94. For the Huang Yu-lin case, see Metzger, "T'ao Chu's Reform," p. 5; and Chiang Yu-hsien, 2:49b. Chiang's punishment arose from the failure of the local salt-administration authorities in Yangchow to control a "surrendered" chief smuggler, Huang Yu-lin. Huang's pardon had been arranged on the promise that he would help catch other, lesser culprits, but he seems instead to have quickly returned to his old ways.

95. For Ch'eng En-tse, see above, note 72. For T'ao Chu's belief that the sea-shipment plan had stirred up a "rumor" (*fu-i*) campaign against its authors, see *TWIK*, 41:29b. Shao I-ch'en, *Shao Wei-hsi*, 61a, in a comment on Chiang written in 1852, sees Chiang's fall as having resulted from the negative effect upon the emperor of his habit of being too "straightforward."

96. For Lin's self-characterization as a Chu-ko Liang (i.e., a loyal minister forced to work without supporters at court), see his *Yün-tso shan-fang wen-ch'ao*, 4:9b–10a.

97. Lin (1785–1850) was a 1811 Han-lin and was 42 at the time of the 1827 fiasco. By contrast, Chiang (a 1781 Han-lin) was 61; and T'ao (1802 Han-lin) was 48.

98. For a detailed account of administrative developments during Lin's term as Kiangnan governor (1832–1837), see Lin Ch'ung-yung, *Lin Tse-hsu chuan*, chapters 9–10. For an excellent monograph on the northern reclamation scheme (details to follow), see chapter 11. That Lin commenced work on the plan as early as 1832 (his first year of office) is confirmed by Feng Kuei-fen, *Hsien-chih-t'ang chi*, 12:25a.

99. *CFSLI*, 18a–24b.

100. For P'an's role, see P'an Tseng-i, *P'an Feng-yü chuang pen shu*, preface and 1a–4a. P'an's discovery of a record of successful irrigated rice agriculture in Shantung in 1834 evidently encouraged Lin to forge ahead. For the role of Feng Kuei-fen (the other local scholar), see his *Hsien-chih-t'ang chi*, 12:25a; and *Chiao-pin-lu k'ang-i*, 25a.

101. Feng, *Chiao-pin-lu*, 26a.

102. *CFSLI*, preface, 1b–2b.

103. Interestingly, in the memorial Lin originally planned for submission in 1836, he had referred quite bluntly to the opposition he expected the scheme to arouse from the bureaucrats, clerks, guards, and trackers, all of whose jobs would be threatened. Such economies as the reform might engender, Lin had written, "would drain way the booty from the sacks of these parasites and deprive even more of them of their perquisites. From the moment [any such reclamation project] is attempted, idle criticisms and attempts at obstruction could be expected to proliferate" (*CFSLI*, 42b). This consideration, obviously, had persuaded Lin to propose only a slow-going conversion to localized grain supply of the capital.

104. For the blockage of the plan by the governor general of the metropolitan

province, Ch'i-shan, and (presumably) by other affected administrators as well, see Lin Ch'ung-yung, p. 157; and Feng Kuei-fen, *Chiao-pin-lu,* 26a. Ch'i-shan's irritation, according to Lin Ch'ung-yung, arose from the fact that the reclamation plan would have required Lin's taking over the metropolitan governor-generalship.

2. The Rise of the Spring Purification Circle

1. Wang Chün-i, p. 225, suggests that the Club had ceased to meet before 1830. His evidence is the internal reference in two poems shared among clubmen before that date to the already lapsed condition of the Club's meetings. If a tight definition of the Club is imposed—i.e., a nine-man group meeting every year on Su Tung-p'o's birthday—it would appear that meetings stopped in 1824. See Chang Hsiang-ho, *Hsiao-chung shan-fang,* 11.1b, 11:17, for the last two references to such a group. However, Clubman Chang was in Peking until the summer of 1828 (see 14a). Chang Hsiang-ho, "Kuan-lung," 3a, records that the author, while serving as a mid-level provincial official in Shantung (1832–1836), sent contributions to pay for Hsuan-nan Club gatherings. However, this and other references to a Hsuan-nan Club of the 1830s appear to confuse the Club with the Spring Purification circle. (Note that Chang lists Hsu Pao-shan as one of the leaders of the Club in the 1830s while, in fact, Hsu was one of the two co-organizers of the Spring Purification group—for which, see below).
2. See note 1.
3. The data on the Spring Purification circle meetings, membership, etc., are culled from Huang Chueh-tzu, *HPSW.* This unusual source, completed in 1849, assembles poems, letters, and other belletristic communications received by the author from his mentors and friends among the elite during the thirty-year period 1816–1846. For the 1829 gathering, see 14:3. This is the first such gathering recorded by Huang himself. However, *CCS,* 14b, says that the meetings had begun under Huang's auspices in the spring of 1826. Chang Chi-liang, 9:1b and 10:4b, shows such meetings as having taken place (under Hsu Pao-shan and under Huang) in 1827 and 1828 respectively. For the probable reason that 1826 was marked as the first year of the Spring Purification meetings, see below, note 22.
4. No printed biography of Hsu Pao-shan exists. For Pi Yuan's secretarial staff as a locus of northern-scholar-clique patronage, see *LCCW,* #2, 8:13a, and *ECCP,* p. 624. For the role of Hsu's father in this group, see Wang Ch'ang, 2:1165; Wu Sung-liang, *Hsiang-su, shih-hua,* 2:1; and Hsu Pao-shan, *Hu-yuan, shih-ch'ao hsuan,* 6:2b, 6a; *tsa-chu,* 4b. Another northern-scholar patronage group in which Hsu's father had participated was the scholarly coterie gathered together by the Yangchow salt commissioner, Tseng Yü (1760–1831; in office 1793–1806), for which see *SJCL,* 41:2a; *LCCW,* #2, 10:5a, 9a; and Wu Sung-liang, 1:15b. For Hsu the younger's reliance on his father's northern-clique connections, see Hsu Pao-shan, *Hu-yuan, tsa-chu,* 4b (discussing his relationship with Tseng Yü and Wu Sung-liang); for Hsu

Pao-shan's mastery of the Wang-Chu school of poetic style, see 8a, and 23a.

5. For Huang's uncle and his connection with Weng Fang-kang, see Ku Ch'un, *Ssu-wu-hsieh-shih wen-chi*, 4:56. For Huang's youthful poems and their conformity with the fashions espoused by Weng, see *Chuan-chi hsing-shu hui-chi*. For Huang's early relationship with Wu Sung-liang, see *HPSW*, 1:9b. For an account of Huang's poetry studies (starting with Wang Shih-chen), see *HPSW*, 6:1a–13a.

6. For Li Yen-pin, see Chu Ju-chen, 6:4a. For Yen-chang as a Weng student, see above; Li Yen-pin is recorded by Huang Chueh-tzu (*HPSW*, 18:14a) as having kept the Su Tung-p'o birthday rites in Peking each winter until 1832, a task he evidently inherited from his elder brother. Chou Chung-hsi (Han-lin class of 1823—see Chu Ju-chen, 6:4b) appears to have been a fourth member of this Han-lin circle. See Change Chi-liang, 9:1b, 10:4b; and *HPSW*, 14:3. No data are available, however, on Chou's familial background or possible ties with the northern-scholar group.

7. For the 1826 beginnings of Huang and Huang's poetry salon, see Hsu Pao-shan, *Hu-yuan, shih-ch'ao hsuan* 3:2b. For Huang's relationship with Tseng Yü, see *HPSW*, 11:3a (congratulatory inscription from Tseng, dated 1826). For Hsu's see note 4, above. Weng was Tseng's examination mentor in the 1780 Shun-t'ien provincial examinations; see Pao Shih-ch'en, 14 *hsia:* 8a; and Wu Sung-liang, *Hsiang-su, chin-t'i-shih*, 3:5a. Tseng shared Weng's devotion to Su Tung-p'o (*LCCW*, #2, 10:5a, 9a), and helped find jobs for the pupils of the northern-clique scholar-official Wang Ch'ang (2:1060). A congratulatory poem from Huang's examination patron, P'an Shih-en, dated 1829, reveals that Tseng and the Weng "student" (and former clubman), Wu Sung-liang, were the poetic judges to whom Huang deferred. See *HPSW* 14:5a.

8. The immediate causes of the problem seem to have been Wu Sung-liang's 1829 departure from Peking, and Tseng's death in 1831. Coupled, these two developments had the effect of leaving Hsu and Huang without elder-generation sponsors in Southern City belletristic society. See Hsu Pao-shan, *Hu-yuan, tsa-chu*, 4b–5a, 33b–34a.

9. Mei and Kuan were students of Yao Nai, the mid-Ch'ing high priest of the so-called T'ung-ch'eng school, a late development in *ku-wen* studies launched, originally, by Fang Pao (1668–1749), of T'ung-ch'eng, Anhwei. (See *ECCP*, pp. 236–237, for Fang and Yao Nai; and *TCFC, I-wei-hsuan wen-chi*, 11:5b–6a, for Mei and Kuan.) For Ma Yuan as a close youthful friend of Mei and Kuan, see Kuan T'ung, *Yin-chi-hsuan wen-chi, pu-i*, 6a. A good summary of the utilitarian and non-conformist values of belletristic evaluation current in early-19th-century T'ung-ch'eng school criticism occurs in the biography of Mei Tseng-liang in Chu Hsuan, *Yao Hsi-pao hsueh-chi*, pp. 185–191. The decline of the *ku-wen* and T'ung-ch'eng traditions in the Ch'ien-lung period seems to have resulted, in part, from the reorientation toward poetry after 1750 (see above, chapter 1, note 14). Fang Pao and the mid-Ch'ing T'ung-ch'eng school held a low estimate of poetry (a medium they regarded as too decorative and formalistic for serious writing), and composed little or none themselves (*ECCP*, p. 237; and *CFTCC, Tung-ming,*

wai-chi, 1:6a, 2:7a; and Ch'en Yung-kuang, *Tai-i-chou wen-chi*, 6:7b). Another reason for the decline might have been the Ch'ien-lung emperor's jealousy of the political influence that T'ung-ch'eng natives had enjoyed under his father, thanks to the position at court of Chang T'ing-yü. (See above, chapter 1.) The marginal status of the *ku-wen* tradition in the Ch'ien-lung period was reflected in the revisionist doctrine of Yao Nai, who taught that belletristic prose (*wen-chang, tz'u-chang*) had to be combined with philology (*k'ao-chü*) and moral philosophy to complete the curriculum. See, for example, Yao Nai, pp. 90–91 (letter to Ch'in Ying). For Kuan T'ung's failures in the examination and his bitterness, see his *Yin-chi-hsuan wen-chi, erh-chi*, 3:4b–5a. Mei Tseng-liang (an 1822 metropolitan graduate) was passed by the influential literocrat Wang T'ing-chen, but was apparently so piqued by his failure to place for a Southern City position that he resigned the magistrate's office to which he was assigned, and stayed away from both Peking and the civil service until 1831. (See Mei Tseng-liang, 2:5a, 3:17b.) All three—Kuan, Mei, and Ma—were employed by the Anhwei authorities as compilers of the 1829 provincial gazetteer (see Kuan T'ung, *erh-chi*, 4:5b; and Mei, 7:18b). Mei was reintroduced into Peking society by Ch'eng En-tse in 1831 (Mei, 7:7b). Ch'eng had been invited by his fellow Hsuan-nan clubman T'ao Chu to lecture at the Nanking Chung-shan Academy. Upon returning to the capital in 1831, he took Mei with him and introduced him to Hsu Pao-shan, a fellow native of She-hsien, Anhwei.

10. For Mei Tseng-liang's *ku-wen* salon in Peking, see Mei, 3:17b; Chu Ch'i, 4:1a; and K'ung Hsien-i, 2:12b. Important participants were Feng Chih-i, Chu Ch'i, Yu K'un, Wang Hsi-chen, Wu Chia-pin, and K'ung Hsien-i, as well as Mei himself.
11. For his relationship with Yao Nai, see *CFTCC, Shih-hsiao-lu*, 6:6a; and *Nien-p'u*, 5b.
12. Ibid., *Nien-p'u*, 6a.
13. Ibid., 7b.
14. For the circumstances of Yao's dismissal, see ibid., 10b.
15. Ibid., 11a–14a.
16. For the trips to Peking, see ibid., 12b and 14a; for the other events, 14a–16a.
17. For Yao as an exemplar, see Chang Chi-liang, *Chang Heng-fu, wen*, 3:1.
18. For Yao's patronage of Fang Tung-shu, see *CFTCC, Nien-p'u*, 15a, and Fang Tsung-ch'eng. For his help for Cheng K'ai-hsi (whom Yao seems to have introduced to his friends in Peking, in 1826), see *CFTCC, Tung-ming, wai-chi*, 1:7; and Chang Chi-liang, 8:12b. Others for whom Yao helped find secretarial or teaching posts during his term as a Kiangsu magistrate and Yangchow salt controller (1832–1837) apparently included Li Chao-lo, Wu Te-hsuan, P'an Te-yü, Lu Chi-lo, and Mao Yu-sheng. See Yao Yung-p'u, 4:20a; and *CFTCC, Tung-ming, hou-chi*, 6:12a, 9:2a, and *Nien-p'u*, 15a. Of these, Cheng and P'an were participants in the Peking meetings of the Spring Purification circle; see *HPSW*, 14:3a, 3b; 15:15a; and 17:10.
19. For the background to Yao's encounter with Chang, see *CFTCC, Tung-ming, wai-chi*, 2:16b–18a; and ibid., *hou-chi*, 11:8a. Yao apparently met Chang in

1823 in Foochow, through the introduction of the master of the Ao-feng Academy, Ch'en Shou-ch'i.

20. For the early influence of the T'ung-ch'eng school of *ku-wen* criticism on Chang, see Chang Ch'i-liang, *wen*, 2:1a; and Ch'en Yung-kuang, *T'ai-i-chou wen-chi*, 4:2b.

21. *CFTCC, Tung-ming, wai-chi*, 2:17b.

22. It is interesting to note that Yao used his connections with the two reigning elders of the Hsuan-nan Poetry Club, Ch'en Yung-kuang and Wu Sung-liang, to help get Chang established in 1826. Through Yao's appeal, Ch'en (who was a fellow pupil of Yao Nai) agreed to lodge Chang at his Peking residence (Chang Chi-liang, 8:20b, 22b) and to present Chang's poems to a certain Lu Yen, who knew two of the examiners overseeing the 1826 examinations in the capital. To Wu Sung-liang, Chang was introduced via Yao's protégé, Cheng K'ai-hsi (ibid., 8:12b, 17b, 10a). Probably through Wu, Chang then met Hsu Pao-shan, one of the two heads of the nascent Spring Purification circle. And Hsu, in turn, brought Chang's poems to the attention of Hsu's examination mentor, Huang Yueh, who endeavored to spread word to *his* "pupils" about his new Fukiense poet-prodigy (ibid. 17:28b, 18:18a). The intermeshing of Hsuan-nan Club and Spring Purification circle connections revealed in this episode might help explain why the two groups were later confused (see note 1 above). Yao Ying might himself have been eager to have Chang make an impression on Ch'en Yung-kuang and his Hsuan-nan Club friends, since Yao was obviously seeking to enlist the support of Chiang Yu-hsien (chief metropolitan examiner for the 1826 examinations) for his own attempt to regain office. See Chang Hsiang-ho, *Hsiao-chung, shih*, 12:9b–10a, 15a.

23. For the episode with Tseng Yü, and Chang's ostracization, see *CFTCC, Tung-ming, hou-chi*, 11:8.

24. For this, see, for example, Chang Chi-liang, 15:28b, 17:28a; and P'an Tseng-shou, *Kai-lan, shih-chi*, 2:6a.

25. For Kung's family background and career, see Wu Ch'ang-shou, *Ting-an hsien-sheng nien-p'u*, pp. 589–631. For his scholarship, see *ECCP*, pp. 431–433. For his bad luck in the metropolitan examinations (which he failed five times consecutively, starting in 1814, and which he passed only in 1829, with a "third"—i.e., in the lowest tier), see Wu Ch'ang-shou, esp. pp. 611, 618. He was placed lowest in 1829, according to this latter source (p. 618), because of his bad calligraphy. Kung's famous satire against the cult of calligraphy in the examination system (*ECCP*, p. 432) was later to become associated with the criticism of the regime of Ts'ao Chen-yung. (See Yü-chai, "Tao-kuang-ch'ao chih chün-hsiang," 1:175–176.) For Kung's pieces on Sinkiang, see *ECCP*, p. 432, and Kung Tzu-chen, pp. 618, 623. In 1839, Kung described himself as a "middle-aged prodigy" (*chung-nien ts'ai-tzu*)—a phrase that remains an excellent description of his style of thought and writing (ibid., 520).

26. For Wang Hsi-sun's biography, see Liu Wen-ch'i, *Ch'ing-ch'i chiu-wu wen-chi*, 9:1a–5b. For his father, Wang Chung, see *ECCP*, pp. 814–815. For Wang's

essays on fiscal reform, see his 1841 (published) *Ts'ung-cheng-lu.* For Wang as the "tongue" of the emerging opposition, see *CFTCC, Tung-ming, hou-chi,* 9:2b–3a (1836 congratulatory preface for Wang Hsi-sun).

27. For Wei Yuan's early (1813) recognition as a poet, see Wang Chia-chien, *Wei Yuan nien-p'u,* 7. Wei apparently did not develop any particular interest in textual-studies issues (such as historical geography or classical philology) until his first (1814) trip to the capital. And he did not become really immersed in either until his protracted post-1821 residence in Peking. See ibid., 8a and 16ff. Wei's failure in the 1826 examinations seems to have been particularly traumatic, since his Classics teacher, Liu Feng-lu, did his best to arrange for Wei's examination paper to win recognition, but to no avail. (See Li Yueh-jui, pp. 54–55.) For his concentration on historical geography and its significance, see *ECCP,* p. 851.

28. Tuan-mu Kuo-hu began his rise into Peking literati society in the wake of his having impressed the Chekiang educational commissioner (and northern-clique scholar-official), Juan Yuan, with an examination poem in 1796. See the 1875 *Ch'ing-t'ien hsien-chih,* 10:12b. For the evolution of his later interests, Juan's attempt to pass him in the metropolitan examinations (in 1799), and Tuan-mu's long wait (until 1833) for Juan to repeat the attempt (this latter time, successfully), see the same source.

29. See *CFTCC, Tung-ming, hou-chi,* 10:11. For Kung Tzu-chen (in 1839) on T'ang P'eng as himself an eccentric, see Kung Tzu-chen, p. 511.

30. For Yao and T'ang P'eng's social role in 1826, see note 29, and Wu Sung-liang, *Hsiang-su,* 12:15a; Hsu Pao-shan, *Hu-yuan, shih-ch'ao hsuan,* 3:7b–8a.

31. For Ts'ao, see above, chapter 1, note 62; and below, chapter 3.

32. For late-19th-century anecdotal materials on Ts'ao as an examiner, see Li Yueh-jui, pp. 59–60 (citing Wen T'ing-shih [1856–1904]), which emphasizes Ts'ao's monolithic and conformity-obsessed repression of scholarly exotica in the examination system. This account perhaps unfairly caricatures Ts'ao's motives. But it reflects quite accurately the amount of influence he exercised over the examinations, and the irritation that anyone enjoying this amount of power would provoke. For a more positive view of Ts'ao's role as a literocrat, see *HCSH,* #3, 10:15b–16a, which notes that he was the first examiner in the Ch'ing to preside over five sittings of the metropolitan examinations. See also Lin Tse-hsu, *Yun-tso shan-fang wen-ch'ao,* 1:6, 2:5. Lin here expresses approval of the kind of centralized influence over scholarship that Ts'ao exercised through his many tours as examiner.

33. Chang Chi-liang (20:33b) notes that Ts'ao could recite from memory the dossiers of all current mid-level (i.e., probationary) provincial officials. Note also that, as of 1837 (two years after Ts'ao's death), all five grand councillors on duty in Peking were Han-lin—an unprecedented state of affairs in the Ch'ing. (See P'an Shih-en, *Ssu-pu-chai pi-chi,* 5:2b.)

34. According to the son of P'an Shih-en, Tseng-shou, Juan Yuan's 1829 recall for an audience with the emperor triggered speculation that Juan was soon to be made an adjunct grand secretary—traditionally the stepping stone for re-entry from provincial office into the Peking political world. See his *Kai-lan,*

shih-ch'ao, 2:2a. In fact, the honor was not gained by Juan until September 1832 (*SL-TK,* 218:17b). P'an Shih-en became a full grand secretary in mid-1833. According to P'an himself, the appointment was announced by the emperor as restoring to P'an his rightful position an an official senior to Juan. (See *Ssu-pu lao-jen shou-ting nien-p'u,* 51a; and *SL-TK,* 235:12a.) P'an gained yet further ground on his rival with an early 1834 appointment as grand councillor, with the usual twelve-month period of apprenticeship waived (P'an Shih-en, *Nien-p'u,* 52b). Juan never did make grand councillor. But he did become an informal adviser after Ts'ao Chen-yung's death in 1835. See below. For more on this competition, see P'an's *Ssu-pu-chai pi-chi,* 1:6b.

35. For P'an as 1828 examiner in the *k'ao-ch'ai* examinations (by which provincial examiners where chosen), see P'an, *Nien-p'u,* 44b. For his relationship as examination mentor to Huang, who was elevated to *pa-kung* licentiate in 1813 by P'an, see *Ssu-pu-chai pi-chi,* 6:4b; and *HPSW,* 11:2a. For more on the P'an-Huang collaboration to promote talent discovered in the 1828 provincial examinations, see *HPSW,* 13:2b–3a.

36. For indirect evidence of this consultation, see *HPSW,* 11:2a, 14:4b, 14:6b; and P'an Shih-en, *Ssu-pu-chai shih-chi,* 3:2. Here we see Huang refashioning an earlier painting of himself (that P'an Shih-en had autographed), this time adding the names of two of his 1828 Kiangnan provincial examination "pupils," P'an Te-yü and Ts'ao Mao-chien. (For whom, see Huang Chih-lin, 3a; and K'ung Hsien-i, *Han-chai wen-kao,* 3:23a.) Presumably, the new illustration would then have been shown again to P'an, with examples of Ts'ao's and P'an's poetry. The other references are to an 1829 poetry discussion meeting to which were invited the two current leading lights of poetry fashion in the capital (Wu Sung-liang and Chang Chi-liang), and P'an Shih-en's two "pupils," Huang Chueh-tzu and Chung Ch'ang, who had been 1828 examiners. See also *HPSW,* 16:5a (letter from P'an Te-yü), which indicates that Huang had undertaken to circulate his "pupil" P'an Te-yü's poetry drafts among unnamed senior officials in the capital.

37. P'an Tseng-shou, *Kai-lan, shih-chi,* 1:7b; and *HPSW,* 14:3.

38. Huang's protégé, Ts'ao Mao-chien, for example, passed the metropolitan examinations in 1832, entering the Han-lin. P'an Shih-en was examiner that year (*Ch'ing-pi shu-wen, hsu,* 3:20a). Also Chang Chi-liang, 17:28b, 18:18a, for Chang's coming to P'an Shih-en's attention in a similar way (probably through Huang Chueh-tzu's recommendation).

39. P'an Tseng-shou, *Kai-lan, shih-chi,* 1:7b; *HPSW,* 13:3b. For the outcome, see Huang Chih-lin, 3a.

40. Ch'iao Sheng-hsi, "Hu-pei-sheng li-shih-shang ti shui-han wen-t'i," pp. 18–19.

41. Huang Chien-hua, "Tao-kuang shih-tai ti tsai-huang tui she-hui ching-chi ti ying-hsiang," pp. 128–130.

42. For the frequency of outbreaks of organized violence as a variable correlating with food scarcity, see C. K. Yang, "Some Preliminary Statistical Patterns of Mass Action in Nineteenth Century China," p. 190, Table 11, columns 7–9. The data in all three columns show the decade 1826–1835 as a watershed in the period 1795–1911. For contemporary commentaries

marking the increase of banditry and its connection with the famine, see, for example, Lu I-t'ung, *T'ung-fu lei-kao*, 3:2b–36, and *shih-ts'un*, 1:8b–10a. According to Lu, who was from the drought-prone Huai-pei region, the banditry that erupted in the winter of 1831–1832 was the worst since 1786.

43. See, for example, *HPSW,* 16:2a, 18:13a–14a, 19:22a, for reports from Huang Chueh-tzu's fellow provincials in Kiangsi on waves of crop- and cattle-stealing in that province in 1831, 1833, and 1834. See also *HCTTS,* pp. 18–20, and *SL-TK,* 238:15a–18a, for the complaint Huang made to the throne based upon this information. (Note that Huang was from I-huang county, where these incidents took place.) See also *SL-TK,* 213:18a–19b, for a mid-1832 general statement of the lettered-elite view on this issue by a censor, Ch'iu Yuan-chün, also of Kiangsi provincial origin. Magistrates with connections in the captial could also be a source of complaints; see, for example, Chou T'ien-chueh, *Chou Wen-chung kung ch'ih-tu, hsia,* 1a–2a, 21b–22a (letters to T'ang P'eng, dated 1832 and 1833).

44. C. K. Yang, p. 209.

45. A survey of censorial impeachments of identified local officials for negligence in arresting and prosecuting criminals, covering the period 1800–1840 for six provinces (Kwangtung, Hunan, Kiangsi, Fukien, Anhwei, and Shantung), shows the following trend (source: *SL-TK*):

    1800–1809   No more than 2 per annum
    1810–1819   Same (except for 1814: 5 cases)
    1820–1829   Same (except for 1822: 3 cases)
    1830–1839   Average of 7.5 per annum (10 in 1830; 8 each
                in 1831 and 1832; and 12 in 1839)

46. *HPSW,* 20:9b.

47. The best general account of the rebellion is Wei Yuan, *Sheng-wu chi,* 7:41a–45a. For Hsi-en's dispatch, see *SL-TK,* 208:9a; for the 10 June penitential proclamation, see 212:10a–11a; for Ch'iu's memorial and response, see 213:18a–19a.

48. For the removal of Li, see *SL-TK,* 218:13a–14b; for the extension of punishment to other, lower-ranking officials in Hunan, see 218:1a–2b.

49. Chang Chi-liang, *Chang Heng-fu, wen,* 3:5b–7a. For other evidence of Spring Purification circle muckraking in connection with the rebellion, see ibid., 15:13b, and Hsu Pao-shan, *Hu-yuan, tsa-chu,* 27b.

50. For Hsu's memorial, see *SL-TK,* 227:24a–25a; and 230:21a–22a.

51. For the 2 February lecture, see *SL-TK,* 227:24a–25a. For the 6 February reinstatement, see Hsu Pao-shan, *Hu-yuan, Kuo-t'ing-lu,* 6b, and *tsa-chu,* 33b–34a.

52. P'an Te-yü, *Yang-i-chai chi, wen-chi,* 22:5b–6a.

53. *SL-TK,* 270:24a–25a (edict of TK 15/8/24, 15 October 1835).

54. Yü-chai, "Tao-kuang-ch'ao chih chün-hsiang," 1:277.

55. For Su Tung-p'o's birthday, see *HPSW,* 18:14a. For Huang T'ing-chien, see ibid., 14:4a. For Weng Fang-kang's role in launching the cult of Huang during the Ch'ing, see Wu Sung-liang, *Hsiang-su, fang,* 4:7a–8a. For the identification with Wang and Chu, it is to be noted that the temple where the Spring Purification circle deposited its most venerated artifact, the Ting-wu-

pen version of the Wang Hsi-chih Orchid Pavilion scroll (see below, note 57) was the Tsao-hua-ssu, where Wang and Chu had planted trees in the late 17th century. (See Chang Hsiang-ho, *Hsiao-chung shan-fang,* 13:3b; Wu Sung-liang, *Hsiang-su, chin-t'i shih,* 11:13a; and *HPSW,* 20:13b.)

56. Called the *Su-mi-chai lan-t'ing kao,* or "Study of the Orchid Pavilion [scroll] by the Master of the Su-mi Studio." See *ECCP,* p. 857.

57. For a translation of the original Orchid Pavilion scroll, see J. D. Frodsham, "The Origins of Chinese Nature Poetry," pp. 88–93. For its subsequent history and the Ting-wu-pen version, see *A Reproduction of the Lan-t'ing Calligraphy Scroll by Wang Hsi-chih,* pp. 9–10, 13. For the hobby of collecting different versions, see, for example, Huang An-t'ao, *Shih-yü-shih shih-chi,* 10:18a; and Liang Chang-chü, *Teng-hua yin-kuan shih-ch'ao,* 7:21b.

58. Kung Tzu-chen, pp. 219, 614; and *HPSW,* 21:13b, 17b, 18b, 24b.

59. For the timing of the Spring Purification gathering to include provincial graduates in Peking for the examinations (*kung-ch'e*), see Wu Ch'ang-shou, p. 619 (entry for 1832); *HPSW,* 21:16a; and Huang Chueh-tzu, *HPSW, wen-lu,* 11:13a. The original Spring Purification banquet of 353 had been held on the 3rd day of the 3rd lunar month, whereas the Spring Purification gatherings of 1829, 1836, and 1838 were held much later in the 3rd (or early in the 4th) month. See above, Table 1, and Frodsham, p. 90. Interestingly, when the Hsuan-nan Club poets Ch'eng En-tse and Liang Chang-chü had convened Spring Purification banquets in 1815 or 1816, they had been more exact in their calendrical choice. See Liang Chang-chü, *Teng-hua,* 7:16b.

60. See note 55 above.

61. For the celebration of Ou-yang Hsiu's birthday (actually on 6/21, but celebrated on 6/16), see *HPSW,* 14:4a. For Ou-yang Hsiu as a consolidator of the *ku-wen* tradition, see Liu Tzu-chien, *Ou-yang Hsiu ti chih-hsueh yü ts'ung-cheng,* p. 88.

62. See, for example, Chang Chi-liang, *Chang Heng-fu, wen,* 3:3a and 3:17b, for Wang's influence on Chang Chi-liang; and *HPSW,* 18:15a, and *Wen-lu,* 6:1a, 9b, for his influence on Huang. For Chu I-tsun as a "mere" Han Learning pedant, see Hsu Pao-shan, *Hu-yuan, tsa-chu,* 8. Chang Chi-liang, 3:17b, criticizes Weng Fang-kang for the same vice: confusing scholarly pedantry with poetry.

63. For Hsu Pao-shan's imitation of and identification with his ancestor, see Mei Tseng-liang, 7:7b; and Chang Chi-liang, 3:16b. For Hsu Ch'ien-hsueh as a scholarly patron, see Lynn A. Struve, "The Hsu Brothers," pp. 260–261.

64. Kung Tzu-chen, pp. 479–480; Huang Chueh-tzu, *Wen-lu,* 6:3a; Tsung Chi-ch'en, *Kung-ch'ih-chai wen-ch'ao,* 7 *hsia:* 8b–9a.

65. For the background of the 1679 examination, see Lawrence D. Kessler, *K'ang-hsi and the Consolidation of Ch'ing Rule,* pp. 158–166.

66. For the determination to request another erudites (by invitation only) examination, see Chang Chi-liang, *Chang Heng-fu,* 19:10b–11b (dated 1834, after the 7th lunar month). For the Spring Purification circle's imitation of the 1679 post-examination banquets, see *HPSW,* 21:12b (Ch'en Ch'ing-yung pref-

ace). See also Liu Ssu-wan, 43:9 (for the original 1679 celebrations). For the 1835 request, see *HCTTS,* p. 44. For the interpretation of the 1679 examinations as a tacit recognition of, or attempt to coopt, the remnant examination-clique networks of the late Ming, see Juan K'uei-sheng, 1:67; and Dennerline, p. 314.

67. For this doctrine, see, for example, Mei Tseng-liang, 2:21 (letter to Sun Ting-ch'en), and Yao Nai, pp. 73–74 (letter to Weng Fang-kang), pp. 77–78 (letter to Wang Hui-tsu), and p. 90 (letter to Lu Shih-chi).

68. For Weng's views on textual-studies learning as character discipline, see *Fu-ch'u-chai,* 7:15b–17b; for his tendency to see parallel developments and virtues in Ch'ing Han Learning and poetic tastes, see 8:10, where he argues that Wang Shih-chen's rejection of the empty formalism of Ming poetics had provided the impetus for the evidentialist stress in Ch'ing textual scholarship. For Weng's fusion of textual studies and poetry, see (approvingly?) Wu Sung-liang, *Hsiang-su, shih-hua,* 1:3a; and (less so) Chang Chi-liang, *Chang Heng-fu,* 3:17b.

69. For statements urging such inclusivity, see, for example, Yao Nai, pp. 90–91 (letter to Ch'in Ying); Weng Fang-kang, *Fu-ch'u-chai,* 4:20b; Juan Yuan, *Yen-ching-shih chi, erh-chi,* 2:30a (citing Chu Kuei); and Ch'en Yung-kuang, "T'ai-i-chou shih-tz'u-ch'ao" (1817 poem, rhymed to poem of Weng Fang-kang).

70. P'an Te-yü, 22:17b–18a.

71. Mei Tseng-liang, 4:16b–17a. See also Chang Chi-liang, *Chang Heng-fu, wen,* 2:32a, for another example of exclusion of *k'ao-chü* (and, interestingly, of *tz'u-chang*) from the curriculum.

72. Mei Tseng-liang, 5:15a, 19a; P'an Te-yü, 3:7b. For the overtone of Neo-Confucian self-cultivation in P'an Te-yü's literary theory, see, for example, 10:2b–4a, which reveals that P'an took his studio name from a phrase in Ch'eng I or Ch'eng Hao. For sincerity as a Neo-Confucian value, see Thomas A. Metzger, *Escape from Predicament: Neo-Confucianism and China's Evolving Political Culture* pp. 89, 285–286.

73. For Huang's memorials, see, for example, *HPSW,* 19:18b (second letter from Kuo I-hsiao), and P'an Te-yü, 18:12b–13a. For P'an's remark, see ibid., 22:13b–14a.

74. See Richard Lynn, "Orthodoxy and Enlightenment: Wang Shih-chen's Theory of Poetry and its Antecedents," esp. p. 248 (for the *shen-yun* theory).

75. Ibid., p. 243.

76. P'an Te-yü, 22:1b, and 22:2b (for the phrase *chang-tan i-li,* or "clarifying and explaining moral principles"). See also ibid., 18:13, for another instance of *hsing-ch'ing* in this (Neo-Confucian) sense. Also Yao Ying, *CFTCC, Tung-ming, wai-chi,* 1:3a–4b (preface for Chang Wei-p'ing), for Yao's use of this standard to criticize the poetry of Weng Fang-kang, Ch'ien Tsai, and the northern-clique scholars.

77. Chang Chi-liang, *Chang Heng-fu, wen,* 3:2a.

78. Ibid., 3:13b ff.

79. For the translation, see Metger, *Escape from Predicament,* p. 40.

80. For the description of the *chih-shih,* see *Chang Heng-fu, wen,* 3:13b–14a; for the quotation, see 3:12b.

81. Ibid., 3:13b–14a, for the quotation. See also 2:12b–13 for another long comment on tragic resonance.
82. *Constitution* hereafter is taken to refer to the larger question of the balance of power between bureaucrats and scholars felt to be desirable by literati commentators. There was, of course, no idea that such a balance should be expressed in the form of a legislative charter.
83. For the *locus classicus* (the *Li-chi*), see Ku Yen-wu in *CSWP,* 8:23a; and Fang Tung-shu in *TCFC, wen-lu,* 6:10b.
84. Some exemplary works are: Yao Ying, comp., *Ch'ien-k'un cheng-ch'i chi.*
85. Kuan T'ung, *Yin-chi-hsuan, ch'u-chi,* 4:1a; and *TCFC, wen-lu,* 6:11a.
86. *CFTCC, Tung-ming, hou-chi,* 6:1b. For the (*ku-wen*) doctrine that the condition of letters mirrors that of the age, see ibid., *Shih-hsiao-lu,* 6:20a.
87. The summary is based on *CFTCC, Tung-ming, hou-chi,* 6:1a–3a. Yao's picture of the *chih-shih* is as a figure "towering above his age and agonizing over its troubles" (ibid., 1a).
88. Kuan T'ung, *Yin-chi-hsuan, ch'u-chi,* 4:1b.
89. Ibid., 2a.
90. Lu I-t'ung, 2:2ff.
91. Ibid., 2:2b.
92. The above is summarized from Lu I-t'ung, 2:2a–5a (letter to P'an Te-yü).

3. The Politics of Opium Suppression

1. *The Times,* 4 July 1840, p. 5, as cited in Chang Hsin-pao, *Commissioner Lin and the Opium War,* p. 251, note 14.
2. Chang Hsin-pao, pp. 85–119.
3. The controversiality of the foreign-trade explanation of (and trade-embargo solution to) the silver price appreciation of the early 19th century has been explored by Willard J. Peterson. (See his "Early Nineteenth Century Monetary Ideas on the Cash-Silver Exchange Ratio," pp. 23–48.) Further evidence of official skepticism on the utility of a trade cutoff follows later in this chapter. But note Pao Shih-ch'en, *An-wu ssu-chung,* ch. 27, 1834 and 1837 letters to Wang Liu, as cited in *YPCC,* 1:540ff., for an example of contemporary opinion advocating the introduction of paper currency as a policy superior to trade interruption. See also Ying-ho, 1:64, for a proposal to deal with silver shortages by increased domestic mining.
4. For a description of the monetary system, see Frank H. H. King, *Money and Monetary Policy in China, 1845–1895,* pp. 42–90. For the failure of the attempt to introduce notes (and large-denomination coins circulated at above their intrinsic value), see Jerome Ch'en, "The Hsien-feng Inflation." See also Wang Ch'ing-yun, *Shih-ch'ü yü-chi,* 5:13, for an 1814 statement of the case against paper money (cited in Peterson, p. 34). For the effect of the sycee shortage on transactions, see *LWCKCS, chia-chi,* 1:15a–22a (Lin Tsehsu memorial of 1833), and *YPCC,* 2:140–141 (Lin memorial of 1838).
5. For coinage debasement, see Peterson, "Monetary Ideas," p. 30. For contemporary awareness of the advantage of foreign coined silver (i.e., Mexican dol-

lars) as a reason for the sycee efflux, see *LWCKCS, chia-chi,* 1:16b–17b, which records a conversation between Kiangnan Governor Lin and local merchants who favored the introduction of Chinese minted silver.

6. For an example of this position, see *WCSL,* 3:23b–24a (Li Hung-pin memorial of 1830). Here, as in arguments on this question later in the 1830s, the native traffickers are referred to in the aggregate as "the distribution system" *(fen-hsiao),* in contrast to "the importing system" *(lai-lu).*

7. For the general problem of the unreliability of civil accusation as a means of identifying smugglers, religious sectarians, and other social criminals, see *SCTI,* 1:360–363 (1836 memorial of Censor Wang Ts'ao), and *SL-TK,* 280: 9a–11a. For official fears of civil accusation resulting in false arrests for opium smuggling, see *HCTTS,* p. 48 (memorial of 1835).

8. An area of inquiry not adequately explored in this chapter is the effect of the ongoing crisis in Chinese Turkestan (Sinkiang) on Ch'ing attitudes toward the military and trade-control questions at stake in its dealings with Great Britain. Starting in 1826 and continuing through 1832, the Ch'ing government attempted to enforce a punitive trade embargo against the non-Chinese merchants of the trans-Pamir state of Kokand. However, the policy boomeranged, and Ch'ing forces suffered a grievous and expensive defeat in 1830, in spite of the capture and execution of the rebel chief, Jahangir, the year before. In 1832, therefore, trade was reopened and peace swiftly returned. One wonders if this episode did not further undercut the appeal of any attempt at closing off the Canton trade. For the episode, see Morris Rossabi, *China and Inner Asia,* pp. 172–176; and Joseph Fletcher, "The Heyday of the Ch'ing Order in Mongolia, Sinkiang, and Tibet," pp. 360–382. Fletcher's fascinating study (pp. 382ff.) in fact sees in the Kokandian settlement a model for Manchu diplomacy along the coast in 1842. To this, however, it must be added that the literati in Peking—as well as Lin Tse-hsu, who had seen service as a supply overseer in the early part of the Sinkiang affray—were firmly against the concessions in Sinkiang, just as they would later oppose those made at Nanking in 1842. See Polachek, "Literati Groups," pp. 198–201; Kung Tzu-chen, p. 618; *LCCW,* #3 10:2a; Hsu Pao-shan *Hu-yuan, shih-ch'ao hsuan,* 3:8b–9a, 10a–11a, 5:7b–8a, and 7:2; *HPSW,* 15:3a; Wei Yuan, *Wei Yuan chi,* 2:802–3; and Lin Tse-hsu, *Wen-ch'ao,* 2:5b–6a.

9. Gerald S. Graham, *The China Station,* pp. 48–49; Chang Hsin-pao, p. 52.

10. Graham, pp. 56–57; Chang, Hsin-pao, pp. 53–55.

11. See *SL-TK,* 255:37. For the quotation, see Graham, p. 57, note 26, citing "A Sketch of Lord Napier's Negotiations With the Authorities at Canton," *Asiatic Journal* (London), August 1837, p. 11. This statement does not appear in published Chinese sources. But see *SL-TK,* 255:37a for the edict issued on the date (TK 14/8/28) that word of the *Imogene* and *Andromache* incident reached Peking. Its tone is conciliatory and anti-military enough to make credible the remark cited by Graham. See also Lo Ping-chang, 7b, for evidence of the emperor's concern over this incident: Lo recalls that he was interrogated about it by the emperor in mid-1835.

12. *SL-TK*, 255:37a.
13. Jonathan D. Spence, "Opium Smoking in Ch'ing China," pp. 150–151, sees this fear as the key catalyst in the turn toward tougher control policies after 1832. *YPCC*, 1:336, contains an interesting account of Lin Tse-hsu's early 1839 audience with the Tao-kuang emperor, which records that it was Lin's remark about the coming ruin of the Ch'ing military by the opium habit that brought the emperor over to supporting Lin's advocacy of an import-interdiction campaign.
14. See above, chapter 2.
15. Spence, p. 150, note 50, citing *SL-TK*.
16. *WCSL*, 3:16.
17. *WCSL*, 4:50a–51b (also *SCTI* 1:239–241).
18. *SL-TK*, 189:19a–21a, for the emperor's agreement with Feng. The *Shang-yü-tang fang-pen* entry for TK 11/5/25 shows that the emperor personally added 24 characters to the draft memorial presented him by the Grand Council, urging Li to exert himself to "eliminate this great evil affecting the entire empire." This suggests that Tao-kuang was personally shaken by Feng's disclosures. For a summary of Li's reply, see *SL-TK*, 205:13a–14a.
19. *SL-TK*, 218:30a–31a. The capitalized section is indicated in the *Shang-yü-tang* to have been added to the edict by the emperor himself.
20. Lu's disaffection with the interdiction policy is established, first, by his agreement with an 1833 (?) essay by the Cantonese academician Wu Lan-hsiu against such a policy; and, second, by his late-1834 plea to the emperor to consider conditional legalization of the drug. See *YPCC*, 1:133, 6:7. The Spring Purificationist Chang Chi-liang, who visited Canton during the winter of 1832–1833, also comments very negatively on Governor General Lu's loyalty to the opium-suppression policy. (See *Chang Heng-fu*, 18:12a, 19a; and ibid., *wen*, 3:6b, 8a–10a.) Chang's source of information seems to have been the Kwangtung circuit intendant, Cheng K'ai-hsi, likewise a Spring Purificationist.
21. The only point at which Lu seems to have been clearly challenged by Tao-kuang was in mid-1834, just before the Napier affair, when his go-soft policies on controlling the drug trade were exposed and laid open to question by the Kwangtung-born censor Tseng Wang-yen. See *SL-TK*, 252:23a–24b, 258:3a–5b. See also *MCSL*, 9:809a–810b, for Lu's reply to Tseng's charges.
22. *SL-TK*, 258:3a–5b. See also Lu K'un's memorial of TK 15/3/14, in *MCSL*, 9:811, which openly espouses the position that attempting to drive the British depot ships from the Lintin anchorage would be useless and that efforts should be concentrated on policing the native smugglers' operations.
23. For Lu K'un's late 1834 attempt to persuade the court to legalize drug imports, see *YPCC*, 1:133–134. For Lu K'un as an examination pupil of Juan, see Liang Chang-chü, *Lang-chi ts'ung-t'an*, 5:4b.
24. For Juan as Liang-Kuang viceroy, see *ECCP*, p. 401. One of Juan's highest priorities had been to bolster the sea defenses of the Pearl River estuary (especially the ones at the Bogue). See *TKHC*, 98:7b. Juan's knowledge of these defenses and of their vulnerabilities might have been one major reason for

his summons to Peking in 1835. For Juan's appointment, see *SL-TK*, 263:5a. Interestingly, the court seems to have had a problem deciding the precedence of Juan and his old rival, P'an Shih-en, now that both were full grand secretaries (*SL-TK*, 263:19a). For examples of Juan as a free-floating deliberative official in Peking, see *Shang-yü-tang*, TK 15/7, pp. 63–82; and TK 17/4, pp. 79–96.

25. For Lu K'un as Juan's (1799) pupil in the metropolitan examinations and for his similar trade polices, see Liang Chang-chü, *Lang-chi ts'ung-t'an*, 5:4b.

26. *SL-TK*, 170:24a–25a. This decree was considered a sufficiently important institutional milestone to warrant insertion into the semi-official encyclopedia of administrative precedents for the late Ch'ing, originally compiled in 1915 (see *WHTK*, 22:8870).

27. *SL-TK*, 270:26a.

28. For Tseng, see note 21 above.

29. For Huang's prior submission to the throne on currency problems in Kiangsu and Chekiang provinces, see *HCTTS*, pp. 23–24 (memorial of 1833).

30. *Chuan-chi hsing-shu hui-chi*, 1b–2a, for Chin Ying-lin's record as a judicial specialist. Consistent with the legal-specialist interpretation of his appointment is the fact that Chin was suddenly drafted for the office of Chihli judicial commissioner in mid-1839 (just as the opium death-penalty provision was coming into enforcement). See ibid., 3a. More evidence of the unusual breadth of the consultative apparatus erected by Tao-kuang in 1835 appears in Lo Ping-chang, 7b, which notes that the Kwangtung-born author was summoned before the emperor in mid-1835 during a reception for all current Han-lin officials, and asked for details about the outcome of the Napier affair. The assumption here evidently was that Han-lin students, like Lo, would have their own sources of information.

31. The best account of the Hsueh-hai-t'ang in English is Benjamin A. Elman, "The Hsueh-hai T'ang and the Rise of New Text Scholarship in Canton." See also Kuhn and Jones, pp. 158–160; and *ECCP*, pp. 401, 510. For the pre-1800 insularity of intellectual life in the southeast provinces of Fukien and Kwangtung (at least in terms of the Peking- and Kiangnan-centered literary and Han Learning fashions discussed in chapter 1), see Chang Chi-liang, *Chang Heng-fu, wen*, 1:16b–17a, 2:9a. For the Hsueh-hai-t'ang as an agent for the introduction of philological studies into Canton, see, for example, Tsung Chi-ch'en, *Kung-ch'ih-chai shih-ch'ao*, 8 *hsia*: 12b, which notes that a certain Yen Chieh (1763–1843), who had helped Juan compile his dictionary of the Classics (the *Ching-chi tsuan-ku* [1800]) in Chekiang, was brought to Canton by Juan explicitly to head up the exegetical projects Juan anticipated launching. For continuing correspondence between Juan and his Hsueh-hai-t'ang students after Juan's departure from Kwangtung, see Juan Yuan, *Yen-ching-shih chi, hsu*, 2 *hsia*: 31b; and 5:6a (Wu Lan-hsiu and Tseng Chao). Another contact at the Hsueh-hai-t'ang who probably figured in Juan's network was I K'o-chung (1796–1838), a Shansi-born scholar who moved to Canton during Juan's years in office, taking his provincial degree in 1832. (See *Kuang-chou-fu t'ung-chih*, 45:26a; and *YPCC*, 6:7.) Pao Shih-ch'en, an administrative

expert and provincial official secretary active in northern-clique circles in the 1820s, records receiving information on conditions in Singapore from I K'o-chung when in Peking, in 1826 (Pao Shih-ch'en, 35:1a). Moreover, I K'o-chung was passed on the 1832 Kwangtung provincial examinations by Juan's close friend, Ch'eng En-tse, and went up to Peking the next year in the hope, it would seem, of benefiting from Juan's assignment as 1833 metropolitan examiner. (See *HCSH*, #1, 11:30b.)

32. For the mercantile support base of the Hsueh-hai-t'ang, see Elman, p. 76, note 29, citing Okubo Eiko, *Min-Shin jidai shoin*, p. 337; Hamaguchi Fujio, "Hō Tō-ju no Kangaku hihan ni tsuite," pp. 174–176; and Tu Wei-yun, *Hsueh-shu yü shih-pien*, p. 135. According to the above, the opium-smuggling activities of the cohong (i.e., foreign-trade monopoly) merchant Howqua II or Wu Ping-chien (1769–1843) paid for the latter scholar's library, and probably for his other philanthropies, which included the Hsueh-hai-t'ang. Apparently, Juan managed to catch Wu in his opium dealings in 1821 and to extort contributions for this and other projects from him as hush money. See *YPCC*, 1:137; and Juan Yuan, 5:28a–30b. The contact between the enemies of Wu and of the Hsueh-hai-t'ang, on the one hand, and the Peking Spring Purificationists, on the other, is revealed in the impeachment of Wu submitted by Huang Chueh-tzu and Yao Yuan-chih in 1835–1836 (see below). Just who helped them obtain this material is unclear. One possible source was Fang Tung-shu, the T'ung-ch'eng scholar who shuttled back and forth between Anhwei, Yangchow, and Canton during the 1830s, never quite at ease with the Han Learning influences that dominated at the Hsueh-hai-t'ang. In an 1842 retrospect, Fang was to recall with some vexation the role of the cohong merchants in lubricating the opium trade. And, in this same memoir, he cites an 1831 tract on the history of British activity in Kwangtung by the Anhwei scholar Yeh Chung-chin, which appears to have been equally anti-cohong in its outlook. (See *YPCC*, 5:589.) In addition, it is to be noted that Huang Chueh-tzu had close relations with two Cantonese academicians apparently hostile to the Hsueh-hai-t'ang: Wen Hsun and Huang Chao; while Yao Yuan-chih, his fellow Spring Purificationist and co-impeacher of Howqua, seems to have been on good terms with a third, Ch'en Hung-ch'ih. For Wen Hsun and Huang Chueh-tzu, see the latter's *HPSW*, 22:1, 4a, and *Wen-lu*, 11:7b. (Wen was associated with the rival Yueh-hsiu Academy and was later to contribute a drug "cure" recipe to Huang's plan for attacking opium consumption: see *YPCC*, 4:341, and Lin Ch'ang-i, *She-ying-lou shih-hua*, 2:18a.) For Huang and Huang Chao, see *HPSW*, 18:16a, and 20:14a. Yao Yuan-chih was an 1805 Han-lin same-year friend of Ch'en Hung-ch'ih and of Li K'o-chiung, two important local advisers to Governor General Teng T'ing-chen, who opposed the plan for opium legalization (see *YPCC*, 6:7). Another possible Cantonese collaborator with the campaign to block legalization was Li P'an-liao, a Kwangtung native (from Tung-kuan county) who was posted as a censor in Peking during the debate of 1836. For Li's objections to legalization, see *TKHC*, 70:11.

33. For Elliot's appointment (he had actually succeeded the successor, Sir George

Robinson, in 1836), see W. C. Costin, *Great Britain and China*, pp. 31–34. For Elliot's information about the legalization maneuver and about Juan's support for it, see Chang Hsin-pao, pp. 88, 190, 150 (note 14), citing *Parliamentary Papers (Blue Books): Correspondence Relating to China* (1840), p. 389. Additional support for the suggestion that Juan supported the legalization idea is found in Liang Chang-chü, *Lang-chi ts'ung-t'an*, 5:5a–6a, which attests that Liang (a close acquaintance of Juan's and a fellow disciple of Chu Kuei) was in favor of such a measure. For Teng's optimism, see Chang Hsin-pao, p. 88.

34. For the Hsu Nai-chi memorial, see Chang Hsin-pao, pp. 85–87.
35. For Wu Lan-hsiu's influence on Hsu Nai-chi's memorial, see Chang Hsin-pao, p. 88; and *YPCC*, 6:6–7 (citing Liang T'ing-nan's *I-fen chi-wen*). For Wu's relationship to Juan, see Juan Yuan, *Yen-ching-shih chi, hsu*, 2 *hsia*: 31b; and 3:15a–16a.
36. For Howqua's activities, see note 32 above. For the suspicions about Juan Yuan's go-soft implementation, see Elman, p. 76, note 29. The Cantonese scholar Liang T'ing-nan believed the Lintin stockpiling began between 1821 and 1822, when Juan Yuan was governor general. (See *YPCC*, 6:5.) In 1837, moreover, the Cantonese censor Li P'an-liao memorialized the emperor about this, claiming that the Lintin anchorage had been used for smuggling since 1821. (See *IWSM-TK*, 1:20b.)
37. *YPCC*, 6:6–7, citing Liang T'ing-nan's extract of Wu's essay (entitled "Ending of the Evils [of Opium]"). Obviously, Wu saw these abuses as arising more out of control efforts themselves than from the drug—a curiously modern view. It might here be added that concern with the abuses within the accusatory system (which relied entirely on civilian complaints) was widely voiced by officials who oversaw the attempts to control distributors. See, for example, Ho Ch'ang-ling's opinion as of 1838 (?), as summarized in Spence, p. 159, note 119 (citing Hsueh Yun-sheng, *Tu-li ts'un-i*, 22:62b–63), and *SL-TK*, 324:10b–12a. For this reason, the new legislation on opium control expressly denied civilians the right to bring accusations against alleged smugglers, and also contained tough laws against public agents (soldiers, etc.) who brought false accusations. See Hsueh Yun-sheng, *Tu-li ts'un-i*, pp. 326–327, and *YPCC*, 1:396, 562–564.
38. For the referral of Hsu Nai-chi's legalization plan to Teng, and his response, see *SL-TK*, 282:28a, and *IWSM-TK*, 1:5b–11b. It is evident, however, from the two days' lapse between Hsu's submission (on 10 June, or TK 16/4/27) and the announcement of its referral (on 4/29) that the proposal had faced severe opposition at court, in spite of Juan's evident support. According to Chang Hsin-pao (p. 88), Teng's reply was sent from Canton on 7 September (7/27). However, the emperor's more-or-less receptive reply to the anti-legalizationist criticisms of two capital officials (Hsu Ch'iu and Chu Ts'un) on 19 September (8/9)—for which, see *SL-TK*, 287:8a—signaled that a decision had been taken prior to the arrival of Teng's memorial in Peking.
39. For Huang's memorial, see *HCTTS*, pp. 49–50. It is possible, however, that the memorial was withdrawn at the last moment: see *HPSW*, 20:11 (letter

from Wang Pi). For Yao's charges and Teng's reply, see *SL-TK*, 284:29a–30a, and 288:1b–3a.

40. See, for example, *SL-TK*, 287:8 (reply to memorials of Hsu Ch'iu and Chu Ts'un).
41. Chang Hsin-pao, p. 91.
42. Ibid., p. 91. See also *YPCC*, 6:209, which records that the rejection of the Hsu Nai-chi legalization plan elicited a string of requests from provincial officials eager to keep in step with the new mood at court.
43. For Kung's proposal (to Lin), see Kung Tzu-chen, pp. 169–170. For other examples of advocacy of this approach by literati in position to influence the views of the Spring Purificationists, see Hsia Pao-chin, *Tung-sheng ts'ao-t'ang wen-lu*, letter to Lin Tse-hsu, 1839; *HPSW*, 23:10a (letter from Ch'en Fang-hai to Huang Chueh-tzu, 1838); *YPCC*, 1:535–539, esp. pp. 538–539 (Pao Shih-ch'en essay of 1820); and Kuan T'ung, *Yin-chi-hsuan, ch'u-chi*, 2:6b–8a (ca. 1820).
44. For the collective composition of the 2 June memorial, see *YPCC*, 1:338, 4:341, and Lin Ch'ang-i, 2:18a. See also Lin Ch'ung-yung, p. 216. These sources make it clear that the Huang memorial was in fact drawn up by the Spring Purificationists and several provincial graduates (including the Cantonese scholar Wen Hsun) in Peking for the 1838 examinations.
45. *HCTTS*, pp. 69–72.
46. The provisions for a one-year moratorium and for the disbursal of drug-cure "medicine" appear in the Huang Chueh-tzu memorial of 2 June (*HCTTS*, pp. 71–72). Huang's 1838 correspondence with his Spring Purificationist friends and other private literati communications from this same period show that the concern with improving the self-confidence of the bureaucracy in making opium-related arrests was a key stimulus in the decision to focus on the more readily identifiable consumer. See *HPSW*, 23:10a (Ch'en Fang-hai to Huang Chueh-tzu, 1838); *YPCC*, 1:321 (Wu Sung-liang, ca. 1838); and Lin Ch'ung-yung, p. 223 (Lin Tse-hsu memorial of 1838).
47. Evidence of a prior arrangement between Lin and the Spring Purificationists for his assignment to Kwangtung is indirect, but substantial. *SLHK*, p. 750, contains a secret memorial of 1838, evidently from a grand councillor (unnamed), that calls for the removal of Governor General Teng and his replacement by a person to be decided by the emperor. The submitter seems to have been P'an Shih-en, a man known to have been a supporter of Lin Tse-hsu in Council debates at least from 1840 onward (*ECCP*, p. 607). The other token of a prior arrangement is the remarkable speed of Lin Tse-hsu's reply to the call for opinions from provincial officials regarding Huang Chueh-tzu's 2 June proposal. Lin Tse-hsu's memorial, which was one of the few to render unqualified support for the death-penalty idea, arrived in Peking on 10 July. By contrast, no other governor general or governor serving in the Yangtze valley returned an opinion before 30 July—a more normal time for arriving at a conclusion on so complex a question as this. (Round-trip communications required between 20 and 30 days between Peking and the key Yangtze cities.) See *IWSM-TK*, 2:20ff. (for Lin); and 3:1ff., and 3:7ff., for the

(much later) arrival of an answer from Lin's subordinate, the Hupeh governor, Chang Yueh-sung, and from the Anhwei governor, Pu-hsing-e. During this interlude, moreover, Lin was in constant communication with his son, Ju-chou (in Peking), whose correspondence enclosed letters from other of Lin's contacts in the capital. (See *LTHJC*, pp. 289–290, entries for TK 18/intercalary 4th/16th, 21st, and 27th days.)

48. Chang Hsin-pao, p. 34, p. 241, note 61, citing Pao Shih-ch'en, 26:5.

49. Wei Yuan, in an 1842 essay on opium control (*Sheng-wu chi*, 14:31a), would later recommend the deployment of special opium-control censors to all (other?) 17 provinces of China proper. However, no mention occurs of any such idea in the 1838 plans put forward by Huang and Lin. For the dispatch of specially commissioned agents to Fukien and Kwangtung, see *HPSW*, 24:1, and *SL-TK*, 329:18a–29b (for Fukien) and 316:16a (for Lin's assignment as commissioner to Kwangtung). The details surrounding Lin's volunteering for assignment to Kwangtung are reviewed exhaustively in Lin Ch'ung-yung, pp. 232–242. For Lin's (post facto) representations on the subject, see *YPCC*, 1:336–338, and chapter 5. According to the first two sources, Huang Chueh-tzu and the Kiangsu education commissioner, Ch'i Chün-tsao, were ordered to Amoy on TK 19/12/21 (or 12/22), to investigate reports of massive smuggling of the drug at Amoy and along the southern Fukien coast submitted by Censor Tu Yen-shih—who was himself a native of this area.

50. For official disapproval of the death-penalty proposal, see *IWSM-TK*, 2:13a– 5:12a, which reveals that, of the 26 high-ranking provincial officials in Manchuria and China proper consulted on the idea, 19 opposed it outright, 5 favored it, and 2 supported it with some qualifications. *HCTTS*, p. 72, suggests that Huang Chueh-tzu and his followers had anticipated that such resistance would materialize, for Huang here asks the emperor to take into account that, in an affair of such magnitude, conventional bureaucratic prudence provides no useful guide to action. For T'ao Chu's objections, see *YPCC*, 1:338. For Ch'i-shan's hostility, see *YPCC*, 1:515ff., and 5:410. The latter reproduces Huang En-t'ung's account of the opium debates, which singles out Lin and Chou T'ien-chueh (the director general of tribute-grain transport) as the only two strong backers of the idea among the ranks of the high-level provincial officials.

51. For the plan to offer rewards for the surrendered opium and to use access to legal trade at Canton as a bargaining chip, see *YPCC*, 2:92, 97. For the destruction of the opium and the effect Lin believed it had upon the foreign community at Canton, see Arthur Waley, *The Opium War through Chinese Eyes*, pp. 49, 51 (citing *YPCC*, 2:155, 160). For the report that Jardine had been intimidated to the point of fleeing Canton, see *YPCC*, 2:143.

52. *YPCC*, 5:584–585. According to Ch'i Ssu-ho (*YPCC*, 6:533), this essay was originally written in 1838 to urge Liang-Kuang governor general, Teng T'ing-chen, to ratify the Huang-Lin anti-consumption legislation (Fang was at the time on Teng's staff as a literary secretary). For another example of this same position, see Hsu Chi-yü, *Sung-k'an hsien-sheng ch'üan-chi, wen-chi*, 1:9.

53. See, for example, Lin Tse-hsu, *Hsin-chi-lu*, pp. 12–13.
54. For details, see above, note 47.
55. For Ju-chou's correspondence with his father during the interlude when the Huang plan was under review, see *LTHJC*, pp. 289–290.
56. *SLHK*, pp. 683–684.
57. Additional evidence of close coordination between Lin and the Spring Purificationists is the extended visit of Chang Chi-liang to Lin's Wuchang (Hupeh) yamen directly after the Huang draft plan had been submitted to Lin and others for their opinion. Chang arrived in Wuchang on Tao-kuang 18/5/14, and, on the following day, moved into Lin's official quarters, where he stayed as a kind of liaison with the literati of the Southern City until Lin was reassigned to Kwangtung. See *LTHJC*, pp. 291, 293, 303 (entries for TK 18/5/14, 6/7, 8/11, and 8/13).
58. *SL-TK*, 320:14b. See also Lin Ch'ung-yung, pp. 157, 160.
59. *SL-TK*, 324:5b–6a; *LWCKCS, i-chi*, 7:1ff (and esp. 18a–20b) for the Peking reclamation project, which recapitulates exactly Lin's 1836 proposal (see above, chapter 1, note 99). According to one source, Lin's securing of imperial interest in the reclamation scheme drew anger from the Chihli governor general, Ch'i-shan, who apparently saw his own job threatened. See *YPCC*, 1:338.

4. The Myth of Victory in Kwangtung

1. For the literati position on these questions, see chapter 5.
2. Reacting to the signs of renewed Chinese militance over the residence provisions of the new treaties in 1849–1850, for example, Palmerston attributed the problem to simple failure of memory. "These half-civilized governments . . . all require a Dressing every eight or Ten years to keep them in order. Their minds are too shallow to receive an Impression that will last longer than some such Period." (Costin, p. 150.)
3. Chang Hsin-pao, pp. 193–194, traces the origins of the Yangtze/Grand Canal blockade plan back to October-November 1839, when the China-trader lobby won Palmerston's support for a war with China, and, likewise, for its own recommendation to attack in central China. For more on the so-called Jardine war plan, see Peter Ward Fay, *The Opium War*, p. 215; and Jack Beeching, *The Chinese Opium Wars*, p. 111.
4. See *LTHJC*, pp. 334–335 (entries for TK 19/2/9, 2/21, and 2/28). For the academy posts of these men, see Liu Po-chi, *Kuang-tung shu-yüan chih-tu*, pp. 230ff. All data on academy posts hereafter cited are based on this source, unless otherwise noted. For Yao Hua-tso, see *PYHC*, 19:12b–13b.
5. For the institutional functions of the Ta-fo-ssu Bureau (known alternatively as the *shen-shih kung-chü*, or "scholar-managed public office" for opium control), see Lin Tse-hsu, *Hsin-chi-lu*, pp. 12, 18, 44–45.
6. For Lin's concern with the problem of identifying distributors, see *YPCC*, 6:13, which notes that a battery of examinations were administered by Lin in mid-1839 to local licentiates in order to give these scholars the opportun-

ity to identify in secret the major brokers and traffickers. Note also the list of dealers Lin brought to Canton with him, based (evidently) on information collected from Cantonese scholars in the capital, in *Hsin-chi lu*, pp. 9–11. For a spectacular case of false arrest that had come to the attention of the authorities in Canton in 1838, see *YPCC*, 1:381, 385.

7. Biographies of local academy pedagogues often contain allusions to anti-Han Learning sentiment or (more rarely) to anti-Hsueh-hai-t'ang sentiment without clarifying the intellectual basis for this disaffection. See, for example, *NHHC*, 14:11a, concerning Chu Tz'u-ch'i (himself a student at the Hsueh-hai-t'ang in the 1820s).

8. The history of the White Cloud Mountain circle in Canton seems to begin with Feng Min-ch'ang (1747–1806: 1778 Han-lin), a Cantonese poet discovered and patronized by Weng Fang-kang in 1765, during the latter's term as educational commissioner for Kwangtung. (See Weng Fang-kang, *Fu-ch'u-chai*, 4:11b; Wang Ch'ang, *Hu-hai*, 2:1009; and Wu Sung-liang, *Hsiang-su, shih-hua*, 1:13a.) According to Yao Ying (*CFTCC, Tung-ming, wai-chi*, 1:4), Feng was responsible for introducing the poetic aesthetic of Weng into Cantonese literati culture. The White Cloud Mountain Club, we might infer, was created to further this purpose. Two of Feng's disciples, Huang P'ei-fang and T'an Chin-chao, figure in the White Cloud circle gatherings. And it is even possible that Feng inaugurated the Club himself, during an 1801–1803 term as head of the Yueh-hsiu Academy in Canton. (See *Ch'ing-shih lieh-chuan*, 73:30.) The fourth name persistently associated with that group is that of Chang Wei-p'ing, who established himself as a poetry fashion-setter in Peking in 1807–1808 under the tutelage of Weng Fang-kang (*HCSH*, #1, 11:4a). The White Mountain Club, originally known as the Yun-ch'uan shih-she, was launched as a formal group in 1812 or 1813 (*ECCP*, p. 58; *SJCL*, 54:3b), and included Chang, Huang P'ei-fang, and Lin Po-t'ung (1775–1845). However, T'an is included in another, overlapping group (*HHHC*, 15:14b; and *Yang-ch'un hsien-chih*, 10:24a). According to Liu Po-chi's list of academy heads, Huang and T'an had held a succession of academy posts outside of Canton before 1839, but had not yet been appointed to the faculty of any of the provincial capital's much more prestigious schools as of this date.

9. *PYHC*, 26:11a–12a. The biographical data on Ch'en are based on the same source. For details on Ch'en's abortive career as a Peking litterateur, see *HCSH*, #2, 7:71a.

10. For the above information on Fang, see *ECCP*, pp. 238–240. In his day, his scholarly reputation rested on a widely read 1824 tract indicting the Han Learning fashion, written while Fang was teaching at the Hsueh-hai-t'ang. (See *ECCP*, p. 239.) For Teng T'ing-chen's patronage of the T'ung-ch'eng school (in his term as Anhwei governor, 1825–1835), see Mei Tseng-liang, 7:18; Chang Chi-liang, *Chang Heng-fu, wen*, 3:5a; and Fang Tung-shu, *TCFC*, 3:21b–23a.

11. For consultation with Ch'en on the legalization question and on a tutor, see *YPCC*, 6:7, 12. For Ch'en Li and the other academy pupils of Ch'en Hung-ch'ih, see *PYHC*, 26:11b–12a. For the appointment of Ch'en Li to the Hsueh-

hai-t'ang, see *Hsueh-hai-t'ang chih*, 23a. Waley, p. 126, notes that Ch'en Li was at this moment serving as tutor to Chang Wei-p'ing's son, and it is possible that Chang was Ch'en Li's patron.

12. Waley, p. 60. For Lin's restriction of the examination students, see *YPCC*, 6:13, and *LTHJC*, pp. 347–349 (entries for TK 19/6/15, 6/27, 7/2, and 7/6). For Lin's residence, see Waley, p. 20.

13. *Hsueh-hai-t'ang chih*, 22.

14. *LTHJC*, p. 334 (entry for TK 19/2/9); ibid., p. 356 (for 9/8); and p. 390 (for intercalary 3/13).

15. *YPCC*, 6:19.

16. *LTHJC*, pp. 373–374.

17. Ibid., p. 374.

18. I here synthesize a variety of Lin's utterances on strategy that will be presented in more detail below. Relevant glimpses into Lin's strategic outlook occur in *YPCC*, 6:22–24, and *IWSM-TK*, 14:41a, 16:20a, and 16:40b. See also Waley, p. 113, which notes Lin's beliefs that the British were compelled to sell opium as they fought in order to pay for their military expenditures. Lin's "state papers" are singularly uninformative with regard to the historical sources of his vision of British maritime strategy (and of its weaknesses). However, Pao Shih-ch'en, who was one of Lin's consultants on strategy, is more revealing, and it is from his and other comments that we can spot the association with the *wo-k'ou* and with Coxinga. For Pao as an adviser, see Waley, pp. 137–138, 153. In his *An-wu ssu-chung* (35:6a, 8a), Pao twice makes the analogy of the British to the *wo-k'ou*. In the same vein, he recommends (35:6a) a well-known text on these anti-pirate campaigns (Cheng Jo-tseng's *Ch'ou-hai t'u-pien*, or *Illustrated Gazetteer of Maritime Defense*, of 1561–1562). Interestingly, this same text on the *wo-k'ou* is put forward by Fang Tung-shu in a poem of late 1841 as a record of an analogous strategic dilemma (*TCFC*, 5:6a), and it even appears as a topic for the examination essay question in the 1841 palace examination (*SL-TK*, 351:20a). Clearly, Lin's strategic thinking conceptions turned on the methods developed against the Japanese invaders, which stressed the enemy's vulnerability to economic and supply problems once theatre-of-action trade opportunities had been eliminated. For the origins of the *Ch'ou-hai t'u-pien*, see Merrilyn Fitzpatrick, "Local Interests and the Anti-pirate Administration in China's Southeast, 1555–1565," p. 30. For an excellent general study of the problem of maritime security in the 16th and 17th centuries, see Wills.

19. For Elliot's decision to comply with the demand for the surrender of the Lintin opium stockpiles, see Chang Hsin-pao, pp. 165–172. For Lin's negotiations with Elliot over the guarantee ("willing bonds") issue, see Chang, pp. 179–185. See also *YPCC*, 2:106–107, and *SL-TK*, 320:41b–42a, for the court's failure to lend Lin full support on this question. For the authorization for Lin to use the embargo weapon (terminating tea and rhubarb exports), see *SL-TK*, 326:30b–31a (29 October 1839). Lin's request for an edict authorizing the permanent termination of British trade and their expulsion from Canton was granted on 13 December 1839 (*SL-TK*, 328:7a–

9a). However, this order exempted other countries from the embargo. Frederic Wakeman, Jr., "The Canton Trade and the Opium War," pp. 193–195, details how Parliamentary war lobbyists were able to exploit Lin's apparent disregard for British commercial and crown property rights in Canton to whip up war sentiment in the lower house.

20. For Lin's confidence that a war of defense and attrition would put the British at a disadvantage, in spite of their acknowledged superiority in fighting on the open seas, see Lin's memorial on strategy of 8 April 1840 (*IWSM-TK*, 10:4a–7b, esp. 5b). This and several later memorials reported the circulation in Canton of rumors that the British were sending a major naval expedition to China, and urged the emperor not to take such rumors too much to heart. (See Waley, pp. 98–100.) Lin also believed Canton to be defensible. For these points, see Liang T'ing-nan's comments on Lin's strategies in *YPCC*, 6:22, 24. The latter citation notes, also, that Lin was unaware at the time (i.e., 1840) of the British war-finance system. Waley, p. 72, points out, however, that Lin's reports about the first naval clashes between Chinese and British ships were incredibly enthusiastic about the Ch'ing performance—a fact that suggests that Lin did not believe he could easily win the emperor over to endorsing the passive defense strategy he personally preferred.

21. For Lin's defense arrangements in the Pearl River estuary, see *LTHJC*, p. 359 (entries for TK 19/9/29 and 10/9), and his *Shih-ch'ao*, 5:15–16. See also Tsung Chi-ch'en, *Wen-ch'ao*, 7:13b. This latter comment, by a Lin supporter and a Spring Purificationist, Tsung Chi-ch'en, observes retrospectively that Lin had made no provision in his initial defense scheme for any kind of active counteroffensive against British forces at Canton or anywhere else. Lin did not explicitly warn the court of an upcoast attack as a real likelihood until the autumn of 1840. (Contrast *IWSM-TK*, 10:5—Lin's first, derogatory mention of the possibility of a major British naval attack—with ibid., 11:23b–25a [3 August 1840]—which, for the first time, acknowledges to the court the possibility that the central coast or the Peking vicinity might be attacked.) See also *YPCC*, 3:363–364, which establishes that Lin's warnings did not reach the Chekiang provincial authorities until 1 August of the same year—nearly three weeks after British marines had occupied Ting-hai in the Chusan Islands. In fairness to Lin, it might be noted that the purchase of some 200 large-bore foreign cannon and of a 34-gun ship (the *Chesapeake*) had been undertaken by Lin in the fall or winter of 1840, in belated recognition that a more aggressive military response might be necessary. See Gideon Chen, *Lin Tse-hsu*, pp. 2–6, 11–23; and Wei Yuan, *Tseng-kuang hai-kuo t'u-chih*, 80:2b–3a.

22. For the size of the British forces, see Jack Beeching, p. 112–113. The dates of all military engagements are based (unless otherwise noted) on Kuo T'ing-i, comp., *Chin-tai chung-kuo shih-shih jih-chih*. For the belatedness of the orders to Ch'i-shan to prepare his defenses, see *SL-TK*, 336:7a–8b; and *IWSM-TK*, 12:7a. For Ouchterlony's observations, see John Ouchterlony, *The Chinese War*, p. 57.

23. For an excellent study of Ch'i-shan's peace intervention and the background

to his attack on Lin, see Hsia Nai, "Ya-p'ien chan-cheng chung ti T'ien-chin t'an-p'an." Some hint of the arguments Ch'i presented to Tao-kuang during the Tientsin crisis of August 1840 can be gleaned from his later investigative reports (sent from Canton) that established the case against Lin. (See *YPCC*, 4:73–5.)

24. *IWSM-TK*, 14:40b–44b, for Lin's memorial and the emperor's response.

25. For Lin's memorial, see *IWSM-TK*, 16:17b–22a; and Waley, pp. 118–121. (Waley believes the memorial to have been sent on 24 September.) For the 11 October (TK 20/9/6) dispatch, see *LTHJC*, p. 371.

26. Lin did not receive the order removing him from office until 20 October (see *LTHJC*, p. 372, entry for 9/25). For Lin's removal, Ch'i-shan's appointment, and the rationale behind these changes, see *SL-TK*, 338:29a, 339:1b–2a, 339:9. For the imperial comment we have quoted, see *IWSM-TK*, 16:21a (the remarks were written directly onto Lin's memorial in the emperor's hand).

27. For the letter to Yü-ch'ien, see *YPCC*, 2:563–566. This document is preserved under the title "family letter" because it was sent to Lin's son (Ju-chou) in Soochow. However, it was clearly intended for Yü-ch'ien. On this latter point, see *YPCC*, p. 566 (editor's note), and Lin Ch'ung-yung, p. 496. I follow Lin Ch'ung-yung's dating.

28. For the Shen Wei-ch'iao letter, see *YPCC*, 2:570–571, which notes that one version of the letter contains a postcript bearing the date "rain-water festival," or 1/27.

29. The role of Huang Chueh-tzu and his allies in the capital in fomenting the movement to sabotage Ch'i-shan's attempt at negotiations can be established from two different sets of evidence. First is the open role of Huang and his fellow "inspectors" in Amoy in lobbying against negotiations as the Tientsin *pourparlers* got under way. See *IWSM-TK*, 12:11b–14a, which reproduces a memorial from Huang and his associates in Amoy that reached Peking on 11 August 1840—anticipating the British approach to the capital and urging that, instead of negotiating, the Ch'ing side prepare for the reconquest of Ting-hai. See also *IWSM-TK*, 17:34b–37a, which transcribes a Huang Chueh-tzu/Ch'i Chün-tsao critique of the negotiations scheme that reached Peking from Hangchow on 11/26. Here, Huang and Ch'i use materials supplied by the Chekiang governor, Liu Yun-k'o, to establish that the British had fortified Ting-hai, thus contradicting Ch'i-shan's claims of an expressed British willingness to evacuate that island. During the remainder of the peace interlude, the critics (following Huang's original argument) continued to dwell on the enemy's presumed intention of remaining on Ting-hai, and to urge upon the court swift military action to prevent this. Second, most of the memorialists who advocated military action instead of negotiations were censors of Kiangsi provincial origin. These were: Wan Ch'i-hsin (see memorials of TK 20/8/6 [*IWSM-TK*, 13:28b–32a], 9/30 [16:5a–6b], and 12/15 [18:40b–41a]); Ts'ao Lu-t'ai (memorials of 11/27 [16:19b–32b], and 11/10 [16:43b–44a]); Ts'ai Chia-k'an (memorials of 11/29 [17:44b–45a], and 11/30 [17:45b–48b]); and Shih Ching-fen (memorial of 12/10 [18:18a–21b]). All

four were from Kiangsi (see Su Shu-fan, pp. 411–413). Since Kiangsi was not itself a war theatre and contained no coastal ports, these censors could only have gotten their information concerning conditions in Ting-hai from the Kiangsi provincial guild—and, ultimately, from Huang, who was himself a Kiangsi man.

30. For Yü-ch'ien's role, see *YPCC*, 3:514–517. That the anti-Ch'i-shan forces hoped that Yü-ch'ien might be appointed commander for Kwangtung is indicated by a letter sent from the Fukien judicial commissioner, Tseng Wang yen (in Foochow) to Huang, early in 1841. (See *HPSW*, 26:7b.)

31. For I-liang's prior relationship with Lin (who had been an approving superior in Kiangsu before the war), see Lin Tse-hsu, *Shih-ch'ao*, 5:6a–7a; *YPCC*, 6:27; and Lin Ch'ung-yung, p. 153. Apparently I-liang's sympathy for Lin had been fueled by resentment against Ch'i-shan's secrecy with regard to the content of his negotiations with Elliot (*YPCC*, 4:209). For I-liang's impeachment of Ch'i-shan and the enclosure of the copy of the proclamation, see *IWSM-TK*, 23:2b–4b.

32. For these imperial objections to territorial concessions and the order for Ch'i-shan's removal, see *IWSM-TK*, 18:17a, and 23:5.

33. Lin was ordered to Chekiang on 15 April 1841 (*SL-TK*, 349:18a), but did not arrive at the front until 10 June (Kuo T'ing-i, 1:108).

34. The account of the demonstration and of its background is based on Liang T'ing-nan: see *YPCC*, 6:33.

35. For Teng's affiliation with the White Cloud Mountain poets and his relationship with Huang P'ei-fang, see *TKHC*, 71:1b.

36. Ch'i Kung was governor of Kwangtung from 1833 to 1838. For this and other details, see Chang Mu's biography of him, reprinted in *YPCC*, 6:389–391. For Ch'i's earlier reliance on the advice of a local scholar, I K'o-chung, see *YPCC*, pp. 7, 35. In an 1835 letter to Ch'i Chün-tsao, however, the Kwangtung educational commissioner, Li T'ang-chieh, would complain that Ch'i Kung was "too realistic" to be able to win the hearts of the Cantonese scholars the way that Lin had (*YPCC*, 5:527). For Ch'i Kung's Han-lin kinsman, see Chu Ju-chen, 5:30a. Ch'i Kung was appointed to Kwangtung on 10 February 1841, to serve as overseer of supply for Generallissimo I-shan (see next note and *SL-TK*, 345:8a). He arrived in Canton on 26 February and was promoted to governor general on 13 April.

37. For the Ch'ing decision to send I-shan to Kwangtung and to mobilize extraprovincial forces for the campaign, see Wei Yuan's account in *SSK*, p. 72. For the size of the extra-provincial army, I have used the estimate provided by Wang T'ing-lan (provincial judicial commissioner), in *YPCC*, 4:25. This does not include locally hired irregulars and regular provincial garrison troops. To pay for this campaign, the court initially ordered the transfer to Kwangtung of 2 million taels from other provinces (*IWSM-TK*, 21:26b).

38. For I-shan's assignment and his previous experience, see *SL-TK*, 344:16, and *ECCP*, p. 391. It is interesting to note that the only Chinese general to be co-assigned to Kwangtung (Yang Fang, 1770–1846) was also a recent hero of the Sinkiang campaigns. See *ECCP*, p. 885.

39. For the background to the siege expedition against Canton and its development, I have followed Peter Fay, pp. 278–302.

40. For Liang T'ing-nan's 1840 appointment, see Liu Po-chi, p. 259. Liang had served as military adviser to Lin before Ch'i Kung's arrival (see *YPCC*, 6:9, 19). For Yü T'ing-k'uei, see *HNHC*, 5:18b. For Ch'i Kung's use of these three advisers, see *YPCC*, 4:599, and 6:35. Note also that the special exam held by Ch'i Kung for city academy students in the spring of 1841 to mark the inauguration of his term excluded the students at the Hsueh-hai-t'ang.

41. For the Li K'o-chiung force (co-headed by two other Fatshan notables, Wu Jung-kuang and Wu Pi-kuang), see *YPCC*, 6:35, and *IWSM-TK*, 331:7a.

42. For the origins of Lin Fu-hsiang's naval militia and its connection with Ch'i and Huang P'ei-fang, see *YPCC*, 4:599. Lin Fu-hsiang's *P'ing-hai hsin-ch'ou* (Thoughts on maritime defense, 1843) is included in *YPCC*, 5:588-605, though its author is misnamed. Lin (1814–1862) was a Hsiang-shang licentiate who had spent some time in Macao in his youth. See Wakeman, *Strangers at the Gate*, pp. 39–40.

43. I.e., at Ni-ch'eng, a position guarding the Canton River near Tseng-pu, or "Tsing-pu" (as it is called in British dispatches). See Lin Fu-hsiang, in *YPCC*, 4:599.

44. For I-shan's behavior, see *YPCC*, 6:83; the remark about bookworms appears on 4:27.

45. For I-shan's attitudes about the Cantonese, see *SLHK*, p. 696; *YPCC*, 4:353; and *SSK*, p. 88. For the decision to recruit "water braves" outside of the vicinity of Canton and the delay this occasioned, see *YPCC*, 4:332-333.

46. The second British expedition northward began in August 1841, after Sir Henry Pottinger (the new British plenipotentiary) had arrived to relieve Charles Elliot of command. Appropriate to its objective of expanding the war, it boasted a much larger complement of men and ships—and especially of steamships—than had the first. All in all, there were 25 warships, 14 steamers, 9 support vessels, troopships, and about 10,000 infantry. See Wakeman, "The Canton Trade," p. 203.

47. The above is summarized from Wakeman, *Strangers*, pp. 14–21. See also ibid., pp. 52–58, for an analysis of the psychology of the actions of the militiamen. Wakeman emphasizes, in this latter section, the role of provincialist xenophobia stirred up by the "invasion" of Hunanese and other elite units from the interior.

48. For the (putatively) genuine San-yuan-li villagers' manifesto, see *YPCC*, 4:21-22; and *WHC*, 2:785-786. The genuinely popular nature of this manifesto's authorship is suggested by the intermittent admixture of colloquialisms into the classical text. Thus, the British are berated for failing to cease their hostile actions "in gratitude for the bit of face that they've been given" by the Ch'ing authorities. Similarly, the fearlessness of the "righteous scholars" and peasants in the face of British threats is depicted in language reminiscent of a street quarrel. "Who's afraid of your big barbarian ships?" is their response to Elliot's alleged warning that he will seek revenge for the disgrace at San-yuan-li (*YPCC*, 4:22). Details on the precise authorship of this document are

not available, but several clues exist. Two of the sources for it noted by the editors of the *YPCC* version mention that, after the attention of the officials and scholars of the Ta-fo-ssu Bureau had been drawn to it, a banquet was held on 8 June (4/9) for the scholar-militiamen presumed to have composed this manifesto (see *YPCC*, 4:21). Among the invited, we find no scholars of rank higher than provincial graduate. Moreover, another document in the *YPCC* collection (an intelligence report prepared for an unidentified official concerning developments in Canton—see *YPCC*, 3:542) confirms that this meeting occurred, and identifies one of the guests as a certain Ho Yu-ch'eng, of the Mu-te-li section of P'an-yü county. Since Mu-te-li is the rural subdivision of P'an-yü wherein the militia league active at San-yuan-li was based, our conclusion must be that the authors of this particular document really were village defense-force chiefs.

49. The three documents I have tentatively identified as products of the urban academy elite are:

(1) "Kuang-chou hsiang-min yü shih-san-hang k'ou hsiao-yu Ying-i shih" (A proclamation addressed to the English barbarians, posted on the cohong offices by the people of the countryside in residence in the city of Canton). *YPCC*, 4:22–23; also in *WHC*, 2:783.

(2) "Chiao-ch'i lu" (Tears of the merman of the Pearl River). *YPCC*, 3:37; also in *WHC*, 2:779.

(3) "Kuang-tung [or Ch'uan-Yueh] i-min yü Ying-i kao-shih [hsi]" (A proclamation from the righteous people of the entire province of Kwangtung, addressed to the English barbarians). *YPCC*, 4:18–21; also in *IWSM-TK*, 31:15b–20b (memorial of Liang Chang-chü, arriving in Peking on 31 August 1841).

The authors of (1) may be inferred from the document's title to be residents of Canton, and thus could not have been the same men that led the peasant bands at San-yuan-li. The writer of (2) is anonymous. But the purpose of the document appears (from a passage near the end) to have been for circulation to literati in Peking or elsewhere outside of Canton. There was no particular reason why the San-yuan-li leaders would have wished their manifesto to circulate in this fashion; whereas, for the scholars of the Ta-fo-ssu Bureau, there were significant gains to be scored by turning Peking's opinion against the regular army and its officers. Thus, I presume that (2) was likewise a city-scholar production. Document (3) is the hardest to attribute. Nonetheless, its text makes pointed reference to plans for the construction of a (Ch'ing) deep-water fleet to be deployed against the British if they are so unwise as to continue the war. This is not the sort of thing that village leaders were likely to have on their minds, since the funding for ship construction (even if perceived as necessary) would have been raised in the city. However, the construction of improved warships was a subject about which both Lin Tse-hsu and the (Tao-fu-ssu Bureau) naval commander, Lin Fu-hsiang, were quite in earnest. (*YPCC*, 4:596.) I therefore suspect strongly that (3) was likewise gotten up by the Tao-fo-ssu Bureau scholars, perhaps in cooperation with Ch'i Kung.

50. *YPCC*, 4:22.
51. *YPCC*, 3:37–38.
52. *YPCC*, 4:20.
53. *WHC*, 2:781. On this point, one might note that Lin Fu-hsiang (the general of the urban militia leadership group) was an open advocate of kicking the "guest soldiers" (*k'o-ping*) out of the Pearl River delta. See *YPCC*, 4:591.
54. For the poem, see *YPCC*, 4:712. For its popularity, see Lin Ch'ang-i, 2:7b–8a. Another local scholar connected with the Ta-fo-ssu Bureau group whose San-yuan-li poem seems to have been broadly circulated was Liang Hsin-fang (*chü-jen* of 1808). See *WHC*, 2:929–930 (for the poem), and *SJCL*, 55:22a (for its citation). (For Liang's relationship to the Lin Tse-hsu-organized militia committee, see *LTHJC*, p. 374.)
55. See *YPCC*, 4:617–619 (esp. p. 619), for Lo's trip home, his observations, and his collection of songs and ballads from the province to take back with him to Peking. See also *IWSM-TK*, 28:24b–25a and 30:8b–9b, for Lo's accusations against the depredations of the expeditionary armies from Hunan stationed at the Canton front.
56. For Fang's poem (quoting the third of the Cantonese placards listed in note 49 above), see *TCFC*, 5:3b. The date of this poem appears from its sequence to be prior to TK 21/9 (1841). The citation of the city manifesto above noted can be deduced from the mention of the placard's warning that death by wind and lightning would be visited upon the British in response to any further outrages by them. This sentiment appears in *YPCC*, 4:20, in the middle of the above-cited document. It appears in no other of the manifestoes. For Sun I-yen's poem—which also makes reference to the expectation of divine wrath descending upon the foreigners—see *WHC*, 1:58. In addition to this version of the San-yuan-li manifesto, others were apparently composed and circulated later on. *YPCC*, 3:173, records that Liu Ch'ang-hua, a scholar living in Nan-t'ung, Kiangsu, saw a copy of a printed set of manifestoes of the "people of Kwangtung." His description of the contents seems to indicate that the manifestoes we have cited were not included. Apparently, the work he saw was that of Ch'ien Chiang and Ho Ta-keng, and had been assembled and printed late in 1842. (See *WHC*, 2:781–784—esp. 784, which records the storing of printing blocks for a small-type version to be circulated outside of the province of Kwangtung.) The text and background of this Ch'ien-Ho version of the San-yuan-li manifesto appear in *YPCC*, 3:353ff., 4:23.
57. For the onset of the autumn 1841 central China campaign and the Ch'ing counteroffensive (which brought 12,000 extra-provincial elite troops into Chekiang), see Waley, pp. 158ff. For the opposition to these transfers by the Min-Che governor general, Yen Po-t'ao, see *IWSM-TK*, 30:15ff. (memorial of TK 21/6/13), esp. 30:18a. Liang Chang-chü was transferred to the Soochow-Shanghai front in mid-1841 (from Kwangsi), and made acting governor (for Kiangnan) and chief of supply operations for Ch'ing operations in Chekiang. The antipathy to the army of extra-provincial regulars (under Generalissimo I-ching) that was current in his office in Shanghai is expressed quite

bluntly in a set of verses exchanged with Liang by one of his secretaries, Chu Chien, in the fall of 1841. (See Huang An-t'ao, *Hsi-keng ts'ao-t'ang shih-chi*, 16:11b–12a.) Liu Yun-k'o, the Chekiang governor, was somewhat more ambivalent on the subject of outside units. In the early winter of 1841–1842, after the initial British successes, Liu actually urged the court to rush more such troops into Chekiang (*IWSM-TK*, 37:20bff.). However, once I-ching's soldiers had begun to run amok in Chekiang, he quickly changed his tune and became averse to the idea. During the weeks after the failure of the Ch'ing counteroffensive in Chekiang (in February-March 1841), Liu even went so far as to deny I-ching's retreating troops access to the provincial capital city of Hangchow (*IWSM-TK*, 3:200). And, around the same time, he urged the emperor to order the withdrawal from Chekiang of all of I-ching's remaining men. (See *IWSM-TK*, 44:27ff., esp. 44:29.)

58. *YPCC*, 4:25–29.
59. For the transmittal of Wang's letter to Yen, see *IWSM-TK*, 30:15b; for Yen's covering memorial, see 30:15a–19b; for Liang's reply (and the enclosure of the manifesto), see 31:13b–15b, and 15b–19b.
60. For the Ch'i Kung request, see *IWSM-TK*, 32:15a–17a (memorial arriving Peking on TK 21/8/7, or 21 September 1841).
61. For the request for the dispatch of more troops to the south, see *IWSM-TK*, 35:30b–33a, esp. 35:32 (memorial of Hai-ling).
62. For the rejection of the request for the southward transfer of more troops from Manchuria, see *IWSM-TK*, 35:33a. The emperor gives as his reason the fact that the troops are needed for the defense of Mukden and of Shan-hai-kuan! More evidence of the throne's increasing concern to concentrate remaining forces at Tientsin and in southern Manchuria comes in the approval, on TK 21/7/19, of a plan to shift 6,000 more elite troops from the interior to Tientsin. (See *IWSM-TK*, 35:33b–35a; note that the planning document is followed by a list of the provinces of the south and the interior from which the 6,000 are expected to be raised. See also *SL-TK*, 357:29, which records an edict of TK 21/7/9, rerouting several Chekiang-bound northern units to Tientsin.) For the 5 November document, see *SL-TK*, 358:12a–15a.
63. For the size of the irregular force at Canton, see *IWSM-TK*, 32:16a; and *SL-TK*, 384:23b. Both of these sources estimate an "army" of some 36,000. Wei Yuan (*SSK*, p. 93) also uses this figure. The nominal quota for Green Standard regulars stationed in Kwangtung was 68,263 (see *IWSM-TK*, 33:35b); however, that figure is doubtless much higher than the actual number of regulars normally under arms.
64. *SSK*, pp. 87–88. The pullback was to a certain Hsia-chin-shan northeast of the city.
65. The effect of the Ch'ing defeat of May 1841 in encouraging bolder behavior by the delta's huge population of smugglers, racketeers, and other "bandits" is stressed by Wakeman (*Strangers*, p. 62). The point is also made very explicitly by Lin Fu-hsiang, the commander of the Ta-fo-ssu Bureau forces, in his 1843 essays on local defense; see *YPCC*, 4:589. Exactly how bad the out-

break was is not easy to say. But officials certainly regarded the problem as serious enough to justify the expansion of the militia. According to Liang T'ing-nan, the cause of the bandit troubles was the partial demobilization of the mercenary forces that had been created during the siege; without work, they turned to crime (*YPCC*, 6:46).

66. For an excellent discussion of how Tanka ("boat people") strongmen and racketeers were absorbed into the fabric of security organization in the reclaimed portions of the delta, see Sasaki Masaya, "Juntoku-ken kyōshin to Tōkai jūrokusa," pp. 186–210.

67. For the fear of a British attack, see *IWSM-TK*, 40:27a (I-shan's memorial of TK 21/11/21). According to one source, the filling of the main channels of the Canton river with stones to obstruct British ships began in the 5th lunar month of 1841, right after the British withdrawal, and was financed and managed entirely by scholar-directors of the militia. (See *YPCC*, 3:20; also *IWSM-TK*, 29:40a.) *YPCC*, 4:264–265, gives some incomplete information on the costs, which came to 10,000 taels for just one of the four locations where the stones were sunk.

68. *YPCC*, 4:338 (citing 1872 Nan-hai county gazetteer) records specifically that in the 7th lunar month of 1841 (in response to a claimed British war threat) the Canton Bureau directors began raising funds for a mercenary force of "20,000 or 30,000." In a memorial reaching Peking on TK 21/8/7, I-shan and Ch'i Kung were already telling the throne that volunteers were inadequate for the mobile war of defense that would have to be fought, and that a professionalized force would be needed. (*IWSM-TK*, 32:16b.)

69. Sasaki Masaya, "Juntoku-ken," pp. 186–210.

70. *IWSM-TK*, 32:16b.

71. *IWSM-TK*, 40:25b–30a (esp. 40:29). Here Ch'i Kung distinguishes clearly between the 50,000 militiamen raised in the countryside by local notables, and a 30,000-man force of mercenaries recruited directly by the Canton militia authority.

72. The best source on the original licensing plan is Liang T'ing-nan (*YPCC*, 6:45–6). To judge from the sequence in which the description of the inauguration of the arrangement is inserted into his narrative, the system began to operate in the fall of 1841. Confirmation of this is given in *SL-TK*, 379:24b–25b (TK 22/8/22), which notes a TK 21/10 fight between some Tanka working in the reclaimed areas of Shun-te county and a body of fighters described as "braves stationed in the provincial capital." The fight occurred when the braves attempted to levy protection fees on the workmen, whom I take to be tenants or squatters engaged in reclamation or farming.

73. The first and only comprehensive report on this outer Bogue reclamation scheme (submitted on TK 23/7/13) is in *IWSM-TK*, 67:33b–39a. Additional information on the origins of the plan appears in *HCSH*, #4, 6:39; *PYHC*, 26:15b–16a; and *YPCC*, 6:390. Two Hsueh-hai-t'ang scholars, Tseng Chao and Fan Feng, appear to have been the individuals responsible for the idea. The scale of the shoal-field holdings policed by the new authority can be roughly estimated from Liang T'ing-nan's observation that 170,000 *mu*

(roughly, 30,000 acres) eventually came under the jurisdiction of the bureau (*YPCC*, 6:45–46). This would amount to about a third of the entire quota of tax-paying shoal fields in all of Kwangtung province (see *CFTCC, Ting-ming, hou-chi*, 12:9, which estimates the latter at 530,000 *mu* in the second decade of the 19th century.

74. See, for example, the emperor's response to Ch'i Kung's and I-shan's report of 21 September 1841 (TK 21/8/7), in *SL-TK*, 355:20a–21a. Here the emperor has drawn the conclusion from what Ch'i Kung has told him that the Cantonese defense forces are capable of joining in a general offensive against the British.

75. For the circumstances surrounding the start of the Chekiang counteroffensive, see *SSK*, pp. 117ff.; also Waley, pp. 158ff.

76. See, for example, the edict in *SL-TK*, 354:9a–10a (TK 21/8/4).

77. *IWSM-TK*, 37:8a–10a; 45:25ff., esp. 26a.

78. For Ch'i-ying's appointment to proceed to Hangchow (in fact, however, to sound out the possibilities for negotiations—though this was not made public), see *SL-TK*, 368:5b. The order for the defeated (ex-) general, I-li-pu, to accompany him (*SL-TK*) indicates, however, that the purpose of the assignment was not to wage war.

79. *YPCC*, 4:262.

5. The Debate Over the Conduct of the War

1. For Yao's (1846) *K'ang-yu chi-hsing*, see below, note 65. For Wei Yuan's (1844) *Illustrated Gazetteer*, see John K. Fairbank, *Trade and Diplomacy*, pp. 178–183; Suzanne W. Barnett, "Wei Yuan and the Westerners: Notes on the Sources of the *Hai-kuo t'u-chih*"; Jane Kate Leonard, "Wei Yuan and Images of the Nan-yang;" and note 40 below. Huang Chueh-tzu's *Hai-fang t'u-piao* is not listed in any library whose holdings have so far been published. It may never have been printed, but did circulate in manuscript. For details about its compilation, see *HPSW*, 26:5b–6b. The *WHC*, 2:926, notes that Huang sent a copy to Tsang Yü-ch'ing at the Chekiang front in late 1841. The definitive study of Hsu Chi-yü's *Short Account* (first published in 1848) is Fred W. Drake, *China Charts the World: Hsu Chi-yü and his Geography of 1848*. For the background and date of Wei Yuan's *Record of the Campaigns* (the text of which is to be found in *SSK*) and Huang En-t'ung's *Record of Pacifying*, see *YPCC*, 6:505–506 (for Wei), and 5:409ff. and 6:513–514 (for Huang). A useful survey of the literature on "maritime defense" and Western geography that developed in the 1840–1860 period is to be found in Hao Yen-p'ing and Wang Erh-min, "Changing Chinese Views of Western Relations, 1840–1895," pp. 145–153.

2. *YPCC*, 4:531.

3. Masataka Banno, *China and the West, 1858–1861: The Origins of the Tsungli Yamen*, p. 7.

4. See above, chapter 4.

5. *YPCC*, 2:570.

6. According to Liang T'ing-nan, Lin had been informed about the dispatch of a large British squadron from India by a tip-off from a certain Chou Yen-ts'ai, a retired Chinese trader and mercenary soldier who had contacts among the foreign trading community through his long-time residence in Annam. Chou told Liang, and Liang passed on the information to Lin in the early spring of 1840 (*YPCC*, 6:22). Lin reported this information to Peking only as a rumor. (See *IWSM-TK*, 10:5a.) Liang then further admitted (*YPCC*, 6:24) that Lin had expected that the embargo at Canton would deny the British the trading profits and supplies they needed to feed their armies, and had not anticipated that the enemy was capable of financing war expenses by a government advance. Putting these two facts together, one comes to the conclusion that Lin believed he did not need to send a dire warning northward at the time. For the 1839 origins of the British plan of attack, the so-called Jardine plan, see Fay, p. 215; and Beeching, p. 111.

7. Hsia Hsieh, *Chung-hsi chi-shih*, 5:13a.

8. Ibid., 5:13a–b.

9. Wang Hsi-chen, *Lung-pi shan-fang wen-chi* (1881) 2:2b.

10. Chu Ch'i, *I-chih-t'ang, shih*, 4:4a. For an example of how remarkably well this version of the Lin/Ch'i-shan story survived in the in-group lore of the literati, see Ko Shih-chün, comp., *Huang-ch'ao ching-shih wen hsu-pien*, 101:6a, citing a memorial submitted in the early 1870s by the middle-rank Southern City official Yin Chao-yung (1806–1883).

11. Wu Chia-pin, *Ch'iu-tzu-te-chih-shih wen-ch'ao*, 4:17b–18b. See also *SL-TK*, 390:3a, for evidence of the submission of this document as a memorial sometime late in 1842 or early in 1843.

12. Yao was one of the handful of provincial officials who supported the 1838 death-penalty idea for opium control. His correspondence with Huang Chueh-tzu on this subject indicates, moreover, that he was fully aware both of the unpopularity of the scheme, and of the arrangement that Lin would support it. See *HPSW*, 24:9a–10a.

13. For this see (in addition to chapter 2, above) *CFTCC, Tung-ming, hou-chi*, 8:1a–2a (1843 letter to Fang Tung-shu). Yao's constant correspondent, Fang Tung-shu, provides an even more vigorous statement of this faith in the power of example and of "urgent words" in his mid-1842 essay on war policy: see *YPCC*, 5:591, 594.

14. *IWSM-TK*, 41:25a–31b (report of Tuan-hua, Mu-ch'ing-a, and Hsu Yu-jen, received in Peking on TK 21/12/9). All dates of battles cited in the following narrative not mentioned in the sources referred to in the footnotes are from Kuo T'ing-i, p.1.

15. *IWSM-TK*, 38:1a–8a (memorial of Yao and Ta-hung-a, received TK 21/10/11).

16. Ibid., 47:10b–13b (memorial of Yao and Ta-hung-a received TK 22/4/5).

17. W. D. Bernard, *Narrative of the Voyages and Services of the 'Nemesis',* p. 301

18. *IWSM-TK*, 63:42a (I-liang's report of TK 22/11/21).

19. Ibid., 41:19b–20a, 31b–32a.

20. Ibid., 38:b–9a (edict of TK 21/10/11).

21. *CFTCC, Nien-pu*, p. 186.

22. Hsia Hsieh, 10:4a.
23. For the Pottinger accusation and the response of Ch'i-ying, I have followed the account in Hsia Hsieh, 10:4a; Liang T'ing-nan's account in *YPCC*, 6:80–81; and Wei Yuan's *SSK*, pp. 156ff. All of these sources are seriously biased against Ch'i-ying, however. Ch'i-ying's final report on the case (*IWSM-TK*, 64:18a–19a) helps redress the balance a bit, as does the account in Bernard, pp. 291–301.
24. *SL-TK*, 386:16a
25. *YPCC*, 6:396 (Wu Chia-pin biography of Yao Ying).
26. For Yao's self-vindication, see his mid-1843 letters to Liu Hung-kao and to Fang Tung-shu, in *CFTCC, Tung-ming, hou-chi*, 7:14a–17b, and 8:1a–2a.
27. Ibid., 7:15.
28. Ibid., 7:1a.
29. Ibid., 8:1a. That Yao was already being hailed in literati circles as something of a hero for his defense efforts on Taiwan—reputedly effective enough to ward off a British attack—even before the *Ann* and *Nerbudda* incidents is evidenced by a poetic tribute to him composed by Fang Tung-shu (in Anhwei) in late 1841. See *TCFC*, 5:3b–4a. See also *WHC*, 2:926., in which Yao appears as the victorious defender of the island in a poem sent in late 1841 from Huang Chueh-tzu to Tsang Shu-ch'ing (then at the front in Chekiang).
30. *CFTCC, Tung-ming, hou-chi*, 8:1b.
31. *YPCC*, 6:596.
32. Hsia Hsieh, 10:8a.
33. Ibid., 10:4a.
34. Lu I-t'ung, 4:34b.
35. For other expressions of literati opinion on the Yao Ying affair (all sympathetic to the point of view here described) see, for example: Shao I-ch'en, *Pan-yen-lu i-chi*, 62a; Wu Chia-pin, 10:1b–2a; and Wang Hsi-chen, (1881), 2:2ff.
36. Yao Yung-p'u, 4:20b.
37. Feng Kuei-fen, *Hsien-chih-t'ang chi*, 12:5. See also Lin Ch'ang-i, 2:4a; and Chu Ch'i, *I-chih-t'ang, shih*, 4:10a–11b, for more records of the activity that took place following Yao's release.
38. For the indebtedness of Wei and Yao (and other literati war commentators) to 16th-century writers on military organization and strategy, see *YPCC*, 5:434. Here Huang En-t'ung, Ch'i-ying's diplomatic adjutant in Canton, criticizes this reliance on such texts rather bitterly. (But see also ibid., 5:556, for Wei's rebuttal.) See above, chapter 4, note 20, for the frequency of references to Cheng Jo-tseng's work (the *Ch'ou-hai t'u-pien*). For the content of Ch'i Chi-kuang's anti-pirate strategy, see Philip A. Kuhn, *Rebellion and its Enemies in Late Imperial China*, pp. 124–126; and Ray Huang, *1587: A Year of No Significance*, pp. 163–174.
39. In the portrait that follows of Wei Yuan's maritime-defense thought, I diverge from the views of Fairbank and others (such as the Chinese scholar Ch'i Ssu-ho) who have seen Wei as the forefather of the realist school of diplomatic strategy that would flourish in the era of self-strengthening (roughly, 1865–1895). See esp. Fairbank, *Trade and Diplomacy*, pp. 179–182. Fairbank's

analysis rests chiefly on the similarity between Wei and the self-strength-eners in advocating the adoption of Western-style armaments. My own inter-pretation, however, stresses Wei's determination to show the feasibility of a militant anti-treaty diplomacy. Such a spirit—central for Wei, inasmuch as his *magnum opus* (the *Illustrated Gazetteer*) was written as an apology for the war party—is simply not to be found in the thinking of the later school. For this reason my account focuses almost exclusively on those aspects of Wei's writings that reveal him as an intransigent.

40. The date of publication of the original version of Wei's *Illustrated Gazetteer* remains something of a mystery. Wang Chia-chien, *Nien-p'u*, p. 82 (citing an unidentified preface), says that it was completed on TK 22/12/13 (roughly, January 1843). *ECCP*, however, gives the date of publication for the first (50-*chüan*) edition as 1844. This latter date tends to find confirmation in a reference to the manuscript version in a poem of late 1844 by Chu Ch'i. Chu, a leading figure in the Ku Shrine Association, and a censor in the Peking bureaucracy, had been requested by Wei to submit part of the manu-script to the emperor. But, according to Chu's own remark, he had declined, noting that the work was about to be printed in any case. (See Chu Ch'i, *I-chih-t'ang, shih*, 4:13b–14a.) Further evidence that Wei and Chu were plan-ning to jointly submit the work to the emperor appears in Lin Ch'ang-i, 24:13b–14a, which contains a copy of the 1843 poetic history of Ch'ing mil-itary accomplishments. The last stanza has obviously been culled from the four introductory essays of the *Illustrated Gazetteer*. To judge from these two bits of evidence, it would seem that the introductory section of Wei's work had been written as a kind of manifesto of the war party's position, and was to have been presented to the emperor in a memorial prior to publication. The actual publication, together with supporting materials, would thus have occurred only after political considerations had ruled out such a direct approach to the throne. The work was expanded and republished in a 60-*chüan* version in 1847, probably in response to the publication of Yao Ying's "Record of an Embassy" the year before (see Wang Chia-chien, *Nien-p'u*, p. 118.) For the publication background of the *Record of the Campaigns*, see the informative comments by Ch'i Ssu-ho (?) in *YPCC*, 6:505–506. According to this latter, the *Record* was originally written as a last chapter for the *Sheng-wu chi* (Military history of the Ch'ing), a work published by Wei in 1842, and republished in 1844 and 1846. Yao Wei-yuan (*SSK*, pref.) states that it was first included in the 1844 edition. But *YPCC*, 6:506, says it was first car-ried in the 1875 edition. Fear of negative official reaction obviously played a part in inducing Wei to postpone the publication, in any case.

41. Comparing the text of the introductory essays ("On Defense") in the *Illus-trated Gazetteer* (see *YPCC*, 5:555–556) with an essay on "pacifying the barbar-ians" appearing in Huang En-t'ung's *Fu-yuan chi-lueh* (ibid., 5:434–435), it is possible to establish that Wei had read Huang's critique of the continue-the-war advocates before writing the critical introductory section of his gazet-teer. In this passage, Wei makes explicit reference to Huang's critique of the war party for failing to perceive the irreversibility of China's naval disadvan-

tage and for relying over much on the "trite texts" of yesteryear as guides to action. Huang's (1846?) *Fu-yuan chi-lueh* (p. 434) also contains a postscript complaining about war-party illusions of exploiting French and American anti-British sentiment and Cantonese anti-foreignism as sources of additional military strength against the enemy and vigorously denounces the Cantonese as "flighty" and "lacking stamina for a sustained fight." Wei's defense of the San-yuan-li militiamen seems to be a response to Huang on this point, too.

42. For Huang's role as an assistant in the Nanking negotiations and his transfer to Kwangtung at Ch'i-ying's behest in late 1842, see Fairbank, *Trade and Diplomacy*, pp. 106, 187.

43. *YPCC*, 5:442.

44. For Ch'ien Chiang—the most spectacular victim of the campaign to bring the militia under control—see *YPCC*, 4:34–37, and Wakeman, *Strangers*, pp. 68–70. Ch'ien was an adventurer from Chekiang who never got along very well with the Ta-fo-ssu Bureau leadership. He was arrested and exiled after helping to foment an unsuccessful demonstration and placard campaign against the authorities (including Huang En-t'ung) in Canton. (See *YPCC*, 6:83–84.)

45. *YPCC*, 5:434.

46. *SSK*, p. 90. Major Becher, General Gough's deputy quartermaster, died of heat prostration during the stand-off near San-yuan-li (Fay, p. 300). Sir Gordon Bremer was commanding officer of the first naval squadron sent out from India in 1840 (ibid., p. 213). I have here followed Yao Wei-yuan's careful study of the mistakes in Wei Yuan's text in *SSK*.

47. *SSK*, p. 92; for the full tale, see pp. 90–99.

48. *SSK*, p. 93. The manifesto here quoted by Wei is clearly the (urban scholars') manifesto no. 3 discussed in chapter 4, note 49 (see *YPCC*, 4:18–19, for the original text). One cannot help but conclude that, for a scholar with a reputation as a serious historian, Wei was being extraordinarily sloppy about corroborating his sources of information. If this was the case in his disposition of evidence pertaining to events that had taken place on Chinese soil, one is inclined to doubt even more the likelihood that he could have entered into an examination of the materials about the British and other foreign powers with anything like the objectivity required to learn anything from his researches.

49. *SSK*, p. 164.

50. Ibid.

51. The maritime defense essays (i.e., the four introductory chapters) of the *Illustrated Gazetteer* are reprinted in *YPCC*, 5:545–582. Wei's praise of civilian irregulars in Kwangtung and Chekiang occurs on pp. 547, 557, 559–562. The phrase *lang-chan* occurs in *SSK*, p. 164, specifically as a critique of I-shan. However, also see *YPCC*, 5:547, for the critique of Yü-ch'ien's decision to contest the Chusan Islands. For Wei's brief service (early in 1841) under Yü-ch'ien in eastern Chekiang, see Wang Chia-chien, *Nien-p'u*, pp. 75–76.

52. An exchange with Pao Shih-ch'en (see *An-wu*, 35:12a–14b; and Wei's *Wei Yuan*

chi, 2:510) reveals that Wei had advised Yü on the feasibility of fighting a war of retreat inside the gates to the Yangtze valley. Yü-ch'ien, however, appears to have been quite stubborn in his conviction that the lower Yangtze front was one place in the Ch'ing defense system where an offensive strategy was required. See Yü-ch'ien, p. 842. (For the critique of I-shan, see *SSK*, p. 164.)

53. *YPCC*, 5:559.

54. Ibid.

55. For the war-of-attrition strategy, see *YPCC*, 5:575 (end of "*i-chan*" essay). Interestingly, Wei discusses the same idea at another point, using as his principal historical model, not the defeat of the *wo-k'ou*, but rather the Russians' defeat of Napoleon and other invading armies (p. 558). In fact, earlier in this essay (p. 552), Wei even argues that the British were more vulnerable than the *wo-k'ou* to a strategy of deep defense, since their military skills were more geared to naval warfare (and presumably less useful on land) than was the case with the 16th-century coastal invaders.

56. *YPCC*, 5:569–571, 573–574. For the legitimation of a Petrine effort to master Western naval architecture (p. 571), Wei poses the precedent of a certain Nan Huai-jen (the Chinese name of Ferdinand Verbiest, 1623–1688; Wei actually meant Michel Benoist, 1715–1774) who was understood by Wei to have instructed the Ch'ien-lung emperor in the science of hydraulic engineering. (For Benoist, see Harold Kahn, *Monarchy in the Emperor's Eyes: Image and Reality in the Ch'ien-lung Reign*, pp. 124–125.) Note also that Yao Ying had been studying Verbiest's maps in 1842 (*CFTCC, Tung-ming, hou-chi*, 7:14a.) This was probably the reason for Wei's confusion.

57. *YPCC*, 5:575ff.

58. For Wei's belief that an anti-colonial revolt might be harnessed to Ch'ing military strategy, see *YPCC*, 5:565. Here Wei argues for using Nepalese and Russian allies in a combined attack on British India should a second Sino-British war erupt. For the date of Yao's book, see Wang Chia-chien, *Nien-p'u*, pp. 113–114.

59. Bernard, pp. 291–292.

60. For the interrogations, see Bernard, pp. 296, 298; and *CFTCC, Tung-ming, hou-chi*, 7:14a, where Yao explicitly notes (in an 1842 letter to Fang Tung-shu) that he had based his estimate of British weakness in India on what he had learned from questioning Denham (Tien-lin) and his other prisoners. According to the *K'ang-yu chi-hsing* (3:4b, 5:1a), details on British weaknesses in India gleaned from the Denham interrogations were reported to the emperor and provoked a request from Peking for information on the state of Russo-British relations along the India border.

61. For Yao's communication to I-liang, see *CFTCC, Tung-ming, hou-chi*, 7:7b–8b. In the copy of this letter that survives in Yao's collected papers, it is dated 1 July (5/23) 1842. According to Yao, a proposal of a similar sort for protracting the war by collaborating with the Nepalese was sent by Yao to Peking in the form of an urgent memorial five days later (on 6 July or 5/28), but was seized en route during the ocean voyage to the mainland. For the Gurkha petition for Ch'ing aid in a campaign against the "Bengals" (by which

was meant the native Indians in the service of the British), see *IWSM-TK*, 17:12a–14b (memorial of TK 20/11/7, from the Ch'ing resident in Lhasa, Meng-pao); and *SSK* (p. 158) for Yao Wei-yuan's explication. See also *IWSM-TK*, 22:27b–28b, for Meng-pao's follow-up intelligence report (received in Peking on TK 21/1/26), which notes that the Gurkhas' enemy–the "Bengals"–might actually be the English.

62. This can be demonstrated from the response to another literati brainstorm, likewise based on a misreading of events in progress in India (as reported in the Macao press). Evidently aroused by rumors then current in Macao of British difficulties in Bengal resulting from the China war's depletion of the India garrison forces, a Kwangtung-born censor, Su T'ing-k'uei, reported to the emperor on 22 May (4/13) 1842, that the "Bengals" had risen against the British and that British ships would soon be withdrawn from the China war to bring the uprising under control. On the basis of this, he maintained that the Ch'ing ought to refuse negotiations. However, when the matter was referred to I-shan in Canton, and when the latter denied that there was any sign of depletion in British maritime activity off the Kwangtung coast, the matter was pursued no further. See *IWSM-TK*, 47:40b–42a (for Su's memorial); 50:39b–40a, 51:1a–4a (for I-shan's reports); and *SL-TK*, 372:36b–37a, 373:1a–2a (for the emperor's response).

63. For Yao's correspondence with friends on the subject of the weakness of the British imperium in southern Asia while he was stationed in Szechuan and Tibet, see *CFTCC, Tung-ming, hou-chi,* 8:16a–17b, 19b–20b, 22b–23a (letters to Mei Tseng-liang, Yü K'un, and Lin Tse-hsu). From this testimony, it would seem that the final impetus for Yao's work was the renewed pressure from the British (in 1846) for the opening of Tibet to direct trade from India. This demand aroused strong antipathy from the Nepalese, since it threatened their own control of the trans-Himalayan carriage trade. (See Fletcher, p. 404; and *SL-TK*, 437:32.) Here, according to Yao, was another opportunity for turning the Gurkhas against the British. It is evident, too, that Yao derived many of his ideas about the precariousness of the British military position in India from an early version of Wei Yuan's *Illustrated Gazetteer,* in which were cited several reports from Macao newspapers concerning Russo-British tensions in Afghanistan. See *K'ang-yu chi-hsing,* 3:4b–5a, for the influence of Wei's views; and *YPCC,* 2:492–494, for the Macao newspaper.

64. Yao Ying repeatedly notes his dependence on the 60-*chüan* version (eventually published in 1847) of Wei Yuan's *Illustrated Gazetteer* for his information on the history of British imperial expansion. See *K'ang-yu chi-hsing,* author's preface, 1a, 5:1a, 8:3b, and 12:2b. The rare bits of information on home government and domestic institutions in England are taken from the same source used by Wei, that is, Hugh Murray's *Encyclopedia of Geography* (London, 1832), a Protestant-inspired semi-religious work that had been translated into Chinese in 1840 as the *Ssu-chou chih* (Gazetteer of the four continents) under the auspices of Lin Tse-hsu. See *K'ang-yu chi-hsing,* 12:6a–8b, esp. 8a–b. Nothing is more revealing of the dogged insularity implicit in

Yao's work than the Sinocentric sequence used for presenting information about the outside world. The first country clearly beyond the bounds of the Ch'ing empire to be discussed by Yao is India (3:2b–7a). Next comes Russia (5:1b–2a), which is treated together with Hindustan and Kashmir—sections of the India frontier where Russian influence might possibly be exploited to threaten the British. It is not until three-quarters of the way through Yao's work that we come upon the first extensive reference to Europe (9:5, 10:2b–3a). And Yao reserves the discussion of the geography and institutions of Britain for the last chapter of his 12-chapter work (12:6ff.).

65. For Ch'en Li's critique, see Wang Chia-chien, *Wei Yuan tui hsi-fang ti jen-shih chi ch'i hai-fang ssu-hsiang*, pp. 151–153, citing *Tung-shu chi* (1892), 2:25–26. Ch'en takes Wei to task for failure to perceive that the Gurkhas had requested a league against the "Bengals" because they believed the Ch'ing had defeated this same people along the China coast. For Wei's addition to the *Illustrated Gazetteer*, see *Hai-kuo t'u-chih*, 13:4b–11b, and 16b–56b. The latter section (esp. 42a–56b) elaborates at considerable length on the feasibility of using Gurkha and Russian armies to attack British garrisons in India. Though no special mention occurs here of Yao Ying's *K'ang-yu chi-hsing*, this latter work is frequently quoted elsewhere in the 1847 revision, and its influence may be assumed. (See Wang Chia-chien, *Wei Yuan tui hsi-fang*, p. 50.) For Yao's influence on Lin Tse-hsu's perceptions of the situation in inner and southern Asia, see *CFTCC, Tung-ming, hou-chi*, 8:17b (letter of 1847).

6. The Ku Yen-wu Shrine Association

1. The events leading to the rise of Mu-chang-a and the influence of military considerations (especially the fear of British conquest) are cogently explored in Fairbank, *Trade and Diplomacy*, pp. 84–86. To Fairbank's analysis, it might be added that Mu-chang-a himself functioned as a prospective diplomatic commissioner for a while, having been sent out to Tientsin to direct defense preparations there in the spring of 1842, when that city was believed to be the next likely target of attack (*SL-TK*, 367:28a). In June 1842, he re-emerged as a central government leader, receiving a special grant of authority over the Board of Revenue (*SL-TK*, 373:35a). He continued to play a leading role in financial planning until his fall, in 1850.

In addition to Mu, at least three other Manchu and Mongol bureaucrats enjoyed prominence as troubleshooters at Tao-kuang's court after the turn away from belligerence in mid-1842, principally because their wartime military experience—and the sense it presumably inspired in them of the need for greater discipline on the Ch'ing side—qualified them for the emperor's fullest trust. These were Sai-shang-a, Prince Ting, and Ch'i-ying. The Mongol Sai-shang-a (*chü-jen* of 1816, d. 1875) was reappointed to the Grand Council in 1841, after a 4-year leave, and was sent twice to inspect the fortifications at Tientsin in 1841–1842. (One reason for his assignment, incidentally, was that he could speak the native tongue of the Mongol cavalrymen on whom the throne relied for its ultimate defense: see *ECCP*, p. 108; and *SL-TK*, 373: 36b.) His name figures after the war as one of the commissioners charged with investigating the Board of Revenue vault-embezzlement case in 1843, of which we shall have more to say below. (See *Chung-kuo chin-tai huo-pi shih tzu-liao*, 1:166; and *SL-TK*, 390:32b–33a.) He also appears as a committee-man in many subsequent financial deliberations during the late Tao-kuang period. Tsai-ch'uan, the 5th Prince Ting (d. 1854), had seen no recorded military service during the war, but emerged as one of the most frequently encountered figures in Peking's financial-planning commissions during the last years of this reign. (The reason for this may have been that he was the only close kinsman of the emperor who had had extensive bureaucratic experience in the capital before inheriting his title.) He too appears on the commissions that dealt with the vault-embezzlement case, and in others later on (see, for example, *SL-TK*, 466:14). Ch'i-ying (d. 1858) was an imperial clansman who had held numerous Peking ministry posts before 1840–1842. During the war, he had been placed in charge of the defenses of the Manchurian coastline (*ECCP*, p. 131). In the final months of the war, he was sent out as negotiator—first to Chekiang, then Nanking. From there he moved to Kwangtung as commissioner in 1843, and was promoted to governor general over that province in 1844 (a post he held until early 1848). Upon being recalled to Peking, he became at once a leading voice in almost all important fiscal and troop-deployment deliberations. (See, for example, *SL-TK*, 464:9a; and *SLHK*, pp. 688–689.) For the displacement of P'an Shih-en and Wang Ting, see *YPCC*, 5:530 (item 6) and 531 (item 10). The office of imperial commissioner (*ch'in-ch'ai ta-ch'en*) was created with Lin's appointment to Canton in 1839, and combined (as later appointments were to continue to do) with on-the-spot powers to conduct negotiations with foreigners, and command local military forces. Ch'i-ying was the first to be granted such powers in the postwar period (Fairbank, *Trade and Diplomacy*, p. 91), when he was assigned to Nanking in mid-1842; this appointment was soon followed by the naming of another Manchu, I-li-pu, to the (then vacant) position of Canton special commissioner, in October 1842 (p. 106); on 6 April 1843, Ch'i-ying replaced the deceased I-li-pu at Canton in the same capacity (p. 109). Sai-shang-a seems to have held a parallel post at Tientsin in mid-1842 (see *IWSM-TK*, 51:26a, 52:6a), which he inherited from Mu-chang-a. But the Tientsin post was not continued past the end of the war.

2. For Juan's relationship with Ho and Chang, see *TCT*, 1:39, 115; and Chang Mu, *Yin-chai wen-chi*, 3:1a. Juan Yuan's support for the Ku Shrine Association is evidenced by his promise to provide a dedication for its first meeting (*HCSH*, #1, 12:6a). His son's membership in the group is based on the association roster (see *KTM*), originally published in facsimile in Soochow in 1887. All statements about Shrine Association membership will be based on this document.

3. See, for example, the interesting quotations from two early British plenipotentiaries (Davis and Bonham) given in H. B. Morse, *The International Relations of the Chinese Empire*, 1:279. See also Fairbank, *Trade and Diplomacy*, pp. 84, 197.

4. *YPCC*, 5:530 (item 9).
5. The information on the movements of Lin and the others is based on Kuo T'ing-i, and on the table of provincial officials (Tables 4 and 5) in *YPCC*, 6:463–477. Ch'i-shan became commissioner for Kwangtung on 17 August 1840, and held this post until his dismissal on 26 February 1841. For I-li-pu's (1842–1843) and Ch'i-ying's (1843–1848) succession, see Fairbank, *Trade and Diplomacy*, pp. 106, 109.
6. Chou T'ien-chueh was promoted to replace Lin Tse-hsu as Hupeh governor general on TK 19/3/9; and reassigned to Foochow as governor general there on 6/2 as war tensions increased. However, he was mysteriously ordered back to Wuchang before he could take up his new seal of office. Then, on 2/17 of the following year, he was impeached for doing favors for a transient scholar (a Spring Purificationist), Chiang K'ai; and on 11/28, was removed from his Hupeh post. (See *SL-TK*, 323:33a; 331:13b–14b; 341:37a.) Part of the difficulty may have been that Chou was a strong supporter of Lin's scheme for enforcing the death penalty against opium addicts. (See *YPCC*, 5:410.)
7. For Chou's assignment to Kwangtung and his actions there, see *SL-TK*, 348:1a, and *YPCC*, 6:39. The recall came at the behest of the (Han-lin) Anhwei governor, Ch'eng Yü-ts'ai, who was, besides Lin and Chou, the third outstanding Chinese military leader during the war. (See *IWSM-TK*, 25:4.) For the seance and the rumor of Chou's 1842 recall to office, see *YPCC*, 3:157, 171.
8. For an astute analysis of the atmospherics surrounding Ch'i-ying's and I-li-pu's Chekiang appointments, see Fairbank, *Trade and Diplomacy*, pp. 91–92. As of the moment the court began to first consider negotiations (February or March 1842), Ch'i-ying was military governor at Mukden, in charge of the defense of the Manchurian coastline. On 28 March he was ordered south, nominally as commandant of the Manchu garrisons at Hangchow and Chapu. However, on 7 April, he was redesignated as special commissioner, and two lesser Manchu officials, formerly under a cloud for having failed to put up a fight in Chekiang (I-li-pu and Hsien-ling), were reinstated as his adjutants. However, the most significant aspect of this new commission is that it did not provide for joint consultations either with the Chekiang governor, Liu Yun-k'o, or with the commander of operations in the lower Yangtze, Generalissimo I-ching. The tensions to which this arrangement gave rise between Ch'i-ying and Liu would be particularly severe—and ironic, too, considering that it had been Liu who had originally pleaded with Peking to send a conciliationist down to Chekiang. (*IWSM-TK*, 44:33a–35b: memorial dated 28 March 1842.) However, once Ch'i-ying arrived and peace discussions were shifted to Nanking (defying Liu's hope that they would take place in Chekiang), Liu turned violently hostile to the commissioners. On 20 August 1842, he went so far as to address a public letter to those commissioners just then starting their talks with the British on a peace treaty, warning them strongly against making "dangerous" concessions. (*YPCC*, 3:112–113, 359–362.) This sort of opportunism had been characteristic of Liu's policies in the earlier days of the war, too. (Contrast

IWSM-TK, 17:25b–29b with 36:18a–19b.) It must have been the distrust this sort of behavior had procured for Liu that caused the emperor to bypass him by appointing outsiders to negotiate with the enemy. Parenthetically, it might be noted that Ch'i-ying and Governor Liu continued to battle each other after the war—now over the naming of lower-ranking personnel to those provincial offices in Chekiang that involved contact with foreigners. (See Fairbank, *Trade and Diplomacy*, pp. 188–191.)

9. On Ch'i Kung's commitment to "popular" government in Kwangtung, see the somewhat ironic report of Li T'ang-chieh (to Ch'i Chün-tsao) in 1843, in *YPCC*, 5:527. For I-li-pu's appointment as *ch'in-ch'ai* for Kwangtung (on 17 October 1842), see Fairbank, *Trade and Diplomacy*, p. 106. I-li-pu died on 4 March 1843. A memorial of Ch'i Kung's that arrived in Peking on TK 23/2/22 (*IWSM-TK*, 65:45ff.) shows Ch'i Kung attempting to guarantee the commissionership for himself. However, on 3/7, Ch'i-ying asked for and got the seal transferred into his own hands (*SL-TK*, 390:6b–8b). Characteristically, his replacement at Nanking (as commissioner and governor general) was Pi-ch'ang, at the time Manchu commandant of the Foochow garrison.

10. Lu I-t'ung, 4:17a; Lin Ch'ung-yung, p. 546; *SL-TK*, 350:10a–11a; *YPCC*, 5:530 (item 8); and *HCSH*, #1, 11:23b–24a. For T'ang as a pupil of Juan, see *TCT*, 1:39–40.

11. For Wang's actions and his removal, see Fairbank, *Trade and Diplomacy*, p. 84. For the rumor literature on Wang Ting's death, see Feng Kuei-fen, *Hsien-chih-t'ang chi*, 7:14a; *LCCW*, #1, 1:17a–18b; *HCSH*, #2, 8:2b–3a; and *YPCC*, 5:531 (item 10).

12. For the background to the Board of Revenue case, see *Chung-kuo chin-tai huo-pi*, 1:166–167, citing Ou-yang Yu, *Chien-wen so-lu*, 5:6–7. For the investigations, see *SL-TK*, 390:32b–34a; 36b–37a; 391:7, 16, 25a–27a.

13. For T'ang Chin-chao's role in supressing the Board of Revenue case earlier, see *Chung-kuo chin-tai huo-pi*, 1:166–167. For the literati protest against the government's disposal of the case, see Ting Yen, *I-chih-chai wen-ch'ao*, 7a–9b, and *SLHK*, 710.

14. For Huang's implication, see *HPSW*, 28:1a. For the removal from office of Tseng Wang-yen (then Fukien financial commissioner), see Wei Hsiu-mei, comp., *Ch'ing-chi chih-kuan piao*, p. 762. For Lo Ping-chang's wartime activities and pro-resistance lobbying, see *SLHK*, p. 708; *YPCC*, 4:617–619; and *IWSM-TK*, 36:1a–3b; for his implication, see his *Lo-kung nien-p'u*, p. 31.

15. For Su T'ing-k'uei as a pupil of Huang Chueh-tzu, see K'ung Hsien-i, 3:23a.For Su's memorial, see *Ch'ing-shih*, p. 4590; *SL-TK*, 390:2b–3b; and the collection of Peking gazettes held by the Office of Manuscripts and Printed Books of the British Museum, Gazette dated TK 23/3/9–10.

16. *SL-TK*, 390:2b–3b.

17. *Ch'ing-shih*, p. 4590.

18. *YPCC*, 5:529 (item 1).

19. Ibid., 5:530 (item 6).

20. Polachek, "Literati Groups," p. 481, Table 3 (based on *SL-TK*).

21. Li Yueh-jui, *Ch'un-ping shih*, pp. 62–63. See also Lo Chü, comp., *Lo Wen-k'o-*

kung (Tun-yen) nien-p'u, 7a. For a listing of Mu-chang-a's previous assignments as examiner, see *HCSH*, #4, 7:2b. Regarding the belief that Mu was undermining scholarly patronage ideals, a mid-century scholar, Li Yang-hua, was later to recall hearing from his elders the opinion that Mu had built upon a tradition of "corrupting" the bureaucracy with rotten examination pupils that had been inaugurated by Ho-shen and carried forward by Ts'ao Chen-yung! (*YPCC*, 1:215.) The association of Mu with Ts'ao in the minds of the examination elite confirms that what really angered the "public" was the tight conformism of Mu's regime, and its exclusion from rewards of more eccentric scholarly types.

22. The feeling of being penalized for scholarly patronage attachments seems to have been particularly intense among the graduates of the 1835, 1836, 1838, and 1840 metropolitan examinations, whose mentors had included (respectively) Ho Ling-han (a Juan Yuan favorite), Juan Yuan himself, and T'ang Chin-chao. For a direct comment on this, see Chuang Shou-ch'i, *Feng-nan shan-kuan i-chi*, 1:2a, which describes the uneasiness felt among the class of 1835 Han-lin. A statistical breakdown (by class cohorts) of metropolitan degree-holders who participated in the Shrine Association during 1844–1848 also helps to confirm the prominence, in that latter body, of the marooned examination clients of the above three examiners. Respectively 7, 5, and 6 members of the classes of 1835, 1836, and 1840 participated in the Association, while earlier classes were represented by much smaller groups of graduates (based on *KTM*).

23. *KTM*, 3b. According to this source, the altar was completed in TK 23/10, and the first gathering for sacrifice to Ku took place on TK 24/2/25, or 12 April 1844. (See also *TCT*, 3:917 for confirmation of this date for the shrine's completion.) However, Ho Shao-chi's poem of 1844, written in commemoration of the opening of the shrine (see *HCSH*, #1, 12:5b–7b), describes the first ceremony as having taken place on 2/14, or 1 April.

24. For Chang and Ho as Han Learning scholars, see *ECCP*, pp. 47–48, 287. In 1844, Chang Mu published a revised chronological biography of Ku Yen-wu, based on an earlier effort by Chu Shou-ch'ien. Ho was an avid collector and intepreter of ancient inscriptions. (See, for example, *TCT*, 1:183, 200.) For the kinship relationship between Ch'i and Chang, see Chuang Shou-ch'i, 7:3b–4a. See also Polachek, "Literati Groups," p. 466, for a diagram of the much larger nexus of marriage ties binding Chang into several prominent Ch'ang-chou (Kiangsu) scholarly families. For the prior membership of the five named literati in the Spring Purification group, see Ch'en Ch'ing-yung, *Chou-ching-t'ang lei-kao*, 12:10b; and *HPSW*, 14:3a, 16:7a, 21:15a, and 23:18a. Chu Ch'i's participation in the Spring Purification circle is not directly evidenced, possibly because he did not settle down in Peking until 1839, when that group was ending its activities. However, his social circle in Peking formed around Mei Tseng-liang's *ku-wen* salon, which had functioned through the 1830s as a center for Spring Purificationist activity. (See Chu Ch'i, 4:1a; and Mei Tseng-liang, 3:17b.)

25. *CFTCC, Tung-ming, hou-chi*, 11:8a–9a, 14:2a.

26. Yang Chi-sheng was murdered in prison for outspoken criticism of the powerful minister Yen Sung (1480–1568), whose policy for reducing tensions between the Ming state and the Mongols had centered on appeasing the latter with generous commerical privileges, most notably the expansion of horse markets (*ECCP*, p. 864). Curiously, his lodgings in Peking (the so-called Sung-yun-an) had become something of a national shrine by the late 18th century, owing in part to the Ch'ien-lung emperor's openly professed admiration for Yang. (Harold Kahn, pp. 130–131; Chu Ch'i, 5:3a–4a; *TWIK*, 59:6a.) In 1829, a year when the debates over whether or not to maintain Ch'ing garrisons in western Sinkiang reached their height (see above, chapter 3, note 8), the Spring Purificationists used this unoccupied villa as a meeting place for protesting the government's current drift away from a policy of tough military confrontation with the rebel state of Kokand. (Hsu Pao-shan, *Hu-yuan, Hu-yuan shih-ch'ao hsuan*, 5:7b–8b.) In 1847, Ho Shao-chi, one of the two co-founders of the Ku Association, raised a subscription to rebuild the villa, apparently so that it could be used for Shrine Association meetings (*TCT*, 2:687).

27. *CFTCC, Tung-ming, hou-chi*, 14:2b–3a.

28. For Yü-ch'ien's clumsy suicide at Chen-hai, see *ECCP*, p. 940. For Hai-ling's death, see Waley, p. 209. Chinese literati sources, it might be noted, did not give Hai-lin a very good press (see, for example, *YPCC*, 3:81), thanks chiefly to his wanton murder of suspected Chinese fifth-columnists during the brief siege of the city in July 1842. Yü-ch'ien did better, perhaps because of his prior wartime cooperation with Lin. See, for example, Lu I-t'ung, *Tung-fu, shih-ts'un*, 2:14a–15a.

29. Brigade General Ko Yun-fei, who was from Shan-yin county, Chekiang (modern day Shao-hsing), had died in the second British seizure of Ting-hai, 1 October 1841. Another Shao-hsing native, Yang Ch'ing-en (a minor local government official), had died in the fall of the Woosung forts, near Shanghai, on 16 June 1842. The shrine (called the Cheng-ch'i ko) was built in 1842 at the villa of the Shao-hsing regional guild in Peking by the former Spring Purificationist Tsung Chi-ch'en, and was dedicated in 1846. (See Mei Tseng-liang, 11:10b–11a; Chu Ch'i, *Wen shih*, 5:3; and Tsung Chi-ch'en, *Wen-ch'ao*, 11:12a.) Interestingly, the shrine also served as a memorial to several prominent Ming loyalist literati from Shao-hsing, such as Ni Yuan-lu (1599–1644) and Liu Tsung-chou (1578–1645)–both of whom had committed suicide when the Ming had fallen. However, both of the latter were high civil degree-holders and serious scholars–a circumstance that could only have reinforced the self-consciousness of the protesters of the 1840s as they looked back on the 1840–1842 war, where there had been no such sacrifices by men of this stature.

30. Contributors to the Chang Chi-liang funeral fund are listed in *CFTCC, Tung-ming, hou-chi*, 11:9. Interestingly, three of the six original contributors were ex-Spring Purificationists (Ch'en Ch'ing-yung, Su T'ing-k'uei, and T'ang P'eng); and two others (Wang Hsi-chen and Chu Ch'i) were Mei Tseng-liang's pupils. The installation of Chang's altar in the Ku Shrine occurred in

TK 24/3 (*KTM*, 3b), and seems to have been financed by a group of Chang's friends from among the cohort of special licentiates (*pa-kung*) who had competed in the 1832 metropolitan examinations, of whom Hsu Han is the best known. For the rebuilding of the Yang Chi-sheng villa (in 1847), see *TCT*, 2:687.

31. For Yao Ying's interest in (and obvious delight over) the Peking literati movement catalyzed by Chang's "suicide," see his 1844 letter to Chu Ch'i (*CFTCC, Tung-ming, hou-chi*, 8:5b–6a). Here he lists with appreciation the (mainly) young literati spirits whom he has just left behind in the capital: Mei Tseng-liang, Shao I-ch'en, T'ang P'eng, Ch'en Ch'ing-yung, Su T'ing-k'uei, Ho Shao-chi, Lu Hsien-chi, Wang Hsi-chen, Lung Ch'i-jui. By no coincidence, all the men on this list were to become Shrine Assocation participants. An 1847 letter from Yao to Chu Ch'i in the same collection also advertises Yao's sympathies for the Shrine Association activists—in this case, for Ch'en Ch'ing-yung, who had been dropped from the censorate for requesting a total pardon for Lin Tse-hsu (ibid., 8:17b–18b). Pupils of Mei Tseng-liang in the association included: Chu Ch'i, Shao I-ch'en, K'ung Hsien-i, Feng Chih-i, Wang Hsi-chen, Tseng Kuo-fan, Lung Ch'i-jui, Sun Ting-ch'en, Pien Yu-li, and Ho Ch'iu-t'ao—to name only the better known. See *KTM*, passim; Chu Ch'i, 4:1a, 6:7b; Wang Hsi-chen, 1881:5:2a, 1883:1:26b; Sun Ting-ch'en, *Ts'ang-lang shih-wen chi*, 3:10a, 12:14; and K'ung Hsien-i, *Han-chai, shih*, 2:12b, 4:4a.

32. The Hunanese contingent included Tseng Kuo-fan and Sun Ting-ch'en (see previous note). The Kwangsi group among Mei's pupils (most of whom were Shrine Association participants) were Wang Hsi-chen, Chu Ch'i, P'eng Yu-yao, Lung Ch'i-jui, and T'ang Ch'i-hua. (See Sun Ting-ch'en, 6:2a; and Wang Hsi-chen, [1881] 5:2a.) A point of interest concerning the special appeal of the T'ung-ch'eng school of *ku-wen* studies in Kwangsi involves its comparatively late diffusion into that part of the empire (during the mid-1830s). The key personality in launching the T'ung-ch'eng school in Kweilin was Lu Huang (1778–1838), a native of Kwangsi who had studied under Yao Nai and under Wu Te-hsuan (1767–1840) in Hangchow—another prominent contemporary exponent of *ku-wen* studies. In 1835 or thereabouts, Lu became head of the Hsiu-feng Academy in Kweilin. He there seems to have made an enormous impression on his pupils, the first and most illustrious of whom was Chu Ch'i. All were routinely sent by Lu to Peking with a letter of introduction to Mei Tseng-liang. See Chu Ch'i, *I-chih-t'ang*, 6:1a, 2b; *shih*, 2:13b; and Wang Hsi-chen, (1883) 4:10b.

33. For Ch'i's alliance with Huang Chueh-tzu during their joint term in Amoy in the latter half of 1840, see *IWSM-TK*, 12:11b–14a, and 17:34b–37a. Both joined Lin's side against Ch'i-shan in the debate over whether or not negotiations with the British should be undertaken. In addition, *LCCW, #1*, 1:19b–20a, records a later joint memorial from Huang and Ch'i on the architecture of fortifications, purporting to show how Chinese batteries could be made impermeable to British shells. Huang Chueh-tzu, *Wen-lu*, 6:9a, records that Ch'i had become his closest poetry companion in Peking on the eve of Ch'i's

appointment to the Council. For Ch'i as a recipient of advice from warmong-ering literati, see Wang Hsi-chen, 2:1a–11a (note that Wang was Ch'i's exam-ination pupil); Pao Shih-ch'en, 35:22a–24a; and Chang Mu, *Yin-chai wen-chi, nien-p'u,* 21b–22b.

34. Chang Mu accompanied Ch'i Chün-tsao to Kiangsu in 1838 as an examina-tion reader or as a literary secretary. (Chang Mu, *Yin-chai, nien-p'u,* 15a–17a; and *shih,* 1:3b.) For a well-documented instance of Ch'i's use of Chang as his examination grader, see Chang Mu, *nien-p'u,* 23. Back in Peking, in 1843, Ch'i underwrote the printing of a carefully annotated chronological biog-raphy of the early Ch'ing scholar Ku Yen-wu, which Chang had authored (ibid., 25a). Miao K'uei was another of Ch'i Chün-tsao's surrogate examina-tion readers during Ch'i's 1837–1839 term as Kiangsu educational commis-sioner. (See *TWC, wen-chi,* 4:26b, and *shih,* 1:3b.) Ch'i subsequently financed the publication of one of Miao's many studies of *Shuo-wen* (an etymological dictionary). See Miao K'uei, *Shuo-wen chien-shou tzu-tu,* Miao pref., 1b. Hsu Han was a *k'ao-cheng* scholar from Anhwei who was a favorite of T'ang Chin-chao. In 1832–1833, he served as examination reader under Ho Shao-chi's father (then educational commissioner in Chekiang), thus becoming close friends with Ho Shao-chi himself. (Chang Mu, 2:19b.) A fourth Han Learn-ing scholar whose following may have been drawn into the Shrine Associa-tion was Yü Cheng-hsieh (1775–1840), for whom Ch'i procured an academy teaching appointment in Kiangyin, Kiangsu, in 1839. (Chang Mu, 3:21; and *ECCP,* pp. 936–937.)

35. See Chuang Shou-ch'i, 1:2a, 7:3b–4a; and Chang Mu, *Yin-chai,* Ch'i Chün-tsao preface, p. 1.

36. See *TCT,* 2:687, for the 1847 reconstruction of the Sung-yun-an; and *KTM,* 3b, for the new altar for Chang Chi-liang.

37. *CCS,* 15b–16a. K'ung Hsien-i, *Han-chai,* 2:5b and 3:23a, records that K'ung placed in the 1837 Shun-t'ien provincial examination, and thus became a pupil of the examiner, Huang Chueh-tzu. K'ung (ibid., *shih,* 1:9a) also records that Yeh Ming-feng was a graduate of this same examination, thereby making him also a pupil of Huang.

38. For the date of the Shrine Association meetings, see *KTM,* passim. An explanatory note appended to a poem in the 1856 Spring Purification scroll observes specifically that the meeting was held that year after the first round of Peking examinations in order to encourage the attendance of provincial graduates visiting the capital for purpose of competing in these examina-tions. See *CCS,* 7a.

39. For the Wan-liu-t'ang (or Chiang-t'ing Pavilion, located in the same com-pound), see Liu Ssu-wan, 43:9; and *HPSW,* 21:12b.

40. See Wu Sung-liang, *Hsiang-su,* 8:6b; P'an Tseng-shou, *Kai-lan,* 4:12a; and Tak-ahashi Kazumi, *O Shishin,* introduction, p. 14.

41. For Ku's relationship with the Hsu family and with Hsu Ch'ien-hsueh in par-ticular, see Willard Peterson, "The Life of Ku Yen-wu (1613–1682), Part 2," pp. 224–226. Ku was the (maternal) uncle of Hsu Ch'ien-hsueh, who had helped clear him of the suspicion of having been a diehard Ming loyalist.

Yet, as Peterson also notes (pp. 225–226), Ku had considerable aversion for his nephew, and was anxious to keep his distance from him.

42. Lin Ch'ang-i, 8:23b–24a. For another reference to the lore concerning Ku's eremitic existence in the Tz'u-jen Temple, see Ch'en Ch'ing-yung, 10:3a. See also *CCS*, 14, for Chu Ch'i's admiring comment on Ku's refusal of the offer to participate in the 1679 examinations.

43. The Chang Mu view of Ku is set forth in his dedicational essay composed for the opening of the Ku shrine: see *Yin-chai, nien-p'u*, 27b–28a. That Chang was particularly interested in Ku Yen-wu's work as a methodological inspiration is suggested by an interesting letter he wrote to Ch'en Ch'ing-yung in 1843 or 1844, setting forth a "corrective" program for the dissolute Ch'en, to involve patient accumulation of information in one or several narrowly focused fields. (See *Yin-chai*, 3:4.)

44. For the issue of attitudes in Ku's political thought, see Philip A. Kuhn, "Local Self-Government under the Republic," esp. pp. 263–264. For Ku's critique of the education and examination systems, see his *Jih-chih lu*, 17:34b, and *Ku T'ing-lin shih-wen-chi*, 1:15a. For the issue of the exclusion of local elites from participation in local administration, see *Jih-chih lu*, 8:9a; and *Shih-wen-chi*, 1:14b (where Ku reflects on the military implications of this exclusion). In the *Shih-wen-chi*, Ku even went so far as to propose the appointment of local magistrates on a hereditary basis, so as to better incorporate their localistic sentiments into administration. Ku's best-known essay on the overpopulation of the lower-degree-holding class is found in his *Shih-wen-chi*, 1:15aff. Imitators of these essays among the members of the Shrine Association include: (1) Wang Po-hsin (1799–1873: see his *Shu-yen* of 1834 and its 1844 sequel); (2) T'ang P'eng (1801–1844: see his *Fu-ch'iu-tzu*, 1844); (3) Sun T'ing-ch'en (1819–1859: see his *Ch'u-yen* of 1860); and (4) Feng Kuei-fen (1809–1874: see his 1861 *Chiao-pin-lu k'ang-i*).

45. *CCS*, 2b. The same point is elaborated at much greater length by Chu in an undated essay entitled, "Distinguishing True Scholarship", in *I-chih-t'ang*, 1:2b–3a. "Unadorned studies" (*p'u-hsueh*) is the phrase commonly used in literati scholastic discourse during the 1840s to denote evidential research.

46. *HCSH*, #1, 12:6.

47. *TCT*, 3:917.

48. For Chu's indebtedness to Kuan's essay, see Chu Ch'i, *I-chih-t'ang*, 6:8b–9b. The original essay by Kuan T'ung from which Chu proceeds is in *Yin-chi-hsuan, ch'u-chi*, 4:1a–3b.

49. *I-chih-t'ang*, 2:1b–2a.

50. Ibid., 2:1b.

51. Ibid., 4:13a.

52. *TWC, tsou-kao*, 1:7a–13b.

7. The End of Manchu Diplomacy

1. *SL-HF,* 6:21a for Lin's recall; 7:8b for Yao's; 7:2b for Ch'en Ch'ing-yung; 6:3a for Su T'ing-k'uei; and 14:7b for Chu Ch'i. Ch'en Ch'ing-yung had been removed from the censorate in late 1845 for demanding punishment for Lin's original accusers (Ch'i-shan?) right after Lin's recall from Ili had been announced in the autumn of 1845. (Chang Mu, 3:9b; *SL-TK,* 423:5; and Ch'en Ch'ing yung, 9:5b.) Su seems to have retired (nominally in mourning) in mid-1844; and then to have decided to extend his leave until 1850 (see *KTM,* 3b–4a). Chu chose to retire early in 1847 out of frustration, apparently, with the political situation in the capital. See Mei Tseng-liang, 2:18a; and *KTM.*
2. *SL-HF,* 20:28b–31a.
3. Ko Shih-chün, 11:4b, contains an 1852 memorial by Lu Hsien-chi that lists all special edicts (inaugural or otherwise) calling for literati opinions on personnel and on policy; Lu traces the practice back to the early Ch'ing.
4. By way of contrast with the liberal wartime policy on militia in Kwangtung, one might note the more conservative line followed in the lower Yangtze front. See, for example, the imperial rescript urging Yü-ch'ien to be cautious in arming the Chusan Islanders in mid-1841 (*IWSM-TK,* 29:34a); and the comments by Chekiang Governor Liu Yun-k'o on the use of "braves" in that province in 1841 (*IWSM-TK,* 35:14b–15a).
5. The use of Mu-chang-a's fall as a cautionary tale to chasten would-be rationalizers of Ch'ing foreign policy seems to have been particularly frequent in the early 1860s, when Southern City groups were challenging Prince Kung's leadership. A specific analogy between Kung and Mu was made by the Peking official Chiang Ch'i-ling on one such occasion. (See Ko Shih-chün, 13:19b–20a.) Apropos of this, it ought perhaps to be noted that Ts'ai Shou-ch'i, Prince Kung's principal assailant in 1864, was a veteran member of the Ku Shrine Association. See *KTM,* meeting roster for Hsien-feng 7/3/3.
6. The authorizing provision was the 6th article of the Supplementary Treaty, signed at the Bogue, near the mouth of the Canton river, on 8 October 1843. See Fairbank, *Trade and Diplomacy,* p. 121.
7. The Canton entry controversy is surprisingly well covered in English. See Wakeman, *Strangers,* pp. 71–80, 91–105; John J. Nolde, "The 'False Edict' of 1849" and "Xenophobia in Canton," for the Chinese side; and Costin, pp. 120–141, and Graham, pp. 239–253, for the British side of the story. The above summary condenses these sources.
8. The crisscrossing trend lines of customs collection at Canton (dropping after 1844–1845) and Shanghai (nearly catching up to Canton by 1852, before the Taiping invasion of the Yangtze valley ruined trade) are shown in the table of customs collections from 1843 to 1855 in Fairbank, *Trade and Diplomacy,* p. 262. According to Lin Tse-hsu (*LWCKCS, i-chi,* 4:20b), Canton's receipts had averaged approximately 1.5 million taels per annum between 1821 and 1843. Shanghai had nearly caught up to that figure by 1852. Coincidentally, empire-wide customs would rise to approximately 22 million per annum by

the early 1890s, most of which was collected in the Yangtze valley. (See Albert Feuerwerker, "Economic Trends in the late Ch'ing Empire, 1870–1911," p. 63, Table 2.) Another feature of the Canton customs that tended to reduce its importance was the traditional attachment of most of its yield by the Imperial Household as a source of revenue. This further limited the disposability of its proceeds.

9. For the late transfer of Ch'i-ying to Canton (to succeed I-li-pu), see above, chapter 6, note 9. It should here be further added that Ch'i-ying, the *primo* in the new Ch'ing diplomatic corps, did not expect to stay in Kwangtung after the completion of the negotiations on a supplementary treaty with Pottinger. His plans were, instead, to return to Nanking (*SL-TK*, 390:13b–14a). He did not vacate his post as Nanking governor general until March 1844 (*SL-TK*, 402:2). Even after his appointment as Liang-Kuang governor general, moreover, his successor, the Foochow Tartar general, Pi-ch'ang, was given only an "acting" designation, indicating that the emperor still wanted to have Ch'i-ying back in Nanking as soon as possible (*SL-TK*, 402:2, 412:14). It is thus clear that the emperor and his close advisers regarded Nanking and the Yangtze as a more important locus for managing foreign relations and defense. Some inkling of why is revealed in an 1847 exchange between the emperor and Pi-ch'ang (*SL-TK*, 438:18a, 442:22), which reveals that the military planners in Peking had been developing a secret plan for making the Yangtze impassable to British ships, and had wished to avoid having the details leaked to the Chinese mandarins in the area. The difficulties that Ch'i-ying encountered in getting sympathetic souls appointed to the higher levels of the regional bureaucracy in Kwangtung are illustrated by the career of Huang En-t'ung. Huang, as mentioned above, was one of Ch'i-ying's star assistants in the Nanking negotiations, and had been sent down to Kwangtung with I-li-pu in October 1842, as a general staff assistant for advising in the impending supplementary treaty negotiations. But Ch'i-ying was not able to get Huang assigned to a local bureaucratic office commensurate with the rank he had held in Kiangsu (i.e., as provincial judicial commissioner) until early in the summer of 1843 (*SL-TK*, 391:3a). Though Huang was soon thereafter to be promoted to governor, as a replacement for the strongly pro-militia, pro-war governor, Ch'eng Yü-ts'ai (*SL-TK*, 413:5a), he did not last two years in that latter post before being abruptly removed by Peking on grounds that look very much like a pretext (*SL-TK*, 437:1; edict of TK 26/12/2). On the same day that Huang lost his job as governor, moreover, a new under-governor was appointed to the province as well, with the latter job now going to a Huang Chueh-tzu examination pupil, Yeh Ming-ch'en.

10. For Ch'eng's appointment and transfer, see *SL-TK*, 387:19b, 413:5a. At the high point of the movement to oust Ch'i-shan during the winter of 1840–1841, Ch'eng had backed the arguments of those who had been urging the throne that paramilitaries and locally recruited irregulars could be used to resume the war (*YPCC*, 4:552). In September 1842, he had sent in a long memorial in support of the idea of protracting the war, which Tao-kuang had ridiculed (*IWSM-TK*, 60:10ff).

11. Hsu Kuang-chin (d. 1858) served as governor from early 1847 to the end of that year, after which he was promoted to succeed Ch'i-ying as governor general. Hsu's father, Hsu Han, was an 1811 *chin-shih* and his elder brother, Hsu Kuang-fu, was an 1829 Han-lin. Hsu himself was an 1820 Han-lin (see *Lu-i hsien-chih* [Honan], 14:14, 15a). For Hsu's complicity with his second-in-command, Yeh Ming-ch'en, to oust Ch'i-ying, see below, and J. Y. Wong, *Yeh Ming-ch'en: Viceroy of Liang-Kuang*, pp. 37, 209 (notes 1, 5). For Yeh's background, see Wong, pp. 1–21. Yeh was descended from a multi-generation Han-lin family, and was himself a Han-lin of the class of 1835—the same Han-lin class from which many of the members of the Ku Shrine Association had been recruited. His father, Chih-shen, had been a colleague of Ch'i Chün-tsao, and, through this connection, Yeh seems to have developed a cordial relationship with that latter leader of the anti-Mu-chang-a coalition in the capital (Wong, p. 8). His brother, Ming-feng, was an examination pupil of Huang Chueh-tzu and was active alike in the Spring Purification and Shrine Association groups. He was leapfrogged into the office of financial commissioner, or under-governor, on TK 26/9/25 (*SL-TK*, 434:22a). However, three days later, the appointment was retracted, and Yeh reassigned to a Peking post. He did not actually take up his position in Kwangtung until several months later (*SL-TK*, 434:26a). The curious withdrawal of the initial appointment probably reflects the discomfiture of Mu-chang-a and Ch'i-ying over the nomination of someone so likely to be sympathetic to the point of view of the opposition. By the same token, however, the emperor's ultimate decision to go ahead with it shows just how limited Ch'i-ying's control actually was.

12. Wakeman, *Strangers*, pp. 97–101, points out the connection between declining trade and rising militancy among the commercial classes in Canton. Fairbank, *Trade and Diplomacy*, pp. 292–293, raises the interesting point that the imperial bureaucracy had secretly enforced a tea-export embargo at the new Fukienese treaty port of Foochow (and would continue to do so until 1854 or 1855), in order to prevent the rerouting of the tea-export traffic. Presumably, the action was undertaken to help limit the effects of trade-route changes on Canton's economy. At the very least, it can be shown that the authorities were exceedingly worried about the dangers (in terms of unemployment and crime) that might result if the inland populations who made their living from the traditional overland shipping of Fukienese teas to Canton were suddenly deprived of a livelihood. (See Wu Wen-jung, *Wu Wen-chih kung i-chi*, 9:1a–4b.) For evidence of Cantonese merchant-class hatred of I-shan for the burdens of the 1841 ransom payments, see *YPCC*, 3:37.

13. See Nolde, "Xenophobia," p. 6, for the placard campaign in Canton in October-November 1842, protesting the terms of the Treaty of Nanking.

14. For the effects of the London financial panic, see Wakeman, *Strangers*, pp. 100–101. The fears of British penetration upriver of Canton after the d'Aguilar raid are revealed in docs. 382, 391, 392, and 395 (urban placards from Canton) collected in Sasaki Masaya, *Ahen*. For the details and documents relating to the real-estate panic, see Wakeman, *Strangers*, pp. 85, 186

(citing Public Records Office [London], F.O. 228/73). The placards record-ing the call for an urban militia are in Sasaki, *Ahen*, items 366–370. Note that permission to constitute the militia was granted (on 20 May, or 4/7) only well after recruitment had begun.

15. For the Manchu military bias against militia, see above, note 4.

16. For I-shan's late conversion to a position of support for the militia, see, for example, *YPCC*, 4:262.

17. A glimpse of Huang En-t'ung's virulently anti-militia views is to be had from several of the papers collected in his *Fu-yuan chi-lueh* (1846): see *YPCC*, 5:410, 419, and esp. 442. The last document is a letter written in 1843 to a friend, Chiang Hung-sheng, who at the time held the office of censor in Peking. The letter is obviously intended to encourage Chiang to complain, through the censorate, to the emperor about the underhanded actions of the Cantonese militia chiefs.

18. *SL-TK*, 379:24b–25a.

19. *SL-TK*, 384:23.

20. After 1842, the names Hsu Hsiang-kuang, Ch'en Ch'i-k'un, Fan Feng, and Tseng Chao turn up with the greatest frequency as go-betweens mediating between the militia leaders and the provincial government in Canton. See *IWSM-TK*, 78:15a; 79:1a; *YPCC*, 6:95, 390; and *PYHC*, 26:15b–16a. The last mention of Huang P'ei-fang that I have been able to unearth has him partic-ipating in the October-November 1842 debates over how and how exten-sively to undertake the rebuilding of the Bogue forts.

21. *YPCC*, 6:46.

22. The role of demobilized patrol-force braves in fomenting the wave of unrest in the shoal-fields is evident from *HHHC*, 22:52b–53a, which describes a complex protection-racket system that grew up between 1844 and 1847 in the northern and northeastern corner of Hsiang-shan county, where cultiva-tion of reclaimed fields was a central part of the economy. In 1847, a certain Chang Tou—clearly an ex-brave—established an illegal "colony-field bat-talion" (*t'un-ying*) headquarters there, to supervise his "10,000-odd" man force of armed followers. The name itself is obviously lifted from the styling of the organizations that had been set up by the Canton militia authorities in 1841. For more reports on this underworld takeover in the shoal-fields, see *TKHC*, 17:15b, which describes the challenge to the scholar-gentry order that developed in the Wan-ch'ing-sha area of the Tung-kuan county, nomi-nally controlled by the Hsi-pei yü she-hsueh. See also Public Records Office (London), "Canton Archive," (F.O. 682), 138/3/21; and *SCTI*, 2:676–681. Similar examples of what looks like a lower-class backlash against the author-ities and against the local elite, prompted by Ch'ing military reverses, are also noted for Chekiang. *YPCC*, 4:433–4, records a rent-refusal movement among cotton-growing tenants in Yü-yao county, during the fall of 1841; and *HPSW* (26:6b) documents a protection racket organized among the same stratum near the fortified town of Cha-p'u in order to extract money and rice from landlords.

23. Ch'eng Yü-ts'ai's report that arrived in Peking on TK 24/3/2, records the

creation of a new, "three-p'ing" militia authority, including the Tung- (east), Nan- (south), and Lung-p'ing leagues, all of which had been modeled after the Sheng-p'ing confederation of San-yuan-li fame (*YPCC*, 4:199–200). However, a close look at Ch'eng's memorial reveals that these new authorities were centered in the Hsin-tsao and Yen-t'ang-hsu townships of P'an-yü county, the traditional administrative centers for the reclamation-intense Sha-wan and Chiao-t'ang subsections of the county (*YPCC*, p. 200). For the history of the Sha-Chiao area (including Hsin-tsao, Nan-ts'un, and Chung-ts'un) as a hotbed of racketeering activity since the 1770s, see Wu Hsiung-kuang, 1:25b; and *SL-CL*, 1109:3a–5a, 1130:3b–6a. For details on the Sha-Chiao militia league in the late 1840s and 1850s, see Public Records Office (London), F.O. 682, items 1971/3, 13, 14; and 279A/6/43. For the activities of this same Sha-Chiao "18-parish" (or "48-parish") militia in the 1847 crisis, see Sasaki, *Ahen*, items 361, 366, and 382. For the later, post-1844 licensing of additional new militia leagues, see *TKHC*, 17:15b (for Tung-kuan county); *Yueh-tung sheng-li hsin-tsuan*, 5:38a (for the Jung-Kuei organization along the Shun-te/Hsiang-shan border); and Sasaki, *Ahen*, item 391 (for the Lung-shan township militia in Shun-te, established in 1847).

24. Part of the problem appears to have been that one of the initial sites chosen by Ch'i-ying for possible rental or sale to the British (a plot of land on Honam Island) lay squarely within the perimeter of the Shuang-chou Academy, a militia and landholding organization that was a member of the Sha-Chiao League. (See Sasaki, *Ahen*, items 361, 366, 368, 370; and Liang T'ing-nan's account in *YPCC*, 6:88–91. According to the latter source, it was the immediate threat to clan corporate holdings and ancestral graveyards that aroused the wrath of the Honam property owners in the first instance.) The Shuang-chou Academy directors met with representatives of the larger Sha-Chiao League on 14 May, 20 May, and 21 May to protest this. Then on 25 May, they met with Governor Hsu Kuang-chin (see item 372), who was reported to have told them he shared their feelings about Ch'i-ying. This in turn seems to have encouraged them to undertake to spread word that the British and Ch'i-ying intended to confiscate much larger tracts in the western suburbs (see items 377, 382, and 386). For the 2 July demonstration, see item 378.

25. For Ch'i-ying's petition to allow scholar participation in diplomatic deliberations, see *SL-TK*, 442:25b–26a. For Ch'i-ying's report on the formation of the commission (received in Peking on 9 September 1847), see *IWSM-TK*, 78:14a–15b. The change in Peking's tone on how foreign affairs should be conducted at Canton is first signaled by an edict of 9 September (in *SL-TK*, 445:2b–3a) that for the first time introduces the requirement that the authorities bolster the people's feelings of solidarity with their officials.

26. For the secret edict of 6 December 1847 (TK 27/10/29), see the list of summaries of secret edicts and memorials concerning the Canton question copied into the *Shang-yü-tang* for TK 30/5, pp. 131–134. The background of this record will be discussed below. No record of the edict survives in *SL-TK* or in *IWSM-TK*. For Ch'i-ying's recall, see *SL-TK*, 450:45b. Wake-

man, *Strangers*, pp. 86–88, argues that the recall of Ch'i-ying resulted from his excessive enthusiasm for conciliating the British in connection with the Huang-chu-ch'i murders case of 6 December 1847 (in which six British hunters lost their lives in the Canton countryside). However, word of Ch'i-ying's handling of that incident did not reach Peking until 28 December, several weeks after Tao-kuang had already begun to treat Hsu Kuang-chin as the de facto plenipotentiary for foreign affairs at Canton. The shift to a commission format earlier that fall thus seems better to explain the reasoning behind Ch'i-ying's removal.

27. On this, see Wakeman, *Strangers*, p. 102, citing *IWSM-TK*, 79:39b–40b, and Nolde, "False Edict," p. 310.
28. *YPCC*, 6:92–100; Wakeman, *Strangers*, pp. 91–96; Nolde, "Xenophobia," pp. 17–20.
29. Most but not all of Hsu's intelligence reports found their way to Peking: see *IWSM-TK*, 79:15a–16b, 17b–19a, 23a–24a, and esp. 31a–32b.
30. See Wakeman, *Strangers*, p. 103, footnote, citing Public Records Office, F.O. 17/188 (Bowring-Granville, Despatch 1, 19 April 1852) for the alleged role of the Americans. For the policy background to the constraints on Bonham, see Wakeman, p. 91, and Costin, p. 138.
31. For the forged edict—which anticipated by several weeks an affirmative response from Peking to the request that it support a refusal of the British entry demand—see Nolde, "False Edict."
32. *IWSM-TK*, 80:9a.
33. Ibid., 6b–7a.
34. Costin, pp. 141–143; Fairbank, *Trade and Diplomacy*, pp. 375–378.
35. The party responsible for provoking Hsien-feng's anxieties about British intentions was apparently the Nanking viceroy, Lu Chien-ying, who had been transferred to the Yangtze post in recognition of his exertions in improving the defenses at Tientsin during the war. Lu forwarded the Bonham Letter to Peking overland (it arrived in Peking on 4/7) together with a covering memorandum that explained that he had wished to avoid giving Bonham a pretext for proceeding to Tientsin. (*IWSM-HF*, 1:9b–10b; see also 10b–13b for the letter.) A later memorial of Lu's indicates he had serious doubts about the strength of Ch'ing defenses near the capital. (*IWSM-HF*, 3:5ff.) This, presumably, was one of the reasons for his desire to keep Bonham happy. Hsien-feng's initial caution is indicated by the fact that an edict responding to the Lu-transmitted letter was not issued until the day after it had arrived. Moreover, on 4/18, when a first response was finally decided upon, the emperor instructed his "foreign secretaries," Mu-chang-a and Ch'i-ying (to whom the letter had been addressed), to prepare a reply that would take due notice of the missive's arrival (rather than refusing it outright), and merely urging the British to take up their complaints with the authorities in Shanghai. (For the text of Mu's reply, see *Shang-yü-tang*, TK 30/4, pp. 265–268.) Finally, on 3 June, after word came from Ta-ku of the *Reynard*'s arrival, Hsien-feng sent elaborate instructions to the Chihli governor general, Norjinga, to insure that there would be no hasty rejection of the peti-

tioners and that Ch'ing soldiers did not open fire first (*HFSL*, 8:18a–19a).
36. The order for a general review of Canton policy and of Ch'i-ying's role in it is noted in *Shang-yü-tang*, TK 30/5, pp. 131–134 (roughly 9th or 10th day), together with the summaries of the relevant memorials and edicts. The cautious line taken by Mu-chang-a and his arrangement of an interview for Ch'i-ying are noted in *SL-HF*, 20:29a (edict of 10/19), when Hsien-feng complained specifically about the actions of these two men during the June crisis.
37. *SL-HF*, 8:18a–19a.
38. *SL-HF*, 9:9b–10a, 13a–15a.
39. The refusal of Hsien-feng to open up foreign-policy deliberations to the censorate and the literati in general during the course of the Bonham Letter crisis was later noted with vexation by the censor Yuan Chia-san in a memorial of 5 August. (See *Hsiang-ch'eng Yuan-shih chia-chi, Tuan-min kung chi, tsou-i,* 1:1b.)
40. Jen Yü-wen, *T'ai-ping t'ien-kuo ch'üan-shih*, 1:187, cites an essay by the mid-century scholar Yen Cheng-chi, which provides much important background on the administrative status of Kwangsi. According to Yen, maintenance of the province's quota of Green Standard troops alone cost 420,000 taels per annum, while the provincial tax quota totaled only 400,000. In addition, some 100,000 was nominally available from inland customs receipts. But this had to be used to pay the salary supplements (*yang-lien*) for civil and military officials of higher rank. Yearly transfers from other provinces had therefore been a necessity, particularly in the postwar years when revenue collection rates dropped to only 50% or 60% of quota. Wong, p. 126 (Table 14), shows that Kwangtung had to bear a large share of the burden of making up for Kwangsi's revenue insufficiencies. Yen Cheng-chi also claims that the provincial governor, Cheng Tsu-ch'en, had "been afraid to ask" for such subsidies because of his awareness that the burdens on other provinces were excessive during these years.
41. For the worsening social conditions in Kwangsi on the eve of the Taiping Rebellion, see Philip A. Kuhn, "The Taiping Rebellion," esp. pp. 264–266; and Jen Yü-wen, 1:175–188. An intriguing glimpse of the itinerant existence of peasant immigrants in Kwangsi in the 19th century is to be found in Ella S. Laffey, "The Making of a Rebel: Liu Yung-fu and the Formation of the Black Flag Army," pp. 87–90.
42. *SL-TK*, 383:17, summarizes a late-1842 report from a Kiangsi-born censor, Huang Tsan-t'ung, complaining of massive unemployment among the Kwangtung and Kiangsi porters who depended traditionally on the trans-Meiling tea freightage for their living; this group must have included the Kwangsi people, too. The problems causing and caused by the inland shift of the dislodged coastal-pirate and smuggler population are discussed in Jen Yu-wen, 1:179–183. For a fuller study, see Laai I-fa, "The Part Played by the Pirates of Kwangtung and Kwangsi Provinces in the T'ai-p'ing Insurrection."
43. The problems caused by the 1847 and 1849–1850 famines in Hunan and Kwangsi and their connection with the Li Yuan-fa rebellion in Hsin-ning are discussed in Kuhn, *Rebellion and its Enemies*, pp. 107–109, and Kuhn

and Jones, p. 185. For more background on this revolt, see *Ch'ing-tai tang-an shih-liao ts'ung-pien*, 2:1–163. See also Ch'iao Sheng-hsi, p. 15, for the effect of flooding in the rice-producing center of Hupeh during these same years. For the 1849–1850 famine in Kwangsi, see Jen Yu-wen, 1:179. Jen, 1:177, cites a mid-1850 memorial by Yuan Chia-san estimating that 70% of the province's population was under bandit control.

44. The Kwangsi scholars' complaints against Cheng's inaction are summarized in Lung Ch'i-jui, *Ching-te-t'ang chi*, 6:4b–5b.

45. For the indemnity payments, see *YPCC*, 5:316. The estimate of the total Ch'ing wartime outlay is taken from *SL-TK*, 391:5b. For the estimate of the cost of repairs for the damage to the Yellow River dikes during 1842 (over 5 million taels, or 25% of the yearly total for expenditures), see *SL-TK*, 382: 22b–23a, and 384:16b–18a. The delays Peking encountered in trying to raise and secure delivery of funding to meet these costs are noted in *SL-TK*, 407:14a, 409:8a–9a, and 455:6a.

46. For the near decision to reduce stipend payments, see *SL-TK*, 390:33b–34a, 391:16, 26b–27a. A document compiled by a Board of Revenue official in 1848 shows 1843 to have been a year of record low payments to Peking of revenue surpluses from the provinces: Only 360,000 taels (less than 7% of the corresponding figure for 1838) were received that year. (See *Chung-kuo chin-tai huo-pi*, 1:172.) For the cavalry and support force at Tientsin, see *SL-TK*, 383:8, and 392:15a. New cannon casting at the Woosung forts (guarding the entrance to the Yangtze) was undertaken by Ch'i-ying in the winter of 1842–1843 in an attempt to produce a 10-thousand catty piece (*SL-TK*, 386: 15a–16a). Ch'i-ying's temporary role as coordinator of fleet construction efforts in the Yangtze is noted in John L. Rawlinson, *China's Struggle for Naval Development, 1839–1895*, p. 27.

47. Several examples of committee-led attempts to tighten the center's control over provincial revenue deposit accounting appear even before the fiscal crisis of 1848. See, for example, *SL-TK*, 400:20b–21b, 401:21b–22b, 405:12b–13b, 436:19b–23b, 443:15b–16b, 446:25b–27a, 450:24b–25b. Ch'i-ying's role as a mastermind of revenue-improvement planning appears to begin at least as early as 1846, when he submitted (from Canton) a comprehensive scheme for reducing the cost and sizes of existing army units to create a surplus for their retraining. (*SL-TK*, 400:18a019a, 433:9a–11b.) The 1848 dunning commission, which also had authority to propose new revenue measures, made its first report on TK 28/11/15 (*SL-TK*, 461:9b–13a). Its members included the grand councillors (under Mu-chang-a) and Prince Ting, as well as Ch'i-ying. However, Ch'i-ying's special influence is suggested by his occasional separate memorials, sent directly to the emperor. (See, for example, his important revision of the 1848 plan proposed on TK 28/12/27, submitted from an inspection tour in Shantung, which is preserved in the Peking Gazette collection of the British Museum under TK 29/2.) An interesting follow-up on the work of this commission is Ch'i-ying's memorial of TK 30/3/10 (see *Wai-chi-tang* entry for that date), which urges the new Hsien-feng emperor to re-open the question of declining remittances to Peking.

48. Lung was an (entering) Han-lin of 1841, who had scored a first on the metropolitan examination of that year. Tu would thus have been his "mentor," since he was one of the examiners.
49. Lung Ch'i-jui, 3:21b–2a.
50. Ibid., 6:5.
51. Two petitions were handed in to the censorate concerning the Kwangsi situation during the early half of 1850, one by the (Hunanese) censor, Huang Chao-lin (on TK 30/5/5: see *SL-HF,* 9:18a–19a), the other by a Kwangsi junior officeholder in the capital named Li Ch'un (on TK 30/5/19: see *SL-HF,* 10:4a–5a). See also 15:3a–4a for Governor Cheng's reply. A third was handed in on 8/29 (see *SL-HF,* 16:15). On TK 30/12/1, and again on HF 1/2/8, two more petitions of this sort were tendered, both of them through the agency of Grand Secretary Tu (see *SL-HF,* 23:1a–3a, and 27:13a–14a). Wang Hsi-chen (1883), 2:6, reports in some detail the consultations of this Kwangsi scholar-leader with high officials in the capital during the winter of 1850–1851 and, in particular, with Tu Shou-t'ien; Wang mentions, also, that Tu agreed to place before the emperor a plan for dealing with the situation in Kwangsi that Wang had drawn up.
52. Sun Ting-ch'en, 6:2b. The poem must have been written before TK 30/5/16, for on that day Lung was ordered to return to the capital.
53. The list of recommendations (together with the names of their sponsors and brief descriptions of character, previous service, and the like) was copied into the *Shang-yü-tang,* TK 30/4, pp. 401–421.
54. The recommendation entries are undated, though in chronological sequence. *SL-HF,* 6:16b, specifically notes, however, that P'an's recommendation of Yao Ying was received on 3/27 (8 May). The one for Lin would have been simultaneous. *SL-HF,* 6:21b, gives the edict for Lin's recall; note that Tu's name is specifically mentioned as the last of Lin's sponsors. The *Shang-yü-tang* (for TK 30/4, p. 417) cites the specifics of Tu's recommendation of Lin and Yao. Both are praised for their success at controlling rebels and bandits, while no mention at all is made of their stance on foreign policy.
55. *SL-HF,* 20:29b–30a, for the 1 December accusation; and 9:9b–10a, for the 12 June second recall.
56. For this, see *SL-HF,* 20:29b–30a.
57. See *Shang-yü-tang* volume for TK 30/10, pp. 11–31. Some of the rhetoric intended against Ch'i-ying may reappear in a later edict (of HF 1/2/28) indicting British missionary activities in Canton as a cause of increasing secret-society and religious-sect activity in China—but in this latter, no specific mention is made of the Taipings (see *SL-HF,* 28:15b–16a).
58. *SL-HF,* 20:29a–30a.
59. Ibid., 20:30.

8. Epilogue

1. See, for example, John K. Fairbank, et al., ed., *The I.G. in Peking: Letters of Robert Hart*, letters 994, 1024; and Liu Kwang-ching, et al., "The Military Challenge: The Northwest and the Coast," p. 209, citing a letter of Charles Gordon.

2. For insightful comments on the pattern of domestic institutional reforms (especially in the military and financial areas), see Liu Kwang-ching, "The Military Challenge," and Rawlinson, pp. 64ff. Liu, p. 206, and Rawlinson, pp. 72–73, document interesting instances (occurring in 1867 and 1878) of maneuvering by central-government financial officials to divert pre-committed revenues away from military modernizers in the name of waterway conservation and famine relief needs.

3. Liu Kwang-ching, "The Military Challenge," pp. 204–206, shows that there was a short-lived effort to train a Manchu-manned Peking Field Force in the use of Western weapons carried out between 1862 and 1870, but thereafter abandoned. The commander, Prince Ch'ün (1840–1891), went on to become the leader par excellence of Manchu resistance to domestic reform.

4. I here follow the excellent account of the politics of the 1861 coup provided in Jason H. Parker, "The Rise and Decline of I-hsin, Prince Kung, 1858–1865," esp. pp. 132ff. Parker (pp. 197ff.) convincingly demonstrates that the Empress Dowager encouraged censorial criticism of Prince Kung in 1865 as a means of signaling to the bureaucracy the limits she intended to place on his power. Another critic who spoke out against Kung in 1863 specifically compared him to Mu-chang-a (Parker, chapter 7, note 5).

5. *ECCP*, pp. 125, 862. For Wo-jen's role in the 1850 campaign to oust Ch'i-ying from office, see Polachek, "Literati Groups," pp. 507–509.

6. The most famous instance of this occurred in 1867, when Kung threw the support of the Tsung-li Yamen behind a plan to grant high examination degrees to graduates of a newly established school of Western languages and sciences. In this case, the accuser was Wo-jen, whose two protest memorials were allowed to circulate in Peking, where they roused a storm of resistance. For an account of this incident, see Liu Kwang-ching, "Politics, Intellectual Outlook, and Reform: The T'ung-wen Kuan Controversy of 1867," esp. p. 94. Prince Kung's response was to publish a huge volume of essays on Neo-Confucian rectitude in statecraft, the *Lo-tao-t'ang wen-ch'ao*, which is analyzed in Parker, pp. 250–318.

7. For this observation, see Lloyd Eastman, *Throne and Mandarins: China's Search for a Policy During the Sino-French Controversy, 1880–1885*, pp. 212–213. The effect of Tz'u-hsi's endorsement of *ch'ing-i* (read Southern City views on foreign policy and domestic reform) may well have been more subtle than Eastman here suggests. Its most important accomplishment seems to have been to lure leading military reformers to compete for influence in Peking by making their own policies look more consistent with literati opinion than those of their rivals. This certainly was the effect on Tso Tsung-t'ang, the Hunan army chief who cultivated support in the capital by stress-

ing the need for restoring the dynasty's "ancestral" control over Ch'ing territory in Central Asia—a move that removed large sums from Li Hung-chang's coastal defense war chest. (See Immanuel C. Y. Hsu, "The Great Policy Debate in China, 1874: Maritime Defense vs. Frontier Defense.") A variation on the same theme was the alignment of the Liang-Kuang governor general, Chang Chih-tung, behind an 1889 plan for an inland railroad linking Peking to Hankow. The trunkline scheme was backed in Peking by conservatives anxious to keep Li Hung-chang from achieving total control over the capital's transportation links to the south through his own Peking-Tientsin railway plan. See Daniel H. Bays, *China Enters the Twentieth Century: Chang Chih-tung and the Issues of a New Age, 1895–1909*, pp. 8, 224 (note 4).

8. I refer here both to the disproportionately large Manchu component within the Peking palace bureaucracy, and to the frequently criticized overcentralization of the Ch'ing system—its tendency, that is, to deny ground-level administration the continuity or independence of action needed for effective local control (a point emphasized in Hsiao Kung-chuan's classic on Ch'ing local government, and, more recently, in F. W. Mote's anatomy of China's pre-modern political system: see Hsiao, *Rural China: Imperial Control in the Nineteenth Century*; and Mote, "Political Structure." M. Zelin's study of fiscal administration in early-eighteenth-century China rejects the notion that the over-centralizing impulse was a perennial factor in Ch'ing government, and suggests instead that it began to debilitate local government finances only in the latter part of the 18th century and thereafter. (See Madeline Zelin, *The Magistrate's Tael: Rationalizing Fiscal Reform in Eighteenth-century Ch'ing China*.) Be that as it may, Hsiao's critique seems highly relevant for the period with which we are concerned in this volume, and helps to explain why tensions between centrist and regionalist viewpoints (the latter usually enjoying strong extra-bureaucratic support) manifest themselves so insistently in the high policy deliberations of our period.

BIBLIOGRAPHY

Atwell, William S. "From Education To Politics: The Fu She." In Wm. Theodore de Bary, *The Unfolding of Neo-Confucianism*, pp. 333–365.

Banno, Masataka. *China and the West, 1858–1861: The Origins of the Tsungli Yamen*. Cambridge: Harvard University Press, 1964.

Barnett, Suzanne W. "Wei Yuan and the Westerners: Notes on the Sources of the *Hai-kuo t'u-chih*." *Ch'ing-shih wen-t'i* 2.4:10–14 (1970).

Bays, Daniel H. *China Enters the Twentieth Century: Chang Chih-tung and the Issues of a New Age, 1895–1909*. Ann Arbor: University of Michigan, 1978.

Beeching, Jack. *The Chinese Opium Wars*. New York: Harcourt, Brace, Jovanovich, 1975.

Bernard, W.D. *Narrative of the Voyages and Services of the 'Nemesis' from 1840 to 1843, and of the Combined Naval and Military Operations in China*. 2 vols. London, 1844.

CCS: K'ung Hsien-i 孔憲彝 and Yeh Ming-feng 葉名灃, comps. *Tz'u-jen-ssu chan-ch'i shih* 慈仁寺展禊詩 (Spring Purification ceremony poems written at the Tz'u-jen Temple in 1856). 1 chüan. 1861.

CFSLI: Lin Tse-hsu 林則徐. *Chi-fu shui-li i* 畿輔水利議 (A plan for water conservancy in Chihli). 1 ts'e. Foochow, 1876.

CFTCC: Yao Ying 姚瑩. *Chung-fu-t'ang ch'üan-chi* 中復堂全集 (Complete works of Yao Ying). Includes *Tung-ming wen-chi* 東溟文集, and supplements; and separately paginated *Nien-p'u* 年譜 (Chronological biography) by Yao Chün-ch'ang 姚濬昌. 98 chüan. 1867. Reprint Taipei: Wen-hai, 1974.

Chang Chi-liang 張際亮. *Chang Heng-fu ch'üan-chi* 張亨甫全集 (Complete works of Chang Chi-liang). 27 chüan. Foochow, 1867.

Chang Chung-li. *The Chinese Gentry: Studies on Their Role in Nineteenth-Century Chinese Society*. Seattle: University of Washington Press, 1955.

Chang Hao. *Liang Ch'i-ch'ao and Intellectual Transition in China, 1890–1907*. Cambridge: Harvard University Press, 1971.

Chang Hsiang-ho 張祥河. *Hsiao-chung shan-fang ch'u-kao* 小重山房初稿 (Collected belletristic works of Chang Hsiang-ho). 5 ts'e. 1826.

————. "Kuan-lung yü-chung ou-i pien" 関隴與中偶憶編 (Memoirs of Chang Hsiang-ho). 1 chüan. In Wang Wen-ju, comp., *Shuo-k'u* 說庫 (Anecdotes). Shanghai, 1915.

Chang Hsin-pao. *Commissioner Lin and the Opium War*. Cambridge: Harvard University Press, 1964.

Chang Mu 張穆. *Yin-chai wen-chi* 殷齋文集 (Collected poetry and prose of Chang Mu). 4 chüan. 1858.

Chao I 趙翼. *Ou-pei shih-hua* 甌北詩話 (Discussions on poetry by Chao I). 12 chüan. Peking: Jen-min wen-hsueh, 1963.

Chao-lien 昭槤. *Hsiao-t'ing tsa-lu* 嘯亭雜錄 (Miscellaneous notes on Ch'ing history). 8 chüan; Supplement, 2 chüan. Taipei: Wen-hai, 1968.

Chen, Gideon. *Lin Tse-hsu: Pioneer Promoter of the Adoption of Western Means of Maritime Defense in China*. Peking: Yenching University, 1934.

Ch'en Ch'ing-yung 陳慶鏞. *Chou-ching-t'ang lei-kao* 籀經堂類稿. 24 chüan. 1883.

Ch'en, Jerome. "The Hsien-feng Inflation," *Bulletin of the School of Oriental and African Studies* 21 : 578–586 (1958).

Ch'en Wei-sung 陳維崧. *Ch'ieh-yen-chi shih-jen hsiao-chuan* 篋衍集詩人小傳 (Short biographies of poets whose works are found in my old papers).

Ch'en Wen-shu 陳文述. *I-tao-t'ang ch'üan-chi* 頤道堂全集 (Complete works of Ch'en Wen-shu). 78 chüan. 1828 (?)

Ch'en Yung-kuang 陳用光. "T'ai-i-chou shih-tz'u ch'ao" 太乙舟詩詞鈔 (Poems of Ch'en Yung-kuang), *Ch'ing-ho* (Shanghai) 3 : 1–24 (16 November, 1934—1 November, 1935), with interruptions.

————. *T'ai-i-chou wen-chi* 太乙舟文集 (Collected prose of Ch'en Yung-kuang). 8 chüan. 1843.

Chiang Yu-hsien 蔣攸銛. *Sheng-i-chai nien-p'u* 繩枻齋年譜 (Chronological biography of Chiang Yu-hsien). 2 chüan. Reprint, Taipei: Wen-hai, 1968.

Ch'iao Sheng-hsi 乔盛西. "Hu-pei-sheng li-shih-shang ti shui-han wen-t'i chi ch'i yü t'ai-yang huo-tung to-nien pien-hua ti kuan-hsi" 湖北省歷史上 的水旱問題及其與太陽活動多年變化的関係 (The historical problem of floods and droughts in Hupei province and their long-term relationship with solar activity), *Ti-li hsueh-pao* (Peking) 29.1 : 14–23 (1963).

Ch'ien I-chi 錢儀吉. *K'an-shih-chai chi-shih kao* 衎石齋記事稿 (Collected occasional papers of Ch'ien I-chi). 10 chüan, 1934; Supplement, 10 chüan. 1881.

Ch'in Ying 秦瀛. *Hsiao-hsien shan-jen wen-chi* 小峴山人文集 (Collected works of Ch'in Ying). 34 chüan. 1817.

Ch'ing-pi shu-wen 清祕述聞 (Civil-service-examination registers under the Ch'ing). 33 chüan. Reprint, Taipei: Wen-hai, 1968.

Ch'ing-shih 清史 (History of the Ch'ing dynasty). 8 vols. Taipei: Kuo-fang yen-chiu-yuan, 1961–1962.

Ch'ing-shih lieh-chuan 清史列傳. (Biographies from the history of the Ch'ing). 80 chüan. Taipei: Chung-hua, 1962.

Ch'ing-tai ho-ch'en chuan 清代河臣傳 (Biographies of river officials of the Ch'ing). Comp. Wang Hu-chen 汪胡楨 and Wu Wei-tsu 吳慰祖 Taipei: Wen-hai, 1972.

Ch'ing-tai tang-an shih-liao ts'ung-pien 清代檔案史料叢編 (Source materials from the Ch'ing archives). Volume 2. Peking: Chung-hua, 1978.

Ch'ing-t'ien hsien-chih 青田縣志 (Gazetteer of Ch'ing-t'ien county). 18 chüan. 1935 revision of 1875 edition.

CHLC: *Kuo-ch'ao ch'i-hsien lei-cheng ch'u-pien* 國朝耆獻類徵初編 (Biographies of eminent figures of the Ch'ing, collected according to categories, first series). 294 ts'e. 1884–1890.

Chou T'ien-chueh 周天爵. *Chou Wen-chung-kung ch'ih-tu* 周文忠公尺牘 (Letters of Chou T'ien-chueh). Reprint, Taipei: Wen-hai, 1968.

Chu Ch'i 朱琦. *I-chih-t'ang wen-chi ch'u-pien* 怡志堂文集初編 (Collected writings of Chu Ch'i, first series). 6 chüan. N.d.

Ch'u Chin (pseud.) 楚金. "Tao-kuang hsueh-shu" 道光學術 (Scholarship of the Tao-kuang period). In *Chung-ho yueh-k'an shih-liao hsuan-chi*.

Chu Hsuan 朱玄. *Yao Hsi-pao hsueh-chi* 姚惜抱學記 (The scholarship and influence of Yao Nai). Taipei: Hsueh-sheng, 1974.

Chu Ju-chen 朱汝珍, comp. *Tz'u-lin chi-lueh* 詞林輯略 (List of Han-lin scholars). 11 chüan. Nanking: Nan-ching chung-yang k'e-ching yuan, Republican period.

Chu Kuei 朱珪. *Chih-tsu-chai shih-chi* 知足齋詩集 (Collected poetry of Chu Kuei). 1805 preface.

———. *Chih-tsu-chai wen-chi* 知足齋文集 (Collected prose of Chu Kuei). 6 chüan. In *Chi-fu ts'ung-shu* 畿輔叢書 (A collection of writings by authors from the metropolitan region). 1879–1892.

Chuan-chi hsing-shu hui-chi 傳記行述彙輯 (Collection of biographic materials). Columbia University Library rare book collection.

Chuang Shou-ch'i 莊受祺. *Feng-nan shan-kuan i-chi* 楓南山館遺集 (Remaining works of Chuang Shou-ch'i). 8 chüan. Kuang-hsu period (1875–1908).

Chung-ho yueh-k'an shih-liao hsuan-chi 中和月利史料選集 (Collection of histori-cal materials from the *Sino-Japanese Monthly*). Compiled by Shen Yun-lung 沈雲龍..2 vols. Taipei: Wen-hai, 1970.

Chung-kuo chin-tai huo-pi shih tzu-liao 中國近代貨幣資料 (Historical mate-rials on monetary policy in modern China). 2 vols. Peking: Chung-hua, 1964.

Costin, W.C. *Great Britain and China, 1833–1860.* Oxford: Oxford University Press, 1937.

CSWP: Ho Ch'ang-ling 賀長齡, ed. *Huang-ch'ao ching-shih wen-pien* 皇朝經世文編 (Our august dynasty's writings on statecraft). 120 chüan. 1826. Reprint, Taipei: Shih-chieh, 1964. 8 vols.

De Bary, William Theodore, ed. *The Unfolding of Neo-Confucianism.* New York: Columbia University Press, 1975.

Dennerline, Jerry. *The Chia-ting Loyalists: Confucian Leadership and Social Change in Seventeenth Century China.* New Haven: Yale University Press, 1981.

Drake, Fred W. *China Charts the World: Hsu Chi-yü and His Geography of 1848.* Cambridge: East Asian Research Center, Harvard University, 1975.

Eastman, Lloyd. *Throne and Mandarins: China's Search for a Policy During the Sino-French Controversy: 1880–1885.* Cambridge: Harvard University Press, 1967.

ECCP: Arthur Hummel, ed. *Eminent Chinese of the Ch'ing Period (1644–1912).* 2 vols. Washington, D.C.: U.S. Government Printing Office, 1943–1944.

Elman, Benjamin A. "The Hsueh-hai T'ang and the Rise of New Text Scholar-ship in Canton," *Ch'ing-shih wen-t'i* 4.2: 51–82 (1979).

Fa-shih-shan 法式善. *Huai-t'ing tsai-pi* 槐廳載筆 (Random notes from the Huai-t'ing Studio). 20 chüan. Reprint, Taipei: Wen-hai, 1968.

——. *P'eng-chiu chi-chien lu* 朋舊及見錄.

——. *Ts'un-su'-t'ang wen-chi* 存素堂文集 (Collected prose of Fa-shih-shan). 4 chüan, 1807; Supplement, 2 chüan, 1811.

Fairbank, John K. "The Creation of the Treaty Port System." In Fairbank et al., *The Cambridge History of China, Volume 10 Part One,* pp. 213–263.

——. "The Early Treaty Port System in the Chinese World Order." In his, ed., *The Chinese World Order* (Cambridge, Harvard University Press, 1968), pp. 257–275.

——. "Synarchy Under the Treaties." In his, ed., *Chinese Thought and Institu-tions* (Chicago: University of Chicago Press, 1957), pp. 204–231.

————. *Trade and Diplomacy on the China Coast: The Opening of the Treaty Ports, 1842–1854.* 1953; reprint, 2 vols. in one, Cambridge: Harvard University Press, 1969.

———— et al., ed. *The Cambridge History of China, Volume 10: Late Ch'ing, 1800–1911, Part One.* Cambridge: Cambridge University Press, 1978.

————. *The Cambridge History of China, Volume 11: Late Ch'ing, 1800–1911, Part Two.* Cambridge: Cambridge University Press, 1980.

————. *The I.G. in Peking: Letters of Robert Hart, Chinese Maritime Customs, 1868–1907.* 2 vols. Cambridge: Harvard University Press, 1975.

Fan-ssu ting-li hui-pien 藩司定例彙編. (Compendium of directives compiled by the provincial financial commissioner of Kiangsi province). 1905. Held at Harvard-Yenching Library.

Fay, Peter Ward. *The Opium War, 1840–1842: Barbarians in the Celestial Empire in the Early Part of the 19th Century and the War by Which They Forced Her Gates Ajar.* Chapel Hill: University of North Carolina Press, 1975.

Feng Kuei-fen 馮桂芬. *Chiao-pin-lu k'ang-i* 校邠廬抗議 (Essays of protest from the Chiao-pin Cottage). 1 chüan. 1897. Reprint, Taipei: Hsueh-hai, 1967.

————. *Hsien-chih-t'ang chi* 顯志堂集 (Collected works of Feng Kuei-fen). 12 chüan. 1876. Reprint, Taipei: Hsueh-hai, 1966.

Feuerwerker, Albert. *China's Early Industrialization: Sheng Hsuan-huai (1844–1916) and Mandarin Enterprise.* Cambridge: Harvard University Press, 1958.

————. "Economic Trends in the Late Ch'ing Empire, 1870–1911." In John K. Fairbank, et al., *The Cambridge History of China, Volume 11,* pp. 1–69.

Fitzpatrick, Merrilyn. "Local Interests and the Anti-pirate Administration in China's Southeast, 1555–1565," *Ch'ing-shih wen-t'i* 4.2 : 1–50 (1979).

Fletcher, Joseph. "The Heyday of the Ch'ing Order in Mongolia, Sinkiang, and Tibet." In John K. Fairbank, et al., *The Cambridge History of China, Volume 10,* pp. 351–408.

Frodsham, J.D. "The Origins of Chinese Nature Poetry," *Asia Major,* n.s. 8.1 : 68–103 (1960).

Graham, Gerald S. *The China Station: War and Diplomacy, 1830–1860.* Oxford: Oxford University Press, 1978.

Hamaguchi Fujio 浜口富士雄. "Hō Tō-ju no Kangaku hihan ni tsuite" 方東樹の漢覺批判について (On a critique of Fang Tung-shu's Han Learning), *Nihon Chûgoku gakkaihō* 30 : 165–178 (1978).

Hao Yen-p'ing and Wang Erh-min. "Changing Chinese Views of Western Relations, 1840–1895." In John K. Fairbank et al., *The Cambridge History of China, Volume 11,* pp. 142–201.

HCSH: Yang Chung-hsi 楊鍾羲. *Hsueh-ch'iao shih-hua* 雪橋詩話 (Poetry anecdotes of the Snowy Bridge). Series 1, 12 chüan; series 2, 8 chüan; series 3, 12 chüan; series 4, 8 chüan. 1913. Reprint, Taipei: Wen-hai, 1975.

HCTTS: Huang Ta-shou 黃大受 ed. *Huang Chueh-tzu tsou-su* 黃爵滋奏疏 (Memorials of Huang Chueh-tzu). Taipei: Ta-chung-kuo, 1963.

HHHC: *Ch'ung-hsiu Hsiang-shan hsien-chih* 重修香山縣志 (Gazetteer of Hsiang-shan county). 1879 edition, 22 chüan; 1923 edition, 16 chüan. Reprinted, together Taipei: Hsueh-sheng, 1968. 8 vols.

HNHC: *Hsin-ning hsien-chih* 新寧縣志 (Gazetteer of Hsin-ning county). 26 chüan. Reprint, Taipei: Hsueh-sheng, 1968.

Ho Ch'ang-ling 賀長齡 et al., comps. *Chiang-su hai-yun ch'üan-an* 江蘇海運全案 (Complete records of the Kiangsu sea shipment). 12 chüan. Tao-kuang period (1821–1850).

———. *Nai-an tsou-i ts'un-kao* 耐庵奏議存稿 (Memorials and other writings of Ho Ch'ang-ling). 22 chüan. Reprint, Taipei: Wen-hai, 1968.

HPSW: Huang Chueh-tzu 黃爵滋. *Hsien-p'ing shu-wu ch'u-chi nien-chi* 仙屏書屋初集年集 (Chronological anthology from the Hsien-p'ing Studio, first series). 31 chüan. 1849. Reprint, Taipei: Hua-wen, 1968.

Hsia Hsieh 夏燮. *Chung-hsi chi-shih* 中西紀事 (A record of Sino-Western affairs). 24 chüan. 1865. Reprint, Taipei: Wen-hai, 1962.

Hsia Nai 夏鼐. "Ya-p'ien chan-cheng chung ti T'ien-chin t'an-p'an" 鴉片戰爭中的天津談判 (Tientsin negotiations during the Opium War), *Wai-chiao yueh-pao* 4.4:43–56 (15 April, 1934); 4.5:95–123 (15 May, 1934).

Hsia Pao-chin 夏寶晉. "Tai-chu-t'ing wen-ch'ao ch'u-chi" 待珠亭文鈔初集 (Collected writings of Hsia Pao-chin, first series). 1812. Unpaginated manuscript, Harvard-Yenching Library.

———. *Tung-sheng ts'ao-t'ang wen-lu* 東省草堂聞錄 (Record from the Tung-sheng Studio). 1839.

Hsiao Kung-chuan. *Rural China: Imperial Control in the Nineteenth Century*. Seattle: University of Washington Press, 1960.

Hsieh Cheng-kuang 謝正光. "Hsuan-nan shih-she k'ao" 宣南詩社考 (A study of the Hsuan-nan Poetry Club), *Ta-lu tsa-chih* 36:4. Reprinted in *Ta-lu tsa-chih yü-wen ts'ung-shu* 大陸雜志語文叢書, second series, Volume 6. Taipei, 1970, pp. 119–126.

Hsieh Kuo-chen 謝國楨. "Chi Hsuan-nan shih-hui t'u-chüan" 記宣南詩會圖卷 (Notes on an illustrated volume of poems from the Hsuan-nan Poetry Club). In *I-lin ts'ung-lu* 藝林叢書 (Connoisseur's anthology). Hong Kong: Commercial Press, 1974.

Hsu Chi-yü 徐繼畬. *Sung-k'an hsien-sheng ch'üan-chi* 松龕先生全集 (Complete collected writings of Hsu Chi-yü). 6 vols. 1915. Reprint, Taipei: Wen-hai, 1977. 2 vols.

Hsu, Immanuel C.Y. "The Great Policy Debate in China, 1874: Maritime Defense vs. Frontier Defense." In his, ed., *Readings in Modern Chinese History*, pp. 258–271.

————, ed. *Readings in Modern Chinese History*. New York: Oxford University Press, 1971.

Hsu Pao-shan 徐寶善. *Hu-yuan ch'üan-chi* 壺園全集 (Complete works of Hsu Pao-shan). 25 chüan. N.d.

Hsu Ta-ling 許大齡. *Ch'ing-tai chüan-na chih-tu* 清代捐納制度 (The system of purchased offices during the Ch'ing period). Peking: Harvard-Yenching Institute Monograph #22, 1950.

Hsueh-hai-t'ang chih 學海堂志 (Gazetteer of the Hsueh-hai-t'ang Academy). 1 chüan. In Lin Po-t'ung 林伯桐, comp., *Hsiu-pen-t'ang ts'ung-shu* 修本堂叢書. Canton: Tao-kuang period (1821–1850).

Hsueh Yun-sheng 薛允升. *Tu-li ts'un-i* 讀例存疑 (Questions on reading the penal regulations). 54 chüan. Peking, 1905. Typeset edition, Taipei: Chinese Research Aids Service Center, 1970.

Hu Ch'eng-kung 胡承珙. *Ch'iu-shih-t'ang ch'üan-chi* 求是堂全集 (Collected works of Hu Ch'eng-kung). 32 ts'e. 1837.

Hu P'u-an 胡樸安. *Pao Shih-ch'en hsien-sheng nien-p'u* 包世臣先生年譜 (Chronological biography of Pao Shih-ch'en). 1 chüan. 1923. Reprint, Taipei: Wen-hai, 1968.

Huang An-t'ao 黃安濤. *Hsi-keng ts'ao-t'ang shih-chi* (Collected poems of Huang An-t'ao), first series.

————. *Shih-yü-shih shih-chi* (Collected poems of Huang An-t'ao), second series.

Huang Chien-hua 黃建華. "Tao-kuang shih-tai ti tsai-huang tui she-hui ching-chi ti ying-hsiang" 道光時代的災荒對社會經濟的影響 (The influence of natural catastrophes on the society and economy of the Tao-kuang period), *Shih-huo yueh-k'an*, n.s. 4.4:127–148 (1974).

Huang Pei. "Aspects of Ch'ing Autocracy: An Institutional Study, 1644–1735," *Tsing Hua Journal of Chinese Studies*, n.s. 1:1–2 (1967). Reprinted in Immanuel Hsu, *Readings in Modern Chinese History*, pp. 105–148.

Huang, Ray. *1587, A Year of No Significance: The Ming Dynasty in Decline*. New Haven: Yale University Press, 1981.

Hucker, Charles O. *The Censorial System of Ming China*. Stanford: Stanford University Press, 1966.

Hunt, Michael. "Chinese Foreign Relations in Historical Perspective." In Harry Harding, ed., *China's Foreign Relations in the 1980s*. New Haven: Yale University Press, 1984.

IWSM: *Ch'ou-pan i-wu shih-mo* 籌辦夷務始末 (A complete account of our management of barbarian affairs). 1929–1931. Reprint, Taipei: Wen-hai, 1970–1971. 36 vols. *IWSM-TK*: Tao-kuang reign. *IWSM-HF*: Hsien-feng reign.

Jen Yü-wen (Chien Yu-wen) 任玉文. *T'ai-p'ing t'ien-kuo ch'üan-shih* 太平天國 全史 (Complete history of the Taiping Heavenly Kingdom). 3 vols. Hong Kong: Meng-chin, 1962.

Jones, Susan Mann. "Hung Liang-chi: The Perception and Articulation of Political Problems in Late 18th Century China." PhD dissertation, Stanford University, 1971.

———. "Scholasticism and Politics in Late Eighteenth Century China," *Ch'ing-shih wen-t'i* 3.4 : 28–49 (1975).

Juan K'uei-sheng 阮葵生. *Ch'a-yü k'o-hua* 茶餘客話 (Compendium of anecdotes on the Ming and Ch'ing periods). 2 vols. Peking: Chung-hua, 1959.

Juan Yuan 阮元. *Yen-ching-shih chi* 揅經室集 (Juan Yuan's literary works). 63 chüan. In Juan Yuan, comp., *Wen-hsuan-lou ts'ung-shu* 文選樓叢書. 100 ts'e. 1842.

Kahn, Harold. *Monarchy in the Emperor's Eyes: Image and Reality in the Ch'ien-lung Reign.* Cambridge: Harvard University Press, 1971.

Kessler, Lawrence D. *K'ang-hsi and the Consolidation of Ch'ing Rule, 1661–1684.* Chicago: University of Chicago Press, 1976.

King, Frank H.H. *Money and Monetary Policy in China, 1845–1895.* Cambridge: Harvard University Press, 1965.

Ko Shih-chün 葛士濬, comp. *Huang-ch'ao ching-shih-wen hsu-pien* 皇朝經世文 續編 (Continuation of our august dynasty's writings on statecraft). 120 chüan. Shanghai, 1897. Reprint, Taipei: Kuo-feng, 1964.

KTM: Ku hsien-sheng-tz'u hui-chi t'i-ming ti-i chüan-tzu 顧先生祠會祭題名第一 卷子 (First roster of the Ku Yen-wu Shrine Association). 1 chüan. Soochow, 1887. Facsimile reproduction, 1908. Held by Library of Congress.

Ku Ch'un 顧純. *Ssu-wu-hsieh-shih wen-chi* 思無邪室文集 (Collected belletristic writings of Ku Ch'un).

Ku Yen-wu 顧炎武. *Jih-chih lu* 日知錄 (Record of daily learning). In Huang Ju-ch'eng 黃汝成, comp., *Jih-chih lu chi-shih* 日知錄集釋 (Record of daily learning and collected commentaries). 36 chüan. Reprint, Taipei: Chung-hua, 1968.

———. *Ku T'ing-lin shih-wen chi* 顧亭林詩文集 (Collected poetry and prose of Ku Yen-wu). Facsimile of K'ang-hsi period (1661–1721) edition; Shanghai: Commercial Press, 1929.

Kuan T'ung 管同. *Yin-chi-hsuan wen-chi* 因寄軒文集 (Collected writings of Kuan T'ung). 18 chüan. Reprint, 1879.

Kuang-chou-fu t'ung-chih 廣州府通志 (Gazetteer of Kuang-chou prefecture). 163 chüan. 1879.

Kuhn, Philip A. "Local Self-government under the Republic: Problems of Control, Autonomy, and Mobilization." In Frederic Wakeman, Jr., and Carolyn Grant, *Conflict and Control in Late Imperial China*, pp. 257–298.

————. *Rebellion and Its Enemies in Late Imperial China: Militarization and Social Structure, 1796–1864.* Cambridge: Harvard University Press, 1970.

————. "The Taiping Rebellion." In John K. Fairbank et al., *The Cambridge History of China, Volume 10*, pp. 264–317.

————, and Susan Mann Jones. "Dynastic Decline and the Rise of Rebellion." In John K. Fairbank et al., *The Cambridge History of China, Volume 10*, pp. 107–162.

Kung Tzu-chen 龔自珍. *Kung Tzu-chen ch'üan-chi* 龔自珍全集 (Complete works of Kung Tzu-chen). Shanghai: Shang-hai jen-min, 1975.

K'ung Hsien-i 孔憲彝. *Han-chai wen-kao* 韓齋文稿 (Collected works of K'ung Hsien-i). 12 chüan. Hsien-feng period (1850–1861).

Kuo T'ing-i 郭廷以, comp. *Chin-tai chung-kuo shih-shih jih-chih* 近代中國史事日誌 (A calendar of events in modern Chinese history). 2 vols. Taipei: Cheng-chung, 1965.

Laai I-fa. "The Part Played by the Pirates of Kwangtung and Kwangsi Provinces in the T'ai-p'ing Insurrection. PhD dissertation, University of California, Berkeley, 1962.

Laffey, Ella S. "The Making of a Rebel: Liu Yung-fu and the Formation of the Black Flag Army." In Jean Chesneaux, ed., *Popular Movements and Secret Societies in China, 1840–1950.* Stanford: Stanford University Press, 1972, pp. 85–96.

LCCW: Ch'en K'ang-ch'i 陳康祺. *Lang-ch'ien chi-wen* 郎潛紀聞 (Miscellany of anecdotes). 3 series. 40 chüan. Ningpo, 1884.

Leonard, Jane Kate. "Wei Yuan and Images of the Nan-yang," *Ch'ing-shih wen-t'i* 4.1:23–57 (1979).

Levenson, Joseph R. *Liang Ch'i-ch'ao and the Mind of Modern China.* Cambridge: Harvard University Press, 1953.

Li Cheng-fu 李正富. *Sung-tai k'o-chü chih-tu chih yen-chiu* 宋代科舉制度之研究 (The examination system of the Sung). Taipei: National Political Science College, Institute of Educational Research, 1963.

Li Yueh-jui 李岳瑞. *Ch'un-ping-shih yeh-ch'eng* 春冰室野乘 (Unofficial record from the Ch'un-ping Studio). Shanghai: Commercial Press, 1926.

Liang Chang-chü 梁章鉅. *Kuei-t'ien so-chi* 歸田瑣記 (Anecdotes remembered in retirement). 8 chüan. Taipei: Kuang-wen, 1969.

————. *Lang-chi ts'ung-t'an* 浪跡叢談 (Collection of random memories and anecdotes). 19 chüan. Shanghai: Chin-pu, n.d.

————. *Shih-yu chi* 師友集 (Collected poetic biographies of mentors and friends). 10 chüan. 1845.

————. *T'eng-hua yin-kuan shih-ch'ao* (Collected poetry of Liang Chang-chü).

————. *T'ui-an sui-pi* 退庵隨筆 (Miscellaneous notes of Mr. T'ui-an). 22 chüan. Taipei: Wen-hai.

————. *T'ui-an tzu-ting nien-p'u* 退庵自訂年譜 (Chronological autobiography). 1875. Reprint, Taipei: Wen-hai, 1968. 2 vols.

Lin Ch'ang-i 林昌彝. *She-yin-lou shih-hua* 射鷹樓詩話 (Poetry anecdotes from the She-yin-lou). 24 chüan. 1851.

Lin Ch'ung-yung 林崇墉. *Lin Tse-hsu chuan* 林則徐傳 (Biography of Lin Tse-hsu). Taipei: Commercial Press, 1967.

Lin Tse-hsu 林則徐. *Hsin-chi-lu* 信及錄 (Record of anti-opium enforcement in Kwangtung). Reprint, Taipei: Hsueh-sheng, 1973.

————. *Yun-tso shan-fang shih-ch'ao* 雲左山房詩鈔 (The poetry of Lin Tse-hsu). 10 chüan. 1886.

————. *Yun-tso shan-fang wen-ch'ao* 雲左山房文鈔 (Prose writings of Lin Tse-hsu). 4 chüan. Taipei: Te-ch'u, 1963.

Liu Kwang-ching. "Politics, Intellectual Outlook, and Reform: The T'ung-wen Kuan Controversy of 1867." In Paul Cohen and John Schrecker, eds. *Reform in Nineteenth Century China*. Cambridge: East Asian Research Center, Harvard University, 1976, pp. 87–114.

———— and Richard J. Smith. "The Military Challenge: The Northwest and the Coast." In John K. Fairbank et al., *The Cambridge History of China, Volume 11*, pp. 202–273.

Liu Po-chi 劉伯驥. *Kuang-tung shu-yuan chih-tu* 廣東書院制度 (The academy system of Kwangtung). Hong Kong: Chi-sheng, 1958.

Liu Ssu-wan 劉嗣綰. *Shang-chiung-t'ang shih-chi* 尚絅堂詩集 (Collected poems of Liu Ssu-wan). 1869.

Liu Tzu-chien 劉子健 (James T.C. Liu). *Ou-yang Hsiu ti chih-hsueh yü ts'ung-cheng* 歐陽修的治學與從政 (The scholarly and political activities of Ou-yang Hsiu). Hong Kong: Hsin-ya yen-chiu-so, 1963.

Liu Wen-ch'i 劉文淇. *Ch'ing-ch'i chiu-wu wen-chi* 青溪舊屋文集 (Collected writings of Liu Wen-ch'i). 11 chüan. 1883.

Lo Chen-yü 羅振玉, comp. *Huang-Ch'ing tsou-i* 皇清奏議 (Memorials of the Ch'ing dynasty). 68 chüan; Supplement, 4 chüan. 1936.

Lo Chü 羅集, comp. *Lo Wen-k'o-kung (Tun-yen) nien-p'u* 羅文恪公(惇衍) 年譜 (Chronological biography of Lo Tun-yen). 1 ts'e. N.d.

Lo Ping-chang 駱秉章. *Lo-kung nien-p'u* 駱公年譜 (Chronological autobiography). Taipei: Wen-hai, 1968.

LTHJC: Lin Tse-hsu chi: jih chi 林則徐集, 日記 (Works of Lin Tse-hsu: diary). Peking: Chung-hua, 1962.

Lu-i hsien-chih 鹿邑縣志 (Gazetteer of Lu-i county [Honan]). 1896.

Lu I-t'ung 魯一同. *T'ung-fu lei-kao* 通甫類藁 (Works of Lu I-t'ung arranged by category). 13 chüan. 1863.

Lung Ch'i-jui 龍啓瑞. *Ching-te-t'ang chi* 經德堂集 (Collected writings of Lung Ch'i-jui). 8 chüan. 1879.

LWCKCS: *Lin wen-chung-kung cheng-shu* 林文忠公政書 (Collected memorials of Lin Tse-hsu). Shanghai: Commercial Press, 1925.

Lynn, Richard John. "Orthodoxy and Enlightenment: Wang Shih-chen's Theory of Poetry and Its Antecedents." In Wm. Theodore de Bary, ed., *The Unfolding of Neo-Confucianism*, pp. 217–269.

MCSL: *Ming-Ch'ing shih-liao* 明清史料. (Historical materials from the Ming and Ch'ing dynasties). Jen-pien 壬編 (series 8). Taipei: Academia Sinica, 1967.

Mei Tseng-liang 梅曾亮. *Po-chien shan-fang wen-chi* 柏梘山房文集 (Collected works of Mei Tseng-liang). 1856. Reprint, Taipei, 1969. 2 vols.

Metzger, Thomas A. *Escape from Predicament: Neo-Confucianism and China's Evolving Political Culture*. New York: Columbia University Press, 1976.

———. *The Internal Organization of the Ch'ing Bureaucracy*. Cambridge: Harvard University Press, 1973.

———. "T'ao Chu's Reform of the Huai-pei Salt Monopoly (1831–1833)," *Papers on China* (Harvard) 16 : 1–39 (1962).

Miao K'uei 苗夔. *Shuo-wen chien-shou tzu-tu* 說文建首字讀. Included in *Miao-shih shuo-wen ssu-chung* 苗氏說文四種 (Mr. Miao's four studies on the Shuo-wen). 8 ts'e. 1851.

Miller, Harold Lyman. "Factional Conflicts and the Integration of Ch'ing Politics, 1661–1690." PhD dissertation, George Washington University, 1974.

Miyazaki Ichisada. *China's Examination Hell*. Tr. Conrad Shirokauer. Tokyo: Weatherhill, 1976.

Morse, Hosea B. *The International Relations of the Chinese Empire*. 3 vols. London: Longman, Green and Co., 1910–1918.

Mote, F.W. "Political Structure." In Gilbert Rozman, ed. *The Modernization of China*. New York: Free Press, 1981.

Naquin, Susan. *Millenarian Rebellion in China: The Eight Trigrams Uprising of 1813*. New Haven: Yale University Press, 1976.

Nathan, Andrew J. "'Connections' in Chinese Politics: Political Recruitment and *kuan-hsi* in the Late Ch'ing and Early Republican China." Paper prepared for the 1972 meeting of the American Historical Association.

NHHC: *Nan-hai hsien-chih* 南海縣志 (Gazetteer of Nan-hai county). 26 chüan. 1910. Reprint, Taipei: Hsueh-sheng, 1968.

Nivison, David S. "Ho-shen and his Accusers: Ideology and Political Behavior in the Eighteenth Century." In D.S. Nivison and Arthur F. Wright, eds, *Confucianism in Action*. Stanford: Stanford University Press, 1959, pp. 209–243.

Nolde, John J. "The 'False Edict' of 1849," *Journal of Asian Studies* 20.3:299–315 (1961).

———. "Xenophobia in Canton," *Journal of Oriental Studies* 13.1:1–22 (1975).

Ou-pei hsien-sheng nien-p'u 甌北先生年譜 (Chronological biography of Chao I). 1 chüan. Hong Kong: Chung-wen, 1974.

Ouchterlony, John. *The Chinese War: An Account of All The Operations of the British Forces from the Commencement to the Treaty of Nanking.* London, 1844.

Oxnam, Robert B. *Ruling from Horseback: Manchu Politics in the Oboi Regency, 1661–1669.* Chicago: University of Chicago Press, 1975.

P'an Shih-en 潘世恩. *Ssu-pu-chai pi-chi* 思補齋筆集 (Anecdotes from the Ssu-pu Studio). In P'an Tsu-yin, *P'an-k'o wu-chung.*

P'an Te-yü 潘德輿. *Yang-i-chai chi* 養一齋集 (Collected writings of P'an Te-yü). 51 chüan. 1872.

P'an Tseng-i 潘曾沂. *Hsiao-fu shan-jen shou-ting nien-p'u* 小浮山人手訂年譜 (Chronological autobiography). 1 chüan. N.d.

———. *Kung-fu hsiao-chi* 功甫小集 (Collected poems of P'an Tseng-i, first series). 11 chüan. N.d.

———. *P'an Feng-yü chuang pen shu* 潘豐谷莊本書 (Manual of the P'an clan estate). Tao-kuang period (1821–1850).

P'an Tseng-shou 潘曾綬. *Kai-lan shu-wu chi* 陔蘭書屋集 (Collected writings of P'an Tseng-shou). 17 chüan. 1828.

P'an Tsu-yin 潘祖蔭, comp. *P'an-k'o wu-chung* 潘刻五種 (Five works by members of the P'an family). 6 ts'e. Kuang-hsu period (1875–1908).

———. *Ssu-pu-chai shih-chi* 思補齋詩集 (Selected poems of P'an Shih-en). 6 chüan. 1850 preface.

———. *Ssu-pu lao-jen shou-ting nien-p'u* 思補老人手定年譜 (Chronological autobiography of P'an Shih-en). 1 chüan. In P'an Tsu-yin, *P'an-k'o wu-chung.*

Pao Shih-ch'en 包世臣. *An-wu ssu-chung* 安吳四種 (Complete works of Pao Shih-ch'en). Reprint, Taipei: Wen-hai, 1868.

Parker, Jason H. "The Rise and Decline of I-hsin, Prince Kung, 1858–1865: A Study of the Interaction of Politics and Ideology in Late Imperial China." PhD dissertation, Princeton University, 1979.

Peterson, Willard J. "Early Nineteenth Century Monetary Ideas on the Cash-Silver Exchange Ratio," *Papers on China* (Harvard) 20:23–48 (1966).

———. "The Life of Ku Yen-wu (1613–1682), Part 2," *Harvard Journal of Asiatic Studies* 24:201–247 (1969).

Polachek, James M. "Gentry Hegemony: Soochow in the T'ung-chih Restoration." In Frederic Wakeman, Jr., and Carolyn Grant, *Conflict and Control in Late Imperial China,* pp. 211–256.

———. "Literati Groups and Literati Politics in Early Nineteenth Century China." PhD dissertation, University of California at Berkeley, 1976.

PYHC: P'an-yü hsien hsu-chih 番禺縣續志 (Revised gazetteer of P'an-yü county). 44 chüan. 1931. Reprint, Taipei: Hsueh-sheng, 1968.

Rankin, Mary B. "'Public Opinion' and Political Power: *Qingyi* in Late Nineteenth Century China," *Journal of Asian Studies* 41.3:453–484 (1982).

Rawlinson, John L. *China's Struggle for Naval Development, 1893–1895.* Cambridge: Harvard University Press, 1967.

A Reproduction of the Lan-t'ing Calligraphy Scroll by Wang Hsi-chih. Taipei: 1961.

Rossabi, Morris. *China and Inner Asia: From 1368 to the Present Day.* New York: Pica Press, 1975.

Sasaki Masaya 佐々木正哉, comp. *Ahen sensōgo no Chū-Ei kōsō: shiryō henkō* 鴉片戰争後の中英闘争：資料編稿 (Anglo-Chinese conflict after the Opium War: documents). Tokyo: Kindai Chūgoku kenkyū iinkai, 1964.

———. "Juntoku-ken kyōshin to Tōkai jūrokusa" 順德縣鄉民と東海十六沙 (The scholar-gentry of Shun-te county and the "sixteen shoal fields of Tung-hai"). In *Kindai Chūgoku kenkyū,* Volume 3, pp. 162–232. Tokyo: Tokyo University Press, 1959.

Schwartz, Benjamin I. *In Search of Wealth and Power: Yen Fu and the West.* Cambridge: Harvard University Press, 1966.

SCTI: Tao Hsien T'ung Kuang ssu-ch'ao tsou-i 道咸同光四朝奏議 (Memorials from the four reigns of Tao-kuang, Hsien-feng, T'ung-chih, and Kuang-hsu). 12 vols. Reprint, Taipei: Commercial Press, 1970.

Shang-yü-tang fang-pen 上諭檔方本 (Grand Council monthly logbook of imperial edicts). Grand Council archives, National Palace Museum, Taipei, Taiwan.

Shao I-ch'en 邵懿辰. *Pan-yen-lu i-chi* 半巖廬遺集 (Remaining works of Shao I-ch'en). 2 chüan. 1908.

———. *Shao Wei-hsi i-wen* 邵位西遺文 (Remaining essays of Shao I-ch'en). 1 ts'e. 1875.

SH-CC: Ta-Ch'ing Jen-tsung Jui huang-ti sheng-hsun 大清仁宗睿皇帝聖訓 (Sacred edicts of the Chia-ch'ing reign of the Ch'ing). 100 chüan. Kuang-hsu period (1875–1908).

SH-CL: Ta-Ch'ing Kao-tsung Ch'un huang-ti sheng-hsun 大清高宗純皇帝聖訓 (Sacred edicts of the Ch'ien-lung reign of the Ch'ing). 300 chüan. Kuang-hsu period (1875–1908).

Shen Chien-shih 沈兼士. *Chung-kuo k'ao-shih chih-tu shih* 中國考試制度史 (A history of the civil-service examinations of imperial China). Taipei: Examination Yuan, 1960.

SJCL: Chang Wei-p'ing 張維屏. *Ch'ing-ch'ao shih-jen cheng-lueh* 清朝詩人徵略

(Anthology of Ch'ing poets). 124 chüan. Reprint, Taipei: Ting-wen, 1971.

SL-CC: *Ta-Ch'ing Jen-tsung Jui huang-ti shih-lu* 大清仁宗睿皇帝實錄 (Veritable records of the Chia-ch'ing reign of the Ch'ing dynasty). 8 vols. Reprint, Taipei: Hua-wen, 1964.

SL-CL: *Ta-Ch'ing Kao-tsung Ch'un huang-ti shih-lu* 大清高宗純皇帝實錄 (Veritable records of the Ch'ien-lung reign of the Ch'ing dynasty). 1,500 chüan. Reprint, Taipei: Hua-wen, 1964.

SL-HF: *Ta-Ch'ing Wen-tsung Hsien huang-ti shih-lu* 大清文宗顯皇帝實錄 (Veritable records of the Hsien-feng reign of the Ch'ing dynasty). 8 vols. Reprint, Taipei: Hua-wen, 1964.

SL-TK: *Ta-Ch'ing Hsuan-tsung Ch'eng huang-ti shih-lu* 大清宣宗成皇帝實錄 (Veritable records of the Tao-kuang reign of the Ch'ing dynasty). 12 vols. Reprint, Taipei: Hua-wen, 1964.

SLHK: *Shih-liao hsun-k'an* 史料旬刊 (Historical materials published every 10 days). 40 ts'e. National Palace Museum, 1930–1931. Reprint, Taipei: Kuo-feng, 1963.

Spence, Jonathan D. "Opium Smoking in Ch'ing China." In Frederic Wakeman, Jr., and Carolyn Grant, *Conflict and Control in Late Imperial China*, pp. 143–173.

————, and John E. Wills, eds. *From Ming to Ch'ing: Conquest, Region, and Continuity in Seventeenth Century China*. New Haven: Yale University Press, 1979.

SSK: Yao Wei-yuan 姚薇元. *Ya-p'ien chan-cheng shih-shih k'ao* 鴉片戰爭史實考 (A history of the Opium War). 1931. Reprint, Taipei: Ku-t'ing, 1975.

Struve, Lynn A. "The Hsu Brothers and Semi-official Patronage of Scholars in the K'ang-hsi Period," *Harvard Journal of Asiatic Studies* 42.1:231–266 (1982).

————. "Some Frustrated Scholars of the K'ang-hsi Period." In Jonathan D. Spence and John E. Wills, Jr., *From Ming to Ch'ing*, pp. 321–365.

Su Shu-fan 蘇樹蕃, comp. *Kuo-ch'ao yü-shih t'i-ming* 國朝御史題名 (List of censors during the Ch'ing period). Reprint, Taipei: Wen-hai, 1967.

Sun Ting-ch'en 孫鼎臣. *Ts'ang-lang shih-wen chi* 蒼莨詩文集 (Poetry and prose of Sun Ting-ch'en). 18 chüan. Hsien-feng period (1850–1861).

Sun Yü-t'ing 孫玉庭. *Yen-li-t'ang chi* 延釐堂集 (Collected works of Sun Yü-t'ing). 8 chüan. 1872.

Suzuki Chūsei 鈴木中正. *Shin-chō chūkishi kenkyū* 清朝中期史研究 (Studies in the history of the middle Ch'ing). Toyohashi: Aichi daigaku kokusai mondai kenkyūjō, 1952.

————. "Shin-matsu no zaisei to kanryō no seikaku" 清末の財政と官僚の 性格 (The nature of the financial administration and the bureaucracy of the late Ch'ing period). In *Kindai Chūgoku kenkyū*, Volume 2. Tokyo: Tokyo University Press, 1958, pp. 189–282.

Ta-Ch'ing hui-tien (t'u-shuo, shih-li) 大清會典, 圖說, 事例 (Statutes of the Great Ch'ing, with illustrations and precedents). 1818 edition, 920 chüan. 1899 edition, 1,220 chüan. Reprint, Taipei: Hsin-wen-feng, 1976.

Takahashi Kazumi 高橋和己. *O Shishin* 王士禎 (Wang Shih-chen). Tokyo: Iwanami Shoten, 1962.

T'ang P'eng 湯鵬. *Fu-ch'iu-tzu* 浮邱子. 12 chüan. 1824.

TCFC: Fang Tung-shu 方東樹. *K'ao-p'an-chi* 考槃集 (Retirement collection). 3 chüan. 1848. In his *T'ung-ch'eng Fang Chih-chih hsien-sheng ch'üan-chi* 桐城方植之先生全集 (Complete collected works of Fang Tung-shu). Kuang-hsu period (1875–1908).

TCT: Ho Shao-chi 何紹基. *Tung-chou ts'ao-t'ang wen-ch'ao* 東洲草堂文鈔 (Collected writings of Ho Shao-chi). 16 chüan. Reprint, Taipei: Wen-hai, 1974. 3 vols.

THHL: *Tung-hua hsu-lu Chia-ch'ing ch'ao* 東華續錄嘉慶朝 (Continuation of the Tung-hua records, Chia-ch'ing reign). 50 chüan. Shanghai, 1909.

T'ien-hsia shu-yuan tsung-chih 天下書院總志 (Register of the academies of the empire). 12 chüan. Reprint, Taipei: Kuang-wen, 1974. 3 vols.

Ting Yen 丁晏. *I-chih-chai wen-ch'ao* 頤志齋文鈔 (Writings of Ting Yen). In *I-chih-chai ts'ung-shu* 頤志齋叢書 (Collected works of Ting Yen). 16 ts'e. 1861.

TKHC: *Tung-kuan hsien-chih* 東莞縣志 (Gazetteer of Tung-kuan county). 1926–1927. Reprint, Taipei: Hsueh-sheng, 1968.

Tsung Chi-ch'en 宗績辰. *Kung-ch'ih-chai shih-ch'ao* 躬耻齋詩鈔 (Collected poetry of Tsung Chi-ch'en). 14 chüan. 1859.

————. *Kung-ch'ih-chai wen-ch'ao* 躬耻齋文鈔 (Collected prose of Tsung Chi-ch'en). 16 chüan. 1857.

Tu Wei-yun 杜維運. *Hsueh-shu yü shih-pien* 學術與世變 (Scholarship and change). Taipei: Huan-yu, 1971.

TWC: Tseng Kuo-fan 曾國藩. *Tseng Wen-cheng-kung ch'üan-chi* 曾文正公全集 (Complete works of Tseng Kuo-fan). 1876. Reprint, Taipei: Wen-hai, 1974.

TWIK: T'ao Chu 陶澍. *T'ao Wen-i-kung ch'üan-chi* 陶文毅公全集 (Collected works of T'ao Chu). 64 chüan. 1840 preface.

Wai-chi tang 外紀檔 (Outer court record book). Ch'ing archives, National Palace Museum, Taipei, Taiwan.

Wakeman, Frederic, Jr. "The Canton Trade and the Opium War." In John K. Fairbank et al., *The Cambridge History of China, Volume 10*, pp. 163–212.

————. *Strangers at the Gate: Social Disorder in South China, 1839–1861.* Berkeley. University of California Press, 1966.

———— and Carolyn Grant, eds. *Conflict and Control in Late Imperial China.* Berkeley: University of California Press, 1976.

Waley, Arthur. *The Opium War through Chinese Eyes.* 1958. Reprint, Stanford: Stanford University Press, 1968.

Wang Ch'ang 王昶. *Hu-hai shih-chuan* 湖海詩傳 (Poetic biographies of friends of Wang Ch'ang). 46 chüan. Reprint, Taipei: Commercial Press, 1968. 2 vols.

Wang Ch'i-sun 王芑孫. *T'i-fu wei-ting kao* 惕甫未定稿 (Incomplete collection of the works of Wang Ch'i-sun). 16 chüan. 1804.

Wang Chia-chien 王家儉. *Wei Yuan nien-p'u* 魏源年譜 (Chronological biography of Wei Yuan). Taipei: Academica Sinica, Institute of Modern History, 1967.

————. *Wei Yuan tui hsi-fang ti jen-shih chi ch'i hai-fang ssu-hsiang* 魏源對西方的認識及海防思想 (Wei Yuan's knowledge of the West and his concept of maritime defense). Taipei: Taiwan University, Institute of Literature, 1964.

Wang Ch'ing-yun 王慶雲. *Shih-ch'ü yü-chi* 石渠餘紀 (Topics in Ch'ing institutional history). 6 chüan. Reprint, Taipei: Wen-hai, 1967.

Wang Chün-i 王俊義. "Kuan-yü Hsuan-nan shih-she ti chi-ko wen-t'i" 關於宣南詩社的幾個問題 (Several questions concerning the Hsuan-nan Poetry Club). In Jen-min ta-hsueh, Ch'ing-shih yen-chiu so, comps., *Ch'ing-shih yen-chiu chi* 清史研究集 (Essays on Ch'ing history), Volume 1, pp. 216–242. Peking, 1980.

Wang Hsi-chen 王錫振. *Lung-pi shan-fang wen-chi* 龍壁山房文集 (Collected writings of Wang Hsi-chen). 1881 edition, 8 chüan; 1883 edition, 5 chüan.

Wang Hsi-sun 汪喜孫 (Wang Hsi-hsun 汪喜荀). *Ch'ieh-chu-an wen-chi* 且住庵文集 (Collected prose of Wang Hsi-sun). Taipei: Shih-chieh, 1971.

————. *Ts'ung-cheng lu* 從政錄 (Essays on governance). 4 chüan. 1841. Reprinted in *Chiang-tu Wang-shih ts'ung-shu* 江都王氏叢書 (Collectanea of the Wang family of Chiang-tu). Shanghai: Chung-kuo, 1925, ts'e 14–17.

Wang Po-hsin 王柏心. *Shu-yen* 樞言. 1 chüan. 1834. Supplement, 1 chüan. 1844.

Wang Shih-chen 王世貞. *Yü-yang shan-jen kan-chiu chi* 漁洋山人感舊集 (Poetic memoirs of old friends of Hermit Yü-yang). 16 chüan. 1752. Reprint, Taipei: Kuang-wen, 1985. 2 vols.

WCSL: Ch'ing-tai wai-chiao shih-liao 清代外交史料 (Historical materials on Ch'ing foreign relations). Volume 2, 4 chüan, Tao-kuang reign. 1932–1933. Reprint, Taipei: Ch'eng-wen, 1968.

Wei Hsiu-mei 魏秀梅, comp. *Ch'ing-chi chih-kuan piao* 清季職官表 (Table of officials of the late Ch'ing). 2 vols. Taipei: Academia Sinica, Institute of Modern History, 1977.

Wei Peh-t'i, "Internal Security and Coastal Control: Juan Yuan and Pirate Suppression in Chekiang, 1799–1809," *Ch'ing-shih wen-t'i* 4.2:83–112 (1979).

Wei Yuan 魏源. *Hai-kuo t'u-chih* 海國圖志 (Illustrated gazetteer of the maritime countries). 60 chüan. 1847. Reprint, Taipei: Ch'eng-wen, 1967. 7 vols.

————. *Ku-wei-t'ang wai-chi* 古微堂外集 (Exoteric collection of the writings of Wei Yuan). 1878.

————. *Sheng-wu chi* 聖武記 (A military history of the Ch'ing). 14 chüan. Completed 1842. Reprint, Taipei: Chung-hua, 1962. 2 vols.

————. *Tseng-kuang hai-kuo t'u-chih* 增廣海國圖志 (Expanded edition of illustrated gazetteer of the maritime countries). 125 chüan. Taipei: Kuei-ting, 1978.

————. *Wei Yuan chi* 魏源集 (Collected works of Wei Yuan). 2 vols. Peking: Chung-hua, 1976.

Weng Fang-kang 翁方綱. *Fu-ch'u-chai wen-chi* 復初齋文集 (Collected writings of Weng Fang-kang). 25 chüan. Reprint, Taipei: Wen-hai, 1968. 3 vols.

————. *Weng-shih chia-shih lueh-chi* 翁氏家史略記 (Brief history of the Weng family). Appendix to *Fu-ch'u-chai shih-chi* 復初齋詩集. 70 chüan. 1814(?). Held at Harvard-Yenching Library.

WHC: *Ya-p'ien chan-cheng wen-hsueh chi* 鴉片戰爭文學集 (Collected literary materials on the Opium War). 2 vols. Peking: Ku-chi, 1957.

WHTK: *Ch'ing-ch'ao hsu wen-hsien t'ung-k'ao* 清朝續文獻通考 (Compendium of documents from the Ch'ing dynasty, second compilation). 400 chüan. Compiled, 1915. Published, Shanghai: Commercial Press, 1936. Reprint, Taipei: Hsin-hsing, 1965, as part of *Shih-t'ung* 十通. 24 vols.

Wills, John E., Jr. "Maritime China from Wang Chih to Shih Lang: Themes in Peripheral History." In Jonathan Spence and John E. Wills, Jr., *From Ming to Ch'ing*. New Haven: Yale University Press, 1979.

Wong, J.Y. *Yeh Ming-ch'en: Viceroy of Liang Kuang, 1852–1858*. Cambridge: Cambridge University Press, 1976.

Wu Ch'ang-shou 吳昌綬. *Ting-an hsien-sheng nien-p'u* 定盦先生年譜 (Chronological autobiography of Kung Tzu-chen). Reprinted in Kung Tzu-chen, *Kung Tzu-chen ch'üan-chi*.

Wu Chia-pin 吳嘉賓. *Ch'iu-tzu-te-chih-shih wen-ch'ao* 求自得之室文鈔 (Collected works of Wu Chia-pin). 14 chüan. 1866.

Wu Ching-tzu. *The Scholars*. Tr. Yang Hsien-yi and Gladys Yang. New York: Grosset and Dunlop, 1972.

Wu Hsi-ch'i 吳錫麒. *Yu-cheng-wei-chai ch'ih-tu* 有正味齋尺牘 (Letters of Wu Hsi-ch'i). 2 chüan. 1909.

Wu Hsiung-kuang 吳熊光. *I-chiang pi-lu* 伊江筆錄 (Anecdotes on administration). 2 chüan.

Wu, Silas. *Passage to Power: K'ang-hsi and His Heir Apparent, 1661–1722.* Cambridge: Harvard University Press, 1979.

Wu Sung-liang 吳嵩梁. *Hsiang-su shan-kuan ch'üan-chi* 香蘇山館全集 (Complete works from the Hsiang-su Retreat). 58 chüan. 1843.

————. *Shih-ch'i-fang shih-hua* 石溪舫詩話 (Notes on poetry from the Shih-ch'i-fair). 2 chüan. In his *Hsiang-su shan-kuan ch'üan-chi.*

Wu Wen-jung 吳文鎔. *Wu Wen-chieh kung i-chi* 吳文節公遺集 (Remaining works of Wu Wen-jung). Reprint, Taipei: Wen-hai, 1968.

Ya-p'ien chan-cheng shih-ch'i ssu-hsiang-shih tzu-liao hsuan-chi 鴉片戰爭時期思想史資料選輯 (Selected materials on the history of thought in the period of the Opium War). Peking: Chung-hua, 1963.

Yamaguchi Michiko 山口廸子. "Shindai no sōun to senshō" 清代の漕運と船商 (Maritime transport and shipping merchants in the Ch'ing period), *Tōyōshi kenkyū* 17.2 : 56–72 (1958).

Yang, C.K. "Some Preliminary Statistical Patterns of Mass Actions in Nineteenth Century China." In Frederic Wakeman, Jr., and Carolyn Grant, *Conflict and Control in Late Imperial China,* pp. 174–210.

Yang-ch'un hsien-chih 陽春縣志 (Gazetteer of Yang-ch'un county). 11 chüan. 1949. Reprint, Taipei, 1971.

Yao Nai 姚鼐. *Hsi-pao-hsuan shih-wen chi* 惜抱軒詩文集 (Collected poetry and prose of Yao Nai). 26 chüan. Taipei: Commercial Press, 1968.

Yao Ying 姚瑩. *K'ang-yu chi-hsing* 康輶紀行 (Record of a mission to Tibet). 16 chüan. 1867 postface. Reprint, Taipei: Kuang-wen, 1969.

————. comp. *Ch'ien k'un cheng-ch'i chi* 乾坤正氣集. 1848. Reprint, Taipei: Huan-chiu, 1966.

Yao Yuan-chih 姚元之. *Chu-yeh-t'ing tsa-chi* 竹葉亭雜記 (Random notes from the Chu-yeh Pavilion). 8 chüan. 1893.

Yao Yung-p'u 姚永樸. *Chiu-wen sui-pi* 舊聞隨筆 (A miscellany of old anecdotes). 4 chüan. Taipei: Wen-hai, 1968.

Yeh Ming-feng 葉名澧. *Ch'iao-hsi tsa-chi* 橋西雜記 (Random jottings from west of the bridge). Taipei: Commercial Press, 1966.

Yen Jung 嚴榮. *Shu-an hsien-sheng nien-p'u* 述庵先生年譜 (Chronological biography of Wang Ch'ang). 2 chüan. 1807.

Ying-ho 英和. *En-fu-t'ang nien-p'u* 恩福堂年譜 (Chronological autobiography). 1 chüan. ca. 1840.

Yoshikawa Kōjirō 吉川幸次郎. *Yoshikawa Kōjirō zenshū* 吉川幸次郎全書 (Complete works of Yoshikawa Kōjirō). 20 vols. Tokyo: Chikuma, 1970.

YPCC: Ya-p'ien chan-cheng 鴉片戰爭 (The Opium War). 6 vols. Shanghai: Shen-chou kuo-kuang she, 1954.

Yü-chai 迂齋 (pseud.). "Tao-kuang-ch'ao chih chün-hsiang" 道光朝之君相 (The ruler and his ministers in the Tao-kuang reign). In *Chung-ho yueh-k'an shih-liao hsuan-chi*, pp. 274–278.

Yü-ch'ien 裕謙. *Yü-ching-chieh-kung i-shu* 裕靖節公遺書 (Remaining works of Yü-ch'ien). 3 vols. Reprint, Taipei: Ch'eng-wen, 1969.

Yuan Chia-san 袁三甲. *Hsiang-ch'eng Yuan-shih chia-chi* 項城袁氏家集 (Works of the Yuan family of Hsiang-ch'eng). Comp. Ting Chen-to 丁振鐸. 1911. Reprint, Taipei: Wen-hai, 1966. 8 vols.

Yueh-tung sheng-li hsin-tsuan 粵東省例新纂 (Revised compendium of Kwangtung province administrative statutes). 8 chüan. 1846. Reprint, Taipei: Ch'eng-wen, 1968.

Zelin, Madeline. *The Magistrate's Tael: Rationalizing Fiscal Reform in Eighteenth-Century Ch'ing China*. Berkeley: University of California Press, 1984.

Americans, 252, 253, 358n30
Amoy, 110, 139, 157, 186–187, 188,
    192, 202, 222, 325n49, 330n29,
    350n33
Andromache, 107, 111, 319n11
Anhwei, 55, 56, 68, 75, 261, 300n50,
    306nn80,81, 311n9, 322n32, 325
    n47, 327n10, 351n34
Ann, 187, 190, 201, 339n29
Ao-feng Academy, 313n19

Becher, Major, 341n46
Benoist, Michel, 342n56
Bonham Letter, 254–265, 267, 270,
    358n35, 359n39
Bonham, Sir George, 252, 253, 254–
    265, 281, 345n3, 358nn30,35
Bremer, Sir Gordon, 197, 341n46

Canton: anti-foreignism in, 6, 8, 10,
    341n41; trade in, 15, 105–108, 109,
    115, 116, 117, 118, 120, 121, 122,
    125, 126, 130, 131, 134, 139; de-
    fense of, 15, 139–141, 149, 152,
    161, 171, 182, 184, 185, 210,
    329n20; academy circles in, 118–
    119, 120, 121, 123, 133, 141, 142,
    144, 145, 146, 149, 158, 159, 172,
    244, 248, 251–252, 254, 281, 282,
    322n32, 327n8, 333n49, 341n48;
    claims of Ch'ing victory at, 138–
    141, 241, 281; 1841 siege of, 142,
    159–169, 172, 197, 281, 332n39;
    embargo at, 151, 338n6; ransom
    at, 166, 247, 355n12; paramilitary
    forces at, 169–175, 180, 195,
    197, 240, 248, 249–250, 252, 253,
    257, 281, 335n63, 336nn66,67,68,
    337n74, 356nn14,22, 357n23; de-
    mobilization of forces at, 196, 250,
    356n22; 1849 British retreat at,
    241, 242–252, 254, 281; and treaty
    concessions, 242, 247, 278; mer-
    chants in, 244, 247, 248, 355n12;
    customs collections at, 245, 353n8;
    1847 British raid at, 247, 248,
    251, 252, 256, 270. *See also* Bonham
    Letter

Catholicism, toleration of, 239, 269

Censorate, 32–38, 65, 80, 81, 82, 83, 95, 99, 116–117, 213, 215, 216, 296n28, 315n45

chan-ch'un chi 湛春集, 63. *See also* Spring Purification circle

Chang Chi-liang, 13, 312nn20,22, 313n33, 314n38, 316n62, 320n20, 326n57; and Spring Purification Circle, 70–71, 78, 81, 224, 226, 283, 309n3, 311n19, 312n23, 320n20; and poetry, 91, 92, 93–94, 97, 219–220, 294n14, 314n36; death of, 218, 220, 221, 222, 224, 349n30, 350n31, 351n36

Chang Chih-tung, 363n7

Chang Fei, 215

Chang Hsiang-ho, 309n1

Chang Hsin-pao, 2, 103, 323n38

Chang Hui-yen, 300n50

Chang Mu, 208, 217, 223, 224, 228, 281, 331n36, 345n2, 348n24, 351n34, 352n43

Chang Shao, 148

chang-tan i-li, 317n76

Chang T'ing-yü, 30, 294n21, 311n9

Chang Tou, 356n22

Chang Wei-p'ing, 143, 146, 148, 166, 167, 281, 327n8

Chang Wen-hao, 307n87

Chang Yueh-sun, 224, 325n47

Chao Chen-tso, 224

Chao I, 299n50

Chao Shen-chen, 302n59

Ch'ao-chou (Kwangtung), 172

ch'ao-k'ao 朝考, 294n14

Chekiang, 167, 182, 183, 223, 259, 313n28, 321n29, 346n8, 356n22; defense of, 140, 158, 174, 175, 198, 199, 279, 329n21, 331n33, 334n57, 337n75, 341n51; governors-general

of, 188, 300n50, 330n29. *See also* Yangtze region

chen 真, 90

Chen-hai (Chekiang), 221, 349n28

Chen-k'ou, 151

Ch'en Chi-k'un, 143, 356n20

Ch'en Chin-fang, 304n68

Ch'en Ch'ing-yung, 217, 237, 349n30, 350n31, 352n43, 353n1

Ch'en Fang-hai, 80

Ch'en Hui-tsu, 35

Ch'en Hung-ch'ih, 147, 322n32, 327nn9,11

Ch'en Li, 147, 203, 327n11, 344n65

Ch'en Shou-ch'i, 312n19

Ch'en Wei-sung, 27, 294n15

Ch'en Wen-shu, 306n79

Ch'en Yung-fu, 300n50

Ch'en Yung-kuang, 44, 47, 69, 70, 299n49, 302n59, 303n63, 312n22

Cheng-ch'i ko Shrine, 349n29

Cheng Hsuan, 49, 84, 86

Cheng Jo-tseng: *Ch'ou-hai t'u-pien*, 194, 328n18, 339n38

Cheng K'ai-hsi, 69, 311n18, 312n22, 320n20

Cheng Tsu-ch'en, 260, 262, 263, 268, 359n40, 360n44, 361n51

cheng-yao 政要, 292n4

ch'eng 誠, 90

Ch'eng En-tse, 51, 58, 305n73, 311n9, 316n59, 322n31

Ch'eng Hao, 317n72

Ch'eng I, 317n72

ch'eng-p'ing chih t'ien-hsia 承平之天下, 97

Ch'eng, Prince, 298n39

Ch'eng Yü-ts'ai, 246, 250, 346n7, 354nn9,10, 356n23

chi-shih-chung 給事中, 296n28

Chi Yun, 49, 295n21, 297n37, 298n47, 300n50, 304n68

ch'i 奇, 70

Ch'i Chi-kuang, 196, 339n38; *True Record of Troop Training*, 194

Ch'i Chün-tsao, 179, 184, 217, 218, 222, 223–224, 275, 276, 325n49, 330n29, 331n36, 347n9, 348n24, 350n33, 351n34, 355n11

Ch'i Kung, 141, 166, 168, 210; as governor of Kwangtung, 159, 162, 169, 211, 246, 279, 331n36, 332n40, 333n49, 335n60, 347n9; and local militia, 160, 161, 168, 171, 172, 173, 174, 240, 281, 332n42, 336nn68,71, 337n74

Ch'i-shan, 82, 130, 141, 223, 307n87, 326n50, 329n22, 331n32, 346n5; vs. Lin Tse-hsu, 61, 139, 149–159, 160, 181, 185–186, 210, 280–281, 286, 309n104, 326n59, 329n23, 330n26, 331nn30,31,32, 338n10, 354n10; and Tientsin negotiations, 156, 157, 181–185

Ch'i Ssu-ho 339n39, 340n40

Ch'i-ying, 6, 191, 192, 239, 243, 244, 248–249, 252, 261, 339n38, 341n42, 344n1, 347n9, 357n25, 360nn46,47, 361n57; and reform, 15, 274; in Hangchow, 175, 337n78, 346n8; and peace negotiations, 189, 195, 210, 211, 245, 339n23; fall of, 206–207, 238, 256, 269, 270, 278, 357n26, 362n5, 355n11; and Canton defense, 246, 247, 248–249, 250–251, 254, 354n9, 359n36; and Canton real-estate panic, 251, 357 n24; and Bonham Letter, 255, 358 n35

Chia-ch'ing emperor, 19, 36–37, 38, 42, 44–46, 298n41, 299n50, 301 nn51,56, 302n58, 303n64

Chiang Ch'i-ling, 353n5

Chiang Hung-sheng, 196, 356n17

Chiang K'ai, 346n6

Chiang-t'ing Pavilion (Peking), 48, 226, 304n66, 351n39

Chiang Yu-hsien, 43–47, 300n50, 301 nn51,52, 303n64; downfall of, 51, 54–55, 58, 59, 308n94, 95, 97; and sea shipment, 56–59, 286, 306n79, 307nn83,85,90, 308n93; protégés of, 285, 302n59, 306n81, 307n89, 312n22

chiao-yü hsing- wen 教育興文, 149

chien-nan chih t'ien-hsia 艱難之天下, 97, 98

Ch'ien Chiang, 196, 334n56, 341n44

Ch'ien Feng, 34, 35–36, 296n33, 302 n59

Ch'ien-lung emperor, 19, 27, 30, 33, 34, 35–36, 38, 85, 294n21, 342n56, 349n26

Ch'ien Tsai, 296n33, 304n68, 317n76

chih-ch'i 志氣, 93

chih-jen chih shih 志人之詩, 92

chih-shih 志士, 93–94, 98, 220, 317n80

Chihli, 61, 81, 82, 130, 156, 181, 182, 255, 256, 261, 321n30, 326n59, 358n35

chih-shih 進士, 75, 76, 146, 246, 293n8, 300n50, 355n11

Chin Ying-lin, 117, 118, 321n30

ch'in-ch'ai ta-ch'en 欽差大臣, 210, 345 n1, 347n9

Ch'in Ch'ing, 34–35, 297n34

Ch'in Ying, 297n37, 299n47, 311n9

Ching-an, governor of Honan, 299n50

ch'ing 清, 292n4

Ch'ing-ch'i Academy, 299n47

ch'ing-hsia 清暇, 21, 292n4

ch'ing-hsing 情性, 92

ch'ing-i 清議, 95–99, 131, 233, 234, 362n7

Ch'ing-shih, 214

Chinkiang, 221

Ch'iu Yuan-chün, 81, 315nn43,47
Chou Chung-hsi, 310n6
Chou T'ien-chueh, 210, 211, 266, 267, 325n50, 346nn6,7
Chou Yen-ts'ai, 338n6
chü 局, 142
Chu Ch'i, 185, 265, 350nn31,32, 352nn45,48, 353n1; and Spring Purification circle, 217, 218, 348n24; and Chang Chi-liang, 220, 222, 349 n30; and Ku Yen-wu Shrine Association, 230, 231, 232–234, 237, 262, 311n10, 340n40, 352n42
Chu Chien, 335n57
Chu I-tsun, 49, 50, 66, 83, 86, 304nn69, 70, 315n55, 316n62
chü-jen 舉人, 21, 120, 223, 292n2, 334n54, 344n1
Chu-ko Liang, 59, 308n96
Chu Kuei, 37, 294n15, 298nn39,45, 299nn49,50, 300n50, 301n50, 323 n33; and northern scholar group, 38, 42, 210, 295n21, 296n33, 297 n37; protégés of, 146, 306n79
chu-shih 主事, 292n4
Chu Shou-ch'ien, 348n24
Chu Ts'un, 323n38
Chu Tz'u-ch'i, 327n7
Chu Yu-ts'un, 224
Chu Yun, 42, 295n21, 296n33, 297n37, 299n49
Ch'ün, Prince, 362n3
Chuang Shou-ch'i, 224
chuang-yung 壯勇, 172
Chung Ch'ang, 314n36
chung-nien ts'ai-tzu 中年才子, 312n25
Chung-shan Academy, 311n9
chung-shu 中書, 292n4. See also *she-jen*
Chusan islands, 152, 153, 182, 329n21, 341n51, 353n4
Costin, W.C., 2

Coxinga (Cheng Ch'eng-kung), 150, 328n18

D'Aguilar, Major, 247, 256, 355n14
Davis, Sir John, 243, 345n3
Denham, Captain, 201, 342n60

East India Company, 106
Elliot, Captain Charles, 120, 124, 138, 151, 152, 155, 160, 170, 186, 189, 322n33, 328n19, 332n46; northern campaign of, 153, 156, 157, 181, 182, 184, 256; and San-yuan-li incident, 163, 165, 332n48
Examination system, 4, 12, 20–23, 50, 76, 84, 206, 226–227, 228, 292n2; and career patronage, 23–29, 41–47, 48, 64, 66, 74, 95, 117, 224, 293nn9,11,12, 296n33, 348n22; and poetry, 27, 294n14, 314n36; and cliques, 30, 35, 40, 75; metropolitan exam, 71, 87, 134, 312nn22, 25; Mu-chang-a's control of, 208, 209, 211, 215, 216, 227, 241, 348n21; and bureaucracy, 233, 241, 265

Fa-shih-shan, 296n33, 297n37
Factionalism, 12–13, 37, 38, 39, 48, 50, 96, 295n24
Fairbank, John K., 2, 4, 339n39, 344 n1, 355n12
Fan Feng 148, 336n73, 356n20
Fang Pao, 310n9
Fang Tung-shu, 96, 167, 322n32, 325 n52, 327n10, 328n18, 334n56; and Yao Ying, 69, 132, 147, 191, 311 n18, 338n13, 339nn23,29, 342n60
Fatshan, 161, 170, 171, 197, 332n41
Fei Ch'un, 299n50
fen-hsiao 分銷, 319n6

Feng Chih-i, 311n10, 350n31
Feng Kuei-fen, 193, 224, 307n85, 308
n100, 352n44
feng-liu 風流, 28
Feng Min-ch'ang, 327n8
Feng Tsan-hsun, 109–110, 111, 117,
320n18
feng-wen 風聞, 32
feng-ya 風雅, 28, 88
Fletcher, Joseph, 319n8
Foochow, 70, 188, 247, 253, 312n19,
346n6, 347n9, 354n9, 355n12
fu-i 浮意, 308n95
Fukien, 69, 130, 138, 162, 167, 187,
188, 190, 210, 257, 259, 321n31,
325n49, 331n30

Gough, General, 164, 165, 341n46
Grand Canal, 174, 221, 260, 279, 303
n64, 307nn84,87,88, 326n3
Grand Council (Chün-chi-ch'u
軍機處), 31–32
Grand Secretariat (Nei-ko) 內閣, 22,
23, 71, 292n4, 293n7
Great Britain: and "opening of
China," 19–20; northern campaign
of, 139–40, 152–158, 181–183,
198; attack on Canton, 152–153,
155, 159–162, 183–185, 252–253;
vulnerability in South Asia, 200–
203, 253, 342nn60,61, 343nn63,64.
See also Canton; Trade; Treaties

hai-k'ou 海寇, 140
Hai-ling, 168–169, 221, 349n28
Han Chinese, 33, 34, 179, 209, 210,
259, 274, 278, 280, 285; vs. Manchus, 12, 224, 244, 302n58; and examination system, 35, 211, 246; and
censorate, 212–213.
Han Learning, 49, 71–72, 84, 86, 89,

119, 123, 223, 317n68, 321n31,
348n24; and Hsueh-hai-t'ang, 145,
147, 322n32; opposition to, 148,
230, 327nn7,10; and Ku Yen-wu,
217, 224, 225, 228, 229–230
Han-lin Academy, 37, 38, 64, 69, 82,
161, 166, 183, 193, 212, 292n4,
310n6, 313n33, 321n30, 355n11,
361n48; and examination elite networks, 22, 23, 314n38, 348n22; and
official appointments, 32, 43, 45, 55,
75, 159, 246, 300n50, 301n52, 302
nn57,58,59; Mu-chang-a's control
of, 215, 216, 217, 223, 232; chauvinism of, 285, 286, 287; examinations for, 294n14, 295n21.
Han Yü, 148
Hangchow, 118, 175, 330n29, 335n57,
350n32
Ho Ch'ang-ling, 306n79, 307nn85,89,
323n37
Ho Ch'iu-t'ao, 350n31
Ho-chou (Kwangsi), 264
Ho Kuei-ch'ing, 215
Ho Ling-han, 348n22
Ho Shao-chi, 208, 217, 227, 230, 231,
345n2, 348nn23,24, 349n26, 350
n31, 351n34
Ho-shen, 36, 49, 232, 295n21, 348n21;
opposition to, 30, 34, 38, 39, 42,
297n35, 298nn42,47, 299–300n50
Ho Ta-keng, 334n56
Ho Tao-sheng, 297n37
Ho Yu-ch'eng, 333n48
Honam Island, 357n24
Honan, 299n50, 301n50
Hong Kong, 155, 157, 158, 160, 169,
174, 175, 178, 254, 255
Howqua II, 121, 124, 322n32
Hsi-en, 80, 82, 109, 315n47
Hsia Hsieh, 184, 192

Hsiang-shan county (Kwangtung), 172, 356n22, 357n23

Hsiao Kung-chuan, 363n8

Hsien-feng emperor, 234, 235, 237, 265, 269–271, 274, 275, 360n47; and Mu-chang-a, 238, 241, 266, 267, 268, 269, 277; and Bonham Letter, 255, 256–257, 358n35, 359 n39

Hsien-ling, 346n8

hsing-ch'ing 性情, 92, 317n76

hsing-t'ien 情天, 92

hsing-wen 興文, 144

Hsiu-feng Academy, 350n32

Hsu Chi-yü: *Ying Huan chih lueh*, 178

Hsu Ch'ien-hsueh, 86, 87, 227, 229, 316n63, 351n41

Hsu Ch'iu, 323n38

Hsu Han, 223, 350n30, 351n34, 355n11

Hsu Hsiang-kuang, 356n20

Hsu Hung-ch'ing, 66, 309n4

Hsu Kuang-chin, 243, 244–245, 257, 282, 355n11, 358nn26,29; and Ch'i-ying, 246, 251–252, 256, 357 n244; and Bonham Letter, 253, 254, 255, 281

Hsu Kuang-fu, 355n11

Hsu Nai-chi, 120, 122, 124, 278, 323 nn34,35,38, 324n42

Hsu Pao-shan, 66, 82, 109, 309n4, 311 n9, 316n63; and Spring Purification circle, 64, 65, 67, 78, 80, 81–82, 86, 87, 309nn1,3, 312n22

Hsu T'ing-k'uei, 249–250

Hsuan-nan Poetry Club (Hsuan-nan shih-she) 宣南詩社, 29, 39–61; as a literati faction, 39–41; as a bureaucratic clique, 41–47; as a brotherhood of connoisseurs, 47–50, 73, 87; decline of, 63–64, 309n1; and Spring Purification circle, 64–

66, 83, 84, 85, 86, 95, 312n22, 316 n59; and literary style, 88, 89; members of, 299nn48, 49, 302n59, 303nn62, 63, 64, 304n69, 305n73, 312n22; and reform, 305n79, 306n81

hsueh 學, 89, 92

Hsueh hai-t'ang, 119, 120, 123, 143, 146, 147, 161, 321n31, 322n32, 332 n40; and drug traffic, 121, 122; and Han Learning, 145, 148, 327nn7, 10.

hsueh-hsi 學習, 292n4

hsueh-jen chih shih 學人之詩, 93

Hsun-chou (Kwangsi), 264

Hu Ch'eng-kung, 49

Hu-Kuang, 127

Huai River, 56, 57, 78

Huang Chao, 322n32

Huang Chao-lin, 361n51

Huang Chien-hua, 79

Huang Chueh-tzu, 66–67, 157, 281, 314n35, 315n43, 316n62, 339n29, 347n14; and Spring Purification circle, 64, 65, 72, 75, 76, 78–79, 80, 83, 85, 87, 91, 117, 213, 222–223, 309n3, 310nn6,7, 323n3; on currency problems, 117, 321n29; and control of opium trade, 118, 119, 123, 124, 125, 126–128, 130, 133, 134, 323n39, 324nn44,46,47, 325 nn49,50,52, 326n57, 338n12, 350 n33; *Hai-fang t'u-piao*, 178; pupils of, 226, 314nn36,38, 347n15, 351 n37, 354n9, 355n11; vs. Ch'i-shan, 330 n29, 331n30

Huang En-t'ung, 195–196, 246, 248, 249, 252, 326n50, 339n38, 341nn42, 44, 354n9; *Fu-yuan chi-lueh*, 178, 340n41, 356n17

Huang Hsi-yuan, 66, 67, 310n5

Huang-Hsu clique, 65, 74, 77

Huang P'ei-fang, 146, 148, 159, 161, 249–250, 327n8, 331n35, 332n42, 356n20

Huang T'ing-chien, 83, 85, 315n55

Huang Tsan-t'ung, 359n42

Huang Yu-lin, 308n94

Huang Yueh, 312n22

hui-t'ui 會推, 31, 296n26

Hunan, 80, 81, 109, 143, 210, 222, 262, 263, 265, 315n48, 332n47, 334n55; famine in, 258, 259, 260, 359n43

Hung I-sun, 298n39

Hung Liang-chi, 37–38, 39, 297n37, 298nn39,47

Hunt, Michael, 7

Hupeh, 60, 79, 297n37, 325n47, 326n57, 346n6, 360n43

I-ching, 199, 334n57, 346n8

I-ching, 72

I-hsin (Prince Kung), 275, 276, 353n5, 362nn4,6

I-huang county (Kiangsi), 315n43

I K'o-chung, 321n31, 331n36

i-li 義理, 89, 90, 91, 92, 93

I-li-pu, 210, 211, 249, 337n78, 345n1, 346n8, 347n9, 354n9

I-liang, 157, 158, 159, 181, 187, 188, 189, 191, 192, 193, 202, 210, 331n31, 342n61

I-mien, 297n37

i-min 義民, 165

I-shan, 170, 247, 249, 286, 332nn44, 45, 343n62; as commander-in-chief in Kwangtung, 141, 160, 161, 162, 165, 166, 168, 174, 175, 197, 198, 199, 279, 281, 331nn36,37,38, 336n67, 337n74, 341n51, 356n16

Imogene, 107, 111, 319n11

India, 201–202, 203, 342nn58,60,61, 343nn62,63, 344nn64,65; and opi-um trade, 15, 151; British forces from, 139, 183, 338n6, 341n46

Jahangir, 319n8

Jardine, Matheson & Co., 131, 325n51

Jardine war plan, 326n3, 338n6

Juan Fu, 208

Juan Yuan, 43, 115–116, 148, 300n 50, 301n51, 313n28, 320nn23,24, 321nn25,31, 322n32, 323nn35,36, 345n2; protégés of, 72, 113, 147, 211, 217, 306n79, 348n22; rivalry with P'an Shih-en, 74, 75, 76, 313 n34, 321n24; and legalization of opium, 119, 120, 278–279, 323 nn33,38; and opium trade, 121, 123, 124, 126; and Han Learning, 145, 208, 223; opposition to trea-ties, 286–287

k'ai-ch'uang chih t'ien-hsia 開創之天下, 97

kan 感, 93, 94

kang-chih 剛志, 99

kang-k'ou 港口, 242

K'ang-hsi emperor, 31, 32, 86, 90, 227, 295n25

k'ao-ch'ai 考差, 314n35

k'ao-cheng 考證, 96, 351n34

k'ao-chü 考據, 49, 89, 90, 304n68, 311n9, 317nn68,71

Keelung (Taiwan), 187, 190

Kiangnan, 54, 55, 59, 60, 75, 78, 134, 286, 306n80, 321n31

Kiangpeh, 54, 134

Kiangsi, 66, 315n43, 330n29, 359n42

Kiangsu, 55, 56, 59, 69, 75, 117, 223, 306nn80, 81, 307n87, 311n18, 321n29, 351n34; and opium con-trol, 127, 325n49; defense of, 140, 199, 261

ko-yun 恪韻, 92

Ko Yun-fei, 221, 349n29

k'o-ping 客兵, 334n53

k'o-tao 科道, 296n28. *See also* Censorate

Kokand, 319n8, 349n26

ku-wen 古文 school, 68, 69, 70, 72, 148, 208, 218, 222, 225, 229, 231, 311n10, 316n61; and Spring Purification circle, 84, 86, 90, 91, 97, 217, 230, 348n24; and T'ung-ch'eng school, 147, 186, 310n9, 312n20, 350n32

Ku Yen-wu, 217, 224, 225, 227, 228, 230, 231, 351n41, 352nn42,43,44; *Jih-chih lu*, 228–229, 352n44; *T'ing-lin wen-chi*, 229, 352n44; Chang Mu biography of, 348n24, 351n34

Ku Yen-wu Shrine Association, 16, 205–235, 238, 264, 266, 268, 280, 281, 282, 287; political organization of, 217–225; ritual and scholastic philosophy of, 225–231; search for political program, 232–235; members of, 237, 246, 251, 262, 340n40, 345n2, 350n31, 353 n5, 355n11; gatherings of, 348n23, 349n26, 351n38

kuan-ping 官兵, 166

Kuan T'ung, 68, 96, 98, 233, 310n9, 352n48

Kuang-shou, 164

Kulangsu Island, 187, 188

kung-ch'e 公車, 76, 316n59

Kung Ching-han, 297n37

Kung, Prince, *see* I-hsin

Kung Tzu-chen, 71–72, 85, 126, 293n4, 312n25, 313n29, 324n43

K'ung Hsien-i, 226, 311n10, 350n31, 351n37

Kuo-t'ai, 34–35, 36, 37

Kwangsi, 43, 115, 168, 210, 222, 258–265, 266, 280, 282, 350n32; social conditions in, 259–260, 359nn40, 41,42,43, 360n44, 361n51; defense of, 260, 359n40; Lin Tse-hsu's appointment to, 268, 270

Kwangtung, 5–6, 9, 110, 117, 118, 139, 247, 253, 258, 259, 260, 279, 321n31; scholar officials in, 5–6, 167, 327n8, 331nn30,36,37; myth of victory in, 15, 137–175; governors-general of, 43, 81, 115, 192, 210, 211, 254, 256, 345n1, 354n9, 355n11; anti-drug campaign in, 111, 123, 124, 125, 127, 128–129, 130, 133, 138, 325nn47,49; First Opium War in, 138, 141, 152–153, 154, 157, 159–160, 167, 168, 169, 174, 194, 195, 196; defense forces in, 140, 141, 169, 174, 182, 183–184, 198, 199, 240, 241, 245, 246, 335n63, 337n73, 353n4, 354n40. *See also* Canton

Kweichow, 75, 115

Kweilin, 222, 260, 261, 262, 263, 264, 282, 350n32

lai-lu 來路, 319n6

lang-chan 浪戰, 198, 341n51

lang-chung 郎中, 292n4

Leichow Peninsula, 110

Li Chao-lo, 311n18

Li Ch'un, 361n51

li-hsueh 理學, 298n45

Li Hung-chang, 363n7

Li Hung-pin, 81, 109, 110, 111, 117, 315n48, 320n18

Li K'o-chiung, 161, 322n32, 332n41

Li P'an-liao, 322n32, 323n36

Li T'ang-chieh, 331n36, 347n9

Li Yang-hua, 348n21

Li Yen-chang, 67, 299n49

Li Yen-pin, 67, 85, 310n6

Li Yuan-fa, 259, 359n43
Liang Chang-chü, 167, 168, 263, 299n49, 303nn59,63,64, 306n81, 316n59, 323n33, 334n57, 335n59
Liang Hsin-fang, 334n54
Liang-Kiang, 55, 57, 129, 130, 134, 306n81, 308n87
Liang-Kuang, 5, 8, 81, 109, 110, 115, 117, 118, 119, 120, 187, 240, 251, 281, 320n24, 325n52, 354n9, 363n7
Liang T'ing-nan, 160, 162, 323nn36, 37, 331n34, 336nn72,73, 338n6, 357n24; and Lin Tse-hsu, 148–149, 152, 161, 183, 329n20, 332n40; on cession of Hong Kong, 158; on demobilization at Canton, 250, 336n65
Lin Ch'ung-yung, 309n104
Lin Fu-hsiang, 161, 332n42, 333n49, 334n53, 335n65
Lin Ju-chou, 134, 325n47, 326n55, 330n27
Lin Po-t'ung, 327n8
Lin Tse-hsu, 182–185, 214, 285, 287, 299n49, 303nn59,64, 319nn5,8, 344n65, 345n1; northern reclamation plan of, 59–61, 133, 308nn96, 97,98,103,104, 326n59; and Spring Purification circle, 102, 127, 313 n32, 326n57; and anti-opium campaign, 128, 129, 130–131, 133–135, 138, 141–149, 284, 286, 320n13, 324n47, 325nn49,50,51, 52, 326n6, 346n6; defense planing of, 139, 140, 180, 194, 195, 199, 203, 208, 328nn18,19, 329nn20, 21, 333n49, 338n6; exile of, 148, 209, 210, 211, 330n26, 350n31; vs. Ch'i-shan, 149–159, 181, 185–186, 280–281, 331nn30,31,33, 338n10, 350n33, 353n1; and siege of Canton, 161, 197; recall of, 237, 238,

241, 257, 265–271, 353n1, 361n54
Lintin Island, 110, 320n22, 323n36, 328n19
Literati, 10–16, 20–23; and ideals of career patronage, 23–29; and constraints on clique politics, 29–39
Liu Ch'ang-hua, 334n56
Liu-chou (Kwangsi), 264
Liu Feng-lu, 313n27
Liu Hung-kao, 190, 339n26
Liu Po-chi, 327n8
Liu Ssu-wan, 299n49, 303n64
Liu Tsung-chou, 349n29
Liu T'ung-hsun, 34, 294n21, 299n50
Liu Yun-k'o, 167, 210, 330n29, 335 n57, 346n8, 353n4
Liu Yung, 34, 295n21
Lo Ping-chang, 166, 167, 213, 281, 319n11, 321n30, 334n55
Lo Ta-kang, 259–260
Lo Tun-yen, 215, 216, 268
Lu Chi-lo, 311n18
Lu Chien-tseng, 298n47
Lu Chien-ying, 358n35
Lu Hsien-chi, 224, 350n31, 353n3
Lu Huang, 350n32
Lu I-t'ung, 96, 98–99, 192, 226, 315n42
Lu K'un, 81, 82, 107, 108, 109, 117, 208, 240, 321n25; and opium control, 110–111, 112, 113, 116, 119, 278, 320nn20,21,22,23
Lu Ping-chang, 33
Lu Yen, 312n22
Lung Ch'i-jui, 262–264, 265, 350nn31, 32, 361nn48,52
Lung-wen, 162
Lynn, Richard, 91

Ma Yuan, 68, 310n9
Macao, 107, 343n63

Manchuria, 56, 168, 169, 210, 245, 307n84, 325n50, 335n62, 345n1, 346n8

Manchus, 52, 159, 160, 161, 179, 181, 194, 195, 206, 319n8, 363n8; and scholar-officials, 14, 15, 16, 18, 19, 20, 29, 30–31, 32, 58–59, 151, 238, 239, 251–252, 295n23, 302n58; peace diplomacy of, 16, 209–210, 215, 216, 239–241, 242, 244, 248, 249, 254, 257, 258, 268, 270, 273, 279, 285, 344n1; bias against militia, 249, 353n4, 356n15; reform leadership of, 273–274, 286; and modernization, 275, 276–277, 362 nn2,3

Mao Yu-sheng, 311n18

Medhurst, W.H., 255–257, 267

Mei Tseng-liang, 68, 90, 191, 310n9, 311n10, 348n24; pupils of, 218, 222, 232, 234, 262, 349n30, 350 nn31,32

Meiling Pass, 259, 359n42

Miao K'uei, 223, 351n34

Ming dynasty, 7, 22, 26, 38, 51, 196, 229, 231, 349n26; politics of, 29, 30, 31, 34, 35, 37, 63, 65, 78, 84, 87, 95, 99, 283, 298nn41,45, 317n66; Tung-lin party, 39, 40, 63, 96; Restoration Society (Fu-she) of, 296 n25; loyalists of, 349n29, 351n41

Mongols, 219, 221, 273, 276, 279, 296n33, 344n1, 349n26

Morse, H.B., 2

Mu-chang-a, 209–217, 218, 234, 274, 275, 280, 286, 307n89, 344n1; fall of, 15, 16, 206, 237, 238, 241, 242, 243, 254, 257, 258, 265, 269–270, 273, 276, 277, 278, 344n1, 353n5; and debate on war, 179, 192; opposition to, 207, 208, 222, 223, 224, 225, 227, 231, 232, 233, 267, 268, 269, 287, 348n21, 355n11, 362n4; and Bonham Letter, 255, 358n35; and Ch'i-ying, 256, 359n36, 360 n47; and Kwangsi, 261–265, 266, 269

Mukden, 335n62, 346n8

nan-ch'eng 南城 (Southern City or Hsuan-nan) set, 21–23, 42, 43–47, 86–87, 88, 95, 203, 280, 283, 353n5; and opium control, 114, 115, 125, 129, 155, 181, 185, 186, 191, 192, 193, 196, 205, 281–282; and postwar diplomacy, 206, 209, 212, 214, 215, 216, 217, 218, 222, 223, 223; and Manchu diplomacy, 232, 241, 242, 262, 266, 271; influence in 1850, 275, 276, 277. *See also* Hsuan-nan Poetry Club

Nan-ning (Kwangsi), 264

Nan-tang (Southern clique), 86–87

Nanking, 186, 189, 192, 195, 210, 219, 245, 311n9, 345n1, 346n8, 347n9, 354n9, 358n35; defense of, 168, 174, 202. *See also* Treaty of Nanking

Napier, Baron William John, 106–107, 111, 112, 114, 120, 321n30

Nei-ko, *see* Grand Secretariat

nei-ko 內閣

nei-ko she-jen 內閣舍人, 23, 71, 292n4, 293n7

Neo-Confucianism, 90, 91, 92, 93, 208, 231, 291n2, 311nn72,76, 362n6

Nepal, 202, 203

Nerbudda, 187, 188, 190, 339n29

Ni Yuan-lu, 349n29

nien-po 年伯, 24

nien-ti 年弟, 24

Ningpo, 188, 253

Norjinga, 256, 358n35

Northern clique, 38, 42–43, 48–49, 51, 67, 298n47, 300n50, 302n59, 310 n6, 317n76, 322n31; leaders of, 38, 295n21, 296n33; patronage network of, 45, 47, 57, 297n37, 309n4, 310n7.

Opium: legalization of, 113–124, 279, 320n20, 322n32, 323n38; and Ch'ing military, 106, 107–108, 109, 111, 112, 113. *See also* Trade: smuggling
Orchid Pavilion scroll, 316nn55,56, 57
Ou-yang Hsiu, 84, 86, 316n61
Ou-yang Hsun, 85
Ouchterlony, John, 153, 329n22

pa-kung 拔貢, 292n2, 303n59, 314n35, 350n30
pa-pen sai-yuan 把本賽原, 111
Palmerston, Viscount, 17–18, 19, 151, 183, 184, 255, 326nn2,3
P'an Shih-en, 64, 65, 125, 133, 206, 267, 310n7, 361n54; and Spring Purification circle, 74, 75–77, 78, 83; and Juan Yuan, 75, 123, 313 n34, 321n24; and examinations, 75, 314nn35,36,38; and Mu-chang-a, 215, 216, 218, 227, 234; and Lin Tse-hsu, 267, 270, 324n47
P'an Te-yü, 82, 89–90, 91, 92, 98, 311 n18, 314n36, 317n72; *Shih-hua*, 92, 93
P'an Tseng-i, 29, 60, 308n100
P'an Tseng-shou, 75, 78, 313n34
P'an Tseng-wei, 218
P'an Tseng-ying, 75
P'an-yü county (Kwangtung), 250, 333n48, 357n23
Pao Kuei-hsing, 302n58

Pao Shih-ch'en, 306n79, 318n3, 321 n31, 328n18, 341n52
Pearl River estuary, 6, 110, 163, 184, 334n53; defense of, 107–108, 139, 141, 159, 160, 162, 168, 170, 250, 320n24, 329n21
Pei-ho, 255, 256, 257, 267
Peking, 6, 21, 60, 70, 85, 95, 153, 260–261
p'eng-tang 朋黨, 12, 29, 30, 37–39. *See also* Factionalism
P'eng Yu-yao, 350n32
Pescadores, 187, 188
Pi-ch'ang, 246, 347n9, 354n9
Pi Yuan, 66, 309n4
Pien Yu-li, 350n31
Ping-lo (Kwangsi), 264
Pottinger, Sir Henry, 175, 189, 332n46, 339n23, 354n9
Pu-hsing-e, 325n47
p'u-hsueh 樸學, 352n45

Rebellions, 2–3, 6, 8, 9, 44, 98, 241, 301nn55,56, 303n62. *See also* Taiping Rebellion; White Lotus Rebellion; Yao Rebellion
Reform, 5, 9, 15, 52, 291n2, 305n79, 306n81, 307n89; and literati, 41, 47, 51, 54, 58, 60–61, 273–277, 286, 291n2, 305n79
Reynard, 255, 256, 257, 358n35
Robinson, Sir George, 322n33
Russia, 342n55, 344nn64,65

Sa-ha-liang, 33
Sai-shang-a, 213, 344n1
San-yuan-li incident, 163–169, 195, 196, 201, 213, 254, 332n48, 333n49, 334nn54,56, 341nn41,46, 357n23; effect on war strategy, 171, 172, 180, 194, 197, 198

Schwartz, Benjamin, 4
Secret societies, 6, 173, 265, 361n57
Sha-Chiao league, 250, 251, 357nn23, 24
sha-t'an 沙灘, 171
Shanghai, 56, 243, 245, 255, 257, 307n84, 334n57, 349n29, 353n8, 358n35
Shansi, 33
Shantung, 34, 297n35, 308n100, 360 n47
Shao I-ch'en, 308n95, 350n31
she 社, 26, 47–48
she-jen 舍人, 23, 71, 292n4, 293n7. *See also* Grand Secretariat
She Pao-shun, 164
shen-chiao 慎交, 28
shen-chiao she 慎交社, 28
Shen-shih kung-chü, 326n5
Shen Wei-ch'iao, 156, 182
shen-yun 神韻, 91–92
sheng-yuan 生員, 293n8
Shensi, 36, 297n37
Shih Ching-fen, 330n29
shih-ta-fu 士大夫, 11, 286
shih-wu 時務, 91
shih-yu 師友, 25, 27
shu-jen 庶人, 96
Shuang-chou Academy, 357n24
Shun-te county (Kwangtung), 172, 336n72, 357n23
Shun-t'ien (Chihli), 310n7, 351n37
Silver famine, 103–105, 108, 109, 279, 318nn3,4,5
Sinkiang, 72, 319n8, 331n38, 349n26
Soochow, 28, 60, 127, 157, 215, 334n57
Southern City, see *nan-ch'eng* set
Spence, Jonathan D., 320n13
Spring Purification circle, 15, 40, 59, 63–99, 157, 216, 316n59, 322n32, 348n24, 349n26, 355n11; as per-

sonal network, 66–73, 312n22; as political faction, 73–83; ritual and symbol in, 83–87; literary and scholastic philosophy, 87–99; and foreign trade policy, 102, 103, 106, 125, 126, 127, 128, 135; and legalization of opium, 113, 117, 118, 119, 121, 123, 124; and anti-drug laws, 129, 130, 131, 132–133, 144, 284; and debate on war, 180, 186, 191, 192, 194, 203, 205–206, 213, 214, 216; and Ku Shrine Association, 207, 208, 217, 218, 220, 221, 222, 223, 224, 225, 226, 227, 230, 233; purpose of 283–284
Ssu-k'u ch'üan-shu 四庫全書, 49, 51, 295n21, 297n37, 304n68
Ssu-en (Kwangsi), 264
Su Kuang-ts'e, 299n49
Su T'ing-k'uei, 213–214, 217, 237, 343n62, 347n15, 349n30, 350n31, 353n1
Su Tung-p'o, 49, 50, 64, 83, 85, 304 nn69,70, 315nn55
Sun Erh-chun, 300n50, 301n51
Sun Hsing-yen, 298n47, 300n50
Sun I-yen, 167, 334n56
Sun Ting-ch'en, 264, 350nn31,32, 352n44
Sun Yü-t'ing, 43, 55, 301n52, 307n87
Sung dynasty, 26, 51, 83, 84, 85, 86, 90–91, 92, 231
Sung-yun, 29
Sung-yun-an villa, 224, 351n36
Szechuan, 36, 189, 202, 303n64, 343n63

Ta-an harbor (Taiwan), 187, 190
Ta-fo-ssu Bureau, 142–143, 144, 148, 158–159, 166, 172–173, 326n5, 333nn48,49, 334n54; and local

self-defense, 160–162, 165, 169, 171, 196, 197, 248, 251, 335n65, 341n44

Ta-hung-a, 189, 190, 269

Ta-ku, 153, 181–182, 183, 261, 358n35

Tainan (Taiwan), 187, 201, 219

Taiping Rebellion, 2, 5, 6, 8, 10, 222, 242, 260, 263, 265, 269, 273, 274, 353n8, 359n41, 361n57

Taiwan, 69, 181, 185–193, 198, 201, 219, 339n29

Tan-shui (Taiwan), 190

T'an Chin-chao, 146, 327n8

T'ang Ch'i-hua, 350n32

T'ang Chin-chao, 211–212, 213, 223, 300n50, 306n79, 347n13, 348n22, 351n34

T'ang dynasty, 7, 26, 84, 85, 148

T'ang P'eng, 72, 214, 215, 217, 313 nn29, 30, 349n30, 350n31, 352n44

tao 道, 296n28

Tao-kuang emperor, 19, 74, 81, 114, 244, 270, 330n23; and literati, 55, 58, 82, 87, 214, 232, 237, 251, 253, 358n26; and opium trade, 103, 110, 112, 115, 116–117, 118, 120, 123, 124, 125, 131, 134, 135, 320nn13, 18,21, 321n30; and Lin Tse-hsu, 154–155, 157–158; and San-yuan-li, 168, 169; and debates on conduct of war, 174, 175, 182, 188, 189, 337n74, 354n10

T'ao Chu, 58, 68, 130, 134, 286, 303 nn59,64, 306n81, 307n89, 308nn95, 97, 311n9, 325n50

T'ao-jan-t'ing Pavilion, 64, 304n66

Temples, 142, 217, 226–228, 230, 315n55, 348n23, 352n42

Teng Ch'un, 158, 331n35

Teng Shih-hsien, 143

Teng T'ing-chen, 68, 147, 148, 161, 187, 302n59, 306n81, 327n10; and opium legalization, 113, 115, 119, 120, 123, 124, 322n32, 323n38, 324 n39; and anti-opium campaign, 125, 133, 278, 325n52; removal of, 184, 210, 211, 324n47

t'i-tiao 提挑, 301n56

tiao-ping 調兵, 199

Tibet, 202, 343n63

T'ien-chou (Kwangsi), 264

t'ien-hsia p'ing 天下平, 97

Tientsin, 110, 206, 243, 256, 270, 330n23; defense of, 140, 152, 153, 169, 261, 335n62, 344n1, 358n35, 360n46; negotiations at, 156, 157, 181–185, 330n29

Ting-hai (Chekiang), 153, 154, 157, 158, 183, 188, 199, 329n21, 330n29, 349n29. *See also* Chusan islands

Ting, Prince, 213, 344n1, 360n47

Trade: and China's monetary system, 2, 18, 103–105, 118, 120; 1839 cut-off of, 15, 103–113, 151–152, 318n3, 319n8, 355n12; coastal shipping, 56–59, 306n79, 307nn83, 84,85,88,89,90, 308nn93,95; smuggling, 101–102, 105–106, 109–111, 115, 122, 126, 128, 140, 144, 259, 283, 319n7, 322n32, 323nn36, 37, 325n49; debates on, 103–113, 115, 120, 121. *See also* Silver famine

Treaties, 6, 10, 239, 269, 275, 278; resistance to, 16, 138–139, 217, 239, 241–242, 244, 246–247, 255, 286, 287, 326n2

Treaty of Nanking, 5, 138, 177, 179, 185, 206, 209, 218, 222, 242, 247, 249, 341n42, 355n13

Tributary system, 4, 7

Ts'ai Chia-k'an, 330n29

Ts'ai Chin-chuan, 143
Ts'ai Shou-ch'i, 353n5
Tsang Shu-ch'ing, 339n29
Tsao-hua-ssu (temple), 316n55
Ts'ao Chen-yung, 46, 47, 71, 74–
75, 83, 232, 303nn62,63, 304n64,
312n25, 313nn31,32,33, 348n21;
death of, 114, 115, 116, 314n34
Ts'ao Lu-t'ai, 330n29
Ts'ao Mao-chien, 314nn36,38
Tseng Chao, 148, 336n73, 356n20
Tseng Kuo-fan, 222, 234, 235, 239,
241, 262, 266, 267, 282, 287, 350
nn31,32
Tseng Wang-yen, 117, 167, 168, 213,
320n21, 331n30, 347n14
Tseng Yü, 67, 70, 220, 298n47, 309n4,
310nn7,8, 312n23
Tso Fu, 300n50
Tso Tsung-t'ang, 362n7
Tsung Chi-ch'en, 329n21, 349n29
Tsung-li Yamen, 275, 362n6
tu-ch'a yü-shih 都察御史, 296n28
Tu Shou-tien, 262, 263, 267, 282,
361nn48,51,54
Tu Yen-shih, 325n49
Tuan-mu Kuo-hu, 72, 313n28
Tuan Yü-ts'ai, 71
t'un-ying 屯營, 356n22
Tung Chiao-tseng, 43, 301n51
Tung-kuan county (Kwangtung), 172,
356n22
Tung-lin Academy, 39, 40, 63, 96, 98,
299n47
T'ung-ch'eng school, 65, 68, 69, 90,
132, 147, 186, 232, 310n9, 312n20,
322n32, 327n10, 350n32; and
Spring Purification circle, 71, 230;
and Hsuan-nan Club, 88, 89. See
also *ku-wen* school
t'ung-hsiang 同鄉, 33
tz'u-chang 詞章, 311n9, 317n71

Tz'u-hsi, Empress Dowager, 275–276,
362nn4,7
Tz'u-jen Temple (Peking), 217, 226,
227–228, 230, 352n42

Wakeman, Frederic, Jr., 5, 164, 329
n19; *Strangers at the Gate*, 5, 332n47,
335n65, 355n12, 358n26
Wan Ch'i-hsin, 330n29
Wang Ch'ang, 28, 38–39, 294n16,
298n47, 310n7
Wang Ch'i-sun, 297n37
Wang Chung, 72, 312n26
Wang Hang, 212
Wang Hsi-chen, 184, 185, 262, 311n10,
349n30, 350nn31,32, 361n51
Wang Hsi-chih, 84, 85, 316n55
Wang Hsi-sun, 71, 72, 192, 300n50,
312n26
Wang I-sun, 291n37
Wang Ju-pi, 300n50
Wang Lin-wang, 35
Wang Liu, 318n3
Wang Po-shin, 352n44
Wang Shih-chen, 49, 50, 146, 227,
304nn69,70, 310n5, 316n62, 317
n68; *Kan-chiu chi*, 27, 294n15; and
Spring Purification circle, 66, 83,
86, 91, 92, 315n55
Wang Ting, 206, 212, 347n11
Wang T'ing-chen, 311n9
Wang T'ing-lan, 167, 168, 213,
331n37, 335n59
Wang Yin-chih, 300n50
Wei Yuan, 72, 202, 284, 306nn79,80,
307n85, 313n27, 325n49, 331n37,
335n63, 339n38, 341n48; *Tao-kuang
yang-sou cheng-fu chi*, 178, 195, 197–
198, 200, 340n40; *Hai-kuo t'u-chih*,
178, 195, 197–198, 200, 202, 203,
340nn39,40,41, 341n51, 343nn63,
64, 344n65; and strategy of defen-

sive war, 194–200, 201, 243, 249, 253, 254, 282, 342nn52,55,56,58, 339n39; *Sheng-wu chi*, 340n40

wen-chang 文章, 89, 90, 91, 311n9

Wen Hsun, 322n32, 324n44

wen-jen 文人, 86

wen-she 文社, 26, 31, 32

wen-tzu chih chiao 文字之交, 25

Weng Fang-kang, 27, 43–44, 85, 88–89, 91, 145–146, 304nn68,69, 305n71, 310n5, 316n62, 317n68; and northern clique, 38, 49, 295n21, 296n33, 298n47; student network of, 42, 46, 66, 67, 75, 299n49, 300n50, 303nn59,62,63,64, 304n64, 310nn6,7; and Hsuan-nan Club, 44, 47, 50, 51, 83, 84, 315n55; and poetry, 294n14, 317n76, 327n8

West River (Canton), 247

Whampoa, 107, 153, 173

White Cloud Mountain (*Pai-yun-shan*) school, 145–146, 148, 158, 166, 327n8, 331n35

White Lotus Rebellion, 36, 41, 43, 297n37, 299n50

Wills, John, 7

Wo-jen, 276, 362n5

wo-k'ou 倭寇, 150, 199, 328n18, 342n55

Wong, J.Y., 5, 6

Woosung forts, 349n29, 360n46

Wu Chia-pin, 214, 311n10

Wu Hsiung-kuang, 297n35

Wu Jung-kuang, 332n41

Wu Lan-hsiu, 120, 122–123, 320n20, 323nn35,37

Wu Pi-kuang, 332n41

Wu Ping-chien, 322n32

Wu Sung-liang, 44, 47, 66–67, 294n16, 299n49, 309n4, 310nn5,7,8, 312n22, 314n36

Wu Te-hsuan, 311n18, 350n32

Wuchang (Hupeh), 326n57, 346n6

Xenophobia, 5, 6, 8, 9, 10, 219, 332n47

Yang-ch'eng Academy, 143, 148

Yang Chi-sheng, 218, 219, 220, 221, 349n26, 350n30

Yang Ch'ing-en, 349n29

Yang Fang, 160, 162, 331n38

yang-lien 養廉, 359n40

Yangchow, 69, 298n47, 308n94, 309n4, 311n18, 322n32

Yangtze region, 8, 74, 187, 194, 195, 198, 211, 221, 246, 259, 324n47, 346n8, 353n4; literati of, 27, 67–68, 78, 117, 118, 224; grain shipments in, 54, 56, 60, 305n76; British threat to, 138, 139, 163, 174, 247, 253, 326n3; defense of, 140, 152, 158, 167, 168, 169, 240, 245, 258, 261, 278, 342n52, 354n9, 358n35, 360n46. *See also* Taiping Rebellion

Yao Rebellion, 80, 81, 109, 259, 263, 315nn47,49

Yao Hua-tso, 143

Yao Nai, 38, 68, 296n33, 304n68, 310n9, 311n11, 312n22, 350n32

Yao Ying, 68–71, 178–179, 283–284, 311nn11,14,17, 313n30, 338nn12, 13; and literati, 51, 72–73, 78, 96, 97–98, 210, 218, 222, 311n18, 312n22, 317n76, 327n8, 350n31, 361n54; and Fang Tung-shu, 132, 147; *K'ang-yu chi-hsing*, 178, 201, 340n40, 342n60, 343n64, 344n65; and Taiwan case, 185–193, 201, 219–220, 339nn26,29,35,37,38; and defensive war, 194, 195, 198, 208; and British vulnerability in South Asia, 200–203, 253, 342nn60,61, 343

Yao Ying (*cont.*)
nn63,64; recall of, 237, 238, 241, 266, 267, 269
Yao Yuan-chih, 124, 322n32, 324n39
Yeh Chih-shen, 355n11
Yeh Chung-chin, 322n32
Yeh Ming-ch'en, 5, 8, 243, 244, 246, 251, 252, 254, 255, 282, 354n9, 355n11
Yeh Ming-feng, 226, 246, 351n37, 355n11
Yellow River, 56, 57, 58, 214, 260, 307 n87, 360n45
Yen-chang, 67, 310n6
Yen Cheng-chi, 359n40
Yen Chieh, 321n31
yen-kuan 言官, 32, 33
yen-lu 言路, 32, 34
Yen Po-t'ao, 167, 168, 210, 213, 334 n57, 335n59
Yen Sung, 349n26
Yen Yü: *Ts'ang-lang shih-hua*, 91–92
Yin Chao-yung, 338n10
Yin-jeng, 31

yin-kung ch'u-fen 因公處分, 301n56
Ying-ho, 46, 47, 55, 57, 303nn62,63, 307nn88, 89
Yü Cheng-hsieh, 351n34
Yü-ch'ien, 155, 157, 158, 183–184, 198, 221, 330n27, 331n30, 341n51, 342n52, 349n28, 353n4
yu-chih chih shih 有志之士, 90
yü-ch'ing 輿情, 81
Yu K'un, 311n10
Yü T'ing-kuei, 161
Yü-yao county, 356n22
Yuan Chia-san, 359n39, 360n43
Yuan dynasty, 51, 72
yuan-wai-lang 員外郎, 292n4
Yueh-hsiu Academy, 322n32, 327n8
Yueh-hua Academy, 143, 146, 147, 148, 161
yung 勇, 99
Yung-cheng emperor, 19, 31
yung-ping 用兵, 199
Yunnan, 75, 115, 297n35

Zelin, Madeline, 363n8
Zen (Ch'an) Buddhism, 91, 92

Harvard East Asian Monographs

1. Liang Fang-chung, *The Single-Whip Method of Taxation in China*
2. Harold C. Hinton, *The Grain Tribute System of China, 1845–1911*
3. Ellsworth C. Carlson, *The Kaiping Mines, 1877–1912*
4. Chao Kuo-chün, *Agrarian Policies of Mainland China: A Documentary Study, 1949–1956*
5. Edgar Snow, *Random Notes on Red China, 1936–1945*
6. Edwin George Beal, Jr., *The Origin of Likin, 1835–1864*
7. Chao Kuo-chün, *Economic Planning and Organization in Mainland China: A Documentary Study, 1949–1957*
8. John K. Fairbank, *Ch'ing Documents: An Introductory Syllabus*
9. Helen Yin and Yi-chang Yin, *Economic Statistics of Mainland China, 1949–1957*
10. Wolfgang Franke, *The Reform and Abolition of the Traditional Chinese Examination System*
11. Albert Feuerwerker and S. Cheng, *Chinese Communist Studies of Modern Chinese History*
12. C. John Stanley, *Late Ch'ing Finance: Hu Kuang-yung as an Innovator*
13. S. M. Meng, *The Tsungli Yamen: Its Organization and Functions*
14. Ssu-yü Teng, *Historiography of the Taiping Rebellion*
15. Chun-Jo Liu, *Controversies in Modern Chinese Intellectual History: An Analytic Bibliography of Periodical Articles, Mainly of the May Fourth and Post-May Fourth Era*
16. Edward J. M. Rhoads, *The Chinese Red Army, 1927–1963: An Annotated Bibliography*
17. Andrew J. Nathan, *A History of the China International Famine Relief Commission*
18. Frank H. H. King (ed.) and Prescott Clarke, *A Research Guide to China-Coast Newspapers, 1822–1911*
19. Ellis Joffe, *Party and Army: Professionalism and Political Control in the Chinese Officer Corps, 1949–1964*
20. Toshio G. Tsukahira, *Feudal Control in Tokugawa Japan: The Sankin Kōtai System*

21. Kwang-Ching Liu, ed., *American Missionaries in China: Papers from Harvard Seminars*

22. George Moseley, *A Sino-Soviet Cultural Frontier: The Ili Kazakh Autonomous Chou*

23. Carl F. Nathan, *Plague Prevention and Politics in Manchuria, 1910–1931*

24. Adrian Arthur Bennett, *John Fryer: The Introduction of Western Science and Technology into Nineteenth-Century China*

25. Donald J. Friedman, *The Road from Isolation: The Campaign of the American Committee for Non-Participation in Japanese Aggression, 1938–1941*

26. Edward Le Fevour, *Western Enterprise in Late Ch'ing China: A Selective Survey of Jardine, Matheson and Company's Operations, 1842–1895*

27. Charles Neuhauser, *Third World Politics: China and the Afro-Asian People's Solidarity Organization, 1957–1967*

28. Kungtu C. Sun, assisted by Ralph W. Huenemann, *The Economic Development of Manchuria in the First Half of the Twentieth Century*

29. Shahid Javed Burki, *A Study of Chinese Communes, 1965*

30. John Carter Vincent, *The Extraterritorial System in China: Final Phase*

31. Madeleine Chi, *China Diplomacy, 1914–1918*

32. Clifton Jackson Phillips, *Protestant America and the Pagan World: The First Half Century of the American Board of Commissioners for Foreign Missions, 1810–1860*

33. James Pusey, *Wu Han: Attacking the Present through the Past*

34. Ying-wan Cheng, *Postal Communication in China and Its Modernization, 1860–1896*

35. Tuvia Blumenthal, *Saving in Postwar Japan*

36. Peter Frost, *The Bakumatsu Currency Crisis*

37. Stephen C. Lockwood, *Augustine Heard and Company, 1858–1862*

38. Robert R. Campbell, *James Duncan Campbell: A Memoir by His Son*

39. Jerome Alan Cohen, ed., *The Dynamics of China's Foreign Relations*

40. V. V. Vishnyakova-Akimova, *Two Years in Revolutionary China, 1925–1927*, tr. Steven I. Levine

41. Meron Medzini, *French Policy in Japan during the Closing Years of the Tokugawa Regime*

42. *The Cultural Revolution in the Provinces*

43. Sidney A. Forsythe, *An American Missionary Community in China, 1895–1905*

44. Benjamin I. Schwartz, ed., *Reflections on the May Fourth Movement: A Symposium*

45. Ching Young Choe, *The Rule of the Taewŏn'gun, 1864–1873: Restoration in Yi Korea*

46. W. P. J. Hall, *A Bibliographical Guide to Japanese Research on the Chinese Economy, 1958–1970*

47. Jack J. Gerson, *Horatio Nelson Lay and Sino-British Relations, 1854–1864*

48. Paul Richard Bohr, *Famine and the Missionary: Timothy Richard as Relief Administrator and Advocate of National Reform*

49.   Endymion Wilkinson, *The History of Imperial China: A Research Guide*

50.   Britten Dean, *China and Great Britain: The Diplomacy of Commercial Relations, 1860–1864*

51.   Ellsworth C. Carlson, *The Foochow Missionaries, 1847–1880*

52.   Yeh-chien Wang, *An Estimate of the Land-Tax Collection in China, 1753 and 1908*

53.   Richard M. Pfeffer, *Understanding Business Contracts in China, 1949–1963*

54.   Han-sheng Chuan and Richard Kraus, *Mid-Ch'ing Rice Markets and Trade, An Essay in Price History*

55.   Ranbir Vohra, *Lao She and the Chinese Revolution*

56.   Liang-lin Hsiao, *China's Foreign Trade Statistics, 1864–1949*

57.   Lee-hsia Hsu Ting, *Government Control of the Press in Modern China, 1900–1949*

58.   Edward W. Wagner, *The Literati Purges: Political Conflict in Early Yi Korea*

59.   Joungwon A. Kim, *Divided Korea: The Politics of Development, 1945–1972*

60.   Noriko Kamachi, John K. Fairbank, and Chūzō Ichiko, *Japanese Studies of Modern China Since 1953: A Bibliographical Guide to Historical and Social-Science Research on the Nineteenth and Twentieth Centuries, Supplementary Volume for 1953–1969*

61.   Donald A. Gibbs and Yun-chen Li, *A Bibliography of Studies and Translations of Modern Chinese Literature, 1918–1942*

62.   Robert H. Silin, *Leadership and Values: The Organization of Large-Scale Taiwanese Enterprises*

63.   David Pong, *A Critical Guide to the Kwangtung Provincial Archives Deposited at the Public Record Office of London*

64.   Fred W. Drake, *China Charts the World: Hsu Chi-yü and His Geography of 1848*

65.   William A. Brown and Urgunge Onon, translators and annotators, *History of the Mongolian People's Republic*

66.   Edward L. Farmer, *Early Ming Government: The Evolution of Dual Capitals*

67.   Ralph C. Croizier, *Koxinga and Chinese Nationalism: History, Myth, and the Hero*

68.   William J. Tyler, tr., *The Psychological World of Natsume Sōseki*, by Doi Takeo

69.   Eric Widmer, *The Russian Ecclesiastical Mission in Peking during the Eighteenth Century*

70.   Charlton M. Lewis, *Prologue to the Chinese Revolution: The Transformation of Ideas and Institutions in Hunan Province, 1891–1907*

71.   Preston Torbert, *The Ch'ing Imperial Household Department: A Study of its Organization and Principal Functions, 1662–1796*

72.   Paul A. Cohen and John E. Schrecker, eds., *Reform in Nineteenth-Century China*

73.   Jon Sigurdson, *Rural Industrialism in China*

74.   Kang Chao, *The Development of Cotton Textile Production in China*

75.   Valentin Rabe, *The Home Base of American China Missions, 1880–1920*

76.   Sarasin Viraphol, *Tribute and Profit: Sino-Siamese Trade, 1652–1853*

77. Ch'i-ch'ing Hsiao, *The Military Establishment of the Yuan Dynasty*

78. Meishi Tsai, *Contemporary Chinese Novels and Short Stories, 1949–1974: An Annotated Bibliography*

79. Wellington K. K. Chan, *Merchants, Mandarins, and Modern Enterprise in Late Ch'ing China*

80. Endymion Wilkinson, *Landlord and Labor in Late Imperial China: Case Studies from Shandong by Jing Su and Luo Lun*

81. Barry Keenan, *The Dewey Experiment in China: Educational Reform and Political Power in the Early Republic*

82. George A. Hayden, *Crime and Punishment in Medieval Chinese Drama: Three Judge Pao Plays*

83. Sang-Chul Suh, *Growth and Structural Changes in the Korean Economy, 1910–1940*

84. J. W. Dower, *Empire and Aftermath: Yoshida Shigeru and the Japanese Experience, 1878–1954*

85. Martin Collcutt, *Five Mountains: The Rinzai Zen Monastic Institution in Medieval Japan*

STUDIES IN THE MODERNIZATION OF THE REPUBLIC OF KOREA: 1945–1975

86. Kwang Suk Kim and Michael Roemer, *Growth and Structural Transformation*

87. Anne O. Krueger, *The Developmental Role of the Foreign Sector and Aid*

88. Edwin S. Mills and Byung-Nak Song, *Urbanization and Urban Problems*

89. Sung Hwan Ban, Pal Yong Moon, and Dwight H. Perkins, *Rural Development*

90. Noel F. McGinn, Donald R. Snodgrass, Yung Bong Kim, Shin-Bok Kim, and Quee-Young Kim, *Education and Development in Korea*

91. Leroy P. Jones and Il SaKong, *Government, Business, and Entrepreneurship in Economic Development: The Korean Case*

92. Edward S. Mason, Dwight H. Perkins, Kwang Suk Kim, David C. Cole, Mahn Je Kim, et al., *The Economic and Social Modernization of the Republic of Korea*

93. Robert Repetto, Tai Hwan Kwon, Son-Ung Kim, Dae Young Kim, John E. Sloboda, and Peter J. Donaldson, *Economic Development, Population Policy, and Demographic Transition in the Republic of Korea*

106. David C. Cole and Yung Chul Park, *Financial Development in Korea, 1945–1978*

107. Roy Bahl, Chuk Kyo Kim, and Chong Kee Park, *Public Finances during the Korean Modernization Process*

94. Parks M. Coble, Jr., *The Shanghai Capitalists and the Nationalist Government, 1927–1937*

95. Noriko Kamachi, *Reform in China: Huang Tsun-hsien and the Japanese Model*

96.   Richard Wich, *Sino-Soviet Crisis Politics: A Study of Political Change and Communication*

97.   Lillian M. Li, *China's Silk Trade: Traditional Industry in the Modern World, 1842–1937*

98.   R. David Arkush, *Fei Xiaotong and Sociology in Revolutionary China*

99.   Kenneth Alan Grossberg, *Japan's Renaissance: The Politics of the Muromachi Bakufu*

100. James Reeve Pusey, *China and Charles Darwin*

101. Hoyt Cleveland Tillman, *Utilitarian Confucianism: Ch'en Liang's Challenge to Chu Hsi*

102. Thomas A. Stanley, *Ōsugi Sakae, Anarchist in Taishō Japan: The Creativity of the Ego*

103. Jonathan K. Ocko, *Bureaucratic Reform in Provincial China: Ting Jih-ch'ang in Restoration Kiangsu, 1867–1870*

104. James Reed, *The Missionary Mind and American East Asia Policy, 1911–1915*

105. Neil L. Waters, *Japan's Local Pragmatists: The Transition from Bakumatsu to Meiji in the Kawasaki Region*

108. William D. Wray, *Mitsubishi and the N.Y.K., 1870–1914: Business Strategy in the Japanese Shipping Industry*

109. Ralph William Huenemann, *The Dragon and the Iron Horse: The Economics of Railroads in China, 1876–1937*

110. Benjamin A. Elman, *From Philosophy to Philology: Intellectual and Social Aspects of Change in Late Imperial China*

111. Jane Kate Leonard, *Wei Yuan and China's Rediscovery of the Maritime World*

112. Luke S. K. Kwong, *A Mosaic of the Hundred Days: Personalities, Politics, and Ideas of 1898*

113. John E. Wills, Jr., *Embassies and Illusions: Dutch and Portuguese Envoys to K'ang-hsi, 1666–1687*

114. Joshua A. Fogel, *Politics and Sinology: The Case of Naitō Konan (1866–1934)*

115. Jeffrey C. Kinkley, ed., *After Mao: Chinese Literature and Society, 1978–1981*

116. C. Andrew Gerstle, *Circles of Fantasy: Convention in the Plays of Chikamatsu*

117. Andrew Gordon, *The Evolution of Labor Relations in Japan: Heavy Industry, 1853–1955*

118. Daniel K. Gardner, *Chu Hsi and the Ta Hsueh: Neo-Confucian Reflection on the Confucian Canon*

119. Christine Guth Kanda, *Shinzō: Hachiman Imagery and its Development*

120. Robert Borgen, *Sugawara no Michizane and the Early Heian Court*

121. Chang-tai Hung, *Going to the People: Chinese Intellectual and Folk Literature, 1918–1937*

122. Michael A. Cusumano, *The Japanese Automobile Industry: Technology and Management at Nissan and Toyota*

124. Steven D. Carter, *The Road to Komatsubara: A Classical Reading of the Renga Hyakuin*

125. Katherine F. Bruner, John K. Fairbank, and Richard T. Smith, *Entering China's Service: Robert Hart's Journals, 1854–1863*

126. Bob Tadashi Wakabayashi, *Anti-Foreignism and Western Learning in Early-Modern Japan: The New Theses of 1825*

127. Atsuko Hirai, *Individualism and Socialism: The Life and Thought of Kawai Eijirō (1891–1944)*

128. Ellen Widmer, *The Margins of Utopia: Shui-hu hou-chuan and the Literature of Ming Loyalism*

129. R. Kent Guy, *The Emperor's Four Treasuries: Scholars and the State in the Late Ch'ien-lung Era*

130. Peter C. Perdue, *Exhausting the Earth: State and Peasant in Hunan, 1500–1850*

131. Susan Chan Egan, *A Latterday Confucian: Reminiscences of William Hung (1893–1980)*

132. James T. C. Liu, *China Turning Inward: Intellectual-Political Changes in the Early Twelfth Century*

133. Paul A. Cohen, *Between Tradition and Modernity: Wang T'ao and Reform in Late Ch'ing China*

134. Kate Wildman Nakai, *Shogunal Politics: Arai Hakuseki and the Premises of Tokugawa Rule*

135. Parks M. Coble, *Facing Japan: Chinese Politics and Japanese Imperialism, 1931–1937*

136. Jon L. Saari, *Legacies of Childhood: Growing Up Chinese in a Time of Crisis, 1890–1920*

137. Susan Downing Videen, *Tales of Heichū*

138. Heinz Morioka and Miyoko Sasaki, *Rakugo: The Popular Narrative Art of Japan*

139. Joshua A. Fogel, *Nakae Ushikichi in China: The Mourning of Spirit*

140. Alexander Barton Woodside, *Vietnam and the Chinese Model: A Comparative Study of Vietnamese and Chinese Government in the First Half of the Nineteenth Century*

141. George Elison, *Deus Destroyed: The Image of Christianity in Early Modern Japan*

142. William D. Wray, ed., *Managing Industrial Enterprise: Cases from Japan's Prewar Experience*

143. T'ung-tsu Ch'ü, *Local Government in China under the Ch'ing*

144. Marie Anchordoguy, *Computers, Inc.: Japan's Challenge to IBM*

145. Barbara Molony, *Technology and Investment: The Prewar Japanese Chemical Industry*

146. Mary Elizabeth Berry, *Hideyoshi*

147. Laura E. Hein, *Fueling Growth: The Energy Revolution and Economic Policy in Postwar Japan*

148. Wen-hsin Yeh, *The Alienated Academy: Culture and Politics in Republican China, 1919–1937*

149. Dru C. Gladney, *Muslim Chinese: Ethnic Nationalism in the People's Republic*

150. Merle Goldman and Paul A. Cohen, eds., *Ideas Across Cultures: Essays on Chinese Thought in Honor of Benjamin I. Schwartz*

151. James Polachek, *The Inner Opium War*
152. Gail Lee Bernstein, *Japanese Marxist: A Portrait of Kawakami Hajime, 1879–1946*
153. Lloyd E. Eastman, *The Abortive Revolution: China under Nationalist Rule, 1927–1937*
154. Irmela Hijiya-Kirschnereit, *Rituals of Self-Revelation: The History and Theory of Shishōsetsu*
155. Richard J. Smith, John K. Fairbank, and Katherine F. Bruner, *Robert Hart and China's Early Modernization: His Journals, 1863–1866*